Tragedy and the Tragic

Tragedy and the Tragic

Greek Theatre and Beyond

✦

Edited by

M. S. SILK

OXFORD
UNIVERSITY PRESS

OXFORD

UNIVERSITY PRESS

Great Clarendon Street, Oxford OX2 6DP

Oxford University Press is a department of the University of Oxford.
It furthers the University's objective of excellence in research, scholarship,
and education by publishing worldwide in

Oxford New York

Athens Auckland Bangkok Bogotá Buenos Aires Calcutta
Cape Town Chennai Dar es Salaam Delhi Florence Hong Kong Istanbul
Karachi Kuala Lumpur Madrid Melbourne Mexico City Mumbai
Nairobi Paris São Paulo Singapore Taipei Tokyo Toronto Warsaw

with associated companies in Berlin Ibadan

Oxford is a registered trade mark of Oxford University Press
in the UK and in certain other countries

Published in the United States
by Oxford University Press Inc., New York

© Oxford University Press 1996

British Library Cataloguing in Publication Data

Data available

Library of Congress Cataloging in Publication Data
Tragedy and the Tragic: Greek theatre and beyond
edited by M. S. Silk.
Includes bibliographical references.
1. Greek drama (Tragedy)—History and criticism.
2. Theater—Greece—History.   3. Tragic, The.
I. Silk, M. S.
PA3133.T73   1966   882'.0109—dc20   95-25867
ISBN 0-19-815259-0

3 5 7 9 10 8 6 4 2

Printed in Great Britain on acid-free paper by
Bookcraft (Bath) Ltd., Midsomer Norton

Contents

List of Contributors

W. Geoffrey Arnott is Professor Emeritus of Greek Language and Literature at the University of Leeds.

Richard Buxton is Professor of Greek Language and Literature at the University of Bristol.

Claude Calame is Professor of Greek Language and Literature at the University of Lausanne.

P. E. Easterling is Regius Professor of Greek and Fellow of Newnham College, Cambridge.

A. Maria van Erp Taalman Kip is Associate Professor of Greek Language and Literature at the University of Amsterdam.

Michael Ewans is Associate Professor of Drama and Music at the University of Newcastle, New South Wales.

Helene P. Foley is Olin Professor of Greek at Barnard College, Columbia University.

Rainer Friedrich is Professor of Classics at Dalhousie University, Halifax, Nova Scotia.

A. F. Garvie is Reader in Classics at the University of Glasgow.

Simon Goldhill is Lecturer in Classics at Cambridge University and Director of Studies at King's College.

John Gould is Emeritus Professor of Greek at the University of Bristol.

Bernard Gredley is Lecturer in Classics at King's College London.

Edith Hall is Tutorial Fellow in Greek and Latin at Somerville College, Oxford.

Stephen Halliwell is Professor of Greek in the University of St Andrews.

Ismene Lada is Lecturer in Classics at the University of Nottingham.

Kevin Lee is Professor of Classics at the University of Sydney.

N. J. Lowe is Lecturer in Classics at Royal Holloway, University of London.

FIONA MACINTOSH is Lecturer in English at Goldsmith's College, University of London.

ROBIN N. MITCHELL-BOYASK is Assistant Professor of Greek and Roman Classics at Temple University, Pennsylvania.

EMESE MOGYORÓDI is Lecturer in Greek Philosophy and Literature at Attila József University, Szeged, Hungary.

THOMAS G. ROSENMEYER is Professor Emeritus of Greek and Comparative Literature at the University of California, Berkeley.

RICHARD SEAFORD is Professor of Greek Literature at the University of Exeter.

CHARLES SEGAL is Professor of Greek and Latin in the Department of the Classics at Harvard University.

BERND SEIDENSTICKER is Professor of Classical Philology at the Free University of Berlin.

M. S. SILK is Professor of Greek Language and Literature at King's College London.

GEORGE STEINER is Emeritus Professor of English and Comparative Literature at the University of Geneva and Extraordinary Fellow of Churchill College, Cambridge.

OLIVER TAPLIN is Reader in Greek Literature at Oxford University and Tutorial Fellow in Greek and Latin at Magdalen College.

MICHAEL TRAPP is Lecturer in Classics at King's College London.

P. J. WILSON is Research Fellow in Classics at the University of Warwick.

General Introduction

The essays that make up this book are new. They are the work of classical scholars, largely though not exclusively. They centre on Greek tragedy and the qualities that make Greek tragedy what it is; at the same time, they bear on tragedy as a whole and the qualities that make tragedy as a whole what *it* is. There is a good deal here about more recent drama, from Shakespeare to Beckett (but especially Shakespeare). There is much reference to theory, and much discussion—and use—of theoretical perspectives, from Nietzsche to Heidegger, from the Romantics to the post-structuralists, from Vernant to Northrop Frye, from Carol Gilligan to René Girard, from Aristotle to Brecht (but especially Aristotle). There is an outward-looking spirit to the discussions, individually or in their cross-relations, which explains the subtitle of the book: Greek Theatre and Beyond.

For all its many contributors and its many topics, the book asks to be read as a coherent volume. It also bears witness to a notable event. The event was a conference entitled 'Tragedy and "The Tragic"', which was held at King's College London on 22–5 July 1993 and brought together around two hundred delegates from twenty countries and six continents. These facts are worth recording, if only because the scale of the event is reflected in the book, and the character of the event too. By this I mean above all that the conference brought together a diverse group of speakers and listeners, not all professional classicists by any means, to address the common question: how best to define or understand Greek tragedy in particular and tragedy in general. It was not so much, though, that a theme or topic served as a point of departure for a series of individual discussions; rather that discussion was dialogic and cumulative, the more so because not only were all sessions plenary, but the majority of them involved a pair of papers, in which the second was a prepared response to the first.

Of the contributors to the book, most were speakers at the

conference, though (for one reason or another) several conference contributions could not be represented here: papers by Gregory Sifakis, Froma Zeitlin, and David Bain, and theatrical presentations and discussions by John Barton and Salli Goetsch.[1] On the other hand, four additional papers are included in the body of the work—those by Halliwell, Silk ('Tragic Language'), Seidensticker, and Ewans, of whom the latter two were to have participated in the conference but in the event could not. Within the book, the editorial arrangement into three sections, the order of the papers within the sections, and the separate short editorial introductions to those sections were not features of the conference; but overall the conference's predominant pattern of argument and counter-argument is preserved: that is, of the twenty-nine papers that follow this introduction, eighteen involve pairs of papers in which the second is a response to, and positions itself with reference to, the first. In these and other parts of the book, however, everything that began as part of the conference (including this general introduction) has been substantially revised in the interests of greater overall coherence—without prejudice, though, to the requisite self-containedness of each paper, or pair of papers, and without prejudice, again, to the diversity of reference and perspective which characterized these debates from the outset.

'Tragedy and the tragic', 'Greek tragedy and tragedy as a whole', 'Greek theatre and beyond': these conjunctions presuppose a set of propositions that deserve to be spelt out.

First: what we know as tragedy, centring on what Frye has called 'the two indigenous developments of tragic drama in fifth-century Athens and seventeenth-century Europe',[2] subsumes some of the most admired and most affecting works in Western literature, the attempt to come to terms with which has animated generations of scholars (classical and other) and has generated a host of theoretical accounts of tragedy—from thinkers as different as Aristotle and Nietzsche and from playwrights as different as Racine and Brecht—which have influenced, and continue to influence, the general understanding of tragedy, Greek and other. Second: in the wake of the theoretical discussions just referred to, 'the tragic' is a concept of central concern to anyone who wishes to come to terms with tragedy, Greek or other. Third: any definition or general

---

[1] On Sifakis and Barton, however, see below pp. 185–6 and 356–7.

[2] *Anatomy of Criticism*, 37.

understanding of tragedy as a whole depends first and foremost on an understanding of Greek tragedy in particular. Indeed, for theorists of tragedy, from Aristotle to our own century, Greek tragedy has been one of the few constants, since virtually all other forms or relatives of tragedy have at one time or another been queried or dissociated from the tragic canon; and to illustrate the point one need only recall Samuel Johnson's remark in his *Preface to Shakespeare* (1765) that Shakespeare's plays are not 'in the rigorous and critical sense' tragedies at all.[3] Fourth: any substantial understanding of Greek tragedy presupposes an understanding of Greek tragedy in its particular cultural context. Fifth: any substantial understanding of Greek tragedy presupposes an understanding of other kinds of tragedy, or non-tragedy, in contrast or comparison with which its particularities take on their particular significance; the tragicness of Greek tragedy can be illuminated by comparison or contrast with the tragicness of non-Greek tragedy; and the feasibility of any theoretical discussion of 'tragedy as a whole' must depend on comparison or contrast of this kind. And sixth: despite, or because of, the wealth of discussions, past and present, under these various headings, there is no current consensus among interested parties on which of these propositions, if any, deserve to be privileged over which. That is, there is no current consensus on how, precisely, tragedy should best be defined or understood, or indeed on how, precisely, *Greek* tragedy should best be defined or understood. Hence the motivation for the present volume, which presents something close to the spectrum of ways in which tragedy in general, and Greek tragedy in particular, *is* currently defined and understood, and offers a series of new interpretations and new readings to help move the process of definition and understanding forward.

Probably the most obvious issue on which consensus is lacking is whether, or how far, to privilege the understanding of Greek tragedy in its own, very particular, cultural context. An emphasis on cultural interpretation brings together important representatives of two otherwise very different positions or clusters of positions: on the one hand, 'traditional' empirical historicism; on the other, positions that tend in the classical world to be vaguely thought of as 'structuralism', but which would more plausibly be

---

[3] Raleigh, *Johnson on Shakespeare*, 15. Cf. Steiner below, p. 540.

described as a species (with various subspecies) of sociological neo-
historicism, except that the neo-historicist label has been appropriated on behalf of one of the particular subspecies in question.[4]
At all events, historicists and (if I may use the term with an uncon-
ventional breadth of application) neo-historicists tend to agree on
two things: positively, to keep their 'tragedy' (and their 'tragic')
Greek; negatively, to take a sceptical, or at least cautious, attitude
towards engaging with any cross-cultural version either of
'tragedy' (with an imaginary capital T) or of that defining set of
qualities by virtue of which tragedy, notionally, is tragedy—that is,
'the tragic'. In the words of one of the contributors to this volume,
any such engagement threatens to involve a 'circular wild-goose
chase';[5] and the awkwardness of the imaginary capital T and the
inverted commas that (in English usage, at least) are never far away
from 'the tragic' (and which indeed figured in the original confer-
ence-title) might well sum up, for many, the problematic nature of
this particular 'chase'.

Both historicism and neo-historicism are well represented in this
volume: both have their distinctive and necessary contributions to
make to the debate. There are no plausible grounds for allowing
either version of historicism to exclude the other; but then again,
there are no plausible grounds for allowing either version of historicism to exclude other perspectives, including the many perspectives of the cross-cultural. Nothing can come of nothing:
everyone must start from somewhere: what matters is where you
get to and, especially, where you get *others* to. However, in saying
this, one inevitably commits oneself to something more than a rel-
ativistic tolerance. One commits oneself to an essentially diaiogi-
cal standpoint, from which it seems neither right nor wrong to
privilege cultural context in the first instance, but right to insist on
the legitimacy, and in the last resort the necessity, of confronting
'tragedy' and 'the tragic' without contextual restrictions—just as
one can also, of course, confront 'tragedy as a whole' through specific, contextually grounded, comparisons between *this* phase or
type of tragedy and *that*. The illumination to be gained from both

---

[4] On which, see e.g. H. A. Veeser (ed.), *The New Historicism* (New York 1989).
[5] Richard Buxton, p. 42 below. On the other hand, *some* neo-historicist ('structuralist') discussions do engage, however briefly, with matters tragic and even
Tragic: see e.g. Vernant on 'Le Sujet tragique: Historicité et transhistoricité', in
Vernant and Vidal-Naquet, *Mythe et tragédie*, 79–90.

kinds of confrontation will, I trust, also be clear from various of the papers that follow. For the time being, a few further theoretical reflections may be helpful.[6]

While caution in confronting the cross-cultural is as proper as caution anywhere else, I would argue that, for the reasons schematized in the six propositions above, the whole conceptual-perceptual apparatus through which any of us beholds Greek tragedy is inevitably, and productively, influenced by a sense of 'tragedy as a whole'—by knowledge of both the tragic practice and the tragic theory that comes after, and in part looks back to, the tragic age of Greece; also, conversely, that any productive discussion of Greek tragedy, whether purportedly 'contextual' or not, inevitably contributes to the wider understanding of 'tragedy as a whole'. None of this makes tragedy (or Tragedy) a fixed, cut-and-dried thing, which it never was, even in its Greek heyday, as a glance at the career of Euripides, or indeed any one of the three tragedians, serves to show.

Wittgenstein's theory of family resemblances reminds us that the specific instances that answer to a generic name like 'tragedy' are wont to show recognizable traits or affinities in the manner of members of a family. The whole set of members will resemble one another in varying degrees, so that in the case of distant relationships the points of resemblance shown by any two members need not be the same as those shown by some other two. One cannot assume that possession of a common name guarantees some fundamental affinity. In a case like drama, certainly, with various sets of variously similar and variously different instances, what tends to happen is that we do (or do not) detect such resemblances as seem to imply a fundamentally 'tragic' affinity and on the strength of that *we decide* (or not) to ascribe the common name, 'tragedy', to the instances in question.

In our endeavour to decide what counts as tragedy, we naturally start with Greek tragedy as the common source and the common point of reference for whatever follows, in the expectation, no doubt, that here at least identification is culturally given and (therefore) unproblematic. Yet consideration of even the seemingly straightforward task of identifying Greek specimens of

---

[6] Part of the argument that follows is developed more fully in my article, 'Autonomy of Comedy'.

'tragedy' serves to show how, here as elsewhere, wider perspectives are, and must be, brought to bear.

Within the dramatic corpus of ancient Greece, we would commonly say we *know* what counts as tragedy. We *know* that Aeschylus' *Agamemnon* 'was' a *tragôidia*, hence 'is' a tragedy. With (say) *Phèdre* by Racine, we count it as a tragedy on several grounds: because its author called it by another derivative of the Greek name *tragôidia* ('tragédie'); because the play is variously evocative of the tradition that goes back to Greek tragedy; and because, above all, *we* perceive that the play resembles Greek tragedy directly. *We* detect affinity. With (say) Shakespeare's *King Lear*, most of us, like most of our nineteenth-century predecessors, are happy to speak of tragedy on the grounds of perceived affinity, ultimately with Greek tragedy, even though we recall that to (say) an eighteenth-century spokesman like Johnson such a play was a hybrid, and even though we may note that this particular 'tragedy' was apparently not at first so labelled, but was first listed as a 'history'.[7] With (say) Chekhov's late plays, we note awkwardly that there is something of 'the tragic' here, because *we* perceive something of the requisite affinity—even though their author insisted on the label 'comedy',[8] and even though in most visible particulars these 'serious dramas' derive from the tradition of Greek New Comedy.

By comparison, the identification of Greek tragedies is in practice less controversial, because we do tend to rely on the testimony left to us by the Greeks themselves, and at least there seems little doubt that the Greeks in all periods knew, or thought they knew, what tragedy (*tragôidia*) was. For Aristophanes at the end of *Frogs*, tragedy is what Aeschylus once epitomized and what Euripides has now corrupted. For Aristotle in the *Poetics*, tragedy is an entity which has shown variations over the course of time, and an entity whose specimens present marked variations, even in their 'developed' form, but nevertheless an entity whose specimens pose no problem of identification, and an entity which can be defined—as a *mimêsis* of an action, and so on. In the first instance, we might wish

---

[7] In the Register of the Stationers' Company (26 Nov. 1607): 'A book called Master William Shakespeare his history of King Lear . . .'.

[8] See e.g. Stanislavsky's testimony about *The Three Sisters*: 'after the reading . . . our impressions . . . amazed Chekhov. . . . He had written a . . . comedy and all of us had considered the play a tragedy and even wept over it': C. Stanislavsky, *My Life in Art*, trans. J. J. Robbins (London 1924) 371.

to say, the Greeks identified tragedy (*tragôidia*) by its immediate festal context: a tragedy is a new play (or, equally, a new performance) at a given Attic festival associated with the god Dionysus, and such plays (or performances) were sooner or later listed in inscriptions and elsewhere on that basis. But then, this is clearly not a sufficient means of identification: partly because new tragedies were sooner or later performed on other occasions elsewhere; partly because old tragedies were sooner or later repeated everywhere; but above all because in the very heyday of fifth-century tragedy the spectator at the tragic festival in Athens would witness, and would expect to witness, not only tragedies, but also satyr-plays.

In the heyday of fifth-century tragedy, tragedies and satyr-plays were commonly presented in a set sequence—three tragedies followed by one satyr-play—and in this sequence, one could argue, the contextual identification of the two types was and remained unambiguous and thus, in a sense, the contextual identification of tragedy is itself maintained. However, the day dawns at the tragic festival, at least as early as the year 438 BC, when a Euripides frustrates, or at any rate complicates, the expectations of his audience by producing a sequence of three tragedies followed by an *Alcestis*, which is certainly not a satyr-play, but is rather a sort of tragedy, or an eccentric tragedy, or a hybrid drama, and is discussed as such by scholars of later antiquity.[9] And their identification (whatever it might be), like our identification (whatever *that* might be), is necessarily founded not, or not primarily, on festal context, but on text: that is, on the perceived affinities, or perceived lack of affinities, of this play with tragedy proper. And if we accept *their* identification, we do so in the knowledge that we make a decision to do so, and not simply in passive acknowledgement of a given. And whether we do accept their identification, or offer one of our own, we are unquestionably, and quite reasonably, influenced by our sense both of what 'tragedy' and 'tragic' mean in Greece and of what they mean beyond Greece as well. We are, that is, likely to hesitate to see *Alcestis* as a tragedy *tout court*, and our hesitation will very likely be prompted by the way *Alcestis* prepares, but

---

[9] See above all the 'Aristophanean' Hypothesis (pp. 34–5 in Diggle's OCT [1984]), whose various characterizations (κωμικωτέραν, σατυρικώτερον, etc.) seem to derive from different sources (cf. A. M. Dale, *Euripides, Alcestis* [Oxford 1954] pp. xxxviii–xl).

averts, a catastrophe. In thus averting catastrophe, *Alcestis* only does what is notoriously done by some Euripidean 'tragedies' (or *tragôidiai*) of a later vintage: *Helen, Ion, Orestes*. We may, some of us, hesitate to call those *tragôidiai* 'tragedies' either, but the Greek label and, in general, the pressure of Greek context probably force our hand. With *Alcestis*, in default of that pressure, we—plausibly—allow our sense of affinity at its widest to determine our response. We sense that *Alcestis* stands with *Helen* and the other 'problem' plays,[10] and stands apart from *Bacchae*, from *Oedipus Rex*, and also from *Phèdre* and *King Lear*, and our hesitation is confirmed. Thus, when we proclaim our right to decide which plays from the seventeenth or later centuries count as 'tragedy' on the grounds of perceived affinity, we are actually only doing on a larger scale what we do even with fifth-century drama itself. In fact, whenever we respond to any play, *tragôidia* or not, as a 'tragedy', we must always be taking such a decision. The process is often tacit. It may involve only a subliminal confirmation that, yes, such-and-such a historical label is just. But the process must take place, and each time it takes place we confirm or modify *our* sense of 'tragedy', and equally of the quality or qualities that make tragedy 'tragic', irrespective of whether, in doing so, we consult the now extensive tradition of theorizing about tragedy as a whole.

Irrespective also—it may be helpful to add—of whether our sense of 'the tragic' is specifically of some quality or qualities central to tragic drama, or of a view of life best embodied in tragedy, or of such a view of life with a characteristic metaphysical dimension. The tragic in that first sense is already familiar to the Greeks. It is what, for instance, Aristotle assumes when, at one point in *Poetics* 13, he suddenly puts aside his composite definition of tragedy (*tragôidia*) as an 'imitation of action'. *That* definition is visibly a definition of *all* tragedies. However, Aristotle now tells us, one might argue that Euripides is 'the most tragic' of the poets (*tragikôtatos*) and his plays are 'the most tragic' of plays (*tragikôtatai*), on the grounds that Euripides favours plays with a certain kind of catastrophic end. Clearly, if some tragedies or tragedians are in any sense *more* tragic than others, it can only be that 'tragic'

---

[10] Thus (e.g.) A. P. Burnett's *Catastrophe Survived: Euripides' Plays of Mixed Reversal* (Oxford 1971) offers a series of discussions of (first) *Alcestis* and (then) *IT, Helen*, etc., without any particular acknowledgement that there is anything noteworthy in associating the earlier 'pro-satyric' play with the other group.

is understood with reference to some central defining quality or qualities—something in this instance to do with catastrophic ends—which not all tragedies possess.[11] There are good grounds for arguing that 'the tragic' as a view of life, and even as a meta-physically defined view of life, also has its Greek antecedents, namely in the philosophy of Plato.[12] Understandably, though, 'the tragic' in these senses is especially associated with the German nineteenth century, where it reflects both the special importance ascribed to tragedy by so many writers and thinkers of that age and their preoccupation with large, ultimately existential, issues.[13] Within that century 'the tragic' is associated most of all, no doubt, with Nietzsche, and it is pertinent to cite, as a representative com-ment on that whole epoch, Nietzsche's retrospective gloss on his own celebrated explorations of Greek drama, and much else, in *The Birth of Tragedy*. That first book of Nietzsche's appeared in 1872. Sixteen years later, in 1888, looking back at his first book, Nietzsche claims that in it he had at long last 'found the concept of "the tragic" and at long last knowledge of the psychology of tragedy'. And he goes on to summarize this 'psychology': 'saying *yes* to life even in its strangest and hardest problems: the will to life rejoicing over its own inexhaustibility even in the very sacrifice of its highest types'.[14] In this existentially accented and (as some may think) lurid late-Nietzschean formula, the metaphysical is implic-itly excluded. 'The tragic' as a metaphysical construct is nowhere more apparent than in that earlier book, where Nietzsche argues that tragedy is incomprehensible in Aristotelian terms as a mere 'imitation of nature'; it is rather (he proposes) that with its creation and destruction of individuals, tragedy offers us a presentiment, terrifying yet uplifting, of that 'primordial unity' which underlies the 'world of phenomena'.[15] This metaphysic—essentially Schopenhauerian and distantly neo-Platonic—is then rejected, along with others, by the anti-metaphysical evangelist of the death

[11] For a different view of this passage, see A. M. van Erp Taalman Kip, p. 132 below; but then again, note also B. Seidensticker's conclusion, p. 393 below, that a sense of the tragic is implicit in Aristotle's notion of *peripeteia*.

[12] See the discussion by Halliwell, pp. 332–49 below; and for a different argu-ment in favour of ascribing a sense of 'the tragic' to Aristotle, see Seidensticker, pp. 377–96 below.

[13] See Silk and Stern, *Nietzsche on Tragedy*, 225–331.

[14] In *Ecce Homo* ('The Birth of Tragedy', §3): Silk and Stern, *Nietzsche on Tragedy*, 125.

[15] *The Birth of Tragedy*, §22.

of God, to whose all-too-human universe belongs the later formula
for the tragic just quoted. 'Saying *yes* to life, even in its strangest
and hardest problems': for the late Nietzsche those 'strangest and
hardest problems' include quite precisely the problem of existence
in a world devoid of metaphysical consolation or meaning. The
point is worth making, then, that here, at the very apex of modern
theorizing about 'the tragic', this elusive 'tragic' itself, though
unquestionably associated with a view of life, is specifically dissociated from the metaphysical.

Some of what I have just argued is controversial. Some of it would
be challenged, on one ground or another, by various of the contributors to this volume. I hope at least, though, that what I have
said helps to clarify the *coherence* of a collection of essays which
variously discuss 'tragedy' or 'the tragic' with or without reference
to metaphysics or a view of life, and Greek tragedy with or without
explicit reference to later tragedy or later theory. Other variations—in perspective, in theme, in conclusion—can speak for
themselves or are better dealt with in the separate introductions to
the three sections that follow. Those sections, it will be seen, move
from specific readings and contextual discussions to the 'beyond'.
To forestall any possible misconceptions, let me stress that this is
in no sense an ascending sequence, but simply what I take to be the
appropriate disposition of material in line with the subtitle and the
spirit of the volume.

Four practical points. First: authors have been encouraged to
cross-refer to each others' papers, where, but only where, particularly appropriate; the indexes at the back of the book should allow
a reader to compare different positions on common or related topics without undue difficulty. Secondly, in the notes to this introduction and the chapters that follow, various modern works are
cited in abbreviated form; full details are to be found in the
Bibliography. Thirdly, in confronting the familiar problem of the
style of representing Greek proper names ('Oedipus', 'Oidipous',
and so on), I have not imposed a uniform style on the whole volume. This is because the variation between Grecizing ('Oidipous')
and Romanizing ('Oedipus') now has an established ideological
significance related to the issues, discussed above, concerning historicism, which it is not for an editor to conceal or distort. Most
readers will be used to the variants. In the indexes Greek names are

usually listed in Romanized form, with other spellings cited alongside. And fourthly, the use of the Greek language itself. In the text, all Greek is accompanied by an English translation (the contributor's own, unless otherwise specified), with the exception of a few single words in general currency in books on Greek literature or culture which will be familiar to anyone likely to read this book, notably: *polis*, 'city state'; *oikos*, 'household'; *genos* 'family, kin'; *dêmos*, 'the people', 'the democratic assembly'; *logos*, 'language', 'argument', 'discourse', 'story'; *muthos*, 'story', 'myth', and also, in Aristotle's terminology, 'plot', versus *êthos*, his term for 'character'; *peripeteia* and *anagnôrisis*, Aristotle's terms for 'reversal' and 'recognition'; and *mimêsis*, his term for 'imitation', 'version', 're-presentation'; *psuchê*, 'spirit', 'life'; *daimôn*, 'god', 'divine power', 'fortune'; *thiasos*, 'company, group of revellers'; *kômos*, 'revel', 'procession of revellers'; *kommos*, a sung antiphonal 'lament'; *agôn*, 'contest'; *rhêsis*, 'speech'; *skênê*, the tragic 'stage'; *orchêstra*, the 'dance floor' on which members of the tragic chorus (*choreutai*) performed; *stasimon*, 'choral song', and specifically one of the 'stationary' songs that followed the *parodos*, the chorus's 'entrance song' (compare the *parodoi*, the 'wings' through which the chorus made their entrance); *chorêgia*, the institutionalized system of 'defraying the expense' of a chorus; *pathos* (a scene of) 'suffering' (to be distinguished from 'pathos'—without italics—in the modern sense). Greek quoted in the text is usually in Greek script, but in some essays there have been particular reasons for preferring transliteration.

Finally, it remains to express my gratitude to all those—speakers and other delegates—at the 1993 conference who helped to generate this book; to those who generously gave me help and advice at various stages of the project, notably Pat Easterling, Bernard Gredley, Edith Hall, Marsh McCall, Oliver Taplin, and Michael Trapp; to Yumna Khan for assistance with the indexes; to Hilary O'Shea and the Oxford University Press for their positive and flexible attitude to the whole enterprise, and equally to the staff of the Press for their meticulous attention to detail; above all, to the contributors to the volume for their forbearance and their willingness to engage in dialogue both with each other and especially with their interventionist editor.

M.S.S.

March 1995

PART I
Greek Tragedy: Readings

INTRODUCTORY NOTE

In this opening section five pairs of readings and counter-readings of Greek tragedy yield ten very different approaches to particular plays.

We begin with Calame, Buxton, and *Oedipus Rex*, partly because, from Aristotle to Nietzsche and beyond, this is for so many admirers of Greek tragedy the model play, partly because the Calame–Buxton debate serves to introduce a series of central issues, from theoretical perspective to the status of tragedy as a theatrical medium, from the importance of mood ('pathos') to the relation between human and divine, from the distinctive role of knowledge to the special importance of the individual's isolation once in a state of knowledge in this tragedy and—ultimately?—in tragedy as a whole. Using as points of reference both Aristotle's *Poetics* and the ideas of the sophist Gorgias, Calame sees in the *Oedipus* a drama which calls into question the premises of dramatic spectacle. The self-blinding in particular is interpreted as the 'annihilation of identity' at the moment of knowledge, as well as the negation of theatrical logic. Buxton's qualifications to this argument lay particular stress on the elusive significance of the 'blind mask', on the problem of knowing what constitutes real knowledge in *Oedipus Rex*, and on the complex meaning of the final gesture of separation in the play.

What *Oedipus Rex* is to Aristotle and Nietzsche, *Antigone* is to Hegel, and the treatments of this play by Foley and Trapp reflect the sense of the centrality of conflict that engendered Hegel's special interest in this tragedy above all others. For Foley the tragic conflict between Creon and Antigone involves not only competing obligations, but competing versions, or articulations, of moral choice, male and female. Quite apart from the clear implications of this argument for contemporary gender-studies (which Foley herself makes explicit), the argument serves as a fresh exemplification of the Vernantian principle that Attic tragedy problematizes civic values and discourse, by undermining Creon, spokesman of the political (that is, male) mode of morality. For Trapp, on the other hand, problematization is indeed of the essence, but what is problematized is moral deliberation as such. Accepting Foley's demonstration of Antigone as would-be persuader (against Creon's 'monotone absolutism') and as representative of the 'morality of care' (against Creon's abstractions), he suggests nevertheless that (more disturbingly than Foley allows) Antigone's moral mode and, for good measure, all other available moral modes, are challenged too.

Lee and Arnott confront the very different conflict, or at least contrastive representation, of Ion and Creusa in one of Euripides' challenging dramatic hybrids, *Ion*. Lee's analysis sets out to reveal the many movements and redrawings of mood in a play which seems at one moment dark, at another humorously light, and at another elusively ironic, and relates these modal shifts to son and mother's contrasting sense of time and, behind that, to their separate struggles with ignorance and knowledge wherein he locates the 'tragic dimension' of the play. *En route* Lee notes the use *Ion* makes of a 'realist' emphasis on the specificities of life. The significance of this emphasis is reconsidered by Arnott, who offers the double argument that, whereas realism activates or intensifies audience involvement in the tragic, in this play, as in Euripides' later plays in general, the disjunction between 'reality' and 'the haloed glories of myth' constitutes an incipient tragic conflict of its own. By way of qualification, though, Arnott points to the 'divine frame' within which the human suffering is placed as at least one significant feature of the play which links it to the bleaker world of *Hippolytus* or *Trojan Women*.

Van Erp Taalman Kip and Garvie focus on our sole surviving connected trilogy, Aeschylus' *Oresteia*. Van Erp Taalman Kip argues that specific contradictions between Clytemnestra's position as presented in *Agamemnon*, on the one hand, and in *Choephori* and *Eumenides,* on the other—its comparative defensibility in the first play as against its total indefensibility in the others—creates a 'dividing-line' between *Agamemnon* and the rest of the trilogy. *We,* however, are predisposed to ignore this division because of our *modern* interest in tragic insolubility, which leads us rather to asso-

ciate *Agamemnon* and *Choephori* (which offer problems) and play
down *Eumenides* (which offers a solution) or else to reaffirm the
'unity' of the trilogy on thematic or other grounds. Central to her
argument is an insistence on the special importance of a cluster of
related issues to the whole of the trilogy: moral responsibility,
guilt, innocence, and divine compulsion. Garvie confronts this
thesis directly, reasserting the more orthodox position that
Agamemnon and *Choephori* do indeed stand together as a coherent
sequence of morally and insolubly complex tragedy, but then
argues that, for all the Athenian 'solution' of *Eumenides,* the logic
of the trilogy as a whole remains essentially unresolved and in that
sense a 'tragic' unity. Against van Erp Taalman Kip, he insists too
that modern notions of 'the tragic' are not anachronistically 'modern' and that most Greek tragedies do in fact bear them out.

Like Calame and Buxton, Segal and Easterling bring to the fore
several of the issues that recur over the whole volume: catharsis
and audience response, ritual and the lament, the individual and
the collective, and (like Garvie) the question of closure. In a discussion that ranges over a number of plays from *Hippolytus* to
Ajax, but that (again like Calame's) comes to rest on *Oedipus Rex,*
Segal makes use of Aristotle's concept of 'catharsis', which he
interprets, or reinterprets, as a collective response of emotional
release that is mirrored, above all, by certain kinds of tragic closure. His particular concern is with closures involving ritual
lamentation on-stage which serve as 'inclusive gestures for the
audience'; such emotional resolution, however, is seen as compatible with intellectual uncertainty, though often in tension with it.
Easterling seeks to clarify Segal's terms of reference by a scrutiny
of closure, ritual, and catharsis in *Oedipus at Colonus, Ajax,* and
Segal's own example, *Oedipus Rex.* Noting that the association of
closure and shared weeping in a ritual context holds good only for
a limited set of Greek plays, and insisting that the norm in any case
is 'incomplete rituals' or 'sketches of ritual', she proposes, in place
of Segal's 'ritual sharing of tears', an alternative and more comprehensive model of communal response: witnessing. On her reading,
it is above all the witnessing chorus, always present at the tragic
closure, which gives the audience its emotional and intellectual
cues.

These particular readings raise—as any purposeful reading
must—large questions of various kinds. One question for any

reader of these readings is the question of their representative status. Can—how far can—what are presented here as significant features or major premises of *Oedipus Rex* and *Antigone*, *Ion* and the *Oresteia*, *Hippolytus* and *Oedipus at Colonus*, be taken as significant features or major premises of Greek tragedy as a whole (to go no further, for the moment)? Lee and Arnott, in the distinctive terrain of 'late Euripides', are in a sense setting out to demarcate the norms of 'Greek tragedy' *per contra*. Van Erp Taalman Kip and Garvie are, for a quite different reason, dealing with the untypical (a connected trilogy), especially untypical in terms of Greek tragedy as we have it. By contrast, Calame and Buxton, and again Foley and Trapp, are focusing directly on particular instances and particular versions of what are certainly taken to be significant characteristics of the genre. Finally, in the case of the 'inclusive gestures' and the 'witnessing' that Segal and Easterling are concerned to articulate, the degree to which these are or are not characteristically tragic features is an explicit item in the debate.

Other issues recur too. One intermittent preoccupation of these readings is with hermeneutics. In particular, the status of Aristotle's *Poetics* for the interpreter of Greek tragedy is a recurrent theme: the value of the *Poetics* in this sense is affirmed by Calame and by Segal, but treated more sceptically by Garvie and Easterling; we shall find both attitudes maintained by contributors later in the volume. Meanwhile the central issue, or problematic, of *what* tragedy or the tragic itself *is* comes into view, notably (and, already, quite variously) in the essays by Calame and Buxton, by Arnott, by van Erp Taalman Kip, and by Garvie.

Vision, Blindness, and Mask: The Radicalization of the Emotions in Sophocles' *Oedipus Rex*

CLAUDE CALAME

As the twenty-first century draws near, one avenue of enquiry remains open to the contemporary student amidst the plethora of attempts to define Attic and Greek tragedy: the return to indigenous theory. However, if we wish to avoid the pitfalls of an image refracted through the lens of classical comedy, we must confront the profusion of readings of Aristotle's *Poetics*. And if we find our way through this forest, we are faced with yet another set of difficulties and paradoxes in the form of a text written on the basis of class notes which appears to be interpreting tragic performances only at a certain remove and from the point of view of the culture of the fourth century, a culture in great part condemned to the written word.[1]

This, at least, is one way of explaining a strange exclusion which we find in the *Poetics*. Let us look briefly at the text in question (1450ᵃ7–ᵇ20). We know that in Aristotelian terms, the specific nature of tragedy is determined by six elements, presented in ranked order as follows: plot, character, thought, diction (or delivery), song, and, finally, the element Aristotle calls *opsis*, which covers everything to do with vision and sight, and which in English is generally translated as 'spectacle'. However, while visual expression complements diction and song, it is definitively excluded from Aristotle's definition of the poetic art; it is relegated to the sphere of the costume designer, not that of the poet. The consequences for Aristotle are clear: tragedy can create its effects outside the context of theatrical competition, even without actors. Ridding tragedy of all elements of *opsis* means reducing tragedy to a text, setting it apart from its public performance in the context of the cult of Dionysus. Indeed, it makes of tragedy a modern literary text, cut off from its enunciative context.

What appears as an exclusion becomes a paradox when Aristotle takes up the problem of vision in his discussion—no longer in the descriptive but now in the normative mode—of the emotions which tragedy is meant to engender.[2] The essence of the poet's art is to arouse fear and pity in the audience, not by means of spectacle, which is, in the end, simply a problem of staging (*chorêgia*), but rather through plot. Aristotle sees in the story of Oedipus as told by Sophocles the model for a plot capable of arousing the emotions as tragedy should—for an audience which Aristotle imagines as auditors, not as readers! It is thus paradoxical that the tragedy Aristotle chooses as a model (oral!) text should be *Oedipus Rex*, a work which is, as many modern readers have pointed out, entirely concerned with the problem of vision.

ARISTOTLE AND SPECTACLE

We must start by returning to Aristotle's text, where we find that the hierarchy of six elements distinctive to tragedy is part of a larger semiotic division at the heart of his reflections on the poetic art. At the beginning of his treatise, the critic posits that every poetic expression can be defined as a product of representation (*mimêsis*). The mimetic procedure can then be divided into three aspects (1447^a13-18): means employed (*en hois*), object represented (*ha*), and mode of realization (*hôs*).[3] In the case of tragedy, diction and song belong to the category of means employed; plot, character, and thought to the object represented; and spectacle to its mode of realization. Aristotle goes on to conclude that, as a mode of tragic representation, the visual aspect encompasses all five other elements! Thus, if spectacle is not part of poetics, this is simply because—in the Aristotelian perspective—it is a technique of a different order. From Aristotle's essentialist point of view, the tragic text itself must be distinguished from its relation with the theatre, that is, from its ritual and dramatic execution.[4]

While the conclusion of this chapter devoted to defining the specificity of tragedy thus excludes the visual aspect of tragic representation from the poetic art, the visual is none the less that mode which best 'seduces the spirit' (*psuchagôgikon*). At this point, then,

Aristotle's theory brings the effect of tragedy under scrutiny through representation. Indeed, Aristotle's whole attempt to define tragedy through its distinctive elements is guided by the themes of representation (*mimêsis*) and effect, which is elsewhere associated with the term *katharsis*. On *katharsis*, central to the essence of tragedy, we note here only what Aristotle himself has noted: by evoking fear and pity, tragedy purges these emotions in the audience. This proposition, object of much commentary on account of its synthetic character, is clearly taken up and developed when the time comes to define the aim of tragedy and the means by which it attains its effects. While emphasizing the role of plot—and in particular, plots in which great men such as Oedipus fall from happiness to misery—Aristotle cannot deny that fear and pity arise as much from the spectacle itself as from the orchestration of the dramatic action. At the same time, however, Aristotle excludes the visual from the poetic art and, as we have mentioned, imagines a rendition of the story of Oedipus the mere listening to which would cause shivers of pity and fear.[5] However, vision makes a sur-reptitious reappearance in the last chapter of the long discussion devoted to the role of plot, when Aristotle asserts that the aim of a correct orchestration of the story-line is, finally, to 'place before the eyes' by means of linguistic enunciation, that is, to transform the listener into a spectator. The images called into being by words should thus coincide with the representation on stage, or, more specifically, with the emotions evoked by the gestures and perfor-mance of the actors ($1455^a22–3$).[6] In the *evidentia* (*enargestata*) assigned to the art of poetry, it is clearly impossible to overlook sight.

THE VISUAL ENQUIRY

From Aristotle's reflections on the paradigmatic nature of *Oedipus Rex* as tragedy, we turn now to the tragedy itself. We begin (as oth-ers have before) with the observation that the entire prologue of the tragedy plays on the theme of sight. The priest opens by inviting King Oedipus to observe with his own eyes the miserable state in which the epidemic has left the city of Thebes (15 and 22). The priest addresses Oedipus as a god from whom divine intervention is required, as indeed Oedipus has intervened in the past to help the city (47–8 and 52–3). In this passage, he evokes the knowledge of the current king of Thebes, knowledge which depends on 'the voice of a god' or the 'vision of a man' (40–5), 'knowledge' (*oistha*) which we may trace etymologically to the root *wid-* designating sight; finally, knowledge which, by the same token, Sophocles' text links to the name 'Oedipus' (*oidi-pous*, 8, during the king's introduction).[7]

In the tension between past and present—between Oedipus' past acts of salvation upon arriving at Thebes and the city's current state of desperation—the theme of vision undergoes two simultaneous narrative transformations operating at the level of the plot as Sophocles has reformulated it.

From Linguistic Knowledge to Visual Knowledge

In the past as in the present of the drama, Oedipus is faced with the task of solving a riddle—that is, he is asked to interpret enigmatic language. In Proppian terms, the test or trial which has made him 'first among men' (33 and 46; cf. 507–11) and that which, by saving the city, should confirm his reign (46–51), both depend on the decoding of speech. However, these oracular pronouncements are of very different origins.

The first was made by the Sphinx, a singer, even a poetess, but also a 'rough-voiced bard' (36), a woman of 'cunning song' (130), a 'bitch of rhapsody' (391), a young 'prophetess with pointed claws' (1199). Independent of the iconography of the day, which represented the Sphinx as a monster with the wings of a bird and the body of a lioness, the text quite plainly portrays the Sphinx in animal terms: while her voice, like that of all bards, can deceive, it is not through its sweetness or charm but by its throaty, beast-like barkings. However, in contrast to literary tradition, which represented the Sphinx as pure monster who devours raw meat and ravages men, Sophocles brings more ambiguous qualities to her poetic voice.[8] It is a voice which contents itself with posing enigmatic questions, a feminine voice usurping the generally masculine role of bard or singer, a voice, indeed, which takes on the deadly qualities of the songs of Homer's Sirens.

By contrast with the bestial voice of Oedipus' first trial, the second trial involves a divine voice, the voice of Apollo, god who reveals (77), god whose arrival strikes the sight (81), god who gives clear orders (*saphôs*, 106). Unlike the voice of the Sphinx, the voice of the god asks no questions; rather, it answers an interrogation.

Furthermore, contrary to its own custom, this voice, now clearly oracular rather than poetic, makes direct reference to knowledge based on visual observation. Without employing his usual enigmatic language, Phoebus the Brilliant orders 'in broad daylight' (*emphanôs*) that the land be rid of the evil which is sullying Thebes (96–8). Creon, questioned by an Oedipus 'eager to know' (*eisomestha*, 84), has no trouble identifying this evil as the murder of the previous king of the city, Laius.

Oedipus, of course, is in a most peculiar position with regard to the experiential knowledge referred to so clearly by the god of Delphi. A newcomer to Thebes, he knows of his predecessor only through hearsay; he has never actually seen him (*exoid' akouôn*; *ou gar eiseidon ge pô*, 105). Unfortunately, we cannot enter into all the details of this rich passage here. What is important at this point is to notice that the entire search which Oedipus conducts on Apollo's orders, as well as the (transparent) oracle of his own fate and that (equally transparent) given to Laius (711–14), all elaborate on the theme of visual knowledge.[9] On the one hand, we find Jocasta stating that the contradictions which she has discovered in Apollo's pronouncement might prevent her henceforth from 'seeing' the oracular statements (851–8; cf. already 720–5). On the other hand, the revelations of Oedipus' origins by the Corinthian shepherd are understood by the king as signs revealed 'in broad daylight' (1050 and 1058–9). Later on, the Theban shepherd, from whom Oedipus demands an answer, looks him straight in the eye (1121) and draws on knowledge which the king recognizes as superior to his own because based on sight (1115–16). As Creon has stated already (119), he is the only one capable of 'showing what he has seen' (*eidôs phrasai*). It is thus doubly ironic when Oedipus himself concedes that 'no one sees the one who has seen' (293). Finally, we may recall Oedipus' conclusion upon hearing what he has been seeking from the shepherd, sole eyewitness to the fateful events:

> Alas, alas, everything becomes evident [*saphê*].
> O, light of day, would that I could see [*prosblepsaimi*] you
>   today for the last time,
> I, shown up [*pephasmai*] as son of those whose son I should
>   not have been,
> Companion of those whose company I should not have kept,
> Killer of those I should not have killed.
>
> (1182–5)

Here we see, then, a narrative reversal expressed on a double level: first, human knowledge, directed by the questions of a creature simultaneously divine, bestial, and feminine, is replaced by divine knowledge, which becomes the object of human questioning; secondly, knowledge based on words is replaced by knowledge founded in sight. Not only does Creon claim that the deceptive songs of the Sphinx have prevented the Thebans from looking 'at their feet', that is, at what was clearly before them, tempting them rather towards the invisible (*ta aphanê*, 130–1); Oedipus himself also declares that the solution to the riddle posed by the Sphinx was merely a matter of language (*dieipein*, 394). Rejecting as mere language this riddle (which, incidentally, Sophocles declines to cite in its well-known formulation), Oedipus provides the backdrop for the pun on his own name which he makes on the same occasion: *ho mêden **eidôs Oidipous***, 'Oedipus who knows | has seen nothing' (397). However we are to interpret this pun, it is clear that the episode of the Sphinx, unnecessary to the narrative logic of the plot, serves to show up by negative example the nature of true knowledge.[10]

On Vision and Blindness

It is precisely this narrative reversal between linguistic knowledge (required by the riddle) and visual knowledge (divine in origin) which brings us to the second narrative transformation on which the drama of *Oedipus Rex* is based.

Let us re-examine here the famous confrontation between King Oedipus and Tiresias, the soothsayer. While recognizing the necessity of what has been made manifest (*exephênen*, 243) in the oracle, and while protesting against Tiresias' prior refusal to reveal his truth (*xuneidôs ou phraseis*), Oedipus himself refuses to see as soon as he is confronted with the truth as the soothsayer finally formulates it. However, no sooner has Tiresias made his revelation (*ekphênô*, 329; cf. 343) than we are taken from the realm of the visual back to the linguistic: the coincidence between 'polluter' and 'Oedipus' is merely a matter of words (*rhêma*, 355; *logos*, 359); it is nothing more than a riddle (439)! Tiresias is also hiding behind words (358, 360, 362, 364, etc.). Oedipus not only takes at face value the soothsayer's blindness; in his anger he then accuses the old man of deafness; it is, in fact, Tiresias' sanity which is put in question (*nous*, 370–1). This echoes the reference to *phronein* which Tiresias had claimed for himself in his first pronouncements at 316–18 and 326–9, as well as, in a *Ringstruktur*, in the last words he utters at 462. The soothsayer has no further reason to withhold the truth. It is not he, spokesman for Apollo, who is blind, but his questioner who 'sees without seeing' (*kai dedorkas k'ou blepeis*, 413) the house he lives in and the people he lives with, who does not know (*oistha*, 415) what parents he is born of. Note that Tiresias' claim is symmetrical with the statement by Oedipus at 1182–5 which effects the play's first narrative transformation. It follows that the voice of the soothsayer announces the outcome of the second narrative transformation which structures the plot of *Oedipus Rex*: he who now can see the light of day will see only darkness (419), the man of sight will become blind (*tuphlos ek dedorkotos*, 454).[11] It is now that Oedipus is revealed (*phanêsetai*, 453 and 457) to be of genuine Theban origin and not a 'metic foreigner', as formerly supposed (*logôi*, 452)—brother and father of his own children, son and husband to his wife, incestuous rival and murderer of his own father.[12]

Thus the transition from linguistic knowledge to visual knowledge orchestrated by the plot causes, in a kind of figurative chiasmus, the material transition from vision to blindness. The vision of mortal men who think they can see through words is replaced by the belief of the blind, whose mutilation puts them in contact with real visual knowledge, that of the gods. It is necessary, therefore, that Oedipus become a new Tiresias so that his literal blindness may be transformed into metaphorical vision, so that the text may move from the domain of supposition (*gnômê*, 398) to that of truth (*alêtheia*, 356 and 369). To rephrase this transformation in the words of the chorus that mark the end of this scene, Oedipus' simple skill (*sophia*) for solving the Sphinx's riddle becomes true knowledge about the affairs of men, comparable to that possessed by Zeus and Apollo (*eidotes*, 497–511).

The Elimination of Sensory Powers

The moment he possesses true knowledge, Oedipus, in one destructive movement, blinds himself. Just as the text, by employing the term 'ankles' (*arthra*), seems to suggest a relation between feet pierced at the moment the child is exposed (1032–6; cf. 718) and the eyes of an adult pierced by two golden hooks (1270), so Oedipus' blinding of himself can be interpreted as the annihilation of an identity, or rather as its substitution. In blinding himself,

Oedipus renounces an identity associating him, through his name, with knowledge and vision (*eidôs*, 397), and takes up instead the identity of a child 'of chance', Oedipus of the pierced feet, Oedipus the Swollen-Foot (1036 and 1080).[13] Readers have, of course, attempted to go further. Thus, paralleling the suicide of Jocasta, this self-mutilation can be seen as expiatory self-destruction consequent on the unspeakable act of incest. Others have associated it with Oedipus' desire to exile himself (1436 and 1452) on Cithaeron, in turn interpreted as the expulsion of the scapegoat. And if we abandon the text altogether for the symbols of which psychoanalytic criticism holds the secret, feet and eyes become signs for the penis and Oedipus' act signifies self-castration, that is, a means of inflicting upon himself the punishment which follows from parricide and incest.[14]

Nevertheless, prudence requires that we return from theories of expiatory suicide, expulsion of the *pharmakos*, and symbolic castration, to the text itself. From a simple narrative point of view, Oedipus' self-blinding provokes an ironic reversal of the initial situation. This king who, from the beginning of the tragedy, insists on his desire to know (*tach'eisomestha*, 84), who wants to conduct his enquiry face to face (1118–20), and who finally submits to the obvious (1182), can, upon his return to the stage, be heard only as a voice emerging from the shadows (1313–15), a voice which sounds strangely like that of Tiresias (1323). Oedipus' voice is also accompanied by heightened auditory perception (1325–6). However, like the soothsayer on his first appearance (324–33), the dethroned king, reduced to a simple voice, refuses—from this point on—all face-to-face encounters. Revealed now in his polluted state, he can no longer look into the eyes of his own parents, whom he expects to join in Hades soon (1371–2), nor can he bear to see his own children (1375–6), nor the city, nor the statues of the gods (1377–9 and 1384–5, in a 'ring structure'). After this rejection of vision (in language bristling with terms denoting sight) the king then expresses his wish to deprive himself of the sense of hearing as well (1386–9). Oedipus the Blind and the Deaf, in his desire to be hidden, rejected, even killed, calls down upon himself a misery far greater than the punishment inflicted on Tiresias: from this point on, he insists that he be seen and heard by no living person (1436–7). This demand confirms, in fact, his refusal of all light at the moment of self-recognition (1183–5).

Deprived of sight, refusing to hear, Oedipus' only link with the outside world is now tactile (1413); it is touch which substitutes for sight when, in the last scene, Oedipus tries to communicate one last time with his daughters (1464–70, where the verb for touch appears three times!): 'Si je les touche, je les verrai', in the translation of André Bonnard. It is also by touching the hand of Creon that Oedipus solicits his protection for Antigone and Ismene (1510). In this way, the blind man, still speaking, accomplishes his last act on stage.[15]

We thus see a progressive self-deprivation of all sensory capacities, ending with the sense of touch. Accompanying this deprivation is an emotional responsiveness clearly activated as soon as Oedipus realizes the truth of his fate. This emotion is apparent not only in the exclamations which punctuate Oedipus' speech (*iou iou*, 1183; *aiai aiai*, 1307; *iô*, 1313 and 1321; *oimoi, oimoi*, 1316; *pheu pheu*, 1324); it is also felt in the use of melic rhythms in the second kommos, and in particular in the melic anapaests (1307–11) and dochmiacs (1314–15 and 1322–3) which mark a part of Oedipus' responses. Indeed, Oedipus can no longer speak of his fate except in melic rhythms as an accumulation of 'misery' and 'suffering' (*kaka, pathea*, 1330).[16] Nothing is left to Oedipus, beyond perception by touch, but to cry over his lot. This is what he declares at two points (1467 and 1486; cf. 1515), at the moment when he becomes aware, through touch, of the presence of his two daughters, also in tears (1473). His own destiny perpetuates itself in the destinies of his daughters, and Creon will twice be called on to take pity on their tragic lot. Furthermore—whether or not the verses are authentic—it is clearly this lesson which the chorus draws when it concludes sententiously that no mortal can 'see' (*idein!*) himself happy unless he is capable of 'seeing to it' (*episkopounta*) that his life comes to its final days without meeting with suffering (*pathôn*, 1530). These are also the play's last words. When the hero of the tragedy deprives himself of his faculties of perception and communication with the outside world, we are left with a residue: the 'pathemic'.[17]

SPECTACLE AND THE PURGING OF THE EMOTIONS

The *pathos* imposed on the hero as the plot unfolds is not without effect on those interacting with him in the tragic fiction constructed on stage. From this point of view, Antigone and Ismene are not the only ones to mirror the tears of their father with their own. In the *stasimon* which follows immediately on the visual revelation of Oedipus' identity, and then again at the beginning of the *kommos* which follows the news of the blinding, the chorus of old men from Thebes clearly anticipate the reactions of the hero himself. In the last strophe of their last ode, the *choreutai* point to the role played by time in Oedipus' self-recognition, time 'which sees everything' (1213); later, by contrast, they voice their desire, analogous to that of the hero, to 'close their eyes' (1220–1).[18] Most notably, when confronted with the spectacle of Oedipus blinded— 'a spectacle the sight of which causes pity' (*theama eisopsei* . . . *epoiktisai*, 1295–6), as the messenger says—the first reaction of the chorus is to cry out in pain at 'a dreadful fate for men to look upon' (*ô deinon idein pathos anthrôpois*, 1297). The chorus cannot look this spectacle of suffering in the face (*eisidein*, 1303), so great is their terror (*phrikê*, 1306). The *pathos* of Oedipus thus rebounds onto the *choreutai*, spectators of the hero's suffering; their emotion is so strong that, like Oedipus, they can neither see nor hear (1312).[19]

Mask, Confrontation, and Emotions

The pathemic of the dramatic action provokes, therefore, corresponding emotions among those who are watching; and the emotions felt by the *koryphaios* and by the *choreutai*—pity and fear—evoke the emotions which make up, for Aristotle, the essence of tragedy's purpose. We may even ask whether the poetician has not chosen the example of the story of Oedipus precisely to illustrate the process of 'purging' the emotions supposedly provoked by the process of dramatization in tragedy?

Of course, this argument should be qualified. In one of the passages from the *Poetics* cited above (1453[b]1–44), Aristotle imagines an affective reaction on the part of the audience, not the chorus; furthermore, he hopes that their emotions will be roused simply by listening to the text of *Oedipus Rex*. But is it then mere coincidence if, for the only time in the *Poetics*, Aristotle does not use the usual *phobos* to designate the sensation of fear, but rather *phrittein*, the same term used by Sophocles (compare *Poetics* 1453[b]5 with *Oedipus Rex* 1306)?[20] The coincidence between the emotions felt by Sophocles' *choreutai* (often taken as representatives of the spec-

tators assembled at the theatre of Dionysus) and the feelings attributed by Aristotle to the audience of a successful tragedy is, at the
very least, striking.[21] As is the philosopher's effort to demonstrate
that merely hearing the text should awaken those emotions commonly provoked by spectacle.

From the point of view of visual communication, the story of
Oedipus as conceived by Sophocles has a very particular impact.
We must not forget that tragic drama in fifth-century Athens
formed part of the cult practices dedicated to Dionysus
Eleuthereus and performed by different groups in the community.
Furthermore, the ritual acts performed for the Great Dionysia
involved, in particular, the wearing of masks. Aristotle himself is
fully conscious of this fact when he banishes all that has to do with
spectacle from the poetic art, placing it in the domain of the
skeuopoios (1450^b20). Pollux's lexicon tells us that assistants to the
director, known in ancient Greece as 'costume designers', prepared not only the clothing but, more importantly, the masks of
the actors.[22] As I have tried to show in two previous studies, the
mask has a function which is central to tragic representation as cultic action.[23] Disguise through the wearing of masks is a crucial element in the celebration of the god who makes possible the
transition from interior to exterior and vice versa. It is the *sine qua
non* for the theatrical dramatization of a narrative belonging to legendary tradition or to the recent past of a civic community assembled in the sanctuary of Dionysus Eleuthereus in the *hic et nunc* of
the spectacle through which the dramatization takes place. The
spectacle confronts the public without mediation, contrary to the
way in which action is usually kept at a distance by fiction and narrative conventions: such techniques as phraseology evoking times
long gone, adverbs that construct an imaginary space quite different from that in which the listeners find themselves, or the persistent use of the pronominal form 'he', in place of the 'I' or 'you' of
direct confrontation. By contrast, here it is only the mask that is
capable of re-creating a certain narrative distance, or, more
exactly, it is only the mask that allows direct confrontation simultaneously with dissimulation. This double function can be traced
to the etymology of the Greek term for mask: *prosôpon* can be
understood both as 'that which is close to the eyes' and 'that which
faces the eyes' (of another). On its own terms, the word for mask
appears to imply the ideas both of appearance and of confrontation

through the gaze.[24] Analysing the actual use of these tragic and comic masks during dramatic representations for the Great Dionysia, we find that the function of the classical Athenian mask is first to dissimulate, and only secondly to identify. Thus, the individual and social identity of the real face of the actor is hidden, without, on the other hand, precisely representing the identity of the character on stage. Far from creating an effect of contiguity or alienation, or even reincarnation—functions commonly, though incorrectly, attributed to masks in general—the tragic mask of the classical period serves to distance a voice and a gaze which one takes to be the hero of the legend, represented live on stage through the dramatization of the narrative action. It 'shifts' the voice and gaze of the hero, for the mouth and eyes are the two organs which correspond to holes in the mask's surface: they let the voice and gaze of the actor appear to the spectators, beyond the hero he is miming. The mask creates a confrontation between the dramatic action and the public, while, by the same token, mediating this confrontation. The mask thus reinforces the mimetic effect of the dramatic fiction.

Emotional Self-destruction, Theatrical Self-negation

Thus Oedipus' self-inflicted blindness has an import beyond the story as reworked and dramatized by Sophocles. It is a gesture that calls into question the very foundations of tragic 'discourse', the conventions of masked representation as performed at the cult of Dionysus Eleuthereus. In appearing on stage masked but deprived of sight, Oedipus negates the possibility of visual (though mediated) communication between actor and spectator, just as his desire to become deaf works as a rejection of the ambivalent effects of speech. Of course Tiresias too appears on stage in a mask without eyes. But his blindness, imposed by a goddess, is a *donnée*, a fact given by tradition. In contrast, Oedipus' self-blinding is an act integrated into the plot as Sophocles has reformulated it. In blinding himself, Oedipus calls into question not only his own identity as actor in the drama, but also that of the wearer of his mask. Oedipus cannot, therefore, take on the role of *pharmakos* or scapegoat which some have wished to attribute to him: what would we make of an expiatory victim who actively wishes to be chased from the city (1289–90, 1380–1, 1436–7, and 1450–1), but finds himself in the end invited to return to his palace (1515)?[25] Rather, it is in blinding himself that Oedipus comes closest to the figure of Tiresias even as he distances himself from him. In the traditional story, the soothsayer is blinded by a deity for having seen a divine body; his blindness confers on him, in return, powers of divination which give him access to the realm of the gods. Of this story, Sophocles' tragedy borrows only the fact of Tiresias' powers of divination (300–1). By mutilating himself at his own hand (*autokheir*, 1331), despite the presence of Apollo behind this act (1329; cf. 1258), Oedipus sanctions knowledge which appears limited to that of his own identity (1183–5), but which in fact grows to be that of his *daimôn*, his *moira* imposed by the gods (1311 and 1458), as the chorus assumes at 1300–2.[26] To know oneself is also to know the foundations of the human condition; it is Delphic knowledge, placed under Apollo's control.[27]

The revelation of the truth guaranteed by the god means the end of the dramatic illusion. If the self-blinding takes Oedipus to the limits of human knowledge, the same gesture brings him to the limits of tragic staging. It has been mentioned that at the end of the play, the hero, instead of going to Cithaeron as he wishes, disappears into the palace. As for his own daughters, Oedipus even thinks that they will no longer be able to attend any festivities in the city without crying (1489–91). If the speech continues for a moment, if there are to be further festivities none the less, it is only to provoke tears. It looks as if Oedipus' drama as staged in *Oedipus Rex* spells out the ultimate implications of a theological truth: no speech is really needed any more, no vision, even no masks. What remains—beyond knowledge of the destiny of mankind, beyond the disastrous consequences of realizing the fate laid out by the gods and revealed by Apollo—is *pathos*, incarnated in the weeping daughters of Oedipus.

Before concluding our enquiry, let us look briefly at the sophist Gorgias, contemporary of Sophocles, who set forth reflections on the power of *logos* which bring us back to those developed by the tragedian in the dramatization of *Oedipus Rex*. While we have no space here to enter into the details of his complex theory, we note that *The Defence of Palamedes*—that epic hero, fooled by the trickery of Ulysses—permits Gorgias to draw a clear distinction between exact knowledge and apparent knowledge (*eidôs akribôs ê doxazôn*). The former is based on sight (*idôn*) and on the direct participation or testimony of a participant; the rest is *doxa*. What, then, is the power of *logos* if not that of arousing or appeasing the emotions? 'Calming fear, relieving affliction, provoking joy, heightening pity', as Gorgias states in his *In Praise of Helen*. It is poetry in particular which can cause in its listeners shivers of fear (*phrikê periphobos*), tears of pity (*eleos poludakrus*), and the sorrow of regret (*pothos philopenthês*). Is this to say that only speech has the privilege of provoking the emotions? This is not where the conclusion to *In Praise of Helen* leads us. In fact, Gorgias affirms, the beautiful Lacedaemonian was not moved by the appearance (*doxa*) of the words addressed to the listener; rather, she was touched by the active visual dynamics of the Greeks' physiological representation of Eros.[28]

Thus, we may posit an analogy between the feelings evoked by Gorgias and those aroused in the actors or *choreutai* at Oedipus' act of self-negation; by proxy, we may take these emotions for those felt by the auditors and spectators of the tragedy. Note, however, that *Oedipus Rex* goes further than *In Praise of Helen*. If, for Gorgias, the emotions belong to the domain of linguistic, even visual, appearance, for Sophocles they are the result of the negation of this same appearance. They are aroused not only by calling into question the power of speech, but even more by the negation of the possibility of distanced communication as offered by the mask. However, while he questions the very foundations of tragic spectacle, Sophocles is not a sophist: beyond the illusions of *doxa*, language and sight make apparent the power of Apollo and of the *daimôn*. It is the dramatic and pernicious revelation of this divine reality which, in the end, causes the emotions described by Gorgias, a revelation which only a being of divine inspiration such as Tiresias (410), with his mask of a blind man, can resist. As far as *Oedipus Rex* is concerned, it is thus to the soothsayer that we must leave the last word, at the moment when he declares to Oedipus:

> I will not leave before saying what I have come for.
> Your face [*prosôpon*], I do not fear it; you cannot destroy me.

> (447–8)

Vision and its negation are so profoundly present in Sophocles' text that, like Aristotle, we might be tempted to overlook the effects of the spectacle itself. In so doing, we would lose sight (!) of the self-negating, and, in this sense, Dionysiac dimensions of the tragedy of *Oedipus Rex*.

Through this questioning of speech, vision, and theatrical illusion, *Oedipus Rex* brings us to the general lesson of an Athenian fifth-century drama: the 'learning through suffering' of something fundamental about the relationship between the human condition and the gods. This is the *pathei mathos* which Zeus concedes to mortals, according to the chorus of Aeschylus' *Agamemnon* (177).

To summarize what is 'tragic' about this learning, we would have to make distinctions between the more local and more general concerns of Greek classical tragedy as performance. First, masks and costume—with their functions of dramatization and confrontation, but also through the particular song of the chorus combined with dance and music—represent the ritual elements of Attic tragedy in cultic local festivals dedicated to Dionysus. Secondly, through plots generally drawn from the Greek heroic tradition, Attic tragedy discusses and questions problems of civic concern like the relationship between *genos* and *polis*: this is the Dionysiac, civic, and in part Panhellenic aspect of classical tragedy. And finally, on a more universal but still Dionysiac level, Greek tragedy confronts us, through the questioning of language and through suffering, with the limits of the human condition and with its metaphysical foundations:

> *ô deinon idein pathos anthrôpois*
>
> O dreadful fate for men to look upon.
>
> (1297)

Notes

1. The fragmented and unsystematic character of the *Poetics* is summed up well by M. Magnien, *Aristote: Poétique* (Paris 1990) 19–24; see also Halliwell, *Aristotle's Poetics*, 1–41.
2. The interlacing of descriptive, normative, and genetic (essentialist) perspectives in Aristotle's reflections on the poet's art is illuminated by J. M. Schaefer, *Qu'est-ce qu'un genre littéraire?* (Paris 1989) 10–25.
3. This distinction is made again with complete consistency in 1448ª24–5. It is applied to tragedy in 1450ª7–14 (a difficult passage which it is advisable to read with the help of the commentary by Dupont-Roc and Lallot, *Aristote: La Poétique*, 199–203).
4. This distinction underlies the point about the perfecting of the form of tragedy at 1449ª7–9. The items not treated in the *Poetics* are discussed by D. Lanza, *Aristotele: Poetica* (Milan 1987) 32–44. On another matter, Taplin, *Stagecraft of Aeschylus*, 477–9, has effectively

demonstrated that *opsis* designates not only straightforward spectacular effects (as described by Plutarch, *Glor. Ath.* 348e–f), but the totality of visual elements; cf. M. S. Silk, 'The "Six Parts of Tragedy" in Aristotle's *Poetics*: Compositional Process and Processive Chronology', *PCPS* 40 (1994) 109, with n. 7.

5. Cf. *Poet.* 1450ᵇ16–18, 1449ᵇ24–8, 1452ᵇ28–30, and 1453ᵇ1–7. If one looks closely at the formulation of 1453ᵇ8–14, it is clear that not only 'spectacle' but, above all, 'actions' must provoke pity and fear in order to induce the pleasure experienced in the performance of tragedy; the expression ἐν τοῖς πράγμασιν ἐμποιητέον may, therefore, refer to the idea of 'l'inscription dans les faits', as proposed by Dupont-Roc and Lallot, *Aristote: La Poétique*, 186–93. Alongside this admirable exegesis of *katharsis* by the French commentators, one may profitably consult the restatements of D. W. Lucas, *Aristotle, Poetics* (Oxford 1968) 273–90 and Halliwell, *Aristotle's Poetics*, 168–201, while noting that in two places (1452ᵇ38 and 1453ᵃ2) fear and pity have as complement τὸ φιλάνθρωπον, the idea of order, of justice being done (on which see Dupont-Roc and Lallot, *Aristote: La Poétique*, 242–3); see also n. 28 below. Lucas (150), argues that at 1453ᵇ6 the expression ὁ τοῦ Οἰδίπου μῦθος could refer equally well to the plot of the *OT* or the whole play, though not to the story of Oedipus.

6. The peculiar problem posed by a form of theatre which has to put before its audience and make 'effective' an action which is being performed by other means on stage is well presented by Dupont-Roc and Lallot, *Aristote: La Poétique*, 278–84. On syntactic grounds the reading ἐναργέστατα is nevertheless preferable to the *lectio facilior* ἐνέργεστατα: see my arguments in this connection in 'Quand dire c'est faire voir: L'évidence dans la rhétorique antique', *Études de Lettres* 4 (1991) 3–22. In her article, 'Les Mots qui voient', in C. Reichler (ed.), *Essais sur l'interprétation des textes* (Paris 1988) 157–82, N. Loraux has perhaps been unduly influenced by J. Lacan, *Le Séminaire VII: L'Éthique* (Paris 1985) 295, when she seems to dismiss this coincidence of visual λέξις and spectacle.

7. The etymological relationship between οἶδα, εἶδον and *video* is reaffirmed by Chantraine, *Dictionnaire étymologique*, 779–80 . In a figure of grating tragic irony, v. 397 offers an etymologizing word-play, undoubtedly explicit, on the name of Oedipus, linking it with οἶδα: see the recent comments by Pucci, *Oedipus and the Fabrication of the Father*, 34, 66–73, 165–6; cf. also n. 13 below.

8. Cf. Aesch. *Sept.* 541 and 776 (ὠμόσιτος, ἁρπάξανδρα); see already Hes. *Theog.* 326 and *Oedipodea*, Arg. (Bernabé), also Pind. fr. 177d Maehler, which mentions the savage jaws of the Sphinx. Further passages are cited by M. Delcourt, *Œdipe ou la légende du conquérant*²

(Paris 1981) 104–40; her interpretation of the Sphinx as not only murderous prophetess, but also demonic she-lover, does not stand up to a comparison of the texts with the visual representations: cf. J.-M. Moret, *Œdipe, la Sphinx et les Thébains: Essai de mythologie iconographique*, i (Geneva 1984) 10–29, 79–91. The ambivalence of the Sphinx's words is considered by Segal, *La Musique du Sphinx*, 110–15, and the tyrannical nature of its mode of speech is defined by A. Iriarte, 'L'Ogresse contre Thèbes', *Métis* 2 (1987) 91–105.

9. The course of the visual investigation conducted by Oedipus, which in fact constitutes the plot of the tragedy, has been traced, step by step, by Seale, *Vision and Stagecraft*, 215–60. His careful study removes the need for a detailed analysis here. One must agree with Segal, *La Musique du Sphinx*, 115, that through the respective figures of the Sphinx and Apollo the *OT* constructs an opposition between 'unintelligibility' and 'intelligible speech', but not that there is 'convergence' (pp. 110 and 115) between the animal's riddles and the god's oracles: to get from one to the other, Oedipus has to be transformed into a seer, a second Tiresias.

10. In two successive studies, narrative and then comparative, L. Edmunds has shown that, from the standpoint of the plot, the resolution of the riddle of the Sphinx is a doublet of the act of parricide in so far as both constitute a means of gaining the power of kingship. The Sphinx episode may thus be considered 'secondary': cf. *The Sphinx in the Oedipus Legend* (Königstein Ts. 1981) 1–39 (reprinted in L. Edmunds and A. Dundes (edd.), *Oedipus: A Folklore Casebook* [New York 1984] 147–73) and 'La Sphinx thébaine et Paul Tyaing, l'Œdipe birman', in C. Calame (ed.), *Métamorphoses du mythe en Grèce antique* (Geneva 1988) 213–27. In the expression πρὸς ποσί it is hard to see any reference to the content of the plot, as suggested indirectly by one of the scholiast's interpretations (*ad OT* 130, p. 170 Papageorgios and p. 106 Longo) and as argued most recently by C. Chase, 'Oedipal Textuality: Reading Freud's Reading of Oedipus', *Diacritics* 9 (1979) 54–68 (reprinted in id., *Decomposing Figures: Rhetorical Readings in the Romantic Tradition* [Baltimore 1986] 175–95): cf. R. D. Dawe, *Sophocles, Oedipus Rex* (Cambridge 1982) 102–3, and contrast Bollack, *L'Œdipe roi de Sophocle*, ii, 72.

11. This transformation is described by Tiresias as a συμφορά (454), a reversal of fortune; reversal is a formative element of the tragic plot according to Aristotle (*Poet.* 1452ᵃ22–9), who cites the *OT* precisely in this connection: cf. Dupont-Roc and Lallot, *Aristote: La Poétique*, 231–2.

12. For the analysis of the 'reversal' in *OT* the classic work remains that of Vernant, 'Ambiguïté et renversement', 101–31. The relationship

between blindness and true vision is correctly stressed by Buxton 'Blindness and Limits', 22–37, while M. Coray, *Wissen und Erkennen bei Sophokles* (Basle 1993) 169–70, insists on the power of φρονεῖν as consciousness.

13. At 1031–6 the text establishes a probable relationship between the piercing of the feet and the name Oedipus (derived in this case from οἰδέω, 'swell'). This is not enough to justify the inclusion of this Sophoclean figure in the set of tyrants marked off by disability, as has been suggested by, notably, J.-P. Vernant, 'Le Tyran boiteux: D'Œdipe à Périandre', *Le Temps de la réflexion* 2 (1981) 235–55 (reprinted in Vernant and P. Vidal-Naquet, *Œdipe et ses mythes* [Paris 1986] 54–78) as well as M. Bettini and A. Borghini, 'Edipo lo zoppo', in Gentili and Pretagostini (edd.), *Edipo*, 215–33: see my thoughts on the subject in 'Le Nom d'Œdipe', in Gentili and Pretagostini (edd.), *Edipo*, 395–407. On the other hand, this new etymologizing word-play on the name of Oedipus does reinforce the sense of the destruction of an identity founded, in a first etymological play, on (visual) knowledge (~*oida*). For the relationship between the two parecheses, see P. Pucci, 'Reading the Riddles of *Oedipus Rex*', in Pucci (ed.), *Language and the Tragic Hero: Essays on Greek Tragedy in Honor of Gordon Kirkwood* (Atlanta 1988) 131–54. On the role played by τύχη in the destiny of Oedipus, see Segal, *Tragedy and Civilization*, 211–14, 227, as well as Pucci, *Oedipus and the Fabrication of the Father*, 70–2, 79–89; see further n. 27 below.

14. The interpretations cited here are those proposed respectively by: N. Loraux, 'L'Empreinte de Jocaste', *L'Écrit du temps* 12 (1986) 35–54; Vernant, 'Ambiguïté et renversement', 114–26; and G. Devereux, 'The Self-blinding of Oidipous in Sophokles: *Oidipous Tyrannos*', *JHS* 93 (1973) 36–49 (which should be read from the sceptical perspective suggested by Buxton, 'Blindness and Limits', 33–4); see also L. Edmunds, 'Il Corpo di Edipo: Struttura psico-mitologica', in Gentili and Pretagostini (edd.), *Edipo*, 237–53 (more thoughts on this subject in Pucci, *Oedipus and the Fabrication of the Father*, 76–8 and 153 with nn. 22–7).

15. V. Di Benedetto, *Sofocle* (Florence 1983) 127–30, points out that, in contrast to the archaic conception of pollution by touching, here these tactile gestures acquire a strongly affecting quality. On this, see also now the remarks of Segal, *Oedipus Tyrannus*, 140–2, who shows how Oedipus is transformed from virtual φαρμακός into a being one can touch.

16. See the metrical analysis put forward by Bollack, *L', Œdipe roi de Sophocle*, i. 314–15, 327–8. On the signification of these various cries of lamentation, see M. Alexiou, *The Ritual Lament in Greek Tradition* (Cambridge 1974) 135–7. J. Gould, 'The Language of Oedipus', in

H. Bloom (ed.), *Sophocles* (New York 1990) 207–22, speaks of the 'total alienation' that separates Oedipus from the chorus in their capacity as citizens of Thebes.

17. The authenticity of these textually difficult closing lines (1524–30) is widely contested: cf. Dawe, *Sophocles, Oedipus Rex*, 247, and Bollack, *L'Œdipe roi de Sophocle*, iv. 1038–54. The 'pathemic' dimension of discourse (understood as 'ensemble des propriétés manifestables de l'univers passionnel') is defined and explored by A. J. Greimas and J. Fontanille, *Sémiotique des passions: Des états de choses aux états d'âme* (Paris 1991) 83–99. H.-T. Lehmann, *Theater und Mythos: Die Konstitution des Subjekts im Diskurs der antiken Tragödie* (Stuttgart 1991) 44–50, notes that the tragic voice is often associated less with dialogue than with the expression of emotion.

18. Commentators on this passage are not sure whether the expression refers to the peaceful sleep enjoyed by the chorus before the fatal discovery, or to a reaction of shame or a wish for death provoked by the revelation: cf. Dawe, *Sophocles, Oedipus Rex*, 220–1, and Bollack, *L'Œdipe roi de Sophocle*, iii. 816–18, who reasonably opts for the second interpretation.

19. Di Benedetto, *Sofocle*, 121–7, has described the sympathetic interaction which arises between Oedipus and the chorus in this essential scene, while Segal, *Oedipus Tyrannus*, 148–53, stresses the complementarity built up between the vision of blinded Oedipus and the words describing what happened in the palace. Stanford, *Greek Tragedy and the Emotions*, 76–90, offers some thoughts on the role of the visual in arousing tragic emotions, especially through gestures.

20. On this, see the remarks of Lucas, *Aristotle, Poetics*, 149–50. On the interpretation of this passage, see the references given in n. 5 above. Segal in the present volume (below, pp. 166–8) shows that the whole closing part of *OT* puts on stage those same emotions that are required of the audience.

21. In the tragedy, the term οἶκτος (ἐποικτίσαι), used by the members of the chorus to express their sense of pity at the sight of the blinded Oedipus (1296; cf. also 1462, 1473, and 1508), is equivalent to the term ἔλεος used elsewhere, notably in Aristotle: cf. Stanford, *Greek Tragedy and the Emotions*, 23–6; according to Segal (in the present volume: below, p. 168), the cathartic effect of the emotions undergone by the leading players in the *OT* is expressed in the tears they shed (1473, 1486). We may recall that it is particularly on the emotional level that the voice of the tragic chorus may coincide with the mood of the audience: see my thoughts on this subject in 'From Choral Poetry to Tragic Stasimon: The Enactment of Women's Song', *Arion* 3 (1994/5) 136–54.

22. Poll. 4. 115; cf. Ar., *Eq.* 230–3, who claims that no σκευοποιός has dared to make a mask representing Cleon. On the ritual and cultic aspects of the tragic spectacle, see the contrasting views of Friedrich and Seaford in the present volume (below, pp. 257–94).

23. See *Le Récit en Grèce ancienne: Énonciations et représentations de poètes* (Paris 1986) 85–100, and 'Démasquer par le masque: Effets énonciatifs dans la comédie ancienne', *Rev. Hist. Rel.* 206 (1989) 357–76. The ritual and cultic aspects of the dramatic performances at Athens have been re-examined by Goldhill, 'The Great Dionysia'; regarding the mask, see also R. Rehm, *Greek Tragic Theatre* (London 1992) 13–14, 39–42.

24. Cf. Chantraine, *Dictionnaire étymologique*, 942, and the complementary observations of F. Frontisi-Ducroux, *Le Dieu-masque: Une figure du Dionysos d'Athènes* (Paris 1991) 9–12, who lays stress on the relationship which the Greek conception of the face has with the gaze, but does not succeed in establishing that the same gaze also animates the theatrical mask; that coincidence would make the mask incapable of 'suppressing and replacing the face which it covers'!

25. This, by way of reaction to the general interpretations of *OT* recently put forward and mentioned above, n. 14. For a critique of the application of the ritual concept of the φαρμακός to the tragic figure of Oedipus, see most recently W. Burkert, *Oedipus, Oracles, and Meaning: From Sophocles to Umberto Eco* (Toronto 1991) 18–21, and also Pucci, *Oedipus and the Fabrication of the Father*, 170–1, and R. D. Griffith, 'Oedipus *Pharmakos*? Alleged Scapegoating in Sophocles' *Oedipus the King*', *Phoenix* 47 (1993) 95–114. This self-referential questioning of the actual ritual functions which the tragic actors take on is no less common on the lips of the chorus: for *OT* see 895–9 with the pertinent discussion by A. Henrichs, ' "Why Should I Dance?": Choral Self-Referentiality in Greek Tragedy', *Arion* 3 (1994/5) 56–111.

26. In this sense, it is no accident, perhaps, that Sophocles does not provide an explicit formulation of the Sphinx's riddle; this (deceptive) knowledge of the physical nature of human life, from childhood to old age, will be set in opposition to the understanding that Oedipus acquires through the action of the play, which bears on the metaphysical nature of his own destiny and that of man in general. Without going this far, Pucci, *Oedipus and the Fabrication of the Father*, 148–59, has judiciously characterized the visual and cognitive reversal which Oedipus' self-blinding represents; cf. also S. Goldhill, 'Exegesis: Oedipus (R)ex', *Arethusa* 17 (1984) 177–200, who traces, on the linguistic plane, the stages whereby search for origins leads to self-blinding. In his comparative study of the different versions of the blinding of Tiresias, L. Brisson, *Le Mythe de Tirésias: Essai d'analyse*

structurale (Leiden 1976) 29–45, has successfully shown that the soothsayer has at his disposal a dispensation which allows him to cross the boundary between human and divine.

27. Through his search for himself, Oedipus may be said to reach the limits of the human condition (cf. Buxton, 'Blindness and Limits', 35–7), but it is not the case that his knowledge takes him beyond them, as claimed by E. A. Bernidaki-Aldous, *Blindness in a Culture of Light: Especially the* Oedipus at Colonus *of Sophocles* (New York 1990) 35–7, 66–70, who relies for corroboration on Reinhardt, *Sophokles*, 139–44: she forgets the incest and parricide which are part of Oedipus' fate as decreed by the gods (1175–85, 1360–5, etc.); see now Segal, 'Sophocles' *Oedipus Tyrannus*', 72–95. The connection between self-knowledge and self-blinding in *OT* has been usefully discussed by A. Cameron, *The Identity of Oedipus the King* (New York 1968) 15–21, and by Seale, *Vision and Stagecraft*, 247–54. The determinative role of Apollo in the working out of Oedipus' destiny, wherein chance (1080) becomes necessity, has been emphasized recently by J. Peradotto, 'Disauthorizing Prophecy: The Ideological Mapping of *Oedipus Tyrannus*', *TAPA* 122 (1992) 1–15, while for F. Ahl (*Sophocles' Oedipus: Evidence and Self-Conviction* [Ithaca, NY 1991], esp. 259–65) Oedipus in his search for himself succeeds only in convincing himself of the reality of a fate which is really a fiction.

28. Gorg. fr. 11a. 2–4 and also 11. 8–10 and 11. 15–19 D–K. It is relevant to note that in the treatise *On Non-Being* (fr. 3. 81–6 D–K) sight and hearing take on a special status: in the context of a physiological conception of the senses, sight and hearing are able to *present*, unlike the *logos*, which cannot be identified with reality and being. But Gorgias says nothing of the status reserved for listening to speech. J. de Romilly, 'Gorgias et le pouvoir de la poésie', *JHS* 93 (1973) 155–62, has shed light on the historical antecedents of the Gorgianic conception of speech and poetry; while among others C. P. Segal, 'Gorgias and the Psychology of the *logos*', *HSCP* 66 (1962) 99–155, makes a connection between Gorgias' ideas on the effects of poetic language and the conception of *katharsis* developed by Aristotle. An analogous theory of the emotions aroused by poetry is developed by Plato in *Ion* 535b–e: cf. R. Velardi, 'Parola poetica e canto magico nella teoria gorgiana del discorso', in *Lirica greca e latina: Atti del Convegno di studi polacco-italiano* (Rome 1990) 151–65. For an overview of these theories on the emotions stirred by poetry, see the classic discussion by H. Flashar, 'Die medizinischen Grundlagen der Lehre von der Wirkung der Dichtung in der griechischen Poetik', *Hermes* 84 (1956) 12–48.

2

What Can You Rely on in *Oedipus Rex*?
Response to Calame

RICHARD BUXTON

THE BLIND MASK

There are many things to admire in Claude Calame's thought-provoking and scholarly paper. I single out three. First, he is right to emphasize the complexity of Aristotle's view (or views) of the relationship between text and spectacle. Secondly, he very properly stresses the importance, for a full understanding of Sophocles' play, of giving due weight to the *pathos* of Oedipus after the self-blinding. It sometimes happens that readers (although hardly audiences) under-interpret *Oedipus Rex* on the false assumption that nothing of importance happens after the messenger's narrative[1]—a view as untenable as that which would locate the effective end of the *Oresteia* at the moment of Orestes' acquittal. Most important of all is Calame's recognition that the theme of knowledge should be central to our appreciation of *Oedipus Rex*. To the first of these three points I shall not return: given the space available, I shall leave aside Aristotle and concentrate on Sophocles. The second point will concern us towards the end of this discussion; the third will form its principal topic. Before addressing the subject of knowledge, however, I propose to deal briefly with the 'blind mask', an issue which, though not decisive for Calame's argument, is perhaps the most striking detail in it.

The thesis about the 'blind mask' has two stages. (1) Thanks to its construction, a tragic mask lets 'the voice and gaze of the actor appear to the spectators, beyond the hero he is miming'. (2) Because it blocks this actor–audience channel, a 'blind mask' subverts normal theatrical communication, with the result that 'in blinding himself, Oedipus calls into question not only his own identity as actor in the drama, but also that of the wearer of his mask'.[2] This thesis, which is typical of the late twentieth century in its emphasis on metatheatricality,[3] is undoubtedly ingenious; but is it convincing?

Now it is true that in some surviving representations of masks the eyes do attain a prominence comparable with that of the mouth.[4] However, our ignorance about the physiognomic realities of ancient 'blind masks' must at the very least cause us to pause before accepting such a hyper-subtle interpretation. Moreover, if we do concede that the effect on an audience of a 'blind mask' would have been to create a sense of blocked, and therefore subverted, communication, we are entitled to ask why the same is not true for *all* wearers of 'blind masks', such as Phineus, Polymestor, Tiresias, and Thamyras. That Calame does not wish us to regard the whole of this category as metatheatrically subversive is evident from the distinction he draws between the blindness of Tiresias ('a fact given by tradition') and the self-blinding of Oedipus ('an act integrated into the plot as Sophocles has reformulated it'). However, it is not clear to me whether the supposedly subversive aspect of Oedipus' act is meant to consist in the fact that this is a *self*-blinding, or in the fact that the play charts a *progress* from sighted to blind, or in the fact that the blindness is *dramatically integrated*. I suggest that this aspect of the argument, intriguing though it is, needs further thought; for the moment it leaves me unconvinced.[5]

But the 'blind mask' is not the pivot of Calame's exploration of the theme of the visual in the play. That pivot is, rather, the link between visibility and knowledge. Calame maintains that *Oedipus Rex* enacts a shift from verbal to visual knowledge, and that this visual knowledge is to be regarded as 'true', 'real', and 'of the gods'. Asking how far these ideas are correct will lead us to the very heart of the play. What is known in *Oedipus Rex*? How is it known? The answers are directly relevant to the wider problems which the present book aims to address.

I shall now examine the extent to which we may indeed talk of 'true knowledge' in *Oedipus Rex*; then stand back in order to relate my findings to 'the tragic'; next consider whether the notion of a *progression* from verbal to visual knowledge is a persuasive one; and finally offer a few brief, general reflections on the play.

'TRUE' KNOWLEDGE?

The frequency of significant verbal repetitions in Sophocles has long been recognized.[6] A striking example in *Oedipus Rex* is the recurring synaesthetic blending of terms for sight and visibility with terms for knowledge and language.[7]

ἔλαμψε . . . φανεῖσα φάμα Παρνασοῦ

the report/rumour/saying appeared and shone out from Parnassus

sings the chorus at 473 ff., referring to Apollo's oracle urging that Laius' murderer be hunted down.

πρὸς τοῦ δ' ἐφάνθη (or: τοὔπος δ' ἐφάνθη)

By whom was it made clear [or, depending on the text: Was the word made clear; sc. that it was through my persuasion that the prophet made these false statements]?

asks Creon a little later (525–6). Jocasta subsequently (848) uses the same trope:

ἀλλ' ὡς φανέν γε τοὔπος ὧδ' ἐπίστασο

Be assured that this [sc. the allegation that there had been several robbers] is the word which was revealed

as does Oedipus himself at 1440:

ἀλλ' ἦ γ' ἐκείνου πᾶσ' ἐδηλώθη φάτις

the god's oracular utterance [sc. to eradicate the father-killer] was made fully manifest.

Of course, it is neither only in this play nor only in the Greek language that 'telling' is expressed in the language of 'revealing' and 'bringing to light'.[8] But what is noticeable in *Oedipus Rex* is the fact that *clarity* is consistently predicated of statements made by humans as well as of those made by gods, and, more significantly still, of statements which ultimately prove false as well as of those which ultimately prove true. The divine oracle, *phatis/phêmê*, which comes from Delphi is a 'clear' injunction to cast out the polluter (86, 96); no less divine than—indeed identical with—the rumour, *phama*, which shone 'clearly' from Parnassus (473–5).[9] On the other hand, when Jocasta observes that the word which was 'revealed' by the herdsman spoke of several robbers (848), this is a word both human and false. But in the world of *Oedipus Rex* such distinctions are notoriously hard to draw. The god's 'clear' oracular command, as cited by Creon (106–7), is reported as enjoining the punishment of the *murderers*—authoritative but false: a god interpreted by humans.[10]

Nowhere is the interference between true and false allegations, between divine and human knowledge, more evident than in the use of the verb *phaskein* ('state', 'allege', 'affirm'). Where will a clue to the murder be found, Oedipus enquires of Creon in their first dialogue (108 ff.):

ἐν τῇδ' ἔφασκε γῇ
he [sc. the god] alleged that it was in this land

What evidence does the sole witness have to contribute, the king wants to know a few lines later (120):

λῃστὰς ἔφασκε
he [sc. a human] alleged [sc. that there were several robbers, not just one, who murdered him]

In this play, to be a *lêistes enargês*, a manifest robber—which is what Oedipus will accuse Creon of being (535)—is no simple matter. The rumour (*phatis*) goes, so Jocasta reassures Oedipus, that 'robbers' killed the former king at a place where three roads meet (715–16). Oedipus echoes this turn of phrase: *lêistas ephaskes*, 'You alleged that the man reported that "robbers" killed him' (842–3). 'Be assured' she replies, 'that this is the word which was revealed' (848).[11]

How, in the world of this play, do humans evaluate these allegations? How do they weigh one *phatis* or *phama*, one act of *phaskein*, against another? The power of a god to reveal what he wishes to reveal is never called into question in *Oedipus Rex*; the problem is to know what the divine will is. Jocasta recalls that 'an oracle came to Laius once—I will not say from Phoebus himself, but from his servants' (711–12). The voice of a god needs translating, and translators can be wrong. The queen's later, more famous remark, 'It is best to live at random' (979), is occasioned not by impiety—for she has just finished praying to Apollo—but by a sense that one simply *cannot know*:

πρόνοια δ' ἐστὶν οὐδενὸς σαφής
there is no clear foreknowledge of anything

(978)

The knowledge associated with the gods is both set apart from the human world, as in the Tiresias scene, and subtly collapsed into it, as exemplified in the linguistic details just highlighted.[12] The insistent framing-devices—'they allege', 'it was said'—constitute seemingly flimsy but actually impenetrable barriers to 'the truth'.

KNOWLEDGE AND 'THE TRAGIC'

Contributors to this volume were encouraged to focus upon 'the tragic', thus continuing a tradition of enquiry sustained by numerous writers, among them persons of great cultural authority.[13] For George Steiner, indeed, seeking out and responding to 'pure' and 'absolute' tragedy is, as he would put it, 'of the essence'. However, the present writer's instincts, shaped by an anthropological approach to literary interpretation, lead him to regard the notion of 'the tragic' with a measure of caution.[14] Indeed, the pursuit of the transhistorical essence of 'the tragic' often seems to resemble a circular wild-goose chase, with the identification of its constituent qualities revealing more about the preconceptions of the beholder than about the characteristics of the beheld.[15] Nevertheless, without in any way committing ourselves to the hunt for 'the tragic', we may, less portentously, agree that (*a*) a number of historically distinct theatrical traditions have generated plays which were described by contemporaries as 'tragedies' (or the linguistic equivalent); (*b*) some of those plays share some characteristics with the dramas which the Greeks called *tragôidiai*; (*c*) certain of these shared characteristics bear on existential issues of great depth and complexity. Which brings us back to knowledge.

A feature of many plays called 'tragedies' is the sense they convey of the presence of a metaphysical structure informing and conferring significance on events, combined with a sense both of the failure of humans to grasp that structure, and of the inadequacy of the structure ultimately to be a comforting and sustaining element in human life. Shakespearean drama illustrates the point: the insistent evocation of the gods in *King Lear*, the uncanny presence of the Weird Sisters in *Macbeth*, the notoriously puzzling ghost in *Hamlet*—these lend a metaphysical dimension to the action which is as unmistakable as it is hard to pin down, and which offers a comfort to the principal characters which is at best limited and at worst illusory. Of course, the emphasis varies, even within a single tradition. In ancient Greece, the metaphysical structure is at its clearest in *Bacchae, Hippolytus,* and *Eumenides,* a good deal more opaque in *Women of Trachis* and *Agamemnon*; variable, too, is the quality of 'sustenance' proffered. But nowhere, I think, is the opacity more enshroudingly present, the solace harder to be sure about, than in *Oedipus Rex.*

For there are no divine pronouncements *ex machina.* It all comes through a glass: for two of the characters, darkly. I imagine that no one but an unreconstructed adherent of the he-knew-it-all-from-the-start theory is likely to deny that all the characters in the play except Tiresias possess more *factual* knowledge at the end than they do at the beginning. But to confer on this acquisition of definitive information about Oedipus' parentage the status of a gaining of access into 'the domain of truth' (Calame's expression) makes a much bolder claim about the kind of insight which is available to mortals. With, once again, the unique exception of Tiresias, access by any mortal to 'real visual knowledge, that of the gods' (again in Calame's phrase) is presented as deeply problematic. Oedipus' assertion that 'it was Apollo who brought about these woes of mine' (1329–30) remains just that: an assertion. Only a true prophet (and how do we identify *him*?) can be regarded as having knowledge contiguous to that of the gods—not the chorus, who can only sing '*If* I am a knowledgeable prophet' (1086); not Oedipus, who, even after the blinding, is only *analogous* to Tiresias.[16]

AWAY FROM LANGUAGE?

I turn now to Calame's reading of the play in terms of a progression from the sphere of linguistic knowledge, to that of visual knowledge, to a state in which the hero's contact with the world is reduced to the tactile. Is this convincing? Largely so, but not, I think, entirely.

Before the revelation of the truth, the play famously abounds in verbal ironies, puns, and riddles, whose effect indeed relates to 'verbal knowledge', whether gained, blocked, or teasingly half-accessible.

γυνὴ δὲ μήτηρ ἥδε τῶν κείνου τέκνων

This woman is the mother of his children
[But also (until the genitive case resolves the ambiguity):]

This wife is a mother
[Or even:]
This mother is a wife
(928)[17]

πατέρα τὸν σὸν ἀγγελῶν
ὡς οὐκέτ' ὄντα Πόλυβον ἀλλ' ὀλωλότα

announcing that your father Polybus is no longer alive, but dead
[But also:]
announcing that your father is no longer Polybus, but a dead man.

(955–6)[18]

For the first three-quarters of the play, terrifying linguistic effects
of this kind build up to generate a kind of cumulative charge
demanding release.

With the revelation that the answers to Oedipus' two questions—Who killed Laius? Who am I?—coincide, verbal irony
becomes pointless; anyway, the scope for it has virtually disappeared. Henceforward, we are largely left with what may and may
not be seen, what one can and cannot bear to look upon, and ultimately, what one must feel. To this extent it makes sense to speak
of a move away from the verbal. But it must not be forgotten that
there is, at the end, a drama of language too. Replacing the tension
of irony and riddle we have the interplay of partially successful and
partially failed persuasion:

OEDIPUS. Cast me from this land at once, to a place where no one shall
    address me.
CREON. You can be sure that I would have done this—had I not first wished
    to learn from the god what should be done.

(1436–9)

OEDIPUS. Above all, let me touch them with my hands and take my fill of
    grief! Please, my king! Grant it, with your noble heart . . .
    Have you pitied me, Creon? Did you send me my dear children? Am I
    right?
CREON. You are right. It is I who brought this about.

(1466–76)

OEDIPUS. Send me from my home, from this land.
CREON. You ask me for what the gods alone can give.

(1518)

OEDIPUS. No! Do not take my daughters from me!
CREON. Do not try to exercise authority in everything.

(1522)

While he may express the *wish* to be unable to hear, Oedipus is in fact neither deaf nor mute: until the very conclusion of the drama, he attempts to affect, even to control, those around him, through speech. The language games have changed, but they are still being played out, to the bitter end.

CONCLUSION

If I had to summarize the impact of *Oedipus Rex*, I would do it like this. What, when it comes down to it, can you rely on? Your own identity? Your parents' identity? The gods? Elementary arithmetic? (But it appears that one can be equal to many, or to nothing.)[19] Your past experience? (As Jocasta puts it at 916, 'judging new things by old'—which was what the priest and the chorus did in placing their absolute trust in Oedipus.) A crucial test is what Oedipus relies on after the self-blinding. He calls the chorus his only friend and companion (1321–2), and he is of course dependent on Creon, but the supreme expression of his reliance on others is in relation to his children. Dependence on touch reduces Oedipus to a state which is almost like that of an autistic child, for whom an embrace is the vital channel for receiving love. ('Almost', because, as we noted above, Oedipus does have language.) There is no moment in the play when what we *see* is as central to the dramatic meaning as it is when, at the very end of the work, Oedipus is compelled to let go of his children. (Here, Calame's stress on the visual is absolutely right.) Indeed if, as some have thought, the last seven lines of exodic choral trochaics are spurious, then that separation is the last sight witnessed by an audience.[20]

In any event, the separation is one of the most overwhelming moments in the Western imaginative tradition, bearing comparison with Priam's kissing of Achilles' hands, or Lear's final entry with Cordelia's body in his arms, or Wotan's Farewell. But it is not a *simple* moment. For the separation is perplexing as well as moving. On the one hand, Oedipus 'should' be distanced from his children, since the play's supreme horror is that he has become too close to his kin; on the other hand, separation means loss of everything which this broken father has remaining to him. Whether we regard this and comparable moments as embodying 'the tragic' comes down in the end to playing yet another language game. More important, I suspect, is our recognition of the complex particularity of these 'simple', searing gestures.[21]

Notes

1. The contribution made by the play's conclusion to the overall dramatic meaning is underlined by M. Davies ('The End of Sophocles' O.T.', *Hermes* 110 [1982] 268–78), and by John Gould (this volume, pp. 231–2).
2. See Calame, above, p. 28.
3. Seaford describes the tendency to see self-reflexivity round every theatrical corner as an 'intellectual fashion of the 1980s' (*Reciprocity and Ritual*, 273). Euripides, more than Sophocles, has been the focus of most critical discussion of metatheatricality. There is a thoughtful example of this type of analysis in ch. 10 of Goldhill's *Reading Greek Tragedy*.
4. For example in the striking bronze mask from Peiraeus, illustrated as fig. 58 in Pickard-Cambridge, *Dramatic Festivals of Athens*².
5. If the notion of subverted mask *is* going to help with the interpretation of Greek tragedy, it is more likely to be in the way suggested a generation ago by John Jones: '[the human interest] of Euripides' work derives from the characteristic penetrative enquiry which, precisely because it forces attention behind the surface show, threatens to destroy the masking convention' (*On Aristotle and Greek Tragedy*, 260).
6. Cf. P. E. Easterling, 'Repetition in Sophocles', *Hermes* 101 (1973) 14–34.
7. See C. Segal, 'Synaesthesia in Sophocles', *ICS* 2 (1977) 88–96, esp. 88–91.
8. For this cluster of metaphors in *Trachiniae*, see P. Holt, 'Light in Sophokles' *Trachiniai*', *Cl.Ant.* 6 (1987) 205–17, with extensive bibliog. If we go beyond both Sophocles and Greek, parallels can be found in many languages. English-speakers may think first of 'illuminate' and 'reveal', with their Romance cognates (cf. Lat. *revelare*, 'to unveil/reveal'). Danish offers *oplyse*, 'to inform' (cf. *lys*, 'light'), Russian *ob"iasniat'*, 'to explain' (cf. *-iasn-*, 'clear'). In Pali and Sanskrit texts there is a close relation between seeing and knowledge, though *hearing* is another common metaphor for/mode of acquisition of knowledge, for instance with reference to the transmission of knowledge of the Vedic hymns. ('Buddha', incidentally, has no linguistic connection with (en)light(enment): it derives from *budh*, 'awaken'.) In any event, it is *not* the case that always and everywhere 'seeing' is the principal metaphor for 'coming to know'. Throughout the whole of Egyptian literature down to the Greco-Roman period, the dominant metaphor to express this process is that of the heart listening rather than of the eye seeing. (I am indebted for advice to Thomas Johansen, Derek Offord, Rupert Gethin, and Mark Collier.)

9. In l. 86, *phatin* is a manuscript variant for *phêmên* (which is a dialectal alternative to *phaman*).

10. R. W. Bushnell (*Prophesying Tragedy* [Ithaca, NY 1988] 79) makes a connection between *phatis* and fallible reporting in *OT*.

11. In his paper 'Λῃστὰς ἔφασκε: Oedipus and Laius' Many Murderers' (*Diacritics,* 8 [1978] 55–71), S. Goodhart argues that what he calls 'the Phocal massacre' was not actually carried out by Oedipus; on the inadequacies of this view, see Segal, 'Sophocles' *Oedipus Tyrannus*', 72–95, at 91 n. 3.

12. Far more attention has been paid to the separation than to the collapsing. An example is the article by G. Ugolini, 'L'Edipo tragico sofocleo e il problema del conoscere', *Philologus* 131 (1987) 19–31. While briefly acknowledging the existence of 'zone d'ombra e interferenze semantiche' (26), this scholar repeatedly stresses 'la distanza impermeabile tra le due forme di sapere' (29), viz. those of the prophet Tiresias and the 'rationalist' Oedipus.

13. Orientation within the Germanic area of this tradition can be found in the first ch. of Albin Lesky's *Greek Tragedy* (London 1967), with bibliog. on pp. 213–14. For recent English contributions to the debate, see Poole, *Tragedy: Shakespeare and the Greek Example*, and Mason, *The Tragic Plane*. Comprehensive rejection of the whole idea of 'essences' is to be found in J. Dollimore, *Radical Tragedy* [2] (New York 1989).

14. In Steiner's view (below, p. 535), I am presumably one of those whose work 'does little to articulate, let alone clarify, the fundamental issue. Which is one of a religious-metaphysical point of view.' Steiner's certainty that he can identify the pure and the absolute commands respect, because that certainty is underpinned by immense breadth of learning. I would, however, make three points. (1) In stating that it is just 'Anglo-American' or 'British' classicists who miss the (= his) point (pp. 535, 545), Steiner is simply wrong. In fact, a huge amount of work has been done in the last twenty-five years *in continental Europe* on the kind of research dismissed by Steiner as 'non-fundamental'. 'Anglo-American' is not a label which immediately comes to mind in relation to Nicole Loraux, Christian Meier, Bernd Seidensticker, J.-P. Vernant, H. S. Versnel, and P. Vidal-Naquet. Nor does it seem appropriate to Walter Burkert (of Zurich), whose reflections on the play (*Oedipus, Oracles and Meaning: From Sophocles to Umberto Eco* [Toronto 1991]) are 'non-fundamental' from beginning to end. (2) It is perfectly possible to make statements about the metaphysical-religious dimension of Greek (Shakespearean/Racinian . . .) tragedy *without* being locked into a cross-cultural pilgrimage in search of *das Tragische*. (3) That is not, of course, to say that readers

of tragedies would not benefit from greater familiarity with the German idealist tradition or (not the same thing) with Steiner's actually rather diverse group of heroes (Hölderlin, Hegel, Schelling, Nietzsche, Benjamin, Heidegger; cf. p. 545 in this volume).

15. Seidensticker (*Palintonos Harmonia*, 12) observes that the use of 'our' concept of 'tragedy' to illuminate Greek tragedies cannot but be anachronistic, importing as it necessarily does the accumulated semantic luggage of generations of reflection upon 'the tragic'. Cf. van Erp Taalman Kip in this volume, below, pp. 131–5.

16. In a previous article ('Blindness and Limits') I should have been more careful to underline the strictly circumscribed nature of Oedipus' 'insight'. Nevertheless, it remains true that Oedipus' enquiry and consequent coming-to-know are in their own way a *success* from the 'methodological' point of view. M. Vegetti pushes this line of approach to paradoxical lengths by observing that 'l'unico sapere *efficace* è dunque quello di Edipo' (*Tra Edipo e Euclide* [Milan 1983] 37); my italics.

17. Dawe, *Studies on the Text of Sophocles*, i. 247, argues that we should alter the text to read γυνὴ δὲ μήτηρ θ' ἥδε, with, presumably, the straightforward meaning: 'This is his wife and the mother of his children.' Lloyd-Jones and Wilson incorporate the change into their OCT. However, a noticeable feature of the text of this play is the fact that its syntax comes under the greatest pressure precisely where it is made to speak the unspeakable. If, *pace* Dawe, we keep the undoubtedly more 'difficult' γυνὴ δὲ μήτηρ ἥδε, we shall have one more instance in this play where the drama plunges towards the abyss, only to veer away from it at the last moment.

18. Cf. Segal 'Sophocles' *Oedipus Tyrannus*', 86.

19. Mathematics: see B. M. W. Knox, *Oedipus at Thebes* (New Haven 1957) 147–58, with important endnotes at 252–5.

20. Dawe (*Studies* i. 266–73) argues vigorously in favour of accepting Ritter's excision of lines 1524–30.

21. I am most grateful to Thomas Johansen for his comments on a draft of this paper.

3

Antigone as Moral Agent[1]

HELENE P. FOLEY

In the *Poetics*, Aristotle defines tragic character in relation to tragic choice. In drama, character, Aristotle argues, reveals a *prohairesis* or a process of undertaking moral commitment in which a person chooses to act or to abstain from action in circumstances where the choice is not obvious (*Poetics* 1450ᵇ8–10).[2] What I would like to begin to explore in this paper is the representation of the making and enacting of difficult moral choices—if not necessarily difficult choices in precisely the Aristotelian sense—by female characters in Greek tragedy, and to examine the complex interrelation between female moral capacity and female social role that conditions, and is articulated in, such choices.

Here, as elsewhere, Greek male writers are using fictional women to think with, and in a challenging fashion.[3] Popular culture often viewed women as either incapable of, or not permitted to make, autonomous moral decisions. Confined largely to their households and to participation in religious events, women had little or no direct influence on the political or military life of classical Athens; even within their houses, their activities were under the legal, if not the daily, supervision of a male guardian. Although fourth-century court-cases make clear that women could have an important informal influence on family affairs, Attic law, beginning with Solon, equates the persuasion of a woman with other deleterious influences, such as sickness or drugs, on a man's reason.[4] Thus, when tragic poets choose to allow an entire action to turn on the moral decision of a woman or to show women taking or urging significant moral positions in a public context, they apparently make at least a partial break from a cultural ideal and use female characters to explore ambiguous and often dangerous moral frontiers. In so far as women are moral agents with a difference, they reveal in a positive sense important social and ethical alternatives, and in a negative sense the social consequences of actions undertaken from a marginal, morally questionable, or socially resistant position.

For this reason, it is not surprising that female characters in tragedy often, and seemingly more often than male characters, violate Aristotle's assumptions about what they should be like. In Aristotle's view tragic characters should be good; elsewhere he endows women with sufficient virtue to maintain *sôphrosunê* ('self-control'), to fulfil their function in the household, and to obey their men.[5] Yet Euripides' Medea makes a deliberate choice to kill her children (*Poetics* 13, 1453[b] suggests that, as dramaturgy, this is less effective than a tragic choice made in ignorance). They should be traditional and consistent—unlike Euripides' Iphigeneia at Aulis, who undergoes, in Aristotle's view, an unconvincing and unmotivated change of heart (*Poetics* 1454[a]31–2). Or, perhaps, like Antigone, whose rationale for risking her life to bury her brother rather than a husband or child is described by Aristotle in his *Rhetoric* as *apiston* ('not credible').[6] They should be appropriate— female characters should not be manly or clever like Euripides' philosophical Melanippe. Melanippe's speech seems to have contained a knowledge of science and philosophy unsuitable for a woman (*Poetics* 1454[a]31). Presumably Aristotle disapproves of behaviour in a tragic character that he would have disapproved of, and/or found to lack verisimilitude in, a real woman. The case of Melanippe makes clear the depth of Aristotle's potential difficulties with female tragic figures, for to eliminate manly or clever heroines would be to purge much of Euripides, to say nothing of Aeschylus' brilliant and androgynous Clytemnestra. For Aristotle, ethical choice plays a critical role in generating tragic action and in producing tragic catharsis. Aristotle argues that an audience cannot experience a sympathetic moral affinity with characters who stand at an ethical extreme; his own views on women severely limit the cases in which ethical choices by women could be categorized as good and appropriate.[7] Autonomous actions by women on the tragic stage thus pose a special set of problems for the philosophical defence of tragedy and for understanding the quality of emotional response produced by tragedy in the predominantly or exclusively male audience for which the plays were designed.

In this paper I confine myself to examining the way that Sophocles' Antigone offers an alternative mode of ethical reasoning to that adopted by Creon. The play exploits this contrast in ethical mode both to make the case for, and to raise questions about, the moral positions adopted by each character. I hope to demonstrate that considering how moral agency is articulated in relation to gender in tragedy offers new avenues for interpreting the relations among tragic character, tragic choice, and tragic catharsis.

Sophocles' *Antigone* makes clear from the start that Antigone and Creon speak in different moral voices, even if they are not precisely representative of their respective genders, as we know from the conflicting views offered by Ismene and Haemon. 'There is nothing in your words that is pleasing to me, and may there never be! And my words are also not pleasing to you', says Antigone to Creon (499–501). 'Are you not ashamed,' says Creon to Antigone, 'to think differently from these men [the Thebans and the chorus]?' (510). As many critics have pointed out, Antigone and Creon use the same moral vocabulary in subtly different ways—the words *philos* ('friend') and *echthros* ('enemy'), for example, develop different connotations in the context in which each character employs them.[8] What has received considerably less detailed attention is their fundamentally different mode of making ethical decisions.[9] The following discussion will stress in particular those parts of the play in which Antigone and Creon explain and defend their actions, and the moral style that each adopts in doing so.

I shall begin with Antigone. Each of Antigone's three explanations and defences of her choice to bury Polynices in the play, although fundamentally the same in content, are aimed precisely at the different audiences that she is addressing: Ismene, Creon, and finally the chorus. Antigone's motive for action is throughout a deeply felt personal responsibility both to bury her *philos*, by which she means a blood-relative in the same household, and to honour the gods below with their due. Initially treating her sister as another self in the first scene, Antigone leads up to her request for help from Ismene by evoking familial bonds and common experiences—shared suffering and dishonour. She takes it for granted that they have the same assumptions about the need to bury blood-kin, and thus she does not try at first to justify her position, but only to stir her sister to act.[10] To Ismene she argues that to perform the act will demonstrate her (and her sister's) noble heritage (37–8), and to fail to perform it would be an act of betrayal

(46). Only when Ismene refuses to join her does she attempt to justify her proposal. She asserts that hers will be a noble death (72, 96–7). She will lie a *philê* ('beloved' or 'relative') to her *philos* (*philou meta*) Polynices (73). Antigone will commit a holy crime (73–4) and *please* those whom she ought to *please* (89), since there is more time to *please* those below than those here (74–5). Finally, Antigone will not dishonour the things due to the gods (τὰ τῶν θεῶν ἔντιμα, 77). In comparison to her usage in her next two scenes, Antigone's language here is narrowly focused to evoke close *philia* in what is staged as a private, familial context (see her terms of affection, her use of the dual, and the frequent possessives that personalize the burial issue).

After Antigone is caught burying her brother, Creon questions her disobedience of the edict. She begins by responding directly to his query. She defends her disobedience by citing Zeus and the unwritten laws (or customs) and the rites due to the gods below. From the unwritten laws Antigone turns to her motives, both social and emotional, for acting. As in the first scene, honour, a principled responsibility to gods and family, and personal pain are given equal weight in her self-defence. She says that she fears, not men's *phronêma* ('attitude'), but penalties from the gods if she does not act (458–60). The painful evils that beset her life (the loss of mother, father, and brothers) make death a gain in her eyes (461–4). By contrast, if she had left her mother's son unburied, she would have grieved (466–8). She expects to win glory for her gesture (502–4). Once again, Antigone's language pointedly personalizes the burial issue. She says that Creon made the edict for Antigone and Ismene (32, see also 45); it is not for Creon to keep her from her own (48). In neither of these first two scenes does Antigone generalize her case beyond the need to act, once Ismene has demurred, in this *particular* situation. It is Tiresias, not Antigone, who universalizes the issue by raising the question of burying the other slain enemies (1080–3).[11] Antigone's language in this *agôn* with Creon more closely matches the public context in which she speaks; it lacks the marks of intimacy, the appeal to shared familial experience displayed in the first scene. Yet the same combination of public and private concerns, of principle and emotional commitment, is used to explain and justify her actions in this specific context.

In a final, and I believe authentic,[12] speech (904–20) defending her burial of her brother to the chorus, Antigone says that she would not have acted against the citizens to bury a husband or a child, who are replaceable. This last justification for her action comes as Antigone departs for death, regretting both the loss of marriage and children and the loss of lamentation for her own death that her courageous act has precluded. In burying Polynices she has not only ignored the claims of the city in favour of familial bonds, but has foregone marital bonds for those with blood-relations.[13] This final attempt at self-defence is addressed to the chorus and introduced by a lyric dialogue with them that, despite the public context, reopens the possibility of a more intimate and sympathetic communication among characters than was possible in her first confrontation with Creon. Only when Creon interrupts this lyric exchange does Antigone begin a self-defence in iambic trimeters.

Antigone apparently turns to this final, formal argument because, as far as she knows, everyone has failed to accept or to understand her position despite her repeated efforts to justify it in other terms.[14] Even Ismene, who finally wants to die with her, to the end thinks Antigone did the wrong thing (555). Earlier, Antigone tells Creon that her act would be pleasing to the chorus (as representative of the people of Thebes) if they were not afraid to speak in front of him (504–5, 509). Antigone's initial use of the lyric mode with the chorus suggests that, as in the first scene with Ismene, she hopes to involve them emotionally in shared values and in the past suffering of her family. Here she has them fully engaged in a dialogue for the first time. Yet, contrary to her earlier expectation (504–5, 509), they do not approve her act (873–5). Although they begin the scene unable to contain their tears at the sight of Antigone (801–5), the chorus do not respond with lamentation to her complaints that she is going to her death unwed and unlamented. Indeed, she feels mocked by them (839).[15]

In contrast to Creon, for whose edict she shows little respect from the start, the chorus (and the city [842–3], to which Antigone appeals once she thinks that the chorus has failed to respond to her) are a source of authority for her. In this final scene Antigone elicits a response from the chorus as citizens and witnesses to her plight (806, 937–44), and addresses them as sources of authority (κοιρανίδαι, 940). Thus it makes sense that Antigone first explicitly recognizes the opposition of the city to her act (βίᾳ πολιτῶν, 907) in this speech, as she refused to do with Ismene or Creon earlier; earlier she concentrated on resisting Creon's edict, which, unlike Ismene, she apparently did not equate with the will of the city, since she thought that the chorus was on her side. (Her assumption is not implausible, since the citizens cited by Haemon do take this view.)

The qualifications that Antigone offers concerning her act in this last speech about her brother are not, as many have argued, inconsistent with the position she has taken at any point in the play;[16] at all times the personal commitment to bury her brother (specifically her brother) and to give the gods their due are her primary motives for action. What differs is the way that she presents her case to a different audience in a different context. Antigone does not in this speech deny the universal validity of the unwritten laws concerning the dead in making clear that *she* would only have risked her life, ignored her obligation and desire to marry and prolong her family line, and disobeyed the citizens for a last brother who had no other family member to bury him. She simply wants to make the chorus understand that, as the last survivor of the doomed Labdacids, she would only have *acted* to bury her brother. Knowing what is right apparently does not require a woman in her position to act on this knowledge in all instances and irrespective of context. Throughout the play she defends an action undertaken in a specific, emotionally concrete instance; the loss of this irreplaceable and known brother to whom she has a deep personal commitment at this time and place has made her willing to accept death and eager to please the dead and to act for the gods below.[17] The whole force of the argument in this last speech develops the contrast between a concrete basis for action and alternatives that would not at this point impel her to act. In short, she would not have challenged the state for a set of relations that are hypothetical to a virgin.

Sophocles is thought to have borrowed in this speech from Herodotus, 3. 119, where the wife of Intaphernes was given the opportunity to *save* the life of husband, child, or brother; she chose the brother, because she could not get another. The adaptation of this story in Antigone's case has been criticized as ill-conceived, because Antigone has no husband and child and chooses to die in a suicidal fashion for a dead brother rather than save a living one.[18] Herodotus' passage contains an implied criticism of Intaphernes' wife; the Persian king Darius, astonished that she does not prefer husband or son, saves both her brother and her eldest son.[19] Antigone's decision is in my view more, not less, defensible and comprehensible, precisely because she does not choose a brother over a family to whom she now has real social obligations as a wife.

Antigone's speech to the chorus, and by extension to the city, relies on the point that there is no other family member left to perform obligations for her blood-kin (Ismene would not act, Creon has denied his responsibility to kin, and her parents and brothers are dead). It seems not unlikely that in classical Attica, as in the modern rural Mediterranean, it was popularly perceived to be the function of a surviving daughter (whether in myth or in reality) to act in the absence of all supporting male relatives and the possibility for future ones (another brother). The modern cases most frequently concern revenge, and here the daughter may choose to take on symbolically the characteristics of a male member of her family and risk becoming an object of vendetta herself. To quote from a study of Corsican blood-revenge:

It is important to stress that while vendetta was both a right and an obligation for men, for women only the former was the case. Only if they wished to undergo the hazards of vendetta would they be placed at direct risk by it. In practice, however, women would become directly involved in the accomplishing of vendetta only if there were no male relatives . . . or if such male relatives declared themselves unwilling to assume responsibility for vendetta. In such cases, either the daughter, or more usually, the sister of the victim would take on the male role of realizing vengeance; having assumed this clearly male function, she would then be fully entitled to all the privileges enjoyed traditionally by males in Corsican society; that is, she would be honoured because of the restoration of clan repute achieved by her. . . . In undertaking the task of revenge she would at the same time expose herself to dangers identical to those suffered by the males. . . . Once she had committed herself to taking a direct part in vengeance procedures, she was counted by the enemy clans amongst the potential victims of vengeance, especially when there were no males remaining to her family.[20]

Gail Holst-Warhaft cites similar cases among the Mani of Southern Greece. A woman named Parsaki is celebrated in a well-known Maniot lament for poisoning her husband, brother-in-law, and father-in-law in revenge for their treacherous killing of her only brother. Her parents welcome her home after the crime. 'You did well,' says her mother, 'May you eat and drink [your inheritance] with the new husband you'll find.'[21] To return to Attic tragedy, Electra proposes to win honour in precisely this fashion by taking revenge on Aegisthus when she thinks that Orestes is dead in Sophocles' play. By contrast, the more conventional Chrysothemis refuses to run the risks involved, to exercise what is for the Corsican daughter or sister a right rather than an obligation. In matters relating to burial, precisely the same options as for revenge seem to obtain both among the Mani and in Sophocles. 'In an act of daring that was repeated in villages all over Greece during the German Occupation [the Maniot woman Costantina Dimaronga] and two other women risked execution by burying their cousin and a group of fellow resistance fighters killed in the battle of Verga-Armyrou.'[22] Dimaronga's later lament for her cousin expressed pride in her action, and anger at those who refused to help the women or collaborated with the Germans. As Sourvinou-Inwood has pointed out, initiating the burial ceremony and interring the body are normally male tasks in ancient Greece (women do pour libations and lament, but under male supervision).[23] Yet in *Oedipus at Colonus* (1411–13), Polynices—a male character—urges his sisters to bury him by predicting that his sisters will win praise (ἔπαινος) if they do so. Although Antigone's actions clearly run counter to normal expectations about female action (as Ismene, or, in *Electra*, Chrysothemis, make clear), the views of the citizens cited by Haemon, who pronounce her act to be worthy of the highest praise, a praise she incurs specifically as a woman (694), must be comprehensible to the play's audience. Antigone's adoption of goals that would normally be appropriate to men, such as the pursuit of honour for her action, would, from this perspective, be understood as part of a special situation that encourages the daughter to act in the interests of her family in the absence of a male relative who is willing to do so—even to the point of a seemingly suicidal heroic death. Although Creon expresses outrage that he is challenged by a woman, and even calls Antigone a slave (479), his insistence both on treating his young and virginal ward as a moral agent responsible under penalty of law for her act and on meting out the prescribed punishment of death by stoning, even for a woman, makes sense in a context where a woman has chosen to act (at least in part) as an honorary male. This hypothesis would also explain why Antigone implies (911–12) that she would not have acted if her parents had been alive, and why she must try to persuade Ismene to act in a case where both sisters agree that Polynices should in principle be buried. In insisting that there was only *one* case in which her action is in her own view fully justifiable, Antigone's speech probably capitalizes on cultural presuppositions about exceptional circumstances—whether these circumstances are real or a tragic topos—in which women could be expected to act autonomously.

To put this another way, in this play a young, unmarried princess (we should not forget that although Antigone is a woman, her affairs have public as well as private importance)[24] wins praise from a substantial portion of the city as the last member of her family willing to act in that family's interest, although she defies men and the state to bury her brother; as was mentioned earlier, even the chorus, who are known for their devotion to the past rulers of Thebes and pointedly disapprove of her disobedience, recognize (unlike Creon) a certain piety in the attempted burial (872), and honour in her mode of death (816–17, 836–9). If such a woman had insisted, especially in the face of the opposition expressed by Ismene, Creon, and the chorus, on her need to act for the full range of hypothetical marital relations to whom she might by public and male standards be obligated by the unwritten laws, Antigone would, I think, have become a cultural monstrosity rather than a subversive yet admirable anomaly.

Many critics have found what they characterize as Antigone's highly contextualized and contingent mode of moral argument in this passage intolerable. Their Antigone is a woman who should consistently have claimed a universal commitment to the gods' laws in all instances, or at the very least to all members of her natal and (hypothetical) marital family, and not risked death exclusively for a dead brother in one context. Other critics have been far too quick to label Antigone as merely intuitive, emotional, primitive, inconsistent, and illogical; or they fail to accord her ethical framework the precise attention that it deserves.[25] We need to examine the assumptions of Antigone's critics, and even of her admirers.

Creon's mode of moral and political deliberation, to be discussed shortly, is more familiar to us; yet we should not permit its familiarity to distort our judgement of his behaviour in Sophocles' play. Nor should we assume that the stance developed for Antigone throughout this play is anything but an equally serious ethical mode that operates on different terms from those adopted by other characters. These less familiar terms have required careful attention to define. It is important to accept the possibility that gender can be a critical factor in defining moral action in Greek culture and literature. General principles dictate the behaviour of both Antigone and Creon, but moral problems arise for each in a contextual framework that eludes an exclusive reliance on abstract reasoning. This is especially the case where the culture does not normally permit adult moral autonomy to the female agent—as Ismene and Creon make clear, women's virtues are traditionally exercised through obedience to men in authority—and defines her above all in relation to the family context in which she is normally inextricably embedded. In Antigone's view, the unwritten laws do require family members to bury their kin. Virgin daughters are apparently last in the hierarchy of those who should undertake this obligation, and the last to undertake risks on behalf of the family, perhaps above all because these risks conflict with their cultural role of producing the next generation. To accept Antigone's argument that there are only specific circumstances in which a virgin daughter should contemplate taking autonomous action in life-threatening circumstances requires her audience to accept that her heroic action cannot serve in any simple sense as a timeless, gender-free model for civil disobedience. At the same time, it does not diminish her heroism and her moral audacity. Within the context of a Mediterranean morality that offers to a woman specific exceptional opportunities to win honour by acting on behalf of the natal family, Antigone's choice to accept a challenge that requires her death still defines her as heroic.

What has been called inconsistency, despite that fact that Antigone remains committed to her act of disobedience throughout, has been shown to derive from her attempt to persuade or to explain her position to three different audiences at three different stages in the narrative of her attempted burial. (The fact that each scene attempts a justification of the same act underlines the role that each audience and each context plays.) In sum, Antigone adopts a range of styles, each suited to a different private or public context and to her interlocutor, to convey a consistent position that repeatedly insists on giving equal weight to concerns of justice and familial responsibility.

Whereas Antigone's ethics derive from a dual responsibility to the unwritten laws and the gods below and to family relations and care for others, Creon's derive from a commitment to general principles as the major determinant of moral action that is entirely familiar in later Western tradition. In his view the interests of the city-state are primary, and enemies to the state should not be buried. He identifies his, and even the gods', interest with that of the city. In contrast to Antigone, emotions and the calculus of pleasure and pain are not cited as supporting motives for Creon's actions. Creon is sure that his principles are best for *all* situations, whereas Antigone, although the unwritten laws play a central role in her decision, develops her position out of her own familial experience and in the specific context of the burial of her brother. Creon will count no one as a *philos* who does not accept his views about the polis and its priorities (182–3, 187–9, 209–10).[26] Blood- and marital relationships, and the responsibilities they entail, are of secondary importance to him, and easily expendable when the interests of city and family (apparently) come into conflict. 'She is my sister's child,' he says, 'but were she child of closer kin than any at my hearth, she and her sister should not so escape their death and doom' (486–9). He will leave his nephew unburied because he fought against Thebes, condemn his nieces to death, and threatens to kill Haemon's bride before his very eyes.[27] Creon defines the self in relationship to others in a hierarchical and contractual fashion. Sons should obey fathers, and prospective wives are interchangeable. If Haemon cannot marry Antigone, Creon asserts, there are other furrows for his plough (569). Yet wives are not interchangeable for the same reasons that a husband and child are to Antigone. He has experienced these relations, and as a male leader he is in a position to choose (for others and himself) among alternatives concerning them. Yet unlike Antigone, Creon will not permit such past personal experience to explain or colour his judgement.

Creon insists that one cannot know the soul, thought, and judgement of a *man* (*andros*) unless he shows his practice of government and law (175–7). Although this statement proves ironically true in his own case, it also means that moral knowledge of women or slaves, or even perhaps the passive citizenry, is fundamentally impossible. No wonder Creon cannot trust any judgement but his own (see 736)—except, finally, that of the chorus, who have demonstrated political loyalty to the ruling house of Thebes in the past, and Tiresias, who has been proved right before. In contrast to Antigone, Creon does not adjust his style of speaking to his interlocutors or to changing contexts; consistent with the ethical stance he has adopted, he presents his case in a public, iambic mode until he reviews his actions in his final lyric laments.

The way that Creon deploys gnomic truths makes his moral range particularly clear.[28] He approaches every dilemma that requires judgement through descriptive and prescriptive generalizations about money, human types, and the behaviour expected from such types; his speeches contain twenty-five such generalizations in 350 lines, in contrast to two for Antigone in 212 lines.[29] Such assumptions about human types and human society may be reasonable in themselves, and even necessary where public decisions must be undertaken without full and reliable knowledge of the circumstances and the characters of those involved in a particular situation. Creon's first speech makes a case for the value of the generalizing mode in a public context. Yet, as is the case with Antigone, his views are immediately put to the test in the following scenes. Because Creon (unlike Antigone) creates the full positive case for his action in this first speech, and the play ultimately exposes the error in his initial stance on Polynices' burial, subsequent scenes serve above all to reveal the limitations of his position and his ethical mode. Thus, where human beings and situations defy his expectations and prove not to be interchangeable, Creon repeatedly fails to register their actual character. To put this another way, in contrast to the moral agent defined by Aristotle in his *Nicomachaean Ethics*, Creon proves deaf to the knowledge of particulars—of place, time, manner, and persons, for example— essential to successful practical reasoning.[30] In short, he does not effectively correlate general principles and specific situations (*Nicomachaean Ethics* 6. 9). By contrast, we will see shortly that Haemon uses generalization in a fashion that is far more responsive to the circumstances than his father. Whereas Aristotle argues that *aisthêsis*, *orexis*, and *dianoia* all play a critical role in this process, Creon does not acknowledge that emotion (in alliance with reason) and perception (or intuition) are as critical to proper moral deliberation as reason.

Unsurprisingly, then, in a sequence of scenes, Creon misjudges and/or fails to respond appropriately to the actions and motives of the guard, Tiresias, Antigone, Ismene, and even to his own son, who, as a young man, should from Creon's perspective accept his father's views without question. His errors are often understandable, but the repetition cannot fail to affect the audience's view of Creon's judgement nevertheless.[31] The guard, like others of his type, must in Creon's view be venal; in fact, as the guard himself remarks, Creon's judgement is in error here (323).[32] Creon initially makes another error of judgement with Tiresias, whereas the chorus put faith in their past experience of Tiresias' reliability (1091–4). Even more telling are Creon's misinterpretations of his close relatives—people whom he presumably ought to know. Creon originally sees the two very different sisters that the audience has observed in the first scene as indistinguishable. He misreads Ismene's distraught appearance within the palace as a sign of guilt (489–92).[33] The chorus, when Ismene appears, immediately interpret her tears correctly as *philadelpha* ('loving towards her sister', 527); later they persuade Creon to renege on his error (770). Creon sees *erôs* as motivating Haemon when Haemon asserts his devotion to Creon's interests, then fatally misjudges both the intensity of Haemon's devotion to Antigone and the girl's unwillingness to live immured in a cave.[34] The chorus, by contrast, take Haemon seriously; they see merit in both Haemon's and Creon's positions and worry over the implications of Haemon's stormy exit. Creon refuses to credit the possibility of a divine role in the first of the two attempted burials of Polynices, despite hints of supernatural happenings at the site that awe the watchman and the chorus (278–303). Ignoring the chorus's advice and the order of Tiresias' words, he buries Polynices before going to rescue Antigone. The disastrous outcome was no doubt unavoidable, but the reversal of priorities is indicative of the judgement that created it nevertheless.

Haemon reveals that Creon's devotion to the state is becoming simply a rigid commitment to his own self-interest and detrimental to civic *homonoia*.[35] Creon ignores the possibility of a conflict between family and state (and among his own family obligations), although we might have expected him to defend himself on these points each time the dilemma arises on-stage in his case.[36] Collapsing the differences between public and private worlds, Creon thinks a man who is 'good', *khrêstos*, in his household is also *khrêstos* in the city (661–2).[37] Here he refuses to consider differences in the two institutions that may require from those representing their interests a different mode of ethical reasoning.[38]

Furthermore, as critics have pointed out, by these very standards Creon demonstrates his shortcomings as a leader, since he repeatedly betrays household obligations (and in so doing also civic obligations, since Polynices' body pollutes the city).[39] He cannot, like the chorus, 'think on both sides' (376). Nor is Creon ultimately willing to look at decision-making in dialogic terms; he aims to enforce his will, not to examine and re-examine his choices in context or, like Antigone and Haemon, to adapt his language and argument to his interlocutors.

When Tiresias frightens Creon into changing his mind, he collapses and asks the chorus to make his decision for him (1099).[40] And in his final laments, where he adopts the lyric mode for the first time in the play, he stresses in particular the failure of his deliberation and judgement: the errors of his ill-thinking mind (φρενῶν δυσφρόνων ἁμαρτήματα), his unfortunate plans (ὤμοι ἐμῶν ἄνολβα βουλευμάτων), and the death of his son through his poor deliberations (ἔθανες, ἀπελύθης, ἐμαῖς οὐδὲ σαῖσι δυσβουλίαις, 1261–9). Creon's own words (and Tiresias and the chorus agree with them) thus raise fundamental questions about the way that he has chosen to deploy the mode of deliberation that he defined and adopted in his first speech. In fact, after the scene with Tiresias he recognizes at first only the validity of the traditional usages (1113–14) that he rejected in Antigone's argument; it takes the loss of his family to bring home to him the full range of his limitations.[41]

Haemon, on the other hand, attempts a genuine if tragically hopeless mediation between Creon's and Antigone's modes of morality. Like Antigone, Haemon tries to frame his position to communicate with his interlocutor. He too uses gnomic generalizations. Haemon cites Antigone's position on the gods below (749) and the glory of her deed (693–8),[42] but he uses other popular wisdom to argue that Creon should be flexible in this instance and bend to the concrete fact of a popular feeling in favour of Antigone. Although Creon denies that public decisions should be influenced by family relationships, Haemon insists on his care for, and relationship to, Creon as his father. 'Father, I am yours,' he says (635). Reasoning as both son and member of the *polis*, he thinks that Creon's own welfare will be served by listening to those who care for him. The father–son relation should be reciprocal to the extent that fathers should hear and consider their sons' advice (or even, by implication, women's advice) when it is good. Public decisions should be reached and re-evaluated in a dialogic, not monologic, fashion. While assenting to Creon's view that the interests of the state are primary and that a son should obey his father (635–8), Haemon argues for a more nuanced view of the city and its governance that is attentive to context (for example, the attitude of the community, the identity of the perpetrator, and the nobility of her act). Haemon's speech makes clear that Creon's mode of generalizing moral reasoning could, if his principles were correct and deployed in a fashion responsive to context and productive of civic concord (ὁμόνοια), provide a satisfactory basis for public morality—even if it will always be vulnerable to chance and human ignorance.

Haemon's speech is critical because up to this point the play has dramatized a clash between modes of deliberation derived from very different social positions and circumstances. Creon seems to assume that 'the wider the system administered to, the less contextually specific interpretations can be'.[43] Haemon, however, takes a position (a position partially approved by the chorus) that even on the level of the *polis*, perception, the bonds of *philia*, and a sensitivity to context can, if deployed in the interest of the city, play as critical a role in public decision-making as reason and principle.[44] Like Athena, who casts her vote for Orestes in Aeschylus' *Eumenides* because of who she is (the motherless daughter of Zeus), Haemon is not ashamed to urge a position on his father and ruler because he is his son. Justice, even civic justice, can be no more detached entirely from the person (or the family) and the circumstance than Haemon in a private context can find another furrow for his plough or Creon can find another wife and son. Pericles implies something similar when he asserts in the Thucydidean funeral oration that those who do not have children to hazard cannot offer fair and impartial counsel to the *polis*. Dinarchus, *Against Demosthenes*, says that a rhetor or a *stratêgos*, in order to get the people's confidence, must observe the laws in begetting children. Both apparently refer to a law (cited in Aristotle's *Athênaiôn Politeia*) that required an archon or a hipparch to have a child over ten. In *Against Ctesiphon*, Aeschines argues that Demosthenes is not fit to be a political leader, because he put on white clothes, sacrificed, and took part in public affairs only seven days after the death of his only daughter. Such a bad father, he argues, could never be a good political leader. Those who do not feel proper affection for those most closely related to them will never value non-kin as they should. Those depraved in private life can never properly direct public affairs.[45] Creon himself adopts a position consistent with these views when he argues that a man not *khrêstos* ('good') in his household cannot be *khrêstos* in the city (661–2), but he fails to put it into practice.

Before concluding, I would like to consider the conflict between Antigone and Creon in the light of questions raised by the cognitive moral psychologist Carol Gilligan. Gilligan's work challenged the theories of Lawrence Kohlberg, who had identified a series of stages in human moral development.[46] Gilligan, initially puzzled by the failure of women to achieve high scores on Kohlberg's tests of moral maturity, came to argue that there is empirical evidence that more than one equally valid mode of moral reasoning and moral agency operates in our society. Those who adopt the second mode, what Gilligan calls a different voice, are often, although by no means exclusively, women. For Gilligan, moral problems arise often for women 'from conflicting responsibilities rather than from competing rights . . . and require for their resolution a mode of thinking that is contextual and narrative rather than formal and abstract'.[47] In her view the morality of responsibility and care differs from the impartial morality of rights, equality, and justice often practised by men, and especially by those acting in public contexts, in its emphasis on connection rather than separation, in its consideration of the relationship rather than the autonomous individual as primary. The moral self is radically particularized, and achieving knowledge of the other persons towards whom we act is a complex and difficult moral task. Moral deliberation in this case is not simply a question of impartially weighing competing claims, but of sustaining connections, expressing emotions appropriate to the relationship and the situation, and including those who require care. The appropriate action for a particular individual to take is not necessarily the right action for anyone to take in that situation. The morality of care and responsibility does not, in Gilligan's view, encompass all morality or replace a morality based on impartiality, impersonality, formal rationality, and universal principle, but remains in dialogue with it. 'Through the tension between the universality of rights and the particularity of responsibility, between the abstract concept of justice as fairness, and the more contextual understanding of care in relationships, these ethics keep one another alive and inform each other at critical points. In this sense, the concept of morality sustains a dialectical tension between justice and care, aspiring toward the ideal of a world more caring and more just.'[48] Gilligan's data in fact show that women subjects do not necessarily ignore considerations of justice in making ethical decisions, but issues relating to care and responsibility tend to predominate or to weigh more heavily with them than with male subjects.[49] At the same time, she does not make clear how the complex dialogue between the two ethical modes might work in practice, and how the tensions between them might be resolved.[50]

I do not have the time here either to do justice to Gilligan's theories, or to contend with the legitimate problems that they have raised.[51] Certainly the charge that her work is ahistorical is relevant here; nor is she sufficiently sensitive to the way that the ethical positions women adopt—actually or prescriptively—are socially constructed by the communities in which they live, not only for women as a class, but for women of different classes, ages, cultural backgrounds, or statuses. Nevertheless, although I am contending that male writers of classical Greece recognized and mobilized for their own ends ethical differences between the sexes, I would not argue that the different voices of tragic women correspond to Gilligan's standards. Antigone acts, in part, out of a sense of responsibility and care for her brother, and contextual and narrative thinking plays a role in motivating and justifying her act. For Antigone, it is her nature to join in love and not in hate (523). She too takes the stance that appropriate actions are not universal or generalizable. Yet the combative, even confrontational, temperament (*autognôtos orga*, 875) and autonomy (*autonomos*, 821) that prove so problematic in the eyes of the chorus, and her assured allegiance to justice in the form of the unwritten laws and to the gods below, make Antigone unlike Gilligan's typical female moral agent. In contrast to Gilligan's different voice, Antigone sees no contradiction between a deeply felt commitment to general moral rules and to familial responsibility, between the dictates of pleasure, pain, and experience and a rational adherence to the unwritten laws and the gods below.[52] Antigone's flexible moral style, despite her unflagging, even obsessive, devotion to principle, her struggle to defend familial concerns in a public context, and her self-consciousness about the way that gender-specific social roles condition moral choice, give her a different voice that must be defined in terms that go beyond Gilligan's current formulations.[53] The play defines its different and gendered ethical voices in a fashion unlike that of Kohlberg and Gilligan, and shows in practice what amounts to an attempt by Antigone to bridge the morality of care and justice that fails to convince Creon as advocate of a principled, impartial morality, even when championed in a more palatable form by Haemon. By staging on slightly different terms the necessary and tension-filled dialectic that Gilligan argues must eventually take place between two different moral modes, it can perhaps open new perspectives on the modern debate. What this paper owes to Gilligan, who served as a catalyst for my own thinking, is a critical strategy. For just as Gilligan has argued in a twentieth-century context that Kohlberg's assumptions about ethical maturity may have been distorted by adopting the practice of a male élite as normative, or by being insensitive to the range of contexts in which ethical choices are confronted and to the differences among moral agents, I have argued that the examination of the ethical stance of the characters in *Antigone* as a whole has been overly conditioned by a set of anachronistic assumptions about what constitutes a valid mode of moral reasoning.

We cannot be sure what range of views Greeks of the 440s might have had about modes of moral deliberation. The age of sophistry and philosophy was at an early stage on these questions. Sicilian rhetoric and Protagoras may have begun to influence Athens in the 450s, and, if so, *Antigone* would have been composed at a period of new self-consciousness about differing modes of discourse and ethical argument. Sophocles rarely shows the enthusiastic receptivity to contemporary rhetoric and philosophy that we find in his younger contemporary Euripides.[54] Nevertheless, I think it is fair to say that in this play Sophocles mobilized remarkably sophisticated and subtle differences in characterization and ethical mode to explore difficult moral issues. Antigone's moral difference in the end serves above all to raise questions about, and expose contradictions in, Creon's mode of morality, and hence indirectly to problematize, as tragedy often does, Athenian civic values and discourse.[55] By emphasizing the importance of the unwritten laws in the public sphere, the play refuses to confine Antigone and her ethics to the world of the *oikos* from which they largely derive, even if it does not go so far as to challenge the relative assessment of justice and care in public morality.[56] Indeed, whereas Ismene initially permits the city and its leader to override her responsibility to her dead brother (and living sister), Antigone attempts to define her responsibility to gods, brother, and city as one. Haemon's mediating speech brings some of Antigone's concerns into play in the context of a justice-oriented morality explicitly attentive from the first to the interests of the *polis*, and hints at a possible and better mode of public deliberation. Both Haemon and Antigone's last speech aim to make her seemingly anti-social female rebellion an intelligible stance that citizens can consider appropriate, and even praise. The disapproving male chorus nevertheless feels pity for Antigone, and Tiresias shows that the interests of family and city are not in fact at odds in this particular situation (and in fact, the public rhetoric of the funeral oration celebrated Athens' willingness to defend the burial of the seven at Thebes on the grounds of traditional usages).[57] The play itself, again in a fashion typical of Theban tragedy, is not optimistic about the possibility of establishing this better mode of public deliberation.[58] In the end Antigone, Creon, and Haemon are all accused of being irrational; each turns on those they profess to care for; each in turn fails to persuade the other. Yet the fact that all the major characters end up experiencing and surrendering to the devastating effects of the loss of family bonds seems to raise questions as well about the morality of the city (both the city of Thebes and the city of Athens, which also privileged in its public rhetoric the concerns of city over that of the *oikos*).[59] The interdependence of citizens central to civic morality fails here to replace the bonds of kin. A *polis* that denies such attachment, that legislates to isolate the family too heavyhandedly, may endanger its mode of deliberation and even its existence.

Aristotle himself seems to be concerned with closely related issues, when he criticizes the watery *philia* that Plato's ideal republic will inevitably create by eliminating familial bonds. And in the *Rhetoric* (1375^{a-b}; cf. 1373^b) he cites with seeming approval the fact that Antigone justifies her disobedience to Creon's *nomos* by referring to the unwritten laws: 'it is the part of a better man to make use of and abide by the unwritten rather than the written law'. Such laws are constant and based on nature, whereas written law (Creon's decree belongs at least in Aristotle's view on this side of the opposition being developed here, even if it is a proclamation), since it varies with time and place, may fail in specific contexts to accord with justice. Haemon's position similarly implies that moral rules (such as the unwritten laws defended by Antigone) have less need to be sensitive to context than moral principles such as those on which Creon bases his stance, and that public rhetoric and public morality need not be based on a rigid refusal to give familial feeling, experience, and responsibility their due.

Notes

1. A version of this paper was first presented at a symposium in honour of Helen North at Swarthmore College. I would like to thank audiences at Vassar, Oberlin, Cincinnati, Wellesley, University of Iowa, Trinity College, Hartford, and King's College, London, and Christopher Gill, Rachel Kitzinger, Page du Bois, Richard Seaford, Michael Trapp, and Christian Wolff for comments on an earlier draft. A fuller version of this essay will appear as part of a book based on my Martin lectures (Oberlin, spring 1995).

2. The formulation here is special to drama; elsewhere *prohairesis* reveals *êthos* for Aristotle. On *prohairesis*, see C. Chamberlain, 'The Meaning of *prohairesis* in Aristotle's *Ethics*', *TAPA* 114 (1984) 147–57; Halliwell, *Aristotle's Poetics*, 151; E. Schütrumpf, *Die Bedeutung des Wortes in der Poetik des Aristoteles* (Munich 1970); and C. Gill, 'The *êthos/pathos* Distinction in Rhetorical and Literary Criticism', *CQ* 34 (1984) 149–66.

3. See further, H. P. Foley, 'The Conception of Women in Classical Athens', in Foley (ed.), *Representations of Women in Antiquity* (New York 1981) 127–68; Just, *Women in Athenian Law and Life*; J. Gould, 'Law, Custom, and Myth: Aspects of the Social Position of Women in Classical Athens', *JHS* 100 (1980) 38–59, and F. I. Zeitlin, 'Playing the Other: Theater, Theatricality, and the Feminine in Greek Dramas', *Representations* 11 (1985) 63–94.

4. Plut. *Sol.* 21. 3. For a recent discussion of the legal position of classical Attic women, see Just, *Women in Athenian Law and Life*.

5. These views are largely represented in the *Politics* and the *Nicomachean Ethics*. For a discussion, see S. Okin, *Women in Western Political Thought* (Princeton 1979) ch. 4.

6. 3. 16.

7. Halliwell, *Aristotle's Poetics*, 154 and 158–9, tends to dismiss these problems of status too readily.

8. On the different languages of Antigone and Creon, see Reinhardt, *Sophokles*, 79 and 87; Goheen, *Imagery of Sophocles' Antigone*, 17; Knox, *Heroic Temper*, 80; J. Dalfen, 'Gesetz ist nicht Gesetz und

fromm ist nicht fromm: Die Sprache der Personen in der sophokleischen Antigone', *WS* 11 (1977) 5–26; D. A. Hester, 'Law and Piety in *Antigone*: A Reply to J. Dalfen "Gesetz ist nicht Gesetz" ', *WS* 14 (1980) 5–11; Kitzinger, 'Stylistic Methods'; D. Porter, *Only Connect: Three Studies in Greek Tragedy* (Lanham, Md. 1987) 61; and Goldhill, *Reading Greek Tragedy*, ch. 4.

9. The bibiog. on the Antigone is so voluminous that any discussion will consist largely of deploying the same chess-pieces to play a new game. I have here attempted above all to cite literature that influenced my own thinking, or the most recent or well-developed version of a particular position. For a summary of the bibliog. on major questions in the play, see Hester, 'Sophocles the Unphilosophical'. Philosophical discussions of the play range from Hegel to several recent, stimulating analyses: G. Steiner, *Antigones* (Oxford 1986); Nussbaum, *Fragility*; Oudemans and Lardinois, *Tragic Ambiguity* (with full bibliog.); and Blundell, *Helping Friends and Harming Enemies*.

10. She is correct in this assumption; see Ismene at 65–7, 99.

11. These lines have been bracketed by many editors.

12. For an excellent defence with full bibliog., see Neuberg, 'How Like a Woman', esp. 59–62.

13. Murnaghan, '*Antigone* 904–920', 195 and 198, Neuberg, 'How Like a Woman', esp. 70, and Blundell, *Helping Friends and Harming Enemies*, 135, all see this speech as arising from Antigone's preoccupation with marriage.

14. See further Winnington-Ingram, *Sophocles*, 141; T. B. L. Webster, *An Introduction to Sophocles* (London 1969) 99. On her isolation here, see Linforth, 'Antigone and Creon', 224.

15. On Antigone's lament here, see H. P. Foley, 'The Politics of Tragic Lamentation', in Sommerstein *et al.* (edd.), *Tragedy, Comedy and the Polis*, 111–13. Antigone has been criticized for abandoning her responsibility to marry and procreate. See Murnaghan, '*Antigone* 904–920', 207; C. E. Sorum, 'The Family in Sophocles' *Antigone* and *Electra*', *CW* 72 (1982) 206–7; Segal, *Tragedy and Civilization*, 189–90; Goldhill, *Reading Greek Tragedy*, 102; Sourvinou-Inwood, 'Assumptions and the Creation of Meaning', 140; Oudemans and Lardinois, *Tragic Ambiguity*, 177. R. Seaford, 'The Eleventh Ode of Bacchylides: Hera, Artemis, and the Absence of Dionysus', *JHS* 108 (1988) 118–36, and 'The Imprisonment of Women in Greek Tragedy', *JHS* 110 (1990) 76–90, discusses the larger implications of such failures to marry in Greek myth. For a detailed response to this and Souvinou-Inwood's charge (above and 'Sophocles' Antigone as a "Bad Woman" ', in F. Dieteren and E. Kloek (edd.), *Writing Women into History* [Amsterdam 1990] 11–38) that Antigone is generally a

'bad woman', see H. P. Foley, 'Tragedy and Democratic Ideology: The Case of Sophocles' *Antigone*', in B. Goff (ed.), *History, Tragedy and Theory* (Austin, Tex. 1995) 131–50.

16. For exceptions, see Blundell, *Helping Friends and Harming Enemies*, 133; Neuberg, 'How Like a Woman', 63; and Linforth, 'Antigone and Creon', 203.

17. As Neuberg, 'How Like a Woman', 69, stresses, Antigone 'describes what she *has* done; and that is all that matters. She *didn't* fail to bury a dead husband, or a dead brother when she had another brother living, and her parents *are* dead, so it is we who construct irrelevant hypotheses if we worry about this; "such was my *nomos* in burying you" is not the same as "such would have been my *nomos* regardless of the situation." '

18. For example, Blundell, *Helping Friends and Harming Enemies*, 134. See further, Hester, 'Sophocles the Unphilosophical,' 37; L. A. MacKay, 'Antigone, Coriolanus and Hegel', *TAPA* 93 (1962) 171; Murnaghan, '*Antigone* 904–920,' 201 and 206; and Winnington-Ingram, *Sophocles*, 143–5.

19. See Murnaghan, '*Antigone* 904–920,' 202–3.

20. H. Deliyanni, 'Blood Vengeance Attitudes in Mani and Corsica', unpub. manuscript, University of Exeter (1985) 95–6. See the similar conclusions of S. Wilson, *Feuding, Conflict, and Banditry in Nineteenth-Century Corsica* (Cambridge 1988) 211–23, esp. 219–20. He quotes a lament by a Corsican woman, Maria-Felice: 'Of so large a family | You leave only a sister, | Without first cousins, | Poor, orphaned and unarmed, | But to accomplish your vengeance | Rest assured that she alone suffices.' On Montenegrin women, who receive more respect than men if they undertake a revenge that is not viewed in their case as an obligation, see C. Boehm, *Blood Revenge: The Anthropology of Feuding in Montenegro and Other Tribal Societies* (Lawrence, Kan. 1984) 46–7 and 55–6. On Albania, see D. E. Cozzi, 'La vendetta del sangue nelle Montagne dell'Alta Albania', *Anthropos* 5 (1910) 654–87.

21. G. Holst-Warhaft, *Dangerous Voices: Women's Laments and Greek Literature* (Ithaca, NY 1992) 81; see further 77–84. She notes (47) that Maniot women frequently demonstrate a stronger allegiance to blood-kin than to the husband's family.

22. Ibid. 91–3.

23. 'Assumptions and the Creation of Meaning'.

24. Blundell, *Helping Friends and Harming Enemies*, 148.

25. As Goheen, *Imagery of Antigone*, remarks, 'Antigone's way of knowing is usually thought less adequate than Creon's'. For Antigone as intuitive and instinctive, see e.g.: ibid. 82; Murnaghan, '*Antigone*

904–920', 195; G. Kirkwood, *A Study of Sophoclean Drama* (Ithaca,
NY 1958) 165; H. D. F. Kitto, *Greek Tragedy*, 131; and Knox, *Heroic
Temper*, 116. For her illogical thought-processes and emotional piety,
see esp. Goheen, *Imagery of Antigone*, 76–9, 98; A. J. A. Waldock,
Sophocles the Dramatist (Cambridge 1951, reprinted 1966) 229; or
G. Norwood, *Greek Tragedy*, 4 (London 1948) 139. C. S. Levy,
'Antigone's Motives: A Suggested Interpretation', *TAPA* 94 (1963)
137–44, esp. 138 and 144, tries to make the case that Antigone combines
reason and instinct. Critics often attribute a serious religious force to
Antigone's supposed intuition (e.g. Reinhardt, *Sophokles*, 76–7: intuition is by the standards of much serious philosophy a legitimate part of
the ethical process); from this perspective the drama pits religious
against political priorities. Yet there are religious and political dimensions on both sides of the conflict (see e.g. Knox, *Heroic Temper*, 75).

26. On this position as exemplary of democratic ideology in Athens, see
    esp. Sourvinou-Inwood, 'Assumptions and the Creation of Meaning';
    Blundell, *Helping Friends and Harming Enemies*, 117; and Oudemans
    and Lardinois, *Tragic Ambiguity*, 164 and 174. For my own views, see
    Foley, 'Tragedy and Democratic Ideology'.

27. See Blundell, *Helping Friends and Harming Enemies*, 118–19;
    Linforth, 'Antigone and Creon', 189; Knox, *Heroic Temper*, 88.

28. On Creon's gnomic language, see E. Wolf, *Sentenz und Reflexion bei
    Sophokles* (Leipzig 1910) 48–53, 126–31; Winnington-Ingram,
    Sophocles, 120 and 126; Gellie, *Sophocles*, 33; Reinhardt, *Sophokles*,
    33; and Kitzinger, 'Stylistic Methods'.

29. The statistics are from Kitzinger, 'Stylistic Methods', 144. The num-
    ber of generalizations is highest in the scene with Haemon, his closest
    philos.

30. Nussbaum, *Fragility*, 80, argues that Tiresias and Haemon, who
    favour flexibility and responsiveness to the natural world and its com-
    plexities, are expressing an Aristotelian sensibility.

31. On Creon's limitations, see esp. Goheen, *Imagery of Antigone*, 75, 83;
    Knox, *Heroic Temper*; and Winnington-Ingram, *Sophocles*, 120 ff.

32. See Gellie, *Sophocles*, 35; and Leinieks, *Plays of Sophocles*, 65.

33. See Linforth, 'Antigone and Creon', 206; and Gellie, *Sophocles*, 40.

34. See Seale, *Vision and Stagecraft*, 99.

35. See further, Blundell, *Helping Friends and Harming Enemies*, 125; and
    Foley, 'Tragedy and Democratic Ideology', 137.

36. Blundell, *Helping Friends and Harming Enemies*, 122; and Nussbaum,
    Fragility, 55.

37. See further, Leinieks, *Sophocles*; H. Musurillo, *The Light and the
    Darkness* (Leiden 1967) 54; Knox, *Heroic Temper*, 11; and C. M.
    Bowra, *Sophoclean Tragedy* (Oxford 1944) 77.

38. See further, Goldhill, *Reading Greek Tragedy*, 99; and Blundell, *Helping Friends and Harming Enemies*, 120.

39. Blundell, *Helping Friends and Harming Enemies*, 122.

40. See Linforth, 'Antigone and Creon', 237.

41. Even at this point, since he does not bring back Antigone's body with him, he leaves the question of her own proper burial puzzlingly open. See W. Calder, 'Sophocles' Political Tragedy, *Antigone*', *GRBS* 9 (1968) 403; and Seale, *Vision and Stagecraft*, 107.

42. On this echoing of Antigone, see A. L. Brown, *Sophocles: Antigone* (Warminster 1987) on l. 745.

43. Porter, *Women and Moral Identity*, 148. As she stresses, 'the emphasis of women's moral agency reflects their historical involvement in small groups'. Yet just habits can be learned in the family, even if the formal claims of justice are less operative there (162).

44. As J. M. Broughton, 'Women's Rationality and Men's Virtues: A Critique of Gender Dualism in Gilligan's Theory of Moral Development', *Social Research* 50/3 (1983) 614, argues, 'while justice requires abstraction, it is intended as the abstract form that caring takes on when respect is maintained and responsibility assumed "for those we do not know personally" '.

45. Thuc. 2. 44. 3–4; Din. *Dem.* 71; Arist. *Ath. Pol.* 4. 2; Aeschin. 3. 77–8. On related issues, see Leinieks, *Sophocles*, 78 and 85.

46. Gilligan, *Different Voice*; and Gilligan, Ward, and Taylor, *Mapping the Moral Domain*; Kohlberg, *Philosophy*, and *Psychology*. In 1984, Kohlberg redefined his position and argued that he was measuring justice reasoning not moral maturity. Justice ideally entails a resolution of competing claims through the impartial application of abstract and universal principles to the situation at hand. Women tend to be arrested at stage three of Kohlberg's six stages. This stage involves mutual role-taking and concern with the approval of others and is linked by Kohlberg to the institution of the family.

47. Gilligan, *Different Voice*, 19.

48. Gilligan, 'Do the Social Sciences Have an Adequate Theory of Moral Development?', in N. Haan, R. N. Bellah, P. Rabinow, and W. M. Sullivan (edd.), *Social Science as Moral Inquiry* (New York 1983) 47. See also Gilligan *et al.*, *Mapping the Moral Domain*, 4–19.

49. As Porter, *Women and Moral Identity*, 156 points out, Gilligan initially tended to ignore women who (like Antigone) use abstract principles and men who (like all of the characters in this play) give a high priority in moral deliberation to social responsibility. Attachment and connection may be felt for units larger than the nuclear family.

50. The best defence of the significance of Gilligan's work for ethical theory is L. A. Blum, 'Gilligan and Kohlberg: Implications for Moral Theory', *Ethics* 98 (Apr. 1988) 472–91. He, too, however, does not show

how moral theory could bridge the gap between these two ethical modes.
51. For representative critiques of Gilligan, see esp. Porter, *Women and Moral Identity*, ch. 6; D. Nails, 'Social Scientific Sexism: Gilligan's Mismeasure of Man', *Social Research* 50/3 (1983) 643–64; M. M. Moody-Adams, 'Gender and the Complexity of Moral Voices', in C. Card (ed.), *Feminist Ethics* (Lawrence, Kan. 1991) 195–212; and Tronto, *Moral Boundaries*, 61–97. The data does not consistently report gender differences in cognitive moral development, and educational, class, ethnic, and economic differences may be equally telling explanatory factors. (See Kohlberg, *Philosophy*; Tronto, *Moral Boundaries*, 82–4; and K. P. Addelson, 'Moral Passages', in E. F. Kittay and D. T. Meyers [edd.], *Women and Moral Theory* [Totowa, NJ 1987] 105.) The care orientation identified by Gilligan may well be the function of setting and dilemma, of private and familial contexts in which certain obligations are presupposed (Kohlberg, *Psychology*). Gilligan's 'theory functions as an account of partial privilege in our society, not as an account of an alternative way to conceive of morality. . . . Gendered morality helps to preserve the distribution of power and privilege' (Tronto, *Moral Boundaries*, 63 and 91).
52. On the unwritten laws as sanctioned by the *polis* and central to its interest, rather than marginal to it, see Creon at 1113 and Blundell, *Helping Friends and Harming Enemies*, 128. At Xen. *Mem.* 4. 4. 14 ff. Socrates suggests that the transgressors of man-made laws may escape punishment, but not those of divine law.
53. Antigone's stance also reflects, however, a female inexperience in undertaking public roles required, at least in Creon's view, of leaders.
54. I do not mean to argue here that we can generalize from *Antigone* about the problem of gender and ethical choice in Greek tragedy.
55. See esp. J.-P. Vernant, in Vernant and Vidal-Naquet, *Tragedy and Myth in Ancient Greece*, 1–27. Haemon's intervention, at least initially, serves to validate public ethics undermined by Creon.
56. Most unwritten laws affirm behaviour sanctioned in the family. Yet I disagree with those critics who see Antigone as consistently aligned with the natural, the supernatural, and the private, as well as devaluing human institutions (e.g. Murnaghan, '*Antigone* 904–920', 200–1).
57. On this issue, see L. J. Bennett and W. B. Tyrrell, 'Sophocles' *Antigone* and Funeral Oratory', *AJP* 111 (1990) 441–56, and Foley, 'Tragedy and Democratic Ideology', 140–20.
58. On Thebes as a tragic anti-Athens, see esp. F. I. Zeitlin, 'Thebes: Theater of Self and Society', in Euben (ed.), *Greek Tragedy*, 101–41.
59. See Sorum, 'Family', esp. 201–2, on the play as a response to the Athenians' appropriation of blood relationships and the household, although my own conclusions differ from hers.

4

Tragedy and the Fragility of Moral Reasoning: Response to Foley

MICHAEL TRAPP

The heart of Helene Foley's closely argued paper is a vindication of Antigone as the occupier of a coherent ethical standpoint and practitioner of a valid ethical style—against those somewhat patronizing, somewhat male, critics (mostly writing before 1965) who have belittled her as an irrational, impulsive female, more lovable for her instincts than exemplary in her clarity of thought. This central vindication is not meant as an end in itself; two paths may be seen leading from it to wider issues. The new view of Antigone, Professor Foley hopes, will prompt an enrichment of our sense of how fifth-century tragedy 'problematizes Athenian civic values and discourse',[1] and a new examination of the workings of the key terms of Aristotle's analysis of tragic poetry, *êthos*, *prohairesis*, and *katharsis*.[2]

In the event, the Aristotelian project is gestured towards rather than developed at any length,[3] though it is easy enough to see how the argument might be allowed to advance. If *êthos* is what clarifies the nature of a *prohairesis*, and if Antigone explains and defends her *prohairesis* in the play from a distinctive, and as yet insufficiently appreciated standpoint, then it follows that attention to that distinctive standpoint will modify our views not only of her *êthos*, but of the possibilities of dramatic *êthos* more generally; and that in turn could affect our understanding of the routes and devices open to the tragedian for inducing (and purging) the proper tragic emotions. This is a line of thought that undeniably has its attractions, but it is also open to some weighty objections. Above all, it seems to me that to make the kind of claim that Foley would want to make about the distinctiveness of Antigone's moral awareness goes outside the terms of reference of Aristotelian analysis. And if that is so, then no new perception of Antigone as the practitioner of a distinctive moral mode can contribute to an understanding of Aristotelian *êthos* and *prohairesis*. Moreover, the difficulties only increase if one attempts to extend the project to include a revised view of tragic *katharsis*.[4]

The second possibility—an enhanced sense of the propensity of tragedy to problematize—is both more substantial and more directly relevant to 'tragedy and the tragic'. Before it can properly be pursued, however, Foley's central claim about Antigone's under-appreciated difference, her 'other voice', needs to be examined. A number of carefully interconnected strands combine to make the case. First, there is the question of the social conventions and understandings relevant to Antigone's unusual status. Foley uses comparative evidence for the workings of vendetta in modern Europe to suggest that the social position from which Antigone speaks is a highly abnormal, yet generally recognized extreme—that of the woman compelled (and licensed) to act on behalf of the family as an honorary man in the absence of surviving male relatives. This Antigone speaks from the far edge of legitimate social organization, dangerously near the boundary, to the central position of political authority so confidently appropriated by Creon. Both the content and the style of what she says from this 'marginal . . . socially resistant position' then call for analysis, again in systematic contrast to both the content and the style of Creon's pronouncements.

There is, of course, common ground between the two antagonists. Both Creon and Antigone have to explain and justify moral choices made[5] in accordance with the commands of an authority they present as supreme (the gods for Antigone, the laws and decrees of civic authority for Creon); and both commend their choices precisely as virtuously obedient to higher principle. Beyond that, their respective terms of reference differ sharply. To Antigone's insistence on the particularity of family relationships, the responsibilities they impose, and their emotional effects on those party to them, Creon opposes a perception of citizenship, collective obedience, and group loyalty, in which individual tastes and emotions can be corrected and directed according to the collective interest, and the function of loyal citizenship takes precedence over individual relationships and membership of subordinate groupings. But this is not all. Creon and Antigone are further held to differ over the way they regard the general principles they act by, and the process of applying them. Creon evinces the belief that right and prudent action will always follow from the (unproblematic) application of principles that are not only general (in the sense of binding on all relevant agents) but also phrased in generalities; individual circumstances, according to this view, are irrelevant to the application of the principles, which *will* always be wholly adequate without modification, and *must* always be acted on. Antigone, by contrast, has a subtler attitude to context and circumstance. This is not so much a matter of her belief that, in the specific circumstances in which she and Creon find themselves, an otherwise serviceable civic principle should yield to another deriving from a different source of authority: that perception might perhaps be inferred from her stance, but it is not explicitly articulated in the play, and does not form part of Foley's reading. The point is rather to do with Antigone's attitude to the principle on which she herself acts. According to Foley, her position is that a general moral principle ('families ought to bury their dead') can exist *without* being automatically binding on all relevant agents; as her last address to Creon and the citizens of Thebes (891–928) makes clear, it is only the specific, abnormal circumstances of the Labdacid line that activate the principle *for her*. Thirdly, and finally, there is a significant difference in the respective ways in which Antigone and Creon set about justifying and recommending their moral choices to others. Creon is happy to urge the same considerations in the same terms to any and every addressee, whether Antigone and Ismene, his son Haemon, or the citizens of Thebes. Antigone, by contrast, varies her presentation according to the nature of her audience, urging purely familial and private considerations to Ismene (1–99), but combining those with more public, political terms of reference in speaking to Creon (443–525) and the city (891–928), and moreover adopting a more respectful and conciliatory tone with the latter than she accords the former.

This is a subtle and challenging analysis, combining a number of elements that need not all stand or fall together. What seems to me to be wholly well-said and immediately acceptable is the initial contrast between Antigone's attention to the particularity of family relationships and responsibilities (her 'morality of care'), and Creon's more abstract, dispassionate talk of civic obligation. This notably refines and enlivens the conventional critical perception of the opposition between the 'claims of the family' and the 'claims of the state' that has become so familiar and ingrained in discussions of the play; in place of that blunt and abstract opposition, we are offered instead a contrast between two different ways of articulating the relationship between individual and group, and thus of understanding the context for moral choice and action. Our view of what is at stake between Antigone and Creon may not be radically changed, but it is appreciably enriched. Equally fruitful is the further contrast between Antigone's more adaptable, rhetorical approach to the communication of her convictions to others, and the monotone absolutism of the political leader. Antigone the Persuader has not so far been a familiar figure in criticism of the play; the emphasis has, if anything, been on her Knoxian-heroic resistance and imperviousness to the persuasion of others. Foley's analysis shows that this is too partial a view, one which considerably understates the complexity and nuance with which Antigone's relationships with the other stage-figures are constructed.

Antigone's readiness to adopt differing persuasive strategies is, however, on Foley's view, demonstrated not only in her exchanges with Ismene and with Creon (in lines 1–99 and 443–525), but also in her last, celebrated address to the chorus in lines 891–928. That same passage is also crucial to her claim that Antigone manifests a distinctively 'contextual' conception of the applicability of moral principles. It is here that my reservations begin. I find it very hard to read the lines in question as they must be read if they are to do the job Foley entrusts to them. For her, these lines constitute an utterance that is in important senses continuous with those of 1–99 and 443–525. In this final speech, as in both of the earlier scenes, Antigone must be read as making yet another attempt to make the grounds for her chosen action clear and convincing to others, and in the process amending and refining the nature of those grounds. Above all, for Foley, it is here that it becomes clear that Antigone would only have done what she did as last (surviving) sister for last (deceased) brother—and thus that her 'moral mode' allows for the existence of moral principles that do not immediately place those involved under an obligation.

What makes me uneasy is the feeling that this reading of the last speech is bought at the price of discounting the surface context and rhetoric of the lines:

O tomb, my bridal bed—my house, my prison
cut in the hollow rock, my everlasting watch!
I'll soon be there, soon embrace my own

. . . .

                    But now, Polyneices,
because I laid your body out as well,
this, this is my reward. Nevertheless
I honoured you—the decent will admit it—
well and wisely too.

. . . .

And now he leads me off, a captive in his hands,
with no part in the bridal song, the bridal bed,
denied all joy of marriage . . .[6]

The overt addressees are not the chorus of citizens, but the tomb,
Polynices, and (implicitly) the gods; and Antigone's words are not,
on the face of it, a quasi-judicial analysis and a commendation of
her motives, but a lament, a *miseratio*, dwelling on the cruelty and
the unfairness of her having to die, unmarried and childless, for no
greater crime than 'honouring' (904, 913) a beloved brother in circumstances which made it emotionally impossible for her not to
choose and act as she did. These are indeed lines full of *êthos*, and
they do indeed again underline Antigone's readiness to give weight
to particular relationships, and the emotions surrounding them, as
determinants of moral choice; but I see in them neither a third
attempt to adapt to a new audience, nor a last refinement of a distinctive view of how moral principles should operate.

My other main reservation concerns the question of Antigone's
social position, and the insight to be gained from comparative,
modern evidence for attitudes to female rights and obligations in
the absence of surviving male relatives. Here too I would be
inclined to tread more tentatively. In the first place, the grounds
for attributing something like the attitudes manifested in the modern evidence to fifth-century Greeks are thin. Secondly, even if
something like those attitudes were current in fifth-century
Athens, one would still have to reckon with the distancing effect of
tragic myth: Antigone is a Theban princess of the distant past, not
a contemporary Athenian virgin, and a social convention that
makes sense for the latter need not necessarily also work in the
imagined world of the former.[7] And finally, I am struck by the
extent to which the play seems to me to shy away from talking in

the necessary terms. Above all, in the opening dialogue between Antigone and Ismene (1–99), no mention at all is made of any new status that events may have conferred on Antigone as representative of her family; indeed, the family seems to be removed from consideration as an arena for choice and action, in order to sharpen the sense of a confrontation between the girls and civic authority (44–8, 59–60, 78–9). Antigone's position is indeed marginal and exposed—as orphaned virgin, as the last representative of a troubled family, and as a woman daring to speak and act in an area to which public, masculine authority claims sole rights—but it is not at all clear that temporary status as an honorary man is also part of the mix.

For all that, more than enough remains of Foley's new Antigone for it to be worthwhile asking how the revised picture might feed back into, and enhance, our sense of the tragic in the play, and thus to return to the proposal that her analysis of Antigone's stance sharpens our awareness of the ways in which Athenian tragedy can and does function to 'problematize . . . civic values and discourse'. This seems to me to be entirely along the right lines, and to work even if the reservations I have entered above are pressed. Creon's 'moral voice' is indeed recognizably akin (though, as Foley shows, not exactly identical) to that of Athenian public discourse, and it is indeed shown up as inadequate by the unfolding of events in the play, both by the abnormal situation in which he finds himself compelled to act, and by the contrast with other actors in the story. Antigone's opposition, both the simple fact of her arguing against him, and the contrasting ethical 'voice' she speaks with, are central to this process, as also is the attempted 'mediation' of Haemon, as son to the one and fiancé to the other.

I am, however, uneasy with the further suggestion that the final effect of the contrast between Antigone and Creon, and Haemon's attempted mediation, is to point towards some 'better mode of public deliberation'.[8] Foley herself qualifies the suggestion by admitting that, given the outcome of the action, the play does not in fact seem to hold out great hopes that such a better mode of deliberation can be realized in practice. But even with this qualification, it seems to me that the balance has been wrongly drawn. For I see a sense in which it is not only Creon's male, public, quasi-Athenian mode of morality that is called into question by the play, but Antigone's (and Haemon's) as well. Because, of course, it is not only Creon's mode which is shown up, in the sense of failing to achieve both a just outcome and one which preserves the happiness and safety of all deserving parties; the same can be said of the other two. I should therefore prefer to see a 'problematization' not simply of civic values and discourse, but of moral deliberation in general, and set this in turn against a picture of the nature of tragedy that stresses the medium's dedication to thinking the uncomfortable thought.

Seen from this vantage-point, the *Antigone* would then appear as an unsettling, destabilizing assault on naïve reliance on human moral resources, on the faith that accepted thoughts and procedures can be guaranteed to yield good decisions, and to ward off harm, in all conceivable circumstances. In a particular, and particularly extreme, moment of mythological time, the *Antigone* finds a set of circumstances, and a set of moral agents, by whom and for whom these comforting convictions are shattered. The first two-thirds of the play (up to line 987) set up a conflict of claims, in which neither claimant can be regarded with complete equanimity: Antigone, for all the instinctive appeal of her position, is at the same time (as Christiane Sourvinou-Inwood argues)[9] a woman out of place, challenging legitimate, male, civic authority; and Creon, for all that he represents legitimate, male, civic authority, worries us by the absoluteness of his confidence in his own judgement and his own rightness. Then, with the arrival of Tiresias in line 988, the play delivers its shock: the authority of the gods themselves, mediated through a human seer, proves Creon to have been wrong and Antigone, if not wholly in the right, at least to have been aiming all along at a right outcome, and to have been more the victim of another's wrong choice than of her own. This is shaking enough in itself, but what redoubles the effect is the fact that (characteristically, tragically)[10] transcendent clarification comes *too late*: too late either for Antigone to claim the security that ought to follow from virtuous impulse, or for Creon to undo the harm he has set in train.

In this perspective, the *Antigone* becomes an illustration of how tragedy 'problematizes' not just civic discourse, but moral discourse in general, by revealing the fragility and fallibility of the available 'technologies of preservation'. Normative moral discourse in Athens (above all, as seen in the formation of the young) enshrined the conviction, or at least the hope, that easily definable virtuous practices and forms of decision-making could be relied upon to keep both individual and community safe and prosperous. This is the conviction we see embodied in such authoritative texts from an earlier age as Hesiod, *Works and Days* 225 ff.:

> For those whose judgements to strangers and citizens alike
> are straight, and who do not diverge from what is right,
> their community flourishes and the people in it blooms;
> peace pervades their land, fostering the young
>
> . . . .
>
> The earth bears them food in plenty
>
> . . . .
>
> and their women bear children that resemble their fathers.[11]

In this context, what tragedy can be seen as doing is undermining such a comfortable assumption, by demonstrating that circumstances can always be found in which the attempted application of normally laudable impulses and principles (civic loyalty, family solidarity, or whatever) fails to yield a safe and pain-free outcome. This can be a matter both of hard circumstances themselves, and of ordinary, familiar kinds of human blindness working to frustrate constructive action. What I think Foley's analysis can be made to add is a further thought to render this sobering vision of unavoidable danger and hurt all the more cruel. For, on her reading, the *Antigone* prompts the realization that moral deliberation itself is not the safely unitary tool that convention pretends: it too can break up into partial, conflicting perspectives, and the conflict between them can play a large part in a particular episode of hurt and loss.[12]

It then becomes an interesting question how far this way of reading the *Antigone* might be extended—to other plays of Sophocles, or to tragedy more generally. Within the Sophoclean corpus, *Philoctetes* would clearly be a promising text to interrogate, with its juxtaposition of the contrasting moral outlooks of Philoctetes, Neoptolemus, and Odysseus; one might also think of the acutely juxtaposed viewpoints of Odysseus and Ajax in *Ajax*. Outside Sophocles, the *Oresteia* inevitably springs to mind, though perhaps misleadingly: the contrast between the deliberations of Clytemnestra and Orestes does not quite seem to be one between alternative modes in the sense required. In Euripides, one might look to such moments as the scene between Heracles and Theseus at the end of *Heracles*. In terms of the analysis of specific texts,

therefore, this looks like a critical manœuvre that will only sometimes yield interesting results. Seen against the wider background
of theories of the tragic, it must also claim only a modest status, but
a real one, as one of several possible determinations of the general
perception that *aporia*, the unsettling inadequacy of human
resources to deal with circumstance, is central to tragic experience.

With an eye still on the tragic, but looking also once more to the
cultural specifics of Sophoclean and fifth-century thought, I conclude with a historical note. Towards the end of her paper, Foley
suggests a connection between the presentation of contrasting
moral modes in the *Antigone* and the growth of fifth-century political and rhetorical theory.[13] As stated, this seems implausible, or at
the very least unprovable. There is nothing in the (admittedly
scanty) record of sophistic thought to parallel the kind of distinction drawn between differing 'ethical voices', or to suggest that the
necessary concepts and vocabulary were even available in the middle of the fifth century. But it might be plausible to claim a connection of a different kind, on the basis of the suggestion made
above, that what is distressing about the conflict of Antigone and
Creon is the very fact that radical disunity and incompatibility
between moral principles is possible. Attacking naïve confidence in
the goodness and effectiveness of conventional justice in his treatise *Truth*, the sophist Antipho gleefully points out how easy it is
for two equally firmly held and central principles of justice to come
into conflict. It is generally agreed to be 'just' both to refrain from
harming those who have not harmed you, and to give true evidence
in court when called upon to do so; but if your true testimony as a
bystander to a criminal act results in the imprisonment or execution of the criminal, then you have, in one and the same act, kept
the second principle but broken the first.[14] Antipho, like
Sophocles, fastens on a set of circumstances where an apparently
stable and coherent system breaks down; but the sophist and the
dramatist draw diverging conclusions. The one sees an opportunity to free the individual from the spell of a conventional morality
that pointlessly shackles his chances of comfort and happiness.
The other sees no such sunny prospect; in its place he articulates
the sobering reflection that no amount of tinkering, even with the
best moral thinking, can ever be guaranteed to yield the comfort of
an agreed outlook, let alone immunity from harm.

Notes

1. Above, p. 66.
2. Above, pp. 49–50 and 68.
3. Although Aristotle is again invoked several times in the later stages of the paper, it is for the light he can throw on the characterization of Creon (p. 60), and for his views of law and civic relationships (p. 67), not for the project initially sketched.
4. It has always been possible for an Aristotelianizing reader to read the scenes Foley analyses as establishing that Antigone's choice of action (to bury her brother in defiance of a formal decree from legitimate authority) is not the choice of a morally defective person: the scenes in question reveal both that the choice itself was informed by deliberation and an awareness of the relevant factors of the situation (*NE* 3. 1–3), and that it was accompanied by an appropriate degree of the appropriate kind of emotion (*NE* 2. 5–6), in such a way that there was no conflict to be fought out between the agent's emotions and her intellect (*NE* 7. 1–8). What Foley's analysis would add is, first, an enhanced sense of Antigone's clear intellectual grasp of the facts of the situation—her awareness of what it is about her unique predicament that obliges her to act; and secondly, the proposition that this same intellectual awareness is of a distinctive kind, not shared by other characters in the play (above all, not by Creon). But this is precisely where it seems that the claim about the distinctiveness of Antigone's moral awareness goes outside the terms of reference of Aristotelian analysis. Neither the *Ethics* nor the *Poetics* provides the language or the concepts to articulate the distinction Foley wants between two different, let alone two equally valid, moral modes. The Aristotelian model of moral perception and moral decision-making is unitary; it simply has no room for such pluralism. And if that is so, then the new perception of Antigone advanced, whatever its other merits, cannot be included in an Aristotelian reading of the play. The further difficulty over tragic *katharsis* arises from Aristotle's stipulation that the misfortunes of the protagonist should be seen to stem from some mistake (*hamartia*) rather than from viciousness of character (*Poet.* 13, 1453ª7 ff.). Antigone does indeed choose, act, and suffer fearfully and pitiably for her action; but the subsequent development of the play shows that it is her adversary—the man who brought it about that her choice and action should lead to suffering—who is the more unequivocally guilty of defective choice. This would seem to make it difficult to isolate a neat *hamartia* on her part. A strict Aristotelian analysis just seems inadequate to the play, and this inadequacy is in no way eased—indeed, it might even be intensified—by any suggestion that Antigone represents a distinctive, and distinctively virtuous, ethical mode.

5. I choose my words carefully here. Foley sometimes speaks as if the play presents moral choices in the making. It does not: the important choices have been made before the action of the play starts (cf. Mogyoródi, in this volume, p. 361); what we see are characters recommending and justifying them, not making them.

6. *Ant.* 891–3, 902–4, 916–18, trans. Fagles.

7. The contrast between the freedoms of movement and initiative enjoyed by tragic women (and the attention given to their choices and perceptions), and the restriction and neglect in Athenian law and public life, is often remarked; given those freedoms, tragic women in their fictive society might be felt to have less need of the honorary masculinity conferred by vendetta. Equally, the way that use of other places and distant times gave Athenian tragedians a medium in which they could examine aspects of contemporary experience, without being obliged to represent it directly, is well-appreciated; this gives a second possible reason for thinking twice before taking a conjecture about fifth-century attitudes as holding also for the world of tragic myth. At the very least, more argument is required to make it plausible that the convention of honorary masculinity is at home in Sophocles' Thebes.

8. Above, p. 67.

9. 'Assumptions and the Creation of Meaning'.

10. Cf. R. B. Rutherford, 'Tragic Form and Feeling in the *Iliad*', *JHS* 102 (1982) 148–9 (also Silk, in this volume, pp. 469–70).

11. Hesiod, *Works* 225–8, 232, 235; cf. also (e.g.) *Odyssey* 19. 108 ff.

12. Cf. Segal's view of tragic *language* as conflict, discussed by Silk in this volume, p. 463.

13. Above, pp. 66–7.

14. Antipho B 44, 2 col. 1 (2. 353–5) D–K.

5

Shifts of Mood and Concepts of Time in Euripides' *Ion*

KEVIN LEE

No play of Euripides shifts mood so challengingly, so aggressively as the *Ion*. Alongside the numerous amusing moments, there stands the figure of Kreousa, whose grief and profound sense of loss are presented with unrivalled power. Our feelings of anxiety at her misguided but quite explicable attempt on Ion's life and at his violent retaliation are not obliterated by the promise of a happy end. Furthermore, it is difficult to agree with interpretations like those of Kitto which see the purpose of the play as nothing more than its own success.[1] A superbly engineered plot, deft touches of irony, and an impressive theatricality certainly make us admire the poet's cleverness. But this virtuosity goes hand in hand with the dramatization of serious themes which are presented too emphatically to be incidental or illusory.

One such theme, which I propose to examine in this paper, involves the varying attitudes to time which are revealed by the characters—Ion and Kreousa in particular. I also suggest that their attitudes to time can be linked with some of the principal changes of mood which we sense as the drama progresses.

The play begins with a typically Euripidean monologue spoken by the god Hermes (1–81). He presents a survey which sweeps from the Erechtheid clan's distant past to the glorious future which awaits Ion. The manner of the boy's conception, birth, exposure, and subsequent rescue are related with an objective precision:

Phoebus had intercourse against her will with the daughter of Erechtheus, Kreousa. . . . Without her father's knowledge (this was the god's pleasure) she carried the child in her womb until its birth. When the time came, after giving birth at home, Kreousa took her infant son away to the same cave where she had slept with the god, and exposed him, seemingly to die,

in a chest deep and neatly rounded. . . . Picking up the wickerwork basket
I brought it here and put the child on the floor of this temple, folding back
the rounded lid of the chest so that the child could be seen. (10 f., 14 ff.,
37 ff.)

In fact, the speech as a whole is devoid of any interest in human
feeling. The significant exception is the Pythia's change of heart:
'She was ready to remove the baby from the temple building; but
pity got the better of her harsh feelings' (46 f.). But this woman
acts, no less than Hermes, as Apollo's agent, and can be seen as an
extension of the supernatural.[2]

The tone of Hermes' speech impresses us with the fact that, as a
god himself and as the agent of the god of prophecy, he can survey
imperiously the past, present, and future. But alongside this, his
speech makes us aware that we shall be looking at events through
the eyes of those whose vision has a narrower focus and for whom
a single event or individual object may be of overwhelming concern. A characteristic of Hermes' prologue is its remarkably
detailed account of places, objects, and circumstances. Kreousa's
rape by Apollo, and her subsequent exposure of her baby, are
exactly located (11 ff., 17); the crib in which the baby was exposed
is mentioned repeatedly and described in a quite precise and elaborate way (19, 32, 37, 39 f.); the circumstances of Kreousa's preg-
nancy and of Ion's rescue by the Pythia are all related with
meticulous care (14 f., 41 ff.). It would seem that from the very
beginning of the play we are meant to be impressed with the
importance of the details of life for those who are immersed in it.

Coupled with this amalgam of the general and the particular is
the fact that the speech has two local foci. We are told, as usual,
where the play is set, and Hermes describes in some detail Delphi
and its oracular fame: 'I have come to this land of Delphi, where
sitting at the very navel of the earth Phoebus sings to mortals, continually explaining in prophecy the things that are and those that
are to be' (5 ff.). But then he turns to a precise picture of Athens
and its acropolis: 'There is a city of the Greeks far from unknown,
which is named after Pallas Athene, who carries a spear of gold
. . . beneath Pallas' hill in the land of the Athenians lie north-
facing rocks called "Long Cliffs" by the lords of Attic soil' (8 ff.).
Hermes' narrative of past events swings between these two places
and we suspect that the play too may shift its locale, since mother
and son, we are told in 71 f., are to be reunited not in Delphi, but in

Athens.[3] The report of Apollo's plan proves to be misleading; nevertheless, it prepares us for the way in which the action is, in a sense, sited in both places. Though it is Delphi that we are meant to see before us, we are repeatedly confronted with images of Athens as we enter the consciousness of characters for whom Athens and events associated with it are an obsessive preoccupation.

In sharp contrast with the god's panoramic perspective is the confined and limited vision of the temple servant Ion, who opens the play proper with a monody accompanying his tasks around Apollo's precinct. Ion is embedded in the present: he has no pedigree, not even a name, and cannot speak with any certainty of his past: 'I know only one thing: I am spoken of as Loxias' property' (311). His age is mentioned as of importance only in relation to the memories of others. Kreousa is distressed to see that he is the same age as would have been the son she has lost (354); later Xouthos reckons with some pleasure that Ion is the right age to have been conceived during a Bacchanalian fling in Delphi (545 ff.). Ion's hold on his past is so tenuous that it is simply a chance meeting with a man desperate for a son that can change his life and lead to his having a name, a father, and even a history which he must accept because it sounds plausible and because he knows nothing to the contrary. He would have had to accept no less readily the marginally different background given to him soon afterwards by the malicious fantasies of the Old Man (817 ff.).

Ion's mode of existence naturally roots him in the present and he is sealed in the almost timeless *now* of service to the god he speaks of as a father: 'In the performance of pious tasks I grow not weary. Phoebus is the father who begat me. I honour him who nurtures me and I call by the name of father my benefactor, Phoebus, god of the temple' (134 ff.). His livelihood and clothes all come from the god and his visitors (323, 326 f.). The entire precinct belongs to him and he feels at home 'wherever sleep takes him' (315). His person is submerged in his activity and so the chorus identify him simply by reference to what he does—as the young man who was sweeping the temple (795).

Ion's involvement with the here and now is brought out forcefully in his opening monody, unique in tone and content. The lowliest of tasks—sweeping, laying dust with water, shooing away messy birds—are accompanied by song in high-flown form and language:

Come, new-grown shoot of fairest bay, instrument of my task, who sweep the steps beneath the temple of Phoebus. . . . Well, I shall stop my work with the trailing branches of bay and shall sprinkle from golden vessels spring water which the streams of Kastalia pour forth. . . . Oh no! The birds are already flocking here leaving their nests on Parnassus. Don't go near the eaves, I tell you, or the temple covered with gold. I shall finish you off too, herald of Zeus, with my arrows, even though with your beak you are the strongest of birds. (112 ff., 144 ff., 154 ff.)

There is no denying that the incongruity has an amusing effect.[4] But I think that the creation of a light-hearted mood is secondary to the main purpose, which is to characterize the singer. Knox compares Ion's activities here to those of Euripides' Electra at the start of her name play.[5] Seidensticker is right, I think, in detecting a different tone.[6] The scene which opens *Electra* is as grimly bitter as Ion's monody is sparkling and flamboyant. But the scenes are parallel to the extent that they are both expressive of character. Electra's gratuitous labour with her water-jug is a flaunting of her sense of disinheritance and is felt as a duty performed out of regard for her husband (57 f., 71 ff.). Ion, on the other hand, embraces his chores, which he sees in an almost sacramental light. The new day finds him performing the only tasks he knows; he has been doing them day after day and prays that he may continue to do so: 'May I never cease serving Phoebus in this way, or may I stop through good fortune' (151 ff.). There is no sign here, as in the case of Electra and others,[7] of any painful dissonance between aspirations and actuality, or between past glory and present deprivation. Instead, there is in Ion's song a sense of complete immersion in the present, with the contentment which that brings. It brings also a tendency to the obsessive, which expresses itself in the attention to the detail of his chores. His various activities are systematically described, with close attention to the precise nature of the broom he uses and to the receptacles for, and source of, the water he sprinkles (112 ff., 146 ff.). The birds which threaten to defile Apollo's temple are carefully distinguished by species and appearance (158 ff.).[8]

That these mundane details are elevated in lyric language which approaches the hieratic is expressive of Ion's almost romantic attachment to his ministry.[9] His pleasure in his humble tasks leads us naturally to the delighted lyrics of the entering chorus. Kreousa's servants connect the sights before them with those of their own city: 'Not in sacred Athens alone then are there courts of the gods with lovely columns and pillars in honour of Agyieus. But also in the domain of Loxias, Leto's son, there is the brightness of beautiful faces shining from twin façades' (184 ff.). They then pick out for elaboration images reminiscent of home: the struggles of Heracles, familiar from stories often told while they work (196 f.); Pallas, whom they call 'my goddess' (211), crushing the Giants.

The holiday mood, as it has been called,[10] of the play's *parodos* is disrupted by the entrance of Kreousa (237).[11] Ion is in the habit of greeting visitors like the chorus who share his pious feelings and for whom Delphi is a source of joy and hope (245 f., 641). But whereas her serving-maids delight in the pleasurable sights around them, Kreousa's eyes are closed with tears as soon as she catches sight of Apollo's shrine: 'You upset me [Ion exclaims], closing your eyes and drenching your noble cheek with tears when you caught sight of the sacred shrine of Loxias. What brings you this anxiety, lady?' (241 ff.). Like the chorus she is reminded of Athens, but for her it is a sad memory of the events in the cave beneath the acropolis. So powerful is the evocation of the past that she seems to lose consciousness of where she is: 'Though standing here, I turned my mind to that place' (251). Kreousa's immersion in past events is further revealed in her highly emotional apostrophes and aporetic questions: 'Unhappy women! The things gods do! What to do then? Where shall we turn for justice if we are going to be ruined by the unjust deeds of those above us?' (252 ff.). But then she seems relieved to engage with the concerns of the kind-mannered stranger.

Two sets of interrogation now follow, with Ion and Kreousa leading in turn. It is often pointed out that the affinity of mother and son is expressed unconsciously in this initial encounter.[12] So too are their differing attitudes to the past and the present. As we have seen, Ion is rooted by necessity in the present. His own past is concealed from him, and so he turns with enthusiasm to the aristocratic stranger's impressive history, and draws on her knowledge of the city in which he displays a keen interest. Kreousa is content to answer each of his questions about her forebears and their connection with Attic soil, but whenever he seems to bring the past too close to home, he meets with an evasive response:

ION. What is it, madam, that brings you sorrow I cannot understand?

KREOUSA. Nothing; I have said all I have to say. I am staying silent about the matter and you worry about it no longer . . .
ION. Is there a spot there known as 'the Long Rocks'?
KREOUSA. Why do you ask about this? You remind me of something! . . .
ION. Have you never ever given birth and are you wholly barren?
KREOUSA. Phoebus knows about my childlessness . . .

(255 ff., 283 f., 305 f.)

When leading the interrogation in 308 ff., Kreousa escapes momentarily from her obsession with events which deprived her of her child, and focuses on the present situation and life-style of the young man in front of her. Ion's ignorance of his place in history is emphasized by contrast with the assurance with which she was able to respond to his queries. This is clearly seen in their parallel exchanges:

ION. Who are you? Where do you come from? What is your homeland? By what name should I call you?
KREOUSA. Kreousa is my name, Erechtheus is my father and the city of the Athenians is my homeland.
ION. Lady, you dwell in a famed city and are born of noble ancestors. How you fill me with admiration!

(258 ff.)

KREOUSA. And who are you? How happy I count the woman who bore you!
ION. I am called a slave of the god, and so I am, lady.
KREOUSA. A slave by public dedication or sold by someone?
ION. I know but one thing. I am called the property of Loxias.
KREOUSA. Then I feel pity for you in turn, stranger.
ION. No doubt because I do not know who bore me and who is my father.

(308 ff.)

On the other hand, Ion is perfectly able to answer her questions on the life he has come to embrace. He is happy to discuss his present circumstances; but talk of the mother who long ago lost and now yearns for him brings a firm closure to the subject:

KREOUSA. Your poor mother, I expect, yearns for you too, stranger.
ION. Ah! Do not prompt me to grieve over what has been forgotten.

(360 f.)

Kreousa's natural attraction to Ion comes out strongly in the next section of their dialogue. She is prompted to share her secret with the sympathetic young man, but αἰδώς ('shame', 'embarrassment') stands in the way (336). The device of the fictitious friend allows her to recount from an assumed distance the events which she felt unable to pursue earlier (283 ff.). The factual tone Kreousa adopts assists her pretended objectivity, but her attachment to her own view of events on the acropolis is clear from Ion's response to her story. His denials are met with firm counter-denials, while his justified scepticism about her inferences is ignored:

KREOUSA. A friend of mine says that she had intercourse with Phoebus.
ION. A mortal woman and Phoebus? Say not so, stranger.
KREOUSA. What is more, she bore a child to the god, unbeknown to her father.
ION. It can't be! It is some man's wrongdoing that causes her shame.
KREOUSA. She claims otherwise, and she has suffered terribly.

ION. If the child is no longer alive, in what way did it meet its death?
KREOUSA. She assumes that wild beasts killed the poor thing.
ION. What evidence does she have for thinking that?
KREOUSA. Going to the spot where she left him, she couldn't find him again.
ION. Was there any trace of blood on the track?
KREOUSA. She says no; and yet many is the time she went over the ground.

(338 ff., 347 ff.)

Ion's concrete, objective approach to the friend's story points the way to the truth, one aspect of which is reached in his suggestion in 357 that Apollo may be secretly rearing the child. But this leads nowhere because Kreousa continues to focus on the sorrow she has felt in the years since Ion's birth. Thus for all their mutual attraction Ion remains nothing more to Kreousa than a reminder of the child she once bore.

The human limitations which are evident in this dialogue are emphasized in its ending with Kreousa's desperate admonition of the god who knows all the answers but who seems determined to keep his distance:

Phoebus, both there and here you do wrong to the absent woman whose story is being told. You neither saved your own child whom you ought to have saved nor, though a seer, will you give an answer to the mother who makes enquiry so that, if the child lives no more, it can have the dignity of a grave-mound, and if it is still alive, it may one day come to find its mother. (384 ff.)

In the light of the predicted happy end this can all be seen as productive of light-hearted irony and as an amusing display of human
failings in the face of a providential and ultimately benevolent
deity.[13] But the characters themselves are unaware that all is to
turn out for the best, and it is their earnest stumbling towards and
away from the truth which encourages us to think seriously about
Apollo's detachment.[14] The reunion of mother and son must wait
for what the god sees as the right moment. The brief delay at this
point is of no more importance to him than the long years since
Ion's birth. But it is precisely the effect of those years which are
brought out in the foregoing dialogue. For Kreousa they are lost
years that have left her embedded in a past event which clouds her
vision of present realities. For Ion they are years spent in the service of his patron, a service bringing contentment which excludes
concern with anything but the present.

Kreousa's hopeless denunciation of the god in 384 ff.—a reprise
of the emotional outburst before her dialogue with Ion—is cut
short by the brief scene involving Xouthos on his way to consult
the oracle after an encouraging interview with Trophonios
(401–28). This excites a fleeting hope for the future, but it is swept
aside in Kreousa's renewed expression of her attachment to the
past. The possibility of good news from Apollo is immediately
related to earlier events. In 410 ff. she prays to Leto for a good outcome so that her previous dealings with the goddess' son may take
a turn for the better. It is with resignation at Apollo's past behaviour rather than any hope for the future that she leaves the stage in
425 ff.:

As for Apollo, if now at last he wishes to make amends for earlier wrong-
doings, he would not become wholly a friend of mine, but his wishes—he
is after all a god—I shall accept.

Left alone with the chorus, Ion concludes the episode with a
speech musing upon Kreousa's words (429 ff.). He has been
shaken by his exchange with the unusual visitor, and it is significant that his immediate remedy for the disquiet occasioned by
Kreousa's story and attitude to Apollo is to find comfort in the
familiar world of temple maintenance: 'But what has the daughter
of Erechtheus to do with me? She is certainly no relation. Well, I
shall go and pour water into the stoups with my golden jugs' (433
f.). But the distraction is short-lived and, even before he can finish

a trimeter, his worry returns and he scolds Apollo: 'But I must admonish Apollo. What has come over him? After taking maidens by force he abandons them? Siring children secretly he then lets them die without a thought? Don't you, Apollo! Rather, since you wield power, pursue virtue' (436 ff.). He exits, like his mother, with deity on his lips. But whereas experience taught her grudging acceptance of the god's superior will, Ion challenges Apollo, among other deities, to prove worthy of his devotion.

The solemn note on which these exits are made is in direct contrast with the comic mood generated in the following scene. The principal amusing effect arises from having Ion misunderstand Xouthos' show of paternal affection as a homosexual advance. This interpretation of the scene was first suggested by Wilamowitz; it was elaborated on by Knox and has been discussed repeatedly since.[15] Less attention has been paid to a further source of humour: the contrast between Ion's matter-of-fact attitude and sober questioning of Xouthos and the latter's euphoric display of ignorance.

In the opening lines, actions speak louder than words. Xouthos approaches Ion with the enthusiatic offer of an embrace: 'My son, greetings! . . . Give me your hand and let me put my arms around you' (517 ff.). But the boy recoils from the stranger and his first thoughts are for the garlands which he wears as signs of his ministry and which Xouthos threatens to ruin: 'Stop! You might break the god's fillets with your rough handling' (522). Further insistence on Xouthos' part elicits a menacing gesture with the bow, used earlier to discourage visiting birds (524). The boy's earnest reaction, characteristically linked with familiar objects, is strongly contrasted with Xouthos' blissful insouciance. In the catechism which follows Xouthos is eager to explain all (529), but Ion's insistence on detailed information, and his carping tone, highlight Xouthos' vague and uninformative replies. The contrast between the speakers is emphasized by the excited use of *antilabe* in the emotionally charged trochaics. In one response after another Xouthos can express only wonder, ignorance, and perplexity:

ION. How did this turn of events come about? XOUTHOS. We both marvel at the same thing.
ION. From what mother am I born your son? XOUTHOS. I am unable to say.
ION. Didn't Phoebus tell you? XOUTHOS. Being delighted with this news, I didn't ask about that. . . .

ION. Well then, was it there you fathered me? XOUTHOS. It does coincide with the time.

ION. How then did I get here . . . XOUTHOS. I am at a loss over this.

ION. . . . . travelling over so long a distance? XOUTHOS. This puzzles me as well.

(539 ff., 547 ff.)

We can sense his relief when in 556 he feels confident enough to say 'Come accept your father, my son', addressing Ion once more as τέκνον ('son', 'child'), a word he used with such exuberance in 517 and with some hesitation in 546. Xouthos entered the play desiring nothing more than a son. Once he thinks that his wish has been granted, he shows little concern for its explanation. But Ion, precisely because of his complete lack of a past, is eager to unearth all that he can. The apparent discovery of his father makes him the more anxious to identify the mother who repeatedly returns to his thoughts (540, 563 ff., and, at the end of the scene, 669 ff.).

The next section of the scene (569 ff.) takes the form of a debate between father and son. But it qualifies in no sense as an *agôn*,[16] since the parties are so unequal in both the vigour and extent of their speeches. Xouthos displays an attitude to the future which is as untroubled as his ignorance of the past; this emphasizes by contrast Ion's serious concerns about life as an outsider in the city whose fame and proud history he has just had confirmed by Kreousa.

Ion's thoughts on these subjects represent a major shift in mood from that which has so far prevailed. The happy temple-slave of the opening scenes experienced a moment or two of concern at the revelations of some visiting woman. This was followed by horrified surprise at the behaviour of her seemingly demented husband. But now Ion feels a much more intense anxiety at the thought of a permanent change to his habits and abode. Delphi and a settled state, with all its uncertainties about the past, seem far preferable to the trials of a prince offered him by Xouthos. Ion's quite cynical assessment of life in Athens scarcely coheres with the unworldly attitude of the naïve temple-slave seen earlier.[17] But the general drift of the speech, which is a negative expression of Ion's attachment to Delphi and the present, seems to me dramatically appropriate. It is part of the irony of Ion's situation that his very contentment with life in Apollo's service stands in the way of his happily accepting Apollo's plan for his future. In the end he agrees grudgingly to Xouthos' proposal. But even then, his closing speech combines the two issues of concern expressed before: the identity of his mother and the prospect of a life in Athens which may be far more servile in fact than his present condition in Delphi:

> If I do not discover the woman who bore me, then my life is not worth living, father. If one must pray for it, may it turn out that my mother is of Athenian stock so that I can enjoy freedom of speech on my mother's side. For if an outsider comes into a city of pure blood, then, though he be a citizen in theory, he acquires the voice of a slave and has no freedom of speech. (669 ff.)

As we shall see, the other obstacle to the god's plan, which will not be so easily overcome, takes the form of Kreousa's attachment to her own version of the past. Before turning to that, I want to say something more about Xouthos' role in the play.

Xouthos' simple-minded and shallow attitudes ensure that we treat him principally as a legal necessity in Apollo's ordering of Ion's destiny.[18] We should waste no time wondering about his future.[19] But some aspects of Xouthos' role throw important light on the theme under discussion. Both Ion and Kreousa, because of their anxiety for the future and attachment to the past, tend to obstruct Apollo's plans. Ion, as we have seen, given the chance of princely rule in Athens by his 'father', unexpectedly prefers to remain in Delphi. Later on, after Apollo's necessary adjustment to his plans, Ion's clinging to familiar uncertainty in the face of learning a possibly unpleasant truth almost prevents his recognition of Kreousa (1380 f.). Kreousa herself, prompted by the chorus's lies and the exaggerated loyalty of the Old Man, almost succeeds a second time in doing away with the boy so carefully protected by Apollo. These obstructive attitudes are highlighted by the compliant reactions of Xouthos. As an outsider he has no attachment to his wife's house and so feels no loyalty to its long history.[20] As a childless man who has just found a son, he has no fears for the future and can lightly dismiss all Ion's misgivings with the cheerful instruction: 'stop this talk and learn to be happy' (650). Thus his behaviour is exactly in accord with Apollo's designs. He obliges even to the point of having been involved in an erotic episode at the right time,[21] and of failing to produce children by Kreousa for just the period necessary to ensure Ion's inheritance, but no longer.[22]

At this, its half-way point, the play arrives at an unsteady

equilibrium. We have every reason to think that Apollo's intentions are well on the way to being realized. At the same time, we
retain our awareness of Kreousa's deeply felt grief, since she is kept
before our minds in Ion's repeated references to his unknown
mother. Further, his fears about sharing a house with Xouthos'
isolated and resentful wife remind us of Kreousa's sense of deprivation, which will prove to be more immediately destructive than
he imagines:

> Moving into a strange house as an outsider to face a woman who is child-
> less and who, after sharing your lot earlier, will have no share in it now,
> but will bear the sting of misfortune all on her own, of course I shall incur
> her reasonable hatred when I stand close by your side while she, still child-
> less, looks with resentment on what you find dear. (607 ff.)

The darker mood which now takes hold is introduced in the following *stasimon*. Despite their master's express orders, this unusually involved chorus debates whether it should inform Kreousa
(695 f.),[23] and goes on to hope that Xouthos and his newly found
son might meet an untimely end (705, 719 f.). Firm commitment
to the Erechtheid cause concludes the song (721 ff.)[24] and introduces the theme which energizes the next movement of the play.

Kreousa enters slowly, guiding the unsteady steps of a very old
man. He is the *paidagôgos* of Kreousa's father, Erechtheus (725),
and as such is a living link with her family's past. The servant has
been brought from Athens to Delphi as a special φίλος ('friend',
'loved one') to share the news, good or—god forbid—bad, that may
come from the oracle (728 ff.). For his part, he sees in Kreousa an
authentic representative of the house he has served for years:
'Daughter, you preserve the worthy traits of worthy forebears and
you have not brought shame upon your family, descendants of
earth-born men of old' (735 ff.). Later on, when he is told of
Xouthos' son and Kreousa's permanent sterility, he is moved by a
mixture of emotions.[25] But his sympathy for his mistress is quickly
overshadowed by rage at Xouthos' perfidy, at his calculated deception of his wife, and at the possibility of a motherless nobody
depriving her of her ancestral rights (808 ff., 837 f.). His abrupt
conclusion is that Kreousa must retaliate: 'For these reasons you
have to do something appropriate to a woman' (843).[26]

The stage is now set for a bitter speech from the long-silent
Kreousa. We might expect that the woman most closely struck by

the news will take further her servants' hopes for the deaths of the intruder and his father. But whereas the Old Man urged her to contemplate some future act of vengeance, Kreousa's quite unexpected reaction is to turn back to the past. Her bitterness at Apollo's apparently continuing lack of concern is so vehement that she can no longer contain her feelings. Overcoming the sense of 'shame' she felt previously, she describes with powerful immediacy her encounter with Apollo and the exposure of her baby. Her monody in 881 ff. is the mirror image of Ion's opening song, with any number of formal and verbal similarities pointing a wide divergence in tone and focus. Ion's almost besotted delight in his present tasks foregrounds Kreousa's vivid representation of the sad events which she has mentally rehearsed for years.[27]

Kreousa's moving aria distracts even the Old Man from his aggressive mood, and it is not for fifty lines that he returns to his earlier demand for revenge: 'Now, daughter, let us no longer cling to cries of distress' (970). After some false starts, Kreousa embraces his idea that Ion should be the target (979). He prefers an armed frontal assault, but she resumes his earlier suggestion (843), and resorts to the typically female approach of stealth and treachery (985).[28] The devious nature of the attack on Ion's life is mirrored in the structure of the dialogue which follows (987 ff.). The seemingly irrelevant details about gigantomachy and aegis introduced by Kreousa puzzle even the Old Man: 'But what harm, daughter, does this mean for your foes?' (998). Hints are given earlier, for example in 1005, but it is not made clear before 1019 that a poisonous drop of Gorgon's blood will be the instrument of Ion's death.

Although Kreousa insisted in her first encounter with Ion that her long family-history and blue blood had been of no help to her (268), at moments of crisis it is her distant past which occupies her mind. When she felt forced as a young girl to abandon her newborn baby, she did not forget, despite her distraught state, to observe the due customs of her ancestors, and equipped the infant with such tokens as were proper to an Erechtheid (20 ff., 1413). In so doing she imitated the action of Athena, who supplied the newborn Erichthonios with a pair of protective snakes. Now she plans to kill Ion with the Gorgon's blood, Athena's gift to Erichthonios (999 ff.) which she has inherited from her father (1007 f.). Her sense of history is made clear in the protracted account of the origin of the fatal liquid and its long-standing link with her family. At the same time she conveys the idea that the intruder will be destroyed by the house itself, which will bring to bear against him both its personal and inanimate forces. The Old Man's delight both at his mistress's cleverness and the aptness of her means is shown in his exclamatory 'O dearest child!' in 1018.[29] Kreousa's almost instinctive return to her heritage is thus presented as associated with destructive, death-dealing actions.

The plotting episode leaves us in an ambiguous mood. Given Hermes' prediction of a happy outcome, we can be hopeful that the plot against Ion's life will fail. On the other hand, it seems clear that events are no longer going according to plan. Even if we feel convinced that all will come right in the end, we must entertain serious doubts as to how the murder plot will be reconciled with Ion's destiny, and how Kreousa's intention to kill Ion forthwith in Delphi will make way for the predicted recognition of mother and son in Athens.

The principal serious theme, however, focuses on the person of Kreousa. Her avowed grief and sense of neglect by Apollo allowed the Old Man to press his earlier demand for revenge, and then it was she who played the leading role in devising the murder plot. Her closing words echo his sneering outrage at the prospect of a δεσπότης ('master') like Ion (1036; cf. 838) and reach a climax in the brutal forecast of what is in store for the upstart boy: 'Once the deadly mixture passes his lips, never will he reach the famous city of Athens, but will stay here, as a corpse' (1037 f.). With relish she speaks of the poisoned drink passing through the boy's λαιμός, a word for throat generally found in the context of savage slaying with a sword.[30] The change experienced by the tender, attractive woman of the first episode and the heart-broken mother of the monody is too grim to be totally overshadowed by our superior knowledge. We are too involved in Kreousa's retreat from unrelieved misery to what, so she is persuaded, is a purposeful defence of her heritage.

After the *stasimon* marking a considerable lapse of dramatic time, a servant enters hastily with the news for which all have been waiting (1106). We may be confident that the plot has not succeeded, but his speech is structured in a way which keeps the fact and manner of Ion's escape a firm focus of interest. The servant's opening statements in reply to the chorus' agitated questions are not incom-

patible with the success of the plot and, while 1118 does suggest
that the attack on Ion has miscarried, we must wait nearly 100 lines
for definite news. Thoughts of attempted murder are dissipated in
the air of ordered festivity, created progressively by the servant's
description of Ion's farewell feast. The comic officiousness of the
Old Man is a further distraction, and it is only after the report of the
dove's death in 1196–205 that we learn definitely of Ion's narrow
escape and discovery of Kreousa's guilt. The retardation of the vital
news, far from creating a delightful effect, as Grube thinks,[31] allows
us to share the horror of the participants. I doubt that we are meant
to find entertaining Ion's narrow escape from a fate which caused
consternation even when suffered by a bird:

[The dove] tasted some of the drink, straightway shook its pretty winged
body in the grip of a convulsion, and gave forth a frenzied cry impossible
to interpret. The whole gathering of merry-makers was astonished at the
bird's pains. Choking for breath it met its end stretching out its reddish
feet. (1203 ff.)

At the same time, it is true, the mood of the speech is predominantly light-hearted. Ion is presented as creating for himself a con-
genial environment which, like Apollo's precinct in the opening
scene, finds him immersed in detail and a sense of order. That he
lives solely in the present seems to be seen, even now at a turning-
point in his life, in the fact that he chooses to decorate the festal
marquee with representations of celestial phenomena which mark
the seasons of the year and belong to different hours of the day.
These are all brought into a timeless amalgam of images.[32] But his
contentment in this setting is unexpectedly shattered as he prepares for an act of worship. His sensitivity to inappropriate language was seen in his instructions to his fellow ministers in 98 ff.,
and now he is naturally disturbed by the profanity of a servant
(1189). Instantly recognizing the ill-omen, he aborts the libation
(1190 ff.). He is just as quick to interpret the death of the dove
which tasted his wine. The rest of the party is thunderstruck by the
bird's convulsions, but Ion, with a vigour seen hitherto only *in
nuce*, drags the truth from the Old Man:

'Who is the man intent on killing me? Answer me, old man. It was you
who was full of bustle and it was from your hand that I took the drink.'
Without further ado, he grabbed the old man's arm and searched him . . .
(1210 ff.)

It is significant that even now he observes the demands of due process and delays his pursuit of Kreousa until after he hears the verdict of the Delphic authorities (1219 ff.).

At the end of the chorus's brief lyric response to the news, we are uncertain as to who will enter next: Kreousa in flight or the towns-folk in pursuit? In fact Kreousa enters first, to be persuaded by the chorus to find asylum at Apollo's altar (1258 ff.). She is soon followed by an enraged Ion, who orders his men to drag her away. But in the end Ion's pious respect for the rules—already well in evidence—gets the better of him and he turns away in disgust.[33] He is stopped by the sudden entrance of the Pythia, who sets in train the *anagnôrisis*, thus bringing to fulfilment the life she gave to Ion long ago:

> ION. Ah! It is a terrible thing that the god has laid down laws for men improperly and without due wisdom. . . . It should be that only those wronged can occupy altars, and not that both noble and base having recourse to this same thing get equal treatment from the gods.
> PYTHIA. Stop, my child! It is I the Pythian prophetess who cross the kerb here after leaving the oracular tripod . . .
>
> (1312 ff.)

After reprimanding Ion for his violent attack on Kreousa, the Pythia explains in a dialogue, during which Kreousa is ignored, that the cradle she carries is the one in which she found Ion as a baby. Advised by the god (1347), she has kept it hidden all this time, but is now prompted, again by divine inspiration (1353), to produce it as a clue to Ion's identity. It is significant that, as in other key events in Ion's life, the entrance of the Pythia is marked by the opportune moment. When Ion was a baby her timely arrival at the temple steps ensured that she was the first one to see the child (41 ff.). Now, like Xouthos earlier (514 ff.), she comes out of the temple just in time to confront Ion at a critical moment. The chance meeting with Xouthos led to the necessary false recognition. The encounter with the Pythia will present him with objects enabling him to begin the search for his mother (1351 f.), the τεκμήριον ('piece of evidence') which he had hitherto lacked (329).

The priestess leaves after a fond embrace (1363), and the *anagnôrisis* moves into its final stage with a speech from Ion which is clearly reminiscent of his mother's earlier utterances. Just as the sight of the Delphic temple had brought her to tears (241 f.), so Ion weeps after taking the cradle from the Pythia (1369). The handling of the cradle triggers his imagination as he reconstructs the circumstances of his birth and separation from his mother. His reverie is introduced with the words ἐκεῖσε τὸν νοῦν δούς, 'taking my thoughts to that place' (1370); the phrase harks back to Kreousa's explanation to Ion for her tears in 251: ἐκεῖσε τὸν νοῦν ἔσχον ἐνθάδ' οὖσά περ, 'though standing here, I turned my mind to that place'.[34]

We might think that this tender reconstruction of his mother's feelings and his own bereft state would make Ion even more determined to find the owner of the cradle. But, no less than before, he feels uncomfortable with the thought of his uncertain past, and decides, with a surprisingly abrupt change of direction, to leave the cradle behind as a dedication to Apollo (1380 f.). But like the Pythia many years earlier on this very spot (46 ff.), second thoughts confront him with the god's providence, which he seems to be opposing (1385 f.). He starts to look more closely at the cradle and is struck by its remarkably untarnished appearance. Again, as we saw in 434 f., disturbing possibilities are put behind him by his absorption in the concrete, by his concentration on immediate, objective reality.

Just as after her first appearance, she had interrupted Ion's work around the temple with her tears, so again Kreousa distracts him from the object in his hands with an emotional cry of recognition: 'What unhoped-for vision is before my eyes?' (1395).[35] For Ion the cradle is suggestive of a past he never knew. In Kreousa's case the crib is evocative of a past all too palpably experienced, with which it affords a tangible, objective link. In fact, one might say that the crib miraculously brings the past into the present because it has not suffered from the intervening years. Ion is amazed at its condition: 'Look how the covering of the beautifully rounded crib has by some miracle not aged and how mildew has been kept from its woven sides' (1391 ff.). Even the olive-branch it contains is still as green as when it was placed there by Kreousa (1435 f.). Quite naturally, Kreousa turns in an instant from the crib, and the moment in her past which it re-creates, to the boy who, though grown, is still the very same infant abandoned by her long ago: 'Don't give me instructions. For I see in front of me the cradle in which one day I exposed . . . you, O my son, while you were just a new-born infant' (1397 ff.). She is thus wrenched from her obsessive and miserable attachment to the past by her delighted realization that her son still lives and is standing before her.

What of Ion and his reaction to the surprising outburst of the woman who had attempted to kill him? Rehearsing his response to the overtures of Xouthos,[36] he assumes that Kreousa is deranged, the victim of some divine impulse. His immediate reaction is a show of force and a rebuttal of her claims (1402 ff.). But while he had no independent means of verifying Xouthos' account of his fatherhood, now he holds in his hands a reliable test of Kreousa's assertions. So he demands from her, with the same detachment seen in his questioning of the overjoyed Xouthos,[37] an itemized account of the cradle's contents:

ION. Is this chest empty, or does it contain something?
KREOUSA. Yes, your baby things which I once put out with you.
ION. Will you be able to name them before seeing them?
KREOUSA. Yes, and if I cannot, I submit to death.
ION. Go on then. Your confidence is really uncanny.

(1412 ff.)

The careful examination of these very significant objects conforms with the emphasis placed on the concrete from the play's beginning. The description of the cradle in Hermes' prologue, Ion's temple routine and his supervision of the work on the festal tent, the chorus's picture of the Delphic statuary, and Kreousa's almost scientific account of the poison in her possession are examples of the play's concentration on life's minutiae. As well as this we find the same contrast between attitudes of mother and son as seen earlier. Ion focuses on the object itself; Kreousa links each item in the cradle with the experiences of years gone by. The weaving is a product of her maidenhood and the time which also produced Ion: 'Look for a piece of weaving which I did while still a child . . . it is incomplete, like a sampler from a loom' (1417 ff.); the snakes are reminiscent of her forebears sprung from the earth: 'a pair of shimmering snakes with jaws all of gold, the gift of Athena, who ordered children to be reared with them, in imitation of Erichthonios of old' (1427 ff.); the olive-branch is a verdant reminder of the spot in which Ion was conceived and abandoned: 'on that day I put around you a garland of olive which first sprouted on the rock of Athena and which, if it is there, has lost none of its colour, but is still green, a shoot of the pure olive-tree' (1433 ff.).

That all these objects are associated with Athena either directly or, in the case of the piece of weaving, by association, is significant. In the foregoing scenes Athena, her city, and its first rulers were associated with death. The acropolis was where the baby Ion was left in a cave as if to die; the branch from the olive planted by Athena was put by the doomed infant's side; the blood of the Gorgon, Athena's victim, was meant to bring about his death later. Erichthonios, to whom Athena in a sense gave birth, was to cause the deaths of Kekrops' daughters (272 ff.); Erechtheus protected Athena's city, but at the cost of his daughters' lives (277 f.), and then later his own (281 f.).[38] These associations, like the crib itself, are now transformed from destructive to salvific. The crib and its contents are the means by which Ion is given a more complete life and allowed to recover his history. Equally, these objects rescue Kreousa from Ion's threats and free her from her morbid fixation on the past. Both these changes are under the symbolic patronage of Athena, who then appears in person to confirm Kreousa's account of Ion's birth and to reveal to him his destiny (1553 ff.).

We can see then that the *anagnôrisis* in this play is more than the mutual recognition of φίλοι ('loved ones'). In fact the recognition re-presents the moment of Ion's birth and exposure. The untarnished crib and the green olive-branch transport us back to the cave on the acropolis so that mother and son, we feel, are reunited where they were parted. Kreousa hoped that Apollo might see fit to make up for his former wrongs by giving her and Xouthos a child (426). The god has gone further. He has not simply made restitution for his supposed neglect of her baby; he has returned Ion to his mother's arms.[39] Thus the *anagnôrisis* marks a new beginning and allows mother and son to confront the future with confidence.

Locked into the present at the beginning of the play, Ion seems gradually to broaden as a result of his experience.[40] The sympathy he feels for Kreousa's story unsettles him, and, after some mechanical observations on the pointlessness of pursuing the gods beyond their will (370 ff.), he goes as far as lecturing Apollo on the need for good example to mortals (436 ff.). His encounter with his pseudo-father encourages further deliberation, on the prospect of life in Athens (585 ff.). His action up to this point has been confined to the temple precinct, but then we see him taking control of his farewell banquet and vigorously pursuing his assailants (1132 ff.,

1208 ff.). Just when Ion seems ready at last for the world beyond Delphi, he is faced with the need to find the mother who, despite his contentment as Apollo's servant, keeps entering his thoughts.[41]

The *anagnôrisis* restores to Ion both his mother and the past from which he has been excluded. But the past is not yet wholly recovered. The exhilaration he wants to share with his newly found father (1468 f.) is replaced by anxiety when Kreousa confronts him again, this time openly, with the story of his conception and birth. Instinctively he turns for confirmation of her account to the god who has been the centre of his life: 'I am not going to deal with the matter lightly like this, but going into the temple I shall ask Phoebus whether I am the offspring of a mortal father or of Loxias' (1546 ff.). But, symbolic of the change before him, it is Athena not Apollo who dispels his fears and in the end accompanies him on his journey to his destined home (1616). It is this blending of progress and uncertainty in the presentation of Ion's persona which is reflected in the swinging moods of the play.

In a way which complements the limitations felt by Ion, Kreousa is obsessed by the dread and fluid memories of past events. Not being youthful like Ion, she cannot grow like him and must escape from her history either by recovering her lost child or finding new children with Xouthos. But there are to be no further children, she is told, and Apollo's apparent gift of a child to Xouthos alone helps to convince her that the child she once bore is certainly dead. With the present unbearable and the future of no account Kreousa retreats further into the past by attempting to kill the interloper who threatens her heritage. She is thus on the point of making permanent the deprivation which Apollo allowed her for a time to feel, and of sealing herself forever in the world of her own memories. But Ion escapes, and in the end his violent interaction with Kreousa leads to an impasse which the god, in the person of the Pythia, resolves in a way which eliminates distorted attachments to the past and the present.

The drama ends in an overtly triumphant mood, signalled by the bright face of Athena: 'What god is this who reveals a face like the sun's?' (1550). The authoritative speech of the goddess envelops the characters with rehabilitating truths and news full of promise. But even here, Apollo's refusal to share in the finale is a pointed reminder that the glories of the divine dispensation have been at the cost of human suffering.[42] Glory notwithstanding, we remain aware, even at the end, of the grief which is a consequence of Apollo's plans. Ion and Kreousa emerge from the years of waiting for the fulfilment of the god's pleasure only after struggling with the demands of lost time. It is the exploration of this theme which lends a tragic dimension to the play and at the same time accounts for its remarkable changes of emotional direction.[43]

Notes

1. Kitto, *Greek Tragedy*[3], 314–17.
2. For the Pythia as a proxy *dea ex machina*, see M. R. Halleran, *Stagecraft in Euripides* (London 1985) 108; H. Strohm, *Euripides: Interpretationen zur dramatischen Form* (Munich 1957) 30.
3. This may be an instance of Euripides' theatrical self-consciousness. In the *Eumenides* a change of scene occurs, again from Delphi to Athens. Could he be inviting the audience to think he may be about to imitate this effect?
4. On the amusing aspects of Ion's monody, see B. M. W. Knox, 'Euripidean Comedy', in Knox, *Word and Action*, 259; Seidensticker, *Palintonos Harmonia*, 217–20.
5. *Word and Action*, 259.
6. *Palintonos Harmonia*, 218.
7. Cf. Hecuba in Eur. *Tro.* 99 ff., 1277 ff.; Andromache in Eur. *And.* 5 ff.; and, most elaborate, Polyxena's speech in Eur. *Hec.* 349 ff.
8. For an interpretation of the bird imagery in the play, see M.-H. Giraud, 'Les Oiseaux dans l' "Ion" d'Euripide', *RPh* 61 (1987) 83–94.
9. The hieratic tone is evident in the repeated use of the *nomen sacrum* Φοῖβος (four instances in the recitative and a further eight in the lyric verses), in the use of a refrain (125–7 = 141–3) and in the repeated reference to the service of the god (θεραπεύω 111; λατρεύων 124, 152; λατρεύω 129; δουλεύσω 182; and θεραπεύων 183). Cf. Barlow, *Imagery of Euripides*, 46–8, and 'The Language of Euripides' Monodies', *Studies in Honour of T. B. L. Webster*, i (Bristol 1986), edd. J. H. Betts, J. T. Hooker, and J. R. Green, 14–15. For Ion as priest, see R. Hamilton, 'Euripidean Priests', *HSCP* 89 (1985) 56–9.
10. Knox, *Word and Action*, 259. Cf. Matthiessen, 'Der "Ion": Eine Komödie des Euripides?', 275: 'Hier dürfen wir einen kurzen Blick auf antiken Tourismus und antikes Fremdenführerwesen werfen.'
11. The suggestion of Lloyd-Jones, printed by Diggle in *Euripidis Fabulae II* (Oxford 1981), that there is something missing before 237 is very likely right. Apart from the linguistic oddities in the *paradosis*, it would be very abrupt for Ion, given his behaviour in the following dialogue, to address a stranger without a formal greeting. For a

contrary view, that fails to convince me, see W. Kraus, 'Textkritische Erwägungen zu Euripides' Ion', *WS* 102 (1989) 38 f.

12. See e.g. A. S. Owen, *Euripides Ion* (Oxford 1939) 89; F. Solmsen, *Electra and Orestes: Three Recognitions in Greek Tragedy* (Amsterdam 1967) 40; Matthiessen, *Elektra*, 139 f.

13. For this view of the scene, cf. D. W. Lucas, *The Greek Tragic Poets* (London 1959) 225. See also Kitto, *Greek Tragedy*³, 316; and G. Gellie, 'Apollo in the Ion', *Ramus* 13 (1984) 94.

14. Cf. Matthiessen, 'Der Ion: Eine Komödie?', 286; A. P. Burnett, *Catastrophe Survived* (Oxford 1971) 126–9.

15. U. von Wilamowitz-Moellendorff, *Euripides Ion* (Berlin 1926) 111; Knox, *Word and Action*, 260 ff. See also Seidensticker, *Palintonos Harmonia*, 225 ff.; Matthiessen, 'Der Ion: Eine Komödie?', 276, 286; R. Rehm, *Greek Tragic Theatre* (London 1992) 138–9.

16. See on this point M. Lloyd, *The Agon in Euripides* (Oxford 1992) 10; and C. Collard, 'Formal Debates in Euripidean Drama', *G&R* 22 (1975) 69.

17. So Owen, *Euripides Ion*, p. xxvii. For possible interpolations in the speech, see D. Kovacs, 'Four Passages from Euripides' Ion', *TAPA* 109 (1979) 116 ff. and 'Tyrants and Demagogues in Tragic Interpolation', *GRBS* 23 (1982) 35 f.

18. The legal requirements are touched on in 72 f. and later by Kreousa in 1535 f. Her view of the matter is confirmed by Athena in 1562. See A. P. Burnett, *Ion by Euripides* (Englewood Cliffs, NJ 1970) 28 f.; W. K. Lacey, *The Family in Classical Greece* (London 1968) 139–46.

19. So e.g. Owen's (*Euripides Ion*, p. xxx) sympathy for Xouthos because of 'what is in store' for him is misplaced, as the fleeting reference to Xouthos' future in 1602 shows.

20. Xouthos' foreign status is stressed repeatedly, both neutrally (63, 290 ff., 592), and with some animus (813, 1070, 1297). I doubt that we are meant to take 542 as a foreigner's deliberate deflation of Athenians' pride in their autochthony. Why should Xouthos make a gratuitous attack on the ancestry of people he is encouraging Ion to rule? I interpret the remark as a typically literal response to Ion's caustic comment on Xouthos' ignorance of his son's origins.

21. Cf. 545 ff., esp. Xouthos' reply in 547. I should apply Occam's razor to Xouthos' love-life and assume that the episode mentioned here is coincident with the fling at Delphi. *Contra*: A. Scafuro, 'Discourses of Sexual Violation in Mythic Accounts and Dramatic Versions of "The Girl's Tragedy" ', *Differences* 2 (1990) 148.

22. The long-standing childlessness of the couple is mentioned in 64 f., 304, 408 f.; that Xouthos should himself father children on Kreousa as part of the divine dispensation is revealed only later by Athena

(1589 ff.). Kreousa's own childlessness is raised by Ion in 305 and then mentioned repeatedly, e.g. 608, 613, 619, 658, 680, 790, 817, 950, 1303.

23. The raising of the possibility here prepares the audience for the chorus's eventual indiscretion in 761 f. For a useful discussion of the chorus's pivotal role, see Gauger, *Gott und Mensch im Ion*, 10 ff. For choral involvement in intrigue generally, see W. G. Arnott, 'Off-Stage Cries and the Choral Presence: Some Challenges to Theatrical Convention in Euripides', *Antichthon* 16 (1982) 37 f.; and Matthiessen, *Elektra*, 45 f.

24. The evident corruption in 722–4 does not obscure this point. The Erechtheid theme recurs even more emphatically in 1055 f., after the chorus has heard Kreousa's monody and prays for the success of her attack on the outsider.

25. His concern is tempered by self-control and he confronts Kreousa's despair with wise caution from the outset. Cf. 763 ff., where the attributions printed by Diggle are cogently defended by M. Huys, 'Euripides, Ion l. 752–755 and 763–765: Kreousa's Reaction to the False News of her ATEKNIA', *Hermes* 121 (1993) 428–32.

26. Diggle's deletion of 844–58 has been supported recently by Kraus, 'Textkritische Erwägungen', 102 73 f. For arguments to the contrary, see Matthiessen, 'Der Ion: Eine Komödie?', 279; and W. Biehl, 'Textprobleme in Euripides' *Ion*', *Philologus* 126 (1992) 20 ff.

27. For a discussion of Kreousa's monody, see J. LaRue, 'Creusa's Monody: *Ion* 859–922', *TAPA* 94 (1963) 126 ff.; Gauger, *Gott und Mensch*, 32 ff.; Barlow, *Imagery*, 48 f.; and, for an interpretation intent on the rehabilitation of Apollo, A. P. Burnett, 'Human Resistance and Divine Persuasion in Euripides' *Ion* ', *CPh* 57 (1962) 95 f.

28. For other examples of this, cf. Eur. *Med.* 384, *Hec.* 884, *IT* 1032, *And.* 911.

29. For ὦ φιλτάτη as an expression of emotion rather than a real form of address, cf. Eur. *Cyc.* 418, 437; *Or.* 1100; *Supp.* 641; *El.* 229. See also D. B. Gregor, "ὦ φίλτατ", *CR* 7 (1957) 14 f.

30. Cf. Eur. *Hec.* 565, *Ph.* 1092, *Or.* 1472; and see N. Loraux, *Tragic Ways of Killing a Woman* (trans. A. Foster: Cambridge, Mass. 1987) 50 f. and 84. The use of the word here may have been suggested by its associations with the severing of the Gorgon's head (cf. Eur. *Ph.* 455, *El.* 459, *Ion* 1054).

31. 'It is the description of a feast rather than a narrative of attempted murder, it is delightful rather than tragic': G. M. A. Grube, *The Drama of Euripides* (London 1941) 272.

32. For discussions of the tent's decoration, see most recently B. Goff, 'Euripides' *Ion* 1132–1165: The Tent', *PCPS* 34 (1988) 42 ff.;

Zeitlin, 'Mysteries of Identity', 166 ff., and the literature cited by her in n. 97.

33. Ion's movements here are problematical. One view is that the Pythia enters to prevent him from attacking Kreousa at the altar. This accords ill with his speech in 1312 ff. and with his general observance of the rules. Cf. on this point D. J. Mastronarde, *Contact and Discontinuity* (Berkeley 1979) 112. Taplin in *Greek Tragedy in Action*, 117 thinks that Ion remains frozen, trapped by indecision. But this is scarcely compatible with the command ἐπίσχες, used elsewhere to put a stop to words, actions, or movement in progress. Cf. Eur. *El.* 962, *Ph.* 896, *Supp.* 397, and, two situations comparable to that here, *And.* 550, *Hel.* 1184.

34. Cf. p. 89 above. The text is that printed by Diggle. For a defence, to my mind unsuccessful, of οἴκοι δέ . . . που, see Kraus, 'Textkritische Erwägungen', 40 f.

35. For φάσμα in connection with the unexpected sight of a sometimes supernatural phenomenon, cf. Eur. *Her.* 817, *IA* 1586, *Alc.* 1127. Kreousa's words here seem to echo those of Ion in 1354 as he takes the cradle from the Pythia.

36. For the parallelism between the two scenes, see Taplin, *Greek Tragedy in Action*, 137 f.

37. As the exchange progresses, however, his emotions are stirred (cf. 1422), and in the end he yearns for Kreousa to give him the right answer (cf. 1432).

38. On the connections between Ion and Erichthonios-Erechtheus, see N. Loraux, 'Kreousa the Autochthon: A Study of Euripides' *Ion*', in Winkler and Zeitlin (edd.), *Nothing to Do with Dionysus?*, 168 ff.; Zeitlin, 'Mysteries of Identity', 150 ff., 170 ff.

39. That this happens literally and is pointed stage business is clear from 1437 f. and 1443 f. We can compare similar situations in Eur. *Hel.* 628 ff., *IT* 843, *El.* 596 f. But in *Ion* the loving embrace takes up the repeated stress on the tangible aspects of the separation of mother from son. Over and over we are reminded that the proper place for a baby is at its mother's breast, cradled in her arms (cf. 280, 318 ff., 962 f., 1375 ff., 1492 ff., and, obliquely, 761 f., 1454 f.). Ion could not enjoy, nor Kreousa offer, this loving nurture.

40. For Ion's growth in the course of the play, see C. H. Whitman, *Euripides and the Full Circle of Myth* (Cambridge, Mass. 1974) 90–3; J. O. de G. Hanson, 'Euripides' Ion: Tragic Awakening and Disillusionment', *Museum Africum* 4 (1975) 27 ff.

41. Cf. 359, 540, 563 ff., 1277 f. (deleted by Diggle), 1370 ff., and, even, obliquely, 1324. Note in particular Ion's closing words in 670 ff., which bring together his two fixations.

42. This emerges from Athena's explanation of Apollo's absence in 1557 f. ('he did not think it right to face you, lest you voice out loud some reproach for his earlier acts') which hints at the god's mishandling of affairs (cf. Matthiessen, 'Der Ion: Eine Komödie', 282). Athena's divine summing-up in 1595 ('Apollo managed everything splendidly') must be set against Kreousa's partial approval in 1609 ('I approve of Phoebos, though not approving of him before'), and her earlier remark in 425 ff. (cf. p. 92 above). For a balanced discussion of Apollo's role in the play, see H. Erbse, 'Der Gott von Delphi im Ion des Euripides', in B. Allemann and E. Koppen (edd.), *Teilnahme und Spiegelung: Essays Rüdiger* (Berlin 1975) 40 ff.

43. For many helpful comments and valuable suggestions I am grateful to Michael Curran, Michael Dyson, and Michael Silk.

6

Realism in the *Ion*: Response to Lee

W. GEOFFREY ARNOTT

Kevin Lee presents a sensitive and observant reading of Euripides' *Ion*, emphasizing its dual perspectives of time and place, and effectively contrasting the adolescent (and at times unworldly[1]) Ion, who lives at Delphi in the immediacy of the present, and the older Creusa, whose view is repeatedly focused on one horrific day long ago in her native Athens. Here I am in total sympathy with Lee's approach, and have virtually nothing to add to, or subtract from, the persuasive analyses with which he supports his interpretations.

The *Ion*, however, is a difficult play to classify. Modern criticism may praise the play's structural virtuosity and individually effective scenes, but it has not found a generally accepted label to define the type of play that it appears to be for today's audiences: melodrama, romance, and tragicomedy have all been suggested, but each of these terms fits only a part of the drama. Yet in terms of the ancient Greek theatre it is simply a tragedy, in both the institutional sense of that word and the Aristotelian glosses attached to it. In fact the *Ion* fits Aristotle's criteria in the *Poetics* for approved tragedies better than most. It has a well-constructed (7, 1450ᵇ24 ff.) and complex plot with recognition and peripety (10–11, 1452ᵃ12 ff.; cf. 13, 1452ᵇ32 ff.); its major πάθη ('the things that are done to a person') involve the relationship of a mother and her son (14, 1453ᵇ19 ff.), and closely parallel the commended incidents in Euripides' *Cresphontes* 'where Merope is going to kill her son, yet didn't kill him but recognized him' (1454ᵃ5 ff.).

If, then, Euripides' and Aristotle's concepts of the tragic differ radically from those with which modern audiences are more familiar after being conditioned by Bradleyan and Nietzschean criticism, we need to look particularly at the plays Euripides wrote in the last twenty-five years or so of his career, in order to identify without prejudice the parameters within which he confined his notions of the tragic, and, if possible, a core essence common to all his later tragedies. It seems to me that his later plays, whether horrendous visions of the abyss like the *Troades*, or exotic fantasies of escape like the *Helen*, generally stress a tragic dichotomy between the bygone haloed glories of the world of myth, where the royal leaders were larger than life in triumph and adversity, and the contemporary realities of ordinary existence in late fifth-century Athens, where the heroic vengeance of an Orestes could be reinterpreted as sordid murder.[2] Unlike *Hippolytus* and *Troades*, the *Ion* does not close in the blankness of death and despair; but its happy ending in no way minimizes the tragic force of Creusa's sufferings in both the events of the play themselves and their Apolline antecedents. Here, as in *Hippolytus* and *Bacchae*, Euripides places the human sufferings of characters like Creusa in a divine frame, which enables the audience to look down on the actions in the play from a dual perspective. Hermes' prologue and Athena's epilogue present a fuller—not always more correct (see 71 f.), certainly not more moral or justified—account of events in the house of Creusa, and thus the two divinities raise the audience to the privileged position of gods by making them privy to facts of which the characters in the play are ignorant. That is one perspective, in which tragedy loses some of its sting by being seen against the wide parameters of the glorious future of Ion's race. The other perspective is provided by the human characters in the play, whose sufferings, although ultimately engendered by Apollo's rape of Creusa long before, are nevertheless greatly increased by their ignorance of essential information and their consequential miscalculations. Virtually all that is tragic in the *Ion*—Creusa's grief over not knowing what happened to her baby, her passionate anger at her husband's claim that Ion was his illegitimate son, the planned poisoning of Ion—springs from human ignorance, and the tragic effect of that ignorance is reinforced by the realistically portrayed background of human life into which it is incorporated. This is a world in which Ion sweeps and sprinkles, and shoos away unwelcome birds (102 ff., 154 ff.), the chorus behave like naïve tourists (184 ff.), and Xuthus' wish to embrace Ion on emerging from the temple of Apollo is misinterpreted as a homosexual advance (519 ff.); and because the human characters operate in situations where their ignorance causes them to misconstrue ambiguous hints, the moods switch from solemnity and misery to tragicomedy and light-hearted irony, just as they do in non-heroic real life.

In describing the means by which creative artists obtain desired effects, Aristotle twice singles out realism as one aspect of *mimêsis*, commenting on both occasions with insight on an audience's reaction to it. In *Poetics* 4 (1448^{b}15 ff.) he claims that 'people enjoy seeing pictures for this reason: by looking at them they find themselves learning and inferring the identity of each thing, e.g. that "this [person] is he" '.[3] The same point is made at *Rhetoric* 1. 11. 23 (1371^{b}4 ff.), with the objects of enjoyment there extended to include poetry and sculpture.

Such realism, aimed presumably at evoking the Aristotelian response 'How like that is to what we know!'[4] in the theatre audience, is a particular feature of Euripides' *Ion*, and Lee repeatedly calls attention to 'the remarkably detailed account of places, objects and circumstances' with which Euripides embellishes song, action, and narrative throughout the play.[5] At key points (towards the beginning of the play, Hermes' prologue [1 ff.], Ion's monody [82 ff.], and the *parodos* [184 ff.]; towards the end, the messenger's speech [1122 ff.] and the recognition scene [1320 ff.]), Euripides paints with vivid, specific, and elaborate detail a series of cameos: the cave of Pan in the northern cliffs of Athens' acropolis, where Creusa was raped by Apollo; the birds that allegedly frequent Apollo's temple at Delphi; the reliefs carved 'on the stone walls' (206 f.[6]) on or near that temple; the pavilion in the Alpine meadows atop the Phaedriades where Xuthus fêted his son; the recognition tokens in the baby's crib. Lee, however, appears to me to take for granted that these cameos not merely create an illusion of reality, but also portray it wherever possible with an uncommon accuracy of detail; he says, for instance, 'the birds which threaten to defile Apollo's temple are carefully distinguished by species and appearance'.[7] Euripides' emphasis here on graphic and illusionistic realism cannot be doubted, but the question whether that realism is an imaginatively deceptive fiction or a portrayal informed by historical, geographical, and biological accuracy merits, I believe, more extended treatment.

Let me begin with the poet's repeated references to the Athenian cave of Pan, which are in fact accurate to the last detail. The scene of Creusa's rape is described as a cave (288, 936) beneath the northern side of the acropolis (11 ff., 936); it is associated with a

sanctuary of Pan (938), in the precipices called the Long Rocks (11
ff., 283, 936, 1400). The detail here is precise and accurate enough
for any visitor in the ancient or modern world to identify the spot.
It is one occasion where we do not need to call on Pausanias for corroboration, which is fortunate, because the passage where he mentions this cave (a sanctuary of Apollo, he calls it, because of its
association with Creusa's rape, which he goes on to mention) is
marred by a lacuna.[8] Euripides' accuracy here is hardly surprising.
He is describing a place under 400 metres from where his audience
was sitting; many of them would have known it and its associations
well, and any imprecisions on Euripides' part here would have
seriously marred the authority of his message.

　But what about Euripides' portrait of Delphi? The details that
he lavishes on it are no less vivid than those of the Athenian cave of
Pan, but are they equally accurate? We do not know how well—if
at all—Euripides knew Delphi from any personal visit, although
his alleged function (presumably when a boy) as πυρφόρος ('bearer
of the sacred fire') in the service of Apollo Zosterios[9] make the
notion of such a visit more plausible. More important is the probability that most of Euripides' audience would not have known
about the place from firsthand experience, and so graphic memo-
rability would take priority over accuracy in any descriptions. Yet
in estimating the accuracy of Euripides' portrayal of Delphi, we are
faced at the outset with a crippling difficulty. There is often little
or no information from other sources, either literary or archaeo-
logical, which would enable us to check the correctness of what
Euripides says. Indeed, if modern archaeologists and historians[10]
themselves sometimes use what Euripides says in the *Ion* about
Apollo's temple and its oracle as unsupported evidence for art and
practices in late fifth-century Delphi, the danger of circular argument arises. It is easy in such circumstances to forget that dramatists are imaginative creators of lifelike fiction, not recorders of
historical fact. So: just how accurate, or how falsely illusionistic, is
Euripides about Delphi?

　In the first place, his geographical descriptions are precise and
authentic. Parnassus has untrodden peaks (κορυφαί, in the plural)
that catch the rising sun (86 ff.); on cloudless mornings the mountain's two summits can be seen by anyone who climbs onto the flat
green Alpine meadows above Delphi and Arachova. Its ridges are
described with equal accuracy as extending over those meadows

where the Bacchants danced to the rocky precipices of the two
Phaedriades directly behind the village (714 ff.; cf. 1126 f.).

Secondly, the temple of Apollo. In the *parodos* (184 ff.) the chorus of Athenian handmaidens sing with the enthusiasm of naïve
tourists about the works of art they are imagined to see before
them. The scene of the *Ion* is Apollo's temple, and so this passage
is usually interpreted as an anachronistic description of the reliefs
on the pediments and metopes of the Alcmaeonid temple in the
poet's own time. The chorus first enthuse about a representation of
Heracles killing the Lernaean hydra with his golden scimitar, and
his brother Iolaus holding a torch at Heracles' side (190 ff.). They
then describe a man on a winged horse slaying a three-bodied fire-
breathing monster (201 ff.): thus the poet presents a chorus art-
lessly ignorant of the myth of Bellerophon, Pegasus, and the
Chimaera. Finally, the chorus identify Athena with her gorgon-
shield, Zeus with his thunderbolt, and Dionysus with his ivy
wand, fighting against the Giants, one of whom (Mimas) is named
(205 ff.).

The Alcmaeonid temple of Apollo, however, was destroyed in
373 BC by an earthquake, and our information about its reliefs is
very much more scanty than that about the reliefs on the building
that succeeded it on the same foundations in the mid-fourth century. A fragment from the Alcmaeonid western pediment appears
to show the lower part of the body of Athena (with mutilated traces
of the aegis) in combat,[11] and this inspired Théophile Homolle, its
original discoverer, to identify the subject of the pediment as the
gigantomachy, using the passage in Euripides' *Ion* as part of his
evidence. The presence of a fighting Athena may on its own make
this identification plausible, but any attempt to reconstruct the
original design is purely hypothetical; as the authoritative discussion of these fragments explains, 'la faute en est à la rareté des fragments, et à leur mauvais état'.[12] Yet the insecurity of the evidence
for a gigantomachy on the west pediment of the Alcmaeonid temple, together with the total absence, anywhere on the temple, of
evidence for portrayal of Heracles' slaughter of the hydra, or
Bellerophon's of the Chimaera, makes questionable the assumption that Euripides' chorus in the *Ion* was accurately describing
known features of the contemporary temple. The poet could, alternatively, have been making his chorus refer to other celebrated
works of art then existing in Delphi—possibly Tisagoras' iron

statue of Heracles and the hydra, if that had already been made,[13] and the gigantomachy portrayed on the north frieze of the Siphnian Treasury;[14] or he could have been—wholly or in part—creating an imaginary artistic scenery made all the more credible to an ignorant audience by the vivid specificity in his detailing, just as he does later with the fictive details of Xuthus' pavilion or Ion's recognition tokens.

When Euripides describes the procedure of the Delphic oracle, he achieves both convincing realism and picturesque colour by the snippets of information which he inserts about its procedures. For instance, the priestess is said to sit on the holy tripod (91 f.); the male temple-attendants wash themselves in water from the Castalian spring (94 ff.) before going to the temple; noble male Delphians, chosen by lot, sit near the tripod (414 ff.). Every detail here appears to be an accurate representation of what actually happened, being confirmed at least partly by ancient scholarship[15] or vase painting.[16]

And finally, Delphi's wildlife, and particularly its birds. This is one area where vividness and accuracy may easily part company. Lee claims that in the *Ion* the birds are 'carefully distinguished by species and appearance'. This is certainly the impression that Euripides intends, but he seems not to have known or cared enough about the birds of Delphi to reinforce with scientific accuracy the vivid cameos that he inserts. In his opening monody Ion describes how he scares away three sorts of bird: Zeus' messenger-bird (Ζηνὸς κῆρυξ), the eagle; the swan (κύκνος) that brings his red foot (φοινικοφαῆ πόδα) to the temple and sings beautifully (161 ff.); and an unspecified bird that plans to nest under the temple eaves (171 ff.). Then later, the messenger's speech refers to a revelling band of doves (κῶμος πελειῶν, 1197) living in the temple of Apollo, one of which drank the poison and in death relaxed its red claws (φοινικοσκελεῖς χηλάς, 1207 f.).

Here the mixture of (mainly) accuracy and (at one point) sheer nonsense is unexpected. Euripides is accurate about the presence at Delphi of Zeus' messenger-bird, the eagle, of birds nesting under the eaves of a building, and of red-footed pigeons; Diodorus Siculus confirms the accuracy of Euripides' report that a flock of pigeons was associated with the temple of Apollo.[17]

That leaves the swan, flying red-footed to the temple, and singing. The only species of swan in this part of Greece during the

nine months of the year when the oracle was operating is the mute
swan, in ancient times a totally wild bird. This swan, as its English
name implies, has no song, although its wings produce a loud
musical throbbing in flight.[18] Although it formerly bred in
Boeotia, its normal habitat is not terrain like the valley of the
Pleistos, but calm or gently flowing waters. And all European
swans have black, not red, feet. In bringing his swan to Delphi,
Euripides was presumably allowing the authority of legendary
associations to override scientific accuracy; the swan was celebrated as Apollo's bird, especially at Delos, with its still lake.[19]

Yet one slip (which few in the audience would doubtless have
noticed) in no way spoils the sum effect of graphic detail in the *Ion*.
Sometimes (and especially when Euripides is talking about
Athens) these details are precisely accurate. Sometimes (and particularly when he is talking about Delphi) they appear to mingle
accuracy and illusionistic fiction. Accuracy and the appearance of
accuracy increase a dramatist's credibility, for an audience will
trust all the more an author who gets his checkable details right and
makes his uncheckable ones plausible. Realistic detail, if carefully
chosen and presented, can be memorable detail, stamping its
impression on the mind of the audience long after the play is over.
Success here for an author requires him to have an eye for tiny
details in everyday life, to describe them with economy and precision, and, by focusing on those details of a scene which have
emblematic or emotive significance, to create the desired empathetic response in his audience.

Euripides' obsession at times with realistic detail may also shed
some light on his relation to the society of his time and its sensibilities. H. Levin's paradigmatic study of realism in the novels of
nineteenth-century France[20] seeks to prove the claim that 'realism
is a literary mode which corresponds . . . to a stage of history and a
state of society'. In writers like Flaubert, Hugo, Balzac, and Zola
their realism seemed to be a characteristic expression of bourgeois,
middle-class society, superimposing contemporary reality upon
romance. If that claim holds for Euripides too, his realism may be
interpreted partly as a reaction, in late fifth-century Athens,
against an obsolescent aristocratic value-system, or as an icono-
clastic attempt to break down the traditional symbols of myth. At
the same time, of course, that emphasis on the significant and
memorable detail makes the audience more at home with the

events and emotions of the play, more moved—even shocked—by what they hear and see, and thus more involved in the tragedy and the tragic.[21]

Notes

1. Cf. A. P. Burnett's sympathetic analysis in *Catastrophe Survived* (Oxford 1971) 104.
2. Cf. W. G. Arnott, 'Euripids and the Unexpected', *G&R* 20 (1973) 198 ff., reprinted in I. McAuslan and P. Walcott (edd.), *Greek Tragedy* (Oxford 1993) 138 ff.
3. διὰ γὰρ τοῦτο χαίρουσι τὰς εἰκόνας ὁρῶντες, ὅτι συμβαίνει θεωροῦντας μανθάνειν καὶ συλλογίζεσθαι τί ἕκαστον, οἷον οὗτος ἐκεῖνος. The awkwardness of the switch from the neuter in ἕκαστον to the masculines in οὗτος and ἐκεῖνος is rightly noted by commentators, but the interpretation of οὗτος ἐκεῖνος (cf. τοῦτο ἐκεῖνο, 'that's it', replacing it in *Rhet.* 1371ᵇ10) itself causes no difficulty (cf. D. L. Page [Oxford 1938] on Eur. *Med.* 98; R. Seaford [Oxford 1984] on *Cycl.* 105; M. S. Silk, 'Aristophanic Paratragedy', in Sommerstein *et al.* (edd.), *Tragedy, Comedy and the Polis*, 477–504, at 488 f.).
4. Cf. Frye, *Anatomy of Criticism*, 136.
5. Above, p. 86.
6. LP's ἐν τείχεσσι λαΐνοισι here is accepted by most modern editors, but Dindorf's τύποισι was preferred by Wilamowitz.
7. Above, p. 88.
8. 1. 28. 4.
9. So the *Euripidis Vita* 2 (p. 2 Schwartz = p. 93 Arrighetti); cf. M. R. Lefkowitz, *The Lives of the Greek Poets* (London 1981) 92, and R. P. Winnington-Ingram, 'The Delphic Temple in Greek Tragedy', in Bremer *et al.* (edd.), *Miscellanea Tragica*, 483–500. Athenaeus 10. 424ef, citing Theophrastus (fr. 119 Wimmer), alleges that Euripides also poured wine for nobly born Athenian dancers involved in the worship of the Delian Apollo.
10. See e.g. P. de la Coste-Messelière, *Fouilles de Delphes* iv. 3 (Paris 1931) 15 ff.
11. Ibid. 17 ff. (fr. A: pl. XXXVI here and, in the separate vol. of plates, pl. III).
12. Ibid. 32. Cf. Winnington-Ingram, 'The Delphic Temple', 500.
13. See Paus. 10. 18. 6, and G. Lippold in *RE* vi. 1. 2 s.v. *Tisagoras*, 1467.
14. Cf. Ch. Picard and P. de la Coste-Messelière, *Fouilles de Delphes*, iv. 2 (Paris 1928) 74 ff.; F. Poulsen, *Delphi*, trans. G. C. Richards (London 1920) 131 ff.
15. For example, Σ Eur. *Phoen.* 224 (bathing in the Castalian spring).

16. For example, J. E. Fontenrose, *The Delphic Oracle* (Berkeley 1978) 205 fig. 2 (the priestess sitting on the tripod).
17. 16. 27. 2.
18. Cf. W. G. Arnott, 'Swan Songs', *G&R* 24 (1977) 149–53.
19. Cf. Christiane Sourvinou-Inwood, 'The Myth of the First Temples at Delphi', *CQ* 29 (1979) 231–51, at 239.
20. *The Gates of Horn* (New York 1963), p. ix.
21. The skills that Euripides deploys to achieve his vividness deserve wider investigation, and I for one should welcome a study of them parallel to that recently published by Graham Zanker on Hellenistic poetry (*Realism in Alexandrian Poetry* [London 1987]).

7

The Unity of the *Oresteia*

A. MARIA VAN ERP TAALMAN KIP

In Aeschylus' *Agamemnon* 1412–20, Clytaemnestra reproaches the chorus for applying double standards: 'Now you sentence me to banishment from the city, to the hatred of the citizens and the loud curses of the people. But then you laid no blame on this man, who without qualms, as if it concerned the death of a sheep—one out of many, in fleecy flocks—sacrificed his own child, my dearest daughter that I bore with pain, to charm away the Thracian winds. Is it not him you should have banished from the land, to atone for the guilt that defiled him?'. Referring to these lines, Rosenmeyer asserts that 'the burden of the tragedy quite simply proscribes any suggestion of Clytaemnestra having done what she did in order to avenge her daughter. The timing of the "explanation", the narrow scope granted to it and the almost throwaway quality of the announcement combine to reduce its importance within the larger scheme.'[1] Vickers, in his turn, remarks on Clytaemnestra's words: 'as if she does not believe it, she does not press it'.[2] Comparable statements have been made by other scholars. In my view, however, their arguments are mistaken.

First of all, it is clear that Clytaemnestra herself can only explain her motives for murdering Agamemnon after the murder has been perpetrated. But the audience was prepared for this explanation as early as the *parodos*. Thanks to their prior knowledge of the story,[3] they knew that Agamemnon was going to be murdered by his wife or her lover or both. Thus they cannot have failed to understand the implications of Calchas' prophecy—quoted by the chorus—concerning the 'child-avenging wrath'. By then they must have realized that in this play the queen's hatred of her husband was fostered by the death of her daughter.

After the *parodos*, the chorus make no further mention of the sacrifice of Iphigenia, but the implications of their general

statements can hardly be misunderstood. When they say that
hubris is used to bring forth new *hubris* (764–5) or that human
blood, once fallen on the earth, cannot be called up again
(1018–21), the audience are clearly being invited to apply these
maxims to the events of the play. Thus they have every reason to
expect that once the deed has been done, Clytaemnestra will plead
the sacrifice as an excuse. And so she does, not in 'a throwaway
fashion', but pressing it with great emphasis.

Her first speech after the murder concludes with the words: 'so
many were the accursed evils this man filled a bowl with in the
house, and now, returning, he himself drains it dry' (1397–8).
What else can she mean here but her daughter's death? Then, during the *kommos*, she refers to it explicitly, not once, but four times.
In addition to 1412–20 she invokes 'Justice accomplished for my
child' (1432); she repeats her accusation in 1521–9, and later imagines with derision how Iphigenia will welcome and kiss her father
in the nether world. This time the chorus finally react: 'Taunt has
now been met by taunt; the case is hard to judge' (1560–1). Even
the chorus, although abhorring the crime of their queen, have to
admit 'that it is not possible for them any longer to throw all the
blame on Clytaemnestra'.[4] This is in line with their horrified
description of the sacrifice in the *parodos*.

Of course, the chorus's reaction does not mean that they con-
done the murder. It has been committed and it has to be avenged.
Moreover, Clytaemnestra's motives are mixed. There is also her
lover, and it was his presence which made it almost necessary to do
away with the husband. But only the sacrifice—and not
Aegisthus—can be considered the motive for the fierce and excessive hatred she displays after the murder. One should not, therefore, ignore or belittle a motive that is given her by Aeschylus and
is nowhere belied.

The sacrifice of her daughter is, in the *kommos* of *Agamemnon*,
Clytaemnestra's first and last defence. For this reason we would
expect her to stress this motive again when, in the next play, she is
confronted with Orestes. This time it is a matter of life and death,
and by calling for an axe just a moment before, Clytaemnestra has
shown that she is prepared to go to any lengths. But once she has
entered into the verbal battle, she meekly allows Orestes to harp on
her adultery, and she makes no mention of Iphigenia. Garvie[5] is
one of the few critics to remark on this silence, observing (on

Choephori 918): 'Aeschylus does not let Clytaemnestra use the much more powerful argument of Iphigenia's sacrifice. Our sympathy for her is not to be aroused too far.' He also deals with this question when discussing Electra's words about her lost sister in *Choephori* 242: καὶ τῆς τυθείσης νηλέως ὁμοσπόρου ('and of my sister who was sacrificed mercilessly'). 'This', so he says, 'is the only direct reference in *Choephori* to Iphigenia, and one of the few reminders that Agamemnon was not a guiltless victim (but see 255 . . .). Not even at 908 ff. will Clytaemnestra plead Iphigenia's sacrifice as her motive for the murder. Agamemnon's crimes are no longer dramatically relevant in *Choephori*, in which Clytaemnestra must be presented simply as the criminal who deserves her punishment. Her discrediting is necessarily balanced by the elevation of Agamemnon'. In both statements Garvie uses verbs that imply necessity: 'is not to be' and 'must'. I should like to examine this necessity a little further.

Since it is my basic assumption that the sacrifice is virtually absent from the second and third part of the trilogy, I must first discuss the one line where it is explicitly mentioned and those passages which, according to a number of critics, contain allusions to it. The explicit reference is to be found in *Choephori* 242. Electra, in welcoming her brother, assures him that for her he represents not only himself but also her father, her mother, who is 'most justly hated', and her sister, who was 'sacrificed mercilessly [νηλεῶς]'. Thus here the sacrifice is not only mentioned, but also, on the evidence of this 'mercilessly', referred to with disapproval. And yet the event is apparently not seen in relation to either the father or the mother. The sacrificer is not named, and hatred for the victim's mother is voiced in the preceding line. Apparently it is mentioned here solely to enhance Electra's past loneliness and present joy. If it were intended primarily as a reminder to the audience, there would be some meaningful follow-up.

Now for the allusions. According to Evelyne Méron there is an allusion to the sacrifice in the very dialogue between Clytaemnestra and Orestes, at *Choephori* 910: ἡ Μοῖρα τούτων, ὦ τέκνον, παραιτία ('Destiny, my child, was in part responsible for these things'). This, so Méron says, must be an echo of *Agamemnon* 1497–1503, 'where Clytaemnestra claimed that she had only been an instrument, chosen by fate to punish Agamemnon and his inexplicable crimes' ('où Clytemnestre prétendait n'avoir été que l'instrument élu par le Destin pour châtier Agamemnon et ses crimes inexplicables'[6]). This paraphrase, however, is inaccurate. In the lines from *Agamemnon*, Clytaemnestra is not referring to the crimes of Agamemnon but to the atrocities committed by Atreus. She considers herself the personification of the 'ancient fierce spirit that takes vengeance for the misdeed of the cruel feaster Atreus'.[7] This same argument may well be implied—as Groeneboom also suggests—in *Choephori* 910, but Iphigenia does not appear in the dialogue.

Other allusions are assumed to be present in Orestes' prayer to Zeus at *Choephori* 245–63, the first in Orestes' comparison of his sister and himself to the young of a dead eagle:

> Ζεῦ Ζεῦ, θεωρὸς τῶνδε πραγμάτων γενοῦ,
> ἰδοῦ δὲ γένναν εὖνιν αἰετοῦ πατρὸς
> θανόντος ἐν πλεκταῖσι καὶ σπειράμασιν
> δεινῆς ἐχίδνης· τοὺς δ' ἀπωρφανισμένους
> νῆστις πιέζει λιμός· οὐ γὰρ ἐντελεῖς
> θήραν πατῴαν προσφέρειν σκηνήμασιν.

Zeus, Zeus, witness what is happening here; behold the young ones bereft of their eagle-father, who died in the coils and wreaths of a terrible viper. They are orphans now and starving hunger bears hard on them, for they are not full-grown and cannot bring home their father's quarry. (246–51)

Winnington-Ingram observes: 'Agamemnon was an eagle and his prey was Troy, but as the omen foreshadowed, Troy at the cost of Iphigenia.'[8] Garvie (on 255) shares his view: 'The whole comparison of the eagle and his helpless children recalls *Agamemnon* 49 ff., 108 ff., where the sacrifice of the hare (θυομένοισιν, 137) leads to the second sacrifice (150, 224), Agamemnon's killing of Iphigenia.' In his Introduction, however, he only mentions the vulture simile: 'The image of Orestes and Electra as the orphan brood of an eagle-father (247 ff.) reverses the picture of the vultures bereft of their nestlings and avenged by the Erinys (*Agamemnon* 49 ff.).'[9] Lebeck,[10] although she brackets the vulture simile and the omen, likewise concentrates on the relation between Orestes' comparison and the simile; indeed, the link with the simile is perhaps more obvious than the one with the omen.

For the audience of *Agamemnon*, the vulture simile cannot have pertained to Iphigenia—not even secondarily, as Lebeck will have it[11]—since at that point they did not know that her sacrifice was to play a role in the further developments. But in retrospect they knew that the vulture simile was followed by the eagle omen, that the victimized birds were succeeded by the aggressive birds. Thus they may have been reminded of the sacrifice in a rather round-about way. Their thoughts may have travelled from the bereaved young of the eagle to the vulture parents bereft of their young, and from there to the eagle omen and the sacrifice. However, I am not convinced that the audience reacted in this way, nor indeed that they were meant to do so.

Another allusion has been noted in the next section of the prayer, where Orestes reminds Zeus of the sacrifices made by Agamemnon, calling his father θυτήρ, 'sacrificer'. Groeneboom[12] agrees with Tucker that he is deserving of this name, as does Winnington-Ingram: 'Those who can believe that, after *tutheisês* ["sacrificed", 242] above, the word *thutêr* ["sacrificer", 255] does not echo a phrase in *Agamemnon* (ἔτλα δ᾽ οὖν θυτὴρ γενέσθαι θυγατρός, ["he brought himself to become his daughter's sacrificer" 224]) are welcome to their faith, which is stronger than mine!'.[13] Rosenmeyer ridicules this view: 'A close reading, fortified with a commitment to unity and its close auxiliary, irony, will pause delightedly over the gruesome implications of the son praising his father and expecting to be honored in turn for the one act of sacrifice with which Agamemnon is burdened in the trilogy, that of the sister of Orestes.'[14] However, it is not unlikely that an audience, watching *Choephori* immediately after *Agamemnon*, were reminded by the word θυτήρ of the shocking sacrifice related by the chorus in the former play. But if so, they undoubtedly soon dismissed the association as irrelevant. For once again, what would be the sense of these two allusions?

According to Winnington-Ingram, the first allusion serves to impress upon us that 'these are children of Agamemnon, that the young eagles will soon show their power to bring home to the eyrie prey such as their father brought'.[15] This construction, however, is not borne out by the text. The similarity between Agamemnon's children and the young eagles is only a general one: the eagle young are not fed, and the children of Agamemnon are deprived of their property. But it is hardly possible to carry the comparison much further. Neither the sacrifice nor Orestes' imminent action can be compared to carrying home a prey. On the contrary, it is the home itself that has to be won, and the prey is waiting within.

The implication of θυτήρ would be, again according to
Winnington-Ingram, that 'the hand that prepares this sacrifice will
be *homoia*'[16]—that is, 'similar' to the hand that sacrificed
Iphigenia. But I doubt whether the audience had any reason to
think of the imminent matricide as a sacrifice. Such an association
would in fact be uncalled for, since in *Choephori*, as Goldhill points
out, 'the killing of Clytaemnestra is not described in sacrificial language' and Orestes 'is not depicted as a corrupt sacrificer'.[17] And
that is not all. Winnington-Ingram argues that these veiled allusions are meant to make it clear that the son is like his father and
that, despite Apollo's command, Orestes' guilt is on a par with
Agamemnon's. Aeschylus, so he thinks, reminds us of the sacrifice
in order to underline the horrible aspects of the matricide.[18]
However, it is implausible that when it came to matters assumed to
be of prime importance for a proper understanding of the play, the
audience had to depend on such barely perceptible references. A
dramatist cannot rely solely on such subtleties; they must be supported by more distinct signals, signals that do not appear in
Choephori. In fact, it is precisely Clytaemnestra's silence on the
sacrifice that proves Winnington-Ingram wrong. If the audience
had been reminded of the sacrifice by the word θυτήρ in 255, the
dialogue between Orestes and his mother would have made it clear
that the reminiscence was incidental and that the death of
Iphigenia was no longer being weighed on the scales of justice. The
closing lines of the play confirm this. Between the meal of Thyestes
and the murder of Agamemnon, there is no reference to the sacrifice of Iphigenia.

In *Eumenides*, too, critics have detected allusions to the sacrifice,
the first in 631–2, where Apollo declares that Agamemnon
returned home ἠμπολημκότα τὰ πλεῖστ' ἄμεινον, 'successful on the
whole'. According to Sommerstein 'this somewhat faint praise (he
does not say ἠμπολημκότα τὰ πάντ' ἄριστα ["wholly successful"] will
remind the audience of certain things about the expedition of
which the jury are not going to be told'. And elsewhere he observes
that, although Agamemnon's faults are largely ignored, 'the audience will not have entirely forgotten the darker side of Agamemnon's victory: Apollo with prudent vagueness will speak of him as
ἠμπολημκότα τὰ πλεῖστ' ἄμεινον ["successful on the whole"]'.[19]
However, this argument is not consistent. Why would Apollo, by
bestowing faint praise on Agamemnon, run the risk of making the

jurors suspicious? Such vagueness would not be prudent at all. But I do not believe that his words are meant to suggest 'faint praise'. The use of ἐμπολάω is, by Groeneboom and others, parallelled with *Ajax* 978, where ἠμπόληκας is considered the equivalent of πέπραγας, 'you fared'.[20] Thus Apollo's words do not suggest any fault on the part of Agamemnon, but at most that he sometimes met with reverse.

According to Winnington-Ingram there is one more allusion to the sacrifice, hidden in 661–2: τίκτει δ' ὁ θρῴσκων, ἡ δ' ἅπερ ξένῳ ξένη | ἔσωσεν ἔρνος, οἷσι μὴ βλάψῃ θεός ('the male is the parent, while she, like a stranger for a stranger, preserves the young plant, unless a god destroys it'). He argues that ἔρνος ('young plant') might be a reminiscence of *Agamemnon* 1525, where Clytaemnestra uses the word of Iphigenia, while οἷσι μὴ βλάψῃ θεός ('unless a god destroys it') is intended to remind us of *Agamemnon* 120 (where the same verb is used of the sacrificed hare), and thus of the sacrifice itself. In his view, it must be understood this way, since otherwise the qualification would be unnecessary.[21] But when may a qualification be deemed unnecessary? I would say: when it adds nothing new. But this qualification does add something new, since it is the final blow to the female role in procreation. This time I quite agree with Sommerstein, who comments: 'Not only is the mother not the genetic parent of the child she bears; she is not even to be honoured with the credit for bringing it safely to birth. That credit belongs to "god".' It is possible that the verbal repetition activated the memory of at least some members of the audience. But once again I find it difficult to accept that if Aeschylus had considered it important to remind his audience of the sacrifice, he would have relied on such faint signals.

It is obvious, in my view, that we are required to think no more of Iphigenia, the more so when we realize how easily explicit reminders (instead of obscure hints) would have fitted into the play. The ghost of Clytaemnestra, who here again might have spoken of her daughter, is silent. The Furies, who are her supporters, might have mentioned her in order to malign Agamemnon and strengthen their own case. Athena, in presiding over the legal procedure, might have enquired about Clytaemnestra's motives for killing her husband, but she does not. Upon hearing of Orestes' case her first question is: 'Why did he do it?', but she displays no such interest in Clytaemnestra's motives. It is remarkable that even the adultery is left out; nowhere is Aegisthus mentioned. The whole issue seems to be reduced to the naked opposition between male and female.

The shift of focus outlined above is initiated in *Agamemnon* itself. Vickers[22] observes correctly that, from the Cassandra scene on, the emphasis changes, but I would challenge his assessment of the change as a final one. The emphasis shifts in that Cassandra does not repeat what the chorus has already told us. She does not evoke the guilt of Agamemnon, but the crime of Atreus, and the imminent murder. The chorus have concentrated on what happened outside; Cassandra concentrates solely on the house. She does not fundamentally alter our former judgement, but rather extends it. The *kommos* is there to prove that we need both her explanation and that of the chorus in order to understand the murder of Agamemnon. It is impossible to disentangle these motives: they have been at work together, and the chorus, though fervently rejecting the murder, acknowledge them both. Clytaemnestra is not discredited—as Vickers[23] argues—by adducing her daughter's death as a reason for her deed or by pointing to the 'avenging spirit' (the *alastôr*: *Agamemnon* 1501) of the cruel feaster Atreus. She is, however, discredited in the final scene. Aegisthus shows himself to be a vulgar, tyrannical coward, and it is he who drags her down. This time the change is final. From now on Clytaemnestra will be cast exclusively in the role of an adulterous murderess or simply a woman who killed her husband, while Agamemnon is the blameless and innocent victim.

Vickers, like Garvie, considers such a reversal to be necessary, but why exactly? And if in the next two plays Aeschylus required a blameless Agamemnon and an altogether blamable Clytaemnestra, why then did he not portray them as such right from the beginning? It is true that such a black-and-white contrast might have impaired the dramatic force of *Agamemnon*. But the same was true of *Choephori*, and there Aeschylus took it in his stride. Why then did he introduce this shift by first presenting the sacrifice as a fundamental issue and afterwards inviting us to ignore it? I think that the answer is to be found in Aeschylus' wish to make sense of the myth. It was the only way to explain, in the moral and theological sphere, why Orestes was allowed to live, while Agamemnon and Clytaemnestra had to die.

The great tales of Greek mythology ended with the sons and

daughters of the warriors who fought at Troy. The myth of the Tantalids ended with the children of Agamemnon and Orestes' act of revenge. The matricide is its last fundamental event; a play about Orestes *not* killing his mother would be a comedy.[24] But apparently the life of Orestes after the murder was more or less virgin soil. The only fixed element seems to be that he *did* live on and was not himself murdered. There was no special sense in this. Mythical events simply came to a standstill; the poets were free to imagine what happened next, and did so in various ways.

However, in an Aeschylean tragedy things are expected to make sense. The acquittal of Orestes, as the overture to a new phase in Athenian history, also concludes the crimes and acts of revenge in the Atreid house. It was, therefore, necessary to explain why such a conclusion was now possible, and why it had not come at some earlier point. In my view, it is for this reason that Aeschylus made a clear-cut distinction between the matricide and the other killings. First of all, in the case of Orestes, there is the divine command. Whatever his personal motives, he is forced to act as he does; the price of disobedience would be his own destruction. To reinforce the idea that Apollo's order must be executed, the murder is amply justified beforehand, and dissenting voices are absent. With the exception of the victim and the servant who warns her, there is not a single character who does not advocate the murder. And even the servant concedes that she will be killed πρὸς δίκης ('at the hands of justice': *Choephori* 884).

Electra, although she asks the chorus whether it is pious to pray for revenge, is soon convinced that it is, and from that moment on she voices no qualms about the matricide. The chorus are fervent supporters of Orestes' case, and it is only after the murder, when they see the corpse of Clytaemnestra, that they begin to fear that suffering is in store for Orestes. But they continue to uphold his cause: he did well 'by cutting off the heads of the two snakes' (*Choephori* 1047). Orestes himself had resolved on killing his mother even before his arrival. He needs the chorus to help him reach the emotional state necessary to commit the murder, but only once does he explicitly express doubt as to whether his resolve is justified. And at that precise moment Pylades, representing the divine will, is there to urge him on.

Since the murder he committed was sanctioned by the gods and approved by men, it makes sense that Orestes is not killed in turn, and that his acquittal is presented as part of a divine design. It is only the Erinyes who oppose him, and they do so for purely 'biological' reasons: a son is never justified in killing his mother. But Apollo points out that there *is* no consanguinity between a mother and a son. And Athena clinches the matter by simply choosing the male principle: 'So I shall not have preferential regard for the death of a woman who killed her husband, the overseer of the household'[25] (*Eumenides* 739–40). By this time Agamemnon and Clytaemnestra have been reduced, so to speak, to representatives of the *genus* husband and the *genus* wife, with no regard for their individual histories.

I believe that Aeschylus was caught on the horns of a dilemma. He could have made his Agamemnon innocent from the beginning, but in that case, why did he have to be killed, while Orestes is allowed to live after committing matricide? Alternatively, he could have made him guilty throughout the trilogy, but how then could the matricide—ordered by a god—be made acceptable, as ultimately it had to be? And how could a simple ideological choice have clinched the matter if things had remained as ambiguous as they were in *Agamemnon*? Neither alternative would do, and for this reason the *Oresteia* is the work it is: in the first play Agamemnon is guilty and Clytaemnestra has at least one valid—though not sufficient—reason to kill him. But when the first play is over, we are required to think no more of this.

It will be clear that this shift of focus is indeed necessary, if we imagine for a moment Clytaemnestra saying to her son: 'You say I *sold* you; but your father *killed* his child.' There would be only one possible answer to that: 'He had no choice, since the war against Troy was necessary and inevitable.' But was it? The elders in *Agamemnon* had very strong doubts, and their misgivings were nowhere disproved. This, too, is a serious issue in the first play which is completely ignored in the other two: the question of whether it was justifiable to send so many Greeks to their death for 'another man's wife'. This note is first struck at *Agamemnon* 62 and gets its full weight in the first *stasimon* from 437 onward. The chorus even consider it a reason for Agamemnon to be punished by the gods: 'for the gods are not unmindful of those who cause much bloodshed' (461). They hope never to become what Agamemnon is, a 'destroyer of cities' (472), precisely the word they later use to greet him (782). They are loyal when he returns, but they tell him openly that they did not approve of his waging war because of Helen. After these lines, however, the subject is dropped completely. My imaginary dialogue would have revived the many ambiguities that haunt the *Agamemnon*, ambiguities that would be unacceptable at the moment of the matricide.

The issue of the Trojan war is not only ignored in the next two plays, there are even downright contradictions. Thus when the chorus in *Choephori* compare the past with the present, they sing: 'Respect for the majesty that once was unconquered, that was irresistible in battle and in war, now turns away, the respect which penetrated the ears and heart of the people' (55–7). But the elders in *Agamemnon* thought differently. According to them there was 'resentful grief against the Atreidae' (450–1) and 'dangerous talk with anger in it' (456). It would make no sense to argue either that the elders in *Agamemnon* or the captive women in *Choephori* are mistaken, or that the elders may be exaggerating while the women are idealizing the past. We are clearly not supposed to compare, let alone to reconcile, the two statements but to accept both of them as 'true' at the moment they are delivered. In the same way, we are expected to accept that ultimately, in *Eumenides*, the war is legitimized by being presented as an exploit of Athena—a goddess who is not even mentioned in *Agamemnon*.[26]

Finally, it may be observed that Cassandra, too, is relegated to oblivion. In *Agamemnon*, on the verge of entering the palace to meet her death, she calls upon the chorus to be her witness 'at the time when for me, the woman, a woman dies' (1317–18), and she prays Helios that the revenge on the murderers may be on *her* behalf as well (1323–5[27]). This leads us to expect that her cruel and moving fate will be referred to at some moment in the course of the next play, but it is not. Her prayer in *Agamemnon* is not answered in *Choephori*, where nobody remembers her fate.

This is in line with my argument. Emphasis on the murder of Cassandra would also remind the audience of the reason for her presence: the fact that Agamemnon took her home as his mistress. And this feature, like the sacrifice and the dubious aspect of the Trojan war, does not fit in with *Choephori*. In the dialogue between Clytaemnestra and Orestes it is clearly suppressed. Clytaemnestra does confront her son with his father's infidelities, but he retorts that she should not blame 'the man who toiled', while she herself sat at home (918–19). Obviously this excuse is valid only for

Agamemnon's behaviour during the campaign, not for his bringing Kassandra into the royal palace. But Clytaemnestra does not
argue the point and merely answers: 'it is difficult for women to be
separated from their husbands, my son' (920). Even this stain on
Agamemnon is removed by silence.

While all this may be necessary within the context of *Choephori*
and *Eumenides*, it reveals a deep rift between the first play and the
other two. If *Agamemnon* had been lost to us, and the other two
tragedies preserved, we would now have a very incomplete and
probably quite mistaken conception of the lost drama, and we
would not be able to imagine its rich complexity. Much in
Agamemnon is equivocal. The justification of the Trojan war, for
the sake of which Agamemnon killed his daughter, may seem
highly dubious to the elders, but they do not deny that it, too, was
a question of justice. *Not* making war for another man's wife
would have meant leaving unpunished Paris' infamous violation
of the law of hospitality and the Trojans' condoning of it. The
chorus roundly condemn Clytaemnestra, but they do not deny
that, up to a point, the murder was justified and that, moreover,
the *alastôr* of the house may have lent assistance. Little of this
ambivalence has found its way into *Choephori* and *Eumenides*.
Even the crime of Atreus, so prominent in the first play, is later
mentioned only in the closing anapests of *Choephori*. Mme de
Romilly remarks on the *Oresteia*: 'The series of crimes here is too
long even for a trilogy.'[28] However, in *Choephori* (but for 1066–9)
and *Eumenides* the murder of Agamemnon seems to be the first
crime of the series.

It is a matter of some dispute nowadays how much unity may be
expected within a connected trilogy. And since the *Oresteia* is the
only example we have, arguments focus on this one. According to
Garvie the three plays 'are bound together in a single dramatic
unity by the tragic situations which they present, by their structure, and by their imagery and language'.[29] And, of course, it is not
to be denied that there is recurrent imagery and that scenes from
Agamemnon are mirrored in *Choephori*. In my view, however, it is
difficult to maintain a claim to dramatic unity when one is required
to forget a number of features that initially carried considerable
weight. Nor is the mere presence of Clytaemnestra in all three
plays any guarantee of unity. This is only the case when there is a
certain consistency in the character's behaviour, a consistency that,

in the *Oresteia*, is destroyed when Clytaemnestra leaves out her most forceful defence.

Other scholars, among them Herington and Rosenmeyer,[30] stress the difference between *Agamemnon* and *Choephori* on the one hand and *Eumenides* on the other. Herington points out that the first two plays are based on traditional tales, while the content of *Eumenides* is mainly fiction. Rosenmeyer observes that *Eumenides* in no way fulfils the Aristotelian maxim that things ought to happen κατὰ τὸ εἰκὸς ἢ τὸ ἀναγκαῖον ('according to proba-bility or necessity'); it is not the logical or inevitable consequence of *Choephori*, while the end of the trilogy has even lost all connection with the house of the Atreids. This is largely true. There is nothing in *Choephori* that prepares us for the role of Athena, for the institution of the Areopagus,[31] or for the Erinyes becoming Eumenides. However, the acquittal of Orestes is an almost neces-sary consequence of the divine command. No spectator of an Aeschylean tragedy would have expected Apollo, who ordered the murder, to let Orestes down. To that extent, there *is* an immediate connection, and in any case *Eumenides* contains no contradictions or inconsistencies in relation to *Choephori*. The true dividing-line runs between *Agamemnon* and *Choephori*.

The Athenian audience must have been aware of this. At the moment they were listening to the dialogue between Clytaem-nestra and Orestes, only about two hours had passed since Cly-taemnestra's derisive words about Iphigenia welcoming her father to Hades. But we do not know to what extent they expected con-sistency and unity of a trilogy. It may well be that these features were less important to them than to us. Similarly, they probably did not ask themselves whether the final play should be considered 'tragic' (or 'a tragedy'), while for modern critics this is an obvious question—a question that, in view of the ending of the play, they will probably answer in the negative. Does this mean that *Choephori*, as a result of the simplifications necessitated by the con-tent of *Eumenides*, is not tragic, too, or at least less tragic than *Agamemnon*? To decide whether a discussion of this issue is mate-rial, a preliminary question ought to be answered first: what exactly do we mean by 'tragic'?

The quotation marks in the title of the conference that generated this volume suggest that there is something that we call tragic, but that it is not a well-defined concept. This is undoubtedly the case.

When we speak of Greek tragedy we mean simply all the plays that were performed at dramatic festivals as tragedies—and not as comedies or satyr-plays. In the same way, we may speak of the 'tragic poets' or a 'tragic chorus', just as the adjective was used, for the most part, by the Greeks themselves. Only Aristotle employs the term in relation to the plot and content of tragedy, and then only occasionally. In *Poetics* 13 (1453ª27–30), for example, he asserts that when staged at the dramatic contests, tragedies ending in disaster prove to be the most tragic, and that Euripides, in this regard at least, proves to be the most tragic of poets.[32] However, at 14, 1454ª1–9 Euripides' *Iphigenia in Tauris*, a play which does *not* end in disaster, seems to be given preference even over *Oedipus Tyrannus*. I will not discuss here the relation between this passage and the earlier one,[33] but I am fairly convinced that Aristotle would not have denied to *Iphigenia in Tauris* the predicate 'tragic' (τραγικόν). And I am equally convinced that Halliwell is right when he assumes that 'For some, this will amount to an ultimate negation of tragedy, a final pulling back from the brink of the "incurable".'[34] Here 'tragedy' is used in the sense of 'a play that is really tragic'.

When in the sixteenth century Scaliger discussed the subject, he saw no problem in tragedies with a happy ending. Such tragedies existed, so apparently a disastrous ending was not necessary. His prime witness is the *Oresteia*: 'The outcome is happy for everyone, Apollo, Orestes, the people, Pallas, and the Furies, so that previous statements that an unhappy ending is a property of tragedy go by the board, provided that it contains within the body of the work frightful events.'[35] But such an uncomplicated view did not persist and, to quote Halliwell once more: 'views on tragedy in the last two centuries have strongly tended to expand from critical or theoretical concerns with certain literary works, to much larger concepts of tragic attitudes towards life as a whole'.[36] Such concepts of the tragic are tied up with the *Zeitgeist*, philosophical systems, and personal preoccupations. They do not derive from Aristotle. They may be inspired by certain Greek tragedies, or even by just one work, but decidedly not by the corpus as a whole, which is far too diverse to yield an all-embracing view.

The ideas on this point are not unanimous, although they do not vary as widely as Greek tragedies do. There are certain shared views. According to Leech[37] tragedy implies 'for us in the last two centuries, an exposition of man's powerlessness in his cosmic setting'. Moreover 'tragic' is often associated with conflicts that cannot be resolved.

Hegel's reading of *Antigone* inspired the notion that a tragic conflict is one between two duties, two equal rights. Nussbaum[38] describes the tragic conflict as follows: 'In such cases we see a wrong action committed without any direct physical compulsion and in full knowledge of its nature, by a person whose ethical character or commitments would otherwise dispose him to reject the act. The constraint comes from the presence of circumstances that prevent the adequate fulfilment of two valid ethical claims.' In the first case the conflicting duties are embodied in two characters. In the second, the valid ethical claims are present in the choice which a character is forced to make. Either way, the absence of an adequate solution reduces one or more characters to powerlessness.

Such notions inevitably lead to a division of tragedies into two groups: those that merely bear the name tragedy and those that are really 'tragic'. But we must be aware that the attribution of this predicate may depend on our interpretation. If we reject (as Goethe so fervently did) Hegel's interpretation of *Antigone*, then the conflict of equal rights is simply not there. Moreover, concepts like these tend to become instruments of evaluation, whose suitability I would venture to question.

Kitto, in discussing Euripides' *Iphigenia at Aulis*, comments: 'Now this is not a bad story, but it is not really tragic.' Agamemnon has no 'tragic choice' and there is no 'tragic illumination', that 'ought to be the justification of this cruel story'.[39] Essentially these are prescriptions deriving from a preconceived concept of the 'tragic'. Admittedly, absence of tragic choice and tragic illumination might perhaps explain why a play does not appeal to *us*. But I do not think this explanation is applicable in the case of *Iphigenia at Aulis*. It is regularly performed and many a critic considers it an impressive and fascinating play, even if Kitto clearly did not care for it.

The word 'tragic' is often used casually, but even seemingly clear descriptions are not easy to apply to individual tragedies. Let me elaborate one example. In his Introduction to *Agamemnon*, Page chooses as his starting-point the famous statement of Goethe: 'All that is tragic rests on an irreconcilable antithesis. As soon as reconciliation is initiated or becomes possible, the tragic disappears' ('Alles Tragische beruht auf einem unausgleichbaren Gegensatz. Sowie Ausgleichung eintritt oder möglich wird, schwindet das Tragische').[40] Page paraphrases the Goethean maxim as 'Solve the problem and there is no tragedy left', and he stipulates that 'in tragedy of this type the beginning is no less inevitable than the end'. Plays that meet this description represent the 'highest form' of tragedy and 'The *Oresteia, Oedipus Tyrannus, Hippolytus* and the *Bacchae* most nearly represent the ideal.' Plays that do not meet the description are of an 'inferior type'.[41]

It is clear, of course, why *Oedipus* was included in the selection, although it has no tragic conflict, no 'conflict of equal or at least irreconcilable rights, of Justice against Justice'.[42] Since Oedipus could not avoid doing what he did, and since the irremediable events occurred before the opening of the play, the problem cannot be resolved. But what of *Bacchae*? Page only comments on the *end* of this drama, but it seems fairly clear that at the beginning the problem can easily be solved. Pentheus has plenty of time and opportunity to welcome and acknowledge Dionysus. It is not the situation, but rather his 'character' (in Aristotle's sense of $\mathring{\eta}\theta o\varsigma$) that prevents him from doing so. This is an insurmountable barrier indeed, and it is perhaps this which Page had in mind— though why did he not then include *Ajax, Antigone*, and *Medea*?

Agamemnon is included by Page, because he is convinced that Agamemnon had no real choice at Aulis, that both alternatives were equally unacceptable. And it is because of the presence of this real tragic conflict that he considers *Agamemnon* a tragedy which meets the criteria of Goethe. But what if Agamemnon *did* have a choice, as other critics (including myself) tend to think? Does this diminish the play for the simple reason that it does not answer to a sense of the tragic which only developed some 2,500 years after Aeschylus wrote his play?

In *Choephori* the insoluble problem seems clearly there, at least at the beginning of the play. If Orestes does not avenge his father, his life will be ruined; if he does avenge his father, he has to kill his mother. But how about the end? While it is true that Orestes runs away in terror, we know that he is going to take refuge with Apollo, and we expect that for him a solution will ultimately be found. In *Agamemnon* the working of the divine is omnipresent, but not clear-cut. In *Choephori* it is: Apollo has ordered the killing, he has

specified the punishments in case Orestes should fail to obey, and
he has promised not to fail him.

But there is more to say. The problem of the matricide may
appear insoluble to us, but is it not also important to consider how
the character himself sees it?[43] Orestes is not racked by despair,
either before or after the murder. He is desperate because of the
pursuit of the Furies, but when—in the next play—he has been
freed from them by his acquittal, his problem has been solved. The
trilogy could not have ended as it does if Orestes, like Oedipus,
were terrified by what he had done, rather than only terrified by the
Furies. In view of *Eumenides* he had to be the very inarticulate
character he is—probably one of the most inarticulate in the whole
of Greek tragedy.

I am aware that most modern critics will not be inclined to create hierarchies in the vein of Page. But I believe that the example
is useful to explain my view that, in a discussion of Greek tragedy,
the concept 'tragic' is essentially unmanageable. One critic may
call a play 'tragic' while another does not, because his interpretation of the play is different, or his specification of 'tragic' is different, or both. The concept is revealing as regards our own ways of
thinking and feeling, and it is an interesting theme in the history of
Western thought. But however we describe it, we cannot lump
together *Oedipus Tyrannus* and *Bacchae*. In the first tragedy we
have a mature man, who in the past has tried, at any price, to avoid
what the god or the gods have destined him to do, who strives to
uncover the truth, and who, when he is utterly destroyed, lives on,
trying to safeguard the future of his daughters and conscious of
other disasters to come. In the second, we see an immature man,
who refuses to ackowledge a god, for reasons that are at least in part
understandable, who is struck with madness and cruelly slaughtered. Where are the similarities? There are virtually none, except
for the working of the divine, very clear-cut in *Bacchae*, much less
so in *Oedipus*. And, of course, both are powerful dramas.

It will be clear by now that I do not think it relevant to describe
the difference between *Agamemnon* and *Choephori* in terms of their
approximation to 'the tragic'. It may be defined in such terms as
'ambiguity' and 'moral complexity', and while I might label the
presence or absence of these features as 'tragic', this would explain
nothing at all, only my own view of the content of the term. Let me
note in conclusion that from *Choephori* onward things narrow

down considerably, and that this reduction of scope may well be the reason why most contemporary spectators seem far more fascinated by *Agamemnon* than by the other two tragedies.

Notes

1. Rosenmeyer, *Art of Aeschylus*, 292.
2. Vickers, *Towards Greek Tragedy*, 385.
3. The story of Agamemnon being murdered at his homecoming must have been familiar, if only because it is told several times in the *Odyssey*.
4. E. Fraenkel, *Aeschylus Agamemnon* (3 vols.; Oxford 1950) iii. 736.
5. A. F. Garvie, *Aeschylus: Choephori* (Oxford 1986).
6. E. Méron, 'Grandeur et misère de Clytemnestre', *REA* 87 (1985) 245–55, 251.
7. Fraenkel's translation.
8. Winnington-Ingram, *Studies in Aeschylus*, 134.
9. Garvie, *Choephori*, p. xxxvi.
10. Lebeck, *Oresteia*, 13–14.
11. Ibid. 9. Silk, *Interaction in Poetic Imagery*, considers παίδων (*Ag.* 50) a 'faint and slightly surreal "proleptic" evocation of Iphigenia', rightly observing, however, that she 'does not form the official topic for some time' (146). This indeed is the most we can say, but we must bear in mind that, at this moment, Iphigenia not only does not form the *official* topic, but no topic at all. Moreover, *two* birds robbed of their nestlings by nameless wrongdoers hardly suggest a mother whose daughter has been killed by her husband. Cf. A. M. van Erp Taalman Kip, *Reader and Spectator* (Amsterdam 1990) 51.
12. P. Groeneboom, *Aeschylus' Choephoroi* (Groningen 1949).
13. Winnington-Ingram, *Studies in Aeschylus*, 134; cf. Garvie, *Choephori*, on 255.
14. Rosenmeyer, *Art of Aeschylus*, 87.
15. Winnington-Ingram, *Studies in Aeschylus*, 134.
16. Ibid. 134–5.
17. S. Goldhill, *Aeschylus. The Oresteia* (Cambridge 1992) 69.
18. Winnington-Ingram, *Studies in Aeschylus*, 135.
19. A. H. Sommerstein, *Aeschylus Eumenides* (Cambridge 1989) on 631–2 and 456–8.
20. P. Groeneboom, *Aeschylus' Eumeniden* (Groningen 1952). Cf. R. Jebb, *Sophocles. The Plays and Fragments*, vii: *The Ajax* (Cambridge 1896), and J. C. Kamerbeek, *The Plays of Sophocles*, i: *The Ajax* (Leiden 1963) on *Ajax* 978.
21. Winnington-Ingram, *Studies in Aeschylus*, 124 n. 107.

22. Vickers, *Towards Greek Tragedy*, 382.
23. Ibid. 385.
24. Cf. Arist. *Poet.* 1453ª35–9.
25. Translation by Podlecki.
26. See *Eumenides* 457; cf. Sommerstein ad loc.
27. The text is corrupt, but this seems to be the gist of her words.
28. J. de Romilly, *Time in Greek Tragedy* (Ithaca, NY 1968) 72.
29. Garvie, *Choephori*, p. xxxviii.
30. C. J. Herington, 'Aeschylus: The Last Phase', *Arion* 4 (1965) 387–403, 392; Rosenmeyer, *Art of Aeschylus*, 341.
31. In view of the aetiological story connected with the Χόϵς, the Athenians may have expected their town to play some part in the third play. But this story obviously implied that *purification* was the aim of Orestes' visit to Athens. In any case, the content of *Choephori* does not prepare us for it.
32. Else, *Aristotle's Poetics*, considers the words αἱ πολλαὶ αὐτοῦ ϵἰς δυστυχίαν τϵλϵυτῶσιν an interpolation and thinks that Aristotle is also referring to other qualities of Euripides' plays. However, editors after him have not adopted this view and the question does not affect my argument.
33. For a recent discussion see S. A. White, 'Aristotle's Favorite Tragedies', in A. Oksenberg Rorty (ed.), *Essays on Aristotle's Poetics* (Princeton 1992).
34. Halliwell, *Poetics of Aristotle*, 137.
35. J. C. Scaliger, *Poetices Libri Septem*, 3.97, 145 b. Trans. C. J. McDonough, in M. J. Sidnell (ed.), *Sources of Dramatic Theory*, i: *Plato to Congreve* (Cambridge 1951), 106.
36. Halliwell, *Poetics of Aristotle*, 126.
37. C. Leech, *Tragedy* (London 1969) 26.
38. Nussbaum, *Fragility*, 25.
39. Kitto, *Greek Tragedy*[3], 362. Kitto calls Aristotle as a witness: 'Aristotle rightly said that the downfall of a bad man is φιλάνθρωπον, but is not tragic; here even τὸ φιλάνθρωπον is wanting, as the play moves right away from Agamemnon.' However, although Aristotle calls it ἀτραγῳδότατον to show bad men passing from bad to good fortune, he does not use the word 'tragic' when discussing the downfall of bad men, and notions like 'tragic choice' are modern, not Aristotelian. Moreover, the reference is irrelevant, since Agamemnon can hardly be qualified as a man who is σφόδρα πονηρός ('very wicked').
40. Goethe to the chancellor von Müller on 6 June 1824.
41. J. D. Denniston and D. L. Page, *Aeschylus Agamemnon* (Oxford 1957), p. xx. Page does not mean, of course, the whole of the *Oresteia*; *Eumenides* is excluded (xxii).

42. Ibid. xxi.

43. Cf. A. Lesky, *Die griechische Tragödie* (Stuttgart 1964) 23; G. Ronnet, 'Le Sentiment du tragique chez les Grecs', *REG* 87 (1985) 245–55. According to Ronnet the substance of the tragic is 'l'affrontement dans une conscience du Destin et d'une liberté' ('the confrontation in a consciousness of Fate and a liberty', 328). She, too, considers *Choephori* an 'authentic' tragedy (together with *Seven against Thebes*, *Prometheus*, *Oedipus Tyrannus*, and *Antigone*), but I cannot really detect such a confrontation in Orestes' consciousness.

8

The Tragedy of the *Oresteia*:
Response to van Erp Taalman Kip

A. F. GARVIE

In her paper on 'The Unity of the *Oresteia*', Dr van Erp Taalman Kip argues that 'the true dividing-line runs [not between *Choephori* and *Eumenides* but] between *Agamemnon* and *Choephori*'.[1] She stresses, quite correctly, that the *Oresteia* is our only surviving trilogy, and it is indeed hazardous to speculate about the rules that normally determined the unity of the Aeschylean trilogy.[2] Aristotle's *Poetics* is singularly unhelpful to anyone trying to make such an attempt. The unity of the *Oresteia* can be discussed in terms of that trilogy alone. Especially problematic is the reconciliation in the final play. In what sense can a trilogy that ends 'happily', whether or not Aeschylus normally wrote trilogies of this kind, be described as 'tragic'? Are we to say that the *Oresteia* consists of two tragedies and a non-tragedy, so that the unity of the whole becomes immediately suspect, or that the happy ending negates, or at least cancels out, the genuine tragedy that has preceded, so that the trilogy as a whole is no longer 'tragic', or that, despite the happy ending, the suffering which the first two plays present is sufficient to impose a sense of tragedy on the whole composition? Here too Aristotle provides no help. Quite apart from *Poetics* 14, 1454[a]1–9,[3] it is extraordinary that Aristotle is able to mention in the same sentence (*Poetics* 16, 1455[a]16–20) *Oedipus Tyrannus* and *Iphigenia in Tauris* as examples of the best kind of recognition, and that he shows no awareness of what seems obvious to the modern reader, that they are very different kinds of plays. But Aristotle is concerned primarily with the external forms of Greek tragedy, and displays little interest in the tragic thinking of the dramatists. If one were to ask Euripides himself to classify *Iphigenia in Tauris*, no doubt he would reply that of course it is a τραγῳδία ('tragedy')—it is certainly not a comedy or a satyr-play—but it is hard to believe that he wrote it under the impression that it was the same kind of play as *Oedipus Tyrannus*, or his own *Medea*, or his, as yet unwritten, *Bacchae*. The concept of the 'tragic', difficult though it is to define, is not exclusively modern. If it were, we should expect to find all three tragedians writing far more plays like *Iphigenia in Tauris* or *Helen*. But most surviving Greek tragedies *do* correspond with modern ideas of the 'tragic', no doubt because such ideas are soundly based, at least partly, on Greek tragedy. It is the others which seem to be anomalous or experimental. This is not to say that Page was right to lay down a hierarchy of tragedies, according to how far they measure up to our definitions of the 'tragic'.[4] But it is unhelpful to deny that there is any difference at all. Most modern readers have felt, like Page, that it is *Eumenides* that differs from the other two plays. Van Erp Taalman Kip's thesis, that the division comes between *Agamemnon* and *Choephori*, is therefore provocative and requires examination.

In the first play Agamemnon is seen as a king who deserves to die because of his crimes, and it is the sacrifice of Iphigenia that Clytaemnestra gives as her principal motive for killing him. I agree entirely with van Erp Taalman Kip, against Rosenmeyer and Vickers, that she is quite sincere, and that we are meant to take this motive seriously. She has, of course, other motives too: Cassandra, whom she mentions, and her adultery with Aegisthus, and her desire for power, which, not surprisingly, she does not mention. In *Choephori* the sacrifice of Iphigenia is almost entirely forgotten,[5] and Agamemnon is presented in a wholly favourable light. In particular, when confronted with Orestes immediately before her death, Clytaemnestra contents herself with referring only to her husband's unfaithfulness (918),[6] and says nothing about her daughter's sacrifice. Van Erp Taalman Kip quotes my remark in my commentary on *Choephori* 918: 'Aeschylus does not let Clytaemnestra use the much more powerful argument of Iphigenia's sacrifice. Our sympathy for her is not to be aroused too far.' More requires to be said about this, and it leads me to a conclusion that is different from that of van Erp Taalman Kip.

I have argued elsewhere[7] that the first two plays of the trilogy are closely bound together, not least by their presentation of analogous, if not identical, situations and moral problems. The dramatic

unity is established by this technique, rather than by the kind of
consistency on whose absence van Erp Taalman Kip focuses. In
Agamemnon, Paris deserves to be punished for his offence against
the laws of hospitality, and Agamemnon is the righteous instrument of Zeus' vengeance. But, as the chorus frequently reminds us
(62, 225–6, 448, 799–804), the war was fought for a mere promis-
cuous woman, and it involves too many deaths (461), as well as the
sacrilege which the Greeks commit at Troy (525–8; cf. 338–42).
The same act is both right and wrong, depending on how you look
at it. From a logical point of view the chorus's ambivalent attitude
to the war makes no sense: does it, or does it not, approve? We
should certainly not try to explain this in terms of the chorus's psychology. Rather, Aeschylus is using the chorus to show the audience that there are two ways of looking at the war. Van Erp
Taalman Kip maintains, in a different context, that 'in an
Aeschylean tragedy things are expected to make sense'.[8] But, if it
is the function of at least one kind of tragedy to present insoluble
problems,[9] sense of this kind is the last thing that we should expect
to find. The world in which we live is one in which there are often
no clear moral answers, and the same act may be both right and
wrong, depending on the way we look at it. When we come to
Choephori, this particular ambiguity concerning the Trojan war is
no longer relevant; for our interest now is entirely in the crime of
Clytaemnestra and her punishment. It will therefore be replaced
by other ambiguities. In *Agamemnon* the sacrifice of Iphigenia is
certainly presented as a crime, but as one which was necessary if
Agamemnon was to obey the command of Zeus to lead the expedition to punish Paris. Van Erp Taalman Kip, like many other scholars, does not, I think, pay sufficient attention to the fact that Zeus
sends Agamemnon to Troy. The verb πέμπω ('send') is used at 59,
61, and 111, in the context of both the vulture simile and the eagle
omen. Just as Zeus sends an Erinys to punish the robber of the vultures' nest, so, by means of the omen, he sends Agamemnon and
Menelaus to punish Paris. Although the 'reference to Zeus Xenios
in no way implies that Zeus must necessarily have approved every
act performed in furtherance of the expedition',[10] it remains true
that, according to the chorus, Agamemnon's first crime was
unequivocally committed because he felt obliged to obey a divine
command, and Aeschylus gives no indication that the chorus's
judgement is unreliable or wrong. This does not mean, in the

famous words of Page,[11] 'that Agamemnon has no choice but to do what he does'. He could have disobeyed. Both alternatives are unacceptable. It is not Agamemnon's fault that he is placed in a situation in which he has to choose between them, but he *is* responsible for the choice that he makes.

Is the situation of Orestes in *Choephori* so very different? Van Erp Taalman Kip argues that 'from *Choephori* onward things narrow down considerably', in that 'whatever his personal motives [Orestes] is forced to act as he does'.[12] He has been commanded by Apollo to kill his mother, so that 'it makes sense that Orestes is not killed in turn'. 'No spectator of an Aeschylean tragedy', says van Erp Taalman Kip, 'would have expected Apollo, who ordered the murder, to let Orestes down.'[13] But it did not work out in that way for Agamemnon, who obeyed the command of Zeus. She dismisses too lightly Orestes' personal motives. As with Agamemnon at Aulis, and with Clytaemnestra in her murder of her husband, Orestes' actions are doubly determined.[14] He too has to make a choice, and whatever he chooses will be wrong. So Electra's despairing cry in the *kommos* (*Choephori* 338), τί τῶνδ' εὖ, τί δ' ἄτερ κακῶν; ('what in this situation is well, and what is free from trouble?'), parallels exactly that of Agamemnon at Aulis (*Agamemnon* 211), τί τῶνδ' ἄνευ κακῶν; ('what in this situation is free from trouble?'). By the end of *Choephori*, I can find little ground for optimism. Orestes' madness and his pursuit by the Erinyes are, despite van Erp Taalman Kip,[15] quite enough to reduce us to despair. μίμνοντι δὲ καὶ πάθος ἀνθεῖ ('suffering in fact bursts into flower for one who waits'), says the chorus at 1009, and at 1020 μόχθος δ' ὁ μὲν αὐτίχ', ὁ δ' ἥξει ('there is trouble now, and more to come'). The last lines of the play (1075-6), ποῖ δῆτα κρανεῖ, ποῖ καταλήξει | μετακοιμισθὲν μένος ἄτης; ('where, then, will it come to fulfilment, where will the might of ruin go to sleep and stop?'), hardly encourage an audience to look forward to the future with hope.

When, after the murder of Agamemnon, Clytaemnestra is justifying herself to the chorus, she naturally says nothing about her husband's moral dilemma at Aulis. It is not in her interests to do so. But the chorus might have reminded her, and us, of that dilemma, and the question why they do not so remind us is perhaps just as interesting as the question why in *Choephori* Clytaemnestra says nothing about Iphigenia. At this stage such a reminder would not have suited Aeschylus' purpose. His concern is now to make as good a case as possible for Clytaemnestra, a case which would only be weakened by the thought that her victim was not entirely guilty. Just as Agamemnon was appointed by Zeus to punish Paris, so Clytaemnestra may claim to be the divinely appointed instrument of Agamemnon's punishment, while at the same time she embodies the curse that makes Agamemnon pay for his father's crimes (*Agamemnon* 1497–1504). What we are to concentrate on now, at the end of *Agamemnon*, is the moral complexity of a situation in which the *rightful* punishment of a criminal is at the same time a further crime, which in its turn will require to be punished. Again the same act is both right and wrong, depending on the viewpoint of the spectator. Agamemnon's death is entirely deserved, because he sacrificed his daughter, but at the same time it is wrong under any circumstances for a wife to kill her husband. Once more we are faced with an insoluble problem, which it is impossible to reduce to logical 'sense', and the chorus's ἀμηχανία at 1530 is not at all surprising. Agamemnon's sacrifice of Iphigenia involved the same kind of moral complexity, but now the characters are different. There Iphigenia was the victim, and Agamemnon the perpetrator, while here Agamemnon has become the victim, and Clytaemnestra is the perpetrator. The difference is that Iphigenia was an entirely innocent victim, but otherwise the situations are analogous.

So is the situation of Orestes in *Choephori*. Clytaemnestra, the perpetrator of her husband's murder, has become in her turn the victim. Again, in the stichomythia at 908–30, it is the concern of Aeschylus to make out as good a case as possible for the perpetrator of the killing. So, to Clytaemnestra's excuse that Fate shared the responsibility for her killing of her husband, Orestes replies, 'it was therefore Fate that prepared also this [his mother's] death' (909–10). And when she complains, 'it seems, my child, that you are about to kill your mother', he responds effectively, 'it is you who will kill yourself, not I' (922–3). Clytaemnestra, like Agamemnon at the end of the preceding play, must be presented as entirely deserving of her punishment, and it would distract from the main issue if we were to be reminded too strongly that she had some justification for what she did in the earlier play. Orestes must emerge as the clear victor from the confrontation, defeating the woman who in the corresponding stichomythia at *Agamemnon* 931–43 (cf. 943, 'be persuaded; the authority is still yours if you hand it over willingly to me'; this must be the sense of the corrupt line) had so easily overcome the man. The complexity lies, not in the suffering of someone who is partly blamable and partly blameless, but in the paradox that it is wrong to give her what she clearly deserves. As Castor puts it at Euripides' *Electra* 1244, δίκαια μέν νυν ἥδ᾿ἔχει, σὺ δ᾿ οὐχὶ δρᾷς, 'what she has received is right, but not what you have done'. Once more we are presented with the moral complexity of a situation in which the *rightful* killing of a criminal is itself a further crime. There is, however, a difference. In *Agamemnon*, Clytaemnestra's attempted justification came after she committed the murder, and was presented to the chorus, whereas in *Choephori* it is the victim herself who, before her murder, in the encounter with her killer, attempts to justify her previous behaviour, and therefore might have been expected to do so more fully. That, no doubt, is why her failure to mention Iphigenia is more obtrusive than the failure of the chorus in *Agamemnon* to remind us that Agamemnon sacrificed Iphigenia as a result of his obedience to Zeus. But this difference is relatively unimportant, and Aeschylus had no choice if he was to bring out the essential similarity between the two situations.

It is *Eumenides* that is different. Such moral complexities are no longer the concern of the play. Motives, whether of Orestes or of Clytaemnestra, are hardly mentioned,[16] and the whole problem of doubly determined actions disappears. At *Eumenides* 199–200 the chorus-leader maintains that Apollo is not μεταίτιος, 'sharing in the responsibility', but παναίτιος, 'wholly responsible', so that Orestes' personal motives are forgotten.[17] The issue resolves itself into the much simpler one of whether it is worse for a woman to murder her husband than for a son to kill his mother. Despite van Erp Taalman Kip, who says that '*Eumenides* contains no contradictions or inconsistencies in relation to *Choephori*',[18] there is a major inconsistency in the relationship between Apollo and the Erinyes. In the earlier play both the Olympian gods and the underworld powers are united in their insistence that Orestes should kill his mother. At *Choephori* 269–305 Orestes describes how Apollo threatened him with his father's Erinyes should he fail to do so. It is only at the very end of the play that the division appears, when Orestes, pursued by the Erinyes, departs to seek Apollo's protection. From now on the emphasis is on the horror of the matricide rather than on the legitimacy of Orestes' vengeance. The shift of focus, already prepared at 931, when the chorus-leader says, 'I

lament even their double fate' (that is, the deaths of Clytaemnestra
and Aegisthus) is comparable to that described by van Erp
Taalman Kip[19] at the end of *Agamemnon*, where the discrediting of
Clytaemnestra prepares us for *Choephori*. Again, the first two plays
are similar in their structure. One might add that Clytaemnestra's
change of mood, her genuine weariness with bloodshed, is balanced by the onset of Orestes' madness in the second play. In
Eumenides the Erinyes twice claim (212, 605) that their function is
restricted to the pursuit of those who murder blood-kin. It is hard
to reconcile this with *Choephori*. It has often been shown too that
in its handling of recurring imagery the third play is set apart from
the other two. There is much less ambiguity, and many of the ideas
which until now have been used to create foreboding and a sense of
perversion, now appear at last in a healthy context.[20] As Colin
Macleod puts it,[21] 'in the *Agamemnon* and *Choephori* there is, both
in the imagery and in the events the play describes, a disturbance
and a distortion of nature, which mirrors or even results from
human crimes. . . . At the end of the whole trilogy these distur-
bances are calmed and the distortions straightened.' The dividing-
line runs between *Choephori* and *Eumenides*, not between
Agamemnon and *Choephori*.

The very fact that there *is* a dividing-line shows, however, that
the unity of the trilogy remains problematical. The first two plays
present a series of insoluble problems that mean as much to us as
they did to the original audience. But in *Eumenides* a solution is
apparently found—one, moreover, that is closely tied to a peculiarly fifth-century Athenian institution, the Areopagus, that
means nothing to a twentieth-century audience. Even if we think
of the Areopagus as standing for the legal process in general, can
we really be satisfied with a solution that finds so simple an answer
to the great problems of human life? In what sense is the *Oresteia*
'tragic'? The trilogy ends 'happily', but it may be that Aeschylus
himself was well aware that the real problems remain unresolved.
Orestes has to be acquitted, because the myth knew of no further
punishment for him. And after the acquittal, Aeschylus changes
the whole direction of the play so that, with Orestes forgotten, an
Athenian audience may enjoy the spectacular and triumphant
reception of the chorus into its new home in Athens. But the question of what Orestes (or Agamemnon) should have done remains
unanswered, and the moral complexities of the first two plays are

given no solution. Orestes is acquitted, but only because the votes
are equal, and Athena has declared in advance (*Eumenides* 741) that
equal votes will mean acquittal. If, as I believe, Sommerstein is
right against Podlecki,[22] that Athena votes together with the
human jurors (735), the latter actually vote for condemnation. But
even if Podlecki is right, the human jurors are unable to reach a
decision, and the support of Apollo for Orestes, on which van Erp
Taalman Kip lays so much stress, is not sufficient to sway them. If
this had been the crucial factor, it would have been easy for
Aeschylus to mark it by producing a decisive majority in favour of
Orestes. But at 795–6 Athena reassures the Erinyes that they have
not been defeated, and that there is no disgrace for them.
According to Kitto,[23] '[the trilogy] does not end in undiluted optimism but with a conditional assurance: the Eumenides, ex-
Erinyes, will give prosperity to a city that reveres *Dikê* [Justice]; a
city that does not will expose itself to their wrath'. But, if that is the
message of the trilogy, even this diluted optimism is false. The first
two plays have shown us clearly that reverence for *Dikê* can itself
be problematic, and in the case of neither cities nor individuals is
good behaviour a guarantee of prosperity. More perceptively,
Goldhill, after discussing the sexual and verbal ambiguities of
Athena, concludes,[24] 'this is a teleology which, as the search for
and postulation of a single parent could not avoid the doubleness
of parentage within the sexual opposition, cannot avoid, despite
the weighty teleology of the *trilogy* itself, a continuing doubling
and opposition. The telos of closure is resisted in the continuing
play of difference. The final meaning remains undetermined.' The
Oresteia as a whole is 'tragic'. At the end of *Eumenides* the tragedy
is no longer uppermost in our minds, but it is not forgotten.

Notes

1. Van Erp Taalman Kip, above, p. 131.
2. See my *Aeschylus' Supplices: Play and Trilogy* (Cambridge 1969)
   183–5; *Aeschylus Choephori* (Oxford 1986) pp. xxvi–xxviii.
3. Cited by van Erp Taalman Kip, above, p. 132.
4. See van Erp Taalman Kip, above, p. 134, citing J. D. Denniston and
   D. L. Page, *Aeschylus Agamemnon* (Oxford 1957), pp. xx–xxii; cf.
   esp. xxii, '*Agamemnon* and *The Choephoroe* are, *The Eumenides* is not,
   the highest form of Tragedy.'
5. It may, however, be significant that the unequivocal reference to it at

Cho. 242, καὶ τῆς τυθείσης νηλεῶς ὁμοσπόρου, 'and of my sister piti-lessly sacrificed'), comes immediately before Orestes, at 247 and again at 256–9, compares himself and his sister to the offspring of the eagle. That comparison recalls the eagles of *Ag.* 114, as well as the simile of the vultures at 49–59, but it is true that the sacrifice of Iphigenia is not emphasized. Rather we are to think of Agamemnon as the great king and military commander, to whom the kings of birds appropriately appear. Orestes is his rightful heir, but he is also the offspring of the snake, with all that that implies, as *Cho.* 248–9 go on to suggest. The occurrence of θυτήρ, 'sacrificer', at 255 should not be pressed, yet it is a rather rare word, which in Aeschylus' surviving plays occurs only here and in the *Agamemnon* passage at 224 and 240. And it is not quite true (van Erp Taalman Kip, above, p. 124) that Clytaemnestra's murder is never described in sacrificial language; see my note on *Cho.* 386–9.

6. I do not see why (van Erp Taalman Kip, pp. 129–30) 919 provides an excuse only for Chryseis, and not for Cassandra. Agamemnon's toil and success in the war may be thought to entitle him to bring home a concubine as a reward.

7. Garvie, *Choephori*, pp. xxix–xxxiv.

8. Van Erp Taalman Kip, above, p. 127.

9. See van Erp Taalman Kip's discussion (pp. 133–4) of Goethe's view, paraphrased by Page (in Denniston and Page, *Aeschylus Agamemnon*, p. xx), that 'tragedy is concerned with problems which are insoluble'.

10. K. J. Dover, 'Some Neglected Aspects of Agamemnon's Dilemma', *JHS* 93 (1973) 65.

11. Denniston and Page, *Aeschylus Agamemnon*, p. xxiii. For my view of the ἀνάγκας λέπαδνον, 'the yoke-strap of necessity' (*Ag.* 218), see my *Choephori*, p. xxix.

12. Above, pp. 135–6 and 127.

13. Above, p. 131.

14. See my *Choephori*, pp. xxxi–xxxiv.

15. Above, pp. 134–5.

16. At *Eumenides* 426 Athena asks the chorus-leader why Orestes killed his mother, ἀλλ' ἦ 'ξ ἀνάγκης, ἤ τινος τρέων κότον; ('but was it of neces-sity, or because he was afraid of someone's anger?'; ἀλλ' ἦ [Page's reading] is Blass's emendation of ἄλλης, which is retained by Podlecki; Sommerstein prints Blaydes' ἀρ' ἐξ), but the chorus-leader dismisses the question as irrelevant, ποῦ γὰρ τοσοῦτο κέντρον ὡς μητροκτονεῖν; ('how could there be so great an incentive as to commit matricide?').

17. Cf. 465, where Orestes calls Apollo ἐπαίτιος, 'responsible', and there is no need to emend, with Weil and Sommerstein, to μεταίτιος. At 579–80 Apollo himself accepts the responsibility.

18. Above, p. 131.

19. Above, p. 126.

20. The whole question of echoes and recurring imagery is one on which scholars hold very different opinions. Some find significance in what others can dismiss as 'barely perceptible references', or as 'faint signals' (van Erp Taalman Kip, pp. 124–5).

21. C. W. Macleod, *Collected Essays* (Oxford 1983) 138.

22. A. H. Sommerstein, *Aeschylus Eumenides* (Cambridge 1989) 221–6; A. J. Podlecki, *Aeschylus Eumenides* (Warminster 1989) 211–13 (both with bibliog.).

23. Kitto, *Greek Tragedy*[3], 93.

24. S. Goldhill, *Language, Sexuality, Narrative: The Oresteia* (Cambridge 1984) 283.

9

Catharsis, Audience, and Closure
in Greek Tragedy

CHARLES SEGAL

TRAGIC THEATRE AND SHARED EMOTION

It is a deeply held assumption among the Greeks of the archaic and classical periods that the sharing of tears and suffering creates a bond of common humanity between mortals. This is the bond that the two bitter enemies Priam and Achilles discover at the end of the *Iliad* (24. 507 ff.). It is also the bond between the survivors and indirect victims of the Trojan war gathered in the house of Menelaus at the beginning of *Odyssey* 4. The bonding between the beggar (Odysseus in disguise) and the swineherd Eumaeus in *Odyssey* 14–15 operates in a lower register of style, class, and situation, but conduces to the same effect, as they share their tales of the misfortunes and vicissitudes of their lives. Sharing these 'woes of life', their *kêdea* (*Odyssey* 15. 399), creates a bond between human beings, for they thus recognize what can happen to all humans as suffering mortals, δειλοῖσι βροτοῖσι (*Odyssey* 15. 408; *Iliad* 24. 525).[1] Even Pindar, in the joyful, celebratory epinician ode, reminds his audience of the community of suffering that unites mortals, and also of the rarity and preciousness of this sharing (*Nemean* 10. 78 f.): παῦροι δ᾽ ἐν πόνῳ πιστοὶ βροτῶν | καμάτου μεταλαμβάνειν ('Few are the trusty mortals amid suffering who take a share of the toil').

Drama effects a concrete, public sharing of grief through the collective response of the chorus, and more broadly through the community of spectators in the theatre. Just as the grief of Telemachus in the palace of Menelaus moves from the single sufferer wrapped in his cloak of privacy and concealment to the whole group (*Odyssey* 4. 113–19, 183–9; cf. also 8. 532 ff.), so the *Hippolytus* moves from the hidden grief, the κρυπτὸν πένθος, of Phaedra's private suffering at the beginning (138 f.), to the κοινὸν ἄχος, the common grief at the end. This shared grief, moreover, is not only that of the Troezenian community within the play, but also that of the community of the theatre that experiences the play. The gestures of lamentation at the end affirm the community of the audience in the shared emotion of the theatre, the 'common grief' among 'all the citizens' (*Hippolytus* 1462). I would, then, extend Aristotle's catharsis, which the *Poetics* seems to envisage as a primarily individual response, to this public participation in the release of emotion in the theatre.

The release of emotion in a scene of formal lament is probably the most satisfying mode of resolution for a 'tragic' work, from the *Iliad* to *Hamlet* ('Absent thee from felicity awhile'), and beyond. The ancient audience too, we should recall, is accustomed to group emotional participation in both public and private rituals, and so would also be accustomed to the resolution of intense emotion through the performance of ritual-like actions within the play. To this aspect of tragedy, as we shall see, the ritual meaning of Aristotle's catharsis as 'purification' would be especially relevant. The presence of death, particularly physical contact with a corpse, as anthropologists like Mary Douglas point out, is a source of disorder and pollution.[2] The rites of lament and burial that frequently end Greek tragedies effect closure by literally putting an end to this disorder. In epic and drama, from the *Iliad* on, such rituals help the audience to achieve a sense of 'purification' from the strong and dangerous emotions through ritual participation and to experience the restoration of order and communal solidarity that rituals produce. Such a resolution is particularly effective in plays where a rite of burial or lamentation is achieved only after great struggle or uncertainty, as in Sophocles' *Ajax* or *Oedipus at Colonus* or Euripides' *Hecuba* or *Suppliant Women*.

Where is Aristotle in all of this? I want to argue that one of the strengths of Aristotle's approach to tragedy is his concern with its ethical issues and with the emotional response of the audience. For all of his attention to the formal features of tragedy—his famous remarks on the structures of reversal (*peripeteia*) and recognition (*anagnôrisis*)—Aristotle also emphasizes that tragedy works on our emotions. Central to this view of tragedy is his theory of catharsis, to be discussed later.

This aspect of Aristotle's view of tragedy is particularly important at the present moment in literary studies. Contemporary literary theory, in the wake of structuralism and post-structuralism, has been particularly concerned with the way in which a work of art fabricates its representation of reality. The emphasis, therefore, falls on artifice, on the power of the communicative medium that the writer uses, and on the production of meaning within that medium. Discussion often focuses on the codes and conventions that make it possible to create an imitation of what a given society will recognize as 'reality' and on the artificiality of that representation of reality. This critical mode is especially interested in the work's self-consciousness of its literary facticity, that is, in the work's implicit recognition that it is a fictive representation of reality. The work indicates this self-consciousness by calling attention to the codes and conventions that make possible this mimetic construction.

The implicit model for the process is an elusive drama of signifiers and signifieds wherein meaning is always uncertain and precarious since there is always a gap between the signifier and the signified. The literary work is viewed as an autonomous verbal structure; but, in contrast to the secure structures posited by the New Criticism of the 1950s and 1960s, the postmodern critical mode emphasizes the precariousness and insecurity of meaning, for meaning is dependent on the arbitrariness of the signs within the signifying system. This model is heavily based on *writing*, particularly in the sense of Derrida's *écriture*, that is, a system of communication that stands under the sign of absence—the absence of the spoken voice behind the written sign, the absence that is always marked by the very fact that reality, presence, the object of existence can be evoked only by a sign.

When applied to tragedy, this approach calls attention to the opacities and ambiguities of language, the uncertainties of knowing the truth of the events, the unreliability of the 'facts' that are reported to us. Recent books in the United States, for example, have examined the *Trachiniae* and *Oedipus Tyrannus* of Sophocles and raised fundamental questions about the events that have generally been taken as a given. Every event in the play, because it is transmitted through language, is reduced to being a purely linguistic phenomenon, a sign-effect, a matter of rhetoric. The author of an otherwise acute study of the *Trachiniae* suggests programmatically:

It cannot, therefore, be safely assumed, as even critics of dramatic technique have done, that the characters in Sophoclean tragedy ever mean what they say, or that Sophocles himself was fully committed to any impression of meaning his plays may seem to produce. The meaning of the plays and their speeches are among the effects of their rhetoric, and may be studied as such.[3]

This approach, when applied to the *Trachiniae*, for example, will not allow us to take any of Deianeira's statements at face value, and so removes or undercuts any sure knowledge about what really transpired between her and Nessus, or about her intentions in using the Centaur's unguent on Heracles' robe:

By showing that the story of Nessus' rape arose not from a rape, but from an anticipation of rape, Sophocles undermines the credibility of the more usual version. He suggests that any verbal account arises from its speaker as an *interpretation of phenomena* rather than from the phenomena it supposedly represents or from a divine authority such as the Muses.[4]

What many have seen as a tragedy of recognition, then, is dissolved into a mass of uncertain suspicions about Deianeira's possible plotting.[5] To take a more extreme example, in a recent interpretation of the *Oedipus Tyrannus* the unresolved contradictions in the various stories of Oedipus' and Laius' past are taken to show that Oedipus may not in fact have committed the acts of incest and parricide for which he blinds himself. He allows himself to be convinced, erroneously, by incomplete evidence. On this view, his tragedy lies not in the unwitting performance of these crimes, their inexorable emergence into the light of truth, and the issues of tragic guilt, but rather in the fact that he punishes himself for crimes that he (probably) did not commit.[6]

I would hardly want to deny the importance of ambiguous language in Greek tragedy, or the value of post-structural approaches. These have the merit of alerting us to uncritical presuppositions about the nature of meaning and signification. Excessive dependence on a critical strategy of purely 'rhetorical' meaning, however, can lead to serious distortions, in part because it neglects the conventions of the form, that is, the unspoken contract between author and audience which enables the audience to accept certain facts as 'true' in order for the story to be told. The telling of the story in Greek tragedy, of course, is rarely a simple matter;[7] but it is important to study its complexities within its narrative conven-

tions and not superimpose ours. Approaches such as those mentioned above run the risk of converting into 'rhetoric' what was
convention for the author and his public, and thereby shifting the
problematical elements in the tragedies to areas where they do not
belong.

ARISTOTLE'S *CATHARSIS* AND AUDIENCE RESPONSE

These logocentric distortions help remind us of one of the great
strengths of Aristotle's approach to tragedy, namely that it recalls
us from the epistemologically oriented rhetoric of post-structuralism to the ethical issues involved in Greek tragedy, and from a
restrictive logocentrism to the affective dimension of the tragic
performance.[8] My discussion focuses on Aristotle's theory of
catharsis, which inevitably involves his definition of tragedy in
Poetics 6 (1449^b24–8): 'Tragedy then is the imitation of a serious
and complete action that has a certain magnitude, using language
that has been embellished by each of the kinds [of adornment] separately in the separate parts [of the play], through persons performing the action and not through narrative, through pity and
fear accomplishing the purification of such emotions.'

This last phrase, δι' ἐλέου καὶ φόβου περαίνουσα τὴν τῶν τοιούτων
παθημάτων κάθαρσιν, is among the most controversial topics in classical studies, and I can enter into its difficulties only very briefly.
In recent years G. F. Else and Leon Golden, among others, have
argued strongly that catharsis refers to an *intellectual* clarification,
either of the events or the emotions, rather than to emotional, medical, or ritual purification or purgation. On this view, the phrase
should be translated 'through pity and fear accomplishing the
purification/clarification of such events'.[9] The word παθήματα,
then, will mean 'events' rather than 'emotions', and Aristotle's
catharsis will be concerned not with the psychology of audience
response but with the interior processes of the work itself. Else
regards the passage as an anticipation of the discussion of the
'proper pleasure' of tragedy discussed in *Poetics* 14, and suggests
that catharsis refers to the way in which the work 'illuminates' the
tragic quality of the events and through this illumination or clarification produces the kind of pleasure that is appropriate to
tragedy, a pleasure that will subordinate emotional excitement to
intellectual clarification.

Both Else and Golden have set forth their interpretations in interesting and effective ways and have carefully documented the usages that they claim for the terms in question. Yet one may continue to have doubts. Else argues that the catharsis applies to the tragic act in some abstract way rather than to the emotions of the spectator: 'The catharsis, that is, the purification of the tragic act by the demonstration that its motive was not μιαρόν, is accomplished by the whole structure of the drama, but above all by the recognition.'[10] Even so, Else cannot entirely eliminate the responses of the spectator, who is still in the position of feeling and so judging. Thus he remarks

> I would argue, then, that the spectator or reader of the play is the judge in whose sight the tragic act must be 'purified', so that he may pity instead of execrating the doer . . . The purification, that is, the proof of the purity of the hero's motive in performing an otherwise 'unclean' act, is *presented* to him, and his conscience accepts and certifies it to his emotions, issues a license, so to speak, which says: 'You may pity this man, for he is like us, a good man rather than a bad, and he is καθαρός, free of pollution.'[11]

The first sentence of this passage brings audience response in by the back door, as it were, and in fact is a roundabout way of speaking about the spectator's emotions: 'The *spectator or reader* of the play is the judge *in whose sight* the tragic act must be "purified", so that *he may pity* instead of execrating the doer' [my italics].

When in *Poetics* 14 Aristotle returns to the emotions of pity and fear that result from the experience of a tragedy, he makes it clear that he is talking of audience response. At the beginning of chapter 14, in defending the notion that the proper tragic effect should result from the structure of the plot and not from the spectacle *per se*, he comments that the shudder of fear and pity (καὶ φρίττειν καὶ ἐλέειν) should result from just *hearing* the story, 'for these are just the things that one would experience in hearing the tale of Oedipus' (ἅπερ ἂν πάθοι τις ἀκούων τὸν Οἰδίπου μῦθον, 1453ᵇ6). This last phrase makes it virtually certain that Aristotle is speaking of the pity and fear that the spectator would feel in watching the play, for he is here putting the reader or hearer of the 'tale' or 'plot' (μῦθος) in place of the spectator.

Else objects that 'purification of such emotions' is too vague, particularly as Aristotle speaks only of pity and fear. What, then, could be the reference of 'such emotions'? For this reason, he argues that Aristotle is speaking of 'events', not emotions, and that therefore his catharsis is not concerned with the spectator's emotional reactions. But a passage in chapter 14, on which Else himself relies heavily for his own 'clarification theory', in fact supports the probability that the catharsis of chapter 6 applies to emotions like those of pity and fear. In chapter 14 Aristotle tries to clarify the 'proper pleasure' that tragedy should produce through its effects of pity and fear and adds the important point that these emotions should be aroused by the *mimêsis* of the action, that is, by the representation rather than the events themselves. He continues, 'Let us then define *what sort of fearful things or what sort of pitiable things* appear from the events' (1453^{b}14: my emphasis). He then goes on to explain that these 'fearful' or 'pitiable' things should be crimes committed between kin or dear ones. The demonstrative 'such emotions' (τῶν τοιούτων παθημάτων) in chapter 6 (1449^{b}27), I suggest, is echoed and resumed in the interrogative phrase 'what sort of fearful or pitiable things' (ποῖα δεινὰ ἢ ποῖα οἰκτρά) in chapter 14 (1453^{b}14). This phrasing also indicates that Aristotle believes the exact type of 'pity' and 'fear' discussed in chapter 6 could be left rather vague at that point and then specified in greater detail at the appropriate place later, in chapter 14.

I prefer, then, to keep the traditional translation, 'through pity and fear accomplishing the purification of such emotions'. With the majority of recent interpreters, I believe that Aristotle is concerned with the emotions aroused in the audience by tragedy.[12] For Aristotle, it is true, the emotions also have a cognitive basis and so presumably can be 'clarified' by intellectual processes.[13] The intellectual pleasures of recognition and learning are fundamental to *mimêsis* (artistic representation), as chapter 4 of the *Poetics* points out (especially 1448^{b}12–19). In the case of catharsis, however, the intellectual function does not seem to be uppermost. Still, it would probably be a mistake to narrow the meaning of the word excessively. We should allow it the full range of semantic possibilities that it has elsewhere in Aristotle's own work.[14] It can include notions of medical purgation, ritual purification, and intellectual clarification. It is possible that Aristotle chose the term precisely because of its range and its reference to a wide area of psycho-physical responses.[15] I am not too troubled, then, by the possible note of vagueness in 'such emotions' in chapter 6, not only because of the later parallel in chapter 14 that I noted above, but also because

Aristotle recognizes that pity and fear are related emotions and can shade into one another.[16]

Two other considerations, often adduced in this connection, support the emotional-affective theory of catharsis. First, Aristotle's frustratingly brief cross-reference to the *Poetics* in book 8 of the *Politics* places catharsis in the context of emotional response and excitation produced by the different musical rhythms and modes, particularly the 'orgiastic' character of flute music.[17] Secondly, there is Aristotle's relation to Plato. Whereas Plato condemns tragedy for its emotional excitation, whereby it feeds the irrational part of the soul,[18] Aristotle regards the emotional impact of tragedy as a positive benefit. Plato specifically includes pity and fear among the dangerous emotions that poetry, including tragedy, inspires in its audience.[19] The terms of this debate increase the likelihood that catharsis refers to the audience's emotional response.

Through his theory of catharsis, as many scholars have argued, Aristotle is attempting to defend tragedy against Plato's criticisms, and specifically to revalidate the tragic emotions. If Aristotle is responding at least in part to the criticisms of Plato, he must address the affective dimension of tragedy that had come so heavily under Plato's attack. He does so by arguing that the emotions of pity and fear are neutralized and so rendered beneficial instead of harmful, whether by purgation, purification, or clarification, or all three together. He goes even further, however, and maintains that these emotions, as experienced within and through the *mimêsis* that tragedy provides of them, are essential to the specific kind of pleasure that tragedy creates, its οἰκεία ἡδονή (chapter 14).

Interpreters of Greek tragedy are generally different from interpreters of Aristotle; but in the case of catharsis (or the interpretation of catharsis that I am arguing for here), Aristotle's view of tragedy does have a close and specific bearing on the performative context of the plays themselves, at least in a few noteworthy instances.[20] A number of Greek tragedies implicitly comment on the emotional response that they intend to arouse. In Euripides' *Hippolytus* and Sophocles' *Oedipus Tyrannus*, for example, a climactic scene not only arouses strong emotions of pity and fear but also calls attention to the desired and appropriate emotional response, cueing the audience, as it were, to this emotion. In these (and other) cases, the cathartic effect is mirrored back to the audi-

ence through the play's stage-action of weeping, either by the chorus or by a major protagonist. In these two plays the response of
tears and pity is marked as a specifically theatrical response: it
implies the response expected of the audience watching the play.
The chorus at the end of *Hippolytus*, for example, marks its closing
lament over the dying hero as a 'common grief' (κοινὸν ἄχος) for 'all
the citizens', that is, an emotional participation that binds 'all' the
members of the theatre together in the collective experience of the
tragic suffering.[21] This experience, I suggest, is akin to that arousal
and resolution of emotions that Aristotle calls catharsis.

CATHARSIS AND THE INTERPRETATION OF GREEK TRAGEDY: VALUE AND LIMITATION

To apply Aristotle's notion of catharsis adequately to tragedy,
however, it must be expanded; for his catharsis, like much else in
his view of tragedy, seems to concern the experience of the spectator as an individual, a tendency perhaps encouraged by the fact
that in his time the tragedies, while continuing to be performed,
also acquire an independent status as written texts.[22] Three other
features of the *Poetics* tend to remove it from its specific theatrical
context: the almost total disregard of the ritual dimension of
tragedy, the disdain for theatrical spectacle, and the view of
tragedy as exhibiting universals (chapter 9).[23] By placing catharsis
in the context of the ritual closure of tragedy, I would go beyond
the *Poetics* and give greater emphasis to the collective and theatrical experience. Ritual is by its very nature a communal experience,
and the ritual closure of tragedy often effects a movement from isolated suffering to some kind of communal sharing. Tragedy, of
course, is not in any straightforward sense ritual; but it makes use
of the ritual practices that pervade the life of the ancient Greek
community.

To begin with a familiar example, the *Oresteia*'s closing ritual
procession is a visual affirmation of Athenian community, in contrast to the accursed house of the Atreids and the isolation of its
sole male survivor, the fugitive Orestes. Similarly, purifying ritual,
miraculous indications of the larger community between gods and
men, and the rites of burial in *Oedipus at Colonus* bring a lonely
sufferer and outcast at the margins of the city symbolically within
its community and protection. In both cases there are important

reservations in the background; but in both cases the communal ritual at the end produces a formal closure to the play and also indirectly refers to, and includes, the audience's emotional experience of release as a dimension of the closing effect.[24]

Conversely, when an expected closing ritual is withheld or postponed to a time and place far from the immediate scene of action, as in Medea's refusal to allow Jason's burial of his murdered sons, the ending seems troubling, bitter, and unresolved. In the case of the *Medea*, Jason's empty hands, reaching in vain to the heroine above him, constitute the sign of a negated ritual, an anti-cathartic closure in which neither Jason nor the spectator can find adequate relief in tears for the murdered children. This refused or incomplete ritual is powerful precisely because it appears so vividly onstage, whereas the future burial of the children in the sanctuary of Hera on Acrocorinth, and the rite which will derive from it, are remote (*Medea* 1378–83). Medea's announcement that she will then proceed straightaway to Athens would probably do little in the way of catharsis for the original Athenian audience (1384 f.).

The suspended, hesitant quality at the end of Sophocles' *Electra* that has been so troubling for interpreters probably has something to do with the absence of ritual and the vagueness about the burial of Clytaemnestra and Aegisthus (1483–90). There is no mention of burial for Clytaemnestra at all, and Electra makes her problematical allusion to the 'buriers' who will attend to Aegisthus while he is still standing alive before her. By contrast, Euripides' *deus ex machina*, Castor, in his *Electra* heals some of the emotional and moral chaos of the matricide with what is virtually a second ending, and this carefully provides for the burial (1276–80).

In Sophocles' *Antigone*, Creon's entrance with the body of his son (1257) seems to point towards a scene of funeral lamentation that would end the play on a ceremonial note and leave Creon with some measure of dignity in his suffering. The chorus's description of the body as a $\mu\nu\hat{\eta}\mu'$ $\dot{\epsilon}\pi\dot{\iota}\sigma\eta\mu\sigma\nu$, 'a conspicuous memorial' (1258), increases our expectation of a solemn funerary ritual. But the second messenger's announcement of the death of Eurydice, of whose burial nothing will be said, interrupts this movement and once more evokes disorder and unresolved loss. Creon's cry to the 'harbour of Hades hard to purify' (1284) in fact brings back the dangers of pollution that he created at the opening of the play by refusing funeral rites. This renewal of pollution, accompanied as it

is by the visual presence of at least one body, and the intense enactment of Creon's agony on the stage are too strong to be fully
resolved in the moralizing verses about teaching wisdom in old age
that end the play.[25] On the other hand, it contributes to the sense
of satisfying closure at the end of the *Oedipus Tyrannus* that, for all
the uncertainties about Oedipus' future, the hero not only completes the movement towards ritual purification but also attends to
the detail of burying Jocasta's body (1446–8), implying the ritual
act of burial that completes her part of the tragedy. Similar is the
effect of the close of Euripides' *Heracles*, where the hero, despite
his horrible pollutions and exile from Thebes, arranges for the
burial of his murdered wife and children and laments over them
on-stage (1360 ff., 1406 ff.).

RITUAL CLOSURE: RESOLUTION AND NON-RESOLUTION

The rituals that end many Greek tragedies often direct the emotional responses of the audience towards resolution in a spirit of
community and continuity. In the *Hippolytus*, Artemis' remote
aetiological account of a ritual that will console Hippolytus for his
suffering (1423–30) is offered by the goddess who, as she says, may
not shed tears (1437 f.). The mortal participants' rite of lamentation within the immediate present and within the circle of the
orchêstra, therefore, defines mortality (in part) as the community of
those who do weep and participate in the collective lamentation for
a tragic loss. The chorus's formal lamentation, in turn, applies by
extension to the audience which experiences and engages in these
emotions within the larger circle of the theatre. The ritual act,
which is by its very nature a collective act, reaches out to the spectators in its inclusiveness. The play thereby directs its audience
towards this appropriate theatrical response, or what Aristotle will
call its οἰκεία ἡδονή.

In the *Andromache*, to take another example, a responsive
thrênos or dirge between the chorus of Thessalian women and the
aged Peleus, father of the slain Neoptolemus, acts out the shared
lament familiar to all members of the audience. Collective lament,
however, gives way to individual miracle as Thetis appears as the
dea ex machina and promises Peleus immortality in the Isles of the
Blest, where he will find his son Achilles. As in *Hippolytus*, the

contrast between the mortal sufferer and the goddess defines the appropriate human response. Even here, however, Thetis' last words point back to, and reaffirm, the larger community of mortals (1268–72): 'For you must accomplish what has been fated, for this is Zeus' will, and cease your pain over those who have died. For *to all humankind* this decree has been established by the gods, and all must die' (πᾶσιν γὰρ ἀνθρώποισιν ἥδε πρὸς θεῶν | ψῆφος κέκρανται κατθανεῖν τ' ὀφείλεται, 1272 f.).

Sophocles frequently achieves a similar sense of community by ending his plays with a rite of burial whose inclusive gesture unites the members of the audience in the emotional resolution that acts of mourning produce. Even one of the most contested burials of Greek tragedy, that of the *Ajax*, ends with the purificatory washing of the still-bleeding corpse.[26] The suicide's lonely walk to the washing-places of the sea for an ambiguous 'purification' by the blood of self-slaughter in the middle of the play (654–6) is made good at the end by a shared, communal purification with fire and the 'holy ablutions' of water (ὑψίβατον τρίποδ' ἀμφίπυρον λουτρῶν ὁσίων, 1404 f.).[27] Solidarity is re-established among the community of the Salaminians, whom Ajax's half-brother, Teucer, draws together, 'all' of them, in their special bond of closeness (*philia, philotês*) to their leader: ἀλλ' ἄγε πᾶς φίλος ὅστις ἀνὴρ | φησὶ παρεῖναι, σούσθω, βάτω ('But come, let everyone who claims to be present here as a friend proceed in haste'). Teucer's call brings us from the intimate, familial *philotês* of the son touching the body of his father (φιλότητι θιγών, 1410) to the broader *philotês* of 'everyone' who would honour Ajax. The outcast and polluted criminal can receive now both heroic monumentalization and the rite of burial (1415–17):

> τῷδ' ἀνδρὶ πονῶν τῷ πάντ' ἀγαθῷ
> κοὐδενί πω λῴονι θνητῶν
> Αἴαντος, ὅτ' ἦν, τόδε φωνῶ.

[Make haste] toiling for this man, noble in every way—no one of mortals grander [than Ajax when he was: I utter this].[28]

The quasi-epitaph that constitutes these near-final lines reinforces the unifying effect of the ritual, for it evokes the value-system in which the hero can now find a place, and it simultaneously suggests the extension of his existence into the future through the social memory, including his cultic status in Athens and elsewhere.[29]

The audience's identification with the lonely hero thus moves from the agony of hopeless, isolating pollution to identification with the forces of solidarity and reintegration available to the community, which in this case comprise both the funeral ceremony and the theatre itself.

In the *Ajax* the resolidification of the hero's community may create an emotionally satisfying closure, but it also re-enacts in miniature much of what is problematical about Ajax. Ritual closure does not necessarily mean complete resolution of the conflicts raised by the play. The exclusion of Odysseus, the mournful nature of the rite itself, and the reminder of the great body still 'blowing out its black force' (1412 f.) continue the mood of conflict, waste, and suffering. These funerary rites for Ajax at the end also say nothing of Tecmessa or female lamentation in general, even though this has been prominent elsewhere in the play (579 f., 624–34, 937–45). The exclusion shifts the emphasis from the ritual mourning *per se*, which might suggest the hero's defeat, to the restoration of his place in his society. What Ajax had valued most was honour among his male peers; and the kind of funerary ritual that he receives at the end, so different from that of Hector in *Iliad* 24 or of Achilles in *Odyssey* 24, confirms his reintegration into that warrior society.[30] He receives a warrior's burial with an entirely masculine focus: his armour, his son, his comrades (ἀνδρῶν ἴλη, 1407), and his bloody wound. This narrowing of vision in the closing ceremony is both his triumph and his tragedy.

In *Hippolytus* too the hero's act of freeing his father of the impurity of shedding kindred blood performs a literal catharsis, in the ritual sense; and this in turn makes possible the embrace of father and son in the closing scene with which the male audience and male judges could certainly identify. And the associations of marriage, funeral, and hero cult, as Richard Seaford argues, bring the ending of the play into relation with the internal structure of marriage rites, and create a heightened civic consciousness.[31] Yet the communal coherence and emotional solidarity celebrated in such ritual closure are often complex, as here, because the ending of a drama may contain many competing voices and because the values involved in the tragedy not only belong to the more controversial areas of social and personal life but are in fact defined by the tragedy as controversial: they emerge only from conflict with other, competing sets of values.

The poet's language may also introduce layers of meaning that complicate, or even work against, the communal closure implicit in the rite. When Artemis, for instance, presents the future marriage-songs as a metaphor (a 'Muse-fashioned concern of maidens') and a grieving that Hippolytus will 'pluck' (πένθη μέγιστα δακρύων καρπουμένῳ | ἀεὶ δὲ μουσοποιός ἐς σὲ παρθένων | ἔσται μέριμνα, κοὐκ ἀνώνυμος πεσών, 1427–9), she pulls them away from their social function as ritual and towards the aesthetic self-awareness of the poet's art. The generalizing and metaphorical language and the phrase 'Muse-fashioned concern of maidens' (μουσοποιός . . . παρθένων . . . μέριμνα), to be sure, evoke the communal commemoration of individual suffering;[32] but this last phrase also reminds us of the artifice and literariness of the poet's own intervention in the myth as one who does the work of the Muses.[33]

Even on the plane of ritual, the metaphorical language pulls us back from collective celebration to individual suffering, and to an awareness of the waste therein, and so to the tragic as an area of loss that ritual cannot solace or resolve. Specifically, the metaphor of 1427 makes the grief to be expressed by these future (and anonymous) performers of cultic song in Hippolytus' honour tangible as a 'fruit' of tears that Hippolytus will 'pluck'—in place of the sexual ripeness of such maidens that he has renounced. He receives his ritual commemoration in just that area of life that he has most intransigently refused, and Phaedra's name will live for ever in the public remembrance of the passion that she had died to conceal in silence (cf. 1429–30, 'Nor will the passion of Phaedra, having fallen upon you, be without name and kept in silence', κοὐκ ἀνώνυμος πεσών | ἔρως ὁ Φαίδρας ἐς σὲ σιγηθήσεται). This cancellation of Phaedra's anonymity is a cruel pendant to Aphrodite's triumph, for it echoes the goddess's opening verse, 'Much among mortals and *not without name* [κοὐκ ἀνώνυμος], I am called the goddess Kypris', and so reminds us of her indifference to her human victim in asserting her own power and 'name'. Hippolytus, conversely, ends as a 'common grief to all the *citizens*', but in life he rejected the normal obligations of 'citizens' (see also 1016–20).

RITUAL AND THE PROBLEM OF CLOSURE

As these examples indicate, Greek tragedy often contains a tension between (on the one hand) the emotional resolution through a ritual that provides a cathartic ending and (on the other hand) the 'anti-closural' elements that emerge when we reflect more intellectually and abstractly on the work, reviewing its meaning in our minds as a total design; that is, when we think of the plays primarily as mythic narratives rather than as dramatic performances.[34] This effect holds true for other tragedy as well. In Shakespearean tragedies like *Hamlet*, *Julius Caesar*, *Antony and Cleopatra*, *Romeo and Juliet*, or *Coriolanus*, for example, a commemorative speech or gesture provides a formal, ritual closure but by no means resolves the problem of waste and suffering. The tension is particularly strong in the case of endings that call attention to their incompleteness. At the end of the *Tyrannus*, for instance, Oedipus' fate is uncertain; at the end of *Trachiniae* we do not know whether apotheosis or painful death awaits Heracles; at the end of *Philoctetes* the abrupt entrance of Heracles only highlights the difficulty of the resolution in strictly human terms, and Neoptolemus is also warned of a future crime of impiety; at the end of the *Hecuba* a version of Polymestor's fearful punishment at the hands of a guileful and vengeful woman awaits Agamemnon back in Greece, and so on.

Such ritual closures, then, are far from simple, and operate on at least two levels. The anti-closural effects occur particularly when we detach ourselves from the living moment of the theatrical experience and reflect intellectually on the play as a whole. The emotional experience of cathartic release and closure in the theatre is doubtless what usually stimulates this intellectual meditation on the mythical narrative; but the two kinds of response need not be simultaneous and often do not coincide.[35] Whatever non-finality the endings adumbrate, furthermore, is more likely to be felt by an audience that experiences the play as a written text rather than as a collective theatrical experience. Both areas of response, the emotional immediacy and the intellectual reflection, however, are equally valid parts of the experience of a tragedy. Confusion of these two levels or areas of experience may have something to do with the ongoing debates about the meaning of catharsis. Audience response to tragedy is as complex as the plays themselves.[36] To compare the serious with the trivial, most of us, I suspect, have had the experience of being moved emotionally by a sentimental B-movie while intellectually we fully recognize its clichés and manipulations.

Aristotle's catharsis should probably not be limited to a *ritual* 'cleansing' or 'purification'; but that ritual dimension is relevant to the collective sharing of intense emotions in the theatre. It is worth noting that the only other use of the word *katharsis* in the *Poetics* is in a specifically ritual sense, namely to describe the ritual cleansing of Orestes of pollution (1455^{b}15). Aristotle may well have felt the affinity between the emotions of group participation in ritual (for example, sacrifice) and the emotions of an audience gripped by the πάθη, the painful events, of a tragedy, especially when these latter often themselves consist in ritual actions, like the sacrifice of Iphigeneia or the sacrificial deaths of Aegisthus in Euripides' *Electra* or of Pentheus in the *Bacchae*.

The ritual and emotional aspects of catharsis come together closely in the formal lament that ends many plays, for these lamentations in themselves, with their release in tears, constitute the cleansing discharge of emotion, and they are also part of a ritual act. Aristotle here, as often, is firmly within Greek cultural practice, in this case the free expression of emotion in weeping. Although he does not speak of tears explicitly in connection with pity, the two are closely associated in Greek views of emotional response.[37] When Gorgias combines pity and fear, for example, in the *Helen* (9), he uses the expression ἔλεος πολύδακρυς καὶ φόβος περίφρικος, 'most tearful pity and most shuddering fear'. Gorgias' language reminds us that Aristotle's notion of pity probably involves a stronger, more violent and invasive emotion than ours, tinged as ours is by Christian notions of mercy and compassion. Aristotle, like Gorgias, describes the companion emotion of fear in terms of the violent physical effect of the accompanying 'shudder' (14, 1453^{b}5).

I referred earlier to the *Odyssey's* depictions of what we would call tragic situations. Odysseus' weeping at Demodocus' song of Troy's fall (8. 521–31) is especially instructive, for the simile that compares his weeping to that of a widow led away into captivity puts him in the place of his erstwhile enemy and suggests a perspective in which the Other's suffering is experienced as his own. The weeping of Achilles and Priam together in *Iliad* 24. 507–17 produces the same effect. Viewing Aristotle's catharsis theory in the light of such passages suggests that the emotions of pity and fear are 'cleansed', that is, purified, made cleaner, in the sense that we feel them vicariously for others.[38] Such emotional participation—that is, the arousal and catharsis of pity and fear and similar emotions—enlarges our sympathies and so our humanity. Aristotle's word for 'humanity' in this sense is τὸ φιλάνθρωπον, another rather controversial term. It has the specific meaning 'moral sentiment' but may also include the wider meaning of 'a general feeling of sympathy with our fellow mortals'.[39] Aristotle associates τὸ φιλάνθρωπον closely with pity and fear in one passage (1452ᵇ38) and with 'the tragic' in general in another (1456ᵃ21).

This expansion of our sensibilities in compassion for others, I would suggest, is also part of the tragic catharsis. The most striking example of this broad sympathy in extant tragedy is Aeschylus' *Persians*, our earliest preserved play (472 BC), which re-creates in the theatre of the Athenians the tearful and pitiable suffering of their recently defeated enemies and invaders, the Persian king Xerxes and his army and family. This play foreshadows the reaching-out to the defeated and degraded hero, some fifty years later, in the endings of Sophocles' *Oedipus Tyrannus* or Euripides' *Heracles*. In the latter, Theseus' sympathy for the polluted murderer and his offer of purification (*Heracles* 1233–8, 1398–1426) may, in fact, be read as a cue for possible audience-response to, and understanding of, this man who has both saved and killed his wife and children. Hippolytus' purificatory gesture towards Theseus at the end of *Hippolytus* asks the audience for a similar kind of understanding for the Athenian king. In any case, it would perhaps have been unwise to leave an Athenian audience with their national hero polluted with kindred blood. Similarly in *Alcestis*, when Admetus can pour forth from his eyes 'springs of tears' in self-pity but then find a sympathetic response from Heracles, greatest of heroes (1067 f., 1079–83), the scene potentially legitimizes a cathartic response of tears in the spectators, especially the male spectators. It sanctions a response of weeping at a 'tragic' loss when such a response might otherwise appear as unmanly, female grieving. In this case, of course, the intense outburst of characteristically tragic emotion is only the build-up for the surprise comic ending that will suddenly turn sadness to joy.[40]

One need not suppose that the audience actually weeps or is explicitly invited to weep, although Herodotus' celebrated anecdote about the weeping of the audience at Phrynichus' *Capture of Miletus* shows that such strong responses were possible (ἐς δάκρυά τε ἔπεσε τὸ θέητρον, 'the theatre burst into tears'); yet, as

Herodotus' account implies, the stirring of such tearful emotions was also disapproved of if the pain came too close to home.[41] More generally, the tears and references to weeping in tragedy serve as a figure or objective correlative for the emotional response and release that the tragic action produces. Aristotle's catharsis points to the same area of emotional response; and, as I observed, he also objectifies this emotional response in a physical reaction, the 'shudder' that accompanies the pity that we feel at the story of Oedipus (*Poetics* 14, 1453[b]5, cited above).

In a different literary genre, we may compare Croesus' pity and forgiveness of Adrastus for killing his son in Herodotus (1. 45. 2). Neither Croesus' initial purification nor his reasoned exoneration of Adrastus from guilt is ultimately successful, and Adrastus commits suicide anyway (1. 45. 3). Adrastus, the 'man of heaviest misfortune', βαρυσυμφορώτατος, cannot escape the 'misfortune', συμφορά, that surrounds and defines his life (cf. 1. 35. 3 and 45. 3). Although Herodotus approximates the mood of tragedy in the inexorable doom surrounding both Croesus and his guest, there is no cathartic experience for his audience because the emotional identification or emotional engagement with the suffering of a single figure is tempered by the variegated, multipersonal, and continuous flow of events in the historical narrative.[42]

CONCLUSION: THE EXAMPLE OF *OEDIPUS TYRANNUS*

I would like to conclude with the example of Aristotle's own favourite model for tragic effects, namely Sophocles' *Oedipus Tyrannus*. This play is almost as explicit as the *Hippolytus* in calling attention to the community of shared suffering created by the theatre. When the messenger arrives with the news of the catastrophe within the palace, he addresses the honoured elders of Thebes and prepares them for the 'grief' (*penthos*) that they will 'take upon themselves' when they hear of their king's sufferings (1223–6):

O you who are always in greatest honour in this land, what deeds you will hear, what deeds you will see, and what great grief you will take on if in noble fashion you still care for the house of the Labdacids.[43]

The lines effectively introduce the chorus to the climactic events now to be reported. But they also serve the same function for the members of the audience, who, in their sympathetic participation in the action of the play, do indeed 'care for the house of the Labadacids' and take on themselves the 'grief' for that house, as if they were the lords of Thebes addressed by the messenger.

In like manner, at the end of the scene, the messenger prepares the real audience of Athenians in the theatre for the visual spectacle, just as he prepares its fictional equivalent, the imaginary audience of Theban elders within the play. So too the messenger's opening words prepared his audience (both in the theatre and within the play) for the verbal narration of the events. In so doing, he also directs them towards the appropriate emotional response to that spectacle, a response of pity (*epoiktisai*) (1292–6):

Yet he [Oedipus] needs strength and a guide, for his sickness is greater than he can bear. He himself will show you. For these gates are opening, and you will soon see a spectacle such as to stir pity even in one who loathes it [θέαμα δ' εἰσόψῃ τάχα | τοιοῦτον οἷον καὶ στυγοῦντ' ἐποικτίσαι].

When these gates are then thrown open, the chorus responds with just the kind of emotion that Aristotle suggests. The messenger had enjoined them to pity, but they respond also with 'fear' or 'terror': 'O suffering *fearful* for men to behold, o *most fearful* sight of all that I have ever come upon' (ὦ δεινὸν ἰδεῖν πάθος ἀνθρώποις | ὦ δεινότατον πάντων ὅσ' ἐγὼ | προσέκυρσ' ἤδη, 1297–9). To this verbal exclamation of terror, they soon add the physical response of a 'shudder' of fear (1306): τοίαν φρίκην παρέχεις μοι ('Such a shudder do you bring upon me'). This 'shudder' of fear is exactly the word that Aristotle himself uses in speaking of the tragic effect of this play, perhaps with this very passage in mind (*Poetics* 14, 1453^{b}5, καὶ φρίττειν καὶ ἐλέειν).

This shudder of fear affects the play's internal audience, the chorus of Theban elders, because they recognize the power of the gods and see the sudden, massive reversal in a human life. As the scene continues, however, the terror is resolved into pity as they change their address to Oedipus from 'wretched one' to 'my friend', 'dear one' (ὅ tlamon, 1299; philos, 1321). They now sympathize with his suffering as they try to understand the reasons behind the self-inflicted pain (1319–21):

καὶ θαῦμά γ' οὐδὲν ἐν τοσοῖσδε πήμασιν
διπλᾶ σε πενθεῖν καὶ διπλᾶ φορεῖν κακά.

And indeed there is no wonder amid so many woes that you feel double grief [*penthos*] and bear double sufferings.[44]

The closing scene with Creon, though still dominated by the struggle between two men of very different temperaments, nevertheless ends in the emotional resolution of pity (1473) as Oedipus hears his 'dear ones' weeping (1472–5): 'By the gods, do I not hear my dear ones weeping? Did Creon take pity [ἐποικτίρας] and send to me my dearest children?' Here too the expression of emotion through tears aids the effect of resolution; and that resolution continues as Oedipus now weeps no longer just for himself but for his children too (καὶ σφὼ δακρύω, 1486).

Viewed in Aristotelian terms, this entire closing movement creates a catharsis, a cleansing release, of those emotions of pity and fear that were so violent at the moment of recognition, when the chorus first looked with horror on their blinded king. Sophocles gradually channels the cathartic effect into the physical expression of tears, shed both by Oedipus and by his children (1473, 1485).

This weeping within the play also provides a cue for the desired and appropriate response of the audience, their participation in the emotional release in the theatre. Whether or not the members of the audience actually join in the weeping, they can join in the emotions it displays. When, in his last extended speech in the *Tyrannus* (1503–9), Oedipus asks Creon to 'pity' his children, he not only shows his own enlargement of concern as he looks beyond his own suffering to the suffering of others. He also enacts that gesture of wider sympathy towards which we as spectators are directed as part of the 'pleasure proper to tragedy', that is, as the appropriate outcome of a successful cathartic experience of a tragic performance.[45]

Notes

1. Odysseus and Eumaeus show their reciprocity of feeling by responding to one another's tales with almost exactly the same pair of lines. 'Ah, wretched among strangers,' Eumaeus says, 'how very much you stirred my heart by relating all the wanderings and sufferings you had' (14. 361 f.). 'Eumaeus, how very much you stirred the heart in my breast,' Odysseus/beggar says in his turn, 'by relating all the sufferings you had in your heart' (15. 486 f.). On these and related passages, see C. Segal, *Singers, Heroes, and Gods in the Odyssey* (Ithaca, NY 1994) 130 f., 174, with the further references there cited.

2. See M. Douglas, *Purity and Danger* (Harmondsworth 1970) 21, 152, 207 ff.

3. Heiden, *Tragic Rhetoric*, 8–9.

4. Ibid. 90; the italics are mine.

5. Cedric H. Whitman, *Sophocles*: *A Study of Heroic Humanism* (Cambridge, Mass. 1951) 103 ff. (among many others) regards *Trachiniae* as a tragedy of 'late learning'.

6. F. Ahl, *Sophocles' Oedipus*: *Evidence and Self-conviction* (Ithaca, NY 1990) *passim*, and my review, *CW* 86 (1992) 155.

7. See e.g. A. Machin, *Cohérence et continuité dans la tragédie de Sophocle* (Haute-Ville, Québec 1981); Roberts, 'Sophoclean Endings', and 'Different Stories: Sophoclean Narrative(s) in the *Philoctetes*', *TAPA* 119 (1989) 161–76; C. P. Segal, 'Drama, Narrative, and Perspective in Sophocles' *Ajax*', *Sacris Erudiri: Jaarboek voor Godsdienstweten-schappen* 31 (1989–90) 395–404 (Festschrift for Hermann Van Looy), reprinted, with revisions, in Segal, *Sophocles' Tragic World*.

8. For a sympathetic recent approach to this aspect of tragedy, see Stanford, *Greek Tragedy and the Emotions*.

9. Else, *Aristotle's Poetics*, 224 ff.; L. Golden and O. B. Hardison, Jr., *Aristotle's Poetics: A Translation and Commentary for Students of Literature* (Tallahassee, Fla. 1981) 133 ff.; also L. Golden, *Aristotle on Tragic and Comic Mimesis* (Atlanta 1992).

10. Else, *Aristotle's Poetics*, 439.

11. Ibid. 437–8.

12. For this view of catharsis, see e.g. Belfiore, *Tragic Pleasures*, 57–60.

13. On fear and pity, for example, see *Rhet.* 2. 5 and 2. 8. For other relevant texts in Aristotle on the cognitive dimension of emotions, see Belfiore, *Tragic Pleasures*, 239 ff.

14. See Else, *Aristotle's Poetics*, 439: 'The great virtue, but also the great vice, of "catharsis" in modern interpretation has been its incurable vagueness.' On this broader view of catharsis, see now Belfiore, *Tragic Pleasures*, 259 f.

15. See Halliwell, *Aristotle's Poetics*, 198, to whose discussion I am much indebted here.

16. For a useful discussion of the problems of 'such emotions' in *Poetics* and various solutions, see Belfiore, *Tragic Pleasures*, 269 f., 354–6. I cannot agree, however, with Belfiore's 'allopathic' interpretation of catharsis: it requires reading a great deal into Aristotle's text that is not there; it does not adequately account for the presence of *pity* beside fear in catharsis; and it does not suit what Aristotle says of his own favourite model in the *Poetics*, the *Oedipus Tyrannus*, as well as the 'homoeopathic' interpretation does. For other reservations, see R. Scodel's review of Belfiore, *BMCR* 4/1 (1993) 1–2.

17. *Pol.* 1339ᵃ50 ff., esp. 1341ᵃ21–6 and 1341ᵇ33–42ᵃ17.

18. *Repub.* 10, 603d–607a; cf. 3, 394e ff.

19. Ibid. 3, 387b–d, 10, 606b.
20. Aristotle, however, does make allowances for the reading of tragic dramas: see *Poet.* 1462ª12.
21. See Segal, *Euripides and the Poetics of Sorrow*, 127 f., 132 f. This affective unity complements the ideological unity that the political themes or implications of the tragedies often created, as in the 'political' plays of Euripides (*Heracleidae, Suppliants, Erechtheus*), or the heavily pro-Athenian elements in Sophocles' *Oedipus at Colonus*, or the hints of Ajax's role as the eponymous hero of the Aiantid tribe in the *Ajax*.
22. On the continuing performances of tragedies in the fourth cent., and their importance, see P. E. Easterling, 'The End of an Era? Tragedy in the Early Fourth Century', in Sommerstein *et al.* (edd.), *Tragedy, Comedy and the Polis*, 559–69, *passim*, esp. 565 ff.
23. On Aristotle's removal of tragedy from its civic and political context, and the movement towards universals, I have profited from the papers of Gregory Sifakis and Edith Hall at the KCL Conference (see below, pp. 185–6, 295–309).
24. One could describe such a closing effect as an enacted figure or theatrical metaphor, or as an aspect of the play's 'metatheatrical' consciousness, a self-referential quality through which the play calls attention to its own function as a work of the theatre.
25. For a detailed discussion of the closing scene of the *Antigone*, see my chapter 'Lament and Closure in *Antigone*', in Segal, *Sophocles' Tragic World*.
26. *Ajax* 1405 f., 1411–13. On this scene and its rituals of purification, see Segal, *Tragedy and Civilization*, 138 ff.; Easterling, 'Tragedy and Ritual: "Cry Woe, Woe" ', 91–8, esp. 97 f.
27. *Ajax* 1393 ff. On the tensions surrounding the ritual at the end, see Segal, *Tragedy and Civilization*, 138–46, 150 f., with the references there cited; Easterling, 'Tragedy and Ritual: "Cry Woe, Woe" ', 97 f.
28. These lines have many difficulties; I follow the texts of R. C. Jebb, *Sophocles. The Plays and Fragments*, i: *Oedipus Tyrannus*³ (Cambridge 1893) and H. Lloyd-Jones and N. Wilson, *Sophoclis Fabulae* (Oxford 1990), but read τόδε in the last line to make translation possible.
29. On the play's reference to Ajax's future cultic status, see P. Burian, 'Supplication and Hero Cult in Sophocles' *Ajax*', *GRBS* 13 (1972) 151–6.
30. Note Ajax's scorn of 'female' lament, 579 f. and cf. 651. His burial at the end seems to fulfil his hope in the martial prowess of Teucer and his injunction to the 'shield-men' of his fleet in 562 ff.
31. In a public lecture at Harvard University in the spring of 1993, based

on his new book, *Reciprocity and Ritual*. See also his chapter in this vol. (below, pp. 284–94).

32. W. S. Barrett (ed.), *Euripides, Hippolytos* (Oxford 1964) *ad* 1423–30 cites Bacchyl. 19. 11, Pind. *Isth.* 5. 27–9, and Eur. (?) *Rhesus* 550; cf. also *Od.* 9. 19 f.; Alcman 3. 74.

33. Cf. e.g. Eur. *HF* 673 ff.; also Pind. *Ol.* 9. 80 f. and 13. 96.

34. See Roberts, 'Sophoclean Endings'.

35. In the Greek theatre too, as Claude Calame and Simon Goldhill observed at the KCL Conference, the effect of closure is rendered problematical by the fact that a play may be only one work in a trilogy, or may be followed by a satyr-play. The experience of reading, like the modern mode of performance, isolates the play from any competition with other works. We cannot gauge the emotional effect of watching a succession of plays of different types (tragedies, satyr-plays, comedies) upon the fifth-century audience. There is no reason to think, however, that the Greek audience would not have been intensely involved in the individual play and have experienced the ending in terms of the integrity of the individual play, especially in the case of non-trilogic plays, such as those of Sophocles. Obviously the effect would have been very different for a trilogy, as is true for modern audiences experiencing the sole surviving trilogy, Aeschylus' *Oresteia*. The levity of the satyr-play may have been necessary to offer relief to an audience that had undergone the intense emotional experience of three tragedies, whether or not they were connected in a trilogy.

36. The reluctance to acknowledge such complexity seems to me one of the limitations of the otherwise fruitful study of M. Heath, *The Poetics of Greek Tragedy*. He rightly emphasizes the importance of the audience's emotional response (8–10 *et passim*), but then insists on an excessively sharp dichotomy between 'meaning' and 'emotion' or the 'didactic' and 'affective' (38 ff.), and this results in treating authorial intention in a highly reductive manner (72 f., 76 ff.). We should keep in mind that we can never be sure how an ancient audience responded, and we should remember that there may be enormous variations among different segments of the audience, from the rude farmer from Acharnae to the friends of Socrates or Agathon. As reader-response critics remind us, we are often creating an ideal or 'virtual' audience when we discuss audience reactions to a remote work of art.

37. On the importance of weeping as a response to tragic events, see ibid. 9 ff.; Segal, *Euripides and the Poetics of Sorrow*, 62 ff.

38. Belfiore, *Tragic Pleasures*, 351–3 (which appeared after I had written this essay), also invokes Homer's scene between Priam and Achilles, but with a different emphasis.

39. On τὸ φιλάνθρωπον see T. C. W. Stinton, '*Hamartia* in Aristotle and Greek Tragedy', *CQ* 25 (1975) 238 n. 2; J. Moles, '*Philanthropia* in the Poetics', *Phoenix* 38 (1984) 328, 334; Halliwell, *Aristotle's Poetics*, 219 with n. 25; C. Carey, ' "Philanthropy" in Aristotle's Poetics', *Eranos* 86 (1988) *passim*, esp. 134 f.; Belfiore, *Tragic Pleasures*, 163.

40. On this scene, see C. P. Segal, 'Euripides' *Alcestis*: How to Die a Normal Death in Greek Tragedy', in S. W. Goodwin and E. Bronfen (edd.), *Death and Representation* (Baltimore 1993) 234, with the further references there cited.

41. Hdt. 6. 21. 2. This story of Phrynichus' play already contains a nascent recognition of the 'tragic paradox', the fact that we derive pleasure from the representation of 'tragic' suffering. It also implies the awareness that there must be a distance between the representation and the reality: see Arist. *Poet.* 4, 1448^{b}10 ff.

42. There is, perhaps, something 'cathartic' in Adrastus' act of suicide, with its overtones of ritual sacrifice in the context; but this non-dramatic text does not call attention to the arousal of emotional response in its audience.

43. For other aspects of this scene, see C. P. Segal, 'Time, Theater, and Knowledge in the Tragedy of Oedipus', in Gentili and Pretagostini (edd.), *Edipo*, 97–9, reprinted with revisions in Segal, *Sophocles' Tragic World*. See also Segal, *Oedipus Tyrannus*, 152 f.

44. With Jebb (*Sophocles. Oedipus Tyrannus*) and other edd., I prefer the manuscript reading φορεῖν in 1320, rather than Nauck's emendation θροεῖν, printed by Lloyd-Jones and Wilson in their OCT.

45. In some portions of this essay I have drawn on, and elaborated, points discussed in Segal, *Euripides and the Poetics of Sorrow*, ch. 2.

10

Weeping, Witnessing, and the Tragic Audience: Response to Segal

P. E. EASTERLING

Charles Segal's rich study prompts discussion from many different angles. I begin with his approach to what Aristotle may have meant by catharsis, which at once takes us beyond strict commentary on Aristotelian usage in *Poetics* and elsewhere and encourages us to range more freely. The broad definition 'cleansing release'[1] conveniently incorporates the ideas of purgation and purification and also recalls the importance for Aristotle of the affective function of tragedy in relation to the spectator. This is a helpful way of making catharsis illuminate modern interpretations of tragedy and the tragic, and Segal's further suggestion, that it should be associated with tragedy's use of ritual action, is also an attractive one. Admittedly, Aristotle says nothing in *Poetics* about the function of laments and other ritual forms, and is notoriously disappointing on the chorus in general, but he may well have taken it for granted that when tragedians made use of the ritual actions familiar in Greek communal life they could expect this to be a potent way of arousing the appropriate tragic emotions in their audiences.[2]

As Segal points out, Aristotle's emphasis is resolutely on the spectator as an individual, not on the audience as a group experiencing the emotions of the collective. This choice of focus may, he thinks, be attributed to the fact that by Aristotle's time the plays had 'acquired independent status as written texts'[3] in addition to the continuing tradition of performance. Of course, it is true that a reading public was developing for tragedy,[4] but, given the immense popularity of performed drama in the fourth century, other explanations need to be considered. For example, one might give weight to Aristotle's very strong stress on the ethical aspect of tragedy and to the fact that the surviving plays most commonly represent the problems of moral choice in terms of the decision-making of individuals, however political the resonances and however strong the communal implications of those decisions. There is another, more formal consideration, relating to language rather than to plot. The texts themselves typically (in the well-established tradition of choral lyric) use the generalizing first person singular in which to express a group's response to painful experience. To take *Oedipus Tyrannus*, which Segal discusses in the latter part of his paper, there is no point anywhere in the choral lyrics at which the elders of Thebes refer to themselves in the plural. For an ancient critic like Aristotle, who must have attended hundreds of theatrical performances, the natural idiom in which the community expressed its response to tragedy must indeed have been the first person singular. 'Alas, generations of men, I count your life as equal to nothing!' (1186–8).

The most telling argument, to my mind, in favour of Segal's general approach is that it relates catharsis closely to structure, which is surely what Aristotle does in laying so much stress on plot, and particularly on *peripeteia* and *anagnôrisis*, in his enigmatic analysis of the way in which tragedy characteristically arouses pity and fear and effects a 'cleansing release' of such emotions. Segal traces a pattern not incompatible with Aristotle's reversal and recognition in stressing that the community's response to the significant deaths that shape the sad stories of tragedy is often expressed in terms of ritual, which powerfully directs the emotional responses of the audience and (in one sense at least) may bring an end to disorder. The difficulty here, if one is looking for a widely applicable theory, is that the notion of closure marked by shared weeping in a ritual context does not suit the whole range of surviving tragedy, and even in plays which do end with a scene of lamentation, both the closure and the ritual may turn out to be hard to pin down precisely. But it certainly stimulates a fresh look at the texts.

Taking *Oedipus at Colonus* as a good example of a play in which ritual is indisputably important, we might ask the following questions: Where does closure begin? What does the ritual consist in? Where should we expect to locate the catharsis?

This play is unusually long for a Greek tragedy (1779 lines), and everything is on an expansive scale. The beginning of the ending is marked 323 lines before the close (at 1456) by a clap of thunder (whether heard directly by the audience or described for them): ἔκτυπεν αἰθήρ, ὦ Ζεῦ, 'Thunder! O Zeus!'. This is the first of the divine signs mentioned by Oedipus at the beginning of the play (94–5), and it is followed by two more before the arrival of Theseus (1463–5, 1478–9). Theseus is present to be a witness to what happens to Oedipus at the 'critical point in his life' (ῥοπὴ βίου, 1508). Oedipus' final 'big speech' (1518–55) sets out the aetiology of what is to be his cult as hero and concludes with wishes for blessings on Athens and the injunction that the Athenians should remember him after his death—an unmistakable farewell, strongly marked in the stage action as the blind Oedipus leads the way, without a guide, to the place where he must meet his end. The chorus sing prayers for his painless passage to the world of the dead (1556–78), and when the messenger returns, he describes what has happened in a speech (1586–1666) full of ritual details—the washing and dressing of Oedipus by his daughters, the water libations, Theseus' solemn pledge to Oedipus that he will protect the girls, and finally the mystery of Oedipus' passing, seen by no one except Theseus and described for the audience only in terms of his gestures (shading his eyes, saluting earth and heaven). Antigone and Ismene return to sing a lament, identified by such words as 'mourning' (γόων, 1668; πενθεῖν 1753), 'lament' (στενάζειν, 1672; στένει, 1710) and 'dirge' (θρῆνον, 1751, 1778), and recognizable from its familiar mourning themes: the bereft state and sense of loss of the mourners, and their direct address to the dead person.[5]

Even so, it is not a typical funeral lament. There are two sharply emphasized features that mark it out as different: first, Antigone's desperate and unfulfilled desire to see the place of her father's death, which suggests the frustration of her ritual needs, and secondly the insistence by both the chorus and Theseus on *ceasing the lament*: λήγετε (1722), παύετε (1751), ἀποπαύετε (1777). 'It isn't right to lament,' says Theseus at 1753, 'for there is punishment', that is, it would provoke divine anger to mourn in a situation where the gods have particularly favoured a mortal. Woven into the girls' expressions of loss and sorrow is the idea of returning to Thebes to help resolve the quarrel between their brothers (1769–72). Thus the play ends in a refusal of ritual: Antigone and Ismene must not weep and must not see the place of Oedipus' death, while the dark reminder of what the future holds for them at Thebes introduces a new temporal perspective and, through a familiar type of

Fiktionsironie,[6] recalls Sophocles' own famous play of more than thirty years before.

And yet the importance of ritual is not denied at the end of the play: this is not a case of straightforward subversion. In announcing Oedipus' orders to him, Theseus says (1760–5): 'Children, Oedipus prohibited any approach to that place and any utterance over his sacred tomb. And he said that if I duly kept this commandment I should always hold the land unharmed.' These simple words summarize all that Oedipus has said about his coming role as a hero-protector of Athens, and at the same time, of course, they recall the language used of the worship of the Eumenides at the beginning of the play: those goddesses whose grove is not to be entered, 'whom we tremble to speak of and whom we pass with eyes averted, without voice, without word' (129–33). It is worth taking note at this point of Burkert's argument[7] that what happens in the last 300 lines of the play translates into action the purification ritual which the chorus describe to Oedipus and which Ismene undertakes to perform (461–509). The cathartic effect of witnessing Oedipus' passing depends on the way in which all these details cohere, not least in the stage action itself, when Oedipus leads the way, 'a strange new [καινός] guide', as he himself puts it (1543). 'This way! here, follow this way, here Hermes the guide and the goddess of the dead are leading me' (1547–8). The significance of this exit is directly related to the emphasis earlier in the play on Oedipus' blind helplessness.

Pinning down both closure and catharsis thus proves to be extremely difficult. Segal summarizes his view of the play as follows: 'purifying ritual, miraculous indications of the larger community between gods and men, and *the rites of burial* [my italics] bring a lonely sufferer and outcast at the margins of the city symbolically within its community and protection. . . . There are important reservations in the background; but . . . the communal ritual at the end produces a formal closure to the play and also indirectly refers to and includes the audience's emotional experience of release as a dimension of the closing effect.'[8] But as I have tried to argue, what we are actually shown at the end of the play is a lamentation which is cut short before its ritual culmination (there can be no 'rites of burial'); and its emotional function is denied to Antigone and Ismene, without, however, negating the significance of the mystery that Oedipus has bequeathed to Theseus.

There is an alternative model which is more comprehensive than that of the ritual sharing of tears, a model within which these scenes of communal grief can be comfortably accommodated. This is the idea of witnessing, which is always a significant function of a watching audience assembled in one place. Audiences are very different from casual passers-by: they are called to watch, and in Greek tragedy the choruses are on hand as built-in witnesses to give them their cues. When stories are enacted for audiences, there is a sense in which the community is required to take cognizance of what the characters do and suffer; and this witnessing function is constant whether the most appropriate emotional response is one of sorrow and tears, or of celebration, or of angry outrage. Sometimes, of course, it will entail conflicting or contrasting emotions,[9] as at the end of *Oedipus at Colonus*, where pity for the desolate Antigone and Ismene may be combined with something approaching hope for Athens.

There are different ways in which the audience may be reminded of its witnessing role. In *Oedipus at Colonus*, Theseus is the privileged witness, as the king of Athens who is to receive Oedipus' secret and thereby keep Athens safe, and it is through him that the chorus and audience are brought as close as possible to the mystery of Oedipus' passing.[10] In *Antigone* the heroine makes a formal appeal to the Theban elders to see what is happening to her as she goes to her death ('Look at me, you rulers of Thebes, the only one left of the royal house, see what I suffer and at whose hands, for revering the duty of reverence', 940–3)[11] and her challenge to them is a challenge to the audience as well; one might compare, on a cosmic scale, Prometheus' appeal, at the end of *Prometheus Bound*, to his mother Gaia and the 'aether that brings round the light shared by all', to see how unjustly he suffers (1091–3).

As Segal points out, tragic texts often give cues to the audience, guiding their emotional reactions and suggesting what might appropriately be the shared response of the community in the theatre. This point could be widened to include the many different signals (not all of them associated with closure) given by the plays—which, after all, are scripts of tried theatrical effectiveness—to help audiences interpret what is going on. 'Look at me now!', 'Pity me!', 'What am I to do?', 'Where will it end?' are signals to the audience in the theatre as well as to the characters in the drama.[12] Commands, questions, appeals guide the response of those witnessing, and it is worth noting that this guidance is given in intellectual as well as emotional terms. Indeed, there is much to be said for not separating the different levels of response, as Segal is tempted to do, into 'the living moment of the theatrical experience'[13] and intellectual reflection on the play as a whole.

There is a particularly telling instance of witnessing in *Oedipus Tyrannus*, which will perhaps illustrate my point. It comes immediately after the climactic moment when Oedipus discovers his identity, and the chorus respond with 'Alas, generations of men, I count your life as equal to nothing' (1186–8). Having witnessed what has happened to their king ('With your fate as my example, *yours*, unhappy Oedipus, I call nothing that is mortal blessed', 1193–6), the men of Thebes reach a new understanding of human nothingness as well as of human achievement: if these disasters could happen to Oedipus, of all people, they can happen to anyone. The form echoes that of a lament (ἰώ at 1186, 1207, and 1217 sets the tone) and the chorus describe their response in terms of sorrowful song (ὀδύρομαι, 'I wail', 1218). Segal does not include this ode in his discussion of the cathartic conclusion of the play, though he does give due weight to the messenger's speech that immediately follows and prepares the elders for the fresh horrors they are to see and hear. But the ode demands to be included: it is arguably the most intense of all the choral passages in the play, and in its placing, immediately after Oedipus' cry of recognition, it offers a clue to Aristotle's stress on the importance of *anagnôrisis*. For Aristotle the cathartic process seems to be a continuous whole: recognition and the painful emotions that it generates, witnessed with pity and fear by the audience, are not separated off, as in the communal weeping model, into immediate emotional release and (often subsequent) intellectual reflection. Aristotle, I suspect, would not much have liked the analogy of the B-movie.[14]

One of the most important points made in Segal's paper is that closing rituals, whose function is often to re-establish a sense of community—even more strongly felt by very large audiences sitting in daylight than by the smaller groups in the darkened auditoria of modern theatres—are not there to solve problems. If a play closes in lamentation, the act of communal grieving may console, but it by no means effaces the sense of loss or the contradictions that have been exposed by the tragic action, just as in off-stage life the function of ritual is to help people to deal with their experiences, not to explain them away. And consolation may depend as much on the recognition that we are all vulnerable—and potentially guilty, too—as on any purely emotional expression of sorrow.

All this is well exemplified by Segal's discussion of the end of *Ajax*, an interesting example of ritual closure on which he and I are largely in agreement,[15] but his analysis of the implicit stage-directions raises a general point worth discussing. Here is how he characterizes the ritual action at the end of the play: 'These funerary rites for Ajax at the end . . . say nothing of Tecmessa or female lamentation in general, even though this has been prominent elsewhere in the play . . . The exclusion shifts the emphasis from the ritual mourning *per se*, which might suggest the hero's defeat, to the restoration of his place in society. . . . He receives a warrior's burial with an entirely masculine focus.'[16]

In order to visualize the stage action, we need to go back to 1168 ff., where Teucer describes what is happening: 'Here they come at the right moment—Ajax's son and wife, on their way to tend the burial of the poor corpse. Child, come here, and taking up your position close by, touch your father's body as a suppliant. Sit in the pose of one who begs protection, holding in your hands three locks of hair, mine, hers, and your own, the suppliant's resource.' Since Tecmessa enters with Eurysaces ('to tend the burial') and shares in the supplication by providing a lock of hair, like Teucer, it is unthinkable that she then withdraws: she must be understood to be part of the ritual tableau and therefore part of the final scene. And what of that scene? It is certainly a military procession, a *pompê*, with all the emphasis on the male domain, but it is not the burial rite itself. All that is shown is the beginning of the *pompê*, and the rest is left for the audience to supply. As the procession leaves, with everyone going to witness the ceremony, one might think of Tecmessa (and her attendants?) taking part in lamentation at some point after the military honours are over, like the women in *Iliad* 24, or one might not; but there is no explicit (or implicit) exclusion of Tecmessa from the end of the play. This open-endedness is, of course, very characteristic of tragedy, a means of ensuring that the audience is left with nothing too sentimental[17] or neatly packaged, which would imply too crude a model of how things might be.

The fact that all the audience sees at the end of *Ajax* is the beginning of the procession should also remind us that these plays do not deal in 'full' ritual events. Incomplete rituals, or mere sketches of a ritual happening, are the most that is usually shown, and I have argued elsewhere[18] that this is as much as one can expect, since drama does not offer literal transcriptions of off-stage experience, but its mode of communication is always in some sense metaphorical. In the end we must gratefully recognize, as Segal notes, that 'audience response to tragedy is as complex as the plays themselves'.[19] Perhaps it is no bad thing that Aristotelian catharsis has always been so hard to define, while so suggestively contributing to our thinking about tragedy and the tragic.

Notes

1. It seems less plausible, though, to take the idea of cleansing as far as Segal does on p. 164, where he suggests that 'the emotions of pity and fear are "cleansed", that is, purified, made cleaner, in the sense that we feel them vicariously for others'.
2. See his well-known discussion of the effects of music in *Politics* 8. 7.
3. Segal, above p. 157. See also Edith Hall's discussion, below, pp. 295–309.
4. Arist. *Rhet.* 3. 12. 2.
5. For these patterns, see M. B. Alexiou, *The Ritual Lament in Greek Tradition* (Cambridge 1974) 161–84.
6. On *Fiktionsironie*, see Rosenmeyer, below, pp. 506–9.
7. W. Burkert, 'Opferritual bei Sophokles: Pragmatik—Symbolik—Theater', *AU* 28/2 (1985) 5–20.
8. Segal, above, pp. 157–8.
9. And the emotions and judgement of the audience may be in a continually fluctuating state; see Mitchell-Boyask, below, p. 434: 'Tragedy's ethical ambiguitites provoke ever-changing responses in its audience.'
10. On Theseus, see my article 'Œdipe à Colone: Personnages et "réception" ', in A. Machin and L. Pernée (edd.), *Sophocle: Le Texte, les personnages* (Aix-en-Provence 1993) 191–200.
11. The translation echoes that of R. C. Trevelyan (Cambridge 1939).
12. Some examples: 'Look at me', Soph. *Trach.* 1076–80, Eur. *Hec.* 807–8 and *Hipp.* 1395; 'Pity me', Soph. *Trach.* 1070–2, Eur. *Hec.* 808; 'What am I/are we to do?', Soph. *Phil.* 895, 908, 963, 974.
13. Segal, above, p. 163.
14. Ibid.
15. Segal, *Tragedy and Civilization*, 109–51; Easterling, 'Tragedy and

Ritual'.
16. Segal, above, p. 161.
17. On sentimentality, see M. S. Silk, 'Pathos in Aristophanes', *BICS* 34 (1988) 84–7.
18. 'Tragedy and Ritual', 17–18.
19. Segal, above, p. 163.

PART II
Greek Tragedy: Contexts

INTRODUCTORY NOTE

The authors of the papers in this second section are concerned to locate Greek tragedy in its Greek context, theatrical, cultural, or socio-political. A series of contextual co-ordinates present themselves.

Taplin and Gredley place tragedy against its Attic 'twin', Aristophanic Old Comedy. Refining an earlier (1986) argument, and with a glance at metatheatrical self-reference and (rather differently from Lee) at tragic laughter, Taplin pinpoints three important indicators that distinguished the two theatrical forms and so helped to establish their self-definition: chorus, gods, and closures. The tragic chorus ('not unlike the tragic mask') is distinctively 'serious but blank'; the tragic gods are distinctively inhuman; the tragic closure (and here Taplin stands apart from Segal in the first section) is characteristically and distinctively open-ended, with *Eumenides* a striking exception under all three headings. Finding (like van Erp Taalman Kip) a solution, therefore a closed ending, in *Eumenides*, Taplin sees in the final procession that incorporates the Erinyes into the city of Athens a comic-like anomaly to be explained. He finds the explanation in a view of the procession as a symbolic enactment of the city's acceptance of the tragic itself, and compares the procession at the end of *Frogs*, where the return of Aeschylus to Athens implies (he argues) a counter-bid by comedy for civic respectability. Reconsidering Taplin's case with reference to the contrasting pair of 'Dionysiac' dramas, *Bacchae* and *Frogs*, Gredley stresses the diagnostic importance for tragedy of a sense of inevitability. He further draws attention to the problems created for comic, as for tragic, self-definition by Euripides' cross-generic experiments, and seeks to clarify the nature of the metatheatre that (on Taplin's reading) closes *Eumenides* and *Frogs*. Stressing the imparities between Aeschylus' and Aristophanes' metatheatrical closures, Gredley insists that in *Frogs* the return of the tragic Aeschylus to Athens means what it seems to mean: an appeal to the image of (and the 'otherness' of) *true* tragedy, which alone preserves the traditional contrast between the genres. His discussion, then, with Taplin's, raises the important issue of comedy's own response to tragedy and the tragic.

Gould and Goldhill pursue the theme of the tragic chorus by debating its relation to the collectivity of the *polis* and the bearing of this relationship on the 'construction of tragic meaning'. Insisting on the significance of the chorus as bearer of communal memory and collective experience alternative to that of the tragic individuals, Gould at the same time questions any ascription to it of the voice of 'the collective citizen-body' or an authoritative voice of any kind. Drawing attention to the marginal or excluded status of most choruses (old men, women, foreigners, slaves), he stresses the specific identity of each choral group, whose voice, however, is always the voice of 'the other': examples discussed include Aeschylus' *Suppliants* and *Seven*, Sophocles' *Trachiniae* and *Oedipus Rex*, Euripides' *Medea, Suppliants, Phoenissae*, and *Electra*. Thanks to this alternative presence, collective and individual experience of the tragic are mutually defined—and Gould notes the contrast with the wholly individualist tragedy of Shakespeare, and then again with the impartial coexistence of individual and collective in Herodotus. In a wide-ranging discussion that looks to *Eumenides* and *Hippolytus*, among many other instances, Goldhill contests the view that social marginality precludes tragic authority: fifth-century tragedy is itself 'the drama of the other', in which Athenian experience is projected through a series of widely alien instances. He concludes that the choral voice, though indeed partial, is also authoritative, serving *both* to mobilize *and* to question collective ('political') wisdom. The chorus is to be seen as a 'key dramatic device for setting commentary, reflection and an authoritative voice in play as part of tragic conflict'; and its voice is central to 'the political engagement of tragedy with the discourse of Athens'.

Attic tragedy had—undeniably—a ritual context, the festival of Dionysus; and from Nietzschean metaphysics to the cultural sociology of Winkler and Zeitlin's *Nothing to Do with Dionysos?*, the meaning of this ritual connection has been a battleground. The battle is reviewed and rejoined by Friedrich and Seaford. For Friedrich the long series of modern attempts to make tragedy intrinsically 'Dionysiac' rest on a gratuitous conflation of the civilized Dionysus of cult (to which the tragic festival belongs) with the savage Dionysus of myth, or else on a misplaced sophistication whereby the 'Dionysiac' label is gratuitously attached to (post)modern preoccupations like fictionality (Vernant) or tragedy's alleged 'interplay between norm and transgression' (Goldhill, whose reading of *Ajax* is considered and rejected). Friedrich acknowledges the pervasive importance of diverse ritual elements *within* individual Greek tragedies, contrasting these with the problematic or limited imprint of Dionysiac 'patterns' or 'ritual elements' *on* tragedy. While largely agreeing with Friedrich's critiques, and (like van Erp Taalman Kip) opposing in particular the prevalent modern linkage of Greek tragedy and the insoluble, Seaford presents a counter-argument that foregrounds the widely ignored aetiological elements of Greek tragedy. Specifically, Seaford contends that the typical patterns of Greek tragedy conform to a pattern established by Dionysiac myth in which kin-killing is terminated by the establishment of communal cult. His examples include *Bacchae*, *Antigone*, *Ajax*, and (once more) *Eumenides*. His conclusions are that Dionysus is a constructive force that 'imposes the emotional cohesion needed for the creation of the *polis*' as against the disruptive autonomy of the household, and that Greek tragedy, accordingly, may be seen as 'the dramatization of aetiological myth shaped by the vital need to create and sustain the *polis*'. As with a number of other contributors (Garvie, Segal, Easterling, Taplin, Gredley, and then Macintosh in the final section), the importance of tragic *closure* to the argument is apparent.

The second section concludes with three sharply focused discussions of contrasting fourth-century responses to Attic tragedy from the great philosophers, Plato and Aristotle, and the (no doubt) less great but (no doubt) more ordinarily representative orators. Hall's discussion of Aristotle was originally framed as a response to Sifakis (cf. above, pp. 1–2). In his conference paper Sifakis stressed that, whereas an explosion of theatrical activity took place in the various capitals of the Hellenistic kingdoms, classical tragedy was an almost exclusively Athenian institution, which reinterpreted for the collective population of the *polis* its mythical traditions, which was judged by the citizens of the *polis*, and which was bound up with the invention and development of the city's democracy. Like many recent interpreters, then, Sifakis insisted on the ideological and historical specificity of tragedy in its collective Athenian context. Unusually, however, he sought to relate these specificities to Aristotle's *Poetics*, offering a striking reassessment of Aristotle's version of the tragic experience as both emotional ('catharsis'), intellectual ('learning'), and, implicitly, political: the philosopher's theory of tragedy is ultimately, despite appearances, a theory conceived with reference to the democratic Athenian audience. Hall's counter-arguments, reformulated to take account of the new, free-standing, nature of her discussion, serve not only to illustrate the problems involved in any 'political' reading of the *Poetics*, but also to bring into focus the transhistorical attitude to Greek tragedy familiar from much modern theorizing about tragedy (and represented in, if not by, the present volume). For Hall, Aristotle's *Poetics*, far from having a theory suited to the democratic *polis*, is an apolitical treatise which ignores both the political context of Attic tragedy and the Athenocentricity of much of its content and thereby prefigures and authorizes the universalizing of Greek *tragôidia* for later ages.

In marked contrast to the Aristotle described by Hall are the orators reviewed by Wilson. Yet if the modern sense of universal tragedy is implicit in the *Poetics*, the modern sense that Greek tragedy means fifth-century tragedy is clearly (on Wilson's evidence) writ large in the orators. Wilson seeks to demonstrate in particular both the special importance of fifth-century tragedy for these fourth-century spokesmen of the *polis* and the ambivalence of their response to the tragic. On the one hand, the orators offer a 'nostalgic' view of tragedy as 'edifying', a view which 'edits out' its more disturbing qualities and sanitizes even Euripides; on the other, when they wish to evoke images of horror and disorder, it is tragedy that supplies them, again and again. Wilson's findings thus suggest that the orators' reading of tragic drama contrasts both with Aristophanes' view of tragedy (as discussed by Gredley) and, in particular, with the modern perception of Euripides (noted by Arnott) as underminer of traditional mythic 'glory'.

Wilson (it might be argued) none the less provides grounds for inferring the currency in fourth-century Athens of a proto-postmodern perception of tragedy's ambivalence—a perception of tragedy as politically supportive yet also (in its violence) subversive. Halliwell, by contrast, surveying Plato's critique of tragedy, offers a revealing interpretation of Plato himself as the first theorist to articulate a proto-modern sense of the tragic, in that he—quite unlike Aristophanes or, again, Aristotle—formulates the perception that underlying tragedy is a world-view, an embodied philosophy and a reading of life. (On this point the editor's argument may be compared and contrasted, above, pp. 8–9.) For Plato, however, this tragic world-view (which he finds in Homer as well as in tragic drama) is untenable and deplorable, because it is pessimistic (and here Halliwell himself cites *Oedipus Rex* in support of Plato's argument) and, more specifically, because (in Halliwell's words) it denies 'the soul's capacity to forge its own moral fate' and precludes the hope which 'nourishes the psychological, ethical, and metaphysical aspirations of Plato's own dialogues', by viewing life as 'governed by external forces'. The editor would note, in amplification of Halliwell's diagnosis, how closely Plato thereby anticipates Schopenhauer in this reading of tragedy's supposed pessimism—and would add that Plato's aversion to tragedy is likewise seen to prefigure the pragmatic anti-tragic stance assumed by Brecht, for whom (as for Plato, on Halliwell's showing) tragedy makes us feel powerless, because misfortune and suffering are indefinitely beyond our capacity to change.

Comedy and the Tragic[1]

OLIVER TAPLIN

I

Theatre is a specially licensed occasion, a time and place for many people to watch a few people enacting things that would not be 'acceptable' in 'real life', outside that time and place. Thus tragedy can look into the 'black hole' (to adopt George Steiner's metaphor[2]), and yet not be irrecoverably sucked into it. But comedy also grew up alongside tragedy at Athens; and the phenomenon of that twin growth may give some leads towards appreciating the nature of 'the tragic'. For, while tragedy and comedy were the twin offspring of the Athenian theatre, they were non-identical twins. And they were not good at sharing their toys: most tellingly, playwrights and actors belonged only to one or the other.[3] Everyone would agree, I think, that the two genres were polarized to some degree, and mutually defined each other by contrasts—though at the same time, as Michael Silk has rightly insisted, this need not mean that they are 'opposites'.[4] Recent critical theory has, however, been mistrustful of 'genres', and scholars have tended to concentrate on generic interference and transgression, breaking down their distinctiveness, and deconstructing their polarities. Swimming against the tide, I shall try to throw some fitful light on tragedy (τραγῳδία) by setting up some of its antitheses with (Old) comedy (κωμῳδία)—not to construct rigid or simple rules, but to salvage some submerged delineations and distinctions. This is far from denying the presence of matter in comedy that is σπουδαῖον (serious)—on the contrary, I would endorse Aristophanes' claims to include it all the way from τὸ γὰρ δίκαιον οἶδε καὶ τρυγῳδία ('trugedy also knows what is right and just', *Acharnians* 500) to πολλὰ μὲν γέλοιά μ᾽ εἰπεῖν, πολλὰ δὲ σπουδαῖα '([let me] deliver plenty that is amusing and yet plenty that is serious' *Frogs* 389–90). Conversely, I would not want to deny the presence on occasion of the γέλοιον ('the amusing') in tragedy, though it is nearly always there to provide a kind of chiaroscuro to set off the surrounding dark.[5] But boundaries are a prerequisite of transgression.

This is not to be a rehash of cold scraps from my 1986 'synkrisis' article,[6] where I concentrated on the omnipresence of overt self-referentiality in comedy, and its absence from tragedy. Tragedy goes out of its way to pre-empt and overwhelm the limiting counter-claim that it is 'only a play', while comedy embraces and exploits this self-subversion. I shall avoid overlap by looking, on the whole, at three areas quite different from those that I approached before: chorus, gods, and closures. I shall, however, try to do something to make good my chief regret about that article: its rigid treatment of self-referentiality in tragedy as something that either is or is not there, as opposed to a feature of widely various intensity and explicitness.

So I do not set out to deny generic transgression, let alone crossfertilization, between tragedy and comedy, but to show the critical value of contradistinctions as well as indistinctions. This point is brought home by the masks, which make a good start, especially since the pair of masks—one grimacing and one grinning—have long been an emblem of the theatre (deriving presumably from Roman iconography). We have enough representations of masks in pottery painting and stone relief, dating from the fifth and early fourth centuries, and made in Athens or Megale Hellas (Magna Graecia), to be quite sure that any spectator waking up in mid-play would immediately have known from the masks alone whether it was tragedy or comedy.[7] It is worth registering, moreover, that at this period the antithesis of expressions was not laughter versus horror. The tragic mask is, in fact, rather blank and expressionless, somewhat solemn perhaps, waiting to take its 'expression' from the events of the play: the predominant characteristic of the earlier comic mask, on the other hand, is clearly not merriment, but *ugliness*.[8] With its furrowed brows, flattened nose, unkempt beard for most male characters, and often balding hair, the keynote is the unbeautiful. The new *Choregoi* vase sets out the contrasting physical appearances of the two kinds of play with unprecedented sharpness.[9] Whatever the best interpretation of the whole scene, Aigisthos surely comes from the world of tragedy. With a life-story encompassing incest, adultery, treachery, and murder, he is hardly a pretty character;[10] yet he is still represented with everything about him handsome. His blankly solemn face is like a tragic mask, except that his mouth is not open, in total contrast with the undignified ugliness of the masks of the other three figures.

Aigisthos' long chiton and tight ornate sleeves are also in strong contrast with the arms and legs of male comic actors, which are characteristically cased in rumpled body-stocking, presumably representing bare skin. Comic actors usually also have bare feet or rudimentary footware with open toes: Aigisthos by contrast confirms that, by 380 at least, the ornately laced boot with thin sole and upturned toe (*kothornos*) was an essential item of the tragic actor's outfit. But most obviously, of course, Aigisthos' body is shapely, while the comic men are heavily padded, before and behind; and they sport the outsize phallic equipment which is as much a signal of comedy as the mask. If it is true that Greek men admired a small member (when unaroused, that is), then these appendages are not only conspicuous but ugly.[11]

Athenian Old Comedy is always ready to expose those basic bodily functions that are not always fully under control. In some ways laughter itself is one such function; and, like yawning or vomiting, this can be quite 'infectious'—that is to say, it can spread by fellow-feeling among a group. Comedy hopes to spread laughter round its audience, and is delighted to be interrupted by it, always provided that it comes at the right places, and that it is exhaled in complicity and not antagonism.[12] Unwanted laughter, however, or laughter in scorn of the play would not be a welcome intrusion into comedy. It would be even less so during a *tragedy*. How often, and how much, tragedy invited *complicit* laughter is an interesting and far from easy question. It is usually answered in the form of an appeal by the critic to the reader's sense of humour: 'surely this would raise a laugh'. It is bad method, I suggest, to approach this issue piecemeal, joke by alleged joke. It needs some overall view of the generic predispositions of the audience. It might be a start to look briefly at how much laughter there is from the actual characters on stage. Performers who want to arouse laughter often enact laughter themselves as a stimulant, like Trygaios at Hierokles (*Peace* 1066), or Herakles confronted by Dionysos (*Frogs* 42 ff.). In tragedy, given that it is likely that any on-stage laughter would be signalled, such indications turn out to be rare and interesting.[13]

Tekmessa at Sophokles, *Ajax* 303, indicates that Ajax laughed during his madness (συντιθεὶς γέλων πολύν); and this may actually have been enacted on stage during the prologue. The chorus at Euripides, *Trojan Women* 406, provide more direct evidence in their comment on Kassandra's speech about her 'marriage' to Agamemnon—ὡς ἡδέως κακοῖσιν οἰκείοις γελᾷς ('how merrily you laugh at your own misfortunes'). In both these cases it is, of course, a kind of mad laughter and full of bitter vindictiveness. When Orestes at Sophokles, *Elektra* 1296 ff., fears that Elektra might betray her joy through laughing or smiling, on the other hand, she reassures him that her sorrow is too ingrained for that. This rarity of on-stage laughter makes Pentheus' behaviour during the scene with Kadmos and Teiresias in *Bakchai* all the more remarkable. He himself speaks of his laughter when he first sees them—πολὺν γέλων (250)—and it is referred to twice more at 272 and 322 (both ὃν σὺ διαγελᾷς, 'whom you laugh to scorn'). This characterizes Pentheus in a way not evident until its unusualness is brought out; and it contributes to the strange uncertainty of tone which is sustained throughout the first two-thirds of this deeply untypical play.[14] In none of these scenes is the audience encouraged to share unreservedly in the mirth, as they are in comedy. The set of feelings through which tragedy captures its audience is generally incompatible with laughter.

II

Both genres have a *chorus*, so how do they compare in this sphere? The chorus in comedy comes on much later in the play, for a start—generally speaking around line 250 or 300, as opposed to about line 100. This is no mere matter of statistics: the arrival of the chorus in comedy is also far more anticipated and built up to than in tragedy, and it is more of an event when it does come.[15] And, compared with Sophokles and Euripides at least, its presence is more obtrusive once it is there. The comic chorus is often alienated from the main 'hero', but tends to establish a certain complicity with the audience, usually taking advantage of whatever its particular identity may be; and often the *parabasis* includes some sort of discourse in praise or defence of its role (birds, clouds, and even, in *Thesmophoriazousae*, wives). Not least, its role is usually unpredictable, ingenious, entertaining, sometimes theriomorphic, sometimes personificatory. As well as those familiar from surviving Aristophanes—clouds, twenty-four species of wild bird, wasp-jurors, opposed half-choruses of old men and women, and so on—we know of many other weird and wonderful choric groups, such as islands (each costumed differently), festivals, goats, dramatic productions, centaurs, and dead poets.[16]

Compared with this menagerie, the identities of the choruses of tragedy are limited and generally predictable. Most are women, women who, whether slave or free, are sympathetic and loyal to the local great house—or occasionally to an estranged or out-of-favour branch (as in *Medeia* and *Herakles* respectively). And when they are not well-wishing women, the tragic chorus tends to consist of old men with similar local loyalties. (This brings out the untypicality of the unsympathetic aliens who comprise the chorus of *Bakchai*.) The observation that the 'guises' of the chorus of tragedy are standard and unsurprising is clearly far less true of Aischylos than of the other two 'greats'. Once *Bakchai* is set on one side (and *Rhesos* also, see below), the least orthodox choruses in Sophokles and Euripides are probably those of *Ajax*, *Philoktetes*, *Trojan Women*, and *Suppliants*. But the Suppliants of Aischylos are a far bolder and more active choice than any of those. And within a trilogy, Aischylos might go for such varied identities as Bassarids, Edonians, and Youths (*Neaniskoi*); or Myrmidons, Nereids (bringing Akhilleus his new armour), and Phrygians (who accompany Priam to ransom Hektor). But it is unlikely that even Aischylos produced another chorus as unpredictable and weird as the Erinyes of *Eumenides*. In fact, many of my generalizations about comedy can be applied to them: they are not fully anthropomorphic; they are hostile to the main characters; their arrival (or at least their first coherent contribution) comes relatively late on in the play; much anticipated, it is quite an event; once they are active, they can certainly not be relegated to the background when convenient; and their identity is in no way subordinate nor (until the end) localized. The Furies are as unlike the loyal conformist old men or slave women of later tragedy as are the weirder choruses of comedy. In a perceptive article some thirty years ago, John Herington went so far as to propose that *Eumenides* was composed under the influence of Old Comedy.[17] The alternative explanation would be that some of the features of early tragedy became assimilated as characteristics of comedy, coming by the same process to be excluded from tragedy; and, unless we suppose that already in the 450s comedy had most of the features of its flowering in the age of Eupolis and Aristophanes, this seems more plausible.

The active centrality of the choruses of *Eumenides* and of the Aeschylean *Suppliants* helps to bring home the point that not one chorus of Sophokles or Euripides (always excepting *Rhesos*[18]) is an indispensable participant in the plot. While many do participate in minor ways, these passing incidents are not integral and are no part of their *raison d'être*—on the contrary their *raison d'être* has something to do with their *detachment* from the plot. Women and weak old men seem to be favoured for choruses partly because of their ineffectuality in action. And it is worth noting that in this respect, at least, *Bakchai* is orthodox, since, contrary to what is often implied, the chorus plays no direct part in the plot or action. Women and old men such as these are not obviously 'on the same wavelength' as the primary audience of male citizens. Paradoxically, the bizarre choruses of comedy set up a closer rapport with the audience than do the docile orthodox humans of tragedy. This is partly because they address the audience directly, advise, flatter and rebuke them, take them into their confidence; also because their guises and their choral identity are thin and permeable—not far beneath the Acharnians or the Initiates or whatever are the audience's fellow-citizens, who are playing the role, and who in some way may 'represent' the playwright. It is above all, though not exclusively, in the *parabasis* (of course) that the Athenian citizens tend to be visible through the cover of the chorus.[19]

These observations run counter to the influential model according to which the tragic chorus is in some sense the representative of the new democracy in a context which sets old-style aristocratic heroes in crisis.[20] Assuming, safely in my view, that the audience consisted overwhelmingly of adult male citizens of Athens,[21] the fact that so many choruses are comprised of women—often not even free women—is striking. Even when it consists of male citizens, it is often emphasized that they are weak and past the age for military action. Aischylos was evidently happy with choruses of younger men, as in *Myrmidons* or *Neaniskoi*, for example[22] (so sometimes is comedy, as in *Knights* and *Peace*), but from all surviving Sophokles and Euripides there are only *Ajax* and *Philoktetes*. *Ajax* is especially interesting since its chorus represents sailors from Salamis—like some of the audience presumably, though it is also emphasized that they are heavily dependent on Ajax.[23] So, holding up the comic choruses as a kind of reverse-mirror or foil, it strikes me how *little* there is in tragedy to assimilate the chorus with the audience as democratic citizens. Two other considerations seem to outweigh any tendency towards this. One is the *helplessness* of the chorus—at least after Aischylos, though this characteristic is already made much of in the death-scene in *Agamemnon*. However emotionally involved and distressed the chorus may be by what is happening, they can do nothing about it—except sing lyrics, of course. On one very important level this *is* like the audience, the audience as spectators, *theatai*: they too are helpless witnesses of the tragic events, who, while they can try to make sense of their thoughts and emotions, can *do* nothing. Secondly, I suggest that the choruses are given relatively weak and unassertive identities so that they can be made to respond malleably to the events. The prominent and peculiar guise of the *comic* chorus becomes one of the determinants of the contents of the play: in tragedy, by contrast, the relatively colourless bystanders respond to, but do not determine, events. The chorus is thus not unlike the tragic mask, serious but blank, with simple indicators of gender and age, waiting for the tragedy to be witnessed.

III

If these sweeping generalizations about the chorus are dogmatic and sketchy, what I have to say about the *gods* is even more so. First, I am primarily alluding to the actual appearances and interventions of the gods on-stage in the plays, not the more general religious or theological dimensions. The antithesis boils down to this: in comedy the gods are all too human, in tragedy all too unhuman. Two incidents may serve to epitomize *comic* divinities: when Dionysos and Xanthias are both flogged in *Frogs*, to discover which is the god, Dionysos feels just as much pain as the human slave (633 ff.); and in *Birds*, when, before the whole pantheon is starved into capitulation, Iris turns up as the Olympian messenger (1172–1261), for all her protests and threats, she is treated roughly, abused, and threatened with rape, as though she were some unprotected female menial. Comic goddesses were presumably costumed with the same robes and ugly masks as human women, though often with some attribute, such as Iris' wings. Male gods sported exactly the same masks, padding, and phallus as human men—at least they do in the comic vase-paintings. Even Zeus appears there, distinguished by crown and eagle sceptre, but otherwise as grotesque and undignified as any comic character.[24]

Contrast the Iris of *Birds* with her non-identical twin at Euripides, *Herakles* 822 ff. The tragic Iris is relentless in her obedience to Hera, insisting that Herakles 'pay the price' (842), even though she omits to specify the crime; and she disdains to give any reply to Lyssa's protest that Herakles has made the earth a fit place for humans to honour the gods (849–54). Generally speaking, the on-stage gods of tragedy are dangerous and unpredictable, most so, perhaps, when they seem most human. As John Gould says of the gods in *Hippolytos*:[25] 'to come face to face with a god is not just to confront a being who thinks and feels like a man but has the power of a divinity; it may be to confront the utterly, destructively alien; impossible, uncanny, sickening, yet undeniably "there" and beyond us to will away'. Athena in the prologue of Sophokles' *Ajax* is a good case in point; and Odysseus' reluctance to go along with her all-too-human-seeming sentiments shows a wise caution in him—he is aware of the mismatch between the human and divine grids. It may be the difficulty of any proper human communication with the gods that tends to push them centrifugally to the less engaged sections of the tragedies, especially the encapsulation of solo prologues and the detachment of 'from the machine' epilogues.

This approach leaves us with two special cases, *Eumenides* and *Bakchai* (leaving aside *Prometheus*, which is a special special case). *Eumenides* is mostly, of course, conducted on the divine plane; and generally the gods seem to be presented at face value, without hidden, incomprehensible agendas. Both Apollo and the Furies wear their weaknesses as well as their strengths on their sleeves; and Athena seems to be both benevolent and relatively 'clean'.[26] At the other extreme, *Bakchai* is the only surviving tragedy which presents a god in human disguise.[27] Moreover, he is on-stage among humans and masquerading as a human for most of the central part of the play (434–518, 604–861, 912–76). But the more human he seems to be, the more misleading this is. Even though the final scenes of the play are severely mutilated, it is clear that Dionysos 'from the machine' was a fully manifest god, and that he speaks in

terms which do not make full human sense. This is especially stark
in his exchange with Kadmos at 1344–51, where the apparent dialogue of stichomythia contains a series of *non sequiturs*. Dionysos is
'uncanny, sickening, yet undeniably "there" '. The attribution of
parts in our *texts* of *Bakchai* may be, I suggest, seriously misleading:[28] the part of 'the stranger' is signalled throughout by the attribution Δι. (= Dionysos), but this textual oversimplification fails to
reflect the ways that the *audience* may be partially lulled into
regarding him as human and humanly intelligible, sharing to some
varying extent the misapprehensions of the characters.

In *Bakchai*, Pentheus thinks that he can control and tie down the
god, because he does not know that he is a god. The 'palace mira-
cles' show how utterly mistaken he is: the apparently controllable
turns out to be amazingly and terrifyingly evasive. In Kratinos'
Dionysalexandros the comic twin Dionysos also disguised himself
as a human; but he did so to try to get his hands on Helen—and he
failed of course! In *Frogs* he shits himself for fear, and decides
between the poets on the strength of an inarticulate impulse. In
comedy the god, phallus and all, is cut down to human size, undignified and unmysterious.

IV

Finally, *closures*. This is a familiar area for generic clichés: as
George Bernard Shaw put it, 'the popular definition of tragedy is
heavy drama in which everyone is killed in the last act, comedy
being light drama, in which everyone is married in the last act'.[29]
While it may have become more applicable in later antiquity, the
happy-versus-unhappy-ending polarity is (of course) far from true
of fifth-century drama. Not all comedies end joyfully, not *Clouds*
or *Frogs*, for example; and quite a few tragedies end more or less
happily —though it is true that *Thesmophoriazousae* raises a kind of
protest against this. What seems to me a more valid generalization
is that Old Comedy tends towards closed, wrapped-up, reassuring
endings, while tragedies tend to reach open, disturbing, unsettled
endings.

The celebratory dance or procession is particularly effective for
smoothing out rumples and overriding reservations. Whatever one
may feel about Dikaiopolis' selfishness in *Acharnians*,[30] there is, so
far as I can see, no encouragement to resist his final victory-parade,

supported by the chorus (1227–34). Whatever the failures of
Philokleon, *Wasps* ends with his choreographic triumph, backed
up by the 'sons of Karkinos' and the chorus. The endings of *Peace*,
Birds, *Lysistrata*, and *Ekklesiazousai* are the most obviously triumphal, incorporating the popular 'real-life' calls that accompany
victory or marriage or both—ἀλαλαὶ ἰὴ παιήων, Ὑμὴν ὦ Ὑμέναι' ὦ,
ὦ τήνελλα καλλίνικος ('*alalai iê paiêon*', '*Humên ô Humenai*' *ô*', '*ô
tênella* for the great victor') and suchlike.

Turning to tragedy, the advocacy of open and unsettling endings
has been predominant in recent times. A case in point is Sophokles,
Elektra, where few would now support an unironically triumphal-
ist reading of the ending.[31] Sophokles could, after all, have ended
the play with both Klytaimnestra and Aigisthos safely dead, finally
sending Orestes off as the reinstated king with a chorus-supported
victory procession. The best strategy for a critic who wanted to
maintain that tragedy normally approached a closed resolution
(and that all this open-endedness is only the product of a critical
methodology which is dedicated to finding it) might be to point to
those tragic closures which enact a funeral procession involving the
participation of the chorus.[32] This kind of unity in sorrow might
plausibly be claimed, for example, for *Seven against Thebes*, where
it is also emphasized that the city is saved.[33] Sophokles' *Ajax*
might be claimed as another instance (though the future is uncertain for Teukros). In *Trachiniai*, however, it seems to me that the
resentful closing sentiments of Hyllos (1266–9), and perhaps also
the foreign pallbearers (cf. 964), are enough to disturb any wish for
a simply redemptive ending, even without involving the question
of how surely an apotheosis on Oita could be taken for granted.[34]
It is, then, interesting to find that there are no such clear examples
of complete or chorally ratified endings from Euripides (apart from
Alkestis, arguably). The nearest is *Suppliants*, which ends without
ado after Athena's 'from the machine' speech. *Bakchai* pointedly
closes with the break-up of both family and polis. It might easily
have ended with a triumphal Dionysiac departure by the chorus,
off to spread the blessings of the god to another city—even to
Athens! It might, that is, have ended with metatheatrical celebration, but it doesn't; and in that it epitomizes tragedy's refusal to
take the easy or comforting way out of the terrors it enacts.

I have reserved till last the great exception to all this: the *Oresteia*
again. While *Agamemnon* and *Choephoroi* are both conspicuously

open and uncertain in their endings, *Eumenides* concludes with a procession which is closer to the endings of Aristophanes than to anything else in tragedy that we know of. Whoever actually participates in this final procession, and whoever sings the final four stanzas of lyrics at 1032–47, it is clear that the procession includes the jurors and everyone else on stage, with no dissenters or reservations of any kind. The second-person-plural-imperative refrains of the processional stanzas are all-inclusive: εὐφαμεῖτε δὲ πανδαμεί and ὀλολύξατε νῦν ἐπὶ μολπαῖς ('sing words of good omen, all you people'; 'raise your cry to accompany our song'). The critical strategies that have been used to break open the ending of *Eumenides* seem doomed to do just the same to *Peace* and *Lysistrata*; and methods that are bound to succeed have lost their vital ability to discriminate. For what more, or what else, could Aischylos have done to create a complete ending, the 'birth of a new era'[35] for the city of Athens? It is the similarity of this closure to those of Aristophanes which brings home how deeply untypical it is of tragedy—or at least of the non-trilogic tragedies of the era of Sophokles and Euripides. This observation has led me towards formulating a way in which the end of *Eumenides* may, after all, be seen as emblematic of the function of tragedy in general.[36]

First, it is characteristic of comedy that its celebratory endings (*Birds*, *Lysistrata*, etc.) represent in some self-referential ways the triumph of comedy over the obstacles of the recalcitrant world outside. Above all, at the end of *Frogs*, with Euripides and Sophokles both dead, it is comedy, and the Dionysos of comedy, that brings back the contemporary equivalent of Aischylos to the city. The torchlight procession, the high-flown language (with subversive lapses, of course), and the echo in *Frogs* 1530 (τῇ δὲ πόλει μεγάλων ἀγαθῶν ἀγαθὰς ἐπινοίας, 'good thoughts for the great good of the city') of *Eumenides* 1012 (εἴη δ' ἀγαθῶν ἀγαθὴ διάνοια πολίταις, 'may the citizens have good thought for good') all add up to a kind of bid for comedy to stand on a civic pedestal beside that of tragedy. The jealous sibling is, in effect, making its characteristically metatheatrical bid for serious attention.

Eumenides thus emerges as the exception that proves the rule for what I have been saying about the differences between tragedy and comedy under all three headings of chorus, gods, and closures. The close analogies between the two closing processions of *Eumenides* and *Frogs* prompts the proposal that the incorporation of the Erinyes represents, on a non-explicit and figurative level of self-reference, the incorporation of tragedy within the city of Athens. Tragedy, like the Erinyes, is fearsome; tragedy, like them, stirs up visions of family conflict, bloodshed, curses, the stuff of nightmares, and not least nightmares about the power of the dangerous female. In *Eumenides* all of these threats are organized and contained within a cult and in a form that will benefit the city and not harm it. So, with this perspective, the procession at the end of the *Oresteia* becomes, at least at one level of reference, an enactment of the triumphal acceptance of the tragic. There is evidence in Aristophanes and elsewhere that the *Oresteia* remained celebrated; and it seems that, after this masterpiece, tragedy did not have to keep pressing self-referential claims for its importance within the *polis*. The connected trilogy was discontinued; tragedies were not set in the centre of Athens;[37] and the closures of the single tragedies became open, cracked and unhealed. Tragedy is strong enough to do this, to contain the unbearable, to resist being sucked into the black hole, while not denying it or turning away from it. After the 'foundation allegory' of *Eumenides*, apology is no longer needed.

Notes

1. I should like to thank Bernard Gredley, Marsh McCall, and Peter Wilson for their comments on drafts of this piece.
2. See below, p. 537.
3. The clear breakdown of this division does not come until Rhinthon, *c.*300 BC, with his Doric φλύακες τραγικοί. See Taplin, *Comic Angels*, 48–52.
4. Silk, 'The Autonomy of Comedy'. This important article is directed primarily at comedy rather than tragedy.
5. It is important to insist on translating γέλοιον as 'amusing' or 'laughter-arousing', not as 'comic'. The modern usage of 'tragic' to mean 'horrific' can be no less misleading than that of 'comic' to mean 'laughterific'.
6. 'Fifth-Century Tragedy and Comedy: A *Synkrisis*', *JHS* 106 (1986) 163–74.
7. The actors' masks were apparently the same for tragedy and for satyr-play, where the chorus was the crucial distinguishing marker.
8. So Dionysos' smiling mask in *Bakchai*, while highly deviant and significant (see esp. Foley, *Ritual Irony*, 205 ff.), is not comic.
9. See A. D. Trendall and A. Cambitoglou, *The Red-Figured Vases of Apulia*, supp. ii (1992) 7–8; also Taplin, *Comic Angels*, 55–66.

10. Cf. P. Wilson below, p. 318

11. See K. J. Dover, *Greek Homosexuality* (London 1978) 124–34; and J. Winkler, 'Phallos Politikos: Representations of the Body Politic in Athens', *Differences* 2 (1990) 29–45. While every male in comedy flaunted his phallus (unless there were special reasons for covering it), genitals are never displayed on-stage in tragedy, and only rarely referred to, with suitable circumlocution.

12. On laughter, cf. N. Lowe below, p. 524.

13. This particular stage-business seems to have been overlooked in the valuable studies by A. Spitzbarth, *Spieltechnik* (Zurich 1946), F. L. Shisler, 'The Use of Stage Business to Portray Emotion in Greek Tragedy', *AJP* 66 (1945) 377–97, and Stanford, *Greek Tragedy and the Emotions*. Bernard Gredley also draws my attention to Medea's children at Eur., *Med.* 1041, where their laughter is poignantly inappropriate.

14. *Bakchai* is sometimes presented as an archetypal or exemplary tragedy (cf. B. Seidensticker, below, pp. 391–2); yet it is through and through untypical. But perhaps this is true of most Athenian tragedies—or at least many of the greatest ones?

15. Full analyses of Aristophanic *parodoi* in B. Zimmermann, *Untersuchungen zur Form und dramatischen Technik der Aristophanischen Komödien*, i (Meisenheim 1985) 6–149.

16. The last three in this list refer to *Didaskaliai, Cheirones*, and to the likely chorus of Kratinos' *Archilochoi*.

17. 'The Influence of Old Comedy on Aeschylus' Later Trilogies', *TAPA* 94 (1963) 113–25. The Oceanids of *Prometheus Desmotes* are, it should be noted, innocuous, the divine equivalent of the standard serving-women. But the Titans of *Prometheus Lyomenos* seem to have been different, to judge from the fragments. And they may have been the inspiration for the chorus of Kratinos' *Ploutoi* (see fr. 171 K–A).

18. *Rhesos* seems to show some kind of reaction or protest against passive choruses. This is especially interesting if (as I believe) it was not the work of Euripides—probably, indeed, dating from after his death.

19. Might it be that the big lyric and recitative structures ('epirrhematic syzygies') that are characteristic of comedy, and are so significantly unlike the choral contributions to tragedy, were somehow also closer to some popular non-dramatic or extra-theatrical performances?

20. On this, see John Gould, below, pp. 217–21.

21. There has recently been new attention paid to non-citizens possibly in the audience—foreigners, children, slaves, and women. Even if women (and slaves) were present, which I personally very much doubt, the claim of Henderson ('Women and the Athenian Dramatic Festivals', *TAPA* 121 [1991] 133–47, at 145) that 'the citizen males

may have been surrounded, perhaps even outnumbered, by the "others" on whose behalf they ran the *polis*' is surely a wild exaggeration.

22. Note also that on the now well-known Basel krater of *c.*480 the six choral dancers are young men (no beards) in corselets.

23. It is interesting that Eur. *Hcld.* and Soph. *OC* both have a chorus of elderly 'guardians' of a specific Attic locality.

24. For gods on comic vases, see Taplin, *Comic Angels*, 60 n. 11. I can add a new vase, with a lasciviously leering, white-haired Zeus, now published as no. 58 in *A Passion for Antiques. Ancient Art from the Collection of Barbara and Lawrence Fleischman* (Malibu 1994). (It is generally accepted that Zeus never appeared in person in tragedy—though his presence is strongly felt in *Prometheus*. See my *Stagecraft of Aeschylus*, 431–2.)

25. In P. Easterling and J. Muir (edd.), *Greek Religion and Society* (Cambridge 1985) 29.

26. Too much can be made, I think, of her reference to her access to Zeus' thunderbolts at 826–9. She does not, after all, claim that, if she resorted to force, it would prevent the Erinyes from poisoning Athens; she is only pointing out that she too, like them, has violent means of vindication (κἀγώ, 826); cf. her next speech of persuasion, where she insists that she too has wisdom (φρονεῖν δὲ κἀμοὶ . . ., 850).

27. It would be very interesting to know how Aischylos handled the god in his Dionysos-plays, since it looks as though he must have been disguised for *Edonoi* fr. 61 Radt. Note that in either *Semele* or *Xantriai* Hera came on stage disguised as a begging, hexameter-chanting priestess, see fr. **168 Radt.

28. A good case of the text being 'only a selection from among the plural potentialities of performance', to adopt and adapt the phrasing of Goldhill, *Reading Greek Tragedy*, 284.

29. I found this quotation in the useful survey of the ancient generic differentia in Seidensticker, *Palintonos Harmonia*, 249 ff., esp. 254–5; cf. also Silk, 'The Autonomy of Comedy', esp. 5.

30. Cf. H. P. Foley, 'Tragedy and Politics in Aristophanes' *Acharnians*', *JHS* 108 (1988) 33–47.

31. For the old, out-of-favour view, see P. T. Stevens, *G&R* 25 (1978) 111 ff.; for a more subtle discussion with shrewd points about the problems of 'irony', see T. Szlezák, *Museum Helveticum* 38 (1981) 1–21. On Sophoclean endings, see Roberts, 'Sophoclean Endings'.

32. Richard Seaford, for example (below, pp. 284–94), wishes to see a civically reassuring aetiology as the goal of each tragedy. But, while often present, this is not often the prominent or predominant *telos* or conclusion. I have been made more aware of the importance of tragic processions by the research of my student Athena Kavoulaki.

33. Provided that it originally ended with the united procession, before the suspect intervention of the herald, which has the very effect of reopening a closed ending; cf. Taplin, *Stagecraft of Aeschylus*, 180–3.
34. The problem is set at its sharpest by T. C. W. Stinton, *Collected Papers* (Oxford 1990) 479–90.
35. Sommerstein ad loc.
36. At the King's conference I argued this case more fully, relating the aetiology of the inclusion of 'the fearsome' in Athens to the later use of Furies as emblematic of tragedy in general, especially in vase-painting. It transpired that these ideas were so much 'in the air' (and partly anticipated by recent publications by R. Padel and E. Belfiore), and were so complementary to the argument of a paper given by Peter Wilson to the Cambridge Philological Society in May 1993, that we have taken the liberty of a more speedy publication of some of the central ideas. This has appeared as P. Wilson and O. Taplin, 'The "Aetiology" of Tragedy in the *Oresteia*', *PCPS* 39 (1993) 169–80.
37. Euripides' *Erechtheus* evidently broke this 'rule'. It would be interesting to know how 'open' or how 'celebratory' its ending was.

12

Comedy and Tragedy—Inevitable
Distinctions: Response to Taplin

BERNARD GREDLEY

Oliver Taplin's paper, which revisits terrain previously explored
in 1986, is soundly based on the conviction that the distinctions
between fifth-century tragedy and comedy matter, and that they
are in no way nullified by the generic transgressions which have
recently attracted critical attention. It is a broad and thought-
provoking analysis, to which this reply does not pretend to be comprehensive. Instead, and focusing particularly on *Bakchai* and
Frogs, I offer a series of related comments on each of his three test-
cases—chorus, gods, and closures—along with a modest development of his remarks about laughter in tragedy.[1]

I

Consider, first, the gods in tragedy and, in particular, the near-con-
temporary images of Dionysos projected in *Bakchai* and *Frogs*. The
tragic Dionysos, accompanied by his triumphal *thiasos*, is 'der kom-
mende Gott', his purpose epiphany, his first words ἥκω Διὸς παῖς
('I, the son of Zeus, have come'), his shape changed, as we are twice
reminded, εἰς ἀνδρὸς φύσιν ('to human form', 4, 53 f.). This is not a
superficial disguise, which might at any moment be discarded, but
a metamorphosis which invites an audience to reflect on the unhuman shape and power beyond and within the figure it sees, namely,
the rejuvenated Dionysos familiar from the middle of the fifth century and transgressively feminine in appearance (353). That the
god's transformation is to be thought of as permanent and complete
is, I suggest, underlined by the way in which the attractions of his
sexuality are communicated mainly by Pentheus' scrutiny of the
features of his smiling face and mask (235 f., 453 ff.).[2] Unlike

costume, which is detachable and may be variously contrasted with the identity and status of its wearer—as with the disguises assumed here by Kadmos, Teiresias, and Pentheus, and, generally, by Euripides' beggar-kings (*Frogs* 1063)—masks have a special status as indicators of identity. They are the essential protection of the actor's ability to impersonate a plurality of roles; that the mask *is* the actor's identity is strongly suggested by the shaving of 'the in-law' in *Thesmophoriazousai* (213 ff.), which implicitly assumes that, whatever else happens to them, characters may not change identity simply by changing masks.[3]

Given the completeness of this transformation, should our text draw a distinction, as Taplin suggests,[4] between the stranger and Dionysos? Can the audience 'be lulled into regarding him as human and humanly intelligible, sharing to some varying extent the misapprehensions of the characters'?[5] It seems doubtful. To look at the same point another way: every misapprehension within the world of the play, and every wrong step taken in consequence, may be seen as reminders of the separateness of the audience's vision and of the privileged, complicit relationship established between it and the god, on an empty stage, when the play begins. For those who know his true identity, the stranger consistently behaves as a god would;[6] his human metamorphosis, when understood as such, underlines the unhuman otherness it conceals from Pentheus.[7] The audience's unremitting perception of the truth mirrors the unremitting ignorance of the characters and helps to generate the sense of detachment and inevitability which is arguably proper to the experience of tragedy.

Dionysos' arrival in Thebes and his arrival in *Frogs* suggest some striking (and indicative) distinctions. Now υἱὸς Σταμνίου ('son of Wine-jar', 22), he has put on a lion-skin and carries a club to play the Herculean role of underworld voyager for which his temperament and physique seem to make him uniquely unqualified. *This* Dionysiac disguise proves a flimsy covering for unheroism, exploded when Herakles opens his door and at once sees the *krokôtos* ('yellow dress') and *kothornoi* ('boots') showing underneath (45 ff.). In contrast to the impenetrable metamorphosis of *Bakchai*, this outfit invites the audience into a running joke directed at the incongruous gap between Dionysos' view of himself and the way others, starting with Herakles, see him. In *Bakchai* the spectators' complicity with the god distances them from the world of the tragic-human characters; in *Frogs* the audience is drawn into the fictive world through its complicity with other characters, especially Xanthias, at the god's expense.

The journeys of the Euripidean Dionysos, whether to Thebes or to the surrounding countryside with Pentheus, are manifestations of unstoppable power, and are accomplished with the eerie effortlessness characteristic of gods. His Aristophanic counterpart comes for help, his baggage and cheeky sidekick in tow, pays two obols and then sweats and farts his way across the lake, demystifying, as he does so, the miracle of descent into the underworld which the likes of Theseus, Herakles, and, more pertinently, Dionysos himself had once made in his search for Semele.[8] It is not surprising, and certainly not jarring, when at the end of *Frogs*, *this* god—Herakles' baby brother, pot-bellied and averse to walking (60, 128, 200)—finds himself lambasted by Euripides as μιαρώτατ' ἀνθρώπων ('the most villainous *man* in the world', 1472).[9] Such a shift, unproblematic in comedy, would be an unthinkable breach of the tragic boundaries which impermeably mark off gods from men.

These two representations of Dionysos point towards a further important distinction between comedy and tragedy. The Aristophanic Dionysos displays the opportunistic flexibility which characterizes the human 'heroes' of Old Comedy, like Euripides' relative in *Thesmophoriazousai* or Strepsiades in *Clouds*; he has an apparently endless ability to change his mind or, when faced with what in realist terms would seem to be the need to make it up at the end of the play, an inability to do so.[10] By contrast, rigid fixity of purpose is a central predicate of the gods in tragedy and one which, allied to their certainty of accomplishment, distinguishes them from most human characters and the emotional vocabulary which gives their cast of mind expression. To persuade a god is a contradiction in terms. Discourse, in consequence, becomes a largely meaningless antiphony, which is perhaps echoed in the tendency Taplin notes[11] for gods to appear only at the detached, non-discussive margins of the play. Fixity of purpose is dispensed *ex machina* at whatever cost in human suffering, as Kadmos discovers when, in reply to his forlorn (and ironically accurate) assertion (*Bakchai* 1348) that 'the passions [ὀργάς] of gods should not be like those of humans', Dionysos intones the unshakeable will of Zeus. Agave recognizes the truth at once: 'It is settled' (δέδοκται) and, as often in tragedy, settled 'long ago' (πάλαι, 1349–50). The comic Dionysos, on the brink of undoing his original purpose, dithers because he does not wish to be on bad terms with either of the competing poets (*Frogs* 1412), indeed looks, almost pantomimically, towards the audience for support (1475). The audience become, or are invited to think they have become, one of the determinants of stage action; their presence can make a difference. The sense of closed, ordered inevitability which in the end often overwhelms the characters and, by implication, the audiences of tragedy, has no place here.

II

HERAKLES. Who banged at my door? He leapt at it like a centaur . . . Tell me, what does this mean?
DIONYSOS. Boy...
XANTHIAS. What is it?
DIONYSOS. Didn't you notice?
XANTHIAS. *What?*
DIONYSOS. How enormously frightened he was of me.
XANTHIAS. Yes, by Zeus, in case you're mad.
HERAKLES. By Demeter, I tell you I can't stop laughing. Mind you, I *am* biting my lip . . . but I'm laughing anyway.

(*Frogs* 38–43)

In *Frogs* Dionysos inhabits a world which is misaligned with that of Herakles, Xanthias, and, to a large extent, the audience. In the context of comic performance, recognition of this discrepancy provokes the kind of laughter Herakles indulgently but unsuccessfully chokes back on first seeing his incompetent disguise (42 f.). His initial incredulity (39), Dionysos' interpretation of it as appropriate terror, and Xanthias' puncturing 'Yes, in case you're mad' (41) all exist within the fissure between 'reality' and a ludicrously mistaken self-view, which in the following scenes will be exploited as a fertile source of comically derisive humour at the god's expense.

On-stage laughter in tragedy is, as Taplin rightly points out,[12] difficult to establish; and I am doubtful that it happens in any of the cases he mentions, including the case of Pentheus in *Bakchai* 250, where his words, πολὺν γέλων ('how laughable', a parenthesis breaking otherwise continuous syntax), are hardly a cue for him to laugh. Nevertheless, Pentheus' reaction is certainly unusual; like

Herakles, he is responding (already in an excited state, 214) to a just noticed and, as he thinks, ludicrous 'disguise'. It would, however, be mistaken to rely on Pentheus' response in evaluating the complex impression made by Kadmos and Teiresias. Viewed through his eyes, the old men dressed as Bacchants are indeed similar to the comic Dionysos posturing as Herakles but, within the tragic frame of *Bakchai*, his is a 'comic' reaction misplaced: not the knowing laughter of a Herakles which spreads itself to a complicit audience, but the isolating sign of a truth misunderstood. Further (and catastrophically), his uncomprehending derision of the old men (248–51) precisely mimics his reaction to the god, the parallel underlined by Teiresias' use of the same words to describe both: ὃν σὺ διαγελᾷς ('whom you mock', 272 = 322; cf. 286).

Pentheus' mockery of Dionysos might be classified as a premature and deluded form of the derisive laughter often anticipated by the characters of tragedy as the reaction of a victorious enemy.[13] In this sense, it is massively repaid when, in his anxiety to avoid the laughter of Agave and the other women (842), he is led in a dress and laughed at through the streets of Thebes—communal derision orchestrated by Dionysos (854 f.), whose own impenetrable smile now assumes another, mocking significance. Pentheus' laughter is therefore not what it seems; it signals not victory over an enemy but deranged incomprehension, as Kadmos and Teiresias see (326, 332, 359). To this extent it resembles the mad laughter which afflicts Euripides' Herakles at the onset of his delusion (*Herakles* 935), when he too stands on the brink of a world of nightmarish fantasy.[14]

The laughter of Pentheus is complex. While it seeks to represent itself as the vindictive derision of a confident and victorious opponent, it is coloured and undermined by hints and accusations of delusion and derangement. Pentheus laughs through a failure to see what he should see: the irresistible power of Dionysos and, metatheatrically, the fact that he lives in the world of tragedy. Laughing in tragedy is like taking oneself seriously in comedy. Both are signs of dislocation and both may be a sign of madness, as Xanthias reminded Dionysos (*Frogs* 41).

Other kinds of incomprehension may also be signalled by laughter. These may be exemplified by the laughter of Herakles' servants (*Herakles* 950), which alternates with fear as they watch him ride imaginary horses and ask each other if it is a joke or madness;

or the laughter of unknowing victims, innocently oblivious of imminent death, like that of Medea's children, apparently secure in their mother's affection (*Medea* 1041): τί προσγελᾶτε τὸν πανύστατον γέλων; ('Why are you smiling at me—your last smile?'). The poignantly skewed effect of their smiling faces is underscored by that πανύστατον, their 'very *last*' smile—a common, almost metatheatrical reminder that tragedy must always stand at the edge of catastrophe. When, just before the death of Astyanax, Andromache notices his tears (*Troiades* 749), she reads them as an incipient recognition of this fact: ὦ παῖ, δακρύεις; αἰσθάνῃ κακῶν σέθεν; ('Are you crying, my son? Do you sense your misfortunes?'). Tragic laughter can never last; so in *Bakchai*, the laughter of Pentheus is a kind of dissonant prelude to the grief (*penthos*) indelibly inscribed in his name and destiny (367 f., 508): τὸ τέλος δυστυχία ('the end is misfortune'), as the chorus predicts in the following *stasimon* (388).[15] It will all, with tragic inevitability, end in tears and the emotional range appropriate to tragedy and felt to be appropriate by the audience of tragedy.[16]

III

In his discussion of the choruses of Attic drama, Taplin[17] properly draws attention to their generally bland and predictable identities in later fifth-century tragedy, compared to the adventurous choices made by comedy and, sometimes, by Aischylos. The most striking Aeschylean instance is, of course, the Furies, and Taplin's explanation of this uniquely unorthodox tragic chorus involves reversing Herington's intriguing but problematic view[18] that *Eumenides* was influenced by Old Comedy, suggesting instead that 'some of the features of early tragedy became assimilated as characteristics of comedy, coming by the same process to be excluded from tragedy; and, unless we suppose that comedy already had in the 450s most of the features of its flowering in the age of Eupolis and Aristophanes, this seems more plausible.

Although our knowledge of both early comedy and early tragedy is so incomplete that proof or disproof of either alternative is impossible, Taplin's proposal seems no more likely than Herington's, and appears to share with it an unattractively polarized view of the way the two genres developed. Among the 'menagerie' of comic choruses Taplin lists, none obviously seems to require Aeschylean Furies as their model; on the other hand, theriomorphic choruses can be traced back to Magnes, are represented on vases as early as the mid-sixth century,[19] and are sufficiently similar to later non-human comic choruses to make it plausible to regard all these comic cho-ruses as a related series and to make it unnecessary to look for influ-ence outside the comic sphere. Secondly, this hypothesis, like Herington's, seems to exclude the possibility of a period, perhaps several decades long, when tragedy and comedy were less sharply differentiated than might, on the evidence of the surviving plays, have been thought. Yet such a period could without too much diffi-culty be inferred from Aristotle's admittedly elliptical description of early (or not so early) tragedy in *Poetics* 4 (1449ᵃ), though without the need to postulate a common origin for the two genres.[20] We might suppose that in 458 BC, at the end of Aischylos' career, the legacy of this period was still visible and that tragedy, like comedy, was still in the process of forming what were to become its defining boundaries and conventions. *Persians* and *Agamemnon* are reminders that Aischylos was as capable as the next tragedian of cre-ating designedly ineffectual choruses of the kind which were to become normative in later tragedy, while *Suppliants* and *Eumenides* serve to show that he felt able to give them pivotal and even com-bative roles within the dramatic action narrowly defined. His work exemplifies a range of choral identities—its outer points juxtaposed within a single trilogy in 458—a range evidentially still available to tragedy in the mid-fifth century but perhaps by then already less exploited by younger dramatists. The contraction of this range is, in my view, less likely to be due to its partial appropriation by comedy than to the increasing popularity of experiments with the kind of actor-oriented structures, themselves already visible in the *Oresteia*, which ultimately conventionalize the marginal status of the tragic chorus—a process parallel to that which in the end also radically affects comedy. The points of contact between the Aeschylean Furies and comic choruses are thus, I suggest, better explained by placing them among what Taplin calls the indistinctions of tragedy and comedy. Yet all such 'indistinctions' do indeed, as Taplin rightly feels, serve to put into sharper relief the significant differ-ences between the two dramatic forms; by the last quarter of the fifth century, Aristophanes' preoccupation with the 'otherness' of tragedy strongly suggests that, in his view at least, these differences had become determinative.

IV

Aristophanic comedy creates a world where anything is possible, especially the impossible; audience expectation, though not always satisfied, is of triumph against the odds and its celebration in a closure centred on the *kômos*. It is a world where almost nothing, except the enactment and aftermath of death,[21] and no one, including the audience, is excluded. By contrast, the world of tragedy is, or becomes, inward-looking, its fixed location a form of intensifying, ordering enclosure, its inhabitants often locked into a rehearsal of key events in their mythic histories, embodiments of their own paradigm, as the old men in *Agamemnon* reflect (1566), 'glued to catastrophe'. The sense of inevitability thus communicated becomes, I have suggested, an important, even defining, aspect of the audience's experience of tragedy, and one quite unlike its experience of comedy; the almost deterministic effect is reinforced by the institutionalized re-enactment of myths at annual Athenian festivals, and reaches beyond the innovations and variations of individual dramatists. The helplessness of the tragic chorus, which Taplin rightly identifies,[22] is a predicate of this inevitability and a reflex of the spectators' experience.

It follows that when, for example, choruses vocalize their anguish at murder behind the *skênê*, and contemplate and then cancel intervention, as in *Agamemnon* (1343 ff.), or when, as in *Hippolytos* (710 ff., 803 ff.), party to a piece of information which might have changed the course of events, they are bound to silence, their imprisonment at the margins of the action should not be seen as more or less fitful nods by the dramatist in the direction of 'realism'. It should instead be read as the deliberate highlighting of crucial moments in an unstoppable sequence, whether present, as in Agamemnon's murder or prospective, as in the abortive attempt to deal with Aigisthos before the return of Orestes (*Agamemnon* 1643 ff.). Cancelled intervention by choruses can be a means of reinforcing an audience's awareness of key links in a chain leading inevitably to catastrophe, and can thus serve as reminders of the kind of construct to which audiences, like choruses, are only witnesses (*theatai*). As such they may be considered as examples of tragic self-referentiality, a kind of structural subset of a phenomenon which Taplin properly describes as of 'widely various intensity and explicitness'.[23]

No such sense of inevitability seems to hang over *Eumenides*. It is perhaps most strikingly absent from the play's processional finale which, in Taplin's words, is 'closer to the endings of Aristophanes than to anything else in tragedy that we know of'.[24] Indeed, so close that the resemblance is sometimes thought to extend as far as direct address to the audience: in Athena's reference to τοῖσδε πολίταις ('these citizens here', 991); the chorus' address to ἀστικὸς λεώς ('townsfolk', 997) and to πάντες οἱ κατὰ πτόλιν ('everyone throughout the city', 1014); and in the closing injunctions of the escorts: χωρῖται ('land-dwellers', 1035); πανδημεί ('the whole *dêmos*', 1039); the repeated ὀλολύξατε ('raise a cry of joy', 1043 = 1047).[25] Whether or not, as Taplin proposes,[26] the Furies' exit from the theatre should be read as an aetiology of the incorporation of tragedy within the city of Athens, the ending of *Eumenides* seems to direct itself beyond the thirty-five or so performers on stage,[27] past the impermeable barrier between play and audience, *de rigueur* in later tragedy, and to implicate its onlookers in a way apparently reminiscent of Dionysos' appeal to the spectators for (vocal?) support at the end of *Frogs*.

Yet the comparison also suggests an instructive contrast. The comic Dionysos explicitly names 'the spectators' (οἱ θεώμενοι) and, in so doing, momentarily identifies the play as a theatrical construct, simultaneously breaking and confirming its frame.[28] Such self-referentiality by direct acknowledgement of its audience is, of course, commonplace in Aristophanic comedy, whose spectators can be singled out by name or referred to by social group or in connection with particular events from 'real life'. Comic performers confront an audience which is located 'out there', a short distance beyond a barrier which can be penetrated, seemingly at will, by both actors and audience. In *Eumenides*, on the other hand, the barrier seems to be, not breached in the Aristophanic manner, but imperceptibly dismantled so as to draw the entire citizen-body of the audience into the tragic-theatrical world and its temporally blurred 'now'. The convergence between play and spectators, though apparently complete as the Furies leave the theatre, nevertheless remains implicit; address to the audience—even, perhaps, incitement to vocal participation—though it may be judged probable, lacks any unequivocal confirmation in the words of the text. The presence on stage of the Areopagites, a group of fictive Athenians who represent and embody all those seated in the

auditorium, effectively seals the fissure between spectators and
performers in the moments when the play projects itself most
strongly into the 'real life' of the city. By this simple strategy, the
audience is implicitly repositioned *within* the performance, the
self-referentiality of Aristophanic comedy is avoided, and the closure, in the manner of later tragedies, remains self-contained and
uninterrupted by recognition of its onlookers. Only in its final
imperatives ('Raise a cry of joy to crown our song', 1043 = 1047),
when the theatrical construct is complete, does *Eumenides* seem to
dissolve into its audience.

A strong case can certainly be made for regarding, as Taplin
does,[29] the closing procession of *Frogs* (1505 ff.) as an explicit reminiscence of that in *Eumenides*. Apart from the close echo of
Eumenides 1012 in *Frogs* 1530, which Taplin mentions, there is the
express injunction of the Aristophanic Plouton to the escorting
chorus (1525 ff.) that they should 'celebrate him [sc. Aischylos]
with his own songs and dances', which suggests a musical and
choreographic homage in the best traditions of Aristophanic nos-
talgia. Thus, to corroborate his view that the end of *Eumenides*
enacts the acceptance of the tragic at Athens, Taplin argues that
the return of Aischylos to Athens in *Frogs* should be interpreted as
a metaphoric counter-bid by comedy for civic respectability: 'With
Euripides and Sophokles both dead, it is comedy, and the
Dionysos of comedy, that brings back the contemporary equivalent of Aischylos to the city.'

For several reasons, this hypothesis is somewhat less persuasive
than his parallel reading of *Eumenides*, not least because metatheatricality in Old Comedy seldom submerges itself so coyly. Like
the Furies, it is true, the Aristophanic Aischylos has a mission to
rid Athens of the symptoms of civic degeneration, which are here
especially associated with the name of Socrates (1491 f.). The particular means of the city's salvation will be the restoration of $\tau \grave{a}$
$\mu \acute{\epsilon} \gamma \iota \sigma \tau a \ldots \tau \hat{\eta} s \ \tau \rho a \gamma \omega \delta \iota \kappa \hat{\eta} s \ \tau \acute{\epsilon} \chi \nu \eta s$ ('the most important qualities of
the craft of tragedy', 1495 f.), *in primis* its capacity to dispense civi-
cally useful advice (1485 f., 1490, 1502 f.; cf. 1008 ff., 1053 ff.).
There are not, I suggest, any compelling reasons to think of this
Aischylos as other than he is here represented to be: the embodiment not, as Taplin proposes, of the spirit of (Aristophanic) comedy but of the kind of tragedy which once gave voice to a
value-system now effectively undermined by Euripides and his

spiritual descendants. The reinstalment of Aischylos in the theatre of Dionysos, if it is to be taken seriously, can be validated only by the patron god of drama and it is pertinent to ask whether it is necessary to follow Taplin in seeing the Dionysos who accompanies him on the journey from Hades as, in a special sense, the 'Dionysos of comedy'. Throughout *Frogs*, Dionysos has, of course, been uproariously 'comic', lately as a humorous foil to two earnest tragedians and before that as a sophisticated connoisseur of the avant-garde, whose self-view is not shared by those around him. Whether as buffoon or enthusiast for Euripides and the flawed values of the late fifth century, the comic Dionysos has been impossibly compromised, and it is therefore notable that, during the closing part of *Frogs*, it is Plouton who, having kept a dignified aloofness during the preceding contest, now injects a new and appropriate tone of sobriety, while Dionysos remains conspicuously silent. Dionysos' silence is, I suggest, a significant one, which stems from the difficulty of aligning his previous 'comic' roles with the more sober demands of the play's ending. This difficulty is perhaps more easily explained if Aristophanes is here viewing Dionysos as primarily the Dionysos of tragedy.

All the same, Taplin is surely right to identify an implicitly theatrical perspective in what is, on first reading, a broadly 'political' closure to Aristophanes' play. The return of Aischylos to Athens emblematizes the rebirth of 'proper tragedy'; it is the reinstallation of the poet who first turned tragedy into an elevated art-form (1004 f.) and who was, or could be represented as, the definer of 'the tragic' and the embodiment of its traditional fixities. A revival of tragedy on the Aeschylean model (and not just revivals of Aischylos) would indeed make Aristophanes' counter-definition of comedy and the comic less problematic, because it would reinstate the generic distinctions made increasingly indistinct by the 'buffoon' Euripides (βωμόλοχος, 1521—itself, appropriately, a comic term); and the permanence of this restored equilibrium is signalled by the arrangements which the Aristophanic Aischylos makes to ensure that Euripides can never again usurp the Throne of Tragedy (1520–3).

Frogs shows a sharp and, in the event, prescient sense of the passing of an era in the civic and theatrical life of Athens. In 405 BC comedy's own self-definition was equally at the point of irrevocable development, albeit towards a strikingly untraditional kind of sobriety, and it was not only tragedy and the tragic whose meaning was coming into question. In this sense, as Taplin has suggested, the closure of *Frogs* is about the future of Old Comedy—or its end.

Notes

1. Taplin, above, pp. 190–1. See further Lowe, below, pp. 522–4.
2. For the smile of Dionysos, see 439, 1021. The smiling mask will itself have been distinctive in tragedy, as is suggested by its discordant conjunction with βρόχον θανάσιμον ('the noose of death', 1021 f.). Unlike the uncomprehending Pentheus, the helmsman in *Homeric Hymn* 7. 14 f. recognizes the smile and dark eyes as sure indications of the identity of the captive Dionysos; with the god's subsequent transformation to animal shape (44 ff.) cf. Eur. *Ba.* 1017 ff.
3. It is therefore probably mistaken to claim, as Taplin does in 'Fifth-Century Tragedy and Comedy: A *Synkrisis*', *JHS* 106 (1986) 170, that the failure of disguise in comedy 'threatens to return the actors to the world of the audience'.
4. Above, p. 196.
5. And, in the aftermath of the 'Palace-miracle' (604 ff.), of the chorus.
6. See e.g. the comments of E. R. Dodds, *Bacchae* 2nd edn. (Oxford 1960) xliv.
7. A terrifying alternative vision is momentarily available to Pentheus in 920–4, when he sees what he 'ought to see'.
8. Paus. 2. 37. 5.
9. Cf. *Birds* 1638, where Herakles addresses Poseidon as δαιμόνι', ἀνθρώπων ('my good man'), and 1642 ff., where Poseidon muses on the succession 'if Zeus dies'.
10. Cf. M. S. Silk, 'The People of Aristophanes', in C. B. R. Pelling (ed.), *Characterization and Individuality in Greek Literature* (Oxford 1990), who argues that Aristophanic character is flexible *because* non-realist.
11. Above, p. 195.
12. Above, p. 190–1.
13. Cf. S. Halliwell, 'Laughter in Greek Culture', *CQ* 41 (1991) 286, who argues that laughter at one's enemies is a reflex of shame-culture, the fear of which is 'voiced with a special intensity in heroic contexts'. He aptly instances Megara's hyperbolic claim (*Her.* 285 f.) that hostile laughter is worse than death itself.
14. I do not believe that either Ajax (*Ajax* 303) or Kassandra (*Tro.* 406) belong in this category, as Taplin claims. (i) Ajax's laughter is the conventional taunting of one's enemies; it happens to take place during the course of his hallucinatory madness but is not *in itself*

deranged, despite later acquiring proverbial status (cf. Leutsch–
Schneidewin, *Corp. Paroem. Graec.*, s.v. *'Αιάντειος γέλως*). In any
case, note that his return to sanity is accompanied by corrective (and
generically proper) laments (308, 310, esp. 317–22). (ii) Kassandra's
laughter is not, as the chorus suppose, an irrational expression of
pleasure at her personal and family misfortunes, but a conventional,
derisive reaction to what she prophetically sees in store for the Greeks
after her marriage. Choral distichs seldom display conspicuous
insights into the speeches they follow, and here the chorus confess to
the puzzling obscurity of her words (407); only Talthybios thinks
them mad (408). As elsewhere, Kassandra sees a world which is real
but as yet hidden from others.

15. Cf. Silk, below, pp. 471–2.
16. This is not to say that innocent laughter, or at least, the joy and plea-
    sure it indicates, is not to be found in tragedy; Helen, for example,
    experiences them in her reunion with Menelaus (*Helen* 625 ff., 632
    ff.). Compared with the cancelled laughter of Elektra in Sophocles,
    discussed by Taplin (above, p. 191), Helen's emotions raise further
    questions about the definition of 'the tragic'.
17. Above, pp. 191–4.
18. J. Herington, 'The Influence of Old Comedy on Aeschylus' Later
    Trilogies', *TAPA* 93 (1973) 113–25.
19. Cf. G. M. Sifakis, *Parabasis and Animal Choruses* (London 1971)
    73 ff.
20. As P. Ghiron-Bistagne, *Recherches sur les acteurs dans la Grèce antique*
    (Paris 1976) 207 ff.
21. Though the frozen action at the end of *Clouds* seems to contemplate
    it.
22. Above, p. 194.
23. For discussion of self-referentiality in tragedy, see Goldhill, *Reading
    Greek Tragedy*, chs. 10 and 11, and, more sceptically, D. M. Bain,
    'Some Reflections on the Illusion in Greek Tragedy', *BICS* 34 (1987)
    1 ff. (esp. 8–12). I suspect that the type of self-reference suggested
    here falls uncomfortably between two of the categories of irony pro-
    posed by Rosenmeyer (below, pp. 497–519)—a kind of systemic
    Fiktionsironie.
24. Above, p. 198.
25. Cf. Wilamowitz, *Aischylos Interpretationen* (Berlin 1914) 185: 'Und in
    die ὀλολυγή, zu der der Chor der Geleiter auffordert, wird das Volk im
    Theater einstimmen.' Similarly A. Sommerstein, *Eumenides*
    (Cambridge 1989), on 1047: 'The singer or singers probably here
    again turn to the audience . . . and thus the *Oresteia* ends with a united
    cry of triumphant joy from over ten thousand mouths as all Athens

hails the birth of a new era.' Taplin's description of the imperatives in
1039 and 1043 = 1047 as 'all-inclusive' implies his agreement with
this view. For suggestive comparisons with the Panathenaea, cf. A.
M. Bowie, 'Religion and Politics in Aeschylus' *Oresteia*', *CQ* 43
(1993) 27 ff.

26. Above, pp. 198–9. Taplin's main arguments for his view of *Eum*. have
been developed elsewhere and are not discussed here: P. Wilson and
O. Taplin, 'The "Aetiology" of Tragedy in the *Oresteia*', *PCPS* 39
(1993) 169–80.

27. The estimate of Sommerstein, *Eumenides*, 278. He takes 1035 and
1043 as directed to the performers, and 1039 and 1047 to the audience,
which suggests a musically reinforced merging of spectators and play.

28. Cf. K. Elam, *The Semiotics of Theater and Drama* (London 1980) 90.

29. Above, p. 198.

13

Tragedy and Collective Experience

JOHN GOULD

My subject in this paper is the tragic chorus. I shall concentrate, in particular, on the contribution that the chorus makes, through its fictive identity and the development of that identity into a dramatic role, to the construction of tragic meaning. In doing so I shall try to bring into focus an issue that I believe has been causing problems in a number of the topics discussed in these papers, namely the fictionality of tragedy and of its chorus, and to point to some important consequences of that fictionality.

Aristotle (notoriously) could define 'tragedy' without reference to the chorus,[1] but we can hardly do so. Despite our proper concern with the 'heroic temper', if we are trying to clarify for ourselves the notions of 'tragedy' and 'the tragic', in their fifth-century Greek context at least, we must inevitably come to grips with the essential and distinctive part played by the chorus in our construction of such terms.

Indeed, in the light of recent research, we are hardly likely to be tempted to do otherwise. New models of 'the tragic' have offered us, among other things, new ways of conceptualizing the role of the chorus, ways which, evidently, have considerably greater attractiveness than what I hope I can take to be the worn-out and never very fruitful notions of 'the ideal spectator' and 'the poet's voice' (though I shall return to the latter).[2] Not only do we have the highly influential model proposed originally by Jean-Pierre Vernant and recently given vigorous expression by Oddone Longo in the opening essay of *Nothing to Do with Dionysus?*,[3] but we have also Jack Winkler's own radical attempt to redefine the dance-song of the chorus as 'the ephebes' song';[4] we have Albert Henrichs's illuminating and important analysis of the ideas of 'choral self-referentiality' and 'choral projection' in two related and recently published papers;[5] and we have Peter Wilson's as yet unpublished

Cambridge doctoral thesis on the tragic *chorêgia*.[6] Moreover, Simon Goldhill has given new impetus to discussion of the perennial issue of the ritual and ceremonial context of the fifth-century performances of drama at the City Dionysia (which Goldhill calls the 'preplay ceremonies').[7] Any discussion of that topic must have major implications (though they are not among those specifically addressed by Goldhill in his article) for our response to the chorus, as to every other aspect of the tragic performances. Winkler, Wilson, and Goldhill have thrown new light on the 'civic ideology' of these performances, Henrichs and Calame on their place in the ritual processes of the *polis*. My own concern here is with the somewhat different issue of the dramatic role of the chorus within the fictional world created by the performances themselves and with our response to that world. But, as Henrichs has convincingly demonstrated, that fictional world is itself interpenetrated by echoes, resonances, and reflections of the 'real', that is, the ritual, functions of the performances, and therefore I cannot pass by these issues altogether without comment.

However, given the constraints of the occasion, it must suffice if I say that my position on the issues of 'civic discourse' and 'ideology' raised by Goldhill is very much closer to his own than it is, say, to that implicit in the characterization of the Dionysia offered by Oliver Taplin in 1978,[8] which Goldhill himself quotes at the beginning of his article. Equally, I share Henrichs's perception that there is a kind of transparency to the fictive world of Greek tragedy which allows us from time to time to perceive the ritual function of the choral dance-song through its boundary walls, while remaining wholly within what we awkwardly call the 'dramatic illusion'. I confess that I have more difficulties with Jack Winkler's model of the choral performances of the tragic theatre as 'rehearsals of manhood' and as quasi-military display: I remain unconvinced by his arguments. But these are questions which for the present I must leave aside.

Instead, I will begin by trying to define the role of the chorus in the tragic experience by what I think it is not. To do so, I will go back to what I shall call (*honoris causa*) the Vernant model, and that will lead me into my central theme of the fictive identity and role of the chorus and what it contributes to our understanding of 'the tragic'.

Oddone Longo's formulation of the Vernant model, which he

puts forward in the context of a general characterization of fifth-century drama as 'the theater of the *polis*', is framed as a simple and trenchant assertion of established fact: 'the essence of the chorus, the essential and distinctive feature of Attic drama, must be recognised in its role as "representatives of the collective citizen-body"'.[9] The account of Vernant and Vidal-Naquet is formulated with greater subtlety and spelt out in more detail: I shall try to summarize. For them, tragedy is for its audience the experience of a double vision of traditional myth, in which the chorus embodies 'the collective truth, the truth of the mean, the truth of the [democratic] city'. This 'truth' is set against 'the excess' of the heroic figures of the tragic fiction, who, by contrast, belong to an 'absent' world, 'separated' from the city, and represent the 'otherness' of the heroic code as it appeared to the fifth-century dramatists of the Athenian *polis* and to their audience.[10]

Now the burden of this paper is indeed that the chorus brings to the fictional world of Greek tragedy an experience alternative to that of the hero, and one that is of its essence both 'collective' and 'other'; that its response to the events enacted in that world is the collective response of a group; and, further, that such a collective response is not a tired survival from remote, putative, 'origins' but of the essence of ancient Greek conceptions of 'the tragic' in the fifth and fourth centuries BC. So far I would agree with Vernant. These are notions which I shall try to elucidate in what follows. But, as I have argued before,[11] this particular formulation of that 'collective experience' has fatal flaws and, I would suggest, must be abandoned. Quite apart from such arguably marginal considerations as the fact that the dance-song of the chorus and its ritual function long antedate the democratic city and that (more significantly) it is the actors who play the heroic roles, and not the chorus, that the *polis* itself collectively pays and equips, through its principal official, the eponymous archon,[12] two more central facts tell decisively against it. The first is that the song of the chorus is expressed in a language yet further removed, in its non-Attic dialectal colouring as well as in its diction and syntax, from the formalized 'speech of the city' given to the actors who play the heroic protagonists: it is, for its Athenian audience, an alien and strangely 'distant' tongue,[13] which could indeed be called the speech of the 'other'.

The second fact, even more crucially central to the issues we are discussing, is that, within the fictional world of the play, the chorus, with only two exceptions in the surviving plays, enacts the response to events, not of representatives of the citizen body, but precisely of those whom the democratic city of Athens and its institutional core of adult, male citizen-hoplites has defined as marginal or simply excluded from the controlling voice of 'the people'. The tragic chorus is characteristically composed of old men,[14] women, slaves, and foreigners (the last often non-Greeks as well as non-Athenians). By combining two or more of these categories to produce a chorus, say, of female non-Greek slaves, the chorus may indeed be perceived by the citizen audience as doubly, or even triply, marginal.

The exceptions are highly instructive:[15] the choruses of *Ajax* and *Philoctetes* are indeed composed of adult males, 'of the city' perhaps, but in both cases they are the sailors who crew the hero's ship and in both they are utterly dependent on the hero and his status, to the extent that in *Ajax* the chorus, helplessly despairing in the face of the hero's loss of honour, are reduced almost to ecstatic incoherence by their momentary and mistaken hope that after all Ajax has escaped the consequences of his mad attack on the Greek heroes,[16] while in *Philoctetes* the chorus show themselves at the outset incapable of acting without the hero's instruction and continue bound to him in dependence throughout the action.[17]

It is surely hard, if not, as I would myself wish to argue, impossible, to imagine a 'civic discourse' which is perceived as giving authoritative voice to the democratic *polis* and its values through the collective utterance of such groups as these.[18] (That, I think, remains true whether or not we believe, as Winkler argues, that such collectivities within the fiction are in reality being performed by a structurally significant segment of the male population, the ephebes, or are in some sense perceived, as Henrichs suggests, as engaged in ritual action on behalf of the *polis*. It is their fictional identity, their dramatic persona within the overall fiction of the play, that must determine our response.)

What I have called the 'marginality' of the chorus requires further definition. I mean, not so much distance from the centre of action and decision in the imagined world of the play, nor distance from the audience's centre of attention (both of these things may be involved in any given play, but they are not of themselves definitive of the choral role). I mean rather a sort of 'social' marginality within the imagined social structure implicit in the world created by the tragic fiction. It is that 'social' marginality that in the first place deprives the chorus of tragic authority (most obviously of the power to initiate or control action, except by the exercise of indirect and often devious pressure).[19] And it is that exclusion from tragic action which in turn surely rules out any reading of the chorus's role as that of expressing the authority of the democratic *polis* and its dominant values in opposition to an alternative and competing value-system, that of the heroic, 'excessive', protagonists.

The two plays called *Suppliant Women* will provide a first illustration of the point that I wish to make. In each play, despite the total difference in the issues involved, the chorus of women are in one sense at the very centre of the play's tragic action: the playwright has chosen to make them the focal point of the dramatic tensions of the play and of its critical decisions. But this is a highly ambiguous centrality. In each case, it is tied to an ultimate and 'socially' defined inability, as women, to determine their own lives. The issue of whether or not they are to be given asylum and protection, whether their claims (in the one case, not to marry their male cousins; in the other, to recover the dead bodies of their sons and give them honourable burial) are to be enforced against the threat of opposition from powerful males, is an issue that they themselves are not, as women, empowered to resolve: they are in the hands of (male) others. They are thus simultaneously central and marginal to the action; in both cases, doubly marginal, since they are not only women but also foreigners and outsiders (seemingly, at least) within the imagined world of the play.

The chorus is thus, even here, not a tragic agent. It is rather the locus of an unresolvable tension between intense emotional involvement in, and exclusion from, tragic action: the chorus are both the prisoners and the passionately engaged witnesses of tragic experience. The two *Suppliant Women* plays present an extreme version of that tension, but in a vitally important sense it is a tension which is everywhere definitive of the choral role within the fictional world of tragic drama.

I am not arguing that the marginality of the chorus, thus defined, precludes it from representing an alternative voice, the voice of the 'other', opposed to the heroic voice, within the dramatic fiction: on the contrary. But the task that now faces us is precisely that of defining the complex nature of the 'otherness' of the chorus. The remainder of this paper will involve an attempt to analyse that complexity.

Let me begin with some representative plays. Among the choral roles which are most revealing of the potential complexities of the chorus's 'otherness' are those of the groups of women, often slaves and captives of war—exiled from their own country and thus deprived of all status within the imagined community of the play—which Euripides increasingly chose to give to his choruses.[20] Such groups, both by gender and by circumstance, stand indeed at the opposite pole of experience to the heroic male figures who are commonly central to the traditional stories, and their songs thus serve to polarize response to tragic action. But while thus confronting two opposing experiences, Euripides simultaneously creates a further perspective, in those plays which place a woman at the centre of the tragic action (and they are the majority of his plays),[21] by setting up a single axis of dramatic tension which aligns, rather than confronts, female protagonist with female chorus and thus enforces a point of view from which the 'heroic' world of men is seen as wholly alien: sometimes frighteningly and violently destructive, sometimes distant and incomprehensible, sometimes despicable and without honour.

But gender alone is not of itself necessary to constitute the 'otherness' of the chorus's voice. More important perhaps (and here we encounter a further aspect of what defines its dramatic role) is the fact that this voice articulates a collective, 'anonymous' experience and response to events. The central, heroic characters of the tragic action struggle to maintain and enforce an individual identity and authority and to impose meaning on the flux of events in terms of that identity, the individual 'I'. The heroic 'I' is focused upon a name; and here it is worth pausing for a moment to register the full significance of naming, and the difference between the named and the unnamed. The hero has a name which is central to his identity: no one who has read or seen the first encounter between Philoctetes and Neoptolemus in *Philoctetes* could forget the fact.[22] The hero fights to maintain his tragic identity in terms of that name: witness the Oedipus of *Oedipus Tyrannus* and his repeated use of an emphatic, ringing 'I', indissoluble from his name.[23] He also has an individual ancestry which is part of his name,[24] and he commonly lives out the 'meaning' of that name.[25]

The chorus, on the other hand, though they too articulate experience in terms of 'I', far more often than as 'we', do so without a name.[26] Their 'I' is a collective first person, not the voice of an individual defining his or her self-awareness in terms of difference. They have only a collective identity and a collective 'name', if we can even call it such. That 'name' is commonly derivative, most often from place (Persians, Women of Trachis, Trojan Women, Women of Phoenicia, 'Corinthian Women'; 'Women of Troizen');[27] from role (Libation Pourers, Bone-Gatherers, Suppliant Women, Bacchants); or from collective ancestry (Danaids, Nereids).[28] They have also a collective, 'social' memory. Their multiple voices thus give single, univocal expression in their songs to a group consciousness and to the experience and memory of that group.

One of the most telling indications of that collectivity of experience and response occurs in a unique moment of its sudden undermining and displacement by the stress of events. In Aeschylus' *Agamemnon* (a play that in most respects might stand as exemplary of the Vernant model) the terrible death-cries of the king, long delayed but now at last heard from within the royal palace, suddenly thrust the chorus (the whole chorus and not just its *koryphaios* or headman)[29] into spoken language and, in an unparalleled moment of formal dislocation of tragic decorum, fractures its unity of response. The familiar, collective voice of the chorus, giving expression to a unified perception of experience, is suddenly broken down into a sequence of diverse, dissonant voices by the stress of traumatic occurence.[30] That much is clear from the adversative language of the pairs of spoken trimeters. The fragmentation of the chorus is ironically introduced by the *koryphaios'* exhortation: *alla koinôsômetha* ('let us take common counsel'). The effect is the more stunningly theatrical because the tragic chorus, unlike the chorus of comedy,[31] is never composed of identifiable individuals.[32] But here the collective voice of the chorus, struggling to make unified sense of the experience of the group, is transformed into a play of separate and opposed voices engaged in a recognizably political argument, which issues not in heroic action (despite the chorus's taking-on of the 'heroic' speech of the protagonists) but in traumatized inaction.

Here surely is the exception that proves the rule. It must seem no coincidence that it is again this particular tragic action which, less than 200 lines later, reduces the collective choral voice to the expression of a numb, almost voiceless, despair: 'I am lost for

thought, stripped of suppleness of mind, lost where I am to turn,
as the house is falling. I am afraid, afraid of the beating of the rain
that is bringing down the house, the bloody rain, as shower gives
way to storm.'[33]

To summarize, then: the 'otherness' of the chorus, its essential
role within the tragic fiction, resides indeed in its giving collective
expression to an experience alternative, even opposed, to that of
the 'heroic' figures who most often dominate the world of the play;
however, they express, not the values of the *polis*, but far more
often the experience of the excluded, the oppressed, and the vulnerable. That 'otherness' of experience is indeed tied to its being
the experience of a 'community', but that community is not that of
the sovereign (adult, male) citizen-body.

Let me return to the issue of complexity. For the 'otherness' of
the chorus, we must acknowledge, takes no single form, and no one
formula will define it for us. It can only be defined in terms of the
very variety of the different perspectives which the playwright may
impose upon his tragic fiction. I shall examine some of these differing perspectives, making use once more of the notion of 'marginality'.

There is more than one way of reading what is 'central', what is
'marginal', within the fictive world of the play. I will take two plays
of Euripides to illustrate the point. It would be difficult, despite its
title,[34] to read *Phoenissae* as having the Phoenician women of its
chorus at the 'centre' of its imagined world. They are unmarried
girls; they are not 'of the place';[35] they are not even Greek: they
refer to themselves and to their language and experience throughout the play as 'foreign'[36] and they stress their non-Theban,
Phoenician origins.[37] Nor indeed are they even resident outsiders
but rather creatures of passage, temporarily caught up in the consequences of the internecine struggle that has led to the attack of
Polynices and the Argive army on Thebes. They are where they are
and come within the ambit of the play's events for the entirely contingent reason that they have been unable to make their intended
way to Delphi and to their designated role as temple-slaves and
sacred dancers in the rituals of Apollo. Euripides has been thorough in making them 'marginal', and theirs is, by any definition, an
alternative experience to that of the protagonists. What is the family of Oedipus and its monstrous experiences to these young, alien
girls?

And yet, of course, the experience of this chorus and the experience of Thebes are bound inextricably together (the two are *koina*: they 'belong' together),[38] and what binds them is ties of kinship and shared ancestry; above all, of collective memory. From the first *stasimon* to the last, the memory of the chorus plays over, and their songs rehearse, the long history of Thebes.[39] They lay before us the unravelling of its tragic inheritance, as they have heard it told 'in a foreign tongue' and another place. But at the same time it is their own inheritance, a part, however distant, of the collective, inalienable memory of their own society and their own ancestry. They heard it 'in our houses'.[40] The long perspectives of violence and suffering that their songs open up to view present them, paradoxically, as far more firmly conscious of the rootedness of the play's events than are the heroic protagonists, who seem without exception so far caught up in the immediacy of new horror as to drift almost unanchored in the present flow of catastrophe, as they respond individually and upon the instant to each new crisis. It is the chorus, 'marginal', transient, and alien though it is, rather than any of the play's protagonists, who bring to this imagined world and its terrible events the ballast of memory. It is that memory which stabilizes and centralizes experience as the experience of a group that exists in and through time: the past is made meaningful by being shared with others who draw on the same collective memory, and it is the past which alone can 'place' and stabilize the present.

The experience that this particular community brings to bear on the play's events is not one that it has lived through and witnessed for itself.[41] What the chorus of *Phoenissae* draws on is social memory, the inherited, collective memory of its ancestry, told and heard[42] as story 'in our houses'; and it uses that memory to assert the rootedness of tragic experience.

Phoenissae thus offers us one model of the 'otherness' of the collective experience of the tragic chorus.[43] The chorus of the Euripidean *Electra* offers us another, wholly different, model. They too are women; probably also unmarried girls,[44] but the 'otherness' of experience that they bring to the world of the play does not derive from alien origins. On the contrary, they are firmly 'of the place', participants as native dwellers in the continuing life and ritual traditions of the community. By contrast, in this play it is Electra who is alien; alien by birth, by change of residence, by the ambiguity of her status (married, but still a virgin) and above all by her repeated refusal to participate in the rituals of the community urged on her by the chorus[45] and by the singularity of her own private ritual of dance and song,[46] addressed to her dead father and her absent brother, which defines her for us on her first entry.

Yet in this play too the chorus and its experience, like the setting of the play itself, is in one sense marginal: marginal, that is, to the great events and bloody killings that take place and have taken place always elsewhere. The chorus can only hear of them, like the chorus of *Phoenissae*, by report and hearsay, as story and as the memory and experience of others. But its social and ritual rootedness none the less here too constitutes the 'other', in contrast to the rootless experience of Electra and Orestes: the chorus belongs and they do not.[47] Its cohesion of response and its participation, even as young girls, in the social memory of the community[48]—these things serve to define the fragmented world of Agamemnon's children as itself uprooted and displaced from its centre.

Here then are two very disparate ways in which the collective experience of the chorus can serve to define, by difference and opposition, the 'heroic' isolation of the protagonists. Both strategies for handling the choral role have analogies in other plays of the fifth-century tragic theatre. The ambiguous 'otherness' of the chorus of Phoenician girls has its parallel in the much earlier chorus of Aeschylus' *Suppliant Women*. That chorus too is a chorus of 'foreign incomers'[49] who yet intimately, even threateningly, share in the traditions and memory of the community to which they have come. They are perceived by those of the place as un-Greek and alien[50] in every aspect of their appearance; as Libyan, Egyptian, Indian, or even, but for their lack of bow and quiver, as the ultimately alien, as Amazons.[51] But these outsiders too prove to be the inheritors of a social memory which tallies at every point with that of the Argive king himself. They too, in their stichomythia with the king, recall the past in the language of oral tradition with which we are becoming familiar in the utterance of the tragic chorus.[52]

Of course, there are differences from *Phoenissae*: in *Suppliant Women* the cause of the chorus, as we have seen, is central to the action of the play, and they have a male *prostatês*, 'a champion', to engage in tragic action on their behalf. But in the end it is the social memory that they embody and deploy, and the collective expression that they give to a single will, the will of the group to press home the ritual force of the act of supplication, that forces the reluctant king of Argos to commit himself to their cause. And, as in *Phoenissae*, the language of the chorus invokes the long reach of inherited memory, which here stretches back to the 'fertile heifer', Io.[53] Repeatedly they recur to that distant past, to Zeus, Hera, and Io, not merely as the grounding of their claim for protection but also because the stability of the certain past stands in reassuring counterpoint with the uncertainties of the present.

In Sophocles' *Trachiniae* we encounter yet another chorus of unmarried girls who, as in Euripides' *Electra*, are representative of the place where the fiction of the play is set, who invoke its landmarks[54] and prepare excitedly to participate in its rituals.[55] They bring to the tragic action of this play and to its fictional world an experience which is altogether 'other' than that of Deianeira, who, born an Aetolian and living once in her father's house at Pleuron,[56] found herself the prey of monstrous, barely human suitors who engaged in single-handed 'contest' to take her. She now lives, in the imagined world of this play, the life of an exile, a passing and rootless presence, with a husband who is himself yet more of an outsider, not sharing her exile in Trachis but always on the move, always in some unknown elsewhere; visiting his wife and children as infrequently as a peasant farmer going to a distant field only to sow and harvest.[57] Against Deianeira's constant, unresting fear and unrootedness of place, against the mobility of her anxiety, the chorus bring to bear, at first, a stable and stabilizing, gnomic wisdom[58] and a decisive certainty in moments of doubt.[59] This certainty is gradually replaced, first by an intense emotional empathy with Deianeira's wholly alien experience[60] and a tragic solidarity of feeling which will ultimately carry this chorus, as the tragic action unfolds before them, to the end-point of praying to be deprived even of their home and community, rather than be forced to see with their own, now terrified, eyes the appalling consequences of Deianeira's gift of death to Heracles. The poignancy of that final wish for displacement is the tragic expression of a new, acquired 'otherness'.[61] It alerts us to the fact that the stance of the chorus towards the action of tragedy may be a shifting one.

The stability of a collective response and of collective memory is again not the only mode in which the chorus may deploy its otherness against the tragic agents of the play. Already in *Seven against Thebes* Aeschylus had chosen to invert this relationship by

opposing the martial order and iron control of Thebes, asserted
from the very outset of the play by Eteocles, to a choral body of
young women in the grip of totally destabilizing fear. This chorus
enters *sporadên* ('in ones and twos'), in a highly theatrical reversal
of audience expectations, in astrophic disorder: the syntax of their
entry-song is marked by repeated asyndeton, by anxious questions
and exclamations piled one upon another, and by gasps of terror
and ritual cries. Their terror is countered, and in some measure
calmed,[62] by Eteocles, the tragic representative of the order of the
polis and its (male) citizens,[63] whose clipped certainties are threatened by the driving force of that panic. But panic and the threat of
(female) disorder soon surface once more in the first *stasimon* and
remain, throughout, the characteristic tenor of this chorus's
response to tragic eventuality.[64] Here is a counter-image of collective experience and group response, one which opposes the threatening instability of the emotions of the group to the assertion of a
claim to represent the *polis* and its order, made (and made explicitly) by the tragic protagonist.[65] We meet its ironical counterpart—
though here, of course, with yet more multiple ambiguities in the
interplay of the ideas of 'order' and 'disorder'—in the opposition
between Pentheus and the chorus of Dionysus' female *thiasos* in
Euripides' *Bacchae*.[66]

We now have the beginnings of a sense of the potential variety
attaching to the chorus's fictional identity and dramatic role, and
of the very different kinds of 'otherness' that it may embody.
There are further aspects to that variety. I referred a moment ago
to Aeschylus having 'chosen' to give the chorus of *Seven against
Thebes* the fictive persona that it has. The reference to choice (like
others earlier in this paper) was deliberate. It was meant to remind
us of an important point, often ignored: that the fictive identity of
the chorus is entirely within the free choice of the poet. Traditional
discussion of the chorus tends to start from, and to focus on, its status as a constituent element in the stylization of the Attic theatre,
as though it could be considered merely as an aspect of the inherited (and sometimes, it is assumed, outmoded) conventions of the
tragic form. As a result its presence is often read simply as one of
the constraining factors within which the playwright had no choice
but to work, however unwilling. This way of speaking is misleading and unhelpful: above all because it may blind us to the fact that
it is precisely the chorus which constitutes that part of the tradi-

tional form that gave the playwright his most open field of choice. There is, after all, nothing in the vast majority of the traditional stories which form the matrix of tragic drama in the fifth century that determines the fictive identity of the chorus. Nothing, for example, in 'the story of Medea' (itself a misleading reification of many disparate stories) that dictated Euripides' choice to make his chorus a chorus of Corinthian women. He could as easily have given the play a chorus of Corinthian male elders, or of Colchian, non-Greek slave-companions of Medea.

The playwright's choice of fictive identity for his chorus is therefore a highly significant one, as the example of *Medea* will make clear.[67] But *Medea* will also bring home to us a further point, that the choice of identity for his chorus is only one aspect of the playwright's range of choice with regard to his chorus.

For, having decided that his play was to have a chorus of Corinthian women (married women, not young girls), it was still open to Euripides to give that chorus any one of a wide range of possible roles within the fiction of the play. It did not at all follow from the choice of social identity (arguably, quite the contrary) that this chorus should declare solidarity with 'the Colchian woman' and her household from their first entry.[68] In the event, Medea's manipulation of that solidarity, with her repeated use of 'we women'[69] and her masterly deployment of the vocative *philai*, 'my friends' (but in Greek the gender is marked), placed with supreme rhetorical skill at each turning-point in her self-explication,[70] provides one of the most powerful emotional strands in the play's action. Moreover, when the chorus, with a theatrically stunning proclamation of that solidarity, sings triumphantly, in the electrifying opening strophe of the first *stasimon*, that nature and the world itself are turned upside down by Medea's declaration of her determination to have revenge on the husband who has abandoned and betrayed her, they too do so in the language of gender solidarity.[71] The wholly unexpected turn which their emotional response to events here takes (and I would stress that it is wholly unexpected)[72] seems to echo Medea's own rhetorical use of *para prosdokian* and crescendo.[73] It is as if they have caught her mood and can now only amplify it by their collective voice.

But in fact they remain within their fictive persona as 'Corinthian women'. Gradually they slip from their stance of amplifying Medea's own moral and emotional position and become indeed (for their male audience, at least) more recognizably Greek citizen-wives of Corinth. They turn, in the second *stasimon*,[74] to deprecation of violent passion; to the expression of fear at the possibility of losing homeland and the support of kin, as Medea has done; later, they make a strikingly firm declaration, face to face with Medea and in the name of human morality, that she must not kill her children.[75] And later still they express a now divided emotion at the immediate prospect of the enacting of Medea's revenge.[76] As that revenge is being enacted, off-stage, they give almost conventional voice to the collective response of women and mothers to the pains and vulnerability of motherhood,[77] and they have, finally, no words to say to Medea when faced, in her presence, with the messenger's horrific report of the accomplishment of her revenge on Jason's new bride.[78] Their last, distracted utterance in song frames the death of Medea's children; it ends by turning away from the intolerable dilemmas of solidarity and involvement, and by taking refuge in memory, in the recalling of the only other murderess of her own children that their collective, social memory can now summon up, the god-crazed Ino.[79] Their song closes with the expression, in another mood altogether from their earlier exultation, of the deadly hurt that women and marriage have in past time created. As the tragic action reaches its final movement, they are seen as no more than the 'women standing at the house-door', whom Jason addresses in the only words he speaks to them in the play.[80]

Euripides' handling of the 'otherness' of the choral role in *Medea* is masterly, as their emotional response to tragic experience is made to move in contrary motion to that of Medea herself. They are presented as a group of women united in their collective experience as women, wives, and mothers, and firmly rooted in the imagined world of the play and its collective perceptions. But they are caught up in events that go so far beyond that experience, and are confronted with so powerful an embodiment of daemonic resolve, that their ability to draw on their experience adequately to respond to what occurs around them is in the end overwhelmed and they themselves are almost swept aside in the final confrontation between Jason and Medea. They represent, in the last resort, neither stability nor disorder but the fragility of humanity, of human culture and human memory, when it is met by cataclysmic events and by overwhelming force of passion: their 'otherness' is the otherness of humanity itself within the field of this particular tragic fiction.

We have perhaps one thing more to learn from the chorus of *Medea*. They remind us of one other essential and definitive fact about the tragic chorus: that it exists always and wholly within the tragic action and that it tries, moment by moment, to respond to, and come to terms with, that action, as it unfolds, by bringing it within the circle of their imagined experience. The chorus's voice is not 'the poet's voice'.[81] They also, like the audience (but also, in important respects, unlike them), have at each point still to learn what only the finality of an accomplished end can show: the shape and 'meaning' of a closed and completed action. We misread them as soon as we think of them as in any sense a privileged presence within the tragic fiction,[82] not bounded by its lack of closure but guiding us, the audience, step by step, in the 'correct' perception of events as yet incomplete. When this chorus sing of Medea, 'you will not be able to wet your hand in blood when your children fall before you in supplication',[83] they voice what their experience tells them, but they are wrong. Deceived by the inadequacies of that experience, it is they who are 'unable', unable to take the full measure of Medea's passionate seeking-after an adequate revenge.

The lesson that we should draw from this passage is a general one: that we must read each choral utterance as the response of this chorus, at this point in the tragic fiction, to what has occurred, a response which is no more protected from fallibility than any other. That is an important lesson. When, for example, the chorus of Theban elders in the fourth *stasimon* of *Oedipus Tyrannus* give collective expression to the private hurt of Oedipus and collective recognition, in the very moment of tragic recognition and of catastrophic loss and destruction, to the precise worth of what they see as now destroyed, they voice that destruction as universal and total, the annihilation of human existence itself and of its claim to significance. They take the experience of Oedipus to be final proof of that conclusion.[84]

But we should be misreading this moment in the play, I am arguing, if we take that response, under the impact of its overwhelming emotional power, as some kind of authorial summation of the play's experience and of the human condition, a summation not bound to its immediate context and the moment of its utterance. That is not the role of the chorus; and in *Oedipus Tyrannus* the sequel (more than 300 lines, a fifth of the play), by restoring precisely what had seemed to dissolve in the moment of discovery, namely the human worth and stature of Oedipus, redefines for us the experience of Oedipus and does so in such a way as to 'deconstruct' that earlier rendering of the play's events. It makes the notion that human achievement is quite simply shown to be mere futility and that the very existence of man 'adds up to nothing' appear now, at the end of the play, as no more than what it was: the instantaneous, collective response of empassioned witnesses to wholly destabilizing experience. It marks, in retrospect, this choral utterance as the expression of momentarily unendurable pain, the pain, even, of association with such happenings.[85]

That the chorus exists wholly within the tragic fiction and its imagined world, and that its 'otherness' does not entail any ability to stand outside that fiction, is a proposition fundamental to the argument I am presenting in this paper. So too is the proposition that the chorus is an essential part of that fiction, and that equally of the essence of the chorus's role is the theatrical and dramatic fact of its collective presence. Having once arrived in the *orchêstra*, the chorus is always there: actors come and go but the dramatic space is never empty. It is inhabited by collectivity. The continuity of fictional experience, the sense that there is something still to be lived through and brought to an ending, is powerfully enacted in this continuous massed presence of the chorus.[86] And their presence constitutes a powerful force within the dramatic space. Silent, often for long periods, they are none the less always there, and the pressure exerted by their presence is always, for the audience, a felt factor in the exchanges between the tragic agents.[87]

The nature of that pressure is not a constant (as we have seen in the plays that I have already discussed), save only in that it is the pressure of a constant presence. After the opening scene (and sometimes in it), nothing is spoken, nothing experienced, within the imagined world of the fifth-century tragic fiction, except in the presence of that collective, emotionally involved witness. There is no privacy in that world, and even the silence of the choral presence can exert a palpable force: the chorus of *Medea*, who address and acknowledge the presence of Medea's nurse, Medea herself, Creon, and Aegeus (the last with warm approval), never acknowledge the several comings and goings of Jason, and speak to him, until the final scene, only to confer a searing rebuke.[88] Inevitably we must read into their silent presence an attitude, a stance towards the heroic figures, who must endure their witnessing.

Let me, by way of conclusion, try briefly to place the account of the chorus which I have been offering in the context of the larger issue: 'tragedy and the tragic'. Clearly the chorus is a distinctive feature of Greek tragedy: the 'Chorus' of Shakespeare's *Henry V* or that of Anouilh's *Antigone* are something else. In the Greek tragic theatre, the presence of the chorus within the tragic fiction, their constant and essential presence (they are not an optional part of that fiction), creates a collective, and in some sense 'communal', dimension for 'the tragic' and sets the tragic experience of an Oedipus or an Electra apart from those of Hamlet, Othello, Macbeth, or Lear.

I have argued that what they bring to that fiction is of its essence the presence of a particular collective experience, the sense of a social group, with roots in a wider community,[89] which draws on the inherited stories and the inherited, gnomic wisdom of social memory and of oral tradition, to 'contextualize' the tragic. That context, the context of the collective 'other', which opposes the group and its shared experience to that of the 'heroic' individual, has, as we have seen, no single way of expressing itself within the tragic fiction. The collective experience and the collective voice of the chorus may oppose that of the individual tragic agent in an almost bewildering variety of ways. The choral experience may constitute an image of stability and rootedness, of threatening disorder, of human vulnerability, to stand against the experience of the protagonists; the axis of its opposition to them can be shifted at will. But it cannot be removed. The sense of difference, the sense that the human condition embraces both the individual and the group, and that all experience, even the ultimate, all-consuming experience of 'the tragic', is to be lived through, perceived, and recollected collectively as well as individually, is so essential a part of the Greek tragic theatre that, in this context at least, we cannot perceive 'the tragic' otherwise.

This perception, and the image of the human condition that it embodies, may put us in mind of other fifth-century images of the experience of men and women. The text of Herodotus, for example, both aligns and opposes the experience of heroic individuals and that of collectivities. These collectivities have sometimes no 'heroic' representatives; they too, like the tragic chorus, may advance no further out of anonymity than their collective persona: 'the Chorasmians', 'the Trausoi', 'the Atarantes'.[90] But all have shared and inherited traditions, stories, cultures. Their collective memories are an essential part of Herodotean *historiê*, and his text abounds in the language of oral tradition that we have already encountered in the dance-songs of the tragic chorus and their evocations of the remembered past.[91] The two worlds, that of the tragic fiction and that of Herodotean narrative, share a common perception that the experience of men, even the 'great and astonishing deeds' of men, binds together the one and the many, heroic individuals and collectivities, in a single universe of discourse; and that 'great deeds' and tragic *peripeteiai* may be experienced and perceived differently, even differently remembered, by the individuals who enact the leading roles in them and by the communities who are caught up in, and witness, them but that in time all will come to take their place in the collective memory of men and societies. They are not private, intimate, personal experiences; they are of the domain of the collective. It is this perception which makes collective memory so central a part of Herodotus' perception of the past and which also makes the chorus an indispensable constituent of 'the tragic'. If there is a difference between the tragic vision of Herodotus and the specific notion of 'the tragic' which characterizes Greek tragedy and which we are considering here, it is perhaps that tragedy focuses its perception of 'the tragic' essentially through the fate of the heroic individual, though always against the perspective of collective experience, while for Herodotus the individual and the collective co-exist in both experience and achievement without either being privileged as against the other.[92]

There are, of course, other ways of reading the role of the chorus in Greek tragedy than the one that I have been putting forward in this paper. We can, for example, read it, as it were, diachronically, as another instrument in the ensemble of tragic performance, an instrument for the solo 'voices' to play with or against. But however we read it, the role of the chorus remains a distinctive and necessary part of the tragic perception in ancient Greek culture. It cannot be discarded, and we diminish our understanding of 'the tragic' if we allow ourselves to overlook it.

It is strange that we should ever have seen it otherwise.[93] It is the chorus, after all, whose performances were from the first recorded,

under the name *tragôidoi*, in the state archives of the yearly celebrations of the festival of Dionysus at Athens;[94] in those same
archives, the man whom we call the tragic playwright appears only
as he who 'trained the chorus'; and it was only when the archon
'gave a chorus' to the playwright that a tragic performance was
commissioned and could take place. [95]

Notes

1. Arist. *Poet.*1449[b]21 ff.
2. See pp. 231 and 240–1. The 'ideal spectator' has had a long run in the
   handbooks from its introduction by A. W. Schlegel in 1809, but it was
   always open to the objection that it ignored far too much in the songs
   that choruses actually sing, and at the very least grossly oversimplified
   the choral role. Some of the uses made of the concept have been more
   reductionist still.
3. Winkler and Zeitlin (edd.), *Nothing to Do with Dionysus?*, 12–19;
   English trans. of an article pub. originally in *Dioniso*, 1978. Vernant's
   formulation of the model appears in Vernant and Vidal-Naquet,
   Tragedy and Myth in Ancient Greece and is developed further in
   Mythe et tragédie II (from which my quotations are taken). A good
   example of the 'seepage' of Vernant's model of the tragic chorus into
   general interpretations of the role of the chorus in Athenian society is
   to be found in G. Nagy, *Pindar's Homer: The Lyric Possession of an
   Epic Past* (Baltimore 1990) 410.
4. *Nothing to Do with Dionysus?*, 20–62; *Rehearsals of Manhood*
   (Princeton, forthcoming).
5. ' "Why Should I dance?": Choral Self-referentiality in Greek
   Tragedy', *Arion* 3 (1994/5) 56–111, and 'Dancing for Dionysus:
   Choral Self-referentiality and Dionysiac Ritual in Euripides' (forthcoming).
6. A paper by Wilson ('Leading the Tragic *Khoros*: Tragic Prestige in
   the Democratic City'), which draws on material from the thesis, is to
   appear in C. Pelling and C. Sourvinou-Inwood (edd.), *Greek Tragedy
   and the Historian* (Oxford, forthcoming). A further important contribution to our understanding of the role of the tragic chorus, particularly in relation to that of the chorus of early lyric, is Claude Calame's
   essay, 'De la poésie chorale au stasimon tragique: Pragmatique de
   voix féminines', to appear in *Métis*.
7. *Nothing to Do with Dionysus?*, 97–129; an earlier version appeared in
   JHS 107 (1987) 58–76.
8. *Greek Tragedy in Action*, 161–2. In fairness, I should add that I doubt
   whether Taplin would offer the same characterization now.

9. Longo, 'The Theater of the *Polis*', in Winkler and Zeitlin (edd.), *Nothing to Do with Dionysus?*, 17.

10. Vernant and Vidal-Naquet, *Mythe et tragédie II*, 21–3, 158–9.

11. *TLS*, 26 Sept. 1986, 1071–2; Hellenic Society London Lecture, 14 Mar., 1991.

12. The point is recognized by Vernant and Vidal-Naquet in *Mythe et tragédie II*, 159.

13. Though one already familiar to the audience of tragedy, as Simon Goldhill points out to me, from the archaic tradition of choral perfor-mances.

14. But not old women, as Richard Seaford points out to me—and that in spite of the widespread ancient perception of old women as transmit-ters of oral tradition and above all as tellers of tales, on which see, most recently, Richard Buxton, *Imaginary Greece* (Cambridge 1994) 18–21, 161. Here too tragedy differs from comedy: see J. Henderson, 'Older Women in Attic Old Comedy', *TAPA* 117 (1987) 105–29.

15. It might be argued that there are two further exceptions, in *Oedipus Tyrannus* and *Antigone*. Both have male choruses who are addressed both as ἄνδρες and as πολῖται (*OT* 512; *Ant.* 162, 806, 842) but who, late in the play, are referred to as old men (*OT* 1111; *Ant.* 681, 1093–4): the ambiguity of these references was pointed out to me by Professor Pat Easterling. They seem to have unusual status and to evoke unusual respect from the 'heroic' characters (*OT* 911, 1223; *Ant.* 940, 988; cf. 164–9, 842). But the tenor of their utterances, I would argue, is still not that of 'civic discourse' or 'democratic ideo-logy'. See further n. 18 below.

16. Soph. *Ajax* 693–718.

17. Soph. *Phil.* 135–68. *Philoctetes* is, of course, an exception in other terms also: it is the only surviving Greek tragedy with an all-male cast.

18. There is also the hardly unimportant point that, when civic and democratic ideology is given expression in Greek tragedy, that expression is characteristically assigned to 'heroic' characters, as it is e.g. to the Argive king and to Danaus in Aeschylus' *Suppliant Women* (365–75, 398–401, 482–5, 517–18, 600–24, 739–40, 942–9, 963–5) and, above all perhaps, to Theseus in Euripides' *Suppliant Women* (403–8, 429–45). By contrast, 'ideological' reflection given to choruses tends rather to take a larger sweep and to be religious and 'cosmic' reflection on the human condition; e.g. Soph. *OT* 873–911; *Ant.* 332–75. The obvious apparent exception is, of course, the chorus of Aeschylus' *Eumenides* (esp. 517–30). But even here (ignoring the fact that this is a chorus of female divinities), when the chorus's gnomic injunctions are repeated, at times almost verbatim, by Athena, it is noticeable (and surely significant) that it is the speech of Athena which is cast in

overtly political and secular language and is part of an explicitly 'civic' discourse, while the chorus's injunction is here too given a cosmic and religious tone and context.

19. Professor Kiso of Osaka University and Professor Oka of Kyoto University have both pointed out to me in discussion of this paper that, in a sense, the choruses of the two plays called *Suppliant Women* do initiate action: they do so by the very fact of their arrival in the imagined world of the play. That is true and important: their arrival does indeed constitute a force which compels tragic decision. But it seems to me that they do so as suppliants and not as women: it is the fact of collective supplication and its ritual significance that in these two plays gives the chorus a power of initiative that the tragic chorus in general does not possess. See J. P. Gould, 'Hiketeia', *JHS* 93 (1973) 74–103, esp. 87–90.

20. Fourteen of Euripides' tragic choruses are female, as against three male (I include *Alcestis* in these figures, but exclude *Cyklops*, *Rhesus*, and the [male] supplementary chorus of *Hippolytus*). For Sophocles, the comparable figures are five male, two female choruses.

21. *Medea, Hippolytus, Hecuba, Andromache, Electra, Trojan Women, Ion, Helen, Phoenissae, Iphigenia at Aulis.*

22. *Phil.* 249–56, 260–3. Cf. Ajax' declaration of his tragic identity (*Ajax* 430–40) which links name and parentage. Nor is the issue of naming central to the perceptions only of human protagonists: we should compare the language of Aphrodite's claim to worth in the opening lines of Euripides' *Hippolytus* (1–2).

23. *OT* 6–8, 396–7: cf. the stress on individual parentage once more in 774–6.

24. For example, the naming of Laius in *OT* 267–8.

25. Ajax (*Ajax* 430–2); Pentheus (*Bacch.* 506–8); Polynices (*Phoen.* 636–7); Helen (*Agam.* 681–716); Hippolytus.

26. See the exhaustive treatment of this question by M. Kaimio, *The Chorus of Greek Drama within the Light of the Person and Number Used* (Helsinki 1970).

27. A preliminary survey of the fragmentary plays suggests that that is true also of the plays that we do not have entire. Of identifiable choruses in the fragmentary plays of Aeschylus (24 out of some 70 plays), 13 derive their 'name' from association with place, 5 from ancestry, and another 6 from their role or 'activity' as chorus. (The figures are not precisely reliable, in part because of uncertainties about which plays were tragedies, which satyr-plays.) The corresponding figures for Sophocles, where even greater uncertainty prevails and the proportion of identifiable choruses to known play-titles is even smaller (only 22 out of more than 120 plays), are: place, 9; ancestry, 3; role, 3.

28. *Danaids* presents a problematic exception to the account of the chorus that I am giving here: one member of the chorus of that play (Hypermestra) must have been named and indeed have acted out an individual identity. Was she in fact a member of the chorus? A. Garvie, *Aeschylus' Supplices: Play and Trilogy* (Cambridge 1969) 206–8, discusses this issue but comes to no firm conclusion. A further anomaly, pointed out by Taplin, *Stagecraft of Aeschylus*, 196, is that two plays of the trilogy (the first and last) seem to have an identically composed chorus, a feature for which no parallel in fifth-century tragedy has been produced.

29. I register here the strong sense that this title is one that calls for further consideration: κορυφαῖος is not a common word and occurs most frequently (four times) in Herodotus, always with reference to 'big men' or to issues of hegemony. Do we have to do with a word specifically of the late sixth and early fifth century, a word perhaps whose origins lie in the language of politics? (After Herodotus, the word is attested only in Plato, Demosthenes [with reference to a dithyrambic chorus], and Aristotle, once each, before the Hellenistic period.)

30. *Agam.* 1348–71. A further, but very different, example of the deformation of the chorus's role by the stress of events occurs in Eur. *Heracles* 252–74. This long *rhêsis* of twenty-three iambic trimeters is presumably spoken by the *koryphaios* (on the attribution, see Bond ad loc.) and is by far the longest iambic speech given to a chorus in the surviving plays. (*Helen* 317–29 is the nearest but far shorter parallel and immediately precedes another gross anomaly in choral behaviour: the chorus leave the acting-area with Helen and go, after a sung exchange and a long aria by Helen, within the *skênê* building. A new 'prologue' follows, on an empty stage.) In *Heracles* it is evident that the murderous threats of Lycus require immediate and 'heroic' response: neither the aged Amphitryon nor Megara, as we have seen, is capable of such a response. Thus the pressure of tragic events of itself thrusts the chorus out of its normal role into filling a theatrical vacuum. The breach of choral decorum gives expression to the anomalous nature of this tragic action. Bond (ad loc.) may be right in thinking that Euripides had the *Agam.* passage in mind in writing this scene.

31. For 'named' chorus-members in comedy, see e.g. Ar. *Ach.* 220; *Vesp.* 230 ff.; *Lys.* 254 ff., 365, 370.

32. But see n. 28 above.

33. Aesch. *Agam.* 1530–4.

34. Which is thus already problematic (not to say deconstructive?).

35. The point is rightly stressed by Calame, 'Poésie chorale'. Contrast *Trachiniae*: see above, p. 227.

36. βάρβαρος, used by the chorus of themselves: *Phoen.* 679–80, 819, 1301; cf. 1509. Tyre is 'my city': 214.

37. Eur. *Phoen.* 202–10.
38. κοινόν: *Phoen.* 239–49; cf. 16, 450, 692, 1016, 1222, 1323, 1483, 1572, 1709. The word and its derivatives haunt and echo through the play.
39. As Calame points out ('Poésie chorale'), the chorus of *Phoenissae*, unlike that of *Seven against Thebes*, do not pray for divine rescue from the present and future threats which menace Thebes: instead their songs are focused on a narrative of the city's past, and narration, not prayer, is the characteristic mode of their songs.
40. Eur. *Phoen.* 819.
41. Not, that is, like the experience of the going of the Argive host to Troy which the chorus of old men in *Agamemnon* recalls from its own collective experience: *Agam.* 40, 72–82, 248.
42. ἀκοή: *Phoen.* 819, 1480.
43. For a sensitive and illuminating reading of the choral songs of *Phoenissae* from a somewhat different standpoint, see M. Arthur, 'The Curse of Civilization: The Choral Odes of the *Phoenissae*', *HSCP* 81 (1977) 163–84.
44. Eur. *El.* 174, 761: see Henrichs, 'Dancing for Dionysus', n. 10.
45. Eur. *El.* 167–212, 310; 859–82 implies at least a partial acceptance.
46. Ibid. 112–66. The dance and prayer together form a strangely 'autistic' ritual act: the stage is empty and the imperatives, apart from the first, appear to be addressed to the dancer/singer herself (see Denniston ad loc.).
47. Eur. *El.* 169–74, 297–9, 452–7, 699–706.
48. Witness their telling of the story of the golden lamb, brought 'once' by Pan to Mycenae, which initiated the destruction of the ruling house: they tell it as a 'report [which] survives in the old stories' (701–2).
49. ἐπήλυδες: Aesch. *Suppl.* 195; cf. 277, 401, 500.
50. Ibid. 234–5.
51. Ibid. 279–89.
52. Ibid. 289–326: φασίν (twice) / φάτις / λόγος / καλοῦσιν . . . οἱ Νείλου πέλας.
53. Ibid. 40–56 (note esp. their characterization of the message that they bring: νῦν ἐν ποιονόμοις ματρὸς ἀρχαίας τόποις τῶν πρόσθε πόνων μνασαμένα), 274–6.
54. Soph. *Trach.* 633–43.
55. Ibid. 205–24.
56. Ibid. 6–9.
57. Ibid. 31–5, 38–41.
58. Ibid. 122–40.
59. Ibid. 385–8, 588–9, 592–3, 723–4.
60. Ibid. 497–530, 647–52, 841–62, 893–5.
61. Ibid. 950–61 (their last song in the play): εἴθε . . . γένοιτ' ἔπουρος ἑστιῶτις αὔρα ἥτις μ' ἀποικίσειεν ἐκ τόπων.

62. Aesch. *Sept.* 203–64.
63. Ibid. 1–20, 30–5.
64. Ibid. 419 τρέμω; 564–7 τριχὸς δ'ὀρθίας πλόκαμος ἴσταται; 720 πέφρικα; 764 δέδοικα; 790 τρέω.
65. See further on this point, P. Vidal-Naquet, 'Les Boucliers des héros', in Vernant and Vidal-Naquet, *Mythe et tragédie II*, 115–47.
66. See 'Mothers' Day: A Note on Euripides' *Bacchae*' (*Winnington-Ingram Papers* [Hell. Soc. Supp. Paper 12], London 1987, 32–9).
67. Just how significant that choice might be we can begin to grasp if we try seriously to imagine *Bacchae*, e.g., with a chorus of Theban male elders or *Antigone* with a chorus of female slaves of the royal household of Oedipus.
68. 'The Colchian woman': *Medea* 132. Solidarity with her household; ibid. 138. Cf. 178 (φίλοισιν) and the explicit statement at 267–8.
69. Ibid. 231, 402–8, 1043; cf. 889–91 for a different but equally rhetorical use of 'we women'.
70. Ibid. 377, 765, 797, 1043, 1116, 1236.
71. Ibid. 415–20: τὰν δ' ἐμὰν εὔκλειαν . . . γυναικείῳ γένει . . . γυναῖκας; cf., with the same implication, ἐμάν 422, ἁμετέρᾳ 423.
72. In contrast to the 'passivity' of their earlier interpretation of Medea's role and theirs as victims, after the scene with Creon: 357–63.
73. Ibid. 364–7, 395–400.
74. Ibid. 627–62.
75. Ibid. 811–13: notice too the chorus's use of γύναι and γυνή in 816 and 818, as they now attempt to reverse the logic of gender solidarity.
76. Ibid. 976–1001.
77. Ibid. 1081–1115.
78. Ibid. 1231–5, followed immediately by Medea's last use to them of the vocative φίλαι.
79. Ibid. 1273–92: NB, once more, κλύω 1282.
80. Ibid. 1293.
81. The 'poet's voice' reading of the chorus's role has had an even longer run than Schlegel's 'ideal spectator': it is already taken for granted, e.g., by the scholiast on Eur. *Med.* 823. The most sophisticated of recent formulations of the 'poet's voice' reading of the tragic chorus is undoubtedly that of T. G. Rosenmeyer's essay, 'Elusory Voices: Thoughts about the Sophoclean Chorus' (*Nomodeiktes: Essays in Honor of Martin Ostwald* [Ann Arbor 1993] 561–71). Rosenmeyer suggests (and here I happily agree with him) that choral songs function, in part at least, as 'free-floating texts . . . statements designed to broaden our horizon, to get us away from the narrow purview of the dramatic agent by folding larger discourses into the tragic design' (ibid. 559). He draws an illuminating analogy between the function

of the choral voice in Greek tragedy and Henry James's use of a 'central intelligence' in his fiction. He goes on to illustrate his argument with a close and perceptive reading of the second stasimon of *Oedipus Tyrannus* (863–910) and concludes that the voice we hear in this song is indeed personal and 'confessional' ('a document of confession'), but that 'whether the speaker is the chorus or the author is beside the point': 'the appreciation of the poetry does not require us, or any audience, to bring in the author's point of view as distinguished from the psychomachy disclosed by the chorus' (ibid. 570–1).

82. A variation on the 'ideal spectator' characterization of the chorus, one which has its roots in Nietzsche, is put forward by Michael Silk in Silk and Stern, *Nietzsche on Tragedy*, 267–8. Silk sees the chorus not as a 'privileged presence' but as a voice whose thoughts have the capacity to be 'disembodied'. In Nietzsche's phrase, they offer 'metaphysical consolation . . . from another world [against the tragic destruction of individuals]', a consolation which carries implications of 'cosmic insight' and which is well exemplified by the first *stasimon* of Sophocles' *Antigone*, the πολλὰ τὰ δεινά ode. The chorus is able to draw on such insight only in its songs, where they become something other than the 'individuated world of the drama proper', to which they belong only when they speak 'in character'. That character is a veneer only: in song and music they are 'something else' and the words that they sing 'seem to have been transmitted from a great and mysterious distance'. Between Silk's 'metaphysical' account of the chorus and the one I present here (which could perhaps be called 'sociological') there is a major difference in reading but no 'empirical' grounds for preferring one to the other: in the last resort the issue is simply one of alternative readings. My own belief is that Silk underestimates the resources of gnomic wisdom in traditional societies when he writes that 'no Theban elders would have had thoughts like these'. But at all events we are agreed as to the 'otherness' of the chorus and perhaps also that we are in some sense dealing with 'ideal' presentations of inherited wisdom.

83. Eur. *Med.* 862–5.

84. *OT* 1186–8 (ἰὼ γενεαὶ βροτῶν, ὡς ὑμᾶς ἴσα καὶ τὸ μηδὲν ζώσας ἐναριθμῶ), 1193–6 (following immediately upon Oedipus' exit).

85. We can hardly fail to respond, e.g., to the emotional thrust of the repeated questions of the second strophic pair (1204–22): τίς . . . τίς . . . τίς | πῶς ποτε πῶς ποθ'; and of their final terrible wish: εἴθε σ' εἴθε σε μήποτ' εἰδόμαν—the ultimate expression on the part of a tragic chorus of the unbearability of the tragic experience. On these repetitions, see Silk in this volume, pp. 487, 496 n. 73.

86. Exceptions to that constancy of presence, of course, occur but they are very rare: the movement from Delphi to Athens in *Eumenides* (234); the search for the hero in *Ajax* (814); the funeral procession in *Alcestis* (746); the procession to consult the seer, Theonoe, in *Helen* (385: cf. 327–9 and see n. 30 above) are the only examples in the surviving plays. I would argue indeed that the fixity of the chorus within the field of the tragic action is another aspect of its 'otherness': the chorus, unlike the heroic agents played by the actors, cannot walk away from tragic experience. It cannot exit. Hence, in part at least, the poignancy of choral songs such as *Trachiniae* 947–70 and of the 'escape' choruses of Euripidean theatre, so often dismissed as 'irrelevant'. The other side of the coin, in this aspect of the chorus's role, is what Professor Sumio Yoshitake, of Seishu University, Sapporo, has called (in discussion of this paper) the 'impunity' of the chorus: however much threatened by the protagonists of the play, the chorus remains at the end intact to speak, in the majority of plays, the final lines: community survives.

87. A point not lost on the poet of the *Iliad*: it is a palpable factor in the extreme ferocity of the quarrel between Agamemnon and Achilles in the first book that it takes place in the presence of the entire army. So too later, in the quarrel between Diomedes and Agamemnon in bk. 9: this time the point is made explicit, in 9. 50–2.

88. *Med.* 576–8; cf. 1232; contrast 1306–7. For the warmth of their farewell to Aigeus on his exit, after remaining silent during his arrival and throughout the dialogue with Medea, see ibid. 759–63.

89. The tragic chorus is never a random, *ad hoc* gathering of unconnected persons: it has the cohesiveness that only consciousness of a group identity, and of a wider community of which it is part, invariably gives it.

90. These last, Herodotus writes, are 'the only people that I know of to have no names': 4. 184.

91. Words such as λέγεται, λέγουσι, λόγος (in the sense 'account', 'report', 'tale': the commonest meaning of the word in Herodotean usage), ἔπος, φάτις, φήμη, κληδών, ἀκοή, μῦθος (the last, in Herodotus, used only on two occasions, each time with the implication of disbelief: contrast Eur. *Ion* 196–7: ἆρ ᾽ὃς ἐμαῖσι μυθεύεται παρὰ πήναις).

92. I owe both the question I address here and in part the formulation of my response to it to a helpful comment by Michael Silk.

93. It is yet another aspect of the central significance of the chorus to the tragic fiction that it is the chorus which largely defines and mediates for us the imagined 'world' of the play. In the *Oresteia*, for example, it is the change of choral identity from one play to the next which redefines the 'world' of each play in relation to the last. The 'political'

world of *Agamemnon* is defined by its chorus of male Argive elders and the pervasively 'political' tone of their collective voice; the shift to the more *oikos*-oriented world of *Choephori* is engineered by the introduction of a new chorus, this time of female slaves of the household; and though in the closing lines of *Choephori* we are alerted to the imminence of a further shift, to a world peopled by divinities, it is only with the new chorus of *Eumenides* that the reality of that world is established. The shifting 'worlds' of the *Oresteia*, which are thus mediated by changes in the fictive identiity of the chorus, may go a long way to answering the anxieties felt by Dr van Erp Taalman Kip about the changing perspectives within which we view characters in the course of the trilogy: see pp. 119–38 in this volume.

94. *IG* ii², 2318 (the so-called Fasti) = TrGF DID A 1 Snell: see also Pickard-Cambridge, *Dramatic Festivals of Athens*² (corrected edn.), 104–7.

95. Cratinus fr. 17 K–A provides the earliest use of the phrase χορὸν διδόναι (as it happens with reference to the archon's refusal of a chorus to Sophocles), but there is no good ground for not believing that it is the *terminus technicus*, for tragedy as well as comedy, throughout the history of the Dionysia. See also Pl. *Leg.* 817d7; Arist. *Poet.* 1449ᵇ1 f.

This paper is a revised version of my contribution to the London conference: it has benefited from the fact that I was subsequently able, first, through the generous invitation of the Japan Academy under its exchange scheme with the British Academy, to read it also at seminars in the Universities of Tokyo and Kyoto; later, while teaching at Stanford University, I was also able to read it to audiences at Stanford, Chicago, and UC Berkeley. I would like to thank Claude Calame, Albert Henrichs, and Peter Wilson for their generosity in allowing me to see unpublished work, and my audiences in Japan and the United States for penetrating and helpful criticism.

14

Collectivity and Otherness—The Authority of the Tragic Chorus: Response to Gould

SIMON GOLDHILL

for John and Jill Gould

Aristotle's startling refusal to consider the role of the chorus in tragedy is a striking demonstration of how a view of the chorus can only emerge from, and in turn inform, a general theoretical perspective on 'tragedy and the tragic'. 'The fundamental premises of Aristotle's theory of poetry and tragedy virtually dictate the devaluation and neglect of choral lyric', writes Halliwell, who may indeed be right to see the confusions of the modern debate on the tragic chorus partly at least as the legacy of Aristotle's strategic exclusion of the collective song from his privileging of agency and causality, practical reasoning and action, as the essence of tragedy.[1] John Gould's refusal of the Aristotelian guide-lines shows his characteristic sense of the scope of a question: I can only agree with his insistence that a treatment of the chorus will be necessary 'to clarify . . . the notion of tragedy and the tragic in the fifth-century context at least',[2] and, what is more, that such a discussion will necessarily involve a wide series of questions about collectivity, authority, ritual, and status. In what follows, I want to pick up three points where Gould's account seems particularly telling, and, secondly, to explore three areas where Gould's position seems to need further development.

The first critical thrust of Gould's argument that I wish to pick up is the challenge he poses to what he calls 'the Vernant model'. In particular, Vernant's construction of the chorus as the collective on stage representing the collective of the audience—which redrafts the formula of the 'ideal spectator' as 'a college of citizens . . . to express the feelings of the spectators who make up the civic community'[3]—is not merely insufficiently sensitive to the different and often liminal roles of the chorus, but also distorts the complexities of the relation between the audience, the chorus, and the action. I will later be raising some questions about the manner in which this critique is developed by Gould, but it is worth emphasizing from the start that the notion of the *ideal* (or idealized) *spectator* plays a fundamental role in the way in which Vernant links his understanding of the chorus both to his general and well-known theories of the polyvalence of tragic language, and also to an idea of 'the tragic' itself. For Vernant follows his discussion of the necessary ambiguity and tension of tragic language with the claim that 'it is only for the spectator that the language of the text can be transparent at every level in all its polyvalence and with all its ambiguities. Between the author and the spectator the language thus recuperates the full function of communication that it has lost on the stage.' For Vernant, the spectator has a clear view of ambiguity, then, and it is through this recognition that he 'acquires a tragic consciousness'[4] (*conscience tragique*), that is, the *anagnôrisis* integral to tragedy and the tragic. The chorus as collective thus mirrors and directs the audience in its role as collective spectator, but it is only the audience that achieves 'tragic consciousness'. There are already, then, fundamental differences that ground the analogy between chorus and audience, the ways in which the chorus can 'represent the audience'. What needs further consideration, however, is the idealization that allows the audience a clear vision of ambiguity. When Cassandra in Aeschylus' *Agamemnon* sings her prophecies to the chorus, a scene of misunderstanding is enacted before the audience, but is it the case that the audience's perception of Cassandra's dense lyric poetry is one of 'full recuperation' of communication? Does the audience not share in a more uneasy sense of the obscurity and power of Cassandra's language? When Ajax delivers the Deception Speech, which is indeed misinterpreted by the chorus, the audience faced by his studied ambiguities may be involved in a more complex process of (failing) interpretation.[5] Tragedy's repeated return to the intractable cannot be fully recuperated by an appeal to the 'clear vision' of the audience (as if *méconnaissance* had no place in *conscience tragique*). Indeed, the *agôn* on stage is mirrored also by an *agôn* in the theatre, not merely in the competition of the festival, but also in the 'strife of warring words' (to use a Euripidean phrase) that tragedy produces in and for its audience. An audience's several and collective relations to a play's language and action involve engagement and negotiation (rereading, misreading, etc.) rather than simply an ideal(ized) spectatorship. The questions Gould poses to Vernant's model open an essential line of criticism, not to retreat from a Vernantian sense of the ambiguities of tragic language into some imagined—idealized—haven of secure meaning, but to develop a more careful understanding of the interaction between the fissured collectivity of the audience and the disseminated language on the stage.

The second point I wish to emphasize is Gould's constant nuancing of what could be called the topography of the chorus, and what Gould calls the chorus's 'social and ritual rooting'.[6] Each element of this phrase seems important. First the 'rooting': choruses typically have a special relationship to the place of the action, whether it is the civic authorities of Sophocles' *Antigone* or the girls of the village in Euripides' *Electra*. When this generalization is not immediately self-evident—say, in Aeschylus' *Suppliants* or *Eumenides* or Euripides' *Bacchae*—there is a specific discourse of topographical placement to define the chorus's role explicitly. In the *Suppliants*, this consists in the appeal for asylum precisely on the grounds of a genealogical and spatial connection, an appeal to be considered 'rooted' in Argos. In the *Eumenides*, the trilogy finds closure precisely by finding a place for the chorus in the ritual, social, and physical topography of the city. (For Aeschylus, what collectivity is becomes a question through such treatments of the chorus.) In the *Bacchae*, the chorus's lack of rootedness, its association with travel from the East, is a central element in the play's articulation of the co-ordinates of inside/outside, city/country, Greek/barbarian. Its lack of rootedness, as with the women of Thebes leaving their houses for the mountain, develops a specific topography of the *polis* and the threat from the outside. So the plays set around Troy—Sophocles' *Ajax* or Euripides' *Trojan Women* or *Hecuba*, say—are specifically concerned with the *loss* of spatial co-ordinates for the chorus.[7] This sense that social identity is grounded in a topography goes back to the *Odyssey* at least, and is one of the major reasons why so many modern performances of Greek tragedy have a difficulty with the chorus: for a modern audience, the connotations and implications of such a rootedness are far harder to articulate, far less easy to appreciate. That this sense of belonging is 'social' emphasizes the correct civic frame for tragedy.

That it is 'ritual' emphasizes the necessary religious and political frame for tragedy. That it is 'social *and* ritual' indicates the necessary overlap between these categories in the *polis*. Above all, what Gould's insistence on 'social and political rooting' requires is a constant awareness of the *place from where a chorus speaks*. All too often in the criticism of tragedy a chorus is treated as a disembodied voice. Gould shows that even when the chorus offers a wide perspective on events, their utterances have a constant framing that cannot be left out of account. The idealization of the chorus as 'the poet's voice' or as the 'privileged spectator' depends on the repression of the place from where the chorus speaks, its rhetorical grounding.

The third strain of Gould's argument I wish to stress is his recognition of the variety in the construction of a choral persona, a variety which Gould places as a subset of 'otherness'. By looking at what he calls the different forms of otherness, he has underlined how difficult it is to come up with a single model to account for choruses in tragedy (at least if that single model is to prove a useful analytical tool). This point, it must be underlined, is not just a retreat from Grand Theory, but rather a comment on the *experimental* nature of tragedy and its leading authors. The existence of a delimited set of extant texts, a *corpus scaenicorum Graecorum*, has too often led to a discussion of the genre of tragedy as if it were a fixed and stable set of rules or expectations. (Aristotle, despite his own developmental schema, is often taken as an authority for this monolithic view of genre.) It is striking that for all the many studies of the origins of the chorus and tragedy itself, all based on negligible evidence, there are so few studies of the generic variation, manipulation, and experimentation in the way a chorus functions. The splitting of the chorus into individual voices in the *Agamemnon*, the exit of the chorus in the middle of the *Ajax*, are well-known and regularly discussed dramaturgic devices. But what other elements of choric dramaturgy need to be discussed? Is there more to be said about the choice of identity and role for a chorus (as Gould suggests), generally as well as for specific plays? Why is there repeatedly a chorus of unmarried, young girls, *parthenoi*, but not of young men, *ephêboi*? (Several non-dramatic factors might be relevant, from the tradition of girls' choral songs to the segregation or isolation sometimes associated with the idea of an ephebe.) Why are choruses specified as 'old men', but never as 'old women'? Although the final procession of the *Eumenides* apparently includes (1027) such a group (*presbutides*: if the line is genuine),[8] is it that old women are not a usual ritual category as a class in the fifth-century *polis* (unlike, for example, 'married, adult women', 'unmarried, young women', 'adult men', *gunaikes*, *parthenoi*, *andres*)—in contrast to the Trojan example of *Iliad* 6. 286–311, and in contrast to the occasional ritual roles for single, specific old women. Indeed, the phrase 'chorus of women' (*choros gunaikôn*) seems to include older and younger women. In the *Lysistrata*, where all editors assume the semi-chorus opposed to the semi-chorus of old men is made up specifically of old women, the ancient Hypothesis gives merely *choros gunaikôn*, and there is no reason to assume that the chorus of the *Hecuba* or *Trojan Women* excludes older women (especially in the light of the example of *Iliad* 6). So too, as Gould suggests, it is possible further to read the chorus as 'an instrument for the solo voices to play with or against',[9] both within particular plays (the relation of Creon and the chorus in the *Antigone*, say) and between different plays (the shifting patterns, say, of support and hesitation between female collective and heroine in the three Electra plays). It is to be hoped that Gould's paper may stimulate further research in this undervalued area.

These three aspects of Gould's argument—the rejection of the 'idealized spectator' model, the awareness of the place from where a chorus speaks, and the awareness of the variety and flexibility of the chorus's functioning—seem to me to be a necessary prelude to what follows, where I wish to explore further and more critically some elements of the central categories of his case, namely, 'the collective' and 'the other'. Gould terms the chorus first 'of its essence . . . collective',[10] and argues that thus the chorus speaks to the privileged place of collectivity as an ideal and practice of democracy (and of the *polis qua polis*). The *response* of the chorus is collective, and thus embodies 'a particular collective experience, the sense of a social group, with roots in a wider community, which draws on the inherited stories and the inherited, gnomic wisdom of social memory and of oral tradition to "contextualize" the tragic'.[11] Thus when the chorus *qua* collective stands in opposition to, or in judgement on, the hero of the drama, this formal tension between group and individual, integral to tragedy, speaks to the tension between individual and collective which is integral to democratic theory and practice. In this general form, Gould's argument is undoubtedly strong and productive. Yet some of the claims that are mobilized in support of this position and some of the conclusions drawn from it seem less well established.

Gould begins the establishment of this position over and against the Vernant model by offering four brief claims, only the last of which is developed at length. Each seems to me to bring problems. First (and least importantly), the ritual dance-song of the chorus is said to antedate the democratic city. Second, the city funds the actors but not the chorus. Third, the speech of the chorus, with its Doric lyricism, is removed from the language of the city. Fourth, the chorus is marginal and 'other' in status and thus cannot speak with authority to or for the city. I shall begin with the first two questions of ritual and funding, and the consequences for the 'representative' role of the chorus. I have three arguments that I think significantly qualify Gould's position.

First, the institution of the *chorêgia* needs a larger place in Gould's economics (and here I draw on the fine study of Peter Wilson, to which Gould also makes reference).[12] Although the city *per se* pays the actors, the act of choosing the playwright, the first task of the eponymous archon in his year of office, is termed to 'grant a chorus', *choron didonai*, and the *chorêgia* is the democratic institution designed to fund this process. The city itself—or the *dêmos*, to use the participants' own rhetoric—required wealthy individuals to support a *choros*. (This was, of course, only one of the many liturgies by which the city's public life from war to celebration was funded.) The resultant conspicuous consumption, culminating in a splendid personal appearance before the greatest collection of citizens in the calendar year, followed by the possibility of the dedication of a victory monument and the celebrations that ensued, invest the role of the *chorêgos* with a particular sociopolitical charge. It is, as Wilson shows, a central element in the contests of status between the male élite to which the law-court speeches bear eloquent testimony. The city as collective *requires* an outstanding individual citizen to fund the collective chorus, and the individual receives the *kudos*, the brilliance (*lamprotês*) of his contribution, displayed before the collective in the theatre, the reward for the burden of the obligation on the individual from and for the collective. The *chorêgia* is, as Wilson has demonstrated, at all levels a way of negotiating the dynamics of individual and collective in the democratic *polis*. So it simply will not do to suggest that the polis's funding of actors but not chorus somehow hinders the chorus from being a representative of the *polis*. From the moment of selection to the moment of performance (and beyond) the chorus is fully inscribed within the politics and economics of power and display that are a foundation of democracy's interplay of individual and group.

Second, the *choros* in the tragedy festival is only one of a range of choral competitions at the Great Dionysia, and throughout the festival calendar of Athens. The civic organization of democracy is strongly in evidence, of course, throughout the festival. In particular, the boys' and mens' dithyrambic events—which involved a thousand people a year merely as performers—were structured as tribal competitions, that is, according to the socio-political divisions of the democratic state. The theatre audience itself may have sat in tribal divisions (tickets and the theoric fund were organized along such lines).[13] In the Great Panathenaia, too, citizens in teams competed in various events as collective representatives of the tribes. The choral singing of the dithyrambic events at the Great Dionysia is thus typically democratic and Athenian in being both tribal and competitive. So are the tragic choruses to be seen as analogous to the other choruses in the festival? To what degree are they different? Masking—a sign of theatrical performance as opposed to dithyrambic performance—is certainly a relevant distancing device, but does it mean that the citizens in the *choros* of a tragedy in the Great Dionysia are viewed in a quite different light from the citizens performing in a dithyrambic chorus in the Great Dionysia? The collective experience of the chorus in this festival is *both* a time-honoured ritual (in that choruses long antedate the democratic order) *and* new and specifically democratic (in that the new organization of the festival is along tribal lines). If the collective response of the chorus is seen as part of the 'essence of the tragic', what happens when the festival is considered as a whole and in its place in the calendar, and the tragic chorus is seen as one of a series of choral performances? 'Ritual' cannot be used as a category to explain away the representative function of the chorus: the festival both democratizes the ritual of choral singing, and requires that the tragic chorus is construed in the light of the culture of choral performance in Athens.

Third, the tradition of choral dance-song as ritual is also, as

Claude Calame's work finely demonstrates, a tradition of educational, ideological performance.[14] The chorus as an educational institution does not disappear with democracy and the *polis*. Indeed, even Plato in the *Laws*[15] says that the standard view of education (*paideusis*) can be summed up as *achoreutos apaideutos*, 'no chorus, no education', no *paideusis* without singing and dancing—and certainly the choral competition of dithyrambs for boys at the Great Dionysia fits into this tradition. Since the performance of tragedy is assimilated to the scenario of the *sophos*, 'the wise man', 'figure of authority', speaking to the *polis*, it is hard not to see the chorus of tragedy drawing on such an educational tradition. (And indeed, learning choral odes is one of the ways that tragedy entered the educational system and the more informal discourse of the educated élite.) The ritual aspect of the choral performance, in other words, far from separating the chorus from any representative or authoritative function, may be thought to draw it towards the position of the authoritative utterance of the *sophos* in the scene of education. I will return to this later. What I hope to have shown so far, however—my first general point—is that neither ritual nor finance can offer a strong case for Gould's central argument that the chorus has no claim to representative or authoritative status.

Let me turn now to Gould's third argument: that the language of the chorus is remote from the city's language by virtue of its Doric colouring and lyric intensity (which is contrasted with the 'formalized "speech of the city" given to the actors who play the heroic protagonists').[16] There is no doubt that the intercalation of choral song and spoken *rhêsis* or stichomythia produces a tension or dialectic fundamental to fifth-century tragedy (and that the iambic metre is said by Aristotle at least to be closest to ordinary speech).[17] But to what degree is choral lyric really 'an alien and strangely "distant" tongue'?[18] It is difficult to judge the effect of tragedy's far-from-thorough-going Doricism. On the one hand, Aristophanes makes fun of dialectal variation, and indeed of Spartans' Doric dialect. On the other hand, choral lyric is traditionally writen in Doric and forms the ritual centre of numerous public and private celebrations—in Athens and throughout Greek culture. When Pindar was hired by an Athenian (as he was on more than one occasion), did the patron expect and receive a poem in 'an alien and strangely "distant" tongue'? Or does the high social class of Pindar's clients already distance them from the *dêmos* to such a degree as to make their example inapplicable? Furthermore, in the classical city tragedy as a genre is already recognized as having a special linguistic register: when Plato has Socrates mockingly regret his own pretentious vocabulary by apologizing for speaking 'tragically', 'like a tragic character' (*tragikôs*),[19] or when Demosthenes attacks Aeschines' bombast as 'putting on a tragedy' (*tragôidein*),[20] there is no suggestion that the perception of the high-flown—alien, distant—element of tragedy is limited to its choral portions. Indeed, when the extensive performances of choral lyrics throughout Greek culture and Athenian society in particular is considered, it seems hard to separate out tragic choral lyric as having an 'alien and "distant" tongue', rather than being one among the many competing tongues of the city of words. My second general point, then, is that the language of choral lyric, despite its difference from other forms of speech in the city, cannot be used to justify the chorus' marginal or non-representative status.

My final general point concerns Gould's fourth and most important claim concerning the marginality or 'otherness' of the chorus. This goes to the very heart of his piece. For central to Gould's argument is the attempt to prove that 'it is . . . impossible . . . to imagine a "civic discourse" which is perceived as giving authoritative voice to the democratic *polis* and its values through the collective utterance of such groups as these',[21] or, in germ, 'social marginality . . . deprives the chorus of tragic authority'.[22] Now, it is certainly the case that the chorus in Aeschylus' *Suppliants* of fifty, half-Greek, black, virgins who claim desperately to be Argives, can be said to embody a range of liminal or marginal statuses, both within the fiction of the play and within the polis of Athens. (It is less clear that the choruses of the *Antigone* or *Oedipus Tyrannus* can be said to have a ' "social" marginality within the imagined social structure implicit in the world created by the tragic fiction').[23] So, too, it is often the case that choruses sing from the 'experience of the excluded, the oppressed and the vulnerable',[24] though what these choruses often sing of is an imagined world of (lost) civic harmony, integration, and fulfilment (as in *Trojan Women*) or a prayer for such political blessings (as in Aeschylus' *Suppliants*). What worries me here is the requirement of a move from social marginality to lack of authority of voice. First of all, there seems to me to be some difficulty in reconciling this position with the further central claim of Gould that the collective voice is used to mobilize 'the inherited gnomic wisdom of social memory',[25] since it is hard to imagine disinvesting such wisdom of all authority. To recognize the authority of such collective, inherited wisdom is not to deny that such wisdom can be shown in tragedy to be insufficient, uncomprehending, and trivial: the chorus often misunderstands the action, and offers generalizations that scarcely account for the actors' torments and violence. Rather, it is to recognize that the mobilization of a collective voice, with its claim to authority, in the democratic theatre is a way of introducing a particular element into the discussions of authority, knowledge, tradition with which tragedy is so concerned. That the chorus can speak with the full weight of a collective authority is crucial to tragedy's explorations of authority, knowledge, tradition within the dynamics of democracy's ethics of group and individual obligations. Second, Attic fifth-century tragedy is played out as 'the drama of the other': there are very few Athenians on stage, and only the *Eumenides* of our extant tragedies reaches the city itself. What difference to the 'otherness' of the chorus does it make that *all* response to tragedy involves projection, sympathy, idealization—a negotiation of 'the other' to find meaning for the self? Apart from the comments in tragedy which explicitly say that wisdom and good advice can come even from servants (and other marginals), and apart from the apparently ironic working of such terms by Euripides, who can have his chorus of Eastern maenadic women—the epitome of otherness—claim to speak for the common man,[26] tragedy's detour through the other is integral to its—authoritative—*sophia*. Third, the ritual role of the chorus, especially when so many choral lyrics return to the resource of the traditions of myth, stands against marginal status, and makes it hard to agree that the chorus cannot have 'in any sense a privileged presence within the tragic fiction'.[27] In short, while Gould is certainly right not to cede the chorus the authority of the poet's voice or of a simple, privileged, determinative view of the action, his rejection of *any* authority or privileged presence inevitably distorts the way that tragedy engages with the question of authority and the collective.

An example will help this final point. When the Furies of the *Eumenides* sing of *dikê* ('justice', 'right')[28] in the second *stasimon* (490 ff.), in a way which presents them in a quite different light from their first wild entrance and violent opening scene, are they singing simply as the Furies at a juncture in the narrative of change

and reversal, or are they drawing on a more general, more authoritative self-positioning, allowing a wider issue to enter the play's
reflection at this point? I take it that the shift between their wild
opening hunting-song and this set of generalizations produces a
productive and interesting ambivalence: the claim to authoritative
status concerning *dikê* will continue to be negotiated in the law-
court and by the final scene's integration of the chorus into the *polis*
precisely as authoritative figures of *dikê*, the *Semnai*, 'The Revered
Ones'. The shift in register of choral utterance between the *parodos* and the second *stasimon* allows the chorus to draw on the privileged position of both the ritual *choros* and a collective (of
divinities), for all that it cannot repress the fact that this is still the
Furies who are singing, and singing at this point in the play. It is
this tension *within* the chorus that the audience is to negotiate. And
since the question of who speaks for *dikê*, in the name of *dikê*, is a
central concern of the trilogy, a question which moves from the
individual household, the *oikos*, to the privileged collectives of law-
court and *polis*, the formal question of voice is never simply a formal issue, but one that goes to the heart of the concerns of the
trilogy. It is, in short, the tension between authoritative, ritual,
mythic utterance and specific, marginal, partial utterance that
gives the chorus its special voice in tragedy.

I will end with an example that will bring together my general
points, and allow me to make my conclusion. In Euripides'
Hippolytus, the nurse uses the example of Zeus' susceptibility to
desire (*erôs*) for Semele as an encouragement for Phaedra to 'bear
up in' or 'dare' *her* 'passion' (*tolma d'erôsa*, 476). The *stasimon* that
follows sings generally of *erôs* and also turns to the example of
Semele, this time as the destroyed female victim. Now here is a
chorus of the women of Troizen singing of that central topic of
desire and of the king of the gods: their account significantly corrects the emphasis of the nurse, in what will be seen to be a highly
prescient way, since Phaedra will turn out to be the female victim
of a divinely plotted tale of desire. How, then, is the difference
between a character's and a chorus's telling of the 'same' story to
be articulated? Is the language of one 'closer' to the language of the
city? Is the logic of fallibility and authority the same in both cases?
By following the sophistic argument of the nurse with a choral lyric
that retells the story, Euripides both uses the authority of the collective chorus to frame the partiality of the nurse's argument with

the traditions of myth, and has a group of women reflect on the dangers of desire in response to their queen's turmoil. As the audience is faced by the question of where desire comes from and how it can be controlled and how it should be talked about, the tension between the *sophia* of the nurse and the *sophia* of the chorus plays a crucial role in the drama.

The collective voice has a particular role to play in the *agôn* of attitudes that makes up tragedy. The chorus requires the audience to engage in a constant renegotiation of where the authoritative voice lies. It sets in play an authoritative collective voice, but surrounds it with other dissenting voices. The chorus both allows a wider picture of the action to develop and also remains one of the many views expressed. The chorus thus is a key dramatic device for setting commentary, reflection, and an authoritative voice in play as part of tragic conflict. This mobilization and questioning of the authority of collective wisdom is one of the most important ways in which tragedy engages with democracy. To make the chorus a central element in 'tragedy and the tragic', as Gould rightly does, is once again to uncover the agonistic, political engagement of tragedy with the discourse of Athens.

Notes

1. Halliwell, *Aristotle's Poetics*, 250; cf., for remarks on legacy, 252.
2. Gould, above, p. 217.
3. Vernant and Vidal-Naquet, *Tragedy and Myth in Ancient Greece*, 10.
4. Ibid. 18.
5. R. Buxton calls this 'bafflement': 'Bafflement in Greek Tragedy', *Métis* 3 (1988) 41–51; Taplin *Greek Tragedy in Action*, 131, notes that this scene 'is deliberately left unclear and unresolved'. For further bibliog. and discussion, see my *Reading Greek Tragedy*, 189–92.
6. Gould, above, p. 226.
7. N. Croally, *Euripidean Polemic: The Trojan Women and the Function of Tragedy* (Cambridge 1994), esp. 174–207, is particularly good on this.
8. See A. H. Sommerstein, *Aeschylus Eumenides* (Cambridge 1989) 280–1, *ad* 1027.
9. Above, p. 234.
10. Above, p. 219.
11. Above, p. 233.
12. P. J. Wilson, 'The Representation and Rhetoric of the Collective: Athenian Tragic *Choroi* in their Social Context' (University of Cambridge PhD thesis).

13. I have recently reviewed this evidence in 'The Audience of Greek Tragedy', in P. E. Easterling (ed.), *The Cambridge Companion to Greek Tragedy* (Cambridge, forthcoming).

14. C. Calame, *Les Chœurs de jeunes filles en Grèce archaïque* (2 vols.; Rome 1977).

15. 654a.

16. Above, p. 219.

17. *Poet.* 1449ᵃ19–20. V. Bers, *Greek Poetic Syntax in the Classical Age* (Yale 1984) 16 n. 42, disagrees.

18. Gould, above, p. 219.

19. *Rep.* 413b.

20. 18. 13; 19. 189.

21. Above, p. 220.

22. Above, p. 221.

23. Above, pp. 220–1.

24. Above, p. 224.

25. Above, p. 233.

26. *Bacch.* 430–1.

27. Above, p. 231.

28. For the different senses of *dikê*, see Goldhill, *Reading Greek Tragedy* 33–56.

15

Everything to Do with Dionysos?
Ritualism, the Dionysiac, and the Tragic

RAINER FRIEDRICH

Dionysos is said to be the 'elusive god' who 'defies definition'.[1] Thus, when we ask the ancient question 'what does tragedy have to do with Dionysos?', we have first to ascertain who this Dionysos might be. Scholarship and Grand Theory since the Romantic era have produced a bewildering plethora of interpretations of this deity. In his important study of the formation of the modern Dionysos (or rather Dionysoi) from Romanticism to post-structuralism, Albert Henrichs observes that 'no other god has created more confusion in the modern mind, nor produced a wider spectrum of different and often contradictory interpretations'.[2] Not only is the resulting picture confusing; it is also depressing. For no other god has been been hitched to more modern ideological agendas than Dionysos. In the process he has suffered a veritable dismemberment—a *sparagmos*—with his *membra disjecta* scattered all over the intellectual landscape in the form of wildly differing concepts of the 'Dionysiac',[3] all redolent of the *Zeitgeist* of modernity (and now of postmodernity). They often reflect the most dubious of our post-Romantic preoccupations: our obsession with the primitive, the savage, the irrational, the instinctual, the collectivist, to name only a few.

Thus, when 'the Dionysiac' is applied as a passe-partout to ancient culture in general and Greek tragedy in particular, as is becoming current in this neo-Nietzschean age called postmodernism, we should be extremely cautious: we must always reckon with the possibility of projecting our modern constructions onto ancient phenomena. Now, Charles Segal has nicely articulated how, in the enterprise of interpretation, construction and projection are hermeneutically inevitable: rooted as they are in their own time, modern critics 'cannot but emerge with a reading that is in some sense contemporary as well as historical'; so there is a 'continual adjustment between the historical uniqueness of an ancient work and the inevitable contemporaneity of subsequent interpretation'; and in this 'lie the incessant changes in our understanding of the past and our constant need for the reinterpretation of the past'.[4] One can take this as a controlling guide or as *carte blanche* for unbridled construction and projection. For us moderns the latter has been true: we have taken extreme liberties with Dionysos and 'the Dionysiac', and clearly upset the balance in favour of the contemporary—with the result that, as Henrichs concludes, 'Dionysus has been so drastically uprooted from his original Greek habitat and transplanted to modern regions where blood is more plentiful than wine that he might not survive.'[5]

Dionysos as the elusive god who defies definition, then, is a post-Romantic phenomenon, the result of the modern confusion arising from claiming the god's good name for various modern ideologies. Henrichs has suggested a way out of this confusion: to go back to the god's original Greek habitat and observe the distinction between the Dionysos of cult and ritual, and the Dionysos of myth. Worshipped as the god of wine and of exuberant life; as the god who instils ritual madness; as the god of the theatre; and as the god of mysteries that promised a happy afterlife, Dionysos was a composite god, like many another ancient deity, and as such not reducible to a unified concept;[6] yet in his original habitat he was well-defined by these well-defined provinces. Within these, Dionysos had his cults, rituals, and festivals, of which the Great Dionysia at Athens was only his most splendid. The notion we form of the god of this festival is that of the genial god of wine, the theatre, and vitality—manifest in ritual wine-drinking, the dramatic *agôn*, and the phallic processions—a notion of Dionysos that has disappeared almost altogether in the bloodshed, cannibalism, savagery, violence, death-cult, irrationalism, and madness in most modern academic conceptions of a rather destructive (and lately deconstructive) Dionysos. The great fallacy, the *prôton pseudos*, of most modern theories of Dionysos and 'the Dionysiac', as Henrichs has shown on several occasions, is their tendency to obscure the distinction between *Dionysiac cult* and *Dionysiac myth*, and base their concepts more or less exclusively on the latter.[7] The two belong together: in general terms, Dionysiac cult and ritual mitigate and tame what is violent and savage in Dionysiac myth. Dionysiac myth usually preserved the memory of ancient tribal savagery,[8] and is in its turn preserved in art and poetry. Modern and postmodern theories of Dionysos derive mainly from Nietzsche's concept of Dionysos, which, in turn, is largely based on the myths and their representations in ancient art and poetry; and these tend to intensify the inherent savagery and violence for artistic purposes. Hence the one-sidedly primitivist, irrationalist, and savage image of Dionysos in many modern theories about him. Henrichs characterizes them as *academic constructs*, deriving ultimately from a *poetic construct*—namely Euripides' representation of Dionysos and maenadism in the *Bacchae*.[9] The academic constructions of Dionysos, not surprisingly, surpass the Dionysos of myth and poetry in savagery and violence. The much tamer and more civilized (and for moderns therefore less exciting) god of cult and ritual who offers his worshippers in his Attic festivals ἀναπαῦλαι τῶν πόνων—'repose from toils'—rather than constant ritual stress and anxiety, has largely got lost sight of.

SETTING THE ANCIENTS RIGHT: FOUR ATTEMPTS AT REINSCRIBING DIONYSOS INTO TRAGEDY

In all that confusion, one of the few certainties about Dionysos is that he was the god of the theatre and that his festival provided the institutional framework for the tragic performances. Yet this certainty is somewhat obscured by the fact that most tragedies had, as the old Greek saying goes, 'nothing to do with Dionysos' (*ouden pros ton Dionuson*).[10] Or so the ancients thought. For them *ouden pros ton Dionuson* ranked as a proverbial platitude and even gave rise to an adjective signifying 'unrelated' or 'inapposite' (*aprosdionusos*).[11] Were the ancients right?

Nietzsche and the Cambridge School

Nietzsche, and many others under his influence, have decided that on this point the ancients needed correcting. For Aristotle, only the beginnings of tragedy had to do with Dionysos. But in Nietzsche's view, Aristotle had thoroughly misunderstood Greek tragedy; and ever since Aristotle had translated his misunderstanding into his theory of the tragic emotions and *katharsis*, aesthetic theory had been out of joint; and Nietzsche was born to set it right. He did so by declaring the Dionysiac the *fons et origo* as well as the essence and the total effect of tragedy. Nietzsche's theory, as the title of *The Birth of Tragedy* signals, follows the genealogical approach: Nietzsche, in Silk and Stern's succinct characterization, 'defines tragedy with reference to its origin and formulates its characteristics *in terms of* that origin'.[12] In genealogical terms, then, tragedy, having originated in the Dionysiac and its ritual, is essentially Dionysiac in vision and substance, tempered and refined by Apolline form.[13] By declaring the tragic protagonists of Aischylos and Sophokles to be masks of Dionysos, Nietzsche has tragedy, even in its Apolline form, remain in essence Dionysiac ritual.[14]

Yet this needs qualifying. Nietzsche was not a ritualist and hardly used the term 'ritual'. He may be said to have produced the first ritual reading of Greek tragedy only inasmuch as he sees the great figures of Attic drama as variations, or as he put it more elegantly, as masks of Dionysos. Nietzsche did not test this view by detailed analysis. This was left to the Cambridge ritualists; and they went about it in a rather technical and un-Nietzschean way. They reconstructed—or shall we say construed?—the ritual pattern of the slain and reborn god (*agôn* [struggle] / *pathos* [suffering] / messenger's report of *pathos* / *thrênos* [lament] / *anagnôrisis* [recognition] / epiphany); and Gilbert Murray tried hard to demonstrate its presence as the shaping force in all extant tragedies, as well as to reveal each tragic hero as a human substitute for the dying Dionysos.[15] Murray's ritual analyses of the Greek plays had to resort constantly to special pleading and, as Kitto put it, to 'endless make-believe'.[16] With a sigh of relief we note that the plays proved recalcitrant to the reduction to the ritual pattern. Imagine the tedium of it all, had the ritualists been right and proved that the history of Greek drama, and of Western drama in general, exhausts itself in the monotonous recurrence of an identical ritual pattern!

Through Murray, ritualist terms such as *pathos*, epiphany, and *agôn* have become part of the general critical idiom and given rise to a fully fledged ritualism in literary criticism that views not just Greek drama but *all drama*, from antiquity to the twentieth century, as ritual.[17] In the 1960s and 1970s the Cambridge ritualist theory even made theatre history when it was translated into the avant-garde movement known under the slogan 'back to ritual'.[18]

Yet in classical studies the ritual theory never caught on. Kitto gave it short shrift, dismissing it as so much 'modern moonshine';[19] and after Pickard-Cambridge's demolition of Murray's analyses, nobody wanted to be seen dead with the ritual theory.[20] So, on the whole, the first modern attempts to correct the ancients by emending 'nothing' to 'everything' and read *pan pros ton Dionuson* ('[tragedy has] everything to do with Dionysos') have not been an overwhelming success. This is, of course, no reason for not trying again. Sure enough, with the current neo-Nietzscheanism, the return of the Dionysiac to the study of Greek drama was inevitable. One of its most interesting results is the inversion of Nietzsche's view of Euripides: once condemned as the decadent rationalist subverter of the healthy Dionysiac culture of archaic Greece, he is now being worshipped as an irrationalist and the *Dionusiakôtatos*, 'the most Dionysiac', among the Greek tragedians: let no one ever say hereafter that scholarly opinion is rigid and inflexible!

Structuralist and Post-structuralist Correctors

The two postmodern attempts I am going to discuss come from structuralist and post-structuralist quarters respectively; they are, of course, more recherché and perhaps more sophisticated than the exalted vision of Nietzsche and the naïve scientism of the Cambridge ritualists.

'The God of Tragic Fiction' is the title of one of J.-P. Vernant's less often cited essays.[21] Here he seeks the Dionysiac in Greek tragedy not in its ritual past but, interestingly, in its modernity. The attempts of the ritualists to pass off tragedy's Dionysiac origins for its essence are dismisssed as 'vain and illusory in principle'. Vernant also rejects the argument that the mask connects tragedy with the animal disguises of troupes of satyrs and sileni dancing for Dionysos: the tragic mask is a human mask, he insists, whose function is aesthetic, not religious, meeting the precise needs of the dramatic spectacle and not the ritualistic needs of translating states of possession by means of a masquerade. The Girardian assimilation—via the *tragos* ('goat')—of tragedy to the ritual of sacrificing a scapegoat Vernant finds more than dubious.

'The "truth" of tragedy', Vernant sums up, 'is not to be found in an obscure, more or less "primitive" or "mystical" past secretly haunting the theater stage.'[22] Rather, he argues, its truth is to be found in the *innovations* which tragedy effected; and these innovations were due to its *break* with its religious and ritual past. First, with tragedy, a new literary genre, drama, was born. Second, the new genre presented the old heroic themes and their inherent traditional virtues and values in a new manner, different from that of epic and choral lyric, where they are presented as given models: in tragedy they are presented as problems and subject to questioning and debate. Third, the *polis*, by making the dramatic contest one of its new institutions, presents itself on-stage as an object of reflection. In these respects tragedy transcends any form of ritual both in morphological complexity and in intellectual force. The religious dimension of the Greek theatre in the fifth century (its being part of Dionysos festivals) is no big deal: in the ancient *polis*, with its civic religion, every institution had a religious dimension—it is something the ancient theatre shared with all the other institutions of the *polis*.

All this is very refreshing and a welcome antidote to the current neo-primitivism. Yet, after having escorted Dionysos politely out of tragedy through the front door, Vernant beckons him to return through the back door. His goal is Nietzschean, but his procedure is not: instead of connecting tragedy and Dionysos via the ritual roots of tragedy (that is, the genealogical way), Vernant associates the god with one of tragedy's innovative aspects that constituted the modernity of the new genre for the fifth century: dramatic illusion and fictionality. In tragic drama characters and events take on the appearance of real existence, although they belong to a completely bygone age: 'the "presence" embodied by the actor in the theater was always the sign, or mask, of an *absence* '.[23] Dionysos is said to be the god who constantly 'confuse(s) the boundaries between illusion and reality, who conjures up the beyond in the here, and who thus makes us lose our sense of self-assurance and identity'. It is in these terms that Vernant reinscribes the Dionysiac into Greek tragedy. When Vernant writes that this is the meaning that a '*modern reader is tempted to give*' the connection of tragedy with Dionysos,[24] is he not projecting here the preoccupation of contemporary theorizing with fiction and fictionality onto the ancient phenomenon? But we can let this pass and ask instead: what does the Dionysiac, thus conceived as a shaping force of Greek tragedy, amount to? Answer: to nothing much. With Vernant the Dionysiac has been attenuated to a mere metaphor: the metaphor for dramatic illusion and fictionality. It is not really a correction of the ancient view; it is rather an elegant rhetorical move, in the precious style of current Parisian theorizing, that brings Greek tragedy in line with a discourse that prizes the Dionysiac.

The other postmodernist move in the business of correcting the ancients is Simon Goldhill's contribution to *Nothing to Do with Dionysos?*[25] Its editors had originally considered the title *Everything to Do with Dionysos*, yet settled in the end for the sceptical question-mark added to the ancient proverb.[26] Even so, the whole enterprise remains a wonderful illustration of *aprosdionusos*; for of its fourteen contributions only one, that of Goldhill, is really to the point.[27]

Goldhill sets out by reprehending as 'fundamentally mistaken' those who accept the ancient view, using Oliver Taplin as *pharmakos*. Yet despite the polemical and censorious tone of the opening, he goes about it in a very constructive and, as we shall see, fruitful way, by reconstructing the social and political context of the performance of Greek tragedy.[28] Goldhill focuses on the civic ceremonies preceding the tragic competition in the theatre: the libations performed by the politically most powerful college in the *polis*, the ten generals; the display of the tributes of the allied cities on the stage in the sight of the allies and foreign visitors present in the audience; the bestowing of honours in the form of a garland upon those who had benefited the *polis*; and the parade of the grown-up war-orphans clad in the panoply of war. In these ceremonies the city celebrates its power and its dignity; and using the occasion to promote civic duties and virtues, the *polis* thereby asserts its priority over the individual citizens and its claim to their loyalty and service to the point of self-effacement and even self-sacrifice.

So far, so splendid. Goldhill succeeds admirably in showing that the four ceremonies preceding the dramatic competition made the Great Dionysia 'fundamentally and essentially a festival of the democratic *polis*'.[29] By directing our attention to these civic and religious ceremonies as the *prelude to the dramatic competition* and by emphasizing the fact that their performance *shares the site with the tragic performances*, Goldhill establishes most effectively the political context of tragedy: the text of tragedy becomes part of the larger text of the civic discourse of the *polis*. This is a significant advance in the understanding of Greek tragedy. Along traditional lines one would now expect that the argument would go on to detail the political nature of Greek tragedy by showing how tragedy shapes, and is shaped in its turn by, the city's civic discourse; how tragedy advances the civic discourse by broadening and deepening it, thereby translating what the pre-play ceremonies simply assert as civic *ideology* into a true civic *discourse* that articulates, and reflects upon, the tenets and presuppositions of the ethical life of the *polis*; by sounding and probing the human condition, placed as it is between the beasts and the gods; by thematizing the anthropology of the *polis*, which defines the human being in terms of active citizenship; and by exploring the tension-ridden union of *oikos* (household) and *polis* and the, at times, conflicting loyalties of individuals to either institution.

Yet for a postmodernist critic this is too predictable and therefore dull. What we get instead is the much spicier fare of paradox, transgression, and subversion. In its particular depictions and uses of myth and language, tragedy is said to display its transgressive force, not only questioning but subverting the dominant ideology put forward in the pre-play ceremonies. We now see: Goldhill reconstructs the political context of the Great Dionysia in order to have tragedy deconstruct it—tragedy was made part of the civic discourse in order to subvert it. The Great Dionysia is presented as one large text that does what any decent self-respecting text is supposed to do: it deconstructs itself, with tragedy as the agent of the deconstructive process.

How does Goldhill arrive at this? In dealing with the pre-play ceremonies, his argument focuses on the parade of the state-educated war-orphans, and then expatiates on developments in military values, virtues, and strategy between Homer and the fifth-century *polis*. In the process the concept of citizenship is strangely narrowed to its military aspects. Soon we see why. His principal example of tragedy's subversive force is Sophokles' *Aias* (*Ajax*); and here the discussion of the protagonist's last address to his son claims much of the space. This connects the play neatly with the orphans' parade of the pre-play ceremonies: a warrior about to die imparts his spiritual legacy to his child, about to become a war-orphan. The play shows Aias dominated by an intense concern with his honour, an excessive *philotimia*, that has made him think, behave, feel, and act in a way that contradicts everything the civic discourse of the *polis*, as espoused in the pre-play ceremonies, demands of, and prescribes to, its warrior-citizens. The *skandalon*, in Goldhill's view, is

that this Aias presents himself as a role-model to his son. It is
through this contradiction that the play is said by Goldhill to subvert the civic discourse, its very own context that sustains it.

Thus, through its pre-play ceremonies, the festival of the Great
Dionysia advertises the civic ideology of the *polis* and has it subverted through its other constitutive component, the dramatic
contest: Goldhill calls this the paradox of Attic tragedy. The subversive paradox is the *via regia* by which Dionysos, conceived as
the god of paradox, triumphantly returns and proves the ancient
proverb wrong. The Great Dionysia, then, represents 'the interplay between norm and transgression'; and it is through paradox,
transgression, and subversion that Goldhill reinscribes Dionysos
into Attic drama—the 'divinity associated with illusion and
change, paradox and ambiguity, release and transgression'. An elegant and forceful argument: but is it tenable?

The *pan-pros-ton-Dionuson* criticism of the Cambridge ritualists
was reductionist. It turned the history of drama into the eternal
recurrence of the same ritual pattern, with the same protagonist,
Dionysos, in numerous disguises (as Prometheus, Oidipous,
Agamemnon, Orestes, Antigone, Medeia, Hippolytos, Macbeth,
King Lear, Hamlet, Dr Faustus, Puntila, etc.); it thereby distorted
the plays and their meanings, and gave rise to the silly hocus-pocus
of modern ritual productions of ancient, Elizabethan, and modern
plays. So its Dionysianism and ritualism were very effective in
doing harm to the reception of Greek drama as well as to the theory, criticism, and practice of the theatre. With Vernant, on the
other hand, the Dionysiac has been attenuated to the metaphor of
tragic fiction; and with Goldhill, to the metaphor of the subversive
paradox of tragedy. The Dionysiac is here a fine rhetorical flourish.
Thus, unlike the ritualism of the Cambridge School and its latter-
day adherents, their Dionysianism seems to do no harm. Does it do
any good?

Paradox, especially in the witty form of the Wildean paradox,
used to be fun. It no longer is. The term has become so loaded with
postmodernist doctrine that all the intellectual pleasure is gone. (It
affects retroactively even the Wildean art of the paradox: Terry
Eagleton has appropriated it by claiming Wilde as a 'proto-
deconstructionist'.) The postmodern fetishism of paradox matches
the cult of subversion; in fact they go together. Paradox, subversive
as it is of the logic and order in texts, is said to liberate the vital

turbulence of language by the creative chaos it engenders in the
texts from what is known in deconstructive parlance as the totali-
tarian regime of logocentrism. The reading of Greek tragedy as a
transgressive Dionysiac force, planting subversive paradoxes in
the civic discourse of the *polis*, is redolent of the current *Zeitgeist*
and has 'postmodern construct' written all over it. Goldhill's
choice of *Aias* and *Philoktetes* for exemplifying this reading implies
the replacement of pious Sophokles by subversive Sophokles. This
is part of the current trend to 'euripidize' Sophokles. Euripidean
drama is often subversive, as Old Comedy knew; and I would concede to Goldhill that much of what he attributes to Greek tragedy
tout court is attributable to Euripides, although one would wish to
use a different terminology.

Maybe it is only Goldhill's terminology that makes Greek
tragedy appear subversive of the *polis*-ethics. For he is quick to
qualify his thesis of tragedy's subversiveness: it implies neither
that in Attic drama the *polis* is seriously questioned as the necessary
basis of civilization; nor that Athens is seriously questioned as the
home of that *polis*-civilization;[30] for Attic tragedy regularly uses
other cities, other *poleis*, as the setting for its subversive tragic narratives, preferably perverse Thebes and wicked Argos.[31] Some
bold subversion! *L'enfer, c'est les autres*: after such qualifications—
what's left of the subversiveness in Attic tragedy?

Nevertheless, let us examine how Goldhill arrives at the thesis of
tragedy as a force that is subversive of the *polis* and its civic discourse. Everything depends on his interpretation of the *Aias*. In
his reading, the plot of the *Aias* focuses exclusively on the opposition between the glory and the awesomeness of Aias' extreme heroism and individualism, and the oppressive and petty vengefulness
of the two Atreidai, posing as the representatives of the *polis*—the
polis at arms, the army—and its civic ideology. Aias' heroism is too
great to fit into the *polis*, and the *polis* unable to do justice to the
great heroic individual. This interpretation raises a host of problems;[32] but leaving them aside I shall focus instead on what I see as
the main problem in Goldhill's interpretation. His deconstructive
reading of the play as subversive of the *polis*-ethics would be tenable if it could be shown to result from the *total effect* of its tragic
action. But it is, as we shall see, the result of a very selective, partial, and in this way reductive, interpretation of Sophokles' *Aias*,
which excludes—has to exclude—one of its chief components.

The protagonist's suicide takes place at verse 865, with more than a third of the dramatic action still to come. In Goldhill's reading, the last part of the play only serves to expose the oppressive pettiness of the two Atreidai as the two representatives of the *polis*, as they discredit themselves and the *polis* by their use of its civic ideology as a means for pursuing their petty vengefulness over the corpse of the great and noble hero—a reading that draws its support largely from Bernard Knox's concept of tragic heroism.[33] In this reading the *polis*-ethics seem to be conceived in terms of Nietzsche's *Genealogy of Morals*: as the translation of the *ressentiment* and envy of the weak, nasty, and mediocre (such as Agamemnon and Menelaos), into a tool to control and humiliate the strong, noble, and magnificent (such as Aias). One figure of the play, second only to the protagonist, who actually dominates the last part of the dramatic action, is missing from Goldhill's reading: there is no word about Odysseus. If it is legitimate to equate the Greek army in this play with the *polis* at arms, then the authentic representative of the *polis* turns out in the end to be Odysseus, and not the two nasty pieces of work whose rhetoric misuses the *polis*-ethics to cover the pettiness of their intended revenge. *Abusus non tollit usum*: neither is the heroic model as such discredited through being perverted by Aias, nor is the civic discourse of the *polis* irredeemably compromised by being made a tool of the commanders' unjust vindictiveness. More important, the *polis* is finally vindicated through the actions and behaviour of Odysseus: they have the effect that the *polis* shows itself able to do justice to the dead Aias. In the end, it is Aias who is honoured by the *polis* at arms by being granted a burial, and, as P. E. Easterling writes, 'it is the Atridae who are isolated, when Odysseus has won permission for a burial which he characterizes, perhaps unexpectedly, as "just in the eyes of all Greeks" (1363).'[34] One could argue: the *polis* can integrate Aias only as a corpse. But this is, in every respect, Aias' own making.

All this tells against Goldhill's interpretation of the play as subversive of the *polis*-ethics. Sophokles' treatment of the Aias story avoids portraying the antagonists in simplistic black-and-white: he attributes greatness to an erring Aias and paints the pettiness of the triumphant archons in vivid colours. But this is a far cry from planting a vicious paradox in the text of the democratic festival with the purpose of subverting the civic discourse of the *polis*. The deconstructive method is here both enabling and crippling. Goldhill needed a larger text which tragedy could subvert: this made him reconstruct the political context of the tragic performances—in which he succeeded admirably, offering, as we have seen, a decisive advance in the criticism and theory of ancient drama. This is the enabling bit. But then, unfortunately, he allows the big deconstructive machine of interpretative free-play to take over and obscure the splendour of his scholarly achievement. Feed any text, any discourse into this machine, and you can be certain that it will come out at the other end with its meaning effectively subverted by paradox and aporia. This is the crippling bit: the deconstructive process designed to liberate the turbulent vital forces of language from the deadening tyranny of logocentrism ends in the paralysis of paradox and aporia: in death. This might be called the tragic paradox of deconstruction.

TRAGEDY'S INSTITUTIONAL TIE TO DIONYSIAC WORSHIP

The attempts to reinscribe Dionysos into Greek tragedy have not totally convinced us that the ancients were so wrong with their proverb. Yet the fact remains that Dionysos' festival provided the institutional framework for the tragic performances. Now, this is an obvious puzzle: tragedy, said to have nothing to do with Dionysos, is nevertheless institutionally tied to Dionysiac worship. How can we satisfactorily account for this?

Why, and how, did Dionysos, who was originally a god of the wild and not of the *polis*, become the theatre-god, the patron god of what can justly be called the greatest cultural achievement of the *polis*, Attic drama? Ah yes, the mask! This is the conventional wisdom: Dionysos is *der Maskengott*; so much so that he was even worshipped in the form of a mask; and *le masque—c'est le théâtre*. Fine. His close association with the mask looked good on his *c.v.* and certainly helped him obtain the tenured position of patron god of the theatre. So his being the god of the mask may be a necessary, yet is not a sufficient reason. For us the mask has become the synecdoche for theatre and drama (thus we may easily be deceived by a rhetorical figure and overrate the significance of the mask). Yet masks play an important role in the rituals of other cultures, too, which have not evolved into drama and the institution of the theatre. Dionysos' association with the mask had a lot to do with his being a nature god. The mask as the idol of the god had a very practical cult-function: it could be mounted on any tree, and, presto, you had a natural shrine for the notoriously mobile god.[35] Now, while conceding a supporting role to his association with the mask, I am more inclined to assume that Dionysos became the theatre-god because his ritual was morphologically complex enough to become the antecedent to Greek drama. Unlike other candidates—as, for instance, Burkert's goat-sacrifice, currently touted as the most likely ritual antecedent to tragedy—the Dionysiac ritual (*drômenon*) was fused with a *legomenon* (myth) that rendered it a fully fledged *mimêsis praxeôs* (a 'representation of an action'). In other words, it had attained a narrative plot whose complexity came close to that of drama.[36] The *Maskengott* Dionysos, then, became the theatre-god chiefly because his ritual, prefiguring as it did the structure of the dramatic plot, gave birth to drama.

Ritual and Drama

We are back at the old question of what relation ritual bears to drama. Here we have to draw two important distinctions. Distinction (1), simply put, is that between: (1*a*) *drama uses rituals*; and (1*b*) *drama is ritual*. Less simply put: (1*a*) rituals are part of drama's thematic and tropic material; and (1*b*) ritual is drama's shaping structure.

As to (1*a*), Greek plays refer to a great variety of rituals belonging to the society in which they originate. These rituals are alluded to in dialogue and choral odes, or prepared and actually performed as part of the dramatic action. In a persuasive essay, 'Tragedy and Ritual',[37] P. E. Easterling has shown, with references to studies by, among others, Burkert, Else, Foley, Seaford, Segal, and Zeitlin,[38] how pervasive and varied the use of ritual language and ritual action is as theme, motif, metaphor, and symbol in Greek drama; and how important for the interpretation of the plays it is to understand how the ritual elements work in dramatic action and imagery, and how the dramatists exploit them for dramatic effect, intensification of verbal images, articulation of the central dramatic theme, highlighting crucial moments of the dramatic action, establishing references connecting past and present, etc. The ubiquity of ritual and the variety of its uses in tragic plot-design (σύστασις τῶν πραγμάτων) and diction (λέξις) are not surprising:

tragedy was, after all, the representative literary art-form of a society whose texture was shot through with rituals and ceremonies. This, and the interpretative uses of the term 'ritual' in dramatic criticism that explores the function of ritual in the extant plays, need no further comment here. However, Easterling concludes her article with an infelicitous speculation. It flies in the face of the general tenor of her argument which emphasizes the 'metaphorical status' of the rituals in Greek tragedy and their being part of the dramatic (that is, artistic) fiction. Her concluding remarks, however, attribute real ritual power to some ritual actions in some plays, such as the finale of the *Eumenides*: they are said to cease being dramatic fiction and become ritual reality. On such occasions, then, she has drama revert temporarily to ritual.[39] As she offers neither argument nor evidence for this view, I set it down for a *pointe d'esprit*, designed to serve as an effective *peroratio* of her splendid piece.[40]

Apart from this last point, Easterling's article clarifies matters by showing that the necessary analysis of the function of *ritual in drama* is quite distinct from ritualism that reads *drama as ritual*. Critical comment will therefore focus on the latter: the reading of drama that posits ritual as its shaping structure. Here we have to draw the other important distinction (2): between (2a) ritual conceived as the *underlying structure* and *informing matrix* that shapes drama; and (2b) ritual as the *morphological antecedent* to tragedy.

The theory of the Cambridge School provides examples for both; and I agree with Richard Seaford that, however unfashionable it may have become, it should not just be ignored.[41] The Cambridge ritualists had originally set out to develop a *genetic* hypothesis which was to explain the ritual *origins* of drama. In this they were guided by the evolutionary historicism of Frazer's anthropology. Under the influence of Nietzschean thinking they succumbed to the fallacy inherent in Nietzsche's genealogy: that the origins of a phenomenon fully explain its essence. This turned their genetically conceived theory of the ritual origins of drama into ritualism, the doctrine that mistakes drama's ritual beginnings for its substance. In this perspective, ritual ceased to be the humble antecedent of drama; and the ritual pattern, as conceived by Harrison and Murray, was passed off as its dominant informing structure. Here ritual functions as a kind of archetype, and individual dramas rank as its 'instantiations'. The implication of this is an odd reversal: ritual, by itself not an aesthetic category but the pre-artistic and pre-literary forerunner of the literary art-form of drama, comes to function in ritualism as an aesthetic category higher than drama. Small wonder, then, that Murray's attempt to demonstrate its shaping force in his ritual analyses of all Greek plays, including those of New Comedy, should have resulted in a débâcle.

In its original genetic conception—before the genealogical fallacy took effect—the Cambridge theory of the birth of tragedy from Dionysiac cult and ritual has much to recommend it. The seasonal ritual of the dying and the reborn god Dionysos has a number of rivals competing for the role of antecedent to drama: Burkert's sacrificial ritual; the scapegoat ritual; shamanistic ritual, with its masks and costumes; the initiation ritual, etc. They all claim to be older, more primal, more *urwüchsig*. Seaford, for one— who favours, with George Thomson, the initiation ritual—thinks the seasonal ritual a by-product, a mere derivation of, and certainly secondary to, the *Pubertätsweihen*.[42] On the other hand, the seasonal ritual of the Cambridge School possesses the necessary complexity for, and can therefore lay greater morphological claim on, being the antecedent to the dramatic genre; while with the others, there would be a morphological gap.[43]

Be that as it may: I do not have to go into this. For my argument enters at an advanced stage in the evolution from ritual to drama: the stage at which ritual has already formed a union with myth, and thus attained a narrative plot; and at which the separation of the participants into performers and spectators has already taken place.[44] It is the stage Seaford calls 'youthful tragedy' whose 'original theme . . . could hardly be other than the [Dionysiac] *hieros logos* which expressed the ritual'.[45] My term for youthful tragedy is *ritual drama*: having already developed a dramatic structure but being still bound to a ritual content, *ritual drama* is no longer pure ritual (actors perform for spectators) but not yet fully fledged drama: it represents an intermediate stage. As the cult-play of Dionysos-worship, its subject was first restricted to the *hieros logos*, presumably involving the god's birth, dismemberment, and rebirth (making for some sort of Dionysiac passion-play); then the repertoire was expanded to include stories about the god's conflict with, and victory over, his adversaries, such as Pentheus and Lykourgos.[46]

In such plots, we must assume, a displacement took place: the focus apparently shifted from the god onto his adversary. After that, it was only a short step towards the final rupture: it occurred when, in Seaford's words, 'developing tragedy turn[ed] its back on Dionysiac themes'[47] and (according to Plutarch) Phrynichos and Aischylos introduced heroic legends and tales of suffering into tragedy (Φρυνίχου καὶ Αἰσχύλου τὴν τραγῳδίαν εἰς μύθους καὶ πάθη προαγόντων).[48] It is the moment when the Athenian spectators are reported by Plutarch to have shouted with dismay or astonishment or both: *Ti tauta pros ton Dionuson?*—'what have these to do with Dionysos?'[49] Their question, presupposing as it does Dionysiac myth as the original subject-matter, marks the point at which youthful tragedy emancipated itself from its cultic foundations, and changed from Dionysiac *ritual drama* to *literary drama*:[50] the Dionysiac cult-myth gave way to heroic myths, and Dionysos ceded the stage to their heroes and heroines.[51] This is the birth of a new poetic genre, the beginning of drama as a universal art-form: it is a qualitative change, a μετάβασις εἰς ἄλλο γένος. By 'universal art-form' I mean a form no longer tied, as ritual drama is, to a particular limited body of cult myths on which it has to draw for its plots. Such drama is universal in the sense that it can appropriate any content as long as this can be shaped into a dramatic action.[52]

The Dionysiac and Tragedy

In this way the tragic plot, though tragedy was performed as part of the Dionysos festival, came to have 'nothing to do with Dionysos'. Dionysiac ritual was secularized and metamorphosed into drama, but the institutional religious framework for the dramatic performances remained.[53] There is nothing extraordinary about this; it has its analogy in almost all the institutions of the *polis*: they all become secularized in the democratic development of Athena's sacred *polis*, yet retain their religious framework. As Vernant has pointed out, religious rituals connected with the political and legal proceedings—oaths, sacrifices—became the formal external framework for political and legal procedures that were secular: 'the rites to which civic officials still submitted on taking office, such as sacrifice and oath-taking, constituted the formal structure and no longer the internal strength of political life. In this sense, there was indeed secularization.'[54]

However, youthful tragedy's ceasing to be Dionysiac cult-ritual and becoming drama did not mean that the Dionysiac disappeared altogether from Attic tragedy. It remained a force in various ways. First, it is only to be expected that its Dionysiac ritual past should have left traces on the new literary art-form.[55] In his recent work Richard Seaford has discerned such traces as 'Dionysiac metaphor' and 'Dionysiac pattern': when youthful tragedy turned its back on Dionysiac themes, the Dionysiac took refuge in imagery and plot-pattern. The 'Dionysiac metaphor' is 'the explicit or implicit comparison of behavior [sc. of *dramatis personae*] to the frenzy inspired by Dionysos':[56] when it is, as it regularly is, connected with the destruction of the household (*oikos*),[57] it can, as it does in *Bakchai* and the Theban plays centring on the Labdacids, expand into the 'Dionysiac pattern', which he describes as 'the salvation of the *polis* . . . linked to the self-destruction of the royal household'.[58] Seaford sees, of course, more in the Dionysiac pattern than just a trace from tragedy's ritual past; the heading of his main section, 'Tragedy: A Dionysiac Pattern', seems to claim for it the status of a pervasive formative structure. However, so far, he can only claim its presence in plays with Theban themes; and plays with such themes are the natural place for identifying Dionysiac residues, given the close association of the god with this city.

Saving the city through the destruction of the *oikos*: this is said, oddly but interestingly, to be Dionysos' way of benefiting the *polis*. It derives from Seaford's concept of Dionysos as a *polis*-god *qua* destroyer of the *oikos*: a complex and most intriguing argument which is of particular interest as it is developed not from forcing fashionable theories on the god but from a thorough discussion and an original interpretation of the available evidence. Here I restrict myself to raising two brief critical points, one general, one specific. Seaford's concept of Dionysos is predicated on his radicalizing the polar distinction between *polis* and *oikos* to a 'contradiction between household and community'.[59] In a convincing piece, Helene Foley has warned against misconceiving the *polis*–*oikos* polarity in terms of a rigid antagonism and dichotomy: both institutions define one another and are interdependent as well as reciprocal.[60] Acting and behaving as if the polarity were a contradiction constitutes the very tragic *hamartia* of both Kreon and Antigone in the Sophoclean *Antigone*, which Seaford adduces as a realization of his Dionysiac pattern. But can the *Antigone* be said to realize the pattern? What brings about the *sôteria poleôs*, the salvation of the *polis*, in this play is the assertion of the right and the duty of the *oikos* to bury its dead: the *polis* is threatened with pollution through the corpse left unburied by the decree of the city's authorities (*Antigone* 998 ff., 1064 ff). In this respect, *Antigone* is the most poignant instance of Sophoclean tragic irony: Antigone, who so exclusively values the *oikos* and its obligations that the *polis* does not seem to exist for her, perishes by carrying out a deed that, though designed to assert the right of the *oikos* against a *polis* arrogating claims in a realm where it has none, nevertheless saves this very *polis*.[61] The *Bakchai* can be said to realize Seaford's Dionysiac pattern only on the assumption that the lost ending showed the restoration of the *polis* through the establishment of the cult of Dionysos. But this is quite uncertain, and even doubtful: the general tenor of the drama suggests a Dionysos acting and behaving as the destroyer of the *polis* as well. Be that as it may: much more convincing are the results of Seaford's earlier piece on ritual elements in the *Bakchai* showing how the pattern of the Dionysiac ritual of mystic initiation is exploited for dramatic effect.[62] Most convincing is Seaford's demonstration that the Dionysiac took its other refuge in the tragic tetralogy's coda—the satyr-play.[63] The Dionysiac nature of this genre is so well established that it needs no further comment.

Thus, when we ask 'what has the tragic tetralogy to do with Dionysos?', the answer is: origins, institutional framework, coda; plus ritual residues and traces, frequently artistically exploited in plot-construction (σύστασις τῶν πραγμάτων) for dramatic effects and in the diction (λέξις) for the imagery. This is quite a lot; but a far cry from tragedy having 'everything to do with Dionysos' (*pan pros ton Dionuson*). 'Nothing to do with Dionysos' (*ouden pros ton Dionuson*), on the other hand, is a bit of a hyperbole. I should therefore settle for Oliver Taplin's rewording which is more precise: 'there is nothing intrinsically Dionysiac about Greek tragedy'.[64]

THE TRAGIC

Ritual, even in the advanced shape of ritual drama (or 'youthful tragedy' or 'proto-tragedy'), is more or less stereotyped. It requires unreflecting participants performing prescribed actions (*drômena*), linked to a restricted body of cult-myths (*legomena*), who feel and act as particles of a collective body bound to the cyclical processes of nature; while tragedy, all *Typik* and conventions notwithstanding, is particularized in form and content, and requires sufficiently individuated agents capable both of making conscious ethical choices with the risk of *hamartia* (tragic error) and of accepting the consequences of such choices.[65] In short, had 'proto-tragedy' not ceased to be Dionysiac ritual drama, and had it not thrown off the cultic yoke, it would have failed to become 'tragic'.[66]

'Tragic' in which sense? In an eminently political sense; 'political' in the larger sense in which Colin MacLeod understood the political in the *Oresteia*[67]—that is to say, in terms of Aristotle's *zôon politikon*; in terms of the hierarchies of *polis/oikos, oikos/*individual, *polis/*individual, hierarchies that also comprise that of divine/human, not only because the anthropology of the *polis* places the human *qua zôon politikon* between the divine and the bestial, but also because the *polis* and its *dikê*, its order of justice, were regarded as the manifestation of the divine and of divine *dikê* in the human world. The choral odes invoke *all* the gods of the *polis*, not just Dionysos; and the *di inferi*, the gods below, which the *oikos* worshipped as its own gods, get their due in tragedy, too. This is a thematic range far outstripping the framework of *rites de passage*, mystery rites, and ecstatic cults: it requires individual actions and actors conscious of themselves as ethico-political beings, members of the *polis* which was viewed as the extension of the divine into the human realm; and for this it needed the medium of the traditional legends that could be shaped in the terms of the city's civic discourse.[68] A 'product of the developing *polis*' (Seaford), tragedy helped articulate the civic discourse and reflected on it by translating its inherent tensions into dramatic conflicts in the medium of heroic myth: these become tragic as they necessitate for their resolutions the suffering of the protagonists, yet in terms of a world-view that grounds the ethico-political in the divine. All this is far beyond the ken of ritual.

Two such political themes are the *polis–oikos* polarity and the relation of *polis* and individual.

The civic discourse projects the harmonious unity of *polis* and *oikos* in the interaction of the public sphere, in which the male predominates, and its natural and material basis, the domestic sphere,

where the female presides over the economic and biological reproduction of life and the care for the family's dead. Yet the rise of the
polis had taken place at the expense of the *oikos*: having been the
institution which once could command the primary loyalty of its
members, the *oikos* came to be relegated to a subordinate institution of the larger *polis*-order, with the role of providing the natural
and material basis of the *polis* and of mediating with the realm of
the dead. Thus to the extent that the *Oresteia* dramatizes the rise
and ultimate triumph of the *polis*, it is also the dramatization of the
defeat of the *oikos* and the loss of its pre-eminence. This is manifest in the universal law and justice of the *polis* superseding the narrow justice of the *lex talionis*, the revenge-law of the tribal *oikos*. All
this makes for a subcutaneous tension operating beneath the harmony that the civic discourse, with its neat hierarchy of *polis* and
oikos, espouses; and here we grasp the basis for Seaford's view of
the contradiction between *polis* and *oikos*. But tension is not contradiction. If the characters of tragedy conceive it as a contradiction, such tension becomes the source of conflicts which grow
tragic because their resolution necessitates the destruction of the
individuals in whose actions the conflicts manifest themselves.

Aias and Antigone are powerful examples of the Sophoclean
lonely individual; and from this, hasty conclusions have been
drawn to the effect that the plays are about the assertion of individuality against the state. This is obviously the projection of a
modern constellation onto an ancient play. But it is not altogether
without a foundation. True, Antigone acts primarily as a member
of the *oikos* defending its rights as protected by the unwritten laws.
Aias' honour-seeking (*philotimia*), too, is primarily *oikos*-oriented:
the traditional hero, by winning personal honour and glory, seeks
to increase the honour and glory of his *oikos* (as the hoplite later
seeks them for his *polis*); so in his first speech after having recovered from his madness and recognizing the full extent of the shame
his deeds have brought upon him, Aias gives expression to his
greatest concern: he cannot bear to face his father, having dimin-
ished, instead of enhanced, the honour (*timê*) and fame (*kleos*) of
his family.[69] On the other hand, Antigone displays an almost jealous insistence on the deed as her very own, and her whole behaviour borders on a stubborn self-will (*authadeia*); and so does that of
Aias when he insists that the claims of his *philotimia* surpass even
those of the *polis*. We see here how the concern for the *oikos* can

become the vehicle for the assertion of an independent individuality against the totalizing claims of the *polis*. Goldhill's interpretation of the *Philoktetes* reveals a similar conflict, which is, as he holds, only artificially resolved by the *deus ex machina*.[70]

This, then, is the other source of potential tragic conflict. The *polis* is the first form of social and political freedom in history. Yet this freedom, being objective in kind and conceived more in terms of duties than rights, did not include subjective or individual freedom; and the rights it accorded its citizens were rights of participation in the ethico-political life of the *polis* which are hard to distinguish from obligations and duties. The *polis* as the first historical form of freedom, then, was predicated on the individual citizens' total subordination of their aspirations, desires, ambitions, and needs to the common good and on their unquestioning compliance with ancestral custom ($\pi\acute{\alpha}\tau\rho\iota\sigma\varsigma\ \nu\acute{o}\mu\sigma\varsigma$): the ethical life of the *polis* had no room for autonomous individuality. On the other hand, the *polis* created the conditions for the rise of subjective freedom—for the rise of a free individuality that claimed independence in thought, feeling, and action, and sought to liberate itself from the total guidance in these matters of the ancestral custom of the *polis*. The *polis*, while creating the conditions of its rise, could not accommodate this inchoate free individuality. On the contrary, it had to regard and to treat it as a source of the corrosion of its ethical life. This inherent dilemma became most pronounced in a real-life tragedy: the deadly collision between Sokrates and the *polis* of Athens, with an outcome that was tragic for individual and *polis* alike.

That's why the *polis* could not last. It created the conditions for the rise of what was to subvert and finally undo it. Euripidean tragedy dramatized this dilemma, Aristophanic comedy tried to resolve it. It was a tragedy in which the classical *polis* was the protagonist.

Notes

1. Segal, *Dionysiac Poetics*, 7 ff.; Henrichs, 'Loss of Self', 209.
2. Henrichs, 'Loss of Self', 240.
3. Henrichs observes that Nietzsche uses 'the Dionysiac' (*das Dionysische*) more often than the name 'Dionysos'; and he comments: Nietzsche 'destroyed Dionysus as a god even as he preserved him as a concept' (A. Henrichs, ' "He Has a God in Him": Human and Divine

in the Modern Perception of Dionysus', in T. H. Carpenter and C. Faraone [edd.], *Masks of Dionysus* [Ithaca, NY 1993] 23). Thus *The Birth of Tragedy* as the birth of the modern concept of the Dionysiac is the death of Dionysos as the ancient god.

4. Segal, *Dionysiac Poetics*, 3.

5. Henrichs, 'Loss of Self', 234.

6. Ibid. 205.

7. For example, A. Henrichs: 'Greek Maenadism from Olympia to Messalina', 121–3; 'Changing Dionysiac Identities', in B. F. Meyer and E. P. Sanders (edd.), *Jewish and Christian Self-definition*, iii: *Self-definition in the Graeco-Roman World* (London 1982) 143–6; 'Loss of Self', 210 (exemplified in Detienne's Dionysos); 'Between Country and City: Cultic Dimensions of Dionysus in Athens and Attica', in M. Griffith and D. J. Mastronarde (edd.), *Cabinet of the Muses: Essays on Classical and Comparative Literature in Honor of Thomas G. Rosenmeyer* (Atlanta 1990) 257–60, see esp. p. 257: 'their [i.e. the modern theorists'] perception of the god is intellectually exciting and consistent with his portrayal in Euripides and, to a lesser extent, in vase-painting, but it is also reductive and threatens to obscure the regional and functional diversity of Dionysus, and the fundamental difference between his mythical and cultic manifestations'.

8. Henrichs, 'Greek Maenadism', 147. There was no *sparagmos* of human victims nor omophagy in the historical cults and their rituals; in official Dionysiac cults and in historical maenadic associations, everything was contained, regulated, and controlled, down to the fees that members had to pay—quite in contrast to the spontaneous violence and ecstatic savagery of the mythical maenads which so excite modern interpreters. See pp. 150–2 on the puzzling phrase ὠμοφάγιον ἐμβαλεῖν in the Milesian inscription of 276/275 as referring to a peculiar type of sacrifice to Dionysos as Raw-Eater.

9. Henrichs, 'Loss of Self', 240 n. 103; see also above, n. 7.

10. Plutarch, *Mor.* 612e, 671e; Cicero, *Att.* 16. 13a. 1; Lucian, *Bacch.* 6. On this proverb, see M. Pohlenz, 'Das Satyrspiel und Pratinas von Phleius', in id., *Kleine Schriften*, ii (Göttingen 1952), 473–96; Seaford, 'On the Origins of Satyric Drama'.

11. Plutarch, *Mor.* 612e, 671e; Cicero, *Att.* 16. 13a. 1.

12. Silk and Stern, *Nietzsche on Tragedy*, 237 (their italics).

13. I cannot go into Nietzsche's theory of tragedy and his doctrine of the Dionysiac and the Apolline; for this we have the exhaustive study of Silk and Stern, *Nietzsche on Tragedy*.

14. 'Up to Euripides, Dionysus remained the dramatic protagonist; all the famous figures of the Greek stage, Prometheus, Oedipus etc. are

but masks of that original hero Dionysus. . . . The one and only
Dionysus appears in the mask of the struggling hero, and enmeshed,
as it were, in the web of individual will. . . . Yet in truth, that hero is
the suffering Dionysos of the mysteries; the god who in himself experiences the pain of individuation [which] should be regarded as the
fons et origo of all suffering and as something to be rejected' (F.
Nietzsche, *The Birth of Tragedy*, trans. F. Golfing [Garden City, NY
1956] 66 f.). See on this R. Friedrich, 'Aristophanes, Nietzsche, and
the Death of Tragedy', *Dionysius* 4 (1980) 8.

15. G. Murray, 'Excursus on the Ritual Forms in Greek Tragedy', in
    J. E. Harrison, *Themis: A Study of the Social Origins of Greek Religion*
    (New York 1962) 341–63; on ritual in New Comedy: G. Murray,
    'Ritual Elements in the New Comedy', *CQ* 37 (1943).

16. Kitto, 'Greek Tragedy and Dionysus', 9 n. 3.

17. Begun by G. Murray in his essay 'Hamlet and Orestes', in id., *The
    Classical Tradition in Poetry* (Cambridge, Mass. 1927) 205–40.

18. See Friedrich. 'Drama and Ritual', 190 ff., 203 ff.

19. Kitto, 'Greek Tragedy and Dionysus', 9 n. 3.

20. A. W. Pickard-Cambridge, *Dithyramb, Tragedy and Comedy* (Oxford
    1927) 329–52. There are exceptions, e.g. J.-P. Guépin, *The Tragic
    Paradox: Myth and Ritual in Greek Tragedy* (Amsterdam 1968).

21. Vernant, 'The God of Tragic Fiction', in 181–8.

22. Ibid. 185.

23. Ibid. 187 (his italics).

24. Ibid. 187 (my italics).

25. Goldhill, 'The Great Dionysia', 97–129 (an article originally pub. in
    shorter form in *JHS* 107 [1987] 58–76).

26. Winkler and Zeitlin, *Nothing to Do with Dionysos?*, preface.

27. The index s.v. 'Dionysos' shows only six entries (though it does not
    seem to be complete). F. Zeitlin's contribution ('The Theater of Self
    and Society in Athenian drama') refers very briefly to Dionysos in
    terms of the title: see Winkler and Zeitlin, *Nothing to Do with
    Dionysos?*, 142 f.

28. In reconstructing the context of the performance of Greek tragedy
    Goldhill is—somewhat surprisingly in view of his purpose of rein-
    scribing Dionysos into tragedy—not interested in the religious com-
    ponents proper of the Great Dionysia (εἰσαγωγὴ ἀπὸ τῆς ἐσχάρης, 'the
    leading in from the sacred hearth'; the πομπή, the procession to the
    sacred precinct of Dionysos, where the sacrifice was performed; and
    the κῶμος, 'the celebratory revel'). For this he is criticized by S. des
    Bouvrie, 'Creative Euphoria: Dionysos and the Theatre', *Kernos* 6
    (1990) 110 n. 161. (I came across this article too late to give it the con-
    sideration it deserves. I intend to respond to it on another occasion.)

29. Goldhill, 'The Great Dionysia', 114.

30. Ibid. 114 f.

31. See Zeitlin, 'Theater of Self'.

32. For instance: do Sophocles and his audience view Aias and his behaviour only in these celebratory terms, and not rather in terms of tragic *hamartia*? This question affects the theme of offering Aias as a role-model—the theme on which the question of the play's subversiveness turns: who is it that offers Aias as a role-model, and to whom? If it is Aias only, and if his son is the only addressee—would not the theme of the role-model then merely be a function of characterization and remain within the confines of the dramatic plot? In that case, how could it have the subversive effect Goldhill says it has on the *polis*-ethics? For the role-model theme to have this subversive effect, would it not have to be the author who offers Aias as a role-model to the sons of the Athenian citizens doing their civic duty by attending the dramatic performances? For a critique of Goldhill's deconstructionist reading of Greek tragedy in connection with the *Oresteia*, see M. C. Clark and E. Csapo, 'Deconstruction, Ideology, and Goldhill's *Oresteia*', *Phoenix* 45 (1991) 95–125.

33. See esp. Knox, 'Sophocles and the *Polis*'.

34. Easterling, 'Tragedy and Ritual: "Cry Woe, Woe" ', 96.

35. A. Schachter, 'Policy, Cult, and the Placing of Greek Sanctuaries', in O. Reverdin and B. Grange (edd.), *Le Sanctuaire grec* (Entretiens Hardt 37, Geneva 1990) 48 f. (see 49 n. 22 for other literature).

36. See Burkert, 'Greek Tragedy and Sacrificial Ritual'. I have discussed Burkert's theory in my 'Drama and Ritual', 167 ff., esp. 170 f.); the case for the morphological complexity of the Dionysiac ritual is made in terms of 'ritual and *mimêsis*' and 'ritual and myth' (see 178–87). See also below, n. 43.

37. Easterling, 'Tragedy and Ritual: "Cry Woe, Woe" '.

38. Burkert, 'Greek Tragedy and Sacrificial Ritual'; Foley, *Ritual Irony*; Seaford, 'Dionysiac Drama'; id., 'The Tragic Wedding', *JHS* 107 (1987) 106–30; id., 'Dionysus as Destroyer'; Segal, *Dionysiac Poetics*; F. Zeitlin, 'The Motif of Corrupted Sacrifice in Aeschylus' *Oresteia*', *TAPA* 96 (1965) 463–508.

39. Easterling, 'Tragedy and Ritual: "Cry Woe, Woe" ', 109.

40. Ritualism of this kind is taken to bizarre lengths in an Ottonian-Dionysiac reading of the *Antigone*, which goes as far as inventing an actual epiphany of Dionysos in the theatre: see A. Bierl, 'Was hat die Tragödie mit Dionysos zu tun?' *WüJbb* 15 (1989) 52: 'In seiner Ekstase ruft der Chor seinen Gott Iakchos-Dionysos als "Feuer schnaubender Sterne Chorführer" (1146 f.) an, der die ganze Nacht von den kosmischen Chören der Thyiaden gefeiert wird. Durch die

Übertragung des Enthusiasmos auf die Zuschauerränge erlebt die versammelte Polis eine Epiphanie des Dionysos als "Chorführer" in der Orchestra.' See also p. 53.

41. Seaford, 'Dionysiac Drama', 263, 269.
42. Ibid. 263 f. 'the rebirth of the youth as adults, which is inherent in initiation, is originally conceived as assisted by the rebirth of nature in the spring, which it may in turn assist; but as the ritual degenerates into a custom the significance of the death and rebirth of the young people is forgotten: the mock death of an individual or of a puppet is conceived entirely in terms of the death and rebirth of nature'. In this view the seasonal ritual is a by-product of the initiation ritual.
43. I have discussed them more fully in my 'Drama and Ritual', 165–74.
44. See ibid. 184 ff.
45. Seaford, 'Dionysiac Drama', 269, 271.
46. Ibid. 269; Friedrich, 'Drama and Ritual', 186 f.
47. Seaford, 'Dionysiac Drama', 271.
48. Plut. *Mor.* 1. 615a. On this see Pohlenz, 'Das Satyrspiel und Pratinas'; 474–8 and Seaford, 'On the Origins of Satyric Drama', 209 f.
49. Plut. *Mor.* 1. 615a.
50. See B. Snell, 'Aristophanes and Aesthetic Criticism', in Snell, *Discovery of the Mind,* 122: 'Attic tragedy succeeded to the status of great literature because it was able to rise above its ancient cult foundation.'
51. Seen in this context Aischylos' quaint statement that his tragedies were mere 'slices from the great banquets of Homer' (τεμάχη τῶν μεγάλων Ὁμήρου δείπνων), i.e. heroic stories derived from the epic, would sound less quaint.
52. That Greek tragedy tied itself initially to traditional myths on which it drew for its plots and characters does not tell against the universality inherent in the new genre; it was a poetic and political convention: in this, tragedy behaved νόμῳ, not φύσει. Comedy devised its own plots from the very beginning, and with Agathon tragedy soon followed suit.
53. It is a secularization of sorts; and by adding 'of sorts', I mean that we cannot really speak of secularization in the modern sense in a society in which everything political was also religious, and everything religious was political.
54. J.-P. Vernant, *The Origins of Greek Thought* (Ithaca, NY 1982) 56 n. 4. See also p. 56: 'The political rationalism that presided over the city's institutions was certainly in sharp contrast to the old religious procedures of government, but still it never went so far as to abolish them.'
55. 'Theatre may be said to be derived from ritual,' Bertolt Brecht wrote,

'but this is only to say that it becomes theatre once the two have separated' (Brecht, *Brecht on Theatre*, 18). Having said that, Brecht does
not tire of pointing to ritual survivals in Western drama, going as far
as stating hyperbolically that the European theatres offer the spectacle of 'human sacrifices all round' (189). On this he agreed with
Walter Benjamin, who spoke of art's 'being founded on ritual' and
formulated the programme of 'emancipating art from its parasitic
dependence on ritual' (W. Benjamin, 'Das Kunstwerk im Zeitalter
seiner technischen Reproduzierbarkeit', in id., *Illuminationen:
Ausgewählte Schriften* [Frankfurt/M. 1961] 155–6). Brecht's epic theatre was conceived as the realization of this programme within the
dramatic arts.

56. Seaford, 'Dionysus as Destroyer', 115.
57. Ibid. 131.
58. Ibid. 138.
59. Ibid. 145; and 145 f.: 'contradiction between *polis* and household'.
60. H. P. Foley, 'The "Female Intruder" Reconsidered: Women in
    Aristophanes' *Lysistrata* and *Ecclesiazusae*', *CP* 77 (1982) 1–21.
61. See Knox, 'Sophocles and the *Polis*', 16.
62. Seaford, 'Dionysiac Drama'.
63. Seaford: 'On the Origins of Satyric Drama', 209–21; 'The
    "Hyporchema" of Pratinas', *Maia* 29 (1977–8) 81–94; 'Dionysiac
    Drama', 271 ff., Euripides, *Cyclops*, ed. R. Seaford (Oxford 1984)
    10 ff.
64. Taplin, *Greek Tragedy in Action*, 162.
65. Segal, *Dionysiac Poetics*, 46, emphasizes other important aspects of
    the difference between ritual and tragedy: 'Ritual tends to be conser-
    vative and affirmative of the cosmic and social order. Tragedy is inno-
    vative, polysemous and deeply questioning of that order. The myths
    embodied or reflected in ritual are basically unitary in their meaning.
    Those of tragedy are complex and problematical, open to new inter-
    pretations, focal points of conflicted points of view and divided val-
    ues.'
66. A. D. Nuttall, 'The Game of Death', *London Review of Books*, 11 June
    1992, 14–16, is very eloquent on this point.
67. C. W. MacLeod, 'Politics and the *Oresteia*', *JHS* 102 (1982) 124–44,
    esp. 131 ff.
68. See on this Knox, 'Sophocles and the *Polis*', 5 ff.
69. *Aias* 434–40; see also 460–6.
70. Goldhill, 'The Great Dionysia', 118 ff. However, the dramatization
    of conflicts inherent in the ethical life and the civic discourse of the
    polis cannot be automatically equated with subversion and the cele-
    bration of transgression: so much *contra* Goldhill. *Pro* Goldhill: it can

be subversive, as it often is with Euripides. His *Medeia* is a case in point: it dramatizes the crisis of the classical *polis* and shows it at the end of its tether, see R. Friedrich, 'Medea *Apolis*: On Euripides' Dramatization of the Crisis of the *Polis*', in Sommerstein *et al.* (edd.), *Tragedy, Comedy and the Polis*, 219–40.

16

Something to Do with Dionysos—Tragedy and the Dionysiac: Response to Friedrich

RICHARD SEAFORD

I am in broad agreement with Rainer Friedrich's criticisms of the four attempts to reinscribe the Dionysiac into tragedy. But I disagree with his belief that there is nothing much Dionysiac about tragedy other than its ritual origins and festival context. That is to say, I believe that tragedy *is* intrinsically Dionysiac in a way that has not been noticed, and that I will begin by summarizing.

Friedrich agrees that tragedy developed out of Dionysiac ritual. But that does not mean, he adds, that there is anything Dionysiac about tragedy itself. After all, he correctly maintains, tragedy is very different from ritual.

However, there is also Dionysiac *myth*. Dionysos is not involved in many myths in the archaic and classical periods. But there is one that is told of various places in roughly the same form. Dionysos arrives from abroad but is rejected by the ruler or ruling family, and so he inflicts on the family a frenzy that results in the females becoming maenads in the wild, in one member of the family killing another in a perversion of animal sacrifice, and finally in the establishment of Dionysos' cult. The best known case is the Theban one, because it was dramatized in the *Bacchae*. I must emphasize here that Friedrich is fundamentally mistaken in thinking of Dionysos in the play as 'destroyer of the *polis*', and that it is virtually certain that Dionysos established his cult in the lost part of his final speech.[1] I would suggest that this *pattern* is common in tragedy:[2] kin-killing, often in a kind of frenzy and involving the perversion of ritual, concluded by the prefigurement or establishment of communal cult.[3]

Not all myth takes this form. For example, myth as told in Homeric epic, which is often thought to be tragic in spirit, is remarkable for the *rarity* of intrafamilial killing, of the perversion of ritual, of frenzy (outside battle), and indeed of Dionysos.[4]

And so I reject Friedrich's attribution of 'universality' to Greek tragedy, his claim that tragedy, as drama, 'can appropriate any content as long as this can be shaped into a dramatic action'. In fact, on the whole the tragic selection and shaping of myth produces the specific pattern of action that I have described.

This pattern is 'Dionysiac' in three senses. First, in that the typical form of tragic myth resembles the central Dionysiac myth, and is indeed most at home in the central Dionysiac myth. The second, stronger claim is that this resemblance comes about because tragic form is influenced by Dionysiac myth. Here we must introduce into the argument the ritual origin admitted by Friedrich. The Dionysiac ritual is also to some extent an enactment of Dionysiac myth. Its development into drama is also the increase in the element of enactment at the expense of the element of ritual. The first themes of tragedy were, ancient sources tell us, Dionysiac. The subsequent selection and shaping of non-Dionysiac myth is then influenced by the Dionysiac pattern, as occurred more obviously in the case of satyr-play. Thirdly, I would add that tragic kin-killing frequently attracts Dionysiac metaphor, as if it were inspired by Dionysos. For example, Klytaimestra is called a maenad of Hades in Aeschylus (*Agamemnon* 1235; cf. *Choephori* 698), and Herakles killing his own children is said to be in a Bacchic frenzy in Euripides (*Heracles* 892–5, 966, etc.).

What does it mean to say that tragedy is (in these ways) Dionysiac? It is a less radical statement than it may seem, once it is realized that by the Dionysiac I do not mean a metaphysical principle. That even now many critics think of the Dionysiac as something like a metaphysical principle, even if they do not call it that, is due in part to the influence of Nietzsche, whose devotion to a metaphysical Dionysiac, in *The Birth of Tragedy*, included the (anti-Hegelian) exclusion from tragedy of 'the politico-social sphere'[5]—one of the silliest features of that marvellously suggestive text.

I take the Dionysiac to be neither a metaphysical principle nor a metaphor for transgressive instability. Much of the activity of Dionysos can be comprehended by regarding him as a force that imposes the emotional cohesion needed for the creation of the *polis*. That is why he comes to the *polis* from the outside, with the outsider's unifying impartiality. That is why he demands worship 'from everybody', 'mixed up together'.[6] That is why he is resisted by the ruling family. That is why he imposes on the ruling family the (necessarily frenzied) *self*-destruction or the exile that are pre-conditions for the peaceful transition to a self-governing *polis*. And that is why he eventually succeeds in establishing his cult in the *polis*. In the process of creating the *polis* against various forms of resistance, the Greeks needed divine agents of the emotions and actions conducive to that process. One of those agents, and a specialist in overcoming a specific kind of resistance, is Dionysos. Such has been the continuing influence of Nietzsche, or of the kind of society that produced Nietzsche, that the profoundly *political* nature of the Dionysiac has been almost entirely ignored.

The specific resistance met by Dionysos comes from the autonomy of the household, especially the ruling household. Historically the *polis* was created out of the demise of ruling households, and could continue to exist only if it claimed some part of the emotional loyalty that might otherwise be devoted to the households of which, of course, the *polis* also consisted. Exclusive adherence to the household is naturally attributed to women, and male control over the females of the household is in Greek myth a frequent expression of the dangerous self-sufficiency of the household. And so when Dionysos draws out the women from their homes onto the mountainside, makes love to the wife of the 'king archon' at the Athenian Anthesteria festival, and so on, these are onslaughts on the autonomy of the household in the interests of the communal cult of the *polis*. Abandonment of exclusive loyalty to the household is crucial for the *polis*, but the loyalty may be so strong that it can be reversed only by frenzy, the frenzy imposed by Dionysos. Moreover, resistance from the *ruling* family may be met with frenzy extreme enough to produce the politically desirable act of royal self-destruction. (Perhaps Dionysos is, at the time of writing, invading Buckingham Palace.)

It will by now be clear that I regard Dionysiac myth and cult as belonging to a social process, rather than as the embodiments of a metaphysical principle. What is basic is not the god but the types of mythic and ritual action which he is sometimes imagined to inspire. This type of mythical action is also characteristic of tragedy. If it is objected that my argument so far is insufficient to permit the separation of the Dionysiac from Dionysos, so that we cannot, after all, call tragedy intrinsically Dionysiac, then I have no completely effective counter—how we choose to define the Dionysiac is a matter of decision, and we may choose to make the presence of the god himself a necessary condition. All I would insist upon is that my mythical pattern expresses (however indirectly) the interests of the *polis*, that it frequently attracts Dionysos, whether in the Dionysiac metaphors of tragedy or in the presence of the god himself, and that tragedy inherited it from Dionysiac myth and cult.

I move now to the consequences of my view for some of the problems raised by Friedrich. I entirely agree with his view that tragedy translates the inherent tensions of the *polis* into dramatic conflicts in the medium of myth. I applaud his emphasis on the tension between *polis* and household. I also applaud his observation that *polis* and household are in certain respects interdependent (though he is wrong to interpret the *Antigone* from this perspective[7]). What I profoundly disagree with is his statement that, as he puts it, 'All this is far beyond the ken of ritual.' In ancient Greece, as in many other societies, a sense of belonging, whether to the *polis*, the household, or any other body, is expressed and reinforced by participation in ritual. And where there is potential contradiction between the bodies concerned, this may have consequences for the representation of ritual. In myth it is specifically by being made to abandon their *homes* that the women participate in the cult of Dionysos. It is while performing sacrifice along with his family that the resistant ruler Lykourgos is driven crazy by Dionysos and, like Agaue, sacrifices his own son rather than the animal. When Herakles does the same in Euripides, it is called a Bacchic frenzy. The self-destruction of the family is poignantly expressed in the perversion of that household ritual of sacrifice which normally expresses its solidarity. In tragedy this is a very common feature, where the perverted household rituals are weddings and funerals as well as sacrifice, to be followed, as in the Dionysiac myths, by the institution of collective cult, which, as everybody knows, will be performed by the *polis* in the proper way. Tragedy uses ritual precisely to represent the *polis*–household polarity.

The Dionysiac complex of myth and ritual from which tragedy developed contained the phenomenon of *initiation* into the Dionysiac *thiasos*. Initiation of this kind involves the (temporary) abandonment of a previous identity and the acquisition of a new one. This is one reason why, although it no doubt pre-dates the *polis*, Dionysiac cult could be deployed to resolve (in favour of the *polis*) the contradiction of loyalties between household and *polis*. Rites of passage involve, and often actually express, a conflict of loyalties. To acquire a new loyalty, you may have to be detached from an old one. With Dionysiac myth in mind, I cannot resist mentioning the Pueblo Indian secret society of women, about which it was believed that initiation involved the woman having to kill one of her own kin. Although it seems likely that the Dionysiac mysteries necessitated detachment from the basic loyalty to the household, the new loyalty was not, of course, to the *polis* but to the *thiasos*. But that is precisely why the Dionysiac *thiasos* became such a central feature of the Athenian festivals of Dionysos, performing rituals 'on behalf of the *polis*', and eventually, I would argue, developing into the chorus of tragedy. For the other feature of Dionysiac initiation that is relevant here is that because it involves a change of identity it is inherently theatrical. In initiation, as in the theatre, you become a maenad or a satyr. And so two basic features of Greek tragedy, the contradiction of loyalties and the assumption of an alien identity, meet in Dionysiac initiation. I would agree with Friedrich that Vernant's conception of Dionysos as a metaphor of theatricality is vacuous, but would add that the only way of saving the point from vacuity is precisely by providing it with the genealogy that Vernant rejects. Dionysos is the god of the theatre, in part because he was god of the mysteries, whose theatricality pre-dates the theatre.[8]

Why was it specifically Dionysiac ritual that gave rise to tragedy? Friedrich's answer is that it was because the ritual was morphologically complex. He has not said very much about what this means. My own explanation would involve both the aspects of Dionysiac ritual that I have raised: the political and the initiatory.

This suggests a solution to the problematic aspects of Dionysos discussed by Friedrich—his contradictory nature, and his embodiment of anti-structure. Those who believe that tragedy is in some sense Dionysiac generally regard these aspects as highly relevant to the understanding of tragedy, and I agree with them in this, although I differ from them in my view of the Dionysiac and of tragedy.

The Dionysiac myths I have referred to are aetiological. They tell of the events leading to the foundation of cult. Tragedy too dramatizes aetiological myth: most extant tragedies (or trilogies) prefigure cult or end in the foundation of cult (or of something similar).[9] Now a general feature of aetiological myth is that the foundation of the cult is preceded by a period of crisis, in which there may occur typically disease, but also confusion of the normal divisions which regulate society. For example, in the events that led up to the foundation of the cult of Artemis Ortheia at Sparta, sacrifice was disrupted by conflict, and humans became sacrificial victims. Such confusions are especially striking in the aetiological myths of Dionysiac cult, partly because of the transformation of identity inherent in initiation. One thinks for example of the initiand Pentheus in Euripides' *Bacchae* becoming both female and sacrificial victim. Imagining a period of aetiological confusion has various functions, of which I here mention two. It may reinforce, by contrast, crucial divisions, say between human and animal, which are ultimately reinforced by the cult. And it may ensure the performance of a cult by representing the crisis that would reappear if the *polis* ever repeated the error of neglecting or resisting the cult.

Hence, I believe, the duality of Dionysos stressed by Friedrich: the contrast between the savagery of Dionysos in myth and the cheerful festivity of his rituals. Dionysos is savage in myth partly because in his secret rituals the initiand would undergo a fictitious death (albeit as a prelude to joyful incorporation), but mainly because the belief that the god will wreak havoc if rejected ensures that his politically vital, peaceful cults continue to be performed.

But modern interpreters, Friedrich points out, tend to concentrate on the myths, and to ignore 'the much tamer and civilized god of cult'. Nietzsche, Albert Henrichs points out, 'was far too preoccupied with the larger antithesis between Apollo and Dionysos to pay much attention to differentiation within Dionysos'.[10] Modern theories of the Dionysiac tend to ignore the eirenic, civic Dionysos because, it seems to me, they do not perceive the significance of aetiology, and in general have no interest in the social functioning of Dionysiac myth and cult.

Even where the orderly, civic Dionysos is *not* ignored, all is not well. Those who note the duality of the god, like Albert Henrichs, are content to ascribe it to his 'elusiveness': 'Dionysos defies definition.' In Simon Goldhill's view, praised and criticized by Friedrich, tragedy tends to subvert the civic discourse of the festival rituals. It is a paradox of this view that the unequivocally Dionysiac element of the festival, namely the ritual, represents the norm, whereas the arguably non-Dionysiac element, namely tragedy, does the subverting. But for Goldhill the Dionysiac resides neither in the one nor in the other. Rather, and I quote, 'It is the interplay between norm and transgression enacted in the tragic festival that makes it a Dionysiac occasion.'[11] In a similar move, Oudemans and Lardinois explain the duality of Dionysos between order and disorder as yet another example of the all-pervasive ambiguity associated with Dionysos. 'For Dionysiac logic', they write, 'there is no harmony and no solving of contradictions in any phase of development. It reveals the coexistence of order and disorder.'[12] From this perspective any contradiction is just one more instantiation of the quasi-metaphysical principle of the Dionysiac—even that contradiction between order and disorder within the Dionysiac which, if properly understood, would in fact provide the key to the social functioning of the Dionysiac. We here come face to face with the historically situated but historically unaware privileging (not to say fetishization) of anti-structure that is (for reasons I leave for the moment to the sociology of knowledge) a central orthodoxy of the postmodern Academy. I am sympathetic to Friedrich in this matter.

This view of the Dionysiac has consequences for the interpretation of tragedy. If there can be said to be a currently prevailing view about the vision of Greek tragedy, it is that it represents insoluble contradiction, poses profound but unanswerable questions, celebrates ambiguity, transgression, the interplay of irreconcilable oppositions. This view is immensely attractive to our culture, for various reasons. And unless we live somewhere like Bosnia, we do not have to think much about the horrors consequent on the ever-present possibility that the *polis* will disintegrate. In the final choral ode of the *Antigone* Dionysos is invoked to come and purify the city, in a way that evokes his role in the *polis* festival of the Eleusinian mysteries. Oudemans and Lardinois admit that in a sense the chorus are right, that Dionysos is indeed the saviour of the city, that the pollution *is* removed from the city. And yet, they go on to say (and here comes the article of faith), 'this should not blind us to the tragic ambiguity which continues to reign'. In what does this irresolvable tragic ambiguity consist? In the fact that 'the city can only continue its existence by sacrificing those who are its

most respected representatives, and there is no end to this persistent self-sacrifice'.[13] The incestuous house of Laios 'most
respected'?! And what is meant here by 'no end'? The need to celebrate the self-destruction continues, but what is celebrated is precisely an end, from which the *polis* benefits in ways too complex to
mention here. The Dionysos of the *Antigone* ode is the civic god
who in tragedy after tragedy presides over the self-destruction of
the ruling families of the mythical past, to the benefit of the *polis*,
the god who has thereby indeed put an end to that introversion and
autonomy of the family which gave rise to tragic conflict. But of
course the benefit can always be lost. Dionysos is indeed for the
Athenian audience 'an elemental agent of inhuman logic',[14] but
only if they omit to honour him in the kind of *polis* festivals evoked
in the final choral ode.

The other tragedy discussed by Friedrich is the *Ajax* (*Aias*).
Without denying the interest of the contrast pointed out by
Goldhill between the civic discourse of the festival and the figure
of Ajax (Aias), I also broadly agree with Friedrich's line of argument. The *Ajax* appears to be an exception to my tragic pattern,
because there is no kin-killing and no cult founded at the end. But
kin-killing is associated by Plato with suicide, on the grounds that
suicide is the killing of the very closest person to you, and by Ajax
himself, who prays that the Atreidai should be, like him,
αὐτοσφαγής ('killed by one's own or self')[15]—which means in his
case suicide and in their case killed by their nearest and dearest.
Ajax also claims that it would have suited his *daimôn* had he, when
in his frenzy, killed his own son. And in fact his suicide is, as
Tekmessa points out, the destruction of his own family. Although
what happens at the end of the play is the ritual of burial rather
than the founding of cult, there are various passages of the play
which prefigure the Athenian cult of Ajax.[16] My purpose here is
not just to extend my pattern to an apparent exception, but rather
to maintain that the tension between heroic household and *polis*
occurs not primarily in the interplay between tragedy and festival,
as Goldhill maintains, but rather *within* the tragedy, and secondly
that this tension consists not of *unresolved* interplay—as is characteristic of aetiological myth, it is resolved, and as is characteristic
of tragic aetiological myth, it is resolved in favour of the *polis*.
Taken as a whole, tragedy reinforces rather than subverts the civic
discourse and civic ritual of the festival. And I should add that the

creation of *polis* cult out of the self-destruction of the heroic family has a marked ethical dimension, not only in Odysseus' rejection of the ethic of vengeance (as discussed by Friedrich), but also in the same rejection by the future recipient of the Athenian cult, Ajax.[17] The fact that Ajax nevertheless later curses the Atreidai is to be explained by the usefulness for the Athenians of his hero-cult. It is useful to have on your side a hero who has suffered unjustly from your enemies, the Dorians, and retains his potent anger against them. The petty and vindictive Atreidai do not, as Goldhill claims, represent the *polis*. They are rather the ancestors of Athens' enemies.

I end with an influential statement of the view whose limitations I am keen to expose. In Greek tragedy, writes Vernant, 'the world of the city is called into question and its fundamental values are challenged in the ensuing debate. When exalting the civic ideal and affirming its victory over all forces from the past, even Aeschylus, the most optimistic of tragic writers, seems not to be making a positive declaration with tranquil conviction but rather to be expressing a hope, making an appeal that remains full of anxiety even amid the joy of the final apotheosis in *Eumenides*. The questions are posed but the tragic consciousness can find no fully satisfactory answers to them and so they remain open.'[18] Vernant is here spreading elegant confusion. The failure to answer questions and the persistence of anxiety are not the same thing. There is no doubt that the ending of the *Oresteia* answers the questions, however much *we* may dislike the answers, the way they are arrived at, or the very idea of questions being answered. But at the same time Vernant is right to say that anxiety persists. The Furies, who have created such havoc in the trilogy, are still there. But this is precisely the salutary anxiety that is vital to the cohesion of the *polis*, because it ensures respect for the Furies and the continued performance of their cult founded at the end of the trilogy.

None of this is intended to deny the importance, in the economy of tragedy, of various forms of ambiguity and anti-structure, which for historical reasons took a new form in late Euripides. But to locate unanswerable interrogation and irresolvable ambiguity at the heart of an ahistorical 'tragic consciousness', as the final destination of analysis, is to place yet another barrier to its understanding, like the barriers labelled 'fate' and 'character'. To help us move on from there to a historical understanding, I end by propos-

ing a definition of Greek tragedy, which is, like all such definitions,
ludicrously incomplete. But it is the one I think we need right now.
Greek tragedy is the dramatization of aetiological myth shaped by
the vital need to create and sustain the *polis*.

Notes

1. (*a*) There is no evidence for D. destroying the *polis*. He has come to
   establish his rites in the *polis* (as occurs in other myths of resistance
   to D.): 20–2, 39–40, 47–50, 61, 320–1, 770, 1295. If there is no *polis*,
   he will have no rites. (*b*) It is normal Euripidean practice for cult (or
   something similar) to be founded or predicated at the end of the
   drama, by the *deus ex machina* if there is one: W. S. Barrett, *Euripides
   Hippolytus* (Oxford 1964) 412. (*c*) We know from the hypothesis to
   the play that part of D.'s speech was directed to everybody (πᾶσι
   παρήγγειλεν). (*d*) After D.'s speech Agaue referred to future maenadism at Thebes (1387). (*e*) Dodds (on *Ba.* 1329) thinks that
   Christus Patiens 1668–9 and 1715 reflect a prediction by D. that one
   day the Cadmeans (i.e. the Thebans) will be expelled from their city,
   and will have only themselves to blame (having rejected D.). This is
   most unlikely. First, there is much from this part of the *Christus
   Patiens* which cannot conceivably come from the *Bacchae*. Secondly,
   the lines explain the guilt of the Jews in crucifying Christ, and their
   consequent diaspora (an idea quite alien to fifth-century Greece).
   Thirdly, it is the royal family (not the *polis*) that rejected D.: 26–31,
   45. If there was, after all, such a prediction, it could refer only to the
   distant future.

2. Certainly it is not confined to plays on Theban themes: note e.g.
   Aesch. *Oresteia*; Eur. *Hipp.*, *IT*, *Med.*

3. See Seaford, *Reciprocity and Ritual*, esp. 275–80, 328–67, 382–8.

4. Ibid. 1§b, 9§§ab.

5. Nietzsche, *Birth of Tragedy*, §7. Silk and Stern, *Nietzsche on Tragedy*
   (68–9) paraphrase: 'We should also reject Hegel's idea that it [the cho-
   rus] represents the populace against the aristocratic heroes of the
   drama proper; in origin and essence, tragedy is purely metaphysical
   and not socio-political.' Elsewhere in *The Birth of Tragedy*, though, a
   political dimension is given to the Apolline (see §21).

6. Seaford, *Reciprocity and Ritual*, 246.

7. Of course in general the *polis* suffers if the household does not bury its
   dead. But the *polis* is threatened in particular by the introversion
   (endogamy), autonomy, and internal conflict of a *powerful* household
   such as the Theban royal household. Nor is it Antigone's action that
   'saves the *polis*', for the consequence of this action, her own entomb-
   ment alive, combines with the continuing non-burial of Polyneikes

(1068–71) in polluting the *polis*. Thirdly, this non-burial has been decreed *not* by the *polis* but by its 'tyrant', Antigone's uncle Kreon (note esp. 60, 693, 734–9, 1056), however much his decree may be, in a sense, political. What does benefit the *polis* is the self-destruction of the ruling household.

8. There is evidence of mystic ritual at the Anthesteria and Lenaia, but not at the other great Attic festival of Dionysos, the City Dionysia—because it was there that the mystic ritual developed into drama: Seaford, *Reciprocity and Ritual*, 262–75.

9. The exceptions are sometimes unusual in other ways, e.g. as having spurious endings (e.g. Eur. *Iph.Aul.*) or being about non-Greek communities (Aesch. *Pers.*, Eur. *Tro.*).

10. 'Loss of Self', 220.

11. 'The Great Dionysia', 127.

12. Oudemans and Lardinois, *Tragic Ambiguity*, 216.

13. Ibid. 159.

14. George Steiner, *Antigones* (Oxford 1984) 101.

15. 841–2. The lines may be interpolated, but this does not much affect my point.

16. Seaford, *Reciprocity and Ritual*, 129–30.

17. *Ajax* 666–80 (reverence for the Atreidai, the realization that an enemy may become a friend). For the possible connection of this speech (the so-called 'deception speech') with the future cult of Ajax, see Seaford, *Reciprocity and Ritual*, 395–400.

18. Vernant and Vidal-Naquet, *Tragedy and Myth in Ancient Greece*, 9–10.

17

Is there a *Polis* in Aristotle's *Poetics*?

EDITH HALL

We should allow the champions of poetry—men who do not practise the art themselves, but are lovers of it—to offer a prose defence on its behalf, showing that poetry is a source not only of pleasure, but also of benefit to communities [πρὸς τὰς πολιτείας].

(Plato, *Republic* 10, 607d6–9)

Correctness in the art of poetry is not the same thing as correctness in the art of politics [οὐχ ἡ αὐτὴ ὀρθότης ἐστὶν τῆς πολιτικῆς καὶ τῆς ποιητικῆς ... τέχνης]

(Aristotle, *Poetics* 1460ᵇ13–15)

In taking up the gauntlet thrown down by Plato in the *Republic*, Aristotle early in his *Poetics* argues that the contemplation of representations in art offers the opportunity for people to come to an understanding of things in a pleasurable way. Moreover, this beneficial function of artistic representations—pleasurable learning—is accessible not only to philosophers, but to all men (ἀλλὰ καὶ τοῖς ἄλλοις ὁμοίως, 1448ᵇ12–14). Visual art is the type of representation Aristotle adduces to prove this point, but it is safe to assume that his theory is meant to apply equally to tragic representations; he seems, therefore, to have thought that tragedy could offer pleasurable learning to everyone. It is tempting to equate this notional 'everyman' with each individual member of the Athenian theatrical audiences during the democratic period, especially since Aristotle's treatise presumes in its implied reader a close acquaintance with Athenian tragedy.[1]

Yet such an identification, though widely assumed,[2] poses a considerable problem. At no point does Aristotle specify the nature or constituency of his imagined theatrical audience. More importantly, no amount of special pleading can alter the fact that the

Poetics goes against the grain of all previous discussions of tragedy in virtually excising from the genre not only the Athenian democratic *polis*, but also the very abstract notion of a *polis*, and of the civic context, consciousness, and function of tragic drama.

This is, of course, not the only striking dimension of classical Greek tragedy which the treatise evades. Particularly problematic is its neglect of the gods. Although kin-killing is acknowledged as a form of *pathos* likely to arouse pity (1453ᵇ19–26), and the use of the god from the machine receives brief attention (1454ᵇ1–6), Aristotle seems almost wholly uninterested in the genre's preoccupation with fate, with death and dying, with mortality and immortality, and with the nature of the divine. In identifying the logic of tragedy as akin to philosophy (1451ᵇ5–6), Aristotle forgets even to identify the 'theological mode of "thought" which the tragedians so ostentatiously pursued through their gods and heroes'.[3] His version of tragedy is quite startlingly anthropocentric, but its focus on humans at the expense of the gods also excludes from consideration the central defining features of the human condition explored in tragedy: that destiny is ultimately beyond human control, and that people die. Aristotle's analysis is 'wholly lacking in metaphysical aspirations, or even in any strongly existential implications for the understanding of "the tragic" '.[4]

The form taken by notions of fate and human autonomy, representations of death, reflections on mortality, and religious beliefs, are culturally variable and culturally determined: they are ideological. And it is ideological aspects of the classical tragedies which Aristotle's analytical and teleological approach excludes. Political concepts are likewise part of ideology. On the assumption that absences in a text speak as loud, if not louder, than its presences, this paper asks a single question—is there a *polis* in the *Poetics*?—by focusing on three particular silences. The treatise almost completely avoids mention of: the political nature of the context of tragic performances at the City Dionysia; the patently Athenian content and latent Athenocentric import of many of the plays; and the civic-didactic function of tragedy, whose consumer in other Athenian authors is emphatically a *citizen*, and specifically a citizen of the Athenian democracy.

It might be objected that even asking this question is anachronistically to project late twentieth-century socio-historicist interpretations back into the past, and irrationally to upbraid Aristotle for not seeing in tragedy what Vernant and Vidal-Naquet, Winkler and Zeitlin, Loraux, Goldhill, and others have documented.[5] Yet the understanding of Greek tragedy as a document of the Athenian civic imagination, undetachable from the historical, topographical, and political contexts of its original production and performance, is by no means an invention of recent decades. In almost every text where tragedy is discussed or quoted in fifth- and fourth-century Athens, including works by Aristotle other than the *Poetics*, such specificity is taken for granted.

THE CIVIC CONTEXT OF PERFORMANCE

It has long been a charge levelled at the *Poetics* that, in contrast with the strong sense of tragedy's public performance in Plato, Aristotle 'seems to sanction a clear separation of the playwright's art as such from its embodiment in the theatre'.[6] The *Poetics* even seems to suggest that reading a tragic text is as critically valid as watching it in performance (1453^b3–7, 1462^a11–18).[7] The usual criticisms of Aristotle's dismissal of the performative aspects of tragedy have focused on his *aesthetic* neglect of the extra dimensions which the visual and aural aspects lend to any dramatic performance: Plutarch called being present at a tragedy 'an outstanding aural and visual experience'.[8] Indeed, in relegating the musical and visual dimensions of tragedy to the places of least importance in his catalogue of its constitutive elements (1450^b15–20), Aristotle not only distorts the nature of the lived experience of tragedy for the ancient spectators. His treatise also ignores the way that the actual meaning of a text can be radically affected, even altered wholesale, by the way in which it is performed. Music, scenery, props, gesture, and delivery are not always mere adjuncts to meaning, but can also be the very media through which meaning is created.[9] But even this neglect is, arguably, secondary to the neglect of the social context of the performances of tragedy.

Recent work has stressed that the context of tragic performances, especially at the City Dionysia, offered an opportunity for Athenian imperial display and a celebration of Athenian citizenship.[10] But such scholarship could not have been produced were the evidence which testifies to its conclusions not explicitly acknowledged by the authors of the texts of classical Athens. Aristophanes makes it clear in *Acharnians* how well his contemporaries understood that performances at the City Dionysia were given before citizens and their allies and were expected to befit such an audience.[11] Cleon could never have prosecuted the comic poet for slandering the city in the presence of non-Athenians were such an assumption not prevalent. Isocrates complains about the convention by which imperial tribute and the city's war-orphans used to be displayed in the theatre during the festival;[12] epigraphic evidence illustrates the practice of conferring honours on individual benefactors of the city at the same time.[13] The descendants of the tyrannicides, heroes of the democracy, were granted rights to seats in the front of the theatre.[14] Demosthenes' *Against Meidias* demonstrates unequivocally the civic importance of the City Dionysia in the fourth century; Meidias' alleged assault on Demosthenes can be characterized as particularly shocking in Demosthenes' speech of prosecution because it took place at the festival.[15] It was also the customary practice of prominent citizens to include in their catalogues of their own civic liturgies (a commonplace in forensic and political oratory) their funding of dramatic choruses.[16]

Yet on this whole subject Aristotle's *Poetics* has absolutely nothing to say. And it is not as though this dimension of tragedy—its civic performance context—were neglected in his other works. Aristotle reveals in the *Politics* that he was perfectly aware of the importance of the connection between the drama festivals and the apparatus of civic administration. When enumerating the many different kinds of official required to administer the civic community ($\pi o\lambda\lambda\tilde{\omega}\nu$ $\gamma\grave{a}\rho$ $\dot{\epsilon}\pi\iota\sigma\tau\alpha\tau\tilde{\omega}\nu$ $\mathring{\eta}$ $\pi o\lambda\iota\tau\iota\kappa\mathring{\eta}$ $\kappa o\iota\nu\omega\nu\acute{\iota}a$ $\delta\epsilon\tilde{\iota}\tau\alpha\iota$: 4, 1299[a]15–16), he names second in order, after the priests but before the envoys, the city's funders of choruses ($\chi o\rho\eta\gamma o\acute{\iota}$: 4, 1299[a]19).[17]

The *Politics* is also replete with analogies from, and references to, tragedy—further evidence that Aristotle did have a sense of the close relationship between this form of poetry and the city-state. When he wants to argue that an association of the same citizens can mutate into a different kind of state by a change in constitution, he significantly uses an analogy from drama: the same chorus 'may at one time perform in a tragedy and at another in a comedy and so be different in kind, yet all the while be composed of the same persons' (3, 1276[b] 4–7). When arguing in favour of the political institution of ostracism, one of his analogies is from chorus training: the choirmaster (χοροδιδάσκαλος) would exclude a singer whose voice was louder and better than those of the other choristers (1, 1284ᵇ11–13).

THE ATHENOCENTRISM OF TRAGEDY

Just as recent scholarship has emphasized the Athenian civic context and arrangements of the performance of classical tragedy, it has also reassessed and come to a better understanding of so-called 'patriotic' tragedy. This dramatizes events from the Athenian mythical past, either set on Attic territory (Aeschylus' *Eumenides* and *Eleusinians*, Sophocles' *Oedipus at Colonus*, Euripides' *Heraclidae*, *Supplices*, and *Erechtheus*), or containing important Athenian heroes and/or Athenian aetiology (see especially *Ajax*, *Ion*, and Theseus in Euripides' *Hippolytus* and *Heracles*).[18] It has also demonstrated the latent Athenocentrism—the Athenian viewpoint, or implicit eulogy of Athens—in other tragedies superficially having little to do with Athens. The tragic Thebes of Sophocles, for example, is characterized as ruled by tyrants, closed in on itself, and liable to internecine strife, which constructs it as the opposite of the idealized tragic Athens, ruled by democratically minded kings, open to suppliants, and free from factional in-fighting.[19] The numerous plays containing barbarians (especially Aeschylus' *Persians*) have been shown to define systematically Athenian civic, ethical, and intellectual values through the medium of dramatized ethnic differentiation.[20]

But again, this perspective on classical tragedy is by no means a modern invention. It is not just that a particularly patriotic function of tragedy is implied by Aristophanes' making Aeschylus claim in *Frogs* that his *Persians* had taught his audience 'always to yearn for victories over their enemies' (1026–7). It is also the case that Athenian oratory similarly demonstrates that the patriotic function of tragedy was a commonplace in the city's public discourse, at least in the fourth century BC. One outstanding example from approximately Aristotle's own time will suffice. Lycurgus, the dominant politician of the 330s and 320s, chose to use the daughters of Erechtheus as exemplars of patriotism in his successful prosecution of Leocrates: his speech accordingly included a performance of the great fifty-five-line patriotic speech by

Praxithea, queen of Athens, from Euripides' lost *Erechtheus*. The same myth was utilized in a similar way by Demades.[21]

It is surely significant that despite the discussion of numerous plays by different poets in the *Poetics*, of which Aristotle's two favourites seem to have been Sophocles' *Oedipus Tyrannus* and Euripides' *Iphigeneia in Tauris*, he fails even to mention any of the famous patriotic plays, or even any tragedy set in or near Athens.[22]

Furthermore, only two of the numerous plays mentioned by Aristotle involve an Athenian mythical figure, and both of these are set elsewhere than Athens. First, Euripides' *Medea*, which is set in Corinth but briefly features Aegeus (1461^{b}20–1). Aegeus is the only Athenian tragic character mentioned by name in the *Poetics*, and his Athenian provenance is not even mentioned. Secondly, Sophocles' *Tereus* (1454^{b}36–7), a famous tragedy featuring the Athenian sisters Procne and Philomela (although Aristotle does not tell us so) being abused by the barbarian king Tereus in Thrace, and misbehaving themselves in turn. Yet Sophocles' *Tereus* is only brought in because of its unusual form of recognition—the famous 'voice of the shuttle'.

In his catalogue of the kind of households 'now' (i.e. 'in his day': *νῦν*) constituting the material for the best tragedies, Aristotle details heroes from Argos, Thebes, Calydon, and Tegea—that is, from nearly every Greek city-state famous in myth *except* Athens: Alcmaeon, Oedipus, Orestes, Meleager, Thyestes, and Telephus (1453^{a}19–21). Besides the obvious masculinism of this list,[23] it is astonishingly un-Athenian: we look in vain for a Theseus, an Erechtheus, a Pandion, an Aegeus, or an Ion. But perhaps we should focus on the use of the word 'now' in the sentence: Aristotle implies that the concentration on the heroes he names is a contemporary development. If we knew more about fourth-century tragedy, it is just possible that we could see his silence on the Athenian-ness of the genre's subject-matter as an accurate reflection of what was really happening in the contemporary tragic theatre.[24] On the other hand, such an argument tends towards circularity: much of what we know about fourth-century tragedy comes from Aristotle himself. Moreover, if the *Poetics* were the only source available for fifth-century tragedy, Aristotle's unrepresentative selection of titles would have suggested, quite wrongly, that tragedy had never been set in Athens or dealt with Athenian issues at all.

THE POLIS IN THE POETRY

Aristotle not only leaves out of his treatise the collective, civic context of the performance of tragedy, and the Athenocentrism of its subject-matter and perspective. His agenda seems to have involved the complete erasure from tragedy of even the abstract idea of the *polis* as an institution—whether Athenian, democratic, or otherwise.

An excursus into lexicography will amply illustrate this point. The word 'citizen' (πολίτης) never occurs in the *Poetics*. The terms 'city-state' or 'city' (πόλις, ἄστυ), 'people' (δῆμος), 'democracy' (δημοκρατία), and 'Athenians' or 'Athens', each occur on only one or two occasions; every single instance is in reference not to tragedy but to comedy, and occurs in the early section on the historical origins of drama. Comedy, says Aristotle, originated in the phallic songs still customary 'in many cities' (ἐν πολλαῖς τῶν πόλεων, 1449ᵃ12). In a tantalizing remark, he suggests just once that he is aware of a connection at least of comedy with democracy: the Megarians claim that they invented comedy, saying that it arose when their democracy was established (ἐπὶ τῆς παρ' αὐτοῖς δημοκρατίας γενομένης, 1148ᵃ31–2). The Peloponnesians likewise claim comedy, saying that they call outlying villages by a cognate term (κῶμαι), while the Athenians call them 'demes'; the Peloponnesians also claim that comic actors wandered among the villages because they were driven in contempt from the 'town' (ἄστυ, 1448ᵃ35–8).[25]

The only exception to Aristotle's renunciation or repudiation of even the vocabulary of the public life of the *polis* occurs with the term 'pertaining to the *polis*', or 'political' (πολιτικός), and the two passages in which it appears may point to an answer to the whole problem of the *Poetics*' missing *polis*. Aristotle tosses off an intriguing remark in his discussion of *mimêsis* of intellect (third in importance after *mimêsis* of *praxis* and *mimêsis* of character); he says that it requires 'political sense and rhetoric [ὅπερ ἐπὶ τῶν λόγων τῆς πολιτικῆς καὶ ῥητορικῆς ἔργον ἐστίν], since the older poets [οἱ . . . ἀρχαῖοι] made their characters speak politically [πολιτικῶς], while contemporary poets [οἱ . . . νῦν] make them speak rhetorically [ῥητορικῶς]' (1450ᵇ6–8).[26] If only Aristotle had enlarged on this chronological schematization, whereby the 'old intellectual content' of tragedy is defined as political, and the 'modern intellectual

content' of tragedy as rhetorical (a change of which he does not seem
to disapprove), we might be able to understand better just why there
is so little about the body politic in the *Poetics*. As it stands, it is not
even clear where the conceptual boundary between old and new
tragedy is meant to be drawn. It is just possible that Euripides is to
be included amongst the modern tragedians (οἱ . . . νῦν) whose characters speak 'rhetorically';[27] I suspect, however, that Lucas is correct in defining Euripides as *both* political *and* rhetorical, and in
seeing Aristotle's chronological dividing-line as approximately
coinciding with the deaths of both Sophocles and Euripides (see also
1453ᵇ27).[28] The ancients were (rightly) less inclined than scholars
today to see Euripides as representing a 'later' stage in the development of tragedy than his near-coeval Sophocles.

In fact, there is one more instance in the *Poetics* of the term
'political'. During the brief discussion of 'Homeric problems'
towards the end of the treatise, Aristotle suggests a principle which
can be used in answering criticisms of Homer: correctness in the
art of poetry is not the same as correctness in the art of politics (οὐχ
ἡ αὐτὴ ὀρθότης ἐστὶν τῆς πολιτικῆς καὶ τῆς ποιητικῆς . . . τέχνης), nor
indeed as correctness in any other art (1460ᵇ13–15). This is
undoubtedly directed against Plato, who had made so much use of
the correctness and incorrectness of poetry, always on the assumption that poetry must be judged by the same criteria as political
questions.[29] To paraphrase Aristotle's crucial formulation, *poetry
is not to be assessed by criteria to do with the polis*. Thus, finally,
albeit in the context of epic rather than tragedy, Aristotle explicitly
cuts the umbilical cord which has tied poetry so firmly to the city-
state in all previous literary criticism. He is, in fact, sidestepping
Plato's request for a demonstration that poetry is both pleasurable
and useful to political communities (πρὸς τὰς πολιτείας),[30] by saying that this is not an appropriate way in which to evaluate poetry:
poetry is a self-sufficient art whose own correctness or lack of it is
immanent, internal to itself, and thus distinct from correctness in
any other sphere of human activity. Aristotle has estranged the
natural bed-partners poetry and the *polis* throughout his *Poetics*,
but he here declares their decree absolute.

The importance of this official separation of correctness in the
poetic and in the political has been little appreciated, probably
because the erasure in the *Poetics* of the civic aspects of tragedy has
itself received scant attention. Hubbard's otherwise excellent

translation, for example, renders Aristotle's 'correctness in the art of politics' here (ὀρθότης τῆς πολιτικῆς . . . τέχνης) as 'excellence in morals', thus obscuring precisely the *polis*-centredness of the kind of literary criticism Aristotle's *Poetics* is repudiating, and which it so extraordinarily and so scrupulously avoids.[31]

What makes this all the more remarkable is that Aristotle's uses of tragedy in his works on rhetoric, ethics, and politics demonstrate that he was as aware of the interpenetration of tragedy and all the other civic discourses as any modern scholar,[32] and, more importantly, as anybody else in classical Athens. Dionysus' mission in Aristophanes' *Frogs*, and the uses to which Sophocles' *Antigone* is put in the battle between Demosthenes and Aeschines,[33] attest to a mutual understanding of tragedy's claim to benefit and educate the *polis*. This understanding is shared by Plato in his *Republic*, even if he emphatically rejects the claim that tragedy is beneficial. Easterling points to the significance of the fourth-century practice whereby old tragedies were revived at the city festivals as 'evidence that the tragedies were felt to have a civic function'.[34] And Aristotle himself, in works other than the *Poetics*, reveals that he was by no means immune to this general perception of the genre. The exclusion from his poetic theory of the idea of the *polis*, of even the very notion of citizenship, must therefore have cost him a considerable intellectual effort. Outside of the *Poetics* the entire ethical system of Aristotle, like that of Plato, turns precisely 'on an investigation of the social order which can generate norms for action; the "moral" question of how one is to act is inseparable from an enquiry into the character of the *polis* to which one does or should belong'.[35]

In texts other than the *Poetics*, Aristotle often quotes tragedy to lend authority to his opinions on social relationships, political behaviour, and the *polis* in general, revealing that although he might in theory take the *polis* out of tragic poetry,[36] he could not in practice take tragic poetry out of the *polis*. Implicit in his other works is the assumption that correctness in the poetical sphere *is* the same as correctness in the political sphere. The *Rhetoric*, of course, a handbook on persuasion, that vital skill of the prominent public man under any kind of constitution, abounds in quotations from tragedy deployed for a wide variety of reasons: gnomic sayings to prove 'truths' about human nature, about natural justice, for use in speeches, and as a form of proof.[37]

But Aristotle uses tragedy to illustrate more transparently *polis*-related matters in the *Nicomachean Ethics*. Correctness in the political sphere is 'proved' by tragic examples of correct social or political thinking. In his treatment of civic consensus (ὁμόνια), when arguing that the existence of two candidates for power leads to stasis, he cites as an example the *Phoenician Women* of Euripides.[38] The discussion of friendship involves two quotations from the same playwright's *Orestes*, a tragedy obsessed with this theme.[39] Practical wisdom, and the difference between the prudent man and the practical politician, who is regarded as an interfering nuisance, are illustrated by a quotation from the Euripidean *Philoctetes*.[40] A similar pattern can be discerned in the *Politics*. Aristotle invokes Euripides' *Aeolus* in order to prove that the ruling class's education should be so designed as to benefit the *polis*.[41] He quotes Euripides' *Iphigeneia in Aulis* to confirm the natural servility of barbarians;[42] a Sophoclean line is adduced to confirm that silence brings credit to a woman.[43]

CONCLUSION: THE DIVORCE OF TRAGEDY FROM THE *POLIS*

There are several reasons for doubting whether it is either correct or advantageous to attempt to integrate the historical Athenian democracy—except by its erasure—into Aristotle's theory of tragedy. But in Aristotle's day the contexts of the composition and performance of tragedy were beginning to alter considerably. During the classical era, which coincided with the Athenian democratic period, Athens held a virtually complete monopoly over the generation of tragedy; despite the occasionally attested productions of exported tragedies in Sicily or Macedonia, it was also the indisputable centre of tragedy in performance. As Plato's *Laches* remarks, anyone aspiring to be a successful dramatist naturally heads straight for Athens.[44] During Alexander's expeditions, however, dramas began to be performed in farflung destinations, even beyond the Greek-speaking world in Tyre, Susa, and Ecbatana.[45] After his death, tragedy began to be both written and performed in earnest in the capitals of the new Hellenistic kingdoms, and theatres were built in almost every town.[46]

The *Poetics*' near-total displacement of the *polis* from tragedy seems to me to be an astonishingly original innovation, which adumbrates the incipient and future status of tragedy as an international art-form. Tragedy was soon to be consumed and appreciated by multifarious individuals, in widely disparate political situations, in physical contexts quite unlike, and in geographical locations at great distances from, the Athenian theatre of Dionysus. Tragedy was about to lodge a petition for divorce from the Athenian democratic *polis*. The *Poetics*, the work of a non-Athenian and of an opponent certainly of *radical* democracy,[47] enacts this divorce on the level of theory, a divorce which was to have a huge impact on the future of ancient literary criticism,[48] quite apart from the direction taken by literary theory in later ages.

Aristotle was an outsider. He was not an Athenian citizen, and was therefore uniquely situated to look at tragedy in a non-political way. We could speculate, of course, on the degree to which the process by which he conceptually depoliticized tragedy was the result of any conscious affiliation with Macedonian expansionism. Unfortunately, it is necessary to remain agnostic about the date of the *Poetics*, which could conceivably have been produced at any time between 367 and 322 BC.[49] I suspect, however, that Aristotle's undoubtedly conscious excision of the *polis* from tragic poetry was the product, rather, of a more subconscious, intuitive, prefigurative grasp of the cultural requirements of the future and of the direction in which tragedy needed to move. In modern cultural-materialist terms, Aristotle can be said to have intuitively identified, been influenced by, and articulated in his poetic theory an 'emergent' rather than 'residual' or 'dominant' strand within fourth-century Greek culture and ideology.[50] But as a divorce of tragedy from the Athenian democratic *polis*, enacted on the level of theory, the treatise has served in the history of the criticism of Attic tragic drama both positive and negative functions.

Aristotle's *Poetics* has certainly played no insignificant part in obscuring precisely those local, historical, and ideological specificities of which its other contemporaries were so aware, and which it has been the task of scholars over the last couple of decades to exhume. But at the same time it can be said to have contributed uniquely to the continued rediscovery, reinterpretation, and re-performance of the tragic corpus, and its constant revivification: in a *transhistorical* and apolitical sense, it has made it accessible to 'everyman', precisely because its reader is encouraged to assess tragedy in complete dissociation from civic concepts. The implied reader of the treatise is not defined by membership of the Athenian democracy or even of a *polis*; it is no longer a requirement of tragedy that it should offer to its consumer any elucidation or confirmation of his civic identity or edification dependent upon its collective consumption. There is indeed no *polis*, concrete or abstract, to be identified in Aristotle's *Poetics*.

Notes

1. Halliwell, *Aristotle's Poetics*, 329.
2. See e.g S. G. Salkever, 'Tragedy and the Education of the *Dêmos*: Aristotle's Response to Plato', in Euben (ed.), *Greek Tragedy and Political Theory*, 274–303.
3. Silk and Stern, *Nietzsche on Tragedy*, 157. They relate the near-absence of the gods from the *Poetics* to Aristotle's own remoteness 'from the now imperilled religious presuppositions of Greek culture' (227).
4. S. Halliwell, 'Aristotle's Poetics', in G. A. Kennedy (ed.), *The Cambridge History of Literary Criticism*, i: *Classical Criticism* (Cambridge 1989) 149–83, at 165–6.
5. Vernant and Vidal-Naquet, *Myth and Tragedy in Ancient Greece*. J. J. Winkler and Zeitlin (edd.), *Nothing to Do with Dionysos?*; N. Loraux, *Les Enfants d'Athéna: Idées athéniennes sur la citoyenneté et la division des sexes* (Paris 1981); Goldhill, *Reading Greek Tragedy*; C. Meier, *Die politische Kunst der griechischen Tragödie* (Munich 1988); Hall, *Inventing the Barbarian*.
6. Halliwell, *Aristotle's Poetics*, 337. See also V. Goldschmidt, *Questions platoniciennes* (Paris 1970) 112–13.
7. On the late fifth- and fourth-century reading public for stage-plays, see L. Woodbury, 'Aristophanes' *Frogs* and Athenian Literacy: *Ran.* 52–3, 1114', *TAPA* 106 (1976) 349–57; Xanthakis-Karamanos, *Studies in Fourth-Century Tragedy*, 8.
8. *De Glor. Athen.* 348c.
9. For example, Taplin, *Stagecraft of Aeschylus*, 25, 477–9.
10. For example, Goldhill, 'The Great Dionysia and Civic Ideology', *JHS* 107 (1987) 58–76; Hall, *Inventing the Barbarian*, 162–4.
11. *Ach.* 377–82, 502–6.
12. Isoc. 8. 82.
13. See Pickard-Cambridge, *Dramatic Festivals of Athens*², 58–9 and 82 n. 2.
14. Isaeus 5. 46–7.
15. Another aspect of Demosthenes' *Against Meidias*, the way Meidias' ethnic origins are constructed on the lines of a tragic narrative, is discussed by Peter Wilson in this volume, pp. 318–19.

16. For example, Isaeus 5. 36, 42–3; 6. 59–61.
17. Interestingly, Aristotle elsewhere in the *Politics* claims that the financing of choruses is a liturgy which not only, like funding a torch-race, is not of public utility, but should actually be prevented under a democracy, a constitution in which the rich must be treated with particular consideration (5, 1309ᵃ14–20). He probably has in mind the system in Crete whereby civic liturgies were defrayed from public funds: see W. L. Newman (ed.), *The Politics of Aristotle*, ii (Oxford 1887) 353.
18. On *OC*, see e.g. M. W. Blundell, 'The Ideal of Athens in *Oedipus at Colonus*', in Sommerstein *et al.* (edd.), *Tragedy, Comedy and the Polis*, 287–306. On *Ion*, see B. Goff, 'Euripides' *Ion* 1132–1165: The Tent', *PCPS* 34 (1988) 42–54, and N. Loraux, 'Kreousa the Autochthon', in Winkler and Zeitlin, *Nothing to Do with Dionysos?*, 168–206.
19. F. I. Zeitlin (1986), 'Thebes: Theater of Self and Society in Athenian Drama', in Euben (ed.), *Greek Tragedy and Political Theory*, 101–41.
20. Hall, *Inventing the Barbarian*.
21. Lyc. *In Leocr.* 100 = Eur. fr. 360 N²; Demad. *On the Twelve Years* 37. For a nuanced study of the uses to which fourth-century orators put tragedy, including the nostalgic patriotism of Lycurgus' quotation from *Erechtheus*, see Peter Wilson's article, pp. 310–31, in this volume.
22. Aristotle mentions many tragedies, and makes numerous other allusions which allow the probable identification of the work he has in mind. These included: Agathon's *Antheus*; Aeschylus' *Choephori*, *Niobe*, and *Philoctetes*; Sophocles' *OT*, *Antigone*, *Electra*, and *Tyro*; Euripides' *IT*, *IA*, *Merope*, *Melanippe the Wise*, *Orestes*, *Medea*, and *Philoctetes*; Astydamas' *Alcmaeon*; Carcinus' *Thyestes* and *Amphiaraus*; Dicaeogenes' *Cyprians*; Theodectes' *Tydeus* and *Lynceus*. He also names plays of unknown authorship, such as a *Helle*, a *Scylla*, a *Phineidae*, an *Odysseus the False Messenger*, a *Phthiotides*, a *Peleus*, a *Phorcidae*, a *Prometheus*, a *Sisyphus*, and a *Mysians*.
23. It is not as though tragedies with female protagonists had ceased to be written: witness Astydamas' *Antigone* and *Alcmene*, Chaeremon's *Alphesiboea*, and Theodectes' *Helen*. The almost complete failure in the *Poetics* to address the issues of the large number of female characters and choruses in tragedy, and the prominence of conflict between the sexes, is further evidence of the treatise's lack of interest in the genre's ideological dimension. The missing perspective on gender in tragedy is particularly surprising in view of (1) the strong views on the 'femininity' of the genre expressed by both Aristophanes and Plato, and (2) Aristotle's own apparent approval of both Sophocles' *Antigone* and Euripides' *IT*, and his familiarity with the latter's

Medea. It is impossible to reconcile the heroines of any of these plays with his prescription that female characters should not be courageous or clever (1454ᵃ23–4).

24. Xanthakis-Karamanos, *Studies in Fourth-Century Tragedy*, 15–16, discusses the mythical characters which were particularly popular in fourth-century tragedy. They included Hector, Antigone, and, significantly, the Salaminian Ajax (who was important to the Athenians) in addition to the heroes catalogued by Aristotle at *Poet.* 1453ᵃ19–21. She does not ask, however, whether Athenian subject-matter had become less popular.

25. To clear up the remaining instances of these terms: the Peloponnesians say that 'the Athenians' use the term πράττειν rather than δρᾶν of 'doing' (1448ᵃ35–1448ᵇ1), and while the plots of comedy came from Sicily, Crates was the first 'Athenian' to construct generalized plots (1449ᵇ7).

26. On this passage, see also J. Gregory, *Euripides and the Instruction of the Athenians* (Ann Arbor 1991) 1 and 12 with n. 1.

27. The view of Xanthakis-Karamanos, *Studies in Fourth-Century Tragedy*, 59–60.

28. D. W. Lucas, *Aristotle, Poetics* (Oxford 1968) 107, 152–3.

29. *Resp.* 10, 601d–e, *Leg.* 2, 653b–60. See G. F. Else, *Aristotle, Poetics* (Ann Arbor 1967) 112.

30. *Resp.* 10, 607d6–9.

31. M. E. Hubbard, in D. A. Russell and M. Winterbottom (edd.), *Ancient Literary Criticism: The Principal Texts in New Translations* (Oxford 1972) 127. The trans. of Halliwell, *Poetics of Aristotle*, 61, 'correct standards in poetry are not identical with those in politics', is much better.

32. See e.g. Loraux, *Invention of Athens*; Ober and Strauss, 'Drama, Political Rhetoric' and E. Hall, 'Lawcourt Dramas: The Power of Performance in Greek Forensic Oratory', in *BICS* 42 (1995).

33. Dem. 19. 246–7.

34. P. E. Easterling, 'The End of an Era? Tragedy in the Early Fourth Century', in Sommerstein *et al.*, *Tragedy, Comedy and the Polis*, 559–69, at 567.

35. T. Eagleton, *Criticism and Ideology* (London 1976) 174.

36. The fragments of Aristotle's lost treatise *On the Poets* (frs. 70–7 in V. Rose, *Aristotelis qui ferebantur librorum fragmenta* [Leipzig 1886]), while suggesting that it addressed the topics of *mimêsis*, sense-perception, and the biographical legend of Homer (see C. O. Brink, *Horace on Poetry* [Cambridge 1963] 120–5), do not indicate that it had any more to say about the civic or ideological dimensions of tragedy than the *Poetics*.

37. *Rhet.* 1. 1371^b = Eur. fr. 183 N^2; 1. 1373^b = Soph. *Ant.* 456–7; 2. 1394^a = Eur. *Med.* 296–7. See North, 'Use of Poetry', 1–33; R. R. Bolgar, 'The Training of Elites in Greek Education', in R. Wilkinson (ed.), *Governing Elites* (New York 1969) 23–49.
38. 9, 1167^{a}32–4.
39. 9, 1168^b, 1169^{b}7-8 = Eur. *Or.* 1046, 665; see also 13, 1155^{b}2–3.
40. 6, 1142^{a}2–6 = Eur. frs. 787, 788 N^2.
41. 3, 1277^{a}19–20 = Eur. fr. 16. 2 N^2.
42. *Pol.* 1, 1252^{b}7–9 = *IA* 1400.
43. 1, 1260^{a}30 = Soph. *Ajax* 293.
44. *Lach.* 183a–b.
45. Xanthakis-Karamanos, *Studies in Fourth-Century Tragedy*, 4–6.
46. See G. M. Sifakis, *Studies in the History of Hellenistic Drama* (London 1967).
47. See e.g. *NE* I 1095^{b}17–20, where 'the many' (οἱ πολλοί) are distinguished by their slavish and bestial lifestyle from men of affairs and philosophers. At *Pol.* 6, 1319^{a}26–8 Aristotle envisages with disapproval degenerate democracies composed largely of craftsmen, hired labourers, and the thetic class. He thinks that the collective opinion of the people (including its manifestations in their judgements of music and poetry) is, in a superior kind of democracy, potentially better than that of each individual (*Pol.* 3, 1281^{b}4–9), yet he expressly qualifies this statement by warning that by no means every kind of *dêmos* (especially not the bestial kind) can make judgements on a par with the highly educated few (ibid. 15–20).
48. At least as practised by the peripatetics (see A. Podlecki, 'The Peripatetics as Literary Critics', *Phoenix* 23 [1969] 114–37) and Horace.
49. This is the conclusion reached by Halliwell, *Aristotle's Poetics*, 324–30, in his appendix on the date of the treatise.
50. For a definition of 'emergent' ideology, see R. Williams, *Marxism and Literature* (Oxford 1977) 121–7.

18

Tragic Rhetoric: The Use of Tragedy and the Tragic in the Fourth Century

P. J. WILSON

One of the starting-points of this paper is an interest in the ambivalent attitudes towards tragedy generated in antiquity: not simply in the contrast between the enormous popularity of tragic drama with the Athenian *dêmos* in the fifth century and the suspicion of intellectuals in the fourth, but in the wider—and largely unrecoverable—attitudes towards tragedy as a cultural institution, and more specifically in speculation concerning the dynamics of Athenian identification with tragedy as an institution. For on the one hand one finds a very high degree of collective and individual self-identification with this leading cultural product of Athens, an energetic contest for the prestige which attaches to it—both within and beyond Attica. Individuals—*ehorêgoi*, poets, and actors—accrued huge stores of cultural capital from their association with the institution of tragedy, as did the Athenians collectively, for whatever its origins, classical tragedy was in practice a thoroughly Athenian phenomenon and drew spectators from all Greece to the festival of the Great Dionysia; while on the other hand, tragedy was by its very nature a troubling performance and it did not require an elaborate theoretical formulation sensitive to the dangers of *mimêsis* in order for doubts to be raised about its introduction into the heart of the city. We have only the texts of extant tragedy and a meagre collection of external evidence to give us any idea of what the perceived relation of tragedy to the life of the *polis* might have been. Much excellent recent work has shown that the relation was one combining displacement, sublimation, and distantiation with an intensely self-reflective focus—a complex interplay of same and other, of proximity and distance.[1] One story from the gloom of the early history of tragedy whose historicity may be given a second glance is that of the theatrical and legislative response of the Athenians in 494 to Phrynichos' *The Capture of Miletos*. According to Herodotos, Phrynichos was fined 1,000 drachmas 'for reminding the Athenians of their οἰκήια κακά', their 'troubles close to home,' and any future use of the drama was forbidden.² At a minimum the story illustrates the sensitivity of the Athenians to the boundary between tragedy and the immediate affairs of the city. Although the story of the destruction of Miletos was indeed a tragic one, it was not the appropriate matter of Athenian tragedy. This lesson, backed by an official legislative intervention, as to the degree and nature of the distance to be maintained between tragedy and the city, seems to have been well learnt. The story thus provides us with a virtually unique insight into the active formulation, under contested circumstances, of the laws of the tragic genre.³

In this paper, however, my focus is on the fourth, not the fifth, century. I want to raise—necessarily in a compressed and somewhat impressionistic manner—some questions about the place of tragedy in the fourth-century *polis*: and I shall be interested not so much in how it functioned in a general way (impossible to ascertain in any case because of the lack of fourth-century tragedy)⁴ as in attitudes to, and appropriations of, the institution of tragedy and of ideas of the tragic—in particular, the way the sensitive boundary between tragedy and the city was manipulated in other civic contexts of public eloquence both to attract the prestige of this leading cultural production and to damn either an opponent in the courts or a course of public policy in the *ekklêsia* by insinuation of the tragic. Is this apparently ambivalent attitude to tragedy in the fourth century—as a potential source, as it were, of both praise and blame—an ambivalence of the same order as that found in the fifth century? Part of the difficulty in answering this question lies in the perennially frustrating mismatch of the kinds of evidence available for historians of tragedy: put crudely, tragic texts of the fifth century, none of the fourth; public rhetoric and various other contextual sources of the fourth century, none of the fifth. One result of this situation is that we are particularly ill-informed as to the rhetorical manipulations that may (or may not) have been worked on tragedy in the period of its greatest efflorescence.⁵ However, I suspect that in the fifth century there was likely to have been a resistance towards taking tragedy from the precinct of Dionysos (back) to the agora, as it were, of a kind not unlike that which kept the 'troubles' that touched the Athenians most immediately from being represented in the theatre.[6]

In turning to 'the orators', one must be sensitive to the aims and context of these texts, which can appear, deceptively, to be transparent windows onto Athenian life and values. The texts have for a long time been ransacked for 'facts' by historians of the Attic stage turning a blind eye to their date of composition or largely ignoring the consequences that follow from their being produced in and for particular rhetorical and political contexts.[7] But as long as one does recognize that the uses of tragedy in these authors are bound to be strategic, and conditioned both by the exigencies of the immediate political *agôn* and the circumstances of public communication, one can in fact perhaps tell rather more from those strategies about changing attitides to, and the uses of, tragedy. It is a focus which also touches upon large issues of the fourth century's relation to the fifth.

To begin with the tip of the iceberg—the direct quotation of tragedy by public speakers:[8] Aischines, Demosthenes, and Lykourgos all adduce the words of the tragic poets to support a line of argument. Sometimes they deliver the lines themselves, with what degree of impersonation one can only guess;[9] but often they order the clerk of the court to read them out, with the characteristic instruction—λέγε.[10] They thus treat these slabs of tragic poetry, varying in length from one to fifty-five lines, as pieces of evidence like any other deposited in the courts—like laws, the written depositions of witnesses, contracts, treaties, or oaths.[11] It is as though these deposited lines of poetry had the relatively self-evident cogency of what Aristotle terms 'non-argumentative proofs'—πίστεις ἄτεχνοι.[12]

All the extant examples of this use of tragedy are confined to a number of speeches delivered in political trials,[13] and the tragedians here often rub shoulders with a range of other poets: Homer, Hesiod, elegy and epigram.[14] And apart from the special motivation for the citation of tragedy that is relevant to the conflict between Aischines and Demosthenes—namely, Aischines' status as an ex-tragic actor—there is little or no apparent difference of attitude to the quality of *tragic* poetry as evidence as opposed to, say, that of Solon's political elegies or an epigram of Simonides. In each instance their citation is an attempt to harness the prestige of poetic *sophia* to an argument, or to deduct it from an opponent's. They are all in the first instance gestures to the authority of an idealized past—an authority tempered in the case of poetry only by the need on the speaker's part to avoid the stigma of élitist learning or 'sophistry'. Ober and Strauss have well analysed the careful balance that had to be observed between 'putting on a good show', as they put it, and avoiding the risk of offending a demotic audience by the signs of an élite education in literary culture.[15]

A lengthy section of the speech *Against Leokrates* of 330 perhaps best illustrates this direct use of tragedy. Its author, Lykourgos, was a politician with a special interest in the theatre.[16] A large part of the speech (see 75–130) is devoted, like so many others of its era, to elaborate appeals to models from the past as protreptics for the present. The tragic poet is represented as a figure of prophetic, and virtually sacred, wisdom: 'Personally I value as the utterance of an oracle these lines, written by ancient poets and handed down to posterity' (92).[17] At 98 Lykourgos turns to the story of Praxithea, the wife of the Athenian king Erechtheus, and her decision to sacrifice her daughter in order to avert the danger of invasion by the Thracian Eumolpos:

And so we should praise Euripides because, apart from his other excellent qualities as a poet, he chose this story as a subject for drama, believing that in the actions of those people the citizens would have a very fine model [κάλλιστον . . . παράδειγμα, 100] which they could look to and contemplate, and so implant in their souls a love of their country. It's worthwhile, men of the court, to hear the iambics which he has depicted the mother of the girl as uttering. For you will see in them a greatness of spirit and a nobility worthy of the city and of a daughter of Kephisos.[18]

There follows a quotation of a full fifty-five lines from a speech by Praxithea in Euripides' *Erechtheus*, copied no doubt from the official text Lykourgos himself was responsible for having established in the state archives.[19] It is full of the tropes of fifth-century Athenian self-glorification familiar in particular from the genre of the *epitaphios logos*: only Athens deserves such a sacrifice, because the people of Athens alone in the world are not newcomers to their land but autochthons—hence they are the only 'true' citizens of Greece; and Athens' greatest glory is the honour derived from putting the collective before the individual, the city before the family.[20]

'On these verses, men of Athens, your fathers were brought

up'—and Lykourgos indulges in only the most self-evident of commentaries on the passage, stressing that 'Euripides' 'shows' (ἐνδεικνύμενος) here that if a woman can act like this, overcoming the innate and universal maternal instinct (φιλοτεκνία) of women (101), then *a fortiori*, men should outdo them in their display of devotion to their country—and not forsake it in a time of peril, the charge for which Leokrates stands trial.[21]

Not only is this a deeply nostalgic view of a glorious past, of a lost ideal of the city nearly a hundred years old,[22] but it is a very nostalgic view of tragedy that virtually assimilates it to the profoundly idealizing genre of the *epitaphios logos*, and edits out, through this decontextualized citation, what might well be considered the most distinctive features of Euripidean tragedy—its irony and its probing, questioning attitude to myth and to accepted values, acknowledged, at least in caricature, as early as Aristophanes—including precisely those features enunciated in Praxithea's speech.[23] It is doubtless the pragmatism of Lykourgos' aims that produces this particularly edifying Euripides, pressed into service for the immediate and not necessarily altogether idealistic purpose of convicting Leokrates. But none the less, its anticipated effectiveness before a mass audience must be based on an assumption that such a view of tragedy would or could be shared by his hearers. Tragedy is here a source of political models for behaviour in keeping with the lost ideals of Athens—ideals which the tragedy that is adduced as illustration had in all likelihood exposed to scrutiny.[24] It has become for a later generation what the power of the *polis* itself was ideally for the citizens of 'Periklean' Athens—an edifying object of contemplation that will seduce its viewers, turning them into its lovers.[25]

In his speech *Against Timarchos* of 345, Aischines cites Euripides, 'a poet than whom none is wiser' (151)—with what is doubtless an affected lack of bookishness (λέγει που, 'he says somewhere')—as the great advocate of an ideal of chaste *erôs*. He does this by quoting two lines from the *Stheneboia* in which a character, unnamed, says 'That *erôs* which leads men to prudence and *aretê* is an enviable gift for mortals; such things I wish for' (ὁ δ' εἰς τὸ σῶφρον ἐπ' ἀρετήν τ' ἄγων ἔρως | ζηλωτὸς ἀνθρώποισιν, ὧν εἴην ἐγώ).[26] This couplet, excerpted from the very play that the Aristophanic Aischylos cites to exemplify the moral damage Euripides had done the city,[27] and which is expressed in any case

in the form of a wish that in all probability found no simple fulfilment within the tragedy, is here sanitized and presented as the wisdom of the great Euripides, guardian of erotic morals.[28]

In these instances fifth-century tragedy is, like Homer, a source
of implicit authority, and a storehouse of edifying moral and political models: an evident desire to appropriate the prestige of the
classics at all costs has led to a rather untragic vision of tragedy.

In his speech *On the Embassy* Demosthenes re-cites lines from
Euripides' *Phoinix* which Aischines had used in his earlier trial
against Timarchos: 'And whoever delights in keeping company
with bad men, I question him not, for I know what kind of man he
is from the company he likes to keep' (245), ὅστις δ' ὁμιλῶν ἥδεται
κακοῖς ἀνήρ, | οὐ πώποτ' ἠρώτησα, γιγνώσκων ὅτι | τοιοῦτός ἐστιν
οἷσπερ ἥδεται ξυνών.[29] Such is the perceived power of the poetic
word that Demosthenes finds it necessary to respond to Aischines'
prior citations. He goes on to reapply these words to Aischines and
his association on the embassy with Philokrates, who was a con-
fessed bribetaker (or at least a convenient scapegoat). By this form
of kledonomancy, reconstruing his enemy's words in a sense hostile to him, Demosthenes as usual has it both ways, disparaging his
opponent's use of tragedy while recovering the value of its citation
for himself.

A key factor in all these cases is that the accredited citations of
tragedy are without exception from Sophokles and Euripides.[30] It
is tragedy of the past, not of the present, that has this power. One
might speculate as to whether anything comparable would have
been possible in fifth-century public speech: it seems to me a manifestation of the peculiarly fourth-century obsession with the fifth,
in which the idealization of tragedy as a monumental icon of lost
value plays an important part.[31] This turning by the fourth-
century makers of public policy to the tragedy of the fifth as a
touchstone of value and a source of potential models for the present
also reflects the generalized sense of crisis and lack of direction that
emerges from a wide range of fourth-century texts, a sense of collective trauma and ideological vacuum that led to a desperate ran-
sacking of the past—or rather of a certain image of the past—in
search of models for the present.[32] I certainly do not wish to reinforce the received ideas about fourth-century tragedy as a story of
decline, of creative sterility, triviality, and empty spectacle, that
Professor Easterling has recently done much to counteract,[33] but

the orators' highly respectful attitude to fifth- and near-to-complete silence as to fourth-century tragedy at least imply an evaluative difference regarding their respective usefulness as persuasive and authoritative paradigms of popular culture. The contemporary tragic theatre was certainly continuing to enjoy enormous popularity and to attract as much, or more, attention from within and beyond Attica; the production of new tragedies seems to have been as vigorous as ever. However, it was also in the 330s that the author of the *Against Leokrates*, Lykourgos, moved legislation to establish the texts of the canonical three fifth-century tragedians and to deposit them in the *polis* archive[34]—pointing to both an enormous degree of official recognition of their importance to the city's identity as a whole and also, in this anxiety about the deterioration of the text, to a perceived need to preserve the great masters of the past from the ravages of the present.[35] This period—between the military defeat of Athens by Philip in 338 and the actual capture of the city by the Macedonians in 322—also saw the building of the new stone theatre and the erection in it of statues of Aischylos, Sophokles, and Euripides. When the re-performance of 'old' tragedies was institutionally recognized at the Great Dionysia,[36] they did not compete in the *agôn* with the new tragedies but were outside and implicitly beyond judgement.

A story told about one of the fourth century's most successful tragedians, Astydamas, presents a fascinating insight into the important—indeed, from the point of view of the poets, it might be termed oppressive—status that fifth-century tragedy held in the fourth.[37] Astydamas had won a victory at the Great Dionysia of 340 with his drama *Parthenopaios*. As a consequence the Athenians granted him the honour of a bronze statue in the theatre. He composed his own epigram for its base, and this earned him a proverbial status in antiquity as a byword for self-praise:[38]

εἴθ᾽ ἐγὼ ἐν κείνοις γενόμην ἢ κεῖνοι ἅμ᾽ ἡμῖν,
   οἳ γλώσσης τερπνῆς πρῶτα δοκοῦσι φέρειν,
ὡς ἐπ᾽ ἀληθείας ἐκρίθην ἀφεθεὶς παράμιλλος·
   νῦν δὲ χρόνῳ προέχουσ᾽, οἷς φθόνος οὐχ ἕπεται.

If only I had lived in their time, or they in mine—
those men who are first in fame for the pleasure-giving craft of words,
so I had been truly judged as a contender from a level start;[39]
but as it is, they have the advantage of time, and envy does not follow
   them.

The impulse to take on and to outdo one's poetic predecessors was always a powerful dynamic of Greek poetics, with a diachronic as well as a synchronic axis to the *agôn*. But this epigram depicts a radical break with the past and is an extreme and explicit case of the anxiety of influence at work—note especially the use of κεῖνος . . . κεῖνοι ('their . . . they') in the first line in chiastic contrast with ἐγὼ . . . ἡμῖν ('I . . . mine'), to convey both the remoteness in time and the illustriousness of the great three. For all its boastfulness, there is a deep-seated frustration here that the masters of the art are now beyond the *agôn*, that the glorious past of tragedy weighs too heavily on its contemporary practitioners.[40] And if any trust can be put in one of the sources which reports this story and tells us that the Athenian council, on hearing this epigram, decided not to let him use it, the Athenians clearly disapproved of even this resentful and frustrated assault on the past masters.[41]

But it is deeply perilous to build up a picture of fourth-century perceptions of tragedy on evidence like this, and I turn to another strand in the rhetoric of tragedy in the orators which suggests that tragedy had not altogether 'lost its sting', as it were: that the power of tragic myth and its disturbing images had not been completely neutralized by an idolizing, 'mummified' view of tragedy.

I am thinking of the use of tragedy to abuse an opponent in public speech.[42] This can be both in explicit terms, via a direct comparison to tragedy or to a figure primarily associated with tragic myth; and in more allusive terms, for example by depicting an opponent in the tones of a tragic tyrant, or by describing his public actions as leading to tragic consequences for the city.

It is striking that speakers are here much less ready to quote directly from tragedy or to mention particular tragedies or tragedians. Given the readiness to announce the citation of the 'wise words of Euripides', when a positive paradigm is to be deposited before his hearers, this reticence might be regarded as significant. If in the case of the edifying example the sense of the tragic has been bleached from tragedy so used, in the case of the appropriation of tragedy for abuse, it seems that the sense of the tragic has to some extent detached itself from particular tragedies.

Relatively early examples can be found in Andokides' *On the Mysteries* of 399.[43] In the latter part of this speech Andokides tells a 'tragic' story about the daughter of Ischomachos and the horrors to which she was subjected by an enemy of Andokides, Kallias. He

hadn't been married to her for a year when he took her mother in
as a mistress (124); the daughter tried to hang herself, but was
stopped in the act; when she recovered, her mother drove her out
of the home and claimed that she herself was pregnant by Kallias,
who denied that the child was his: when he was presented with the
child at the Apatouria, 'he took hold of the altar and swore that the
only son he had or had ever had was Hipponikos . . . otherwise, he
prayed that both he himself and his house might perish utterly—as
they surely will', adds Andokides (126). This whole scenario, with
its motifs of disordered sexual relations, of attempted suicide and
the self-curse at the altar, has clear tragic overtones, though, as
often in these usages, they are tinctured with the comic, as though
the object of attack were not worthy of the full 'dignity' of a tragic
portrait: later, Kallias 'fell in love with the abandoned old hag
again' and now claimed the son as his; 'What ought a son like that
to be called?' asks Andokides, 'Oidipous? Aigisthos?' (129).
Oidipous and Aigisthos are here surely emblematically tragic figures rather than figures from particular tragedies: this shift to the
general and iconic is an especially marked feature of the abusive
rhetoric of tragedy.

   Demosthenes is even more explicit when he attacks the *genos* of
his enemy Meidias in Speech 21 (149–50):

   'His high birth, by Zeus?! Well, every one of you knows the
secret; it's like something in a tragedy, this man's origins. Two
complete opposites are involved in his case:[44] his real mother, the
one who gave birth to him, was the most sensible person in the
world, while his supposed mother, who took him as her child, was
the stupidest of all women. The evidence: the former sold him as
soon as he was born; the latter could have bought a better one at the
price, and this is the one she purchased! And so for this reason he
has got possession of wealth which doesn't belong to him, and has
become a citizen of a city where the rule of law probably prevails
more than in any other; and I suppose he's completely unable to
tolerate or make use of these circumstances, but the truly barbarian and god-loathed part of his nature is overwhelming and violent,
and makes it obvious that he uses what he has as though it belonged
to others—as indeed is the case.'

   The depiction of Meidias' origins as reminiscent of something
from tragedy forges an overt link between the social drama of this
legal conflict and the foremost civic forum for the representation of

social conflict and disorder, tragedy. This topos from the tragic stage, a place from which Athenian citizens are markedly absent but where issues of origins, birth, and status are paramount, becomes in the arena of the courts a topos of abuse.[45] The rhetorical movement in this passage from a denial of Meidias' high birth to a denial of his civic status *tout court* is reminiscent of the Oidipal shift from god-like king to what is worse than a slave; while the powerful climax of 150, with its allegation that Meidias is an imposter, a counterfeit citizen who has utterly overturned the stabilizing hierarchies of society, also evokes the reversals of Sophokles' Oidipous, ἴσα καὶ τὸ μηδὲν ζώσας, 'equal with those who live not at all'.[46] A cutting edge is here given to that familiar 'game' of public speeches—the allegation of foreign or servile birth against an opponent—by this rhetorical insertion of a tragic intruder into the heart of civic life.

Consider another passage from a speech ascribed in antiquity to Andokides, though probably not by him—the *Against Alkibiades*.[47] Its context of production is obscure, but its author is clearly of oligarchic sympathies, in spite of its often tinny democratic rhetoric. None the less, the text affects to address itself to a demotic audience in assembly on the occasion of an imaginary *ostrakophoria*. In 20–1 the writer describes Alkibiades' physical assault on a rival *choregos* at the Great Dionysia, Taureas, whom he beat up and drove out of the *orchestra*: an appropriation, typical of Alkibiades—or at least of antiquity's representations of Alkibiades[48]—of that most public and visually oriented of all civic forums in Athens, the theatre during the festival, in order to demonstrate his own status and unofficial power:

You are the ones responsible,[49] because you don't punish perpetrators of *hubris*; you chastise those who do wrong in secret, but adore those who flagrantly commit acts of violence. That's why the young don't spend their time in the *gymnasia* but in the lawcourts, and why old men fight our battles while young men make speeches[50]—they take this man as their model, who carries his criminal excess so far that, after recommending that the Melians be sold into slavery, purchased a woman from among the captives and has had a child by her—a child whose birth is more transgressive than Aigisthos', since his parents are each others' bitterest enemies and his family is divided between those who have committed and those who have suffered the most extreme wrongs. It's worth clarifying his recklessness still further: he has a child by this woman whom he turned from a free woman into a slave, whose father and male relatives he killed, and whose *polis* he has obliterated, so as to make the son as bitter an enemy as possible to himself and to the *polis*: so powerful are the constraints of hatred that bind him. When you watch such things in tragedies you regard them with horror, but when you see them taking place in the *polis* you think nothing of them. Yet in the case of tragedy you don't know whether the events have actually taken place or were fabricated by the poets; but with these you have a clear knowledge that they were committed in this transgressive manner, yet you treat them with casual indifference. [And.] (4. 21–3)[51]

Like the passage of Demosthenes, this is a subtle manipulation of the tragic and of what one might term the *tragedic* (that which relates to tragedy as a theatrical institution) to represent Alkibiades as the tragic Other within the civic scene and to harness the powerful emotional effects of tragedy to galvanize his audience into action against the 'real' tragedy taking place in the *polis*. Aigisthos is again an emblematic figure of transgressive tragic origins,[52] while Alkibiades is the model—the παράδειγμα (22)—for the tragic inversion of the proper order of civic life; his actions cause a deterioration in the norms of behaviour appropriate to the generations; he himself has destroyed an entire *polis*, murdered its citizens, broken the fundamental polarity between free and slave, and in his offspring brings into hideous alliance utter opposites and extremes—the child's parents are bitter enemies, one the most deadly criminal, the other his most wretched victim; and he has produced the deeply tragic scenario of a son being the avowed enemy of his father and of his *polis*.

This is a powerful mobilization of an idea of the tragic which is close to Vernant's model of social transgression and of the boundary between tragedy in the theatre and tragedy in the *polis* against an individual. The distinction drawn at the end of 23 is particularly fascinating for my concerns: when 'contemplated' (θεωροῦντες) in tragedies, the kind of behaviour exemplified by Alkibiades is recognized and feared, but when 'witnessed' (ὁρῶντες) in the *polis*, it is thought nothing of, though the former is a fiction, or at least its basis in fact is open to uncertainty; while the latter is the object of clear knowledge.[53] This distinction in the *dêmos'* alleged responses to tragedy in the theatre and 'tragedy' in the city equally implies a confusion, or a sense that the power of fictive representation is for the *dêmos* more real than its knowledge of immediate reality. Behind the deeply tendentious and polemical thrust of this argument is perhaps an implicit critique of the dangers involved in the public institution of tragic representations of a kind reminiscent of Plato, or indeed of what Solon, in Plutarch's biography, claimed to fear when he saw Thespis' novel creation in action—that 'Very soon, if we give this sort of playing so much praise and honour, we shall find it in our most solemn affairs.'[54]

A theme of this text, as of others of this period, is that tragedy, or the tragic in its more troubling manifestations, has in a sense entered the realm of the *polis* and is now at home there.[55] Many more examples could be cited: for instance, the account given by Demosthenes (19. 130) of Aischines' behaviour at a feast hosted by Philip after the destruction of the Phokians describes him joining in the libations and prayers, and so 'he cursed his own fatherland', a topos which, while not apparently alluding to a particular tragic scenario, is certainly tragic in tone. Or consider Demosthenes' description of Aischines later in the same speech (314), in a passage that superbly vilifies his alleged transformation from a public secretary slavishly thankful for his lowly office to a land-owning anti-democrat: 'he marches through the agora with the stately stride of Pythokles, his long robe reaching to his ankles, his cheeks puffed out, as though to let you know that here is one of Philip's most intimate friends'. This description seems to draw on a kind of symbolic lexicon of tragic gesture and behaviour, referring both to the form and to the matter of tragedy: a *himation* or *chitôn* that reaches to the ankles is a staple garment of the tragic stage,[56] and the puffing-out of the cheeks in arrogant pride suggests the gestures of a tragic tyrant.[57] This 'tragic' behaviour in the agora is that of a friend of Philip and an aspiring subverter of the democracy.[58]

The line between theatre and politics became increasingly blurred throughout the century. As a civic space the theatre itself had come to be used for more narrowly 'political' purposes at significant moments from the late fifth century on. It is most interesting that the first of these that we know about seem to have been situations of emergency or revolutionary politics—as though there were a natural connection between this site of heightened dramatic action, especially of tragedy, and the drama of such politics: it was in the *orchêstra* of the theatre of Dionysos that the conspirators to the mutilation of the Herms supposedly met at night,[59] and the theatre is also associated with the seismic events in the life of the city of both 411 and 404;[60] while Demetrios, when he came to garrison Athens, entered the theatre on his arrival, not the Pnyx or agora—like a tragic actor, adds Plutarch.[61]

Even the issue concerning the crowning of Demosthenes for his public benefactions—and the more widespread phenomenon of which it is an example—can be seen to represent a certain displacement or readjustment of the spheres of theatre and politics: it is surely significant, and it is a fact frequently emphasized by Aischines and corroborated by inscriptions, that it is precisely the moment prior to the *tragic agôn* which is chosen for the conferral of crowns.[62] The theatre had, according to Aischines, displaced the *ekklêsia* as the place for this allegedly illegal, transgressive form of public display—which in itself seems a testimony to Athens' desire for a saviour in the guise of a tragic hero. And the procedure now made all Greece its audience, not just the Athenian *dêmos*:[63] a matter very much of domestic concern, the conferral of crowns, had thus become spectacle for all Greece—and again, it is hardly fortuitous that the moment for this show was that just prior to Athens' most prestigious and highly charged symbolic performance of tragedy. It is ironic that this alleged conversion of Athenian politics into a spectacle for all Greece should have been so intimately connected to the institution of tragedy, just as Athens' own history was coming more and more to resemble a political tragedy and, moreover, as tragedy itself was ceasing to be an exclusively Athenian performance.[64]

Aischines certainly made much of the proximity of these events to tragedy, though in *his* narrative Demosthenes is the reckless tragic villain, not the epiphanic saviour. At *Against Ktesiphon* 152 ff. Aischines enjoins his hearers to remember the fallen of Khaironea, men whom Demosthenes sent to their deaths despite the inauspicious indications of the sacrifices (152)—a clear tragic colouring to his representation of Demosthenes and his alleged role in the final military defeat of Athens. Will this monster, the 'plague of Hellas' whose evil fortunes—*daimôn* and *tuchê*—are destroying the city (157), be crowned 'for the disasters of the city'? (ταῖς τῆς πόλεως συμφοραῖς, 152): 'I ask you to imagine for a moment that you are not in the courtroom but in the theatre, and to imagine that you see the herald coming forward to make the proclamation . . . consider whether you believe the relatives of the dead will shed more tears over the tragedies and the sufferings of the heroes soon to enter the stage, or over the blindness of the city'

(153). The easy imaginary shift Aischines asks his audience to make between courtroom and theatre, and between theatre as a place of political tragedy and of theatrical tragedy, is a powerful rhetorical strategy—but it rests on something more than pure rhetoric. In this deft management of different fictive scenarios, the 'tragedy' of Demosthenes' proposed award in the theatre, in the here and now of the *polis*, is figured as a greater source of grief for the parents of the dead (πλεία δάκρυα ἀφήσειν, 153) than tragedy's own images of horror. The point is made again with the added weight of a moralizing 'historical' contrast: 'a Greek, brought up in the ways of freedom' (154), would feel pain as, sitting in the theatre, he remembered the glorious past of Athens, and the days when the moment prior to the performance of tragedies was given over to the display of the orphaned sons of the war dead, nurtured by the *polis* until their coming of age and dressed by it in a set of hoplite armour—the most noble proclamation and a great protreptic to virtue (προτρεπτικώτατον πρὸς ἀρετήν, 154). Yet as things are, the herald will today bring forward a man who is himself responsible for making orphans of many children (155). Aischines supplicates his audience: 'by Zeus and the gods, do not set up in the *orchêstra* of the theatre of Dionysos a memorial of your own defeat' (μὴ πρὸς Διὸς καὶ θεῶν, ἱκετεύω ὑμᾶς, ὦ ἄνδρες Ἀθηναῖοι, μὴ τρόπαιον ἵστατε ἀφ' ὑμῶν αὐτῶν ἐν τῇ τοῦ Διονύσου ὀρχήστρᾳ, 156), and exhorts them to envisage yet another tragic scene, the destruction of the Thebans—'imagine that you see their city taken, the razing of their walls, the burning of their homes, their women and children led into captivity, their old men, their aged matrons, late in life learning to forget what freedom means, weeping, supplicating you, angry not so much at those who are taking vengeance as at the men who are responsible for it all' (157).

The theatre has become the place of the tragic politics of Athens, and the disasters of Athenian international affairs of state are depicted in the shape of tragic scenarios.[65] I might not go so far as to say, with Zoe Petre, writing of the fourth century: 'The theatre was still there, but with mere remakes, and even the names of Athenian triremes evoke only past glories of the fifth-century drama; as if the city was staging its own past. Instead of tragedy, which was questioning the political order, they now privilege self-praising rhetoric, patriotic allegory, and political propaganda.'[66] However, more distance could scarcely have been travelled from the attitude implied by the Athenian response to Phrynichos' *The Capture of Miletos*, when the Athenians policed with the force of legislation the boundary between tragedy and Athens' own public troubles. Whatever may have been happening in fourth-century tragedy, tragedy of the past was being called upon in an effort to explain, improve, exhort the present of the troubled city—and in the end to represent it.[67]

Notes

1. I think in particular of the work of Vernant, Vidal-Naquet, Loraux, Zeitlin, Goldhill.

2. Hdt. 6. 21. 2. See Rosenbloom, 'Shouting "Fire" '. The Athenians of the classical period tended on the whole to prefer not to remember or be reminded of their misfortunes. N. Loraux, 'L'Oubli dans la cité', *Le Temps de la réflexion* 1 (1980) 213–42 has analysed some ways in which Athenian political discourse employed selective forgetfulness in the interests of an ideal of unity. E.g. in 401, after the expulsion of the thirty tyrants, loaded with all the crimes of which the Athenians needed to be freed, there was an official, institutional decision to forget: μὴ μνησικακεῖν (see Xen. *Hell.* 2. 4. 43), 'not to remember troubles'. The attitude implied by the response to Phrynichos' dramatization of *oikêia kaka* seems consonant with this.

3. Rosenbloom, 'Shouting "Fire" ', esp. 183, has an excellent discussion.

4. With the probable exception of the *Rhesos*; for discussion of the fourth-century tragic fragments, see Xanthakis-Karamanos, *Studies in Fourth-Century Tragedy*.

5. In their excellent article devoted largely to this topic, Ober and Strauss, 'Drama, Political Rhetoric', down-play the significance of this mismatch in our evidence. See esp. 240: 'there was political rhetoric in the fifth century and drama in the fourth'. Granted, but we must be attentive to their potential differences over a period of 200 years. For some helpful remarks on fifth-century rhetoric, see M. Nouhaud, *L'Utilisation de l'histoire par les orateurs attiques* (Paris 1982) 40–3. There is no sign of anything comparable in the speeches of Thoukydides; while the evidence of comedy is inconclusive—the passage frequently cited is Aristophanes, *Wasps* 579–80: when the tragic actor Oiagreus is a defendant at law, says Philokleon, he is not let off πρὶν ἂν ἡμῖν | ἐκ τῆς Νιοβῆς εἴπῃ ῥῆσιν τὴν καλλίστην ἀπολέξας. See Dorjhan, 'Poetry in Athenian Courts', 86. Bers, 'Tragedy and Rhetoric', 190, has recently argued that Antiphon's 'experiment' with introducing tragic affect into dikanic *logos* (he is referring to Antiphon

1. 17 ff.) was not well received: 'My guess is that other speechwriters, and even Antiphon himself, seeing that the jurors did not want to be treated to a spectacle too reminiscent of tragedy, which they demonstrated by derisive hooting and then their vote, made an adjustment in the direction of more constricted affect.' Arist. *Rhet.* 1. 15. 13 includes Kleophon as one who used the poets in oratory against Kritias. He specifies Solon's elegies, however, and is thus not strong evidence of another (late) fifth-century example of 'tragic rhetoric'.

6. One (late) fifth-century figure who I suspect—though the suspicion must sustain itself largely on evidence from the fourth century or later—*was* very possibly depicted in 'tragic' colours in his own lifetime in public contexts is Alkibiades. See below n. 48 and Wilson, 'Leading the Tragic *Khoros*'.

7. In focusing on the orators, I shall be overlooking the way historians, philosophers, and, of course, tragedy's alter-ego, comedy (both 'Old' and 'New'), appropriate tragedy and the tragic, although I hope to consider aspects of this elsewhere. Comedy in particular is clearly a crucial site for the formulation of the very category of 'the tragic' through its critical and competitive relation to the genre. Comedy's extensive use of tragedy must have paved the way for the forensic use by having made it a familiar object for quotation and discussion. Cf. M. S. Silk, 'Aristophanic Paratragedy', in Sommerstein *et al.* (edd.), *Tragedy, Comedy and the Polis*, 477–504.

8. Cf. North, 'Use of Poetry'; S. Perlmann, 'Quotations from Poetry'; J. Ober, *Mass and Elite in Democratic Athens: Rhetoric, Ideology, and the Power of the People* (Princeton 1989); Ober and Strauss, 'Drama, Political Rhetoric'; Bers, 'Tragedy and Rhetoric'; E. Hall, 'Lawcourt Dramas: The Power of Performance in Greek Forensic Oratory' (forthcoming), discusses the affinities between Athenian legal speeches and drama in some detail.

9. Hermogenes in his *On Types of Style* (2. 338) prefers this form of citation, sometimes called *kollêsis*; see North, 'Use of Poetry', esp. 23–4.

10. E.g. Dem. *Emb.* 247; Aischin. 1. 47–8, 150. A practical advantage in having the clerk read them out was that their recitation would thus not impinge on the time allowed for the speech, since the *klêpsydra* was stopped when depositions were made: Dem. 45. 8. Dorjhan, 'Poetry in Athenian courts', 92, points out that Aischines generally quotes Euripides and Hesiod himself, leaving the Homer to the clerk; he suggests this may have given the clerk the opportunity to cite from memory, and so demonstrate the popularity of Homer in a way that would reinforce Aischines' own argument. A passage of Sophokles would presumably carry special weight in the mouth of Sophokles himself, but the anecdote that he defended himself by citing all or part of the

Oid. Kol. is generally regarded as ahistorical: see J. G. F. Powell, *Cicero Cato Maior: De Senectute* (Cambridge 1988) 150 f.

11. In the surviving speeches, only non-lyric passages are quoted (ἰαμβεῖα or ῥήσεις); that is, those parts of tragic diction which are closer to 'ordinary speech': Arist. *Poet.* 4, 1449ᵃ26–7: πλεῖστα γὰρ ἰαμβεῖα λέγομεν ἐν τῇ διαλέκτῳ τῇ πρὸς ἀλλήλους. It is, I would suggest, a gauge of the different relationship of the *dêmos* to tragedy that in the fifth century references to citation of tragedy outside the theatre—as in the quarries of Syracuse (Plut. *Nikias* 29. 3) or the comic image of 'conservative education' (Aristoph. *Clouds* 961 ff., 1364 ff.)—are generally to choral parts. This change may be related to a possible decline in civic participation in *choroi* and increased professionalism in the fourth century.

12. *Rhet.* 1355ᵇ35 ff., 1375ᵃ22 f. In the latter passage, discussing πίστεις ἄτεχνοι, Aristotle classes the poets among 'ancient witnesses' (μάρτυρες παλαιοί), and deems them more credible than recent witnesses because they are incorruptible. At the same time, however, the use of these 'ancient witnesses' could allow an opponent to allege a lack of contemporary witnesses, as at Dem. 19. 243. In praise of the educative value of poetry in the courts and in general over the terseness of law, Lykourgos, *Against Leokrates* 102, says that the latter gives orders while the former gently persuades through argument and demonstration. Modern historians of Greek law have tended to ignore the use of poetic depositions in their discussions of evidence.

13. Perlman, 'Quotations from Poetry', 162.

14. For example, Lyk. *Against Leokrates* 92–110. Quotation from or allusion to *comedy* is virtually non-existent.

15. Ober and Strauss, 'Drama, Political Rhetoric', esp. 251–2.

16. Cf. Carrara, *Eretteo*, 11 n. 4. Hermogenes, *On Types of Style* 2. 389, says that Lykourgos frequently digressed into the world of myth, history, and poetry.

17. The lines then quoted are *TrGF* 2. 296 Kannicht–Snell (adespota).

18. Plut. *Lives of Ten Orators* 843e (cf. *Mor.* 841b) says that Lykourgos' own *genos* derived ultimately from Erechtheus. Lykourgos himself may well have made political capital from this relation to so noble a 'tragic' family; a possibility made to seem all the more likely after the discovery of the long papyrus-fragment from the end of the play, which gives 'something close to a foundation-charter for the Eteoboutadai and explain[s] their claim to the priesthood of Athena Polias': P. MacKendrick, *The Athenian Aristocracy 399 to 31 B.C.* (Cambridge, Mass. 1969) 73.

19. The fragment is Nauck fr. 360.

20. See Loraux, *Invention of Athens*; Carrara, *Eretteo*, 64.

21. 17–27. Cf. Demades 1. 37.
22. The *Erechtheus* is generally dated to c.425–422. See Carrara, *Eretteo*, 13.
23. See Bers, 'Tragedy and Rhetoric', 190.
24. Note that in Aristophanes' *Frogs* a similarly nostalgic—and comic—view of tragedy as simple moral, political edification is expressed by 'Aischylos' at various points. Cf. N. Loraux, *Tragic Ways of Killing a Woman*, trans. A. Forster (Cambridge, Mass. 1987) 47 on the *Erechtheus*: 'But when one is dealing with a tragedy of Euripides, who would expect one unambiguous reading? The confusion of genres, institutions, and languages is very typical of Euripides in practice, whatever his "intentions" may have been—whether he was being ironical or not, whether he did or did not mean to expose to the judgment of the spectators these armies of men who find their salvation in the blood of virgins.' Cf. H. Kuch, 'Continuity and Change in Greek Tragedy under Postclassical Conditions', in Sommerstein *et al.* (edd.), *Tragedy, Comedy and the Polis*, 545–57, for a rather different view: 'Love for the fatherland . . . was to be developed by the actions in the story. This is Lycurgus' way of articulating his understanding of Euripides, and he seems to be right in interpreting the tragedian's aspirations.'
25. I refer of course to Thouk. 2. 43. 1, where the verb is θεωμένους: 'You must day by day fix your gaze upon the power of the *polis* and become its lovers.' Cf. θεωροῦντας in 100 in Lykourgos; and the same verb used in the passage of [And.] 4 cited below of the *dêmos* watching tragedy, where it is, so the author asserts, similarly 'seduced' by tragedy.
26. Nauck fr. 672.
27. *Frogs* 1043 ff.
28. Cf. K. J. Dover, *Aristophanes: 'Frogs'* (Oxford 1993) 35–6.
29. Nauck fr. 812.
30. The same tendency appears in Aristotle's quotations of tragedy in the *Rhetoric*: Euripides (× 17), Sophokles (× 5); also Agathon (× 2) and Theodektes (× 2), but no Aischylos.
31. See n. 5 above. Note too that some have seen at Aisch. *Against Tim.* 190–1 an allusion to Khairemon's *Akhilleus Thersitoktonos* (of before 350), though neither poet nor play is explicitly named: see M. Meulder, 'Timarque, un être tyrannique dépeint par Eschine', *LEC* 57 (1989) 321 n. 53; L. Séchan, *Études sur la Tragédie Grecque dans ses rapports avec la céramique* (Paris 1926) 529–31. If this can count as a genuine reference to a fourth-century tragedy, however, it is most telling that this is also the only example of the *rejection* of a tragic tale: 'For don't imagine, men of Athens, that the impulse to wrongdoing is from the gods—but instead it is from the wickedness of men; nor that

impious men are, as in tragedies, driven and punished by Poinai with blazing torches.' For the association of the Erinyes/Poinai with tragedy, see O. Taplin and P. J. Wilson, 'The "Aetiology" of Tragedy in the *Oresteia*', *PCPS* 39 (1993) 176.

32. See e.g. E. Lévy, *Athènes devant la défaite de 404* (Paris 1976), esp. pt. 3; and P. Cartledge's review, *Gnomon* 50 (1978) 650–4; cf. also Loraux, *Invention of Athens*, esp. 126 for the conviction, evident after Khaironea in various texts, including Demosthenes' Epitaphios, that the history of Athens had finally come to an end.

33. P. E. Easterling, 'The End of an Era? Tragedy in the Early Fourth Century', in Sommerstein *et al.* (edd.), *Tragedy, Comedy and the Polis*, 559–69.

34. Plut. *Lives of Ten Orators* 841f: καὶ τὰς τραγῳδίας αὐτῶν ἐν κοινῷ γραψαμένους φυλάττειν καὶ τὸν τῆς πόλεως γραμματέα παραγινώσκειν τοῖς ὑποκρινουμένοις· οὐκ ἐξεῖναι γὰρ παρ' αὐτὰς ὑποκρίνεσθαι. P. Ghiron-Bistagne, *Recherches sur les acteurs dans la Grèce antique* (Paris 1976) 204; Pickard-Cambridge, *Dramatic Festivals of Athens*[2], 100; on Lykourgos, see C. Mossé, 'Lycurge l'Athénien: Homme de passé ou précurseur de l'avenir?', *QS* 30 (1989) 25–36.

35. Whether or not, as some have deduced from the passage of Plutarch, the perceived threat was primarily from actors' interpolations. R. Thomas, *Oral Tradition and Written Record in Classical Athens* (Cambridge 1989) 49, notes that the transmission of the tragic texts effectively remains oral, since the law prescribed that the secretary should read them out to the actors.

36. Theatre audiences had been used to 'repeats'—predominantly of the three 'classics'—from 386, and of Aischylos from the fifth century, and so they would in some sense have been acclimatized to the notion of their iterability in a way that must have helped the forensic development. See Pickard-Cambridge, *Dramatic Festivals of Athens*[2], 86, 99–100, whose discussion of the relevant epigraphical evidence (*IG* ii[2], 2318, 2320) at 124 suggests that the performance of old tragedies may have only become a regular part of the programme in 341–339, bringing it closer in time to Lykourgos.

37. See *TrGF* 1. 60 Kannicht-Snell; the *Souda* says he wrote 240 dramas and had 15 victories.

38. Astydamas [II] *TrGF* 1. 60 T2a; cf. 2b.

39. I follow Page, *Further Greek Epigrams*, 33–4 on this difficult line, esp. on ἀφεθεὶς παράμιλλος, of which he writes at 34: 'This is the language of the stadium. ἄφεσις is the start of a race, the man who is παράμιλλος is competing side-by-side (*LSJ*'s rendering, "*beyond rivalry*", is nonsense). The author wishes that he could have *started level with* his competitors, ἀφεθεὶς παράμιλλος; in fact his rivals start in

a lead . . . given by Time, which outruns the jealousy of contemporaries.'

40. Cf. the closely comparable annoyance of the fifth-century epic poet Choirilos of Samos that the *tekhnai* had reached their peaks before his time, and he had no team to enter the race. It is interesting that Aristotle in the *Rhetoric* (3. 1415) cites this as an example of *captatio benevolentiae* taken from dikanic prooimia (*Suppl. Hell.* 317): ἃ μάκαρ, ὅστις ἔην κεῖνον χρόνον ἴδρις ἀοιδῆς | Μουσάων θεράπων, ὅτ' ἀκήρατος ἦν ἔτι λειμών· | νῦν δ' ὅτε πάντα δέδασται, ἔχουσι δὲ πείρατα τέχναι | ὕστατοι ὥστε δρόμου καταλείπομεθ', οὐδέ πῃ ἔστι | πάντῃ παπταίνοντα νεοζυγὲς ἅρμα πελάσσαι.
Cf. S. D. Goldhill, 'The Naive and Knowing Eye: Ecphrasis and the Culture of Viewing in the Hellenistic World', in Goldhill and R. Osborne (edd.), *Art and Text in Ancient Greek Culture* (Cambridge 1994) 197–223, at 206 f.

41. Zenobios 5. 100. Page, *Further Greek Epigrams*, 33, is cautious in the extreme: 'It would be an act of blind faith to accept the truth of the tale or the authenticity of the epigram.'

42. In some works of Isokrates (although these can hardly count as public speech), τραγῳδεῖν is used to mean virtually 'to eulogize'—see *Antidosis* (15). 136 of c.354, where an idea of tragedy as the heroic memorialization of 'Great Men' appears; cf. *Euagoras* (9). 6. This is perhaps the more fascinating for being a 'positive' view of tragedy that comes from a self-styled élite. See n. 58 below.

43. For discussion of another in this speech see Ober and Strauss, 'Drama, Political Rhetoric', 255–8; an earlier example is to be found at Antiphon 1. 17, on which see n. 5 above.

44. Note the explicit emphasis in this 'tragic' context on the *co-presence of opposites* (esp. 149 ᾧ δύ' ἐναντιώτατα συμβέβηκεν εἶναι)—an implicit recognition of the *paradoxical* qualities of tragedy highlighted by modern critics from Nietzsche on? Cf. also [And.] 4. 22, quoted below.

45. Fuller discussion in P. J. Wilson, 'Demosthenes 21 (*Against Meidias*): Democratic Abuse', *PCPS* 37 (1991) 164–95. Cf. J. K. Davies, 'Athenian Citizenship: The Descent Group and the Alternatives', *CJ* 73 (1978) 111–14.

46. Soph. *OT* 1187–8; cf. Vernant and Vidal-Naquet, *Myth and Tragedy in Ancient Greece*, ch. 5.

47. Cf. W. D. Furley, 'Andokides IV ("Against Alkibiades"): Fact or Fiction?', *Hermes* 117 (1985) 138–56. Further discussion in Wilson, 'Leading the Tragic *Khoros*'.

48. Among many similar anecdotes, that told about Alkibiades' return to Athens from exile in 408/7 is particularly fascinating for its

connection between Alkibiades and tragedy: Duris of Samos (*FGrH* 76F70) reports that he came into the Peiraieus after subduing the Hellespont for the Athenians with the prows of his triremes garlanded, many full of spoils. His own trireme had purple sails—a colour elsewhere frequently associated with tragedy (cf. the purple fabric in Aischyl. *Agam.* and Philemon fr. 105 (K–A): τὰ δ᾽ ἀργυρώματ᾽ ἐστὶν ἤ τε πορφύρα, εἰς τοὺς τραγῳδοὺς εὔθετ᾽, οὐκ εἰς τὸν βίον); keeping the time for the rowers was Chrysogonos the Pythian victor on the *aulos*; while giving the orders was Kallipides the *tragic actor*, fully dressed in his costume: Καλλιπίδης δ᾽ ὁ τραγῳδὸς ἐκέλευε τὴν ἐπὶ τῆς σκηνῆς στολὴν ἠμφιεσμένος. One would hesitate to accept the simple historicity of such an event, especially when related by a third-century historian associated with the new so-called 'tragic' style of historiography (see F. Walbank, 'Tragic History: A Reconsideration', *BICS* 2 [1955] 4–12, and L. Torraca, *Duride di Samo: La maschera scenica nella storiografia ellenistica* [Salerno 1988] 69), but it is illuminating for the connection it makes between this famously transgressive political individual and tragedy.

49. Note the remarkable and perhaps deliberate echo here of the famous passage of Thouk. 3. 38. 4, Kleon's speech on the second debate over Mytilene: αἴτιοι δ᾽ ὑμεῖς κακῶς ἀγωνοθετοῦντες, οἵτινες εἰώθατε θεαταὶ μὲν τῶν λόγων γίγνεσθαι, ἀκροαταὶ δὲ τῶν ἔργων. This criticism of the Athenians as 'spectators of words' is also very relevant to the distinction made in 23 of the [Andokides] passage.

50. For the antithesis of old warriors and young orators cf. incidentally (*mutatis mutandis*) Aristoph. *Ach.* 676 ff.

51. αἴτιοι δ᾽ ὑμεῖς . . . ἀλλ᾽ ὑμεῖς ἐν μὲν ταῖς τραγῳδίαις τοιαῦτα θεωροῦντες δεινὰ νομίζετε, γιγνόμενα δ᾽ ἐν τῇ πόλει ὁρῶντες οὐδὲν φροντίζετε. καίτοι ἐκεῖνα μὲν οὐκ ἐπίστασθε πότερον οὕτω γεγένηται ἢ πέπλασται ὑπὸ τῶν ποιητῶν· ταῦτα δὲ σαφῶς εἰδότες οὕτω παρανόμως πεπραγμένα ῥαθύμως φέρετε.

52. Taplin, *Comic Angels*, 62, argues that Aigisthos is an emblematic representative of tragedy on the important 'Choregoi' vase.

53. Precisely the same distinction is made in Isok. *Panegyrikos* 4. 168: no one has ever protested at the dreadful evils afflicting society (man-made war and *staseis*; people being put to death contrary to the law in their own countries, others wandering with their women and children in strange lands, etc.), but they see fit to weep over the disasters fabricated by the poets, while viewing complacently the many real and terrible sufferings that are taking place because of the war.

54. Plut. *Solon* 29. 4–5. Though in all likelihood this story is told through a Neoplatonic screen.

55. In this process the changing role and increased public profile of the

actor play an important part, in an era when *mimêsis* has become a key term of political discourse—a topic I hope to discuss elsewhere.

56. Pickard-Cambridge, *Dramatic Festivals of Athens*², 180 ff.

57. Cf. Eur. *IA* 125, 381; Soph. *Elektra* 1385.

58. In Hyperides' fragmentary speech *On behalf of Lykophron* of some time before 338 (12), we find an explicit association between behaviour represented as 'tragic' and the subversion of the democracy. In this speech τραγῳδίας γράψαι is used to describe his opponent's lurid forensic allegations—largely concerning adultery, it seems; cf. the use of the verb τραγῳδεῖν in Dem. 18. 13 and 19. 189 to mean something like 'to tell in lurid, tragic style'. One final example, especially interesting for its apparent status as a piece of proverbial discourse, is the expression preserved from a speech of Lykourgos: τοὺς ἑτέρους τραγῳδοὺς ἀγωνιεῖται—'he will act in tragedies made for others' (fr. 21 Sauppe)—to describe people who seek to adapt themselves to a role in life beyond their powers.

59. See And. 1. 38.

60. Thouk. 8. 93—the pro-democratic hoplites hold an assembly in the Peiraieus theatre in 411; Lys. *Against Agoratos* (13) 32 (404); see U. Albini, *Nel nome di Dioniso: Vita teatrale nell'Atene classica* (Milan 1991) 115.

61. See Plut. *Dem.* 34. 3–4. The spectacular assassination of Philip under the most theatrical circumstances should certainly be added to this list.

62. For example, Aisch. *Against Ktesiphon* 34, 152–3; cf. H. J. Mette, *Urkunden dramatischer Aufführungen in Griechenland* (Berlin 1977) 94–102.

63. For example, Aisch. *Against Ktesiphon* 34.

64. Cf. G. O. Rowe, 'The Portrait of Aeschines in the *Oration on the Crown*', *TAPA* 97 (1966) 404, on Athens depicted as tragic protagonist in the *Crown*.

65. Not that 'tragic' representation of Athenian fifth-century politics was not possible, as Thoukydides shows it was. What was in Thoukydides primarily the historian's ironic perspective on past events has become, in the public discourse of the orators, one sign of a rather more disillusioned and brittle attitude to the present.

66. Z. Petre, 'How to End *Stasis* at Athens', (unpub. paper delivered at a colloquium 'Democracy and Citizenship', Darwin College, Cambridge, May 1992).

67. My warm thanks to Michael Silk, Oliver Taplin, Simon Goldhill, Chris Pelling, and Pat Easterling for helpful comments and criticism; and to all who offered suggestions in the discussion following my paper at the KCL conference.

19

Plato's Repudiation of the Tragic

STEPHEN HALLIWELL

> There is something which, for lack of a better name, we will
> call the tragic sense of life, which carries with it a whole con-
> ception of life itself and of the universe, a whole philosophy
> more or less formulated, more or less conscious.
>
> (Unamuno)[1]

Theories of the tragic are only one species within the genus constituted by concepts of tragedy. The existence of such theories has
become especially associated with a line of thought which goes
back to German Idealism and Romanticism, and one commonly
drawn corollary of this connection is the claim that while ancient
Greece created the first and most intense tradition of dramatic
tragedy, it lacked anything that can be classified as an explicit
notion of the tragic.[2] But distinctive as are the existential and spiritual accounts of the tragic produced by theorists from Schelling
onwards, we run the risk of unduly constricting our reading of the
history of ideas if we take these accounts as an exclusive paradigm
of the concept. I propose in this essay to develop this consideration
by arguing that there are important grounds for ascribing the first
conscious delineation of the tragic, at any rate outside tragedy itself
(a complex reservation), to Plato. To make good this thesis I shall
work with a distinction between what can broadly be termed pragmatic theories of tragedy, and theories which, by contrast, contain
a central emphasis that qualifies them for the category of the tragic.
While pragmatic theories can incorporate generic characteristics of
diverse kinds—formal, material, psychological, ethical—they
remain separable from approaches which diagnose an essential and
metaphysical significance at the core of tragedy. I take it, accordingly, as a necessary condition for a conception of the tragic that it
should suppose tragedy (at least in its ideal form) to intimate some
ultimate insight, of profound spiritual and moral consequence,

into reality, even if the nature of such insight may have to be characterized as inherently mysterious. As that condition perhaps already implies, where the tragic is framed in metaphysical or quasi-metaphysical terms, the dramatic genre of tragedy will become subsumable under, rather than representing the exclusive carrier of, the larger vision or world-view.

The case which I wish to put attributes the first theoretical formulation of the tragic to a thinker whose special motivation was to challenge and contest it on the deepest level of philosophical belief. But as regards the purely factual question of Plato's historical priority in articulating an understanding of the tragic, we might reasonably wonder whether it is accidental that we possess no view of a comparable kind elsewhere in fifth- or fourth-century sources. Classical Athenian culture must, after all, have fostered a rich and widespread discourse of attitudes to tragedy: this inference is pressed upon us not just by the sustained tradition of performance at civic festivals, but also by the size of audiences and the attested explicitness of their reactions (both positive and negative) to plays, the creation of a theatrical system which involved preselection of plays and official competition between staged works, and, last but not least, the survival of two documents, Aristophanes' *Frogs* and Aristotle's *Poetics*, which in their very different ways give us glimpses of available critical assessments of tragedy. Yet if we look for traces of a strong conception of the tragic in the evidence for Athenian responses to tragedy before, or indeed anywhere outside, Plato, it is hard to find much of salience. In the first place, it is only a wide and vague idea of tragic qualities which is conveyed by most classical uses of the adjective *tragikos* itself. When not purely technical, in reference to poets, costumes, choruses, and the like, the word's connotations are of high-flown solemnity or ostentatiously lugubrious subject-matter. Plato aside, there are very few cases indeed in which we have reason to discern more extensive implications than this, and the same is true of metaphorical senses of *tragôidia*, *tragôidein*, etc.[3] Perhaps the most striking of such cases is Aristotle's famous remark at *Poetics* 13, 1453ᵃ29–30, that Euripides 'is found the most tragic of poets' (*tragikôtatos* . . . *phainetai*) in the theatre.[4] It deserves emphasis, since it is so often ignored, that Aristotle is not pronouncing directly on Euripides, but on the impression which many of his plays—those ending in extreme and unmitigated misfortune—make on contemporary

audiences. This is important in part because it means that
Aristotle's phrasing can be taken to attest at least an instinctive
inclination, within Athenian culture of the mid-fourth century,
towards identifying the manifestation of unqualified pessimism as
an archetypally tragic phenomenon. However, this is not at all the
same as inferring that Athenian audiences always expected or
wanted this kind of experience from the genre: Aristotle's further
observation, just two sentences later in the *Poetics* (1453^a33-5),
that audiences prefer plots which end with a moral resolution
(rewards for the virtuous, punishment for the evil), is sufficient to
block this further inference. But if this inference is not open to us,
that is in itself tantamount to saying that Aristotle's reference to
the impact of particularly bleak Euripidean endings is not compelling evidence for a strongly articulated conception of the tragic
within fourth-century Athenian responses to tragedy.

This conclusion from the *Poetics* as a broad reflector of contemporary theatrical values is complemented by the work's own stance
towards tragedy. All the major features of Aristotle's treatment of
the genre bear out the proposition that his interpretation of tragedy
is independent of, and in some ways actually inimical to, what we
might now deem to be a developed notion of the tragic. These features include an analytical framework (the 'six parts' model) which
stems from a general theory of poetic art and could consequently
be applied equally to comedy, as well as a fundamental concern for
issues of structure, unity, and coherence which are likewise much
larger than tragedy, or even than poetry, in their scope. Of course,
Aristotle erects on these foundations a specific account of tragedy
which incorporates a combination of elevated action and characters, the arousal of pity and fear, and the motif of movement or
transformation (*metabasis*) between poles of prosperity and adversity. The *Poetics* thus elaborates a concept of tragedy which recognizes the centrality of acute suffering and vulnerability, and this
aspect is further refined in the positing of human fallibility (*hamartia*) as the key factor in great changes of fortune. But it is legitimate
to hold that this theory of tragedy yields something appreciably
different from a sense of the tragic, not least because Aristotle's
discussion of mutability repeatedly leaves open the possibility of
movement from adversity to prosperity, as well as the reverse. In
this respect, the *Poetics* adopts a position which is true to long-
established patterns within Attic tragedy, and that alone should

prevent us from thinking here in terms of an Aristotelian short-coming of sensibility. In a further respect, namely the down-playing of religious explanations of human suffering, Aristotle does markedly diverge both from the tragic tradition and, for dif-ferent reasons, from the Platonic views which I shall presently dis-cuss. But that important point, while complex in its entailments for Aristotle's approach to tragedy,[5] need not deflect us from drawing the crucial inference that the evidence of the *Poetics* as a whole, at the level of both documentation and theory, permits us to believe that it was entirely feasible within classical Athenian culture to speak about the nature and experience of tragedy without speaking in terms of the tragic.

This observation receives some oblique confirmation from the earlier evidence of Aristophanes' *Frogs*. There are many poten-tially separable strands in the fabric of the comedy's contest of tragedians—among them, Aeschylus' militaristic ethos, dramatic silences, choral refrains, and verbosity; Euripides' beggar-heroes, 'democratic' realism, devotion to new gods, and stereotyped pro-logues. But the competition is unified by an overlapping interest in, broadly speaking, stylistic and ethico-political factors. This pairing of subjects and criteria is signalled by the agreement between Aeschylus and Euripides, at the outset of the *agôn* (1008–10), that a poet should be judged for both 'skilfulness' (*dex-iotês*) and 'edification' (*nouthesia*), which between them constitute the artistic excellence (*sophia*) that is at stake in the contest.[6] But this much-quoted passage can be used to underscore a provision-ally negative inference. The leading themes of the debate, precisely because revolving around a generalized conception of the fine poet, bring with them no genre-specific standards of distinctively tragic qualities, let alone a more abstract consciousness of the tragic as a form of *Weltanschauung*. The competition naturally contains ref-erence to features, such as prologues and choral lyrics, which have a definable place within the conventions of tragedy; and there are various allusions to the particular heroes and myths which provide the stuff of the tragedians' works. But what is conspicuously miss-ing—conspicuously even from the perspective of the *Poetics*, and still more so from that of Plato—is any prominent attention to the emotional states, other than general pleasure, aroused by tragedy, the heroically heightened sense of suffering embodied in many tragic agents, or the intense aura of religious meaning in which the

lives of these agents are characteristically shrouded. The nearest
the discussion ever comes to such topics is perhaps in Dionysus'
reminiscence about scenes of communal grief in *Persians* (1028–9),
Aeschylus' comment on the shame-impelled suicides of Stheno-
boea and similar heroines (1050–1), or Dionysus' and Aeschylus'
sarcastic remarks, *à propos* Euripides' quotations from the start of
his *Antigone*, about the illusory happiness of Oedipus (1182–95).

There can, of course, be no question of relying uncritically on
Frogs as a close image of contemporary Athenian attitudes to
tragedy. Comic selectiveness and distortion rule out the feasibility
of detailed inferences about what were no doubt the complicated
habits of thought which informed late fifth-century experience of
tragic theatre. In particular, it is impossible to suppose that audiences of this period were blind to the religious ideas or the heroic
values by which tragedy's mythical materials were typically satu-
rated, though that is not to imply that awareness of these ideas and
values would in itself suffice to constitute a strong sense of the
tragic. An alternative hypothesis, which would allow us to integrate the partial evidence of *Frogs* and of other fifth-century
sources[7] without resorting to implausibly extreme conclusions
about Athenian audiences of tragedy, is that certain major elements of tragedy, however fundamental to the type of experience
which it offered, were nevertheless left largely unvoiced in the general terms in which individual plays were discussed and the categories by which they were judged. This view has a positive
corollary which I would now like to develop, namely that it was
part of Plato's project to bring to the surface of argument, and to
open up for reflective evaluation, dimensions of tragedy which had
not previously received sustained recognition in the culture's critical discourse.

Indirect support for this thesis can be derived from the observation that while, as already noted, the terms *tragôidia*, *tragikos*, etc.
had developed a range of metaphorical usage by the first half of the
fourth century, we encounter in Plato a much more thought-provoking set of figurative applications of these words than in any
other author of the period.[8] Since these applications occur mostly
outside contexts in which the significance of tragedy is directly
addressed, and since they have rarely been given connected consideration, it will be worthwhile to examine them before turning to
other, fuller Platonic materials. As the first of these passages

reveals, however, the employment of tragedy as a trope cannot be disentangled from its status as an object of philosophical criticism. Towards the end of the discussion in the *Philebus* of mixed experiences of pleasure and pain, of which tragedy is held up as an instance, Socrates declares: 'So our argument shows that pains and pleasures are mixed together in lamentation and in tragedies and comedies—not only in stage-plays, but in the entire tragedy and comedy of life.'[9] Metaphors of this species have become so familiar a topos, even a cliché, that it is easy to underestimate the force of Plato's point.[10] Whether or not the imagery is original to him, its implication is that tragedy (as well, of course, as comedy) can be perceived as the vehicle of a highly distinctive sense of life—so much so, indeed, that it becomes equally possible to regard tragedy as an interpretation of life, and life itself as a quasi-aesthetic phenomenon possessing the kinds of properties which are exhibited in their most concentrated form in theatrical works.

The content of tragedy's sense of life is left entirely unspecified at *Philebus* 50b, but we edge a little closer to it in the playful yet eloquent etymologizing of *Cratylus* 408b–d. Here, the double nature of the god Pan is linked to that of speech or language (*logos*), which has the capacity to signify 'everything' (*pan*), both truth and false. While truth is 'smooth and divine', falsehood represents the lower, 'human' side of Pan, with the 'harsh and tragic' (*trachu kai tragikon*) features that go with human existence: 'for it is here [i.e. in the human world] that very many stories and falsehoods belong, in connection with the tragic life' (408c7–8). The self-conscious wit of the passage depends principally on the etymologizing recuperation of the goat (*tragos*) element in tragedy, so that what is 'harsh and tragic' in human life can be correlated with the 'rough and goat-form' side (*trachus kai tragoeidês*) of Pan's nature. But the verbal punning, for all its factitious ingenuity, contains a kind of philosophical enigma. Not only do we have the reference to a conception of life, 'the tragic life', which could be construed either as life in general seen in a tragic light (as at *Philebus* 50b) or as a specific pattern of life (that of the tragic individual). We also have the unmistakable insinuation that, on either construal, this conception is a matter of myth and falsehood/fiction: in other words, that it *is*, in some as yet undefined respect, a myth and a falsehood, tied up with a harsh humanness—an incorrigibly human view of things— which is sharply opposed to the 'truth' of the 'divine'. The key to the enigma, as we shall see, can be found elsewhere in Plato, in those very passages which elucidate philosophical reasons for repudiating any adherence to 'the tragic life'.

If *Cratylus* 408 hints in playfully allusive terms at a possible critique of tragedy, an express contrast between 'tragic' and 'philosophical' interpretations of life is supplied by a well-known passage of *Laws* 7. Here, the Athenian envisages an encounter between the well-governed city's collective lawgivers (the persona of himself and his companions in philosophical discussion) and a travelling troupe of tragic actors who request permission to perform in the city. The lawgivers' imagined response to the request is notable for its metaphorical and symbolic extension of the concept of tragedy, in a manner which is continuous with, but much clearer in its implications than, the idea of the 'tragic life' in either the *Philebus* or the *Cratylus* passages already considered: 'Honoured visitors, we ourselves aspire to be poets/makers [*poiê-tai*] of the finest and best tragedy; our whole state/constitution [*politeia*] is constructed as a representation [*mimêsis*] of the finest and best life—which is what *we* count as the truest tragedy. So you and we turn out to be poets using the same materials, and we are your rivals and competitors in producing the finest drama' (7, 817b1–8). This passage could be claimed to disclose, in a highly pregnant way, more than almost any other about the nature of Plato's engagement with tragedy, since it indicates how that engagement is not simply an opposition but an active attempt to transform and overcome tragedy within a new kind of philosophical writing. At first sight Plato's terms may look paradoxical, since it would be bizarre to suppose that Attic tragedy offers overt and unconditional paradigms of 'the finest and best life'. But the point is deeper, and very powerful. It can be provisionally adumbrated (along lines that we shall shortly see corroborated by other Platonic texts) by saying that philosophy perceives tragedy as inescapably committed to the affirmation of certain values, precisely in virtue of what it mourns and grieves. If tragedy's values are followed through, then the genre must surely be the expression of nothing less than a 'life'—a conception of what is supremely worth living *for*: to lament what is lost or destroyed in suffering is implicitly to cling to a certain sense of what is worth having and preserving in life. And that is why, in this the boldest of self-referential figures in Plato's writing, tragedy—'the truest tragedy'—can become the ultimate trope for philosophy itself and for its efforts to create an alternative vision of what 'the finest and best life' might be.

There is one further passage, from the *Phaedo*, which deserves to be added to those in which Plato exploits the idea of tragedy in at least a semi-figurative fashion. Though the *Phaedo* as a whole can be justifiably regarded as a kind of tacit response to, and transcendence of, tragic drama, it contains only one direct reference to tragedy. This is the moment where, as the time to drink the hemlock approaches, Socrates tells his companions, with the gentlest of ironies, that they will follow him on some future occasion, before adding: 'but as for me, "fate" [*heimarmenê*], as a tragic man would say, now summons me' (115a5–6). Commentators have mostly treated *anêr tragikos*, the 'tragic man', as meaning a character in tragedy. But it could equally, I think, mean a person possessing or adopting a tragic view of (his) life, so that *tragikos* here would be parallel to the 'tragic life' of *Cratylus* 408c8 and the 'tragedy' of life at *Philebus* 50b3. At any rate, Socrates' remark involves the transferability of a tragic attitude from the theatre to one's own life: if he were to behave with the convictions of a 'tragic man', he would interpret the situation of his death, and thus feel about it, in a very different way from the philosophical equanimity and acquiescence which he has displayed throughout the dialogue. The ramifications of the point embrace not just Socrates as an imagined individual, but the nature of Plato's depiction of him and the response which this depiction both invites from and encourages in a reader. Just as a tragic presentation of a hero's death could convey a whole 'world' of value, so the *Phaedo*'s dramatization of Socrates' death opens up a transvaluation of the tragic construal of the event. To achieve this, it must allow the tragic reading to be heard, and it does that by its dramatic unfolding of a scene in which everyone *except* Socrates exhibits impulses towards tragic grief:[11] that is, towards the experience of Socrates' death as an evil done to the fabric of human value, because an irreversible loss of something supremely treasured.

The passages so far adduced from *Philebus*, *Cratylus*, *Laws*, and *Phaedo* have brought to light, mostly through metaphorical and figural applications of the idea of tragedy, what I take to be four overlapping elements of a Platonic conception of the tragic: first, tragedy's perceived function as the medium for a world-view or overarching sense of life; secondly, tragedy's alleged dependence on a restrictedly human, embodied perspective (symbolized by the lower, harsher part of Pan's nature) which excludes the truth of the divine; thirdly, tragedy's implicit expression of ultimate values and commitments ('the best life'); fourthly, tragedy's obsession with death, not as a raw datum about the world but as something whose interpretation is central to the outlook on life itself. In the texts already considered, these elements are present only as hints and pointers; for a fuller articulation of them we need to refer to the two great treatments of poetry in Books 2–3 and 10 of the *Republic*. Of these, I shall concentrate in greater detail on Book 10, but after first drawing attention briefly to some pertinent aspects of the argument in the earlier context.

The discussion of poetic stories (*muthoi*) in Books 2–3, from 376e to 392c, is guided by a concern with the ethics of fiction in an educational setting, and deals predominantly with Homeric texts. Of more than thirty quotations in this stretch of the work, over three-quarters are Homeric and only four (all Aeschylean) from tragedy.[12] But while these proportions may reflect something of note about the paramount status of the Homeric poems in Athenian education, they do not reduce the relevance of the passage's main lines of thought to Plato's delineation of the tragic. This relevance, which becomes strongly foregrounded in Book 10, can be most readily appreciated by reminding ourselves of four primary propositions, or quasi-propositional attitudes,[13] which the argument identifies and condemns in the images of 'gods and heroes' (377e1–2, 392a5) projected by many poetic *muthoi*: first, that gods are responsible for evil (379a–c; cf. 391d6);[14] secondly, that death is to be feared (386a–387c); thirdly, that the greatest heroes regard the death of those they cherish as an ultimate loss (387d–388d); finally, that justice and happiness cannot be correlated (392b). All four of these ideas can be seen to trace out components of a mentality which finds the structure of the world—governed by divine powers capable of ruthless destructiveness, and limited by the inevitability of death—to be fundamentally hostile to human needs and values, and irreconcilable with a positive moral significance. The rejection of this mentality, the mentality of an Achilles or a Niobe, is a prerequisite for the assertion of a religio-ethical interpretation of reality, as Socrates' proposals for educational and cultural censorship make entirely clear. Notwithstanding its wider frame of reference, it is possible to discern that the critique of poetry in Books 2–3, when put together with the strands which I have already gathered from Plato's deployment of tragedy as a trope, provides an analysis and rejection of a specifically tragic sense of life. In the overall structure of the *Republic*'s argument, this conclusion is confirmed by the return to poetry in the last book of the dialogue.

As in Books 2–3, the approach to tragedy in Book 10 is intertwined with a critique of Homer. But since a conception of the tragic like the one I have already sketched out has an intrinsic tendency to run beyond the genre of dramatic tragedy as such, the Homeric material in both these parts of the *Republic* accentuates and enhances the scope of what Plato understands by a tragic sense of life. The tenth book's famous description of Homer as 'teacher and leader of the tragedians' (595c1–2), and 'first of the tragedians' (607a3), establishes that the Homeric epics themselves matter to Plato in this context primarily as texts which justify a tragic reading. This implication of the conjunction of epic and dramatic tragedy is corroborated at 602b8–11, where Socrates refers to those 'who put their hands to tragic poetry, whether in epic hexameters or in iambics' as 'tragic artists *par excellence*'. This sentence, together with another mention of tragedians at 597e6, helps to suggest that tragedy, *qua* vehicle of the tragic, not only is in the argument's sights throughout the first stretch of Book 10 (up to 605c), in which mimetic poetry in general is convicted of a shallow manipulation of appearances, but is actually the chief target of this argument.

If that is so, there is an incentive to ponder afresh the relationship between the book's earlier arguments, with their condemnation of *mimêsis* as 'twice removed from the truth', and the 'greatest charge' argument which is presented at 605c ff. and whose relevance to tragedy (once more, both Homeric and Attic: 605c11) is explicit and intense. Approached from this angle, tragedy will be the paradigm, however paradoxically, *both* of the limitation of mimetic poetry to the 'surfaces' of life, *and* of poetry's capacity to corrupt the mind by encouraging ethically inappropriate responses to its dramatic images. Some scholars have found this combination of emphases—on mirror-like simulacra, and on severe psychological harm—to be incongruous; but while that might be so in terms of the rhetorical contrast between art as speciously trivial and as darkly dangerous, it need not be so on the deeper level at which tragedy is the unifying object of attention. If poetry is a play with illusions or simulations, then it will become most dangerous at just the point at which those illusions involve things that are taken with the greatest seriousness. The thrust of the critique will therefore be that tragedy is the poetic form, indeed the representational art-form, which most potently brings together the falsehood of *mimê-sis* and the gravity of the most important human beliefs and commitments.

Before seeing how this critique is brought to a head in the 'greatest charge' argument, it is worth looking at the character of the immediately preceding passage, 603c–605c, in order to reinforce the claim that tragedy can be read as the major target throughout the treatment of poetry in Book 10. For it is here that the dialogue effectively makes a transition from the idea of poetic illusion, which has predominated since the start of the book, to the ethical anxieties which lead to the 'greatest charge' itself. It does so by a sequence of thought which seems, at first sight, curiously elided. After a general statement, reminiscent of Aristotle's definition of tragedy in the *Poetics*, about poetry's (ethical) occupation with patterns of success and failure, joy and grief, in human life (603c4–7),[15] Socrates at once turns, without any direct reference to poetic characters, to the psychic conflict between reason and emotion that can affect any 'good person' struggling to come to terms with the loss of something of supreme importance, such as a loved one (603e3–4). Two observations are required, to make sense of this apparent elision. The first is that tragic poetry is recognizably the *subtext* of the argument. The example of bereavement at 603e3–5, though applying in the first instance to ordinary psychology not to poetic figures, looks back to the third book's critique of displays of grief by Homeric-tragic heroes.[16] The emphasis on *pathos*, which is simultaneously the objective cause and the subjective experience of 'suffering', demarcates a fundamental feature of the material of tragic poetry, and one soon to be picked up in the 'greatest charge' argument itself (606b1–8).[17] Finally, the suggestion—supposedly part of what *nomos* (law/tradition) prescribes—that 'nothing human merits great seriousness' (604b12–c1) alludes to the idea, cited ironically in several Platonic passages, that tragedy is above all the genre of portentous 'seriousness' (*spoudê*).[18] The presence of tragedy as a subtext to the remarks on the general psychology of grief is in due course clinched by the reference to Athenian theatre-audiences at 604e.

But there is a second observation which further clarifies the allusions to tragic poetry in this passage. Plato's argument can move, without warning, from poetic images to general human psychology, and then back again to poetry, because the ground is being prepared for the claim, already touched on at 604e and to be developed in the 'greatest charge' section, that the psychology of tragic audiences is involved in a mutual interplay with that of tragic characters: that is, tragedy *appeals* to powerful grief-directed instincts in the psyche; and the psychology of audiences can in turn be influenced by, *assimilated to*, that of tragic heroes.[19] Furthermore, we can connect this point with the conception of the tragic which I outlined in the first part of this essay, namely as a sense of life which finds its most potent expression in tragic poetry but is not confined to the particular forms of literary art. Both the appeal and the influence of tragedy reflect propensities of the human soul which are prior to the creation of tragic art-forms. On the Platonic view, 'the tragic' could and would have existed as a response to life even if tragic poetry had never come into being. None the less, the focus of the argument at this point is not on the structure of the psyche as such but on poetry's control over it, and it is this theme which comes to a climax with the 'greatest charge' at 605c6 ff.

The greatest charge against poetry is just this, that it has the psychological power to 'maim' or 'impair' the souls even of the good,[20] and to make the lives of those exposed to it 'worse and more wretched' (606d6–7). The charge potentially covers all kinds of poetry (606c2–d7), but its main statement applies specially to tragic epic and drama, whose capacity to open up the emotions, and to free them from rational inhibition, affects even 'the best of us' (605c10–11). As this last phrase intimates, a key aspect of this famous passage is its acknowledgement that the force of tragedy is not something artificial or aberrant: its secret is that it taps a universal and ever-present possibility within the psyche. Tragedy can elicit what is described at 605d3 as emotional 'surrender' precisely because the impulse to yield to grief (for oneself) and pity (for others) is entirely 'natural' (606a5), and calls for actively *repressive* measures to keep it in check (606a3). Because it is taken for granted that the impulse to grief (*to thrênôdes*, 606b1) and to pity (*to eleinon*, 606b8) is one and the same, it is implicit in the greatest charge that the passions aroused by tragedy involve the same values, the same attachments to life, that are expressed in the personal sorrows of bereavement. The tragic heroes envisaged at 605d1–2—Plato has no need to mention such names as Achilles, Ajax, Eteocles, Heracles, Oedipus, Priam, and many others, especially given the third book's citation of some prominent cases—are ones whose uncompromising acuteness of anguish, projected by all the means available to poetic artistry, destroys the canons of moderation and self-control that were ascribed to the 'good man' at 603e3 ff. They are ultimate embodiments of a sense of life which makes grief an imperative, and which releases a pressure towards rage at the world's (the gods') coldness to human aspirations.[21] To sympathize with these figures, to share their suffering (*sumpaschein*), is consequently to accept the valuation of life which they represent.

The dynamics of psychological-cum-ethical influence posited by this argument are not uncontestable. Even in Plato's own time there were some Athenians who noticed a disparity between responses to tragic theatre and reactions to sufferings in the real world,[22] and subsequent thinkers have frequently generalized such observations in relation to aesthetic experience as a whole.[23] But it is important here to draw a distinction between claims of an automatic or simple transference from art to life, and a more subtle recognition of the involvement of art in the shaping, modification, and reinforcement of attitudes which can inform patterns of behaviour. There is no good reason to take the 'greatest charge' argument as an example of the first rather than the second. Although Plato's case refers to the inevitability of 'infection' between our imaginative responses to tragic characters and the place of emotion in our own lives, there is an explicit appreciation that such responses represent no ordinary frame of mind but a heightened receptiveness, commensurate with the idea of 'surrender' (605d3), to the dramatic projection of feeling (606a7–b8). The point is not that aesthetic experience has easily calculable or immediate consequences for our mental lives, but that a strong yielding to emotions expressed in a work of art amounts to the enactment and acceptance of an underlying valuation. It is hard to see how such a judgement could be confidently discarded without at the same time depriving tragedy, or any other art, of its 'seriousness' (a recurrent motif, as we saw, in Platonic references to tragedy) by severing its links with the realities of emotion as a psychological determinant of action.[24] That still leaves quite open, of course, the possibility of dissenting from the Platonic argument at the level of the proposition that the emotions are intrinsically 'irrational' and dangerous, and therefore badly in need of the control of the 'higher' function of reason. But an objection on that front would do nothing to diminish, and might even tend to strengthen, the suggestion that emotional responses to tragedy are the carriers of implicit values and thus hold the potential to generate, or intensify, a tragic sense of life.

The psychological issues raised by this section of *Republic* 10 would evidently warrant a separate and extensive enquiry of their own. But it is worth emphasizing that in one fundamental respect Plato's position is aligned with a perspective sometimes explicitly assumed by tragedy itself. It is an obvious but far-reaching fact that tragic suffering is almost always witnessed and responded to within the dramatic context of tragedy, most usually by the chorus. This means that suffering is not just shown in its rawness, but already to some extent *interpreted*, in the immediate environment of the events. And one distinctively tragic interpretation of suffering—the interpretation which Plato has in mind both in *Republic* 10 and in other passages mentioned earlier in this essay—is the translation of a particular *pathos* into a symbol of the limits on the human condition in general. Perhaps the aptest example of this idea is the final stasimon of *Oedipus Tyrannus*, where the chorus treats Oedipus as in every respect a model, a *paradeigma* (1193), for their understanding of man:

> O generations of mortals,
> I count your lives as equal
> To nothingness itself.
> For who, tell me who,
> Has happiness that stretches further
> Than a brief illusion
> And, after the illusion, decline?
> Considering you as my model,
> Considering your *daimôn*, yours alone,
> O wretched Oedipus,
> I count no mortal blessed.
>
>   (1186–96)

Oedipus is interpreted as a model in terms equally of what he had appeared to achieve, and of what he has now lost: the curve traced by his rise and fall, and beneath which the agency of a god (*daimôn*, 1194) can be felt, is held up as a pattern definitive of the human condition. Regarded in this paradigmatic light, his case encourages the chorus to extrapolate to all 'generations of mortals', and to conclude that all happiness, *eudaimonia*, is a mirage. The mentality of the chorus, in universalizing the implications of Oedipus' catastrophe, perfectly bears out the diagnosis which *Republic* 2–3 provides of tragedy's tendency to deposit a corrosive pessimism about human possibilities. The mind which surrendered to this pessimism in a permanent way might indeed find itself living a 'worse and more wretched' life (*Republic* 606d6–7), since it would be condemned by its own beliefs to abandoning any hope that its highest endeavours could be meaningfully satisfied by the world. Such permanent surrender is part of what Plato elsewhere evokes by the notion of a 'tragic life'. If such outright pessimism really is the heart of what tragedy offers, and if the experience of it can be consistently translated into sustained patterns of thought and feeling, then the Platonic critique will continue to raise penetrating questions about its psychological consequences (however short it may fall of refuting its metaphysical basis). But both of those conditionals contain permanently disputable propositions, whose validity is surely relative to individual and cultural variables that are not encompassed by the terms of Plato's argument. Even in the *Oedipus Tyrannus*, tragic pessimism is not necessarily definitive of tragedy; the play's final stasimon is not its last word.

It may well be, then, that the most basic objection to the Platonic critique of tragedy is that it ignores the *manifold* nature of what tragedy can and does offer. Yet this objection may itself be, in a sense, beside the point, in so far as it addresses precisely what makes the critique, so I have argued, into a conception of the tragic. If, as I originally suggested, theories of the tragic, as opposed to more general perspectives on tragedy, are characterized by their perception of an essential, defining vision, the content of this vision need not be discoverable in all *de facto* members of the genre of tragedy. Equally, anything which qualifies as a definition of the tragic will do so by virtue of supplying not so much a useful framework for the analysis of tragedy, but something akin to the 'whole conception of life itself', the 'whole philosophy more or less formulated', to which Unamuno refers in my epigraph.[25] This point is especially pertinent in the case of Plato, and allows us to regard in a richer light the idea—an idea explicitly prompted, as we earlier saw, by *Laws* 817b—that his response to tragedy, his repudiation of the tragic, is a vital dimension of his own philosophy. The Platonic disavowal of the tragic reflects an awareness, paralleled in antiquity only by the later and partly platonizing views of the Stoics, that the tragic itself is a philosophy in embryo. And it is precisely the strength of this awareness which makes tragedy, from the Socratic imperturbability of the *Apology* to the overt terms of *Laws* 817b itself, a permanently important 'adversary' to be engaged by the voices of Plato's own writing.

If we return, with that claim in mind, to *Republic* 10, it should appear appropriate that the book not only conveys direct antipathy to a tragic conception of life, but also completes the entire work with a myth which has specifically anti-tragic resonance at several stages. The myth of Er is, more than anything else, an allegory of the soul's responsibility for its own life. The Thyestes-like tyrant who finds that it is his 'destiny'[26] to eat his own children and commit other execrable deeds, proceeds to grieve in the uninhibited manner characterized earlier in the book as tragic, and to blame 'fortune and the gods and everything *but* himself' (619c2–6). By this externalization of his self-imposed destiny he shows himself unable to grasp or face up to the supreme denial of the tragic incorporated in the earlier pronouncement to the souls, 'the responsibility lies with the chooser; god is blameless' (617e4–5). His case is therefore a stark emblem of the Platonic contrast between two ultimate hypotheses about the world—the first that human lives are governed by external forces which are indifferent to, and capable of crushing, the quest for happiness; the second that the source of true happiness is located nowhere other than in the individual soul's choice between good and evil. To embrace the first of these is to open the flood-gates to (self-)pity, and to interpret the world as a stage made for the tragedy of life. To follow, on the other hand, a belief in the soul's capacity to forge its own moral fate, is to entertain a hope which nourishes the psychological, ethical, and metaphysical aspirations of Plato's own dialogues. Whatever else may need to be said about the nature of this dichotomy, the Platonic consciousness of it is as remarkable for its identification of one version of the tragic as for its pursuit of a philosophical rationalism by which tragedy might be transcended.

Notes

1. M. de Unamuno, _The Tragic Sense of Life_, Eng. trans. J. E. C. Flitch (London 1921) 17.
2. See e.g. A. Lesky, 'Zum Problem des Tragischen', id., _Gesammelte Schriften_ (Berne 1966) 213–19.
3. Some classical additions to LSJ's examples of figurative or semi-figurative uses of these terms are: Men. _Sik._ 262–3 (_tragôidia_), _Asp._ 329 (_tragôidein_); Ar. _Peace_ 136; Arist. _Rhet._ 1406^{b}8, _Meteor._ 353^{b}1 (_tragikos_).
4. Aristotle's other uses of _tragikos_ etc. in the _Poetics_ are, when not plainly technical, unrevealing: 13, 1452^{b}37 appeals to the criteria of pity and fear, 14, 1453^{b}39 to the requirement of _pathos_; 18, 1456^{a}21 is deeply obscure.
5. See my _Aristotle's Poetics_, ch. 7, and cf. Edith Hall in this volume, above p. 296. The counter-considerations adduced by M. Heath, 'The Universality of Poetry in Aristotle's _Poetics_', _CQ_ 41 (1991) 389–402, at 395–7, suggest that there are ways in which divine involvement in a tragic plot could be consistent with Aristotle's general theory, but they do not require a serious amendment to the claim that the _Poetics_ neglects the religious dimension of the genre.
6. See K. Dover, _Aristophanes: Frogs_ (Oxford 1993) 12–15. For _sophia_, see e.g. 882.
7. See ibid. 25–7, for other fifth-century references to tragedy, none of which contains any overt indication of a conception of the tragic.
8. In addition to the cases which I discuss, see those cited by D. Tarrant, 'Plato as Dramatist', _JHS_ 75 (1955) 82–9, at 83.
9. _Philebus_ 50b1–4: I leave aside, for present purposes, the possibility that 'tragedy and comedy of life' denotes a hybrid concept of tragicomedy.
10. Later imagery of this kind is cited by (e.g.) E. R. Curtius, _European Literature and the Latin Middle Ages_, Eng. trans. W. R. Trask (London 1953) 138–44, H. A. Kelly, _Ideas and Forms of Tragedy from Aristotle to the Middle Ages_ (Cambridge 1993) 23–6, 79–81.
11. I have given one view of this side of _Phaedo_ in 'Plato and Aristotle on the Denial of Tragedy', _PCPS_ 30 (1984) 49–71, at 56–8.
12. The tragic quotations are at 380a3–4, 381d8, 383b1–9, 391e7–9.
13. Plato's argument does not draw any distinction between these two things; it focuses on _muthoi_, 'stories', as bearers of _logoi_ (see esp. 376e11, 378a7 and d3 [_logopoiein_], 380a8), and the latter could be glossed as propositionally expressible views. This typifies a broader Platonic tendency, which I discuss in an as yet unpub. essay, 'The Subjection of Mythos to Logos: Plato's Citations of the Poets'.

14. The argument about divine metamorphosis and deception (380d–383c) can here count as a variation on the theme of divine responsibility for evil.

15. See my note in *Plato Republic 10* (Warminster 1988) ad loc.; here, as elsewhere in bk. 10, Plato may be recalling Gorgianic ideas (see fr. 11. 9).

16. 603e4 refers back to 3. 387d–388e.

17. On *pathos* see T. Gould, *The Ancient Quarrel between Poetry and Philosophy* (Princeton 1990), with the reservations stated in my review in *CP* 87 (1992) 263–9.

18. Compare *Gorgias* 502b, *Laws* 7, 817a2, 8, 838c4.

19. This is also a return to one of the dominant psychological and educational topics in the treatment of poetry in bks. 2–3: for one interpretation, see my 'Plato and the Psychology of Drama', *Drama* 1 (1992) 55–73.

20. *Lôbasthai* at 605c7 echoes 595b5: the greatest charge has been in view since the return to poetry at the beginning of the book.

21. The element of rage, and the part of the soul which feels it or responds to it in others, is *to aganaktêtikon* (604e1–2, 605a5; cf. 604b10).

22. See the rather similar passages at Andocides 4. 23, Isoc. 4. 168; *Republic* 606b5–6 claims that understanding of the psychological influence of art on life is not widely recognized. One might recall here Nietzsche's idea that Athenian audiences of tragedy were hard, warlike men who were taken temporarily out of themselves in the theatre (*Morgenröte*, § 172): this section can be read as a revision of Plato's position in the 'greatest charge' section of *Rep.* 10, to which it goes on to refer.

23. One recent occurrence of this point is in G. Steiner, *Real Presences* (London 1989) 144, though Steiner proceeds to endorse the strength of the Platonic challenge.

24. A forceful statement of a quasi-Platonic position in this area is W. C. Booth, *The Company We Keep: An Ethics of Fiction* (Chicago 1988).

25. It is curious that while Unamuno himself frequently cites Plato, he does so always as a paradigm of the yearning for immortality, and nowhere as the repudiator of a tragic sense of life: note, however, the passing acknowledgement of Platonic complexities where Unamuno refers to 'the serene Plato', before adding 'but was he serene?' (*Tragic Sense*, 45).

26. *Heimarmenê* (619c1), exactly the same term used by Socrates in his deprecation of a tragic gesture at *Phaedo* 115a5–6 (see my text, above); its use here is subtly ironic.

PART III

Greek Tragedy and 'Tragedy as a Whole': Perspectives and Definitions

INTRODUCTORY NOTE

The papers in the third and final section are the most diverse. What they have in common is a specific orientation towards one or other of the relationships between the tragedy of Greek antiquity and the serious drama and theoretical perspectives of the modern world in and since Shakespeare. And if many of the issues and preoccupations of earlier essays are once again to the fore, one special recurrent theme is a commitment to definition, not least the definition of tragedy 'as a whole' itself.

The three opening papers confront Greek tragic practice with Continental theory, philosophical and dramatic. On one level, Mogyoródi's essay recalls the preoccupation with issues of moral responsibility and choice that informs the papers by Garvie and van Erp Taalman Kip, Trapp and Foley, and the major question of 'freedom' that is touched on by Friedrich, among others. Yet Mogyoródi's concern with these issues differs radically from theirs, just as her reading of *Antigone* differs radically from Foley's or Trapp's, not only in its emphasis or its detail, but in its fundamental alignment. Behind her discussion is an engagement with the tradition of thought—moral and existential—that runs from Kierkegaard to Heidegger and beyond. Seeking in effect to reappraise the notion of tragic 'fate' that is stigmatized by several contributors, from Goldhill to Ewans, she contends that the widely disregarded 'family curse' in *Antigone* (along with its equivalents in other tragedies) plays a crucial role in the tragic 'complicity of freedom and necessity' and thereby in the tragic itself. In her argument that Antigone 'appropriates necessity', Mogyoródi offers a new perspective on a series of classic discussions—by Dodds (on the 'false alternative' between necessity and freedom), by Lesky (on 'double determination'), and by Vernant (on 'the will').

Seidensticker's concern is with Aristotle and Euripides, but also with the classic German tradition of argumentation about the tragic and, in particular, the reassessment of this tradition by Peter Szondi. For Szondi the 'dialectical' quality of the tragic is to be seen as the basis of the concept and, although (like most critics) he denies Aristotle a philosophy of the tragic, he still detects its germ in the *Poetics*. After a review of Szondi's argument, of Aristotle, and of Euripidean tragedy from *Medea* to *Bacchae*, Seidensticker affirms the importance of Szondi's dialectic as an essential characteristic of tragic drama, but (in qualification of Szondi's argument) finds a clear anticipation of the principle in Aristotle's notion of *peripeteia*. More specifically, he proposes a modified version of the dialectical principle as a handle on the tragic qualities of Sophocles (a thesis argued elsewhere) and as a way of distinguishing between the tragic and the non-tragic elements in Euripides. The revised dialectic is defined in terms of a paradoxical, but inevitable, reversal that arises from the nature, intentions, or actions of the tragic characters. Such a reversal is found to be central to the tragic quality of *Medea*, *Hippolytus*, and *Bacchae*; in *Hecuba*, *Trojan Women*, and *Heracles* catastrophe is produced by other means; in the 'tragicomedies' dialectical elements confront others (and here Seidensticker's findings might be set against Lee and Arnott's readings of *Ion*).

A concern with the problem of audience response unites discussions as different as those of Calame, Lee, Segal, Gould, and Halliwell. Lada's paper puts the problem in a new light by bringing together the dramatic theories of Bertolt Brecht and the psychology of Greek tragedy as represented by the response of the ancient audience in the ancient theatre. Adducing evidence from, above all, Aristophanes' *Frogs*, and pointing also to tragic *exempla* from *Antigone* to *Bacchae*, she argues that tragic performance in Greece implies a response both emotional and intellectual, both empathetic and socially committed. In this it fundamentally contradicts Brecht's theory of 'traditional' ('Aristotelian') theatre as empathetic through and through. Lada, in fact, promises to illuminate Greek theatre through the perspective of Brechtian theory and in turn challenges Brechtian theory—and its premise that empathy militates against intellectual awareness and social commitment—by a discussion of Greek theatre itself.

The connection of tragedy and ritual, discussed by Segal and Easterling, and especially by Friedrich and Seaford, is presented in a different light by Macintosh. Her concern is the centrality of death to tragedy and to the tragic effect, a nexus explored through the unexpected affinity she finds between Greek tragedy and the modern Irish drama of Yeats, Synge, and O'Casey. The affinity is represented by two common features of these theatrical traditions, the 'big speech' of the dying heroes and the lament of their mourners. These two formal elements are seen to be parallel to each other and, in their parallelism, to reflect ritual relationships between mourners and mourned. Drawing on such plays as *Antigone*, *Trojan Women*, and *Trachiniae*, Yeats's *Death of Cuchulain*, Synge's *Deirdre of the Sorrows*, and O'Casey's *Juno and the Paycock*, Macintosh argues that the big speech and the final lament, though special articulations associated with special individuals, tend away from the individual. Their ultimate significance is that of the collective gesture (and here the argument points back to the debates initiated by Gould and Calame, as well as Segal): in its stylization the gesture appeals to a 'shared inheritance' beyond the personal, while its repetitive qualities are a prerequisite for the elusive 'pleasure' associated with the tragic experience.

The theme of ritual, among others, is picked up by Mitchell-Boyask. His paper, along with those by Ewans and Silk that follow it, brings to the foreground the major relationship between Greek tragedy and Shakespeare. Like Foley and Trapp, van Erp Taalman Kip and Garvie, and, in very different ways, Mogyoródi and Halliwell, Mitchell-Boyask directs his argument towards character and ethical issues, but in his case in a literary-theoretical frame of reference associated with discussions of Shakespeare by Kenneth Burke, Harry Berger and René Girard. His starting-point is Girard's controversial theory of 'mimetic desire' as the undifferentiating force between individuals, good or bad, which is reversed by the differentiating effects of 'scapegoating', an essentially arbitrary process dramatized and disclosed by tragedy. Noting the problems involved in discussing dramatic individuals in isolation, and especially in mechanically assimilating the individual characters of Shakespeare to those of Greek theatre, Mitchell-Boyask constructs a modified Girardian theory that takes account of Burke's concept of 'victimage' and Berger's insistence on the psychological and ethical interactions between the members of a play's 'community', a community which includes audience as well as stage figures. Thus tragedy, from *Coriolanus* to *Hippolytus*, is seen to enact a process in which the audience accepts the culpability of, yet is disturbed and moved by, the victimized individuals. If the tragic is located in mimesis, yet *our* 'mimetic desire' (so Mitchell-Boyask argues, against Plato) stops before we succumb too far.

Ewans too picks up several of the volume's major themes: not only Greek tragedy and Shakespeare, but also religion (compare, variously, Calame and Lee, Taplin and Gredley, Seaford and Halliwell), tragedy and the 'tragic' *Iliad* (compare Lowe, later in this section), freedom and necessity (compare, above all, Mogyoródi), and Aristotle. In the *Iliad* Ewans finds a central principle whereby the lives of the leading characters—their *moirai* (usually translated 'fates')—'take shape' in accordance with the operations of immanent divinity in us and in nature around us. Older Greek tragedy, he argues, depends on this principle and articulates the inevitability of the 'taking shape' in various ways: by appeal to mythological tradition, by the dynamic of pollution (which must be rectified) or prophecy (which must be fulfilled), and by the logic of story-pattern. This is the tragedy of necessity, exemplified by *Trachiniae* and *Oedipus Rex*, in which patterns of 'necessity' connect human actions with each other and with the actions of the gods. On the Shakespearean side *Macbeth* and *Hamlet* follow essentially the same patterns. By contrast, much of the drama of the later fifth century—like the Euripidean drama pondered by Lee and Arnott—is based on suspense, surprise, and chance. This is the tragedy of 'probability'; and Ewans suggests that Aristotle's formula of 'probability or necessity' is a disjunctive principle that points, differentially, to the two contrasting modes. His argument thus invites comparison, as well as contrast, with Seidensticker's.

Drawing freely on Greek and Shakespearean examples from *Bacchae* to *Oresteia* and *Antony and Cleopatra* to *Othello*, Silk's paper accepts, but seeks to move beyond, the Aristotelian principle that tragic language is elevated and complex. Rejecting both Aristotle's further demand for linguistic clarity and the postmodern postulate of incommunicability, he argues that on the evidence of Greek tragedy and Shakespeare, tragic language is 'propelled by three irreducible determinants': compulsion, excess, and identity. In linguistic terms, tragedy tends to foreground *must*, *too*, and the *name*, or else their equivalents on the stylistic level. These linguistic and stylistic markers, in any event, tend to cluster at particular moments of crisis for the striving individuals on whom the tragedy depends, namely at moments of decision or collision before the catastrophe, or at moments of recognition afterwards. From the categories of this discussion various connections might be made: to Mogyoródi, Ewans, and Gredley on 'necessity'; to Calame and Buxton on tragic knowledge and isolation; to Seidensticker on critical moments of reversal; to Friedrich on norms and transgressions.

In Rosenmeyer's paper the range of reference is extended over the whole front of 'serious drama', as we return to the problem of mood and the relationship of drama to audience that exercises Lada and Macintosh in this section and so many others before. Rosenmeyer's particular concern is with the concept of irony, widely used and widely questioned. He sets out to reappraise and rehabilitate the concept by means of a new taxonomy. After a critical review of modern theories of irony, from the 'dramatic irony' of the Romantics to the postmodern extension of the word to cover virtually any gap, fracture, resistance, or deferral, he offers a fourfold classification of irony in drama: forensic ('the irony of attack and defence'), blind irony (involving unintentional revelation), structural irony (the 'irony of tension', beloved by the New Critics), and the more disturbing *Fiktionsironie* (the irony of 'skewed orders of reality'). His wide-ranging discussion touches on such central issues as the conflict of voices and the 'creative participation' of the tragic principals—but 'as dupes'—in the tragic experience; and the argument is particularized by a further series of subdivisions and a wealth of examples, from Sophocles to Seneca and Goethe to Ionesco. As Lowe makes clear in his response, which concentrates on the Greek experience, Rosenmeyer's classification not only clarifies the distinctive place of irony in drama, but also brings into focus two relationships of special importance to the present volume: between Greek tragedy and Greek Old Comedy and, particularly, between Greek tragedy and Homeric epic. Under the first heading, Aristophanic comedy is seen to be dominated by forensic irony, and the 'assertion of power relationships' that goes with it, and by *Fiktionsironie*, with its acknowledgement of the arbitrary constructedness of the text, whereas in tragedy blind and structural irony predominate; here, clearly, is a contrast supplementary to, but in line with, those discussed by Taplin and Gredley. Lowe's own main concern, however, is the clarification of 'tragic irony'—that is, blind and structural irony—by reference to the Homeric perspective. From the *Iliad* tragedy derives an 'ironic image of the universe' that centres on a perceived 'gap between individual and cosmic value', from the *Odyssey* a sense that 'the hermeneutics of deception' are built into the world. The tragic, then, is located in 'the fifth century's reading' of Homer, 'concentrated into *mimêsis*'. Stressing (like, but also very unlike, Seidensticker and Mitchell-Boyask) the *dramatic* qualities of tragedy, Lowe notes such 'concentrating' features as 'the elision of the authoritative narratorial presence' and the complex simultaneities of other kinds of presence (spectatorial, divine, human) in the theatre. An example from *Ajax* is used to help elucidate 'the special role we feel for classical tragedy in the anatomy of irony and for irony in the anatomy of tragedy'.

There could hardly be a more appropriate end for a book with the scope of 'tragedy and the tragic' than an essay by George Steiner. Revisiting territory first covered in *The Death of Tragedy* (1961) and more recently in *Antigones* (1984), and against the background of his long engagement with the possibilities of art in an age of modern barbarity, Steiner offers his view of tragedy 'as a whole'. 'Tragedy'—that is, 'tragedy, pure and simple'—is rare: it is confined to a few Greek plays, a few by Racine, a few others. Tragedy in this special and restricted sense is 'a dramatic enactment of a highly specific world-view', namely that 'human life *per se*, both ontologically and existentially, is an affliction'. This, for Steiner, is the burden of *Bacchae*, *Timon of Athens*, *Bérénice*—and *Bérénice* above all provides the representative image of the 'economy of the absolute' in its uncompromising final moment when the universe is 'brought to a single point of total compaction'. At which juncture, those present at the conference that generated this book might well think back to the talk given then by that most distinguished of contemporary theatrical directors, John Barton (see above, pp. 1–2). Explaining his long-standing interest in dramatic cycles, represented not least in *The Greeks* (1979), a trilogy of trilogies based on Euripides, Barton discussed the ambition of such 'epic tragedies' to 'tell the whole story'. The provocative implication of his project for fundamental questions of definition, and the contrast with Steiner's category of 'pure' tragedy, could hardly be more apparent. For Steiner, a concern for 'the whole story' is the mark of Shakespeare—the Shakespeare who knows that 'the facts of the world are hybrid'—and points precisely to the reason why most Shakespearean 'tragedy' is no more 'pure' tragedy than it was for Dr Johnson in an earlier age.

Steiner's reading of tragedy—Greek and other—is hardly without its controversial aspects. Buxton, for one, questions its trans-historical premises (p. 42). Steiner's 'dark' reading of such dramas as *Bacchae* would be contested by, for instance, Seaford, whose own constructivist 'Dionysiac' reading of that and other Greek tragedies is—in Nietzschean terms—as Apolline as Steiner's itself is Dionysiac *tout court*. As against this, Steiner's continuing endorsement of the special status and value of tragedy—Greek and other—and, above all, perhaps, his closing insistence on the 'strangeness' of tragedy, the challenge it constitutes to us and our everyday comfort, are affirmations which in their many different ways the great theorists from Aristotle to Nietzsche would endorse, and the other, diverse, contributors to this volume too.

20

Tragic Freedom and Fate in Sophocles' *Antigone*: Notes on the Role of the 'Ancient Evils' in 'the Tragic'[1]

EMESE MOGYORÓDI

In memoriam Éva Ancsel, not 'from' but 'of' whom I have learnt

In Greek tragedy 'the tragic' is distinctively brought about in the mythical context of a doomed family or, in Aristotelian language, of those ἐν μεγάλῃ δόξῃ ('with a great reputation'). The adverb, 'distinctively', of course, makes all the difference. I do not wish to imply that Greek tragedy could in any way be subsumed under this one heading, or that the concept of 'the tragic' (as embodied in the Greek tragedies that have come down to us) could be exhausted by a simple pattern associated with the presence of a family curse, as, very simply, in most of them this is missing. Yet it may not be quite by chance that in the three most distinguished tragedies that have been handed down to us, the tragic family doom, together with curses or oracles that go with it, is certainly present—and here I have in mind the *Oresteia* (counting Aeschylus' trilogy as one tragedy), *Antigone*, and *Oedipus Rex*. I would like to maintain, however, that in all three of these plays the 'ancient evils' constitute a dominant presence and that, unless we determine in what way they contribute to the heroes' and heroine's fate, the core of the tragic remains inscrutable. But what about other tragedies, such as *Supplices*, *Prometheus*, *Ajax*, *Philoctetes*, *Trachiniae*, and, indeed, a great deal of Euripides? Let us say that these tragedies that we consider paradigmatic are the outcome of a relatively long process of experimentation with the tragic, and that the hard core gradually crystallized into the pattern from elements that are present in scattered and somewhat undifferentiated form in virtually *all* the tragedies.[2]

On the basis of the thesis indicated above, I could be expected to
argue for the pervasiveness of necessity, as opposed to freedom, in
Greek tragedy. But the case is quite the contrary: I agree with
Dodds in considering the 'necessity versus freedom' debate a
debate about false alternatives, but I wish to stress the importance
of both the 'ancient evils' (unlike Dodds) and yet *also* the element
of freedom.³ The Greeks were well aware of superhuman forces of
causation, striking at the very heart of human endeavours, yet 'vigorous, self-assertive, emulous, ambitious, they pursued their aims
in some confidence that they could attain them. And freedom, as
individuals and as communities, they valued above most other
things.'⁴ I do not think it would be much of an overstatement to say
they valued freedom above all. By exploring in what way freedom
is operative despite the inevitable workings of some external determination, I hope to provide reinstatement for freedom, as against
views that overemphasize the determination.⁵ Conversely, by
stressing the role of an external contingency, I would like to argue
for the importance of determination, as against views that may lead
to an undue exaltation of freedom.⁶ Without seeking in any way
even to outline a relevant development that has run its course in
Continental philosophy since the critics of Kantian morality
attempted to come to grips with the idea of 'radical evil' and examine its consequences for the issue of human freedom, I would like
to note that the notorious 'false alternative' is the result of a conception of freedom which has remained unaffected by these developments. I cannot attempt here to do justice to an appreciation of
what Heidegger, whose philosophy represents in this regard one of
the crucial steps, called 'finite freedom', yet I must note that this is
the kind of conception of freedom that I have in mind when trying
to go beyond the 'false alternative'.⁷

For such an attempt, the *Antigone* seems to be particularly suitable in a number of respects. The 'evils that stem from Oedipus'
are in Antigone's thoughts when she enters the stage; they provide
a most painful overture to the play and recur on several occasions.⁸
They are recalled at times of puzzlement or when they seem to be
expected to throw some light on the misfortune. We may gather, as
the chorus does,⁹ that what happens and, consequently, our heroine's fate (even if not her guilt, for the time being) has something
to do with that sinister background. Yet it seems unlikely that she
should be falling victim to a monstrously unjust doom that strikes

down the members of the Labdacids by perfunctory blows. But, again, with a ghastly automatism in the background, there seems to be no room for choice, and thus for freedom.[10] But what about Ismene? She is also a member of the family and, of course, it cannot be denied that she gets her share of afflictions. But could we, by the same token, also contend, with some cogency, that her fate is tragic in the same sense as her sister's, or that she is a tragic 'heroine'? If nothing else, this could be ample evidence that *there is* an alternative, *there is* room for choice and thus for freedom, since their fates take markedly diverse paths, as is emphatically indicated by Sophocles. I would like to argue that whereas what happens to Ismene is, from the point of view of dramatic construction as well as poetic design, a simple case of 'ordinary' misfortune, Antigone's fate is tragic in a decisive sense whose meaning is determined precisely by the way she relates herself to the contingency (the external fatedness) represented by the family doom. I detect an unfolding contrast between their differing responses to the predicament occasioned by Creon's edict.

The play opens with the confrontation of the last two descendants of the famous, or ill-famed, Labdacid family with a serious moral predicament occasioned by Creon's edict that one of their brothers should be left unburied. Ever since Bruno Snell expounded his view that Aeschylus 'discovered' an 'archetype of action' in Pelasgus' 'soul-searching' and choice, the issue of tragic decision has been subjected to heated debates.[11] But whatever the problems arising from a philosophically or theoretically undifferentiated[12] conception of choice, freedom, will, or free will among the Greeks, the dramatic setting, discourse, textual organization, and vocabulary underline the fact that in this play, too, we are presented with a genuine 'situation of choice'.[13] True enough, there is no 'weighing' of alternatives, no 'sustained period of indecision, leading up to a final choice', no 'reasoned speech' in which the sisters explore 'the pros and cons in detail',[14] but there is a gradually unfolding divergence and separation of courses of actions to be taken through an unparalleled dramatization of decision-making.[15] It is in the course of *the process* of this unfolding separation that a discernment of what we would call 'choice' arises through their encountering an alternative course of action represented by the other.[16] It appears as though one of them, Antigone, has gone a step further in encountering the impasse, if only because she has come to know about the indictment earlier. Ismene appears to know nothing about the news, yet seems not over-anxious to hear why Antigone has sent for her in such haste. We may suspect that Ismene's ignorance is not wholly innocent, and we may see it as at least appropriate that Antigone should be the first to know about it. Thus, it appears as though Antigone has already made a decision, which may account for the impression here of that impatience or impetuousness which is thought to be so characteristic of her. In her opening address to Ismene, however, there is no indication of a definitive intention or even reference to an alternative. Yet there is a straightforward allusion to anguish both old and new[17] and a palpable indication of an indignant tone ('for me, I tell you' [Grene]: λέγω γὰρ κἀμέ, 32)[18] only intensified by Ismene's evasive attitude. True enough, at the end of her attempt at elucidating for Ismene the true source of her indignation, she does outline an alternative, puzzling as it may seem to be to her sister ('There you have it; soon you will show yourself | as noble both in your nature and your birth | or yourself as base, although of noble parents' [Grene]: οὕτως ἔχει σοι ταῦτα, καὶ δείξεις τάχα | εἴτ' εὐγενὴς πέφυκας εἴτ' ἐσθλῶν κακή, 37–8). Should we conclude, then, that her decision has *already* been made, prior to her encounter with Ismene? A positive answer to this question would disregard the dramatic significance and import of the two sisters' encounter, the fact that the prologue is to comprise preliminaries and foreshadow what is to come. This apart, we may ask why Antigone should turn to seek help from her sister once she has assumed a choice and is, therefore, confident about what ought to be done?[19] I do not intend to deny that her consciousness of the impasse and, by implication, awareness of choice is the key to her tragedy. On the contrary, what is often perceived as impetuousness or harshness in her I consider prerequisite for tragedy to be induced. The contrast with Ismene in this regard is substantial, for were she ready to collaborate with Antigone in the first place, there would certainly be no tragedy, or at least it would not be the tragedy of Antigone alone. Yet a trait of character alone does not suffice to make a tragedy; decision, choice, and action in the sense of Snell's 'archetype' are also required. Antigone, then, is aware of the danger, and thus knows there is a safer alternative. She 'recognizes' both alternatives but the one she eventually 'chooses' *is not yet her own.* That the one way open for her is exclusively hers, that it is something apportioned to her alone, is disclosed for her only in the course of the confrontation with the opposite choice made by another.

But why should we insist on emphasizing a gradually unfolding decision instead of one made prior to action? There are several reasons for this. First of all, such a conception of choice and decision-making assumes a far more organic mental structure and, in my view, one that is closer to the Greek understanding of mental activity than the modern conception of deliberation and will, without, however, depriving the Greeks of any awareness of the issue.[20] For what critics often take as a trait of character (impetuousness, harshness, unswerving adherence to her principles, etc.) is an initial *impetus* in Antigone which, being impeded or obstructed by a negativity embodied in Creon's edict,[21] splinters into alternatives. Were it not for this primordial impetus, alternatives would not arise, any more than they do for Ismene. Conversely, were it not for an obstacle in the path of a passionate drive by which the course of that drive is barred, there would be no alternatives either. But although the primordial impetus (whose source is still to be detected) pushes her in the direction of defying the decree, it needs to be 'recognized' and *assented to* in order to constitute a choice for Antigone. She thus becomes the 'accomplice'[22] of an elusive force that remains hidden until the encounter with a diametrically opposed attitude and decision. Secondly, once we have discerned a categorical difference between an accidental trait of character and a more substantial impulse which establishes a closer bond between decision and action,[23] we can start gaining a deeper insight into the true source of indignation observable in the very first lines. For tragedy, as we learn from Aristotle's suggestive yet rather cryptic observation, is not a question of character ($\mathring{\eta}\theta os$) but of action ($\mu\hat{v}\theta os$). It is totally in accord with Antigone's character that she should defy the edict, but how could one find that out if she did not *act* that way? Action, however, should have a momentous sense, assuming an existential gravity that is able to affect and determine a whole course of life, the personal fate of the agent. Thirdly (and this is intimately related to the crucial determinants of the tragic—that is, to *hamartia*, *peripeteia*, and *anagnôrisis*), such a description of choice allows for a far less conscious agent, leaving room for an inscrutable causation both internal and external to character and action. For if, *pace* Hegel, Antigone 'interiorizes' external contingency to the extent that she is aware in what, and to precisely what extent, she is guilty by transgressing a law—in Hegel's words, if she 'wittingly commits her crime'—she will either qualify as one of the σφόδρα πονηροί (the 'extremely evil' characters) of Aristotle or as a victorious Romantic 'heroine' who falls victim to a tragic doom or to the accidental workings of human law.[24] In both the latter cases her own contribution to fate would be inorganic and the tragic quality of her fall inexplicable, since her deed would be completely determined from outside. We must, at this point, anticipate another basic insight gained from our description of tragic choice, which is that her guilt can no longer be thought of as constituted by the simple transgression alone, since she is every bit aware of that: in her own words, she has 'done wrong', but 'in a sacred cause' (ὅσια πανουργήσασ', 74).

In contrast with Antigone, then, Ismene fails to choose in the sense determined above. Since she lacks the impetus (and not impetuousness) of an Antigone, no alternatives arise for her; and although eventually she is clearly informed of what is at stake, her evasive attitude, anxious reservations, and submissive perturbation preclude her from recognizing the alternatives. But can we really contend that she fails to *choose*? Is there a sound reason for denying her what is explicitly stated by Antigone, reproachful as it may be, that she has chosen to live ('Life was your choice, and death was mine.' [Grene]: σὺ μὲν γὰρ εἵλου ζῆν, ἐγὼ δὲ κατθανεῖν, 555)? If we are to see the reasons for refuting Antigone's claim and expand the meaning of tragic choice, we need to examine our second major passage, which reveals the consequences of what happened in the sisters' first encounter.

Antigone has been brought in front of Creon to plead guilty for her deed and to be sentenced to the proclaimed punishment. Ismene enters the stage at the very moment Creon's rage reaches its highest peak, when, having made sure the transgressor is—in his eyes—an utter reprobate obdurately boasting about her crime (480–3) and having been humiliated both by Antigone's relentlessness and his own procrastination about saying the last word,[25] he finally gives in and turns his thumb down, making at the same time one of his several assertions of masculine authority (524–5). Ismene immediately pleads guilty, which may be partly because of her general submissiveness, partly because of some kind of heroic or desperate self-sacrifice by which she hopes to save Antigone. But either way, her motives are rather confused.[26] She may have the best of intentions, but her behaviour only makes it clear that the two sisters' separation is now complete. Late as it may seem to be, she would now like to share the punishment and thus the 'honour' (544–5). But what amends could she make now that the dice have long been cast? It is not only the punishment for a deed she has not committed (546–7) that she cannot incur; she is dispossessed of a fate whose choice she has deferred. She is thus literally *bereft of* Antigone's fate, while, at the same time *guilty* of her sister's isolation and fall, because she has failed to undertake a crucial existential challenge for herself ('And shall I have no share in your fate?' [Jebb]: καμπλάκω τοῦ σοῦ μόρου; 554).[27] She is thus guilty of a fault she did not incur, subject to a fate she did not choose. It would be erroneous to contend that she undergoes some kind of reversal, since her blindness to the truth of the situation is almost pathological. When Antigone has exhausted her explanation of why the 'fate' Ismene has induced cannot be undone (538–9, 555), and has spurned all the futile and confused efforts Ismene makes to establish the opposite 'argument',[28] the latter still insists that their 'guilt is nevertheless the same' (καὶ μὴν ἴση νῷν γ' ἐστιν ἡ 'ξαμαρτία, 558), to which Antigone can only make the somewhat resigned remark, 'pull yourself together' (θάρσει, 559) and repeat that they have chosen two contrary paths. If the prologue had left us with any doubt that the lives and fates of the last two descendants of the Labdacids have been painfully severed, that doubt would be completely dissolved by now.

Ismene, then, is dispossessed of Antigone's fate. But does that mean that she has no fate at all? Are not her worries about her sister, her personal suffering, and her desperate attempt to help genuine enough? No doubt they are. But suffering as such, however genuine and profound it may be, does not suffice to merit the title of 'the tragic'. Just think of the characters of Homer, including the most tragic of the epic heroes, Achilles.[29] There is suffering, then, and there are consequences for Ismene's choice or rather, *non-choice*.[30] But is there a *fate*? And, what will prove to be the same question, is it *tragic*? If it is true that she has chosen life, why is she 'destitute' (λελειμμένη, 548)? She is dispossessed of both life and death and can only end up with a similarly destitute soul, Creon (cf. 548–9). She becomes what could be called an *idiôtês*, a completely isolated individual, the puppet-like subject of another *idiôtês* who could only be 'a fine dictator of a desert'.[31] What remains for her is a non-tragic *fatum*, a sheer external necessity holding sway over her from outside. Her life is no longer hers, because she has failed to choose it. Her suffering, or even death, can no longer be her own possession, because she has not chosen them either. She is disinherited from the family not only because she has not chosen to unite symbolically with it, but also because she has not chosen at all. For the common bequest of the members of this particular family is precisely an ability to come into possession of their own fates, which is, at the same time, their common bequest.

In clear contrast with Ismene, then, Antigone chooses in the sense defined above: she discerns the alternatives and assents to one of them; or rather, by the very act of discerning, she assents to one and acts accordingly. We may ask, however, why it is that Antigone assents to one of the alternatives and not the other? We may say, as it is often the case, that 'she is like that', or that she acts the way she does because she is 'determined' to do so. But this is precisely the kind of misinterpretation we should seek to avoid. By ascribing action to character or to determination, we construe these as modes of causation essentially external to action. Determination commonly understood is opposed or detrimental to some 'internal' faculty which counteracts the predictable element in what has been 'determined' and is thus considered to be the repository of freedom. On account of its internal construction, this faculty then appears to fall within the domain of 'character', which thus assumes the role of the real adversary of determination. But clearly, there can be no true fate where there is character either, since fate in this sense involves the choice of the contingent and the unpredictable, whereas 'character' thus understood presupposes a degree of generality which is incompatible with such contingency and unpredictability.[32] Character understood as a closed and predictable totality of internal qualities is just internalized determination. Antigone is not 'like that' *before* and *without* responding to the situation the way she does, but *by* responding to it that way, she *becomes* one of the tragic characters. This is how Aristotle's statement, that action 'reveals' character, may be understood. Yet there still remains something preceding, something external in the background of her deed, but it is not alien either to action or to character; on the contrary, what appeared as a primordial impetus pushing her towards the 'discovery' of choice is a *conative* aspect of action lying behind 'the primal unity of mind' so characteristic of the Greeks' conception of mental processes.[33] Noting that the closest equivalent to the Greek connection of ideas with actions is the 'ideo-motor' theory of modern psychology, which asserts that a tendency to movement inheres in a state or act of knowing, R. B. Onians propounds the view that the emotion may even precede the idea, 'may be vaguely felt before taking definite shape in consciousness and being "intellectualized" '.[34] We may add that the more vivid an emotion is, the more likely it is to precede its being 'intellectualized'—the reason why we talk about someone being 'carried away' by a feeling or an emotion. While there is no sign of a decision having been taken by Antigone prior to her encounter with her sister, there is a vital emotion 'carrying her away' up to the point of deciding. In order to see the full depth of Antigone's tragic choice, we need to enquire into the nature and source of that emotion and see precisely how it functions.

The vital emotion at issue, the impetus, as we called it above,[35] is clearly some mixture of sorrow about past and present unhappiness (1–8) and an indignation induced by the outrageous injustice of Creon's edict.[36] Yet if our description of a gradually unfolding process of decision holds true, and if the impulse precedes Creon's edict, so that it could be obstructed by it and splinter into alternatives, we need to sever the two components of this mixture of feelings. What matters from the point of view of 'the unity of mind', the conative aspect of action that we are looking for, must obviously be different from what is induced by the obstacle and must precede any emotion felt over Creon's indictment. If in the end we found, however, that the preceding emotion is not essentially different in kind from what is provoked by the obstacle itself, it would only prove the truth of Onians's suggestion that the emotion precedes the idea, since in taking a more definite shape, the very same emotion may well be transferred to the immediate response to the obstacle. This is, in fact, what we do find if we look closer into Antigone's language. Her indignation is not directed towards Creon's edict alone. It is present right from the start, when she recalls 'the evils that stem from Oedipus' (2) and connects the new 'evils' by a co-ordinating conjunction to them ('and now, again . . .': καὶ νῦν . . . αὖ, 7).[37]

The question is thus the following. What is the source of the indignation she feels about the 'the ancient evils' and in what way does this impetus determine the quality of action it induces? With this question we can now return to 'the ancient evils' or 'family curse', which figure so collusively behind the scenes. Their first major evocation is put into the mouth of Ismene, who recalls them when Antigone's intention has, at long last, become clear for her (49–57). It is not by chance that Antigone's reference to the sorrows that have afflicted the family is only tentative, whereas Ismene goes through its story in all its details. This may also be an indication of the emotional difference that ultimately determines their different decisions. Apparently, Antigone has already 'thought' the situation over, whereas Ismene needs to linger on the conditions as well as the consequences. Certainly, she argues against disobedience on sound political, religious, and general moral grounds, such as that one should obey the ruler and live in compliance with the law (53–60, 78–9); that for women it is unseemly not to obey the stronger (61–4); and that in general, to be 'overbold' is foolish (67–8). But all this taken together still does not suffice to account for her horror at the thought of defiance, and it still leaves such a detailed reference to the family story totally unwarranted. Rather than being related to the *mode* of their impending execution, the intensity she attaches to the words referring to their death ('think how we shall perish, *more miserably* than all the rest' [Jebb]: ὅσῳ κάκιστ᾽ ὀλούμεθ᾽, 59) serves to reveal the *contextual* horror of their death, in that it is not just any death, but that of the members of a family struck by a dreadful succession of unnatural ends. That Antigone is aware of this singular horror and that it incites a deep indignation in her is attested by the repetitive allusion to her sufferings (4–6) engendered by the phrase, 'for us while we yet live' (Grene: νῷν ἔτι ζώσαιν, 3). But why the indignation and whence its overwhelming force? Given the gradual differentiation of what we called choice and the special *in medias res* construction of the drama, which entails as pre-given not only Creon's edict but, even more fundamentally, the myth of the Labdacids, it is important to note that what we are now seeking to ascertain as Antigone's thoughts and emotions are *ex post facto*: they are retroactive to whatever ran its course in her before she spoke to Ismene.

What unsettles both Antigone and Ismene is the wretched family history of Oedipus' horrendous fate, Iocaste's suicide, and their brothers' deaths, dealt 'by mutual hands' (49–57). But in contrast with her sister's anxiety at the thought of defiance, because it would extend this murderous story over yet another generation, Antigone's feelings are provoked by something else. It is not worry she feels at all, but righteous anger, and not, in the first place, over an indictment that assaults her moral principles, but over the burden of a history whose consequences she has to endure simply by being what she is, a descendant of the family:

Ὦ κοινὸν αὐτάδελφον Ἰσμήνης κάρα,
ἆρ᾽ οἶσθ᾽ ὅ τι Ζεὺς τῶν ἀπ᾽ Οἰδίπου κακῶν
ὁποῖον οὐχὶ νῶν ἔτι ζώσαιν τελεῖ;
οὐδὲν γὰρ οὔτ᾽ ἀλγεινὸν οὔτ᾽ †ἄτης ἄτερ†
οὔτ᾽ αἰσχρὸν οὔτ᾽ ἄτιμόν ἐσθ᾽, ὁποῖον οὐ
τῶν σῶν τε κἀμῶν οὐκ ὄπωπ᾽ ἐγὼ κακῶν.
καὶ νῦν τί τοῦτ᾽ αὖ φασι πανδήμῳ πόλει
κήρυγμα θεῖναι τὸν στρατηγὸν ἀρτίως;

Ismene, my dear sister,
whose father was my father, can you think of any
of all the evils that stem from Oedipus
that Zeus does not bring to pass for us, while we yet live?
No pain, no ruin, no shame, and no dishonour
but I have seen it in our mischiefs,
yours and mine.
And now what is the proclamation that they tell of
made lately by the commander, publicly,
to all the people?

(1–8)

The uneasiness caused by Creon's decision is yet another reason for despair amid her severe afflictions.[38] What exasperates her is that the two of them are 'still alive' and yet seem to be condemned in their very existence because, as far as their own individual courses of life are concerned, an exogenous power presides over their being. Thus it looks as though this were a clear case of determination external to their own volition. But Antigone, for one, does not despair; on the contrary, she acts in a crucial sense where her sister fails to. Several of her later assertions (notably 460–6, 559–60) seem to underline that she has accepted that external determination, that she has bent her head under 'the yoke of necessity', to recall the *Agamemnon*. But by emphatically choosing determination, she ambiguously asserts her freedom to determine her own fate. She 'knows' well enough that it is precisely by taking on the transgression and being punished by death for it that she activates necessity—that is, incarnates the tragic family doom— and yet, paradoxically, there is no other way for her to avow her own self-sufficient initiative than by passionately choosing: that is to say, by joining in with the alien force that threatens her sponta- neous creativity.[39] This surplus of compliance with the inevitable is what ultimately distinguishes fate from *fatum*. By passionately desiring and choosing necessity, Antigone 'appropriates'[40] that sinister agency, and thus it is no longer an alien force, no longer an external contingency, but an integrated dynamism expedient to her own inalienable fate. Ismene, on the other hand, fails to expose herself to the complicity of that alien force, evades action and with it any 'Dionysiac descent into the divine depth'[41] even when the alternative is clearly presented to her, and is therefore broken by sheer necessity, a *fatum* completely external to anything she might possess.

Within modern criticism, the conception of tragic fate closest to the one just presented is obviously Albin Lesky's 'double motiva- tion' theory.[42] I cannot enter here into a comparison of Lesky's tar- get figures (Agamemnon, Eteocles, and Orestes) with Antigone, yet a brief remark may suffice for the purpose of rounding off my discussion.

In Antigone's case there is obviously no compulsion of the sort Agamemnon or Orestes face, no fatal alternative involving bad or worse. Compared with Agamemnon, or even Orestes, she freely chooses to transgress, and if the force of an 'unwritten law' is com- pelling for her, it is certainly in a far less forcible way than the cor- responding compulsion on these two figures.[43] Yet there is something behind the mere transgression or obedience, if you like, that makes her situation similar to that of Aeschylus' heroes: her deed is charged with the weight of a past that seems to deprive her of all the spontaneity with which she might determine her own course of life. Lesky, in fact, failed to explore the full significance of his idea of 'double motivation' in the case of tragic figures. He was looking for the source of personal responsibility, and rightly found it in his heroes' 'passionate desire' for what is fated, since without a surplus of willingness to undertake the deed at issue, per- sonal responsibility would not avail. But he was content with the quasi-Hegelian idea of a totally balanced working of two equally powerful forces and did not realize that there is a paradoxical but palpable primacy of one of them over the other. For without the heroes' surplus of willingness, without what could certainly be called their freedom in the sense of spontaneous creativity, necessity or determination would not be activated or reinvigorated; consequently 'overdetermination' is no longer determination in the strict sense, but also the assertion of freedom. From this it follows, however, that freedom, in turn, is no longer pure, but is affected, as it were, by itself. The real complicity of freedom and necessity consists in the paradox that without the act of 'appropriation', necessity does not manifest itself with all its mythical profundity. Without Antigone's re-enactment of the common fate of the Labdacids, that fate would and could no longer be 'common'—that is to say, the chorus could not and would not refer to it as the ultimate explanation of what has happened. Ismene is not mentioned in this context, because she excludes herself from that common heritage. Equally, however, without the background of a mythical past, Antigone's new deed would merely be a transgression, and not an act that induces a tragic *fate*. It follows, therefore, that while it is an appropriated necessity, her deed is also a *disappropriation* of the common doom: while she partakes of the common lot of the family, her fate is also her own inalienable portion in life. She has a fate, and this is why she must feel destitute (876–82). But the cause of her destruction is her own appropriated freedom, which, by the very act of appropriation, comes to be revealed as *non-freedom*. Her fate may thus be reinstated by the paradoxical formula that *she falls victim to her own freedom to fall victim to her own non-freedom*. Ambiguity prevails and the complicity of freedom and necessity remains unavailable for further rational analysis. Yet Antigone compares herself to a goddess (823–33), because she has forged her own fate (αὐτόνομος, 821) and was *only thus* struck down by it.

Notes

1. I would like to acknowledge my indebtedness to the TEMPUS Foundation, which made my stay at University College Dublin possible, where I wrote the first draft of this paper. I must also express my gratitude to Dr Brendan M. Purcell for his constant stimulus and encouragement over that period. Finally, my warm thanks to Professor M. S. Silk for his invaluable criticisms, corrections, and tolerance of different versions, Professor Zsigmond Ritoók for his

precious comments, and Tamar Nelson for our discussions of the topic and for correcting my English.

2. Among these elements could certainly be included oracles (conditional or unconditional), the topoi of φθόνος and ἄτη, and the inscrutable 'situation of choice'. Diverse as these elements may seem to be, they share the characteristic that they constitute a *contingency* that is markedly external to the heroes' drives and motives.

3. Cf. E. R. Dodds, 'On Misunderstanding the Oedipus Rex', in id., *The Ancient Concept of Progress* (Oxford 1973) 70.

4. Winnington-Ingram, *Sophocles: An Interpretation*, 153–4.

5. The classic advocate of this view is H. Lloyd-Jones in his 'The Guilt of Agamemnon', *CQ* 12 (1962), esp. 187–99, and in *Justice of Zeus*, esp. 104–28. More recently, see also Rosenmeyer, *Art of Aeschylus*, 284–307.

6. These are, of course, two extreme possibilities, which are rarely found in a pure form. For a list of views that reject the importance of the family curse, see Lloyd-Jones, *Justice of Zeus*, 104 ff.

7. For Heidegger's term, see his *Being and Time*, trans. J. Macquarrie and E. Robinson (Oxford 1962) 436; for the broader context of the concept, see esp. chs. 58 and 74. I do not wish to imply that the conception of freedom that lies in the background of my discussion is Heideggerian. In borrowing his term I would like to refer also to a range of other thinkers who have dealt with the problem along similar lines. In my eyes these pre-eminently include: Kierkegaard, who foreshadowed Heidegger's conception of guiltiness and freedom to a far greater extent than Heidegger himself ever dared to admit; and Jean Nabert, the unduly forgotten French philosopher, who, as Ricoeur noted with admiration, took the implications of Kant's conception of radical evil to their logical conclusion with regard to an understanding of freedom; see P. Ricoeur, *Fallible Man* (New York 1986), pp. xlvi–xlvii.

8. The topic is re-evoked by Ismene in the prologue, when she, at long last, brings herself to the realization of what Antigone has in mind, viz. the burial of Polynices; it is passingly referred to by the chorus in the second *epeisodion*, at 470–1; it reappears in the second *stasimon* as an enigmatic conclusion to the second and a premonitory introduction to the third *epeisodion*; it is present, again, in the *kommos* and with more general overtones in the fourth *stasimon*; finally, it is also referred to by Tiresias at 1017–18. Concerning the 'ancient evils' in our play in particular, virtually all the important studies on Sophocles and/or Greek tragedy could be cited. A few major examples: C. M. Bowra, *Sophoclean Tragedy* (Oxford 1965) 87 f.; T. B. L. Webster, *An Introduction to Sophocles* (London 1969) 31; Linforth, *Antigone*

and Creon, 212, 214–15, 223–4; Winnington-Ingram, *Sophocles: An Interpretation*, 167 ff.; Segal, *Tragedy and Civilization*, 18, 189–90, 191–2, 197, 200.

9. 471–2, 582–625 (second *stasimon*), and 856.

10. Cf. the clear formulation of Winnington-Ingram: 'Antigone did not choose to be the daughter of Oedipus or to inherit the hardness which was both her death and glory' (*Sophocles: An Interpretation*, 178).

11. For Snell's classic analysis, see *Discovery of the Mind*, 101 ff. For its criticism, see A. Rivier, 'Remarques sur le "nécessaire" et la "nécessité" chez Eschyle', *REG* 81 (1968) 5–39. For a response to both, and an original discussion of the problems of 'free will' and decision in Greek tragedy, see J.-P. Vernant, 'Intimations of the Will in Greek Tragedy', in Vernant and Vidal-Naquet, *Tragedy and Myth in Ancient Greece*, 28 ff.

12. In using this term I am relying on Voegelin's comprehensive study of the 'differentiation of consciousness' from Homer to Plato and Aristotle. See Voegelin, *Order and History*, esp. i and ii.

13. The lack of philosophical terminology does not mean that the *issues* themselves were not present to the minds of the Greeks. See e.g. H. Fränkel, *Early Greek Poetry and Philosophy* (Oxford 1975), p. xi; Lesky, *Göttliche und menschliche Motivation*, 9; Dodds, *Greeks and the Irrational*, 20 n. 31; and Winnington-Ingram, *Sophocles: An Interpretation*, 154. That the two sisters' situation is that of a significant choice is made clear by several factors. First of all, there is a feeling of 'helplessness' (ἀμηχανία) (cf. Snell, *Discovery of the Mind*, 43 ff., esp. 53–4, 62, and 100; cf. *Ant.* 79, 90, and 92) occasioned by the impediment represented by Creon's edict, which 'arises in the path' of 'expectations or demands' (Snell, *Discovery of the Mind*, 55). Further, the very fact that the confrontation of this impediment awaits *two* sisters whose reactions will eventually represent contrary alternatives reinforces the gravity of choice. At the level of discourse, this is expressed by antithetical constructions (εἴτ'... εἴτ', 38; λύουσ' ἂν εἴθ' ἅπτουσα, 40; ἐγὼ μὲν... τὸ δὲ, 78; σὺ μὲν... ἐγὼ δὲ, 80), conditionals and imperatives, a verb and a construction of deliberation (σκόπει, 41, and ποῦ γνώμης ποτ' εἶ, 42), and a verb of volition (θέλῃς, 45, and θέλοις, 69).

14. Cf. Rosenmeyer, *Art of Aeschylus*, 302. His remarks on choice concern the *Agamemnon*, but as regards a general evaluation of the idea, his analysis is highly relevant.

15. Started by the plural note (expressed by the word κοινόν, the unique prefix to -αδελφον and the dual) emphatically struck by Antigone (ὦ κοινὸν αὐτάδελφον Ἰσμήνης κάρα, | ἆρ' οἶσθ' ὅ τι Ζεὺς τῶν ἀπ' Οἰδίπου κακῶν | ὁποῖον οὐχὶ νῷν ἔτι ζώσαιν τελεῖ; [Dawe, 1–3]) and continued

by a gradually unfolding diversion (expressed first by Antigone with the indignant aside, λέγω γὰρ κἀμέ, 32, which is re-echoed in Ismene's reply, τί δ᾽, ὦ ταλαῖφρον, εἰ τάδ᾽ ἐν τούτοις, ἐγὼ | λύουσ᾽ ἂν εἴθ᾽ ἅπτουσα προσθείμην πλέον, 39–40), the process of their ultimate separation reaches its extreme point with the exchange: ΙΣ. ἦ γὰρ νοεῖς θάπτειν σφ᾽, ἀπόρρητον πόλει; | ΑΝ. τὸν γοῦν ἐμόν, καὶ τὸν σόν, ἢν σὺ μὴ θέλῃς, | ἀδελφόν· οὐ γὰρ δὴ προδοῦσ᾽ ἁλώσομαι (Jebb, 44–6). They isolate themselves from one another as a result of another isolation (from Polynices) which is simultaneously occurring. Ismene disengages herself from *her* brother by not choosing to unite symbolically with him in an act of tribute, whereas Antigone unites herself with *her* brother by the opposite choice.

16. Cf. Rivier's 'recognition' quoted by Vernant in Vernant and Vidal-Naquet, *Tragedy and Myth in Ancient Greece*, 31, which does not, in my view, exclude a sense of 'choice' that is comprehensible to the modern mind. It is Ismene's dull-witted indifference whereby she fails to conceive of the urgency of the situation and the disconcerted hesitation whereby she responds to the vaguely envisaged κινδύνευμα (42) that prompt Antigone's proclamation that no one can 'divert' her from 'her own' (48) with the double implication of her family and her intention. Her 'decision' is resumed in line 45 (and 46, if it is authentic) and proclaimed in lines 48 and 69–77. It is noteworthy that both proclamations contain the verb θέλω (θέλῃς, 45 and θέλοις, 69) referring to Ismene and the first person singular referring to herself (ἐμόν, 45 and ἐμοῦ γ᾽, 70). This indicates that Antigone has separated herself from her sister, because she has recognized in her a 'will' contrary to hers. It is again significant that for Ismene her own decision becomes conscious after Antigone's proclamation (78–9), that is to say, with reference, again, to the opposite choice, and that the ultimate formulation of their mutual detachment as well as the course of action Antigone is about to resume follows thereupon (ΑΝ. σὺ μὲν τάδ᾽ ἂν προύχοι᾽, ἐγὼ δὲ δὴ τάφον | χώσουσ᾽ ἀδελφῷ φιλτάτῳ πορεύσομαι, 80–1).

17. Oedipus' κακά, 2–3 and Creon's κήρυγμα, 7–8.

18. The Greek text I have used is mostly R. D. Dawe, *Sophocles: Tragoediae* ii (Leipzig 1985), but also R. C. Jebb, *Sophocles: The Plays and Fragments* iii (Cambridge 1891) where indicated. There are also references to Müller's commentary. Translations are taken from Jebb and from D. Grene, *Sophocles* i (Chicago 1991) where indicated. A few phrases have been translated by myself.

19. Her reason could be that she is, on her own, physically unable to 'lift the corpse' (cf. 43). But if the symbolic act of spreading dust on the corpse is—in the drama—enough to represent burial and incur Creon's punishment, why could it not have sufficed for her *prior to*

speaking to Ismene? The obvious answer is that she wanted to do it *together with her sister*. Her opening speech underlines this hope: she strikes the plural note and hopes for collaboration. Her fallacy, in the end, concerns not the existence of an alternative and thus a decision but the fact that she is to face it *on her own*, because a significant decision induces a *fate* which is the sole 'possession' of its 'creator'.

20. For a series of conditions that determine a differentiated conception of will, see Vernant and Vidal-Naquet, *Tragedy and Myth in Ancient Greece*, 32.

21. Cf. Snell's analysis of Sappho's 'discovery of the soul': 'It is the obstruction which makes the wholly personal feelings conscious, and annihilates the normal values' (*Discovery of the Mind*, 53 ff.). My interpretation of tragic action only seeks to make the bond between Snell's analysis of 'the rise of the individual' in the lyricists and that of the tragic 'archetype of action' stronger.

22. Cf. Vernant and Vidal-Naquet, *Tragedy and Myth in Ancient Greece*, 49.

23. That the concepts of knowledge—or in our case, discernment of choice—and action are integrally connected for the Greeks has been noted by several distinguished scholars. See Vernant and Vidal-Naquet, *Tragedy and Myth in Ancient Greece*, 39 and 58; Onians, *Origins of European Thought*, 16–18; and Dodds, *Greeks and the Irrational*, 16–17.

24. For Hegel's argument, see *Hegel on Tragedy*, ed. A. and H. Paolucci (New York 1962) 279. I am not, of course, debating Hegel's interpretation of the *Antigone* here.

25. Cf. Antigone's (for Creon) bitingly ironic and (from her viewpoint) straightforward remark at 499. That Creon is, despite his gradually growing anger, deferring any decision is clearly shown by the several attempts he makes to bring Antigone around (473–96 and 508–22) or to proclaim the sentence (485 and 498). Note how he finally urges the guards to lead Antigone away (577), which is, psychologically speaking, a clear example of transfer.

26. See Müller, *Sophocles: Antigone*, 108.

27. The meaning of this line is thus even more complex than Müller points out (*Sophocles: Antigone*, 130).

28. In a way, Ismene is *arguing* that she has something to do with the fateful deed. See 540–1, where she claims her share of the deed on the ground that she accepts its consequences. Antigone's point at 538–9 and 555 is that there is no way Ismene could now undo the fact that she failed to do something in the past. It was *action* that the tragic situation required and not words either then or now (see 543 and 556).

29. For a thought-provoking study of the tragic aspects of the epic, see

R. B. Rutherford, 'Tragic Form and Feeling in the Iliad', *JHS* 102 (1982) 145–60.

30. Relying on Snell's 'archetype of action', Voegelin in his succinct but substantial chapter on tragedy goes as far as denying the status of action to the evasive attitude we found Ismene 'guilty' of: 'Not every type of conduct, therefore, is action. We can speak of action only when the decision was reached through the Dionysiac descent into the divine depth. And conversely, not every situation is tragic. . . . A negative decision, an evasion through utilitarian calculus, or a mere insensitiveness toward the issue, would not be considered action' (*Order and History*, ii. 251).

31. 739. The term *idiôtês* has an important role in Voegelin's analysis of the Heraclitean 'exploration of the soul' and 'philosophy of order' (*Order and History*, ii, ch. 9, esp. 232–3). I would call Ismene and Creon a private and a public *idiôtês*, respectively.

32. Cf. Walter Benjamin, 'Schicksal und Charakter', in *Gesammelte Schriften*, ii/1, edd. R. Tiedmann and H. Schweppenhäuser (Frankfurt/M. 1980) 171–9, esp. 172–3.

33. Cf. Onians, *Origins of European Thought*, 16 ff. Note that it is precisely on the basis of 'the primal unity of mind' that Onians stresses a closer bond between character and cognition (ibid. 18), which is the corollary of a closer bond between character and action.

34. Ibid. 17.

35. With reference to the idea of 'the primal unity of mind', which envisages mental states in terms of an inherent tendency to movement, I would characterize what is widely considered to be some kind of emotion or feeling (for example impetuousness, harshness, indignation, etc.) in Antigone as an impetus rather than an emotion, unless the latter is understood etymologically in terms of *moveo* or *emoveo*.

36. See Antigone's indignant aside, λέγω γὰρ κἀμέ, 32.

37. Her indignation is attested by the emphatic repetition of the words νῷν ἔτι ζώσαιν (3) in the form of a co-ordinated construction of the first- and second-person singular personal pronouns (6 and 31–2). It is, again, a sign of the process of decision-making and the resulting separation that the dual should be replaced by the singular. Her aside, λέγω γὰρ κἀμέ (32), is the first and unconscious indication of this separation.

38. The conjunction καὶ νῦν . . . αὖ (7) is echoed in Ismene's words, νῦν δ' αὖ (58). She also views the impasse resulting from Creon's decision as just another component of the afflictions that derive from their ancestors. And yet (as her detailed reference to the story of the family indicates), she is also aware of the uniqueness of this particular situation. For if any one of them decides now to act against Creon's edict, the

family's tragic doom will be once and for ever sealed. By opposing Antigone and obeying Creon, therefore, Ismene expresses her protest against accepting what seems to be predetermined by the family doom.

39. From the perspective of a primordial desire to which the acts of an autonomous personality like Antigone attest, a desire by which the personality seeks to assert an irresistible claim for self-sufficiency, it follows that in the last analysis it is Antigone, and not Ismene, who thus protests against accepting 'the tragic family doom'.

40. Vernant's apposite term (Vernant and Vidal-Naquet, *Tragedy and Myth in Ancient Greece*, 31).

41. Cf. n. 30.

42. See Lesky, *Göttliche und menschliche*, and 'Decision and Responsibility in the Tragedy of Aeschylus', *JHS* 86 (1966) 78–85: cf. e.g. Dodds, *Greeks and the Irrational*, 7; N. G. L. Hammond, 'Personal Freedom and its Limitations in the Oresteia', *JHS* 85 (1965) 42–55; Winnington-Ingram, *Sophocles: An Interpretation*, 177; and Vernant, 'Intimations', *passim*. Within the context of what Lesky called 'double motivation', however, the theory of tragic fate is likely to remain less exploited than it should be: its full potential can only be seen if we lay bare its philosophical affinities (see n. 7).

43. Cf. Vernant's observation that the Greeks had no clearly differentiated conception of law or duty (Vernant and Vidal-Naquet, *Tragedy and Myth in Ancient Greece*, 3 f. and 14 ff.).

21

Peripeteia and Tragic Dialectic in Euripidean Tragedy

BERND SEIDENSTICKER

In 1961 Peter Szondi, one of the most distinguished and influential of recent German literary critics, published a short book on the nature of the tragic.[1] In the first part of his discussion, which is certainly one of the most important modern treatments of the subject, Szondi analysed selected passages from major philosophical and aesthetic discussions of tragedy and the tragic from the end of the eighteenth century to the twentieth. As the common denominator of the approaches of philosophers and poets as different as Hegel, Schopenhauer, and Nietzsche, Hölderlin, Goethe, and Hebbel, he proposed the 'dialectical structure or modality of the tragic', defining the tragic itself as a 'dialectical modality of impending or actual destruction'.[2]

The title of my paper juxtaposes and links two concepts: Aristotle's *peripeteia* and Szondi's tragic dialectic. Recently I attempted to relate these two concepts to one another, despite the two-thousand-year gap between them, and to apply them to the interpretation of Sophoclean tragedy. Since Szondi's tragic dialectic is also the theoretical basis of my thoughts on Euripidean tragedy, I would like briefly to outline the main arguments of the earlier paper.[3]

At the beginning of *Poetics* 11 (1452ª22–9) Aristotle defines and explains *peripeteia*:

Ἔστι δὲ περιπέτεια μὲν ἡ εἰς τὸ ἐναντίον τῶν πραττομένων μεταβολὴ καθάπερ εἴρηται, καὶ τοῦτο δὲ ὥσπερ λέγομεν κατὰ τὸ εἰκὸς ἢ ἀναγκαῖον, ὥσπερ ἐν τῷ Οἰδίποδι ἐλθὼν ὡς εὐφρανῶν τὸν Οἰδίπουν καὶ ἀπαλλάξων τοῦ πρὸς τὴν μητέρα φόβου, δηλώσας ὃς ἦν, τοὐναντίον ἐποίησεν· καὶ ἐν τῷ Λυγκεῖ ὁ μὲν ἀγόμενος ὡς ἀποθανούμενος, ὁ δὲ Δαναὸς ἀκολουθῶν ὡς ἀποκτενῶν, τὸν μὲν συνέβη ἐκ τῶν πεπραγμένων ἀποθανεῖν, τὸν δὲ σωθῆναι.

A *peripeteia* ['reversal'] is a switch [μεταβολή] of actions to the contrary, as described, in which the change involved is also probable or necessary in the way specified. For example, in the *Oedipus*, the man who came to comfort Oedipus and free him from his fear about his mother in fact did the opposite by revealing who Oedipus was. Again, in the *Lynceus*, Lynceus was being led off and it seemed he would be put to death and that Danaus, who was with him, would kill him, but the earlier actions resulted in Danaus' death and Lynceus' release.

A survey of the complex history of the reception of Aristotle's definition since the Renaissance shows that almost every single element in the definition has been given different interpretations.[4] The great variety of translations, paraphrases, and explanations can, however, be reduced to two alternative views, which eventually turn out to be the result of two different interpretations of the phrase which I have translated 'actions', τῶν πραττομένων. According to one view, πραττομένων is basically identical with γιγνομένων, 'happenings'. Many critics accept this interpretation and consequently understand *peripeteia* in a wider sense as 'a change in the events of the play as it develops', that is, 'a change in the dramatic situation or plot'.[5] Yet the problems this reading presents are considerable.[6] Logic as well as linguistic usage[7] rather suggest the meaning: 'change of the actions into their own opposites'.

The 'wider' interpretation of *peripeteia* becomes still less persuasive as soon as one considers the two examples that Aristotle adduces. Both of these evidently illustrate not—or at least not explicitly—a switch in the plot, but rather a switch of single actions (πραττόμενα); both clearly describe the change as a change of particular actions into their opposites (that is, the opposites of what they were intended or expected to accomplish); in both cases, finally, the wording plainly underlines the point that the particular actions lead to an outcome which is precisely the opposite of what they were intended to achieve or seemed to be achieving.[8]

Two supplementary phrases in Aristotle's definition specify what precisely is meant by the idea of actions turning into their opposites. 'As described' (κάθ' ἅπερ εἴρηται) probably alludes to the end of *Poetics* 9, where Aristotle insists that 'tragedy portrays events which are fearful and pitiful' and adds that 'this can best be achieved when things occur contrary to expectation, yet still on account of one another'.[9] The unexpected turn of events must develop cogently out of the premises of the action, as in this way the ironic effect of the paradox will be most telling. This stipulation is further specified by Aristotle in a second supplementary phrase: like all other elements of the plot, *peripeteia* too must follow the rules of 'probability and necessity' (κατὰ τὸ εἰκὸς ἢ κατὰ τὸ ἀναγκαῖον). The ironic-paradoxical structure of the reversal evidently does much to heighten the tragic effect of single scenes as well as of whole plays, and Aristotle emphasizes this quality explicitly. In *Poetics* 6 (1450ᵃ33–5) he points out that both 'reversal' (*peripeteia*) and 'recognition' (*anagnôrisis*) evoke pity and fear in a special way. Hence, as one of the fundamental elements of the emotional function of tragedy, *peripeteia* plays a crucial role in his theory.

The Aristotelian thesis assumes that the intensifying tragic effect is produced by the paradoxical (yet natural and compelling) transformation of an action (undertaken with a particular purpose or expectation) into its opposite (that is, the opposite of its purpose or expected result). This appears to coincide, despite some significant differences, with the thesis of Peter Szondi's essay on the tragic. Szondi analyses the metaphysical and aesthetic writings of German idealists and post-idealists with the declared aim of revealing, among 'the most diverse definitions of the tragic', a 'more or less hidden element' which is 'common to them all', and finds the common element in his 'dialectical structure', which he sees as the 'sole constant' in all the rich variety of 'definitions of the tragic from Schelling to Scheler'.[10] In order to clarify this thesis I would like to recall just two of the theories discussed by Szondi. In Hegel's theory of a 'dialectic of morality' ('Dialektik der Sittlichkeit'), the dialectical movement is activated by that momentous principle of 'individuation', to which everything is subject and through which, as Hegel points out in the *Aesthetics*, 'moral forces, like the characters of the action, are differentiated in respect of their content and their individual appearance'. It follows that every individual action in its one-sided isolation, in its attempt to achieve its own purpose, 'inevitably engenders the emotion opposed to it and thereby brings in its train unavoidable conflicts'.[11] Scheler's definition of the tragic, the most recent of the theoretical positions analysed by Szondi, displays major differences from Hegel's, but as regards the dialectical structure, there are striking similarities: ' it is in the most unqualified sense tragic . . . when a thing is made the embodiment or catalyst

['Realisierung'] of some exalted value and, in the act of . . . achieving this, the very power that succeeds in achieving it *itself* becomes
the cause of the destruction of the thing as a bearer of value'.[12]

Szondi tries to underpin the universal significance of the dialectical mode with a reference to Aristotle. It is quite surprising that
he appeals to two passages in the *Poetics* which are in fact off the
point,[13] while overlooking the obvious reference to Aristotle's
peripeteia. This might be due to the fact that Szondi's understanding of the *Poetics* was strongly influenced by Max Kommerell,
whose interpretation of *peripeteia* as 'change of fortune' ('Glücks-
wechsel') may have prevented him from realizing the dialectical
significance of Aristotle's definition.[14]

By way of anticipating an obvious misunderstanding, let me
stress that I do not wish to ignore or water down the fundamental
differences between the two approaches. Aristotle's theory of
tragedy and its underlying philosophical tenets have little in common with the tragic philosophy of German idealism, as analysed
by Szondi; and the two concepts *peripeteia* and 'tragic dialectic'
possess a rather different emphasis and orientation. Whereas
Aristotle concerns himself with an effective structural element of
the dramatic action, Szondi defines his tragic dialectic in a highly
abstract way as 'mode of action which follows on a unity of opposites', as 'conversion of one state of affairs to its opposite'
('Umschlag des Einen in sein Gegenteil'), as 'self-division' ('Selb-
stentzweiung')—a principle which, in its dramatic realizations,
may take on many different forms and shapes.[15] But having said
this, one must insist that the two concepts do have a common
denominator: they both emphasize the importance of a paradoxical
yet inevitable shift of a (dramatic) movement to its exact opposite.
In addition, when Szondi applies the abstract concept that he
extracted from the various philosophical systems to the concrete
analysis of individual tragedies, he stresses (like Aristotle) the special significance of dramatic action.[16] As Szondi himself makes
clear, the value of his concept can only be tested by a detailed study
of individual dramas. The only Greek tragedy among his eight witnesses is Sophocles' *Oedipus Tyrannus*, a play which in fact offers
the most impressive exemplification of his thesis.[17] In the *Oedipus*
the dialectical structure of the tragic is constitutive of all levels and
elements of dramatic form, of single scenes and the structure of
the whole plot, no less than of such aspects as characterization,

language, and dramaturgy.[18] But this paradigm is not an isolated case. In the paper mentioned above I have tried to show that tragic dialectic can be regarded as an essential characteristic of the whole of Sophoclean tragedy. The present essay concentrates on the question if and to what degree Sophocles' younger contemporary Euripides makes use of the principle. In answering this question, I shall use the term 'dialectic' in a sense that is at once narrower than Szondi's 'tragic dialectic' and wider than Aristotle's *peripeteia*. In my usage 'dialectic' will refer to any reversal that appears to arise paradoxically, yet naturally and inevitably, out of the nature of the *dramatis personae* or out of their intentions, plans, or actions.

If one considers the range, variety, and particular quality of the Euripidean *œuvre*, which in many respects does not display the same homogeneity as Sophocles' seven extant plays, it is not at all surprising that the dialectical mode cannot be found everywhere. Where it is found, it manifests itself both in different degrees of intensity and in a variety of forms. But it is precisely the absence, or rather the reduction, of the concept which confirms, albeit indirectly, Szondi's thesis of the special tragic effect of the dialectical mode. For it is demonstrable that the very scenes and plays that have always been regarded as particularly tragic by all the critics are characterized by this feature, whereas elements and dramas which, in modern terms, one would rather assign to genres such as 'historical play', 'melodrama', or 'tragicomedy', are free from it, either largely or entirely. Thus, the two suppliant plays, *Heraclidae* and *Supplices*, are not relevant to our discussion; and plays such as *Alcestis* or *Ion*, the particular quality of which might be best described as 'tragicomedy', bear the hallmark of the dialectic only in those elements which are definitely tragic.[19]

But even among those dramas which, according to modern criteria, belong to the genre of tragedy, there are significant differences. Thus a brief look at the *Troades* shows that Euripides creates the tragic effect here (as he does again in the *Hecuba*), not primarily by means of the dialectical mode, but through the presentation of the sheer boundless suffering that overwhelms the innocent—Hecuba and her daughters—from the outside. Even so, the destruction of Troy and the enslavement of the aged queen and her daughters is presented in ever new antitheses as a total reversal of their former happiness;[20] and right in the middle of the play the downfall of the Trojans appears as a sudden dialectical reversal of their hopes and expectations. The chorus evokes the fatal night when the Trojans, in the first flush of victory, dragged the wooden horse into the city and thereby brought ruin on themselves. Suddenly the rejoicing, the dancing and the singing, are interrupted by cries of murder and the iron step of Ares; the altars at which the Trojans were offering sacrifices for their victory are now drenched in the blood of human victims; the young girls who were dancing for Artemis are now raped by Greek soldiers (511 ff.).

Moreover, the tragic fate of the individuals is intensified by the ironic way that their hopes and expectations are put into reverse, and it is here that Euripides more than once confers particular poignancy and bitterness on the tragic turn of events by stressing the dialectical quality of the reversal. Thus Andromache complains that it is precisely her high reputation as exemplary wife of Hector which has now rebounded against her: her husband's murderer has chosen her as his 'gift of honour' precisely because of her reputation (643 ff.). In a similar way Astyanax is ruined by the nobility of his birth (743 f.); and his mother must stand by and watch helplessly while her young son, who was destined to rule Asia, falls victim to the Greeks. Hecuba, too, perceives the Trojans' downfall as a bitter reversal of all her dreams: 'the daughters I fancied I would bring up to marry the noblest of husbands— I have brought them up for the enemy' (484–6). Eventually she herself must prepare for burial the corpse of her grandson Astyanax, who so often promised to bury *her* with all traditional honours (1180 ff.). At the end the tragic bitterness of the play is intensified by the dialectical twist that it is Hecuba, of all people, who urges Menelaus to listen to Helen's plea (906 ff.): thereby she offers the woman she wants dead, the woman she hates more than anyone else, the chance to present herself to her husband in all her physical beauty and so save her own life.

Finally, Euripides has given a special complexity to the dramatic structure of the dialectic in the *Troades* by planting a second reversal underneath the first. This time the reversal will be inflicted on the Greeks, who, after ten long years, are looking forward to a triumphant voyage home. The prologue points unambiguously ahead to the punishment of the hybristic victors:

> The man who sacks a city is a fool,
> Who gives the temples and the tombs, the hallowed
> Places of the dead, to desolation. His own ruin must come.

(95–7)

And soon afterwards, in her great vision of the future, Cassandra prophetically announces the suffering in store for the Greek heroes, especially Agamemnon and the house of Atreus (308 ff.). From the beginning, therefore, the victors are marked out as future victims. To be sure, their 'bitter home-coming' is not the retribution for what they have done to the helpless Trojan women, but punishment for defiling the temples of Troy. Nevertheless, by announcing the punishment in a prologue and not in a *deus-ex-machina* scene at the end, Euripides does create the impression, erroneous though it is, that their brutal actions against the Trojan women will recoil on them. However, as with the reversal of Troy's fate, the internal link between doing and suffering is not conceived dialectically.

In the *Hecuba*, the second of the two Trojan tragedies, Euripides once more presents the tragedy of Troy as the complete transformation of splendour and happiness into suffering and slavery.[21] As in the *Troades*, he stresses the suddenness of the catastrophe that annihilates all the Trojans' hopes and expectations, when the chorus lament the fatal night that the wooden horse was brought into the city (905 ff.); and as in the *Troades*, Euripides focuses entirely on the victims, not the victors. It is only in the last part of the play, when the frail and helpless victim Hecuba turns into an awesome agent of punishment, that the rather static plot gains dramatic momentum, and it is here that the dialectical element of the Polydorus theme unfolds its full force. When Troy seemed doomed to fall, Priam and Hecuba sent Polydorus, the youngest of their sons, to Polymestor, an old Thracian guest-friend, and with him went large amounts of gold (1–15). However, this attempt to save Polydorus' life and to secure the wealth of their surviving children turns unexpectedly, and yet with compelling logic, into its exact opposite. In his greed for the gold, 'the first of all the guest-friends' of the royal house of Priam (as Hecuba calls Polymestor in 793 f.) kills the boy who has been put in his custody (21–7). With the punishment of this crime, the dialectical movement repeats itself by means of the same compelling logic. For Hecuba successfully inveigles the greedy Thracian king into her tent by promising to show him where the treasures of Priam's house are hidden (998 ff.); in this way she is able to blind the traitor and kill his young sons. Just like Priam and Hecuba, Polymestor suffers the opposite of what he has been hoping for. The tragic irony of the reversal is obvious. The greed for gold, which seduced Polymestor into committing a crime against the divine law of hospitality, is now responsible for his destruction, and his fate overtakes him in the seemingly safe context of hospitality.

Like the plot of the *Troades* and the *Hecuba*, the overall dramatic structure of the *Heracles* is not dialectically conceived. As in the Trojan tragedies, Euripides relies for the emotional impact of the play primarily on a detailed and poignant elaboration of the reversal, or rather the series of reversals, which arise from outside causes without inner dialectical coherence.

When he set out for his last great adventure, the descent into Hades, Heracles left his wife, Megara, and their children in the tutelage of his old father, Amphitryon. During the hero's long absence, Lycus has taken possession of the Theban throne; in order to stabilize his fragile power, he plans to destroy the family of Heracles. The opening scene of the play presents the first total reversal. Amphitryon and Megara have taken refuge at the monument which the Thebans erected for Heracles in honour of his victory over the Minyans (44 ff.). Time and again they lament the way that all their hopes have been overturned.[22] Only at the very last moment, when any prospect of defying Lycus or escaping his murderous assault has gone, when Megara, with wreaths and black robes (442 f., 526 f.), has already prepared herself and the children for their impending death, when the audience at any moment expects the entrance of the executioner Lycus—only now does Heracles appear and kill the usurper. This sudden *peripeteia* is in exact accordance with the second of Aristotle's examples. As in the *Lynceus* of Theodectes, the events develop in such a way that one who wanted to kill is killed, while those who appeared to be doomed are saved (728–31).

Yet now, at the very moment of rejoicing at the unforeseen turn of events (735, 765 f.), Iris and Lyssa break in, turning the dramatic action back in the opposite direction yet again (815 ff.). Now the gods destroy the victor (τὸν εὐτυχῆ μετέβαλεν δαίμων, 884). The messenger-speech (922 ff.) presents the second, sudden, radical reversal. The hero who has triumphed over Hades plunges into a second and far worse Hades, the dark night of madness. At the altar where he means to celebrate his victory over Lycus, the putative saviour of his family kills his wife and children with the very same weapons he has just used to save them (1098 ff.).

Theseus' arrival leads to a third and final reversal (1153 ff.). The king of Athens succeeds in persuading Heracles that he can and must go on living. But Theseus actually came to rescue the family of his old friend Heracles from the assault of Lycus and thus, in effect, has arrived too late. The bitterness of the tragic pattern is almost unrelieved. Over and over again in the last part of the play, Euripides stresses the utter reversal of Heracles' greatness and fortune: the greatest of all the Greek heroes is finally ruined by Hera's wrath (1356 ff.); all his toils and labours have ended in suffering; all his glorious victories have only led to a final horrible murder (1266 ff., 1353 ff.). For all the help and comfort that Theseus can offer him, his plans and his life's work are in ruins (1367 ff.).

In the reversals embodied in the two Trojan tragedies and the *Heracles*, one can only detect hints or isolated elements of tragic dialectic. By contrast, the other three great tragedies of the preserved *œuvre*—*Medea*, *Hippolytus*, and *Bacchae*—are deeply imbued with the tragic dialectic of human doing and suffering.

In the *Medea* both the more distant and the closer antecedents of the play are already dialectically structured. Pelias has sent Jason off to get the golden fleece, hoping to get rid of the dangerous son of a brother he once deprived of the throne, and thinking thereby to consolidate his reign. But the ingenious plan rebounds on him. Jason brings back not only the golden fleece but also Medea, who makes Pelias the victim of a sinister revenge. These antecedents are of very little importance for the play; however, the starting-point of the dramatic action, as presented by Medea's nurse in the prologue, is also clearly a dialectical *peripeteia* in its own right. Medea has sacrificed everything for Jason: her country, her family, and her own security. Right at the moment when her whole well-being in a foreign country depends on the man she loves, he forsakes her. All her deeds which were designed to create and strengthen the bonds of endearment have ended in hostility (16); her nearest and dearest has turned out her worst enemy; the woman who betrayed for love is now herself betrayed—and, as she surmises, for love again.

The revenge that springs from this situation is conceived dialectically in its entirety. This already holds true of the starting-point of the play. Creon, king of Corinth, has decided to drive Medea out of the country because he fears that, in her anger at Jason's new marriage, she may hurt his daughter Creusa (271 ff.). But the aggravated situation—the prospect of sudden expulsion on top of the loss of her husband—compels Medea to react. The king's prudent attempt to head off a potential revenge precipitates the catastrophe and thus contributes to the death of his daughter and his own end. The effect of this dialectical movement is further intensified by the peculiar tragic irony of the scene in which Medea finally succeeds in persuading the hitherto obdurate king to let her stay an extra day, by an appeal to his love for his daughter (340–7). Yet it is precisely this filial love, which moves the king first to act and then to give in, that is destined to destroy his child and himself.

What is true of the deuteragonist Creon and his fate applies equally to the way the fatal clash of the two central figures is shaped. The conflict between Medea and Jason gains its particular tragic poignancy from the dialectical movement in which their intentions and actions rebound on them and destroy them. Jason had preferred Medea to all Greek women and thus in a sense himself determined, or at least contributed to, his subsequent misfortune. What once saved his life—Medea's love, determination, and intelligence—now destroys it. As Jason freely explains, the intention behind his decision to marry the Corinthian king's daughter was the hope of ensuring the future of his house and a high position for his two sons (593 ff.) But as he endeavours to persuade Medea of the integrity of his intentions, both his arguments and the way he presents them cannot but intensify her anger. More important, they supply her with her scheme of revenge.[23] When she has reached her final decision and secured a refuge in Athens, she proclaims in triumph:

> With heaven's help he'll pay me for his crime.
> Those sons he had from me he'll never see
> Alive again, nor on his new bride
> Will he beget another child.
>
> (802 ff)

In the following scene Medea's appeal to filial love sways Jason as it swayed Creon (938 ff.). The hope of keeping his two sons for himself makes him blind to Medea's cruel plan that turns the children, for whom he lives and plans and acts, into the gruesome instrument of her revenge.

In the end Jason has to realize that his life, as he planned it, is completely destroyed:

To mourn my fate is all that's left for me;
I'll have no pleasure from my new-wed wife.
The sons I fathered and brought up, I'll never
Speak to alive. I have lost them.

(1347 ff.)

Medea's answer to Jason's accusations translates the dialectic of his designs and their failure into a simple and concrete form, when she declares that it was not she, but Jason, who killed the children:

JASON. Children, what a wicked mother you had!
MEDEA. No, your father gave you the disease you died from.
JASON. I tell you it was not my hand that killed them.
MEDEA. No, it was your wantonness, and your virgin wedding.

(1363–6)

JASON. Your sons live on, to bring down curses on you.
MEDEA. The gods know who was the author of this sorrow.

(1371 f.)

When Medea finally prevents him from either touching or burying his two sons, the play ends with a cry of outrage from Jason that pointedly summarizes the dialectical reversal of all his dreams and plans:

Would I had never fathered them
Only to see them slaughtered by you.

(1413 f.)

The true emotional centre of the play, however, is hardly the tragedy of the weak Jason, but the tragedy of the mother who brings herself to murder her children. As in the case of Jason, one can clearly recognize the dialectical movement by which Medea's plans and actions not only affect her antagonist, but also turn against herself. The tremendous dramatic tension of the play, which reaches its climax in the famous—and much disputed—decision-monologue (1021–80),[24] derives from the way that Euripides leads Medea, step by step, towards the tragic realization that she cannot fully punish Jason unless she kills their own children. The punishment of the traitor, so desperately desired, turns agent into victim at the very moment of the agent's victory. The wreck of Jasons's life inevitably wrecks Medea's own hopes and dreams:

Yet I must go to exile in another land
Before the joy of seeing you in your happiness,
Before I've dressed your brides and made your marriage beds
And held the torch up at your wedding.
What misery: my own self-will has caused it.
Children, I brought you up for nothing,
And suffered pain and wore myself away
In cruel labour when I gave birth to you.
Yes, once I had great hopes of you. I thought
You would look after me in my old age,
And when I died your hands would dress me for the grave
And the world would envy me. Now that sweet thought
Is gone. Once I am left without you,
Bitter my life must be, and full of sorrow.

(1024 ff.)

Whereas Jason falls victim to his own inner weakness, Medea's tragedy is the logical consequence of her strengths. The play is the tragedy of a heroine with pride and self-esteem both as woman and princess, and with strong religious, social, and moral convictions that will not allow her to tolerate the outrage inflicted upon her;[25] and Euripides' Medea is too intelligent not to find the most effective revenge, and too determined and strong not to carry it through, despite the fact that in the course of her revenge she must hurt herself as much as the man she hates. Thus it is the best in her which—by way of a dialectical volte-face—turns against her and forces her to destroy in a single act not only her enemy, but herself.

The same is true—*mutatis mutandis*—for Hippolytus, who is brought down by the peremptoriness of his nature and by the determination with which he pursues his chosen life. His uncompromising devotion to Artemis and her ideals of purity, chastity, and self-control inevitably calls forth the divine counterweight in the shape of Aphrodite. The prologue leaves no doubt that Phaedra is the instrument and victim of the goddess of love, but this does not mean that dramatic action and tragic conflict lose their natural force and their inner compulsion. Hippolytus' extraordinary piety and self-control get the tragic mechanism going and drive it on towards the catastrophe. What is not said explicitly in the text, though there are clear indications of it,[26] is that, besides the exceptional beauty of her young stepson, and his inaccessibility, it is the purity and rigour of his nature and ideals that made Hippolytus desirable to Phaedra in the first place; and in large measure it is these same qualities that further the dramatic development of the action. Thus it is inevitable that Hippolytus' excessive (albeit understandable and justifiable) resentment of the nurse's proposal should trigger Phaedra's fear that her unholy love for her husband's son will be made public; it is this fear of loss of honour which, in her eyes, leaves her no option but suicide and at the same time requires that Hippolytus be destroyed. Hippolytus must react the way he does, because the proposal violates his most sacred convictions and feelings; because he cannot bring himself to give up his ideals, he is forced to keep his silence, when at the crucial moment he could have answered Theseus' accusations and been safe. This honourable silence, however, and the self-assured and self-righteous assertion of his purity (993 ff.) naturally intensify his father's anger and thus render the catastrophe unavoidable. Hippolytus himself sees this clearly when, in words that are bound to seem enigmatic to Theseus, he declares:

> Virtuous she was, when virtue could not be hers;
> Virtue was mine, but I have used it badly.
>
> (1034 f.)

A particular dialectical irony lies in the fact that it is precisely Hipppolytus' steadfast adherence to piety and self-control which earns him the stigma of pollution because of his supposed unholy love (Theseus actually uses the technical word for pollution, *miasma*, 946), and brings him under suspicion of being the servant not of Artemis, but of Aphrodite (947 f.).

The chorus see Hippolytus' fate only as a paradigm for the 'fall of the mighty' and understand the catastrophe as an example of divine arbitrariness and the fragility of all happiness (1104 ff.). Euripides, however, leaves no doubt that Hippolytus' nature and actions have contributed decisively to his downfall. In the messenger-speech (1173 ff.) the indissoluble fusion of two kinds of causation, internal and external, self and other, human and divine, is symbolized by the form in which the catastrophe unfolds. Euripides presents its instrument as the huge bull of Poseidon, but he also stresses more than once that it is Hippolytus' *own* chariot that undoes him, and that he is finally dragged to his death by his *own* horses.[27] All in all, Euripides intensifies the tragic quality of Hippolytus' fate by presenting it as a dialectical reversal of intentions and actions that are guided by positive ideals and goals. The

cogency and inevitability of the dialectical process, in which
Hippolytus is destroyed by his one-sidedness and refusal to compromise, is reminiscent of Hegel's principle of tragic individuation: 'Under specific conditions, individual action will realize an
objective or a character . . . which necessarily engenders the emotion opposed to it, because it occupies a position of unique isolation
by virtue of its self-sufficiency; thereby it brings in its train
unavoidable conflict.'[28]

It has already become apparent that the fate of Phaedra is insep-
arably linked to that of Hippolytus, and that her tragedy, as well as
his, is dialectically conceived. But in the case of Phaedra, the
dialectic cannot be seen as issuing primarily from her nature or
ideals; rather, it seems to involve the logical inversion of all her
intentions and actions. In the first part of the play Phaedra's desperate attempt, if not to overcome, at least to suppress and conceal
her fatal passion, combined with the physical effects of this
endeavour, naturally and inevitably rouses the compassion and
curiosity of the nurse and the chorus. When Phaedra's resistance is
finally broken, the nurse, who only wanted the best, has achieved
the worst (353 ff.). To her mistress, whose life she wanted to save,
death is now the only means of salvaging her honour (419 ff.).
However, even Phaedra's decision to avoid imminent disgrace by
killing herself unavoidably produces the opposite result. For the
nurse, of course, again tries to save her mistress's life (433 ff.); and
her second attempt, again undertaken with the best intentions,[29]
costs Phaedra not only her life, but also her honour. After the nurse
has talked to Hippolytus (565 ff.), Phaedra, bitterly complaining
that now she cannot even die with honour (687 f.), is forced to protect herself and (as a means to that end) to take Hippolytus down
with her.[30] But her double reaction to her impasse—suicide and
slander—is born out of an impure mixture of honourable and
unworthy impulses and therefore does not achieve the preservation
of her honour, which is her chief objective. Thus at each stage—
both before the action of the play begins, and at its beginning, as
well as after the nurse's disastrous intervention—all her efforts
naturally and inevitably produce the contrary result. Like her
antagonist Hippolytus, she is a victim of Aphrodite, but none the
less she contributes substantially to her own destruction and does
so specifically by means of the positive elements of her own intentions and actions. Schiller's statement in his essay 'On the Tragic'

can be applied to both of the main characters in the play: 'not only is the cause of misfortune in no way at odds with morality; it is only through morality that it becomes possible'.[31]

Finally, the last of the three great tragedies of Euripides, the *Bacchae*: it would be easy to show that this play too is dialectically conceived, right down to the level of linguistic, dramatic, and thematic detail, though only a brief sketch is possible here. The general dialectical movement of the play is already spelt out unambiguously in the prologue. Pentheus' resistance to Dionysus will lead only to the triumphant revelation of the new god in all his power and glory:

> Pentheus is at war with god in me,
> Thrusts me from his offerings; forgets my name
> In his prayers. Therefore I shall prove to him
> And every man in Thebes that I am god indeed.
>
> 45–8

Everything the unbeliever does turns against him. All his attempts to fetter the beautiful young stranger and his proselytes lead only to ever more impressive signs and demonstrations of the god's liberating power. In the tragicomic dressing-scene, the dialectical movement reaches its visual climax (912 ff.). The general, who, only a few minutes before, was committed to leading his army against the maenads that threaten the order of the *polis* (809), is now persuaded to go alone, in secret, as a spy, to the woods of mount Cithaeron (811 ff.). The rationalist, who until this very moment has measured everything with the yardstick of human intelligence,[32] is now smitten with madness (850 f., 918 ff.). The misogynist, who has scorned and ridiculed the effeminate stranger and his women acolytes, now makes a point of looking like a maenad himself (925 ff.). The man who insists that no one should see him (816, 840) finds himself in full view on top of a fir-tree (1063–75) and is finally torn to pieces by the women he has derided as the weaker sex all along (1076 ff.). The dialectical *peripeteia* turns the watcher into the watched, the hunter into the prey, the enemy of the god into his victim, to be sacrificed by the maenads.

The outer dramatic action, in which every measure Pentheus takes against Dionysus leads only to an ever more powerful epiphany of the god, can be seen as the symbol of the inner dialectical movement of the tragedy. The psychological truth of the play lies in the fact that at the crucial moment of the *peripeteia* Pentheus is not, or not only, overpowered from the outside, but is, or is *also*, undermined from the inside.[33] The more rigorously the Dionysiac instinct in Pentheus is repressed, the more powerfully it breaks through, until in the end it overwhelms him and destroys him.

The dialectical rhythm of the tragic development in the *Bacchae* is no less evident than in the *Medea* and the *Hippolytus*. The dramatic and emotional effect of these three great tragedies of Euripides rests squarely on the dialectical mode that structures their characters and their plots. At the same time, the dialectical connection between what the characters are and do and what they suffer allows the tragic events of the three plays to seem natural and inevitable, and thereby comprehensible and bearable. In the two Trojan tragedies and in the *Heracles*, on the other hand, the tragic catastrophe does not arise from the nature of the victims or from their intentions, plans, or actions; instead, catastrophe overwhelms and destroys them from the outside. This is deeply disturbing.

It would certainly be instructive—if only as a kind of cross-check—to submit the rest of the Euripidean *œuvre* to the terms of this enquiry. At the end of his life Euripides produced a number of dark and bitter problem-plays, whose peculiar tragic quality has always worried critics: *Electra* and *Orestes*, *Phoenissae* and *Iphigeneia at Aulis*. A detailed analysis of these four late plays would show that here Euripides makes a far less extensive use of the effective possibilities of tragic dialectic and, in so far as he employs the dialectical mode, he does so in a way that is quite different from what he does in the great tragedies. I would wish to argue that the worrying effect of the late plays can be explained, at least in part, precisely by the absence of, or the different use of, the dialectical mode. In the *Orestes*, for instance, Euripides dramatizes Orestes' desperate expedients to escape the consequences of matricide; and instead of edifying tragic decisions and actions, he offers a sobering look at a series of dishonourable and unsuccessful attempts on Orestes' part to save his own skin. The only reversal takes place at the end of the play, where, however, the intervention by Apollo (which puts the derailed situation back on its traditional mythical tracks) has no meaningful connection with the dramatic action that precedes it; rather, by the glaring absurdity of the 'solution' that it represents, this intervention only serves to intensify the general impression of senselessness and futility.

And then there are the tragicomedies, *Alcestis*, *Iphigenia in Tauris*, *Ion*, and *Helen*, four plays which offer a welcome confirmation of the special tragic effect of the dialectical mode as defined in this paper. As a matter of fact, they bear the marks of tragic dialectic, if at all, only in those dramatic and thematic elements that are clearly designed to produce a tragic effect. This is particularly evident in the last scenes of the *Ion* and in that complex tragicomedy, the *Alcestis*. In this play the 'tragic' action is indeed conceived dialectically: it is natural and inevitable that Admetus' attempt to save his life by relying on Alcestis' willingness to die for him should actually destroy his life instead. By contrast, the action that culminates in the rescue shows no trace of the dialectic, but instead works according to the 'comic' principle of poetic justice: Admetus' hospitality simply earns him the gratitude of Heracles, who duly brings Alcestis back.[34]

Interpretation of the problem-plays and the tragicomedies, however, must be reserved for another paper. The present analysis has shown: that Peter Szondi's definition of the tragic as a 'dialectical mode of impending or actual destruction' is a valuable aid to the understanding of Euripidean tragedy, as, arguably, of tragedy in general; that if our interpretation of *peripeteia* is sound, Aristotle has made some allowance for the importance of this principle for Greek tragedy; from which it follows that the much-quoted sentence with which Szondi opens his discussion—'Since Aristotle we have a theory of tragedy, but only since Schelling do we have a philosophy of the tragic'[35]—is not quite correct. It would rather seem that, when it came to recognizing the essence of the tragic, Aristotle was more perceptive than many modern critics have been willing to concede.

Notes

1. *Versuch über das Tragische*.
2. Ibid. 209.
3. Seidensticker, 'Peripetie und tragische Dialektik'.
4. For the literature, see ibid. 260–3.
5. See e.g. Else, *Aristotle's Poetics*, 344.
6. For full discussion, see Seidensticker, 'Peripetie und tragische Dialektik', 246–8.
7. In particular, the 'wider' interpretation must take the supplementary

phrase εἰς τὸ ἐναντίον as meaning a 'change from good fortune to misfortune or misfortune to good fortune', but ἐναντίον (against all expectation) would then refer not to the πραττόμενα which are undergoing a μεταβολή, but rather to the opposite of some sort of fortune, εὐτυχία or ἀτυχία, which is never mentioned in the definition. One would have to suppose that Aristotle spoke of a change from *x* (i.e. the πραττόμενα) into the contrary of *y* (i.e. either of the two opposite states of fortune). Another problem for the 'wider' interpretation is the position of τῶν πραττομένων, which (as the word order indicates) is related both to μεταβολή and to εἰς τὸ ἐναντίον: cf. Vahlen, *Beiträge zu Aristoteles' Poetik*, 6.

8. *Poet.* 1452ª26 (ἐναντίον ἐποίησεν). This 'narrower' interpretation of *peripeteia* was originally put forward by Vahlen in 1866. Understanding πραττόμενα as ἃ πράττεται [ἐπράττετο] ὑπὸ τῶν πραττόντων and taking into account the precise meaning of πράττειν in Aristotles's theory of *praxis*, Vahlen, *Beiträge zu Anstoteles' Poetik*, 6 concluded: 'Bei πραττόμενα ist nicht an πρᾶξις und πράγματα, an Ereignis oder Situation zu denken, sondern gemeint ist das, was man that oder thut zu einem bestimmten Zweck, das allerdings nicht diesem, sondern den gerade entgegengesetzten zur Folge hat.' It is undeniable that this interpretation is open to criticism as well, but the questions that arise are much easier to answer than is the case with the 'wider' interpretation; cf. Seidensticker, 'Peripetie und tragische Dialektik', 249–50.

9. See e.g. Else, *Aristotle's Poetics*, 344–5; for the various explanations of the supplementary phrase, see D. J. Allan, 'Peripeteia quid sit, Caesar occisus ostendit', *Mnemosyne* 29 (1976) 338–41.

10. Szondi, *Versuch über das Tragische*, 205: 'die verschiedensten Bestimmungen des Tragischen auf ein mehr oder weniger verdecktes Strukturelement hin durchsichtig zu machen, das allen gemeinsam ist'.

11. Hegel, *Sämtliche Werke*, xiv. 529: 'die sittlichen Mächte wie die handelnden Charaktere unterschieden sind in Rücksicht auf ihren Inhalt und ihre individuelle Erscheinung'; 'notwendig . . . herbeileitet' (see n. 28 below).

12. M. S. Scheler, 'Zum Phänomen des Tragischen', in *Gesammelte Werke*, ed. M. Scheler (Berne 1955) iii. 158: 'Im ausgesprochensten Sinne tragisch ist es . . . wenn ein und dieselbe Kraft, die ein Ding zur Realisierung eines hohen positiven Wertes (seiner selbst oder eines anderen Dinges) gelangen lässt, auch im Verlaufe dieses Wirkens selbst die Ursache für die Vernichtung eben dieses Dinges als Wertträger wird.'

13. 1453ª7–17, 1453ᵇ14–22; cf. Seidensticker, 'Peripetie und tragische Dialektik', 242–4.

14. M. Kommerell, *Aristoteles und Lessing* (Frankfurt/M. 1940 [1984]) 178 ff.

15. Szondi, *Versuch über das Tragische*, 209.

16. 'Da sich nämlich der Begriff des Tragischen aus der Konkretheit der philosophischen Probleme in die Höhe des Abstrakten zu seinem Unheil erhebt, muss er sich in das Konkreteste der Tragödie versenken, wenn anders er gerettet werden soll. Dieses Konkreteste ist die Handlung. Gerade in der Reflexion auf das Tragische wird sie freilich gern über die Achsel angesehen. Und doch ist sie das wichtigste Konstituens des Dramas, das seinen Namen nicht zufällig ihr verdankt': Szondi, *Versuch über das Tragische*, 210.

17. The other seven plays are: Calderón, *La Vida es sueño*; Shakespeare, *Othello*; Gryphius, *Leo Arminius*; Racine, *Phèdre*; Schiller, *Demetrius*; Kleist, *Die Familie Schroffenstein*; Büchner, *Dantons Tod*.

18. Szondi, *Versuch über das Tragische*, 213–18; Seidensticker, 'Peripetie und tragische Dialektik', 253–6.

19. See above, p. 393. To avoid excessive annotation, references to secondary literature on these and other Euripidean plays are kept to a minimum.

20. See e.g. *Tro.* 615, 639 ff., 820 ff.

21. See e.g. *Hec.* 1 ff., 285, 490 ff., 765 ff.

22. See e.g. (Megara) 60 ff., 457 ff., 480 (!), and (Amphitryon) 1 ff., 508 ff. (!).

23. On the development of her scheme, cf. B. Manuwald, 'Der Mord an den Kindern', *WS* 17 (1983) 27–61.

24. See B. Seidensticker, 'Euripides' *Medea*: An Interpolation?', in M. Griffith and D. J. Mastronarde (edd.), *Cabinet of the Muses* (Harvard 1990) 89–102 (n. 1 lists the most important discussions of the problem).

25. Cf. E. B. Bongie, 'Heroic Elements in the *Medea* of Euripides', *TAPA* 107 (1977) 27–56; P. E. Easterling, 'The Infanticide in Euripides' *Medea*', *YCS* 25 (1977) 177–91; and esp. B. M. W. Knox, 'The *Medea* of Euripides', *YCS* 25 (1977) 193–225.

26. E.g. the suggestive lines 198 ff.

27. *Hipp.* 1166, 1240 ff., 1355 ff.

28. Hegel, *Sämtliche Werke*, xiv. 529: 'Das individuelle Handeln will dann unter bestimmten Umständen einen Zweck oder Charakter durchführen, der unter diesen Voraussetzungen, weil er in seiner für sich fertigen Bestimmtheit sich einseitig isoliert, notwendig das entgegengesetzte Pathos gegen sich aufreizt und dadurch unausweichlich Konflikte herbeileitet.'

29. *Hipp.* 496 f., 596 f., 699.

30. Phaedra, of course, destroys Hippolytus not only to protect her honour, but also because of the injury to her pride and self-esteem.

31. F. Schiller, *Kleine prosaische Schriften* (Leipzig 1802) iv. 210: 'Diese Gattung des Rührenden wird noch von derjenigen übertroffen, wo die Ursache des Unglücks nicht allein nicht der Moralität widersprechend, sondern sogar durch Moralität allein möglich ist.'

32. H. Diller, 'Die Bakchen und ihre Stellung im Spätwerk des Euripides', *Abh. Akad. Mainz* (1995) 5: 45 ff. (= *Kleine Schriften* [Munich 1971] 369 ff.); B. Seidensticker, 'Pentheus', *Poetica* 5 (1972) 35–63.

33. R. P. Winnington-Ingram, *Euripides and Dionysus* (Cambridge 1948); E. R. Schwinge, *Die Stichomythie in den Dramen des Euripides* (Heidelberg 1968) 342 ff.; B. Seidensticker, 'Comic Elements in the *Bacchae*', *AJP* 99 (1978) 303 ff.

34. For the complex tragicomic structure of the *Alcestis*, see Seidensticker, *Palintonos Harmonia*, 129–52.

35. Szondi, *Versuch über das Tragische*, 151: 'Seit Aristoteles gibt es eine Poetik der Tragödie, seit Schelling erst eine Philosophie des Tragischen.'

22

Emotion and Meaning in Tragic Performance

ISMENE LADA

This paper examines Greek drama from the perspective of audience-oriented criticism. I hope to explore some aspects of the communicative channel between the Greek plays and their original spectators, focusing primarily on the interrelation of affect and understanding as part of the response of classical audiences to a theatrical event. I deal with this issue through a test case, namely through a comparison of ancient drama with Brecht's revolutionary 'epic theatre', where thought and critical appreciation are set at the opposite extreme of an emotional response, and where the sole prerequisite for understanding is the viewer's 'disengagement' or 'alienation' from the stage-world. The range of firsthand information on the response of classical Greek audiences to the theatrical event is lamentably restricted.[1] Nevertheless, a very interesting, albeit largely unexplored, type of evidence is *implicit* in the dramatic (both tragic and comic) texts themselves, in so far as they are self-consciously concerned with their own conditions of creation and performance. It is this 'metatheatrical' dimension of Greek drama that I propose to concentrate on, with special reference, of course, to tragedy. Such an 'internalized' perspective, I suggest, can open up new ways of understanding of the possible impact that classical Greek tragedy could work upon its first spectators.

In Brecht's evaluation, Western dramaturgy, which he terms comprehensively 'Aristotelian' drama, effects a kind of 'hypnosis': the actors 'go into a trance and take the audience with them'.[2] The kernel of this type of theatre is the notion of *Einfühlung*, the spectator's tendency to empathize with characters and action:

Everyone (including every spectator) is then carried away by the momentum of the events portrayed, so that in a performance of *Oedipus* one has for all practical purposes an auditorium full of little Oedipuses, an auditorium full of Emperor Joneses for a performance of *The Emperor Jones*.[3]

The consequences of this empathetic way of attending the theatrical event are, in Brecht's evaluation, alarming. For empathy blocks the viewer's understanding and blunts his/her critical alertness, producing an audience which 'hangs its brains up in the cloakroom along with its coat'.[4] Brecht's own 'epic' theatre, on the other hand, appeals first and foremost to the viewer's reason:[5]

The essential point of the epic theatre is perhaps that it appeals less to the feelings than to the spectator's reason. Instead of sharing an experience the spectator must come to grips with things.[6]

Thought and critical appreciation is diametrically opposed to emotional response:[7]

Sorrow is hostile to thought; it stifles it; and thought is hostile to sorrow.[8]

The indispensable prerequisite for understanding is the spectator's 'alienation' from the stage-world:

The spectator was no longer in any way allowed to submit to an experience uncritically (and without practical consequences) by means of simple empathy with the characters in a play. The production took the subject-matter and the incidents shown and put them through a process of alienation: the alienation that is necessary to all understanding.[9]

My purpose, then, is to address the issue of 'emotion' and 'meaning', emotion and cognition, principally by raising the question whether Brecht's appreciation of the 'Aristotelian' theatre as 'emotionalist' and 'hostile to thought' can be considered an adequate qualification of fifth-century Athenian drama. My main thesis is that although Greek theatre *justifies* Brecht's conception of the 'Aristotelian' auditorium as a space where 'everybody feels',[10] emotion within the Greek dramatic frame is *a privileged way of attaining understanding, self-realization, and socio-cultural self-definition.*

The first text I shall consider is Aristophanes' *Frogs*, a play renowned for its metatheatrical insights into the impact of Athenian tragedy upon society. The comic stage dramatizes a theoretical conflict where cognition and emotion are presented as irreconcilable. These two contrasted modes of audience participation are juxtaposed through the figures of Aeschylus and Euripides and the respective publics they have allegedly created.

Euripidean drama demands an audience alert and critical throughout the theatrical performance, capable of exercising its mental faculties of 'thinking and understanding', νοεῖν and ξυνιέναι (957). Boasting, as he does, about the *intellectual* dimension of his drama, Euripides draws close to a 'Brechtian' dependence on an audience 'capable of thinking and of reasoning, of making judgments even in the theatre'.[11] The older dramatist's performance, on the other hand, creates a communicative channel which results in 'snatching people out of their senses'. Euripides accuses him in 961–2: οὐκ ἐκομπολάκουν | ἀπὸ τοῦ φρονεῖν ἀποσπάσας, οὐδ' ἐξέπληττον αὐτούς, 'I didn't talk big, | thrusting them out of their wits, nor did I astound them.' Now, the notion of *ekplêxis* in particular deserves considerable attention, for whether it refers to Aeschylus' astounding theatrical devices or to the flights of his pompous *logos*, it designates the complete bewilderment of the experiencer which blunts his readiness for critical evaluation or even leads him to irrational response. To narrow the focus on the effect of verbal discourse and performance, *ekplêxis* or *kataplêxis* conveys the power to 'unhinge' men's minds, thrusting them under the domination of affect.[12] In the Platonic *Ion*, for example, *ekplêttesthai* at the singing of the rhapsode[13] is explained as the listeners' emotional engagement, their imaginative projection into the fictive epic world,[14] while a text as late as Polybius' *Histories* conceives of *ekplêxis* as the goal (τέλος) of tragedy and as an experience inherently intertwined with the captivation of the soul, ψυχαγωγία.[15]

Nevertheless, the semantic field of *ekplêxis* is broader still. As can be inferred from the Platonic dialogues, *ekplêxis* as the soul's response to *logos* is such an all-pervasive feeling that it may even be compared to an experience of religious possession. Many a time, the bewilderment of those overwhelmed by amazing *logoi* is conveyed through metaphors drawn from the areas of orgiastic trance. Thus, the *ekplêxis* of Socrates by Phaedrus' words is elucidated as a state of Bacchic trance,[16] while Alcibiades in the *Symposium* attributes to the *logoi* of Socrates himself the power to make the listeners *ekpeplêgmenoi* and possessed:[17] Socrates is compared to the mythical Marsyas, for even 'without instruments, by mere words' (*Symposium* 215c) he is able to emulate the flute's insuperable possessing power.[18] Alcibiades, correspondingly, conveys his own experience of *ekplêxis* with the image of the wild ἔκστασις (entrancement) of the Korybantic rites: 'for when I listen to him my heart is leaping much more than the hearts of those possessed by Korybantic frenzy, and tears stream forth from my eyes at the sound of his speech' (*Symposium* 215e). The parallelism just quoted is all the more important for its direct bearing on the realm *par excellence* where *ekplêxis* is operative—that is, the sphere of mystic rites, where the neophytes have to undergo the emotional ordeal of overwhelming terror: 'just like in the most sacred initiation-rites [ἐν ταῖς ἁγιωτάταις τελεταῖς], before the sight of the mysteries, the initiands are overcome by terror [*ekplêxis*]'.[19]

If this wider semantic frame of *ekplêxis*, then, is taken into account, Euripides' dismissal of Aeschylus' technique acquires a richer range of implications: as the re-presentation (or mis-re-presentation?) of a playwright's voice enunciated from the theatrical *skênê* itself, it testifies to the ability of drama to refer to its own spectacle in the language of a mystical event. Besides, the interpretation of tragic *ekplêxis* in terms of the word's mystical associations has powerful contextual support: not only is initiation-symbolism the primary force which holds the play's imagery and plot together, but also, in the *agôn* of the *Frogs*, the older dramatist emerges as an Eleusinian/Bacchic poet.[20] Demeter herself had nourished his mind,[21] while, as Angus Bowie suggests,[22] the Euripidean distorting lens seems to cast the Aeschylean figures in the role of initiands in the Demetrian mystic rites: sitting on the stage veiled and in silence under the sway of choral songs sung around them,[23] they could have easily recalled for the initiated among the audience the pivotal initiation-rite of the *thronôsis* ('enthronement'). In this respect then, it would seem that in a dramatist's perception of a stage-performance, the spectacle can work upon its audience an emotional impact of an extreme intensity. Through its participation in the Eleusinian/Bacchic nature of the *Frogs'* discourse, *ekplêxis* is invested with the signs of a mystic initiation: that is, that 'unspeakable' (ἄρρητος) experience of the soul which can only be compared to its suffering (*pathos*) at the hour of death[24] and which entails such a thorough remoulding of identity that it ultimately amounts to a rite of rebirth.[25]

The captivating power of the theatre informs another Euripidean accusation against Aeschylus' technique, namely the *apatê* (deception) that he practises at the expense of the spectator (908–10):

τοῦτον δὲ πρῶτ' ἐλέγξω,
ὡς ἦν ἀλαζὼν καὶ φέναξ οἵοις τε τοὺς θεατὰς
ἐξηπάτα.

But first I will prove that he was a rogue and an impostor and (I will show) with what tricks he deceived [*exêpata*] the audience.

Now, at first glance Euripides simply charges his antagonist with fooling his spectators, cheating them by creating plays deficient in artistic structure. Nevertheless, all the key words of this passage are fraught with connotations which can be activated *par excellence* within the frame of a literary context: *alazôn* (rogue) and *phenax* (impostor) seem to be closely interwoven with enthralment and bewitchment produced by various kinds of discourse, ranging from the misleading power of sophistic *logos* to the realm of magic[26] or to the confusion of the listener through a style convoluted and ambiguous to the extent that it becomes reminiscent of an oracular response.[27] As for *apatê*, it is quite possible that in fifth-century literary debate it could acquire the nuance of 'illusionism'; this would most probably have centred on the illusionist power of drama, such as is vividly expressed in Gorgias' famous dictum[28] that tragedy

offers through its myths and sufferings 'illusion' [*apatê*] . . . whereby he who deceives [*apatêsas*] is more just than he who does not deceive, and he who is deceived [*apatêtheis*] is wiser than he who is not deceived.

Thus, for the informed spectators, able to appreciate the subtle quality of intellectual humour upon which the whole passage rests, it is Euripides rather than Aeschylus who seems to be unable to comply with the requirements of a game in which the deceiver is ultimately more just than the non-deceiver. Dionysus' reply, on the other hand (916–17),

ἐγὼ δ' ἔχαιρον τῇ σιωπῇ, καί με τοῦτ' ἔτερπεν
οὐχ ἧττον ἢ νῦν οἱ λαλοῦντες

But I, for my part, rejoiced in the silence, and this device pleased me no less than those who now chatter

testifying to the 'rejoicing' and 'pleasure' of a spectator at the dramatic spectacle that Aeschylus created, obliquely acknowledges the power of Aeschylean theatre to bewitch and cast a spell: the silence of the protagonistic figure together with the 'strings of odes' that the chorus sang[29] created a sublime and transcendental atmosphere inducing the spectator to surrender.

Ismene Lada

The presence of Dionysus, however, raises an important question. Does his choice of the poet who 'deceives', over the intellectual, cold-minded craftsman, carry any force *outside* the limited, fictitious time and space of the play? In other words, how important for our understanding of a Greek performance is the fact that the patron god of theatre himself succumbs to tragedy as an emotional, spellbinding event? In my view, the comic Dionysus' *emotional* response to an *emotionally* laden performance does actually deserve to be considered at face value, in so far as it can be shown to correspond to real patterns of response embedded in Greek culture and to the social parameters which shaped a Greek theatrical event. For, as I have argued at length elsewhere,[30] important strands in Greek culture privilege an *emotional* response to all performative enunciations of *logoi*: whether we are confronted with the gratifying discourse of poetry or with the implacable and truthful voice of philosophical enquiry; whether we are dealing with the explicit theatrical frame of a stage-production or with the implicit and 'hidden' theatricality of oratorical displays in the Assembly and the lawcourts, it is primarily the *soul* as an emotive substance which is envisaged as the first and foremost addressee of *logos*. Furthermore, if social parameters are taken into account, pride of place should be given to the Dionysiac nature of the ancient drama. For at the core of the Dionysiac psychology lies the experience of 'becoming other', the vicarious bridging of the gap between oneself and a variety of different personae. The 'Aristotelian' spectator, then, becomes participant in a performance whose archetypal symbolic action is to 'step out of himself' and to relinquish temporarily the safe contours of social identity. As a Dionysiac spectator, he is therefore culturally prone to extend himself sympathetically towards new frames of existence, to appropriate rather than to shun the emotional experience of the 'other'.

Returning now to the *agôn* of the *Frogs*, the sharp polarization between reason and emotion should make us pause. For how were the play's *original* spectators supposed to interpret this elaborately contrived poetic clash? A variety of avenues, sometimes irreconcilable, are open for investigation. The possibility that I propose in this paper may be summarized as follows: given that Aeschylus and Euripides exemplify consecutive phases of the same theatrical tradition, namely the tragic spectacle of the Dionysiac festivals of Athens, the juxtaposition of their tactics acquires a clear metatheatrical dimension: it can be read not only as the illustration of a 'Brechtian'-like opposition, but also as an indication of the theatre's self-conscious exploitation of its power to elicit *both* intellectual *and* affective modes of response.

Judging on the basis of our everyday experiences, most of us tend to envisage affective and rational reactions as entirely separate processes, or even as mutually exclusive. Yet, in the last decades there has been a broad consensus among researchers in the fields both of psychology and of philosophy that in all cultures cognitive processes are a most significant—if not the sole—means of eliciting emotion.[31] The central tenet of such a cognitively oriented theoretical approach is that feelings 'issue from cognitive interpretations imposed on external reality, rather than directly from reality itself'.[32] In other words, 'each emotional reaction, regardless of its content' is thought to be 'a function of a particular kind of cognition or *appraisal*'.[33] As far as the Greek world is concerned, the first full-scale theoretical appreciation of emotions in a cognitivist perspective takes shape already with Aristotle.[34] To narrow the focus on the inherently 'tragic' emotions of 'pity' and 'fear', the 'ability to reason well',[35] together with a multitude of cognitive considerations, are *sine qua non* parameters in the determination of an individual's proneness to the emotive state of pitying;[36] fear, correspondingly, not only is elicited on the basis of a rational evaluation of the reality, proximity, and imminence of danger,[37] but also leads to further deliberative and mental action.[38] Now, of course one should beware of uncritically assuming that the philosopher's insights were shared by wider circles.[39] Nevertheless, the poetically expressed feeling of the interdependence of affect and reason can be traced as early as the Homeric epics, where the Sirens' song is not only the epitome of pleasure and enchantment,[40] but a source of knowledge as well.[41] Even a play like Euripides' *Medea*, which is renowned for its exploitation of the *clash* between passion and reason, implies that emotion is perceived as the result of a cognition or evaluation: in the Nurse's account of Medea's situation at the play's opening scene, Medea is in grief and anger[42] *because* she perceives her honour as slighted.[43] As Fortenbaugh has put it, 'the nurse's remarks do not suggest a dichotomy that locates all cognition on the side of deliberation. Part of being angry is perceiving or thinking oneself outraged.'[44]

Nevertheless, this interplay of emotions and cognitions is by no means a simple, 'one-way' traffic. For emotion often redirects or interferes with cognitive activity or, to quote Carroll Izard, emotions 'constitute a powerful motivational system that influences perception, cognition, coping, and creativity in important ways'.[45] Fifth-century Athenian drama is actually a privileged field where the transmission of knowledge and communication of ideas can be shown to implicate to a great extent a set of psychological processes. Thus, in Greek tragedy knowledge is often an achievement which comes only through the torture of emotion, the extremity and the intensity of suffering, such as grief at someone's death. Some very obvious cases could be sought in Euripides' *Alcestis*[46] and the Sophoclean *Antigone*, where Creon's speech of lament to the chorus is replete with mistrust of reason, of rational argumentation and beliefs,[47] laying bare the shortcomings even of 'the best thought out plans' (τῶν ἀρίστων βουλευμάτων, 179) he has been previously so proud of. It is only through the painful experience of loss, amid the lamentations of grief, that he ultimately 'learns': οἴμοι, | ἔχω μαθὼν δείλαιος, 'Alas, I have learnt it to my bitterness' (*Antigone* 1271–2).

In Greek theatrical experience then, a fundamental channel of communication between author, performer, and their addressees is sustained through the transfusion of emotion, the identity of shared feelings. Moreover, in contrast to Brecht's—and Plato's!—evaluation that poetry's appeal to emotionality jeopardizes the individual's attempt at rational control,[48] emotion is a privileged way of getting access to the truth, of reaching both understanding of others and, most importantly, self-realization. Besides, if, as many studies have persuasively argued, there are reflections of initiatory patterns in Greek drama, one might say that Greek theatre preserves its ritual antecedents, where the emotional ordeal of the initiand is the *sine qua non* for his/her attainment of the light of truth.

Nevertheless, I should now explain that within the frame of theatrical representation, cognition takes on an added layer of signification: it does not merely refer to the agent's understanding of a sequence of events or to moral, aesthetic, social evaluations; it also extends to the viewer's realization of the idiomorphous relation of the 'self' to the dramatic frame—that is, the awareness that one's spectating position lies by definition *outside* the pageant of the represented world. A few metatheatrical examples are relevant here,[49] but I shall only discuss Dicaeopolis' para-tragic performance in the *Acharnians*, where tragedy and its impact are filtered through the comic lens. More specifically, I wish to focus on *Acharnians* 441–4, where Theatre reflects upon its own status as both an experience of 'translation', a narcotic dulling of the mind, and a frame where the viewer may keep his/her cognitive integrity intact.

In his wish, or rather plan, as expressed in lines 442–4

τοὺς μὲν θεατὰς εἰδέναι μ' ὃς εἴμ' ἐγώ,
τοὺς δ' αὖ χορευτὰς ἠλιθίους παρεστάναι,
ὅπως ἂν αὐτοὺς ῥηματίοις σκιμαλίσω

The audience must know me for who I am, but the chorus must stand there like imbeciles, so that I can give them the long finger with my little phrases

Dicaeopolis acknowledges explicitly the simultaneous existence of two distinct audiences of his performance: the 'theatre-audience' of the Aristophanic comic play, and the 'internalized' audience of the para-tragic speech, which is the comic play's chorus. And this differentiation goes hand in hand with the assignment to them of different reactions: penetration into the metamorphosis and awareness of the role-playing (εἰδέναι) versus mental inactivity (ἠλιθίους παρεστάναι) and potential persuasion or *apatê* through the fiction—(ὅπως ἂν αὐτοὺς ῥηματίοις σκιμαλίσω, 444). Now, of course, one may read into these verses a metadramatic comment on fifth-century generic differentiation in audience-response: the *critical*, more readily responding viewer of *comedy*, versus the *bewitched* spectator of the *tragic* drama who succumbs to the stage magic. However, I would lay more stress upon the fact that, in purely dramatic terms, the reactions of the actor's 'double' audience are actually assumed to be exemplified in the unified response of the Aristophanic play's real, single audience: the Athenian spectators, in front of whom both the 'theatre' and the 'metatheatre' of the *Acharnians* are played. In other words, it seems to me that in this scene Greek theatre self-consciously exploits its awareness of empathy and enthralment as compatible with cognitive processes, as it constructs for itself an 'implied' spectator who is both 'engaged' in the fiction and capable of penetrating it.

To sum up then, Brecht's conception of empathy as lying at the opposite extreme of reason is dangerously misleading when applied to the workings of the classical Athenian drama. Nevertheless, in Brecht's perspective, there are also some broader consequences of the 'Aristotelian' spectator's identification with the world of fiction, and my purpose now is to touch upon the question of whether the connotations of aesthetic *Einfühlung* as a whole are applicable to the fifth-century Athenian drama. For Brecht saw empathy as the principal obstacle to the spectator's social understanding: by enwrapping the spectator in the web of empathy, the 'Aristotelian' type of drama functions as a pacifier, inducing him to accept unquestionably the play's world and the reality that it reflects:

The dramatic theatre's spectator says: Yes, I have felt like that too—Just like me—It's only natural—It'll never change—The sufferings of this man appal me, because they are inescapable.[50]

Furthermore, emotional response causes individuality to merge with the prevailing mood of the spectating body: losing perspective on himself as a social entity, the viewer tends to forget what differentiates him from his fellow-spectators. In other words, Brecht conceives of the 'Aristotelian' audience as boiled down 'to a shapeless dumpling in the stockpot of the emotions'.[51]

In view of the above considerations, then, I will now very briefly touch upon three closely related issues.[52]

1. It is one of Brecht's main theses that the Aristotelian drama's empathic orientation is irreconcilable with the 'engagement' of the viewer's social 'self' in the performance. This thesis cannot be justified when tested on the classical Greek drama, where *emotional* response is inevitably a *social* response, contextually determined and culturally dependent. Pity and awe at Medea's infanticide, for example, are ultimately inseparable from an entire cluster of culturally determined questions, such as the meaning of the feminine voice 'speaking out' for herself on stage, the meaning of the male viewer's witnessing the usurpation of his own male/heroic code by the feminine 'other', and so on.

2. The premise of that first thesis is inherently interwoven with one of the most pervasive concerns in Brecht's writings on the theatre, namely the association of empathy with social passivity. Empathy within the playhouse acts as an impediment to one's prosocial motivation: 'coming to terms with' through identification inhibits one's willingness to act in order to alleviate the ills of

the world;[53] emotional reaction in the theatre is harmful, as it substitutes for real action in communal life.[54] How does Greek society understand its double function as a passive—that is, spectating—body in the theatre, and as a politically active—that is, decision-making—organ in the city's public life? It would seem that the sundering of roles and responsibilities which worried Brecht was indeed recognized, but actually condemned as deviant and intolerable. Orators take political spectators to task for the discrepancy between their social and theatrical response: the overflow of emotion at the stage dramas should ideally transmute itself into altruistic action:

Against these ills no one has ever protested; and people are not ashamed to weep over the calamities which have been fabricated by the poets, while they view complacently the real sufferings, the many terrible sufferings, which result from our state of war; and they are so far from feeling pity that they even rejoice more in each other's sorrows than in their own blessings. (Isocrates 4. 168)

3. Cross-cultural studies of a variety of civic performances have shown that any public spectacle can be construed in a variety of ways by different groups of the onlooking community. I should like to believe that there is solid ground for arguing that in the Greek theatrical event as well, the richness of perspectives reflected in the tissue of the text and scenic spectacle entails a variety of voices of dissent within the space of the auditorium. Consider, for example, the conservative Athenians, nourished with values such as those upheld by the Just *Logos* in the *Clouds*. Their sympathy for those tragic heroes who are driven to despair by the Calliclean principle of might is right[55] may tend to enhance their awareness of the bedrocks of their own education, which is irreconcilable with the disruptive moral relativism of sophistic discourse. Furthermore, it cannot be emphasized too strongly that the challenge which arises from the male viewer's empathy with characters who incarnate an 'other' mode of being, such as females, ephebes, heroes, and so on, is a twofold process: while putting to the test the limits of the onlooker's 'vision', it may also work in such a way as to consolidate his own identity as *different* from the object of his empathy on the stage. In other words, although the empathetically aroused challenge is certainly synonymous with destabilization of identities, it may also lead to the reinforcement

of self-definition and of culturally formed self-conception. To generalize even more, many a time in the plays, shifting points of view, and therefore shifting focuses of polarization, create a mechanism through which empathy becomes a social exercise in constructing, deconstructing, reconstructing, the difference between categories of 'us' and 'them'.[56]

Greek drama, therefore, disproves Brecht's evaluation of the 'Aristotelian' theatre as a channel of communication which is neither socially oriented nor successful in sustaining a diversity in its audience's response. In other words, there are some very important respects in which Greek tragedy itself approaches Brecht's own ideal of dramaturgy and stage-representation. Nevertheless, at least one fundamental difference sets the classical Greek model radically apart.

Although, within the frame of Greek culture, stage and civic life amply cross-fertilize one another, the tragic vision, however challenging, disturbing, and unsettling it may be, does not fulfil Brecht's ideal of materializing on the social plane in radical, subversive action. Indeed, it can be argued that a Greek audience's emotional participation in the fictive construction of social alternatives on-stage serves the distinctively anti-Brechtian aim of reaffirming, strengthening, revitalizing the civic 'status quo', as the spectator is many a time required to share in this peculiarly ambiguous experience of simultaneously undermining and reasserting or, to put it in Bakhtinian language, of 'burying' and 'reviving' at once. In other words, there is a strong sense in which, by celebrating the negative, Greek drama clarifies the positive, and this again is a function of the audience's empathic identification. For example, to identify with protagonists who operate through deceit and guile—transcribing therefore onto the civic space the inverted models of ephebic marginality[57]—or to experience an emotional *sparagmos* at, say, Pentheus' dismemberment—thus annihilating and subverting the civic sacrificial code—is to participate vicariously in a picture of confusion and disorder. Yet, the utter havoc wreaked through calling the established civic frameworks into question has precisely the function of heightening the awareness of the rule, of reinforcing the very structure which has been violated by making explicit one's unconscious assumptions about the indispensability of categorization, discrimination, and order. Besides, the very idea of heroism which furnishes the plots of all the tragic dramas is inextricably interwoven with transgression and subversion, as—by definition—a hero does not and cannot tidily conform to socio-cultural classifications. Lying precariously on the margins between 'nature' and 'culture', and therefore flouting restrictions, breaking rules, violating taboos at will, the classical dramatic hero—and by consequence the actor who incarnates him on-stage—cuts across the most important categories by which Greek culture organizes itself into a coherent whole: bestial and human, human and divine, male and female, barbarian and Greek, and so forth. But, if the emotional process of empathizing with such a stage-figure is a *challenge* to the male Athenian self, it is also a process which forces back an *intensified awareness* of the implied positive model: that is, the one-dimensional, integral, masculine citizen-self.

No single portion of this paper can claim to constitute a straightforward, representative piece of evidence. Nevertheless, each one of the perspectives offered so far, even if not conclusive in itself, lends support to my initial proposition and encourages us to challenge on all sides Brecht's disjunction of affect and intellect, as expressed, for example, in his famous aphorism '[dramatic characters] are not matter for empathy; they are there to be understood'.[58] And, if Martha Nussbaum is right in believing that Aristotelian *katharsis* is the spectator's intellectual experience effected 'through the emotions themselves',[59] it is actually the founder of the allegedly 'non-cognitive' Western theatrical tradition who gives the strongest blow to the theoretical assumptions upon which the Brechtian model rests. Against Brecht, therefore, we may conclude that, whatever may be said of tragedy or serious drama in other socio-cultural contexts, tragic performance in ancient Greece implied a model of audience-response wherein affect and intellect, 'emotion' and 'meaning', were inextricably interwoven.

Notes

This paper makes some use of material published in the *Proceedings of the Cambridge Philological Society for 1993* and *Arethusa* for 1996 (see nn. 1 and 52 below). I am grateful to the editors of *PCPS* and the Johns Hopkins UP for permission to reuse this material here.

  1. For a survey of the existing evidence, see Lada, ' "Empathic Understanding" '.

2. Brecht, *BT* 26. In my quotations from Brecht I shall be using the abbreviations Brecht, *BT* and Brecht, *MD* in order to refer to Brecht, *Brecht on Theatre*, and Brecht, *The Messingkauf Dialogues*, respectively.

3. Brecht, *BT* 87.

4. Ibid. 27.

5. Cf. ibid. 14, Brecht, *MD* 50.

6. Brecht, *BT* 23.

7. However, many times, and especially in his later writings, Brecht emphasizes that he does not wish a complete banning of emotion. See e.g. Brecht, *BT* 23, 125, 173 (reflecting, according to Willett, a 'new qualification of Brecht's view of empathy'): 'Only one out of many possible sources of emotion needs to be left unused, or at least treated as a subsidiary source-empathy.'

8. Brecht, *MD* 47.

9. Brecht, *BT* 71.

10. Ibid. 26.

11. Ibid. 79. Cf. Nietzsche's attitude to Euripides (undoubtedly influenced by the Aristophanic 'Euripides') and the comment in Silk and Stern, *Nietzsche on Tragedy*, 360.

12. Cf. e.g. Soph. *Trach.* 385–6 (λόγοις . . . ἐκπεπληγμένη κυρῶ), Eur. *Alc.* 1125, Thuc. 2. 65. 9 (λέγων κατέπλησσεν), Gorg. *Hel.* 16.

13. Pl. *Ion* 535b.

14. Ibid. 535e.

15. Pol. *Hist.* 2. 56. 11 (ἐκπλῆξαι καὶ ψυχαγωγῆσαι).

16. Pl. *Phdr.* 234d.

17. Pl. *Symp.* 215d.

18. Pl. *Symp.* 215b–d.

19. Procl. *Theol. Plat.* 3. 18, p. 64 Budé. Cf. Procl. *In Remp.* vol. 2 (Kroll), p. 108, 21–2: 'so that some of the initiands are struck with amazement [καταπλήττεσθαι], as they become filled with sacred fears'; Arist. 22. 2 (Keil); Procl. *In Remp.* vol. 2 (Kroll), p. 181, 5–8 (on Dionysus who 'is the leader of many apparitions', whose function is 'to terrify the souls', καταπλήττειν τὰς ψυχάς), etc. See also Strabo (10. 3. 7) who, treating collectively the *teletai* of Kouretes, Korybantes, Kabeiroi, Idaean Dactyloi, Telchines, presents them as 'in the guise of officials who inspire terror at the celebration of the sacred rites [ἐκπλήττοντας κατὰ τὰς ἱερουργίας] by the flute and loud cries'. For ἔκπληξις as extreme terror, see e.g. Soph. *Trach.* 24: ἐκπεπληγμένη φόβῳ.

20. For the *Frogs* as a reflection of Dionysiac initiation as well as for the Bacchic characteristics of Aeschylus in the *agôn*, see Lada, *Initiating Dionysus: Ritual and Theatre in Aristophanes' Frogs* (Oxford, forthcoming).

21. *Frogs* 886.
22. A. M. Bowie, *Aristophanes: Myth, Ritual, and Comedy* (Cambridge 1993) 247–8.
23. *Frogs* 911–15.
24. See Plut. fr. 178 Sandbach.
25. For the symbolism of 'death' and 'resurrection' as lying at the core of initiation rituals, see e.g. V. Turner, *The Forest of Symbols: Aspects of Ndembu Ritual* (Ithaca, NY 1967) ch. 4; M. Eliade, *Initiation, rites, sociétés secrètes, naissances mystiques: Essai sur quelques types d'initiation* (Paris 1959); W. Burkert, *Ancient Mystery Cults* (Cambridge, Mass. 1987) 99–101. For fifth- and fourth-century Greek evidence, see the famous Orphic/Bacchic gold leaves, especially G. Zuntz, *Persephone: Three Essays on Religion and Thought in Magna Graecia* (Oxford 1971), tablet A1, vv. 7–9 (with A. J. Festugière, 'Les Mystères de Dionysos', in id., *Études de religion grecque et hellénistique* [Paris 1972] 48–62); Zuntz, *Persephone*, tablet A4, vv. 3–4 (with Seaford, 'Dionysiac Drama', 262 and 254 with n. 28); v. 1 on the recently discovered Pelinna tablets (K. Tsantsanoglou and G. M. Parássoglou, 'Two Gold Lamellae from Thessaly', Ἑλληνικά 38 [1987] 3–16); see further S. G. Cole, 'New Evidence for the Mysteries of Dionysos', *GRBS* 21 (1980) 223–38 and ead., 'Life and Death: A New Epigram for Dionysos', *Epigraphica Anatolica* 4 (1984) 37–49; F. Graf, 'Dionysian and Orphic Eschatology: New Texts and Old Questions', in T. H. Carpenter and C. A. Faraone (edd.), *Masks of Dionysus* (Ithaca, NY 1993) 239–58. For the Eleusinian circle, see Burkert, *Homo Necans: The Anthropology of Ancient Greek Sacrificial Ritual and Myth*, trans. P. Bing (Berkeley 1983), esp. 256–97.
26. See primarily Burkert, 'ΓΟΗΣ: Zum griechischen "Schamanismus" ', *RhM* 105 (1962), esp. 50–1 (with nn. 74–5); for a list of sources and discussion, see Lada, ' "Empathic Understanding" ', 99 (with nn. 41–2).
27. See e.g. Arist. *Rhet.* 1407ᵃ35–7.
28. Fr. B23 D–K.
29. *Frogs* 911–15.
30. See Lada, ' "Empathic Understanding" '.
31. For some useful overviews of the debate, emphasizing the heavy contribution of *cognitive* factors to the emotion-eliciting process, see: R. S. Lazarus *et al.*, 'Towards a Cognitive Theory of Emotion', in M. B. Arnold (ed.), *Feelings and Emotions* (New York 1970) 207–32; Lazarus *et al.*, 'Emotions: A Cognitive-Phenomenological Analysis', and R. Plutchik, 'A General Psychoevolutionary Theory of Emotion', in Plutchik and H. Kellerman (edd.), *Emotion: Theory, Research, and Experience*, i: *Theories of Emotion* (New York 1980) 189–217, 3–33;

C. E. Izard, 'Emotion–Cognition Relationships and Human Development', in Izard *et al.* (edd.), *Emotions, Cognition, and Behavior*, 17–37, also 'Introduction', ibid. 1–14, and P. J. Lang, 'Cognition in Emotion: Concept and Action', ibid. 192–226; R. I. Levy, 'Emotion, Knowing, and Culture', in R. A. Shweder and R. A. LeVine (edd.), *Culture Theory: Essays on Mind, Self, and Emotion* (Cambridge 1984) 214–37, also R. C. Solomon, 'Getting Angry: The Jamesian Theory of Emotion in Anthropology', ibid. 238–54; H. Leventhal and K. Scherer, 'The Relationship of Emotion to Cognition: A Functional Approach to a Semantic Controversy', *Cognition and Emotion* 1/1 (1987) 3–28, also K. Oatley and P. N. Johnson-Laird, 'Towards a Cognitive Theory of Emotions', ibid. 29–50; Ortony *et al.*, *Cognitive Structure of Emotions*.

32. See Ortony *et al.*, *Cognitive Structure of Emotions*, 4.

33. See Lazarus *et al.*, 'Cognitive Theory', 218: my italics.

34. See primarily W. W. Fortenbaugh, *Aristotle on Emotion: A Contribution to Philosophical Psychology, Rhetoric, Poetics, Politics, and Ethics* (London 1975); and id., 'Aristotle's *Rhetoric* on Emotions', in J. Barnes, M. Schofield, R. Sorabji (edd.), *Articles on Aristotle, 4: Psychology and Aesthetics* (London 1979) 133–53; S. Halliwell, 'Pleasure, Understanding, and Emotion in Aristotle's *Poetics*', in A. O. Rorty (ed.), *Essays on Aristotle's Poetics* (Princeton 1992) 241–60, also J. Lear, 'Katharsis', ibid. 315–40; Belfiore, *Tragic Pleasures*, esp. ch. 7. For the implications of Aristotle's 'cognitivist' psychology for our understanding of classical dramatic audience-response, see further Lada, ' "Empathic Understanding" '.

35. Arist. *Rhet.* 1385ᵇ27: εὐλόγιστοι γάρ.

36. See *Rhet.* 1385ᵇ11–1386ᵇ7. For a brief discussion of the cognitive considerations involved in the generation of pity in Aristotle, see Nussbaum, 'Tragedy and Self-Sufficiency', 133–7.

37. See *Rhet.* 1382ª20–1383ª12.

38. Ibid. 1383ª6–7.

39. Cf. Halliwell, *Aristotle's Poetics*, who emphasizes that 'the relationship between Aristotle's understanding of emotions and the ordinary Greek conceptions of the same emotions is not an easy one to settle' (172).

40. See *Od.* 12. 37–52.

41. See ibid. 12. 188 (τερψάμενος νεῖται καὶ πλείονα εἰδώς, 'then goes on, well pleased, knowing more than ever he did'). This peculiar amalgam of *thelxis* with mental alertness and receptiveness can be exploited in a variety of performative and other contexts; consider e.g. Luc. *Salt.* 85; Timocles, fr. 6 K–A, 5–7; Gorgias *Hel.* 10.

42. See esp. *Med.* 16, 24 ff.

43. Ibid. 20–3, 33.
44. W. W. Fortenbaugh, 'On the Antecedents of Aristotle's Bipartite Psychology', *GRBS* 11 (1970) 243 n. 18.
45. 'Four Systems for Emotion Activation: Cognitive and Noncognitive Processes', *Psychological Review* 100/1 (1993) 86. Cf. Lazarus *et al.*, 'Emotions', 191; Izard *et al.*, *Emotions*, 33–4, 285–6; R. G. D' Andrade, 'Cultural Meaning Systems', in Shweder and Le Vine (edd.), *Culture Theory*, 98–101.
46. See esp. *Alc.* 144–5 and 940.
47. *Ant.* 1261–9.
48. See primarily *Rep.* 605b–d, 606a–d.
49. See further Lada, ' "Empathic Understanding" ', 121–2 (on Ar. *Thesm.* 846 ff. and Eur. *Bacch.* 912 ff.).
50. Brecht, *BT* 71.
51. Ibid. 143; cf. 60.
52. For a detailed argument, see Lada, ' "Weeping for Hecuba: Is it a "Brechtian" Act?', *Arethusa* (forthcoming, 1996).
53. See esp. Brecht, *MD* 27.
54. Cf. Jean-Jacques Rousseau's *Lettre à M. D' Alembert*, as in Rousseau, *Du contrat social et autres œuvres politiques*, introd. J. Ehrard (Paris 1975) 141.
55. Consider e.g. Andromache as manipulated by Menelaus/Hermione (Eur. *Andromache*), Megara as bullied by Lycus (Eur. *Heracles*), etc.
56. Cf. S. Goldhill, *The Poet's Voice: Essays on Poetics and Greek Literature* (Cambridge 1991) 188.
57. e.g. Odysseus in the Sophoclean *Philoctetes*, or Orestes in the plays wrought around his mythical persona. For a typology of plays revolving around ephebic themes, see J. J. Winkler, 'The Ephebes' Song: *Tragôidia* and *Polis*', *Representations* 11 (1985) 32–8.
58. Brecht, *BT* 15.
59. See Nussbaum, 'Tragedy and Self-Sufficiency', 144; cf. Nussbaum, *Fragility of Goodness*, 390–1.

23

Tragic Last Words: The Big Speech and the Lament in Ancient Greek and Modern Irish Tragic Drama

FIONA MACINTOSH

More, perhaps, has been written about tragedy than about any other dramatic form, and yet two of the mainstays of tragic drama—the big speech and the lament—have received relatively little attention. This is surprising not least because death, even if it does not always constitute 'the necessary action', is always present as 'a necessary actor' in tragic drama.[1] And death as 'action' and death as 'actor' receives, of course, its fullest articulation through the big speech and the lament respectively. This paper will demonstrate, with comparative evidence drawn from Greek tragedy and modern Irish tragic drama, that a consideration of the last words uttered by both the dying characters and the chief mourners alike must be central to any discussion concerning the effect of tragedy.

It might seem surprising to compare the Greek tragedies with Irish plays written some two and a half thousand years later, but there are a number of reasons that make such a comparison both valuable and instructive. First, the mythical material which forms the basis for many Irish tragedies written during the Irish Literary Revival, and indeed many aspects of rural life at the time they were written, reflect a strong traditional outlook which makes such a comparison useful. Secondly, the writers of the Irish tragedies— notably W. B. Yeats and J. M. Synge—explicitly turned to the Greek tragedians as exempla in their attempt to found a national theatre. And the Irish hero Cuchulain was regularly compared to Heracles and Achilles by Celtic scholars no less than by the playwrights themselves. But the benefit of the comparison works, I hope to show, in both directions, throwing light on the ancient texts as well as providing insight into the complex interrelationships of text and audience.[2]

The close connections between mourner and mourned in societies where elaborate death-rituals are required to usher the dead from this world to the next have long been noted by structural anthropologists. The suspension of normal activity that is demanded of the mourners during the course of the burial rites indicates that the living are understood to share to a very considerable extent in the transitional state to which the dead relative is temporarily confined. The Greek mourning gestures such as the ritual cutting of the hair are performed, as Aristotle explained, in 'homoeopathy' with the deceased.[3] And according to Synge, in his account of life on the Aran Islands, the Irish keen not only provides an outlet for personal grief, it is the medium through which the mourner can communicate with the dead. Synge writes:

Each old woman, as she took her turn in the leading recitative, seemed possessed for the moment with a profound ecstasy of grief, swaying to and fro, and bending her forehead to the stone before her, while she called out to the dead with a perpetually recurring chant of sobs.[4]

We will find that these parallels between mourner and mourned that are reflected in everyday Greek and Irish death-rituals are strikingly re-enacted in the plays through the parallels between the big speech and the lament.

The process of the characters' death begins early in the tragedies—indeed, it could be maintained that the cost of tragic status is exclusion from the full process of living. During the course of the big speech, it becomes clear that the dying characters have only the most tenuous of links with their immediate surroundings; it is as if they already occupied the liminal world beyond the world of the living that the chief mourners themselves are understood to occupy during the course of the burial rites.

There is a very real sense in which the formal features of the big speeches serve to make them intrinsically separate from the action proper. Time in these interludes is qualitatively different from the linear logic normally associated with the episodes, and much closer to the timelessness characteristic of the choral odes of Greek tragedy. The action is very often frozen in the background whilst the preoccupations of the dying character dominate the scene.

Sophocles' *Antigone* offers a striking example of how the last

words of a character doomed to die are spoken beyond the confines
of the dramatic present. As David Bain has pointed out,[5] Creon
enters at line 883 and orders Antigone's immediate dispatch; but
his order is ignored during the course of Antigone's penultimate
speech (891–28) until it is repeated with renewed vehemence some
fifty lines later (931). Antigone's penultimate speech contains some
notoriously disputed lines (904–20); and although the tendency
today is to accept them as authentic, even if one were to follow earlier commentators and excise them as an interpolation,[6] there are
some twenty or so lines between the impetuous tyrant's first order
and his second intervention. There is no logical explanation for
Creon's uncharacteristic reticence: it is artistic licence that curbs
the tyrant, and Bain is clearly correct to see this episode as a freezing of the action. It is most probable that Antigone's words
(891–928), which are in iambic trimeters and anapaests, are delivered from a fixed position somewhere in the *orchêstra*; and Creon's
threats to the guards (931–2) refer to the slow, and undoubtedly
reluctant, march that begins with the choral anapaests of the previous two lines. In a play in which absence of movement is clearly
associated with fixity of purpose, it is highly appropriate that the
freezing of the action should accompany the boldest statement of
that fixity. Antigone's last words are foregrounded here by being
uttered both within and without the dramatic present.

There is a similar example in Euripides' *Trojan Women*, where
almost an entire scene of 'last words' is permitted despite the
apparent urgency of the character entrusted with the task of trans-
porting the victim to her 'death' (294–461).[7] Talthybius orders his
attendants to fetch Cassandra immediately (294–6); he renews his
order some 120 lines later (419–20), but this is apparently ignored
for a further twenty lines (until 445), when Cassandra pronounces
her own departure and demonstrates her full acceptance of her fate
by her symbolic discarding of Apollo's wreaths (451–4). Some
sixty lines have elapsed since the first order was issued, and in the
interim Cassandra has dominated the scene.

The extraordinary power of this interlude derives in large measure from the marked shifts in register and tempo. The vibrant
energy of Cassandra—her untameable, supra-human presence—is
conveyed through the variety of modes of expression: the wild
rhythms of the dochmiac metre which accompany her maniacal
travesty of the hymeneal (310–41); the iambic trimeters in which

she prophesies the destruction at Argos and lucidly argues that the victim rather than the victor has better fortune on this occasion (353–64); and, finally, the recitative trochaics which contain her passionate disavowal of Apollo (444–61). The cumulative effect of the various modes of expression is to convince the audience, at least during her presence on the stage, of the strength of her arguments. As with the big speeches in the *Alcestis* (244–392), the interplay between lyric and spoken metres makes the dramatic time in this episode qualitatively different from that normally associated with the linear logic of other episodes. Cassandra's last words acquire an expressionistic force that sets them apart from the action proper.

In the Irish plays too we find that various formal features are employed which set the last words of the dying characters apart from other utterances. In Yeats's *The Death of Cuchulain*, for example, Cuchulain's last words are contained in discrete episodes that have been compared to the dream sequences associated with the Expressionist plays of Ernst Toller.[8] But they are also frozen tableaux of the kind associated with the big speech in general. In Synge's *Deirdre of the Sorrows*, it has been noted that some of Deirdre's speeches bear a strong resemblance to 'arias [where] the movement of the plot is suspended to allow a lyrical outpouring of feeling in which pain is taken up into melody and beauty'.[9] These frozen tableaux, which are particularly evident towards the end of Synge's play, are also found in his sources; and Synge's version is the only one of the various treatments of the Deirdre legend during the Irish Literary Revival to enjoy an intimate relationship with the original saga-material.[10] It is, without doubt, Synge's adoption and adaptation of certain highly stylized set speeches from the original that make Deirdre sound surprisingly similar to her Greek counterparts on the verge of death.

Deirdre's lament over the brother's corpses—the prelude to her big speech—begins with a freezing of the action that recalls the *kommos* of the *Antigone* and the threnodic hymeneal in the *Trojan Women*. In her speech, the linear logic of the dramatic present is subsumed by a rhythmical ebb and flow of the syntax, whose circularity is reinforced by the swaying of her body. Deirdre begins:

It's you three will not see age or death coming, you that were my company when the fires on the hill-tops were put out and the stars were our friends only. I'll turn my thoughts back from this night—that's pitiful for want of pity—to the time it was your rods and cloaks made a little tent for me

where there'd be a birch tree making shelter, and a dry stone: though from
this day my own fingers will be making a tent for me, spreading out my
hairs and they knotted with the rain.[11]

The use of repetition and echo, the lateral (as opposed to sequential) thought-patterns, together with the typical Hiberno-English
features—the suppression of the relative pronoun and the dependence on continuous forms—combine to arrest the linear flow of
action and to establish the plangent tone and tempo of the final part
of the play.[12]

It is not simply, however, that the formal features of the big
speech effect a serious disruption in the immediate action as they
usher a new temporality into the scene. It is also that the attitudes
adopted by the characters in the face of death serve to heighten the
sense of displacement that the formal features of the scene have
already generated.

Whilst the contents of the last words have traditionally been
considered special, tragic last words are rarely profound or immediately consolatory; more often than not, the truths they contain
are of the most perfunctory kind. In Greek tragedy, in particular,
the formulaic ring to the last words—where the conventional
farewell to the light is couched in strikingly similar language across
the plays[13]—means that the contents of these words are not themselves of intrinsic interest. Paradoxically, what makes the last
words in tragedy interesting is the speakers' apparent inability to
come up with anything new: different characters with (otherwise)
different outlooks—and, moreover, from different cultural backgrounds—express astonishingly similar sentiments before their
exits for death. In this sense, tragedy makes the exit for death the
individual's own merely in name.

The dying characters in both the Greek and Irish plays frequently turn away from their immediate surroundings in order to
address the environment.[14] This is far more than mere pathetic fallacy: it is a sign of a radical reorientation towards the world
whereby the concept of 'home' has been displaced and extended to
include the whole sphere of organic life. There is a concomitant
personification of objects which serves as the dramatic correlative
to the characters' psychological isolation: so Ajax's sword becomes
both his friend and enemy;[15] Cassandra's fillet and wreaths
become incarnations of Apollo himself;[16] and wives, isolated from

their husbands on the threshold of death, invoke the marriage bed instead.[17] That the characters occupy a liminal space is clearly evidenced by the imagined audience: it is the dead themselves to whom their words are commonly addressed, not their living auditors.[18]

The most concrete enactment, however, of the characters' absence from the immediate environment in the final speeches is their use of the third person to refer to themselves. In the Greek tragedies, this marked fissure between mind and body—in which the self is viewed as both subject (*psuchê*) and object (body) simultaneously—has nothing to do with the so-called primitive fragmented consciousness that Snell identified in the Homeric poems.[19] Instead, the use of the third-person self-address in the big speech is, I suggest, the linguistic equivalent of the separation of *psuchê* and body at the point of death. As the *psuchê* in Homer is barely thought of when the individual is alive and well,[20] so the *psuchê* only becomes prominent in tragedy when the character is on the threshold of death.

Heracles in the *Trachiniae*, for example, displays the hyperconsciousness of self that is characteristic of the dying character of tragedy when he views himself as the object, rather than the subject, of suffering at the end of Sophocles' play: παῦλά τοι κακῶν | αὕτη, τελευτὴ τοῦδε τἀνδρὸς ὑστάτη, 'This is rest indeed from evils, the final end of this man' (1255–6). He directs his final words to his *psuchê* (1259–63), ordering it to overpower his body with brute force: it is to provide a bit of steel to muzzle his cries (χάλυβος . . . στόμιον, 1262–3). With the personification of the *psuchê*, and the reification of it through the vivid image of the steel bit, we have a powerful illustration of Heracles' passage to another sphere: the *psuchê* is now in charge, and it is the *psuchê* that will carry out the joyful, though enforced, task of definitive separation in death (1262–3).

The hyperconsciousness of self that the characters display on the threshold of death in the plays of Synge and Yeats is clearly related to the attainment of full mythical status that comes with death. Deirdre in Synge's play, for example, does not merely witness herself in the throes of performing the duties of chief mourner for her dead lover, she also foresees herself as an affective focus in the future ('But who'll pity Deirdre has lost the lips of Naisi from her neck, and from her cheek forever.')[21] In Yeats's *The Death of*

Cuchulain, the obliqueness of Cuchulain's perspective on himself is so marked that we are offered a kind of posthumous re-enactment of his final moments. Cuchulain observes:

> There floats out there
> The shape that I shall take when I am dead,
> My soul's first shape, a soft feathery shape,
> And is not that a strange shape for the soul
> Of a great fighting man?[22]

When we turn to the laments, we find formal features that distinguish these interludes even more sharply from other utterances in the plays. Whilst the Greek laments very often culminate in song and may well be accompanied by highly formalized movement (often a funeral procession) involving the chief mourners and the chorus as well, the Irish laments adopt a highly stylized idiom and incantatory rhythms (or, in the case of Yeats's *The Death of Cuchulain*, a dance) to express the heightened emotions of the scene.

The chief mourners in both the Greek and Irish plays display a distracted air that recalls the dying characters' own abstraction from their immediate surroundings during the course of the big speech. Whilst the mourners might not share the dying characters' attendant attachment to the environment, they do share with them a preference for dead or immortal (as opposed to living) interlocutors. And the deployment of stage properties to represent absent loved ones during the course of many laments is strongly reminiscent of the personified objects upon which the dying characters themselves depend. In Aeschylus' *Choephori*, for example, the tomb of Agamemnon that is situated in the *orchêstra* is the focus of the action during the first part of the play (1–652). And although the incantatory invocation of Agamemnon over his tomb marks the first step in Electra's and Orestes' arduous passage back into ordinary society (315 ff.), the use of a stage property as another actor in the immediate action is a powerful means of underlining the chief mourners' alienation. When the object deployed is portable—as is the urn containing the ashes of the supposedly dead Orestes in Sophocles' *Electra* (1126 ff.), or Hector's shield in the *Trojan Women* (1194 ff.)—it elicits a powerful and deeply poignant evocation of the deceased that makes the mourner's dual perspective even more acute. And sometimes—as with Michael's clothes in

Synge's *Riders to the Sea*[23]—the stage property is handled with a deeper, suprapersonal awareness that the object itself embodies more of the dead person than the absent, and thoroughly mangled, corpse ever could. Furthermore, if the most concrete enactment of the dying characters' absence from the immediate surroundings is their oblique perspective on their earthly selves, it receives a striking parallel in the mourners' similarly heightened perspective on reality, which affords shifts from personal to general, and finally to universal, considerations in quick and easy succession.

I would like to look at an Irish lament in some detail—the lament of Juno Boyle at the end of Sean O'Casey's *Juno and the Paycock*—because it is a particularly illustrative example. It contains many typical features of the lament in general, including both the bereaved mother's traditional memory of the pangs suffered in childbirth as she is forced to endure the far worse pains of having to bury her offspring, and the common realization that death entails a terrifying loss of individuality. But what makes this particular lament representative is not so much its content as its highly allusive style.

In order to understand the significance of Juno's lament, it is important to consider the earlier lament by Mrs Tancred which occurs in the middle of Act II. When Mrs Tancred and her fellow mourners loom out from the dismal hallway and stand on the threshold of the Boyles's living-room, it is not simply the party that is interrupted; the action too is suspended as the music-hall turns give way to an interlude in which the framework of the traditional antiphonal lament is clearly discernible. At the climax of the lament for her die-hard Republican son who has been killed in an ambush, Mrs Tancred invites us to see her lament as a mirror image in political terms, and an echo in personal terms, of an earlier lament intoned by another mother whose son died as a Free-State soldier. Death has not only levelled out any differences between the two sons, it has united them as well. It is not, however, simply the connections between these two laments that are notable here; other associations are also called to mind as Mrs Tancred's accusatory prayer

O Blessed virgin, where were you when me darlin' son was riddled with bullets, when me darlin' son was riddled with bullets![24]

reproduces both the words and cadences of Shelley's elegy for Keats when the poet demands,

> Where wert thou, mighty Mother, when he lay,
> When thy son lay, pierced by the shaft which flies
> In darkness?[25]

The rhythms and sentiments of the King James Bible are also
caught in her final plea:

Sacred Heart of the Crucified Jesus, take away our hearts o' stone . . . an'
give us hearts o' flesh! . . . Take away this murdherin' hate . . . an' give us
Thine own eternal love![26]

When Juno Boyle delivers her own lament for her dead son
towards the end of Act III, before she makes her final exit with her
daughter, her lengthy monologue moves away from a vernacular to
a highly ritualized idiom. And just as Mrs Tancred's lament is
made up of a dense tissue of allusions to other utterances, and to
previous threnodic utterances in particular, Juno's own lament
reproduces not only the sentiments already expressed by Mrs
Tancred but the identical words as well:

Maybe I didn't feel sorry enough for Mrs Tancred when her poor son was
found as Johnny's been found now—because he was a Die-hard! Ah, why
didn't I remember that then he wasn't a Diehard [*sic*] or a Stater, but only
a poor dead son! It's well I remember all that she said—an' it's my turn to
say it now: What was the pain I suffered, Johnny, bringin' you into the
world to carry you to your cradle, to the pains I'll suffer carryin' you out
o' the world to bring you to your grave! Mother o' God, Mother o' God,
have pity on us all! Blessed virgin, where were you when me darlin' son
was riddled with bullets? Sacred Heart o' Jesus, take away our hearts o'
stone, and give us hearts o' flesh! Take away this murdherin' hate, an' give
us Thine own eternal love![27]

It has already been noted that the self-conscious echo is an effective means of aligning Juno with Mrs Tancred, and in turn with all
bereaved mothers, including the Blessed Mother herself.
However, the content of the speeches has not always met with the
same commendation: the reliance on biblical and literary allusions,
it has been alleged,[28] is simply a cheap theatrical contrivance
designed to elevate subjects and subject-matter that are otherwise
unworthy of such elevation. But these criticisms seem to overlook
a vital point. By remembering all that Mrs Tancred and others
have said before her, O'Casey's character is evocatively aligned
with other mourners; and indeed in adopting such a highly allusive

mode of address, Juno Boyle might be appropriately termed *the* archetypal mourner.

Like Juno's lament in O'Casey's play, all tragic laments are, in the strictest sense, never entirely the property of one individual. For the lament in tragedy remains the collective response that it is recognized to be in Homer, and that it continued to be until late in the nineteenth century in Ireland. The hallmark of the lament is its allusiveness: its allusiveness in relation to earlier laments, and equally, and especially (as we have seen), its allusiveness in relation to the big speech.

Therefore, what is most distinctive (and indeed most noteworthy) about the last words in general is not their uniqueness, but their highly stylized nature, both in terms of form and content. The stylization of the big speech and the lament, I suggest, grants the speakers access to a shared inheritance that is recognized by the members of the audience no less than by the dramatic characters themselves. It is not simply that particular pains have been absorbed into the generality of human suffering, but that the audience respond to the repetitions and allusions with pleasure.

Dionysiac truths, as Nietzsche maintains in *The Birth of Tragedy*, are only made bearable if the Apolline pleasure in patterning is satisfied at the same time.[29] In Book I of the *Rhetoric*, Aristotle reminds us that lamentation and mourning involve pleasure as well as pain because they include the pleasurable experience of recalling an absent loved one. And in the *Poetics*, he maintains that the pleasure derived from *mimêsis* is essentially a joy in recognition and learning.[30] For Freud, studies in children's play-patterns reveal that repetition is *per se* an intensely pleasurable activity.[31] And even in our day, when novelty has such a high premium, the delight obtained from watching a film for the tenth time would suggest that repetition and recognition are still felt to be inherently pleasurable.

Repetition, recall and recognition: these three intrinsically pleasurable activities—pleasurable, one must stress, for both participant and spectator—must be central to any discussion of the big speech and the tragic lament. The characters repeat and echo words and gestures that others have made before them, and will, we trust, make after them; whilst the audience, for their part, recall and recognize those repetitions and echoes, and derive considerable pleasure from them. For as Ronald Gaskell reminds us:

Repetitions of phrase and gesture suggest that experience has, if not any meaning that we can formulate, at all events a pattern to which we can assent: our lives are ordered, not random.[32]

In this sense, I suggest, the big speech and the lament are more than incidentals: they constitute the hallmarks of tragic drama and provide a key to that thorny paradox, 'tragic pleasure'.

Notes

This paper makes use of material published in my book *Dying Acts* (see n. 2 below). I am grateful to my publishers, Cork University Press, for permission to reuse it here.

1. So R. Williams, *Modern Tragedy*, rev. edn. (London 1979) 58.
2. For an extensive comparative study, see F. Macintosh, *Dying Acts: Death in Ancient Greek and Modern Irish Tragic Drama* (Cork 1994).
3. Arist. fr. 101 Rose *ap*. Ath. 675a. See R. Parker, *Miasma* (Oxford 1983) 64.
4. Synge, *Collected Works*, ii: *Prose*, 74.
5. D. Bain, *Masters, Servants and Orders in Greek Tragedy* (Manchester 1982) 25.
6. For a recent discussion, see Neuburg, 'How Like a Woman'. Cf. R. C. Jebb, *Sophocles: Antigone*[3] (Cambridge 1900), ad loc. See further Foley, in this volume, pp. 52–8.
7. Cassandra's exit here is analogous to other exits for death because her passage to Argos is, of course, a journey to death.
8. R. A. Cave, *Yeats's Late Plays: 'A High Grave Dignity and Strangeness'* [= *Brit. Acad. Proc.* 68 (1982) 299–327] (Oxford 1982) 320–2.
9. K. Worth, *The Irish Drama of Europe from Yeats to Beckett* (London 1978) 125.
10. Synge made a translation of the 18th-cent. version of the Deirdre story by Andrew MacCuirtin. See D. Kiberd, *Synge and the Irish Language*[2] (Dublin 1993) 176–95.
11. Synge, *Plays II* 261.
12. Ibid. 261–9.
13. See the Aristophanic parody in the *Acharnians*: ὦ κλεινὸν ὄμμα νῦν πανύστατόν σ' ἰδών | λείπω φάος γε τοὐμόν, οὐκέτ' εἰμ' ἐγώ ('O Eye of glory, now having looked my last on thee I leave the light—of my life. I am no more', 1184–5). This contains the three recurrent words—πανύστατόν, φάος, οὐκέτι—which are generally found in close conjunction, although sometimes in slightly modified form, in all the 'big speeches'.
14. E.g. Aesch. *Ag.* 1157–61; Soph. *Aj.* 412–27, 859–63, *Ant.* 844–6, 891–2, 937; Eur. *Alc.* 244–5, 248–9, *Hipp.* 672, *Tro.* 458, 1277–80.

15. Soph. *Aj.* 815–22, cf. 678–83.
16. Aesch. *Ag.* 1264–8, esp. 1269–70, when Apollo becomes the force who tears the trappings from her body; and Eur. *Tro.* 453–4.
17. Soph. *Trach.* 920–2, cf. *OT* 1242–3, 1249; Eur. *Alc.* 177–82.
18. Aesch. *Ag.* 1305; Soph. *Ant.* 869–71, 897–904; Eur. *Tro.* 459–60, cf. *Alc.* 263, 266 (addressed not to the dead, but to Hades or his agents).
19. Snell, *Discovery of the Mind*, 1–21.
20. J. Bremmer, *The Early Greek Concept of the Soul* (Princeton 1983) 74–5.
21. Synge, *Plays II*, 257–9.
22. W. B. Yeats, *The Collected Plays* (London 1952) 702.
23. Synge, *Plays I*, 25.
24. O'Casey, *Complete Plays*, i. 55.
25. *Adonais*, 2 (l. 10).
26. O'Casey, *Plays*, i. 55. Cf. Ezek. 11: 19, 'And I will give them one heart, and I will put a new spirit within you; and I will take the stony heart out of their flesh, and will give them an heart of flesh.'
27. O'Casey, *Plays*, i. 87.
28. By e.g. R. Ayling, *Continuity and Innovation in Sean O'Casey's Drama* (Salzburg 1976) 96; and cf. S. Deane, 'Irish Politics and O'Casey's Theatre', *Threshold* 24 (1973) 5–16.
29. Nietzsche, *Birth of Tragedy*, §§1–14.
30. Arist. *Rhet.* 1. 11. 11 ff., *Poet.* 1448^{b}12–19.
31. S. Freud, *Beyond the Pleasure Principle*, trans. J. Strachey, *The Standard Edition* (London 1955) xviii. 14–17.
32. R. Gaskell, *Drama and Reality: The European Theatre since Ibsen* (London 1972) 104.

24

Dramatic Scapegoating: On the Uses and Abuses of Girard and Shakespearean Criticism

ROBIN N. MITCHELL-BOYASK

> Ich studiere wieder die Geschichte der Revolution. Ich fühlte
> mich wie zernichtet unter dem grässlichen Fatalismus der
> Geschichte. Ich finde in der Menschennatur eine entsetzliche
> Gleichheit, in den menschlichen Verhältnissen eine unab-
> wendbare Gewalt, Allen und Keinem verliehen.
>
> I am studying the history of the Revolution again. Under the
> horrible fatalism of history I felt as if I was destroyed. In
> human nature I find a dreadful sameness, in human relations
> an irrevocable power—bequeathed to all and none!
>
> (Georg Büchner)[1]

In recent years comparative approaches have enriched the study of
Greek drama, but the increasing congruity of Renaissance and
Hellenic studies might surprise many classicists. Proponents of the
'New Historicism' would recognize how the stimulating collection
Nothing to Do with Dionysos?[2] also investigates what Stephen
Greenblatt calls 'the circulation of social energy',[3] the societal
forces engaged by the text. The two fields have been adopting ever
more similar interpretive strategies as part of a more general movement to recontextualize literarary studies in history. While scholars of Renaissance culture have been trying to disabuse us of
reading Shakespeare with our own cultural assumptions, and thus
assuming the characters are just like us, classicists might now recall
with irony John Jones's warnings thirty years ago about treating
Oedipus like Hamlet, which dissolved the perceived kinship
between our two major bodies of tragic drama.[4] Now we discover
that not only is Oedipus not Hamlet, but Hamlet isn't Hamlet
either. I hope that recognizing the dangers of reading Greek alongside Shakespearean tragedy can allow us again to build bridges
between Renaissance and Greek drama, for, as one recent critic

observes, 'tragedy demands comparison'.[5]

Here I shall bring together the ideas of two theorists, René Girard and Kenneth Burke, whose work has also involved Shakespeare and Greek drama, and a theoretically inclined Shakespearean, Harry Berger, to approach Greek tragedy by stressing the ethical and psychological implications of the loss of character-differentiation in drama. Each Greek tragedian, as Girard observes of Shakespeare, 'in the portrayal of certain characters seems to oscillate between two opposite, really incompatible poles. On the one hand he makes these characters quite distinctive, especially as "villains"; on the other hand he shows these same characters behaving and thinking exactly like their antagonists.' 'The dynamics of human conflict, the reciprocity of retribution and revenge,' Girard argues, lead to *un*differentiation.[6] Great theatre is thus a play of differentiation and undifferentiation.

Homologous with this dramatic process is what Girard calls the 'sacrificial crisis'.[7] Over the last twenty years, Girard, most notably in *Violence and the Sacred*, has demonstrated the tension between culture as a structure of differentiation and the moments of instability when humans oppose one another, a conflict generated from what Girard has termed 'mimetic desire' in which 'the subject desires the object because the rival desires it'.[8] During rivalry, the imitation of the other's desire destroys the differences among individuals, heightening antagonisms, creating a mechanistic monstrosity feeding on itself until a scapegoat is found to recreate difference in self and community by assigning blame arbitrarily to one person. Sacrifice generates difference. Because the sacrificial crisis is the loss of distinctions, and Girard often uses 'sacrifice' in the context of cultural order in general, it can denote more than literal sacrifice in Girard's work. Scapegoating is thus the structuring mechanism of civilization, but its efficacy depends on its participants deceiving themselves about its true nature. Myth and literature often present this phenomenon in concealed form, but tragedy, which questions its society's structures, actually discloses, albeit partially, the arbitrary nature of victimage, while in the Gospels victimage is disclosed more completely.

Despite a notorious controversy over Girard, some classicists, following Girard's own use of Greek tragedy, have evoked some of his ideas, but usually without any sustained development. Still others have attacked Girard savagely, in arguments evoking the wider controversy, either for his sweeping anthropological claims, the eschatological ambitions of his thought, or his loose approach to Greek texts.[9] Girard repeatedly asserts the universality of the scapegoat phenomenon, the efficacy of his theory to explain all cultural phenomena, and the historical reality of the collective murder at the beginning of human society. The anthropological and historical arguments are beyond this essay's scope, but I shall provide a response to the concerns about his reading of Greek tragedy. Briefly, as Livingston observes, Girard's claims that the Gospel uniquely reveals victimage, and his insistence on the original scapegoat's historical reality, are logically separate from the theories of mimetic desire and scapegoating. Similarly, as Griffiths argues, Girard's ideas would not have surprised the Greeks, as Girard claims, because tragedy betrays an awareness of surrogacy and because institutions resembling scapegoating, such as the *pharmakos*, existed in Greece and were reflected in Greek tragedy.[10] I propose to develop Girard's theories as a heuristic practice for understanding the dynamics of Greek tragedy, but by looking beyond the more spectacularly overstated *Violence and the Sacred*, his most (in)famous work, whose flaws Girard himself has subsequently admitted. While maintaining that work's stress on mimetic desire and violence's societal function, I emphasize his later essays on Shakespeare, which develop his theories in readings of specific texts, thus shifting the focus from anthropology back to literature.[11] Girard can be an outstanding reader of texts, and his own readings, which usually become lost in the controversies over his sweeping theories, can point the way towards a more rigorous Girardian study of Greek drama.

Mimetic desire and scapegoating serve to structure drama, which, as Aristotle was the first to observe, represents human beings in action. To avoid both the rather dry analyses of Aristotle's descendants and the excessively character-based studies focusing on Hamlet's dietary habits, one needs to keep both character and action in mind: tragedy is about what happens to characters and how they respond. *Muthos* is unintelligible without *êthos*. The pressure a tragic plot exerts on characters changes them into their opponents, thus erasing the identity that initially marks them as 'good' or 'bad'. Girard argues that tragic violence symmetrically eliminates differences between good and evil. This loss destabilizes both stage and theatre, and leads to scapegoating, which occurs not just within the stage community, but between stage and audience. Everyone becomes equally guilty of this violence, but only one is blamed, the tragic protagonist. Departing from Girard, I would argue that because the characters in a play engage our sympathy once they have become scapegoats, the play reveals the reality of victimage. The disaster incurred by this subversion of the hero's identity arouses pity, which in turn restores the hero's identity, thus allowing for a more general restoration of communal order. The hero can emerge from the ordeal as himself again, but only because he has become the scapegoat who attracts the violence of the play's community.

Any attempt to restore character in a specific sense to the study of drama must confront John Jones's criticisms of earlier discussions of Greek tragedy that were influenced by A. C. Bradley's type of character analysis. For all the Hegelian affinities of Bradley's own thinking, his and other analyses tended to look back to Goethe and Coleridge in treating literary figures like people with lives outside what is pertinent to the text. Bradleyan analysis imposed such a conception of character onto Greek drama, where, however, action, not psychology, matters most. Since Girard questions the basis of human subjectivity, his ideas avoid naïvely projecting casual notions of the modern self back on to Sophocles. And since Shakespearean critics have revised the relationship between character and action, it might be useful to consider the applicability of a modified character-in-action approach to Greek tragedy. Despite the different psychological frameworks of Greek and Renaissance drama, perhaps certain overarching, shared qualities to character interaction, self-presentation, and patterns of action provide legitimate grounds for comparison. This approach avoids the earlier problems because it examines not an individual character, but the character's function in, and relation to, the whole text. Allowing for cultural differences, the character's behaviour must make sense in terms of his or her circumstances, which include both the culture that produces the drama and the play's specific setting: Clytemnestra should not be assimilated to Lady Macbeth, because fifth-century Athens differs enough from sixteenth-century England to demand dissimilar responses to the two characters. However, with these differences in mind, we can turn to an informed consideration of similarities. Even Aeschylean

drama—where psychology is subordinate to action—foregrounds
the motivation for, and the circumstances of, an action as much as
the action itself.[12] And by not restricting analysis to a single character, we can attend also to the dramatic community's psychology
or ethos.

This approach, emphasizing character as a member and function
of community, derives from Harry Berger's studies of the complexities of relationships among characters, and of language's role
in representing these relationships in Shakespeare.[13] Berger delin-
eates two main differences between his character-and-action
approach and Bradley's, which I shall briefly summarize, showing
also their pertinence for Greek tragedy.

In the first place, Berger stresses the relationships between characters and how certain psychological or ethical themes express
these interactions. Berger sees significance not in the number of
Lady Macbeth's children, but in how their absence affects her
relationship with Macbeth 'as it reveals or betrays itself in the language they speak'. Because the Macbeths' marriage antedates the
play's action, their words thrust us into the middle of two lives and
one relationship that are about to change very suddenly, and so 'we
are expected to assume, and so to reconstruct, a generalized past as
the locus of stable or settled relationships'.[14] Similarly, in
Euripides' *Hippolytus*,[15] Phaedra's marriage to Theseus and passion for Hippolytus both precede the play's action. Understanding
Phaedra depends on knowing (*a*) how Greek drama and myth con-
ventionally represent women, (*b*) Greek marriage-custom, and (*c*)
what to reconstruct from what she and Aphrodite tell us. Although
Aphrodite's announced need for revenge causes Phaedra's desire
for Hippolytus, we remain partly in the nurse's position in trying
to determine exactly what Phaedra's crazed desires mean and how
they affect the drama's human dynamics. Hippolytus emphasizes
his sexual purity, his illegitimacy, and the loss of his mother, but
the text does not connect the three for us as determining his behaviour during the play. Thus, the play exerts an interpretive pressure
on its audience to construe this character from the information the
text provides. Similarly, in Sophocles' *Ajax*, the anxiety the mere
thought of Telamon produces in Ajax and Teucer entails consideration of his role in their selves and actions. Greek drama so frequently mentions family structures and histories that a text's
coherence requires us to consider how events antedating a play

determine the actions in it and the characters' reactions to them. A character, the locus of a set of cultural roles, myths, and traditions, depends on other characters for intelligibility. Therefore, one examines psychological and ethical forms of action not in an individual character but in the play's community, which Berger defines as

a group of speakers placed in relation to each other by differences of gender and generation, of social rank and political status, and positions in households, families and extended families. Their interactions are mediated by these roles, their attitudes and projects heavily influenced by the assumptions and expectations, the constraints and opportunities that adhere to the roles.[16]

Berger's stress on the individual as a function of the whole recalls Jones's argument that 'there is something wrong in our critical isolation of the protagonists, and something wrong with our sealing-off of the principal figures . . . from the lyric commentary they live in'.[17]

In the *Hippolytus* the even distribution of parts stresses the agents' interactions, on which the pressure of the past and of structured social relationships weighs heavily. Hippolytus is a hero's son, a frequently problematic type of relationship in Greek myth, and his self-consciousness about his illegitimacy and his Amazon mother help determine his behaviour towards his father, and the way we read or expect such actions. This information is all in the text. Greek drama uses myth, which socially encodes the roles and expectations of its agents, and tragedy arises in the violation of these structures.

Berger's other significant argument about character centres on the fact that the language the characters speak provides our access to these considerations of self and community, but it often suggests more than the characters realize about their actions and psychology. Berger calls this process 'redistributing complexities,' the way the play's language 'carries the burden of redistribution'. Generally, characters enter displaying their particular ethical affiliation, after which two things may occur. 'The characters may shift position on the ethical spectrum; and the play may offer the audience a model of the ethical range that differs from any particular character's version of it.'[18]

Let us take these two points separately. (*a*) Characters change in some way; otherwise there would, quite simply, be no action, since the driving force of the tragic action—that is, of the shifts in ethical affiliation—is mimetic desire. Clytemnestra's murder of Agamemnon takes the form of a perversion of sacrifice similar to Iphigenia's death, thus imitating Agamemnon's violent behaviour.[19] The long-suffering Hecuba responds to her innocent children's deaths by killing other innocent children. These characters hold our interest to the extent of our sympathy or antipathy towards them or to the extent that our sympathies change. (*b*) Characters do not see the ethical poles between which they move, nor realize the meaning of what they say. A drama presents a range of words, phrases, and values that the characters attempt to seize as their own for self-definition, but that ultimately indicate primarily their mimesis of each other, their lack of identity. Hippolytus and Phaedra both lay claim to *sôphrosunê* ('control of passion') while denying it to the other in ways that decidedly deny its existence in themselves, and Creon and Antigone symmetrically assert their visions of *nomos* ('law') and *dikê* ('justice'). In both tragedies the attempt to assert difference leads to similarity. Berger calls this 'structural irony': 'a character intends to communicate one message, but his language, speaking through him and in spite of his effort to control it, conveys another which he didn't intend'.[20] Differing from intentional irony, where characters say one thing and mean another, in structural irony characters mean one thing and say another. Structural irony indicates how characters' positions as speaking subjects change in relation to their community. Hippolytus intends his language to be moderate, controlled, and pious, but it continually signifies excess and impiety. In Euripides' *Hecuba*, Polyxena's speech at her sacrifice proclaims the admirable preference for dying well and gloriously to living a base life of slavery, while simultaneously valorizing the same warrior-ethos that kills her. Language determines the relation of one character to another, of one character to itself and to the community, and also to the audience. When characters' language says something other than what they mean, we perceive purposes, qualities, and meanings that cast them in a different, often less favourable, light.

Such reinterpretation necessarily requires us to pass judgement. Critics like Richard Levin accordingly object to this 'ironic' approach because it engages in 'character assassination,' as cynical readers, imposing their suspicions on the text, vilify noble characters.[21] Berger, for example, elicits some dissonant aspects in Cordelia's self-presentation, such as 'her persistent habit of publishing her unpublished virtues'.[22] While Berger rightly corrects, I think, the tendency to damn exclusively Goneril and Regan and praise Cordelia, a judgemental tone does sometimes creep into his language, and latterly he admits this. Berger's consequent correction re-emphasizes the dramatic community, and he argues that the reader should avoid judging the characters because, while they act as accomplices to their own fates, the real trial involves the community at large and its ability to endure evil and suffering. And since the process of judgement occurs inside both the play and the theatre, that community ultimately includes us. By presenting agents who continually shift all over its ethical spectrum, Euripides' *Hecuba* forces these characters, the original audience, and us to confront wrenching questions about human identity and to judge the characters themselves. Beyond the stage community, tragedy tests *our* willingness to become accomplices in scapegoating. The stories 'good' and 'bad' characters tell about themselves may differ from their community's reality and require a process of judgement embedded in Greek drama's social function. Since, as Ober and Strauss observe, 'like legal trials and assembly speeches, Athenian theatrical performances and dramatic texts were closely bound up in the mediation of conflicting social values', and since the spatial organization for the mass assemblies in Athens, the Pnyx, and the theatre of Dionysus resembled one another,[23] Greek tragedy continually forced the audience into the position of judges deciding proper and improper behaviour in plays that problematized such questions.

Tragedy levels differences, destroying indifferently both good and bad, making good people act in bad ways through mimesis. It is not character assassination to locate 'the tragic' in mimesis. Tragedy involves action, action creates conflict, and conflict breeds change, which its audience must judge. Berger quite eloquently describes the audience/reader's part in this:

The play, that is, tests us by tempting us to adopt the unpleasant perspective of the ethical judge who voyeuristically penetrates the speech of the 'good' characters and searches out the wickedness that flaws the heart . . . The play puts us in jeopardy so that we may discover our own complicity, our kinship with what we condemn, and come to 'see feelingly' without, however, refusing to see critically.[24]

Tragedy's ethical ambiguities provoke ever-changing responses in its audience. The *Hippolytus*, *Hecuba*, *Oresteia*, and many other tragedies represent humans imitating each other, yet still consciously rejecting these imitations, until the character held responsible for the crisis of difference falls as the scapegoat. Thus, the 'good' become culpable within the community and dissociated from the audience's sympathy, which prepares the victimage. But the shock of the actual violence against the protagonist/scapegoat divorces us from the emotional community on-stage, and, as we realize our complicity in scapegoating, the text reveals dramatic victimage. Euripides especially pursues such transformations, suddenly presenting, for example, the vile Polymestor as the voice of judgement and truth at the *Hecuba*'s end.

The dramatic scapegoat must be someone the audience accepts as a victim and who still brings the audience to pity. Because of the metonymic relationship between stage and audience, the tragic protagonist/scapegoat provokes emotional reactions in the audience that reflect the social dynamics on the stage, a process Kenneth Burke's essay on victimage in *Coriolanus* can help elucidate:[25]

The character to be sacrificed must be fit for his role as victim; and everything must so fit together that the audience will find the sacrifice plausible and acceptable (thereby furtively participating in the judgement against the victim, and thus even willing the victimage).

While Burke's focus on Coriolanus, the most dislikeable Shakespearean protagonist, presents the strongest case for the plausible victim, Othello, Antony, Lear, Hamlet, and Macbeth similarly incur not only their communities' wrath but the audience's as well. Greek tragedy likewise appears to enact the interplay of scapegoating on-stage and between stage and audience. The *Agamemnon*'s *parodos* and first *stasimon* narrate Agamemnon's revenge against Troy, the waste of human life there, and his sacrificial murder of Iphigenia. Agamemnon arrives on-stage with so many negative associations that his death at the hands of Clytemnestra seems plausible and, arguably, justifiable to the audience and to Argos. Similarly, Sophocles' masterpiece would have differently affected the democratic *polis* if Oedipus did not act at times like a *tyrannos*. Without generating some amount of hostility in the audience, the tragic victim will fail to excite the appropriate range of reactions. Tragedy engages the most deeply irrational part of ourselves, subjecting it to a violence analogous to that experienced by the protagonists and their community.

Burke stresses that the victim must play on the tensions of the audience's society: 'If we are going to "dramatize" such a tension, we shall want first of all a kind of character who in some way helps intensify the tension.'[26] As in the case of Coriolanus, Hippolytus' proclamations of his own superiority sit well neither with his community nor with the audience (or not, at least, with a fair percentage of it). By 428 BC, the plague has ravaged Athens, Pericles is dead, factionalism is increasing in Athenian politics, the colonies are in upheaval, and a youth arrives on-stage proclaiming his purity, his virginity, superiority, and separation from society, which would all make him suspect to an audience living in a *polis*. Hippolytus' neglect of proper sacrifice and the accusations of incest would have further excited social tensions in the audience, preparing it for his victimage. Burke thus provides a literary dynamic for the social tensions enacted in Greek drama between the individualistic, aristocratic heroes and the democratic *polis*.

I have tried to present a composite theory that, instead of projecting a Romantic idea of a unified self back on to Greek tragedy, shows how, as Adrian Poole observes, 'tragedy affirms with savage jubilation that man's state is diverse, fluid, and unfounded'.[27] In *Republic* 3, Plato argues against tragedy because its heroes act unheroically, and because the actors' imitations of these bad characters destabilize their own souls. If heroes come to imitate each other in conflict, and the actors in turn imitate them in performance, then these imitations, given the drama's emotional power, could indeed continue to spread contagiously out into its audience. However, the scapegoating of the protagonist not only stops the dramatic violence, but also through catharsis puts a brake on our own involvement. Plato, who sees the tragic poet as a dangerous maker of an imitation that represents further imitations, would literally expel the poet as a scapegoat, 'with myrrh poured over his head and crowned with wool'.[28]

Notes

1. *Georg Büchner: Werke und Briefe*, ed. K. Pörnbacher *et al.* (Munich 1980) 256. This paper is part of a much larger project on Euripidean

drama, and thus it can only sketch many ideas that need much greater elaboration.

2. Winkler and Zeitlin (edd.).
3. *Shakespearean Negotiations* (Berkeley 1988).
4. *On Aristotle and Greek Tragedy.*
5. A. Poole, *Tragedy: Shakespeare and the Greek Example* (Oxford 1987); p. viii.
6. 'Hamlet's Dull Revenge,' *Stanford Literature Review* 1 (1984) 159–200. ' "To Entrap the Wisest": A Reading of the Merchant of Venice,' in E. Said (ed.), *Literature and Society* (Baltimore 1978) 100–19.
7. Girard, *Violence and the Sacred.* For further bibliog., see my article, 'Miasma, Mimesis and Scapegoating in Euripides' *Hippolytus*', *CA* 10 (1991) 98–122, and P. Livingston, *Models of Desire: René Girard and the Psychology of Mimesis* (Baltimore 1992).
8. *Violence and the Sacred*, 145.
9. See Mitchell, 'Miasma', for bibliog. (esp. H. Foley), both for and against Girard. Segal, in *Dionysian Poetics*, develops some of Girard's principal ideas about the *Bacchae*, but without a sustained critique of Girard's approach. More recently, see the special issue of *Helios* (spring 1990), 'René Girard and Western Literature'. On Girard and Roman epic, see P. Hardie, *The Epic Successors of Virgil* (Cambridge 1993).
10. Griffiths, 'Girard on the Greeks'. On the *pharmakos* ritual, see J.-P. Vernant, 'Ambiguity and Reversal: On the Enigmatic Structure of *Oedipus Rex*,' in Vernant and Vidal-Naquet, *Myth and Tragedy in Ancient Greece.*
11. These essays have been collected in *A Theatre of Envy: Shakespeare* (Oxford 1991).
12. On action and psychology in Greek tragedy, esp. Aeschylus, see Rosenmeyer, *Art of Aeschylus*, esp. 211–55. Rosenmeyer also remarks with regard to the circumstantial mutability of character in Brecht: 'In Brecht's case, characters change as social circumstances demand it of them; capitalism forces the human amoeba into wayward shapes, and the drama traces the process with mirrorlike quality.'
13. See in particular: '*King Lear*'; 'Text against Performance: Gloucester'; 'Text against Performance: The Example of *Macbeth*,' *Genre* 15 (1982) 49–79. Recently, Berger has produced two valuable books: *Imaginary Audition: Shakespeare on Stage and Page* (Berkeley 1989), and *Second World and Green World: Studies in Renaissance Fiction-Making* (Berkeley 1988), selected and arranged, with an introd. by J. P. Lynch.
14. '*King Lear*', 348.
15. These and other remarks here on the *Hippolytus* rely on my article, 'Miasma'.

16. 'Text against Performance: Gloucester', 213–14.
17. *On Aristotle and Greek Tragedy*, 82.
18. '*King Lear*', 349.
19. For a Girardian reading of the *Oresteia*, see C. Rubino's review of *La Violence et le sacré*, *MLN* 87 (1973) 986–98, and Griffiths, 'Girard on the Greeks'.
20. 'Text against Performance: Gloucester', 212.
21. See 'The New Refutation of Shakespeare,' *MPh* 83 (1985) 123–41 and *New Readings vs. Old Plays: Recent Trends in the Reinterpretation of Renaissance Drama* (Chicago 1979).
22. '*King Lear*', 367–72. Berger draws on S. L. Goldberg, *An Essay on King Lear* (Cambridge 1974).
23. 'Drama, Political Rhetoric', 238.
24. 'Text against Performance: Gloucester', 212.
25. Kenneth Burke, 'Coriolanus and the Delights of Faction', in Burke, *Language as Symbolic Action*, 81. Girard acknowledges a kinship with Burke in 'Levi-Strauss, Frye, Derrida and Shakespearean Criticism,' *Diacritics* 3 (1973) 34–48.
26. *Language as Symbolic Action*, 82.
27. *Tragedy: Shakespeare and the Greek Example*, 2.
28. 398 a–b.

25

Patterns of Tragedy in Sophokles and Shakespeare

MICHAEL EWANS

I

The *Iliad* is demonstrably akin to the later genre of tragedy not just in the means used to evoke pathos, but in its feeling-tone or effect.[1] In Book 6 Hektor soothes Andromache's anxiety before returning to battle; his speech sets out the grim but consoling vision of human life and death which underlies Homer's epic:

> Strange one, do not grieve overmuch for me;
> for no one will hurl me to Hades beyond my *aisa*;
> but I say that no one has escaped from his *moira*,
> coward or brave man, *epên ta prôta genêtai*.
> Return to our house, go on with your work.
>
> (6. 486–90)

To interpret *aisa* and *moira* correctly, and translate the clause in 489 in a way which is true to our experience both of the poem and of Athenian tragedy, are crucial tasks which turn out to be surprisingly hazardous.

Aisa and *moira* are synonymous, and represent the Greek concept closest to our 'fate' or 'destiny'; they are often so translated, although their literal meaning is a lot, portion, or share. The linguistically most obvious rendering of the clause is 'when once he has been born';[2] if this reading is correct, Hektor is clearly saying that each human being has an immutable death-day, prefixed by destiny at or before the moment of birth; no one can be hurled to Hades before that day, but everyone will inevitably die when it arrives.[3]

However, this reading does not respond to the way in which the poem proceeds towards the climactic moment when Hektor dies at the hands of Achilleus in Book 22. We learn in 9. 410 f. that Thetis has told Achilleus his *aisa* will either be a long life without glory if he returns home, or a short but glorious one if he remains before Troy.[4] At first, both alternatives seem open; until Book 9, Achilleus' response to Agamemnon's appropriation of Briseis appears to be developing towards a complete withdrawal from the war against Troy. As the events unfold, however, this perspective is gradually modified. The battle flows in favour of the Trojans over the span of Books 5–15, up to the first great climax of the poem, the moment where Hektor gets hold of and sets fire to a Greek ship; this forces Achilleus out of his complacency. Unable to tolerate the loss of face involved in rejoining the combat himself, he devises the expedient of sending Patroklos; but Patroklos, carried away by the zest for combat, goes beyond the safe limits which Achilleus foresaw (16. 85 ff.)—and dies at Hektor's hands.

When Thetis brings the news of Patroklos' death in Book 18, the events have precluded Achilleus' return to a long life in Phthia. We hear the alternative, now made more precise as Thetis' increased perception allows her to see his *moira* in a new, sharpened form:[5] the if-clause which is at the centre of the poem's tragic weight. *If* Hektor dies, Achilleus' own *moira* will follow soon after.[6] The tragic turning-point is reached as Achilleus embraces this fact, and brings down his *moira* upon himself;

> 'As it is, you will have a thousand sorrows
> when your child is dead, whom you will not receive again
> returning to our house; my spirit tells me not to live,
> and not to share the world of men, if Hektor does not first
> lose his life struck by my own spear, and pay
> in his own blood because he killed Patroklos.'
> Thetis in answer said, tears pouring down:
> 'Then you will meet your *moros* swiftly;
> for your end is ready, and will follow Hektor's death.'
> Greatly disturbed, Achilleus of the swift feet said to her:
> 'May I die soon, since I could not be there
> to help my friend when he was killed.'

(18. 88 ff.)

Hektor's moment of death at Achilleus' hand was therefore not predestined since his birth. It only became his *moira* when he killed Patroklos, and this act was not in any way inevitable; it only took place after Patroklos voluntarily went beyond the limits of his ability—and then only because of the strength of Achilleus' feelings for Patroklos. Similarly, the death of Hektor 'dooms Achilleus' (if you like) to what emerges—later, in Hektor's dying prophecy at 22. 356 ff.—to be a humiliating death; but only because Achilleus chose freely in Book 18 to kill Hektor.[7]

It is therefore necessary to adopt a different interpretation of 6. 486 ff. unless we are willing to assume that Hektor's consolation encapsulates a vision of the world totally at odds with the rest of the poem. The first essential is to stop all talk of fate, doom, or destiny, and insist that *moira* and *aisa* bear always in Homer their root meaning of a lot or share in life—sometimes extending to mean a whole life-span;[8] the second is to opt for a more difficult reading of the *epên*-clause, taking *moira* as the understood subject, and translate, for example, 'once it has first taken shape'.[9] The passage then fully reflects the fundamental narrative pattern of the *Iliad*. As the poem unfolds, the *moirai* of the principal characters gradually 'take shape'; its tragic power is given by the spectacle of Hektor and Achilleus—who in different ways have greater insight into this process than any other human characters in the poem—openly accepting such a world, and deciding that they will fight on none the less, despite the imminence of death.[10]

II

In the acknowledged masterpieces of Athenian drama, the dramatist creates the tragic effect not primarily by selecting a particular kind of hero, subject-matter, or type of imagery, but by shaping a serious story to conform with the same pattern as that of the *Iliad*; a *moira* gradually takes shape as the drama unfolds from beginning, through middle, to end,[11] as a result of the actions of human beings who are perceived as choosing freely. I have argued elsewhere[12] that this pattern is central to the *Oresteia*: four times (in the first choral ode of *Agamemnon*, and at the climaxes of each of the three dramas) Aischylos exhibits a central character choosing freely between two disastrous alternatives, but in a context where the consequences of earlier events have developed to a point where only one of them is possible and therefore must be and is done; I turn now to two dramas by Sophokles.

Classical Greek tragedy, like the *Iliad*, moves in a world where the forces of a fully animate natural surround are personified.[13]

Until around 430 BC tragic playwrights could assume in the Athenian audience a shared cultural belief in the element of *to theion*, the divine or marvellous. The Greek gods represent not discrete forces interfering with us from outside, but powers which are immanent both in mankind and in the processes of nature which surround and interpenetrate us.[14] Such a belief is an essential precondition for producing the characteristic effect which we call 'tragic', since it provides a vocabulary for expressing the role in life of elements beyond direct rational experience. These elements bind human actions together as action and consequence, and express the ways in which our *moirai* take shape. Analysing their role enabled the playwrights to explain how and why human beings, in a world which lacked any concept of predestination or a mechanistic fate, find themselves in situations where they make disastrous choices and commit monstrous actions.

Taking advantage of this feature of their culture, Aischylos and Sophokles made recurrent use of a limited number of methods to set in motion and achieve the gradual narrowing-down from an opening situation, in which a wide range of alternative possibilities is available, towards the point where a *moira* has taken its full shape. The plots of tragedies were structured so that the Athenian spectators increasingly realized that the drama is heading towards one particular outcome, one set of variants on and from the previous epic, lyric, and dramatic versions of the particular myth being dramatized.[15] Three additional methods were frequently used. One of the most common ways of shaping a tragic story (both ancient and modern) is to show a pattern of disorder rectified, but at terrible cost; for this reason several Greek tragedies begin with a *miasma*, a literal and psychic pollution which indicates that the community has in some way violated the normal order of the world and incurred the displeasure of the gods.[16]

Many tragedies are based on an oracle or prophecy whose full meaning, exact application, and truth are revealed as the action unfolds.[17] In addition tragedies frequently make use of a 'story-pattern' (in Richmond Lattimore's unjustly neglected terminology[18]) which underlies the plot and provides the spectators with a familiar sequence of events, whose development intensifies the feeling that the action is proceeding in a particular direction.

In *Women of Trachis*, the main theme is the destructive power of beauty and love, *erôs* (24–5 etc.; cf. especially 441–4, 488–9).

Sophokles makes this emphasis possible by his ordering of the myth,[19] and reinforces it by stressing the precarious nature of our universe, in which everything is in that state of flux which John Jones refers to as mutability.[20]

In the plot, this theme, and this vision of human existence, are exhibited through the use of a story-pattern, and dramatized by superimposing on that pattern an oracle which is gradually narrowed down and made specific. The pattern is, as in *Agamemnon*, the sequence of events surrounding the *nostos* or homecoming of a king; Sophokles' story shows how the normal pattern of events, from the first rumours that Herakles is about to return after his labours, via the arrival of the advance herald Lichas, right through to the king's actual return, is perverted by Herakles' infatuation with Iole. Her presence reinflects the arrival of the herald in a literally fatal direction, when it disastrously induces Deianeira to welcome her husband with the gift of the (poisoned) robe.

The sequence is explained by the gradual revelation of the oracles about the homecoming of Herakles. Deianeira tells Hyllos a loose version of the main oracle at 79 ff.;

> He would either come to fulfil the end of his life,
> or live for the rest a fortunate life,
> once he had taken on and won this contest.

After the entry of the women of Trachis, Deianeira gives them a fuller, more explicit version (155 ff.), in which Herakles instructed her to divide up his property

> since he would either die exactly at this time,
> or if he ran beyond it, he would live
> hereafter in a life which had no grief.
> And this, he said, the gods had fixed
> to be the end of Herakles' torments;
> so, he said, the ancient oak had told him once
> at Dodona through the twin Doves.
>
> (166 ff.)

The drama shows the action of the critical time during which this 'either/or' is becoming clarified.[21] The oracle is the framework within which Sophokles requires us to understand the subsequent action—the return of Lichas with Iole, Deianeira's decision to use the 'love-potion',[22] and its appalling consequences. Once those are known—with Deianeira dead, and Herakles dying—the prediction is brought to the surface once again to explain the action. The women of Trachis gain full wisdom, and are able to realize how— and how completely—the ambiguous oracle, which appeared to offer a pair of alternatives, has come true (824 ff.):

> that when the twelfth year came to an end,
> it would fulfil release from toils
> for Zeus' true-born child;
> and truly this comes back to harbour now,
> complete.
> For how can he who sees no more
> still have a toilsome servitude
> when he is dead?

The dying Herakles reads this oracle in the same way, and realizes that he is the victim of a sick pun[23] by the gods on the Greek phrase *apallagê ponôn*—'release from toils':

> my father's oak that speaks with many tongues
> told me that at this present, living time
> I would achieve release from all the toils
> imposed on me. I thought this meant good fortune—
> but it was nothing else than death for me;
> for when you're dead no toils come near to you.

(1168 ff.)

Now, in the phrase which almost redeems Ezra Pound's extraordinary translation[24]

> 'Come at it that way, my boy, what
> SPLENDOUR,
>   IT ALL COHERES.'

This coherence near the end of the drama is formed in and by the narrowing of two alternatives to one, the recognition and understanding of how and why terrible events have happened.

Oidipous the King begins with a clear indication of divine displeasure with Thebes, the plague. Its general cause is soon clarified by Kreon's message from Delphi—'drive out the murderers of Laios'—and very soon specified precisely, as a result of the quarrel between Oidipous and Teiresias, in the hideously explicit forecast of the events which the prophet unleashes in his departing lines (447 ff.). After that, the divine recedes, and human choices lead to the revelation of the truth—just as they did in the past, as narrated by Oidipous at 787 ff. Oidipous' free choice led him to parricide and incest when, horrified by the oracle's prediction, he forgot why he originally came to Delphi, headed north (away from Korinth, where his supposed parents were)—and so encountered Laios on the road to Thebes.[25]

Aischylos and Sophokles normally provide only broad initial hints at what will actually happen.[26] In *Oidipous*, however, the cause of *miasma* is narrowed down rapidly, and fully spelt out to the audience by Teiresias before a third of the drama is over. This pattern places the main theme of the drama—Oidipous' movement to the discovery of who he is and what he has done—within a framework which ensures that the successive results of his attempt to disprove the truth of Teiresias' accusations only intensify the searing credibility of the prophet's exit speech.

None the less, even Teiresias and Apollo *could* be wrong: both Iokaste and the elders actively contemplate this possibility towards the midpoint of the drama, and the elders are appalled by it (897 ff.).[27] For a time Oidipous has no doubt that they *are* wrong, and the plot seems to have been shaped to emphasize a movement from initial piety, through tortured disbelief, to a terrible *peripeteia*, a sudden reversal in which the whole truth becomes known. Within this movement, a particular pattern recurs to generate the momentum of the drama. Well-intentioned people try to help the king to discover the cause of the *miasma* in Thebes; but, simply because of the limitations of human knowledge, their inadequate information makes them at the same time lead Oidipous towards realizing the truth of Teiresias' prophecy.[28] The central instances are Iokaste's attempt to prove that no prophet—including, of course, Teiresias—is ever right (707 ff.), and the Korinthian messenger's desire to capitalize on his success in convincing the royal pair that Oidipous' father is dead, when he intervenes at 989 in their conversation and frees Oidipous also from his fear about making love to Merope—so precipitating Iokaste's recognition of who Oidipous is and what he has done. (Appalling pathos is then lent to the final touch of natural human goodness—the Theban herdsman's pity for the infant Oidipous—at 1178 ff.)

As a result, Oidipous' search becomes increasingly fanatical as his resistance to the truth becomes increasingly untenable; and the climax is an archetypal moment at which Oidipous, by the strange paradox which is at the heart of 'the tragic', recognizes the inevitability of choosing to know.:

OIDIPOUS. Was it a slave, or his true child by marriage?
HERDSMAN. O god, I am on the brink of terrible speaking.
OIDIPOUS. And I of terrible hearing; but I must hear.

(1169 ff.)

In that 'must' lies all the force of the tragedy.[29] What Oidipous accepts is not an externally imposed necessity, but a now irresistible human compulsion to know. His search is over, and suddenly the tempo changes, as he slows, and *chooses* to accept into himself the truth. He takes the step which the audience by now deeply expects—and indeed, almost perversely, desires.[30]

In *Oidipous the King*, as in *Women of Trachis*, the plot unfolds to a point of revelation and of need for tragic action, where all the elements cohere: the traditional myth of Oidipous, the Sophoklean rhythm of sudden change or mutability, the *miasma* and the steps towards its removal, the story-pattern of riddle and decipherment, and the momentum of the plot, which has unfolded through a particular pattern of action.

III

Tragedy turned from a living Athenian culture into a Panhellenic showcase for star performers as the result of an increasing disbelief in the existence, or at least in the efficacy, of the gods, during the last thirty years of the fifth century.[31] The new climate is amply documented in our other Athenian sources—especially the comedies of Aristophanes and Thoukydides' *History*.[32] In tragedy it is reflected not simply in sceptical outbursts by individual characters,[33] but by a different pattern of plot-construction to reflect a different vision of the world. A new kind of *tragôidia* emerged, in which there is no feeling that a *moira* is taking shape as the action unfolds; a tragedy, to use Aristotle's repeated and precise terminology,[34] of 'probability' rather than of 'necessity'. Interpretation is very difficult; but I doubt whether the orthodox contention[35] that these are logical terms, with nothing to do with the sense of tragic inevitability, can be sustained. In each context, Aristotle is discussing the feeling of necessity or probability created in the spectator by the unfolding plot of a tragedy. And the disjunction between the two terms is at the heart of understanding the effects produced by Greek *tragôidia*.

The Greeks make purist critics uncomfortable by including under that last name not only those charismatic works of 'high tragedy' which we comfortably rank among the summits of the genre alongside Shakespeare's finest tragedies, but also numerous surviving works which modern taste disqualifies either for excessively 'melodramatic' content (e.g. *Orestes)* or because much suspense and surprise is generated during the course of the action, and then dissipated in and by a 'happy ending'. I suspect that Aristotle's repeated appeal to two particular, favourite plays as examples—*Oidipous the King* and *Iphigeneia among the Taurians*—is not primarily due to their similarity, the masterly handling of recognition and reversal.[36] These two dramas are paradigms of two opposed types of *tragôidia*. *Oidipous* represents 'necessity'; it is the classic drama of a gradually shaped *moira*, where there is almost no suspense about the outcome and the one major surprise—the arrival of the messenger from Korinth—leads directly to revelation of the deeply expected. *Iphigeneia* is based on 'probability', and is a supreme example of the new dramas which emerged in the late fifth century:[37] full of suspense, unpredictable fluctuations, and true surprises because they operate in a climate of chance where no patterns of necessity, connecting human actions with each other and with the actions of the gods, are present. Under such conditions there cannot be a medium comparable to the 'classic' or 'high' Greek tragedy of Aischylos and early to middle Sophokles.[38]

I V

Macbeth has frequently been felt to be the most 'Greek' of Shakespeare's tragedies. The affinity goes beyond the concision, the absence of subplot, and the theme of the rise and fall of an illegitimate ruler.[39] Shakespeare handles the role of prophecy in his tragedy in a manner analogous to middle-period Sophokles, and uses natural and supernatural elements to create the feeling that a *moira* is taking shape as the drama unfolds.

Shakespeare's representation of the oracular powers in *Macbeth* as 'traditional Scottish witches, with withered skin, beards, and a native love of mischief'[40] has led to a common view that they personify evil, and to readings of the play as centred 'on a struggle between the individual and the recurrent forces of demonic possession'.[41] This interpretation echoes Banquo's earnest warning to Macbeth that

> oftentimes, to win us to our harm,
> The instruments of darkness tell us truths;
> Win us with honest trifles, to betray's
> In deepest consequence.
>
> (I. iii. 122 ff.)

For Banquo as for Hamlet,[42] it is vital to establish whether 'supernatural solicitings' (I. iii. 129) have been sent by heaven, as true prophecies, or by the Devil to cause their undoing. However, the supernatural has a rather different function in *Macbeth*. Like the Delphic oracle in *Oidipous*, the Weird Sisters merely predict; human beings create the fulfilment of their predictions. Macbeth fulfils the correct prophecy that from Glamis he will become first Cawdor and then King by being allured by it[43]—that is, by a feature of his own nature, his desire for greatness.[44] The *miasma*, the inversion of the natural order which the witches detect in I. i,[45] is the consequence of unnatural human ambitions which go (as the Greeks would put it) *huper moron*—beyond the Macbeths' due place and station in life.

Shakespeare establishes from the outset a climate in which his plot will rapidly be understood by its audience as conforming to a story-pattern familar from history and from other medieval and contemporary fictions[46]—the establishment and overthrow of a usurping regime. In Greek terms, the murder of Duncan is a violation of the bonds of *philia* (kinship), and *xenia* (the rights and obligations of guest and host). It is so seen by Macbeth, in the soliloquy at I. vii. 12 f. Accordingly, the *miasma* which it causes is far less easily removed than that of murder outside these bonds. Shakespeare establishes this by means which a Greek audience would immediately have understood: the Lady's confident prediction that 'a little water clears us of this deed' (II. ii. 67) is shown to be false in the famous sleepwalking scene (V. i), where Shakespeare boldly treats the Christian concept of an internalized guilt as if it were an externalized Greek *miasma*.

After Macbeth is crowned king, the plot continues to unfold in a manner familiar from Sophokles. Macbeth's undoing, and the fulfilment of the witches' prophecies, result from natural human responses to the developing political situation in the kingdom of

Scotland. For example, Macbeth's decision to appoint a third murderer to superintend the assassination of Banquo goes awry, as do, in *Libation Bearers*, Klytaimestra's attempts to propitiate Agamemnon's spirit, and send a messenger to Aigisthos—and for the same reason: the mistrust engendered by tyranny is itself the tyrant's downfall. Similarly, Fleance's escape is an accident, no more divinely *caused* than the arrival of the Korinthian messenger in *Oidipous*; but like that arrival, it is the crucial step towards the fulfilment by human action of the prophecy made by divine agents earlier in the play. The flights first of Malcolm and Donalbain (II. iii *fin.*), then of Macduff (III. vi), are, equally, natural and prudent human responses to the increasingly murderous character of Macbeth's reign.

In *Macbeth*, the supernatural reappears after the opening scenes. Shakespeare studies the development of Macbeth's feeling of guilt in a manner parallel to Aischylos' dramatization of Orestes' conscience. The apparition of Banquo makes Macbeth realize the inevitability of action and consequence ('blood will have blood', III. iv. 121); and also drives him, painfully aware, through spies, of the increasing defections from his regime, to seek out the Weird Sisters once more. The decision to make them reappear creates a dramatic development similar to the sequence in *Iliad* 18–19 where Achilleus learns his precise *moira* from Thetis and Xanthos, to the Kassandra-scene in *Agamemnon*, and to the sudden appearance of the messenger with Kalchas' prophecy in *Aias* (*Ajax*). In each case, the late additional revelation, clarifying just how far the central figure's *moira* has now taken shape, clinches the feeling of the inevitability of his death.

Here, in IV. i, comes the one major opposition in *Macbeth* to normal Greek procedure.[47] The 'sprites' of future Scottish kings, Hecat tells the witches, 'As by the strength of their illusion | Shall draw him on to his confusion' (III. v. 28–9). Greek oracles often shroud the truth in ambiguous or euphemistic language—as in *Women of Trachis*, and in the famous oracle given to Kroisos that if he attacked Kyros' Persia, he would destroy a great empire;[48] but in the surviving tragedies they are never deliberately misleading. The prophecies in IV. i. 78 f. are by contrast designed to give Macbeth false confidence. Though his method is not classical, Shakespeare's purpose here is thoroughly Aristotelian; to set up a powerful pattern of recognition coupled with reversal at the

climax, when Macbeth realizes he has been deluded (v. vi. 59–61).
Malcolm rightly notes that 'Macbeth | Is ripe for shaking, and the
powers above | Put on their instruments (IV. iii. 237–8). The
'instruments' which fulfil the divine pattern, the restoration of
kingship to Duncan's son, and the witches' prophecies, are human
beings—Malcolm, Macduff, and their army; as in *Libation
Bearers*, god helps those who help themselves.[49] So, when
Malcolm makes Birnan Wood come to Dunsinane, and the 'man
not of woman born' confronts Macbeth, the audience observes a
classically Greek pattern in which the freely chosen actions of men
have fulfilled the prophecies given by *to theion* that certain things
will inevitably happen. And, like our Greek examples, both the
prophecies about the fall of Macbeth's kingdom are if-clauses.
Macbeth cannot be harmed, unless . . .

In v. vi, these potentials are actualized, and so Macbeth's personal *moira* has now taken its full and fatal shape. His response precisely fulfils the model of heroic acceptance—defiance, not
submission, now that death is imminent—which was laid down for
tragedy by the *Iliad* itself; and in a way which transcends moral
judgement, and establishes his stature directly as a ' tragic hero'.

> Though Birnan Wood be come to Dunsinane
> And thou opposed, being of no woman born,
> Yet I will try the last. Before my body
> I throw my warlike shield. Lay on, Macduff;
> And damned be him that first cries, 'Hold, enough!'
>
> (v. vi. 69 ff.)

So too Hektor, when he stood abandoned and alone before the
walls of Troy to face Achilleus

> from long ago this must have been more dear
> to Zeus and to his son the archer god, who in the past
> protected me; but now my *moira* is upon me.
> Still, I will not die without a struggle, without glory—
> only when I've done some deed that even future men will hear.
>
> (22. 301 ff.)

V

Hamlet is a revenge tragedy, based, like *Richard III* and *Macbeth*,
on the familiar sequence of unlawful usurpation and eventual

re-establishment of order; but it is grounded upon the concept of *miasma*, brought out in the early exchange between Marcellus and Horatio: 'Something is rotten in the state of Denmark.' | 'Heaven will direct it' (I. iv. 90–1). As Hamlet recognizes immediately (I. ii. 256–8), the appearance of the ghost (like that of the witches in *Macbeth* and the plague in *Oidipous the King*) is a divine response to human disruption of the natural order of the realm. It precipitates a sequence of human responses which end when Hamlet, for all his despair ('O cursed spite', I. v. 188–9) becomes the main agent through which Heaven 'directs' (sets right) the rottenness of Claudius' Denmark, in a manner parallel to that of the other dramas studied in this essay. 'There's a divinity that shapes our ends, | rough-hew them how we will' (V. ii. 10–11): as the final scene begins, Shakespeare makes his spectators see that the denouement fulfils this pattern.

Like *Libation Bearers*, *Hamlet* is dominated by images of a city-state whose body politic is being consumed by the consequences of incest, regicide, and usurpation—a kingdom which is 'out of joint' (I. v. 188). Even Claudius is aware of this ('O, my offence is rank. It smells to heaven', III. iii. 36);[50] and the process by which it is set right is the fundamental pattern underlying *Hamlet*. The importance of this pattern was first argued by Kitto;[51] but his interpretation of *Hamlet* as 'religious drama' is flawed, as F. R. Leavis acidly noted, by extending that concept so far that it is almost meaningless.[52] The reading is also excessively moralistic; for Kitto this play, like the major Greek tragedies, works out an inexorable moral law that 'evil, once started on its course, will so work as to attack and overthrow impartially the good and the bad'.[53] In Shakespeare as in Greek tragedy, *dikê* is nearer to a simple recompense or payment for past actions than to any Christian, post-Platonic ideal of justice. It is overtly manifested in V. ii, when Laertes recognizes that 'the fearful potion has turned itself on me', and that in being made to drink his own poison '[Claudius] is justly served' (V. ii. 307, 320).

However, as L. C. Knights recognized,[54] Kitto's stress on the importance of what—to avoid the pitfalls of the term 'religious'[55]—I would prefer to call *to theion* provides an essential counterweight to the Bradleyan tradition of humanistic, secularized, and psychological readings, which has bulked unfortunately large in English readings of Shakespeare.[56] Recent British studies now rightly emphasize the central imagery of order and disorder.[57]

Within the framework of this pattern, successive acts by the eight main characters—including, most importantly, of course, Hamlet's own oscillations between rashness and procrastination—develop by v. ii a situation which gives tragic pathos to the central figure. The climactic moment of Aristotelian *anagnôrisis* comes when, after finally accepting that he must avenge his father's death (v. ii. 63 ff.), Hamlet attempts revenge, and recognizes that he has achieved it only at the price of his own death (v. ii. 326 ff.). It would be foolish to deny the complex psychological interplay which Shakespeare has built upon this framework in *Hamlet*; but equally, it is essential not to deny that the tragedy operates within it.

The four dramas studied in this essay achieve the characteristic effect of high or classic tragedy partly through their formidable deployment of rich and complex poetic language; partly because the Greek and Elizabethan theatre-shapes served supremely well as metaphors for dramatizing subject-matter relevant to the closest concerns of their cultures; but above all because Athenians and Elizabethans both believed in the kind of animate, surrounding forces in nature which I have termed *to theion*.[58] Such beliefs permit the possibility of ordering the action of a drama, for example by introducing *miasma* and its inbuilt need for expulsion and purification, so the events show a *moira* taking shape; each successive scene increases the inevitability of a particular outcome. Then at the climax comes a moment of illumination, in which the drama 'makes sense of experience'[59]—in particular of human suffering. Such a climactic revelation is the essential effect of true tragedy.

Notes

1. Cf. C. Macleod (ed.), *The Iliad: Book XXIV* (Cambridge 1982) 1–8, 'The *Iliad* as a Tragic Poem', citing Plato's description of Homer as 'the pathfinder of tragedy' (*Republic* 598d).

2. This is adopted by a majority of interpreters, editors, and translators, including e.g. Adkins, *Merit and Responsibility*, 19 (an otherwise good discussion of *moira*), G. S. Kirk, *The Iliad: A Commentary*, ii (bks. 5–8) (Cambridge 1990), ad loc., and *Homer: The Iliad*, trans. R. Fitzgerald (Oxford 1984) 111.

3. Cf. e.g. J. Griffin, *Homer* (Oxford 1980) 36–7, where the poem's 'genuinely tragic view of the world and of human life' is regarded as growing from the fact that Zeus loves Hektor and Achilleus 'because they

are doomed'. To my mind, the spectacle of doomed creatures going to a predestined destruction has nothing to do with tragedy or the tragic; cf. Taplin, *Greek Tragedy in Action*, 165.

4. This explains in retrospect both the depth of Achilleus' anger in bk. 1, when Briseis is taken from him, and Thetis' depression at 1. 414 ff. when it temporarily appears that Achilleus' *aisa* will be both short *and* miserable.

5. For the way in which divine and prophetic insight into the future become clarified as events unfold, cf. Kalchas' two visions in the opening choral ode of *Agamemnon*; first he fears lest divine anger may darken the expedition (126 ff.), and then, when the winds have come, he realizes that it has, and becomes aware of the sacrifice which will be needed to propitiate the angry goddess (198 ff.). Cf. M. Ewans, 'Agamemnon at Aulis: A Study in the *Oresteia*', *Ramus* 4 (1975) 21–5.

6. Adkins's analogy of the game of snakes and ladders (*Merit and Responsibility*, 19) is a helpful but partially misleading guide to the nature of *moira*. *Moirai* often take the form of 'if *x*, then inexorably *y*'; but human beings do not land on *x* simply by an accident analogous to the throw of the dice; in Homer and in Greek tragedy, *x* is an action, which they choose to do.

7. This point is so important that, to make it, Homer permits Achilleus' immortal horse Xanthos temporarily to overcome the limitation (*moira* again) which normally confines speech to humans (19. 404 ff.). Xanthos sees Achilleus' death as inevitable—but only *after* the decision made in bk. 18, since he links it directly with Patroklos' defeat.

8. When Athena, arguing that Zeus should not break the barrier between gods and humans by prolonging Hektor's life, says at 22. 179 that as a mortal man Hektor is 'long marked down for this *aisa*', she means not that he has long been doomed to die now, but that it is long established that he must die (sc. once his *moira* has taken shape), simply because he is mortal.

9. Cf. *The Iliad of Homer*, trans. R. Lattimore (Chicago 1951) 166: 'once it has taken its first form'.

10. See 19. 421 ff. (Achilleus), and 22. 297 ff. (Hektor)—on which cf. M. Mueller, *The Iliad* (London 1964) 63–4.

11. Aristotle's insistence (*Poet.* 6–9, *passim*) on the importance of the arrangement of incidents, the *muthos* or plot, which he regards as 'the foundation and so to speak the soul' of tragedy (50^{a}38), and on the linear unfolding of tragic action through time (50^{b}26 ff.), provide the essential starting-point for any effective analysis of 'the tragic' in Greek drama. Cf. Jones, *On Aristotle and Greek Tragedy*, 21 ff., esp. 26.

12. M. Ewans, *Aeschylus: Oresteia* (London 1995).

13. J. Herington, *Aeschylus* (New Haven 1986) 5–14.

14. Cf. Lloyd-Jones, *Justice of Zeus*, 160.

15. The extent to which previous treatments of the legend shaped audience expectations when they were watching a new tragedy is a crucial topic; cf. M. Ewans, *Wagner and Aeschylus* (London 1982) 56–9. The lack of evidence has led to a reluctance to discuss it; for a comprehensive but relatively superficial treatment see W. Flint, *The Use of Myth to Create Suspense in Extant Greek Tragedy* (Diss. Princeton 1923).

16. This pattern is first seen in the *Iliad* (1. 43 ff.; notice that Agamemnon orders the troops to undertake ritual *katharsis*, purification, at 312 ff., after Chryseis has been returned to her father). In tragedy cf. e.g. *Libation Bearers* and *Oidipous the King* for an opening situation which is specifically established in the dialogue as *miasma* in need of *katharsis*, and *Aias* and *Eumenides* for an opening situation—in both cases within the building represented by the *skênê*—which has brought pollution upon the place where the action is set, and is such a major disturbance of the natural order that it has forced a god or gods to become visibly manifest to human beings.

17. Cf. esp. *Agamemnon* (and therefore the *Oresteia* as a whole), *Women of Trachis*, *Aias*, and *Oidipous the King*.

18. Lattimore, *Story Patterns in Greek Tragedy, passim.* I analyse the action of *Agamemnon* in terms of the *nostos* (homecoming) story-pattern in M. Ewans, 'The Dramatic Structure of *Agamemnon*', *Ramus* 11 (1982) 1–15.

19. The key feature is the decision to place Herakles' marriage to a young Deianeira early in his career, so that she is approaching (Greek) middle age—i.e. over 35—at the time of the sack of Oichalia; this version of the legend enables the arrival of Iole to cause Deianeira's predicament. For a concise account of the relevant myths in literature before Sophokles, see P. Easterling, *Sophocles: Trachiniae* (Cambridge 1982) 15–19.

20. First choral ode, 94 ff. Cf. Jones, *On Aristotle and Greek Tragedy*, 174–7; Easterling, *Sophocles: Trachiniae*, 2–3; and Winnington-Ingram, *Sophocles: An Interpretation*, 330–1. The opening allusion in this drama (cf. also 945–6), like the closing allusion in *Oidipous*, to the 'Solonian' proverb 'count no man happy until he is dead' is designed to reinforce this vision; cf. Easterling, *Sophocles: Trachiniae*, 71.

21. Cf. the twenty-four-hour period of Athena's wrath inside which the action of *Aias* takes place: 719 ff.

22. Sophokles emphasizes her freedom of choice by having her first resist and then (after exit and re-entry) succumb to temptation: 436 ff., 531 ff.

23. The joke is not even mediated through Apollo at Delphi, but given directly by Zeus' own oracle at Dodona. Its sickness is worthy of

Aristophanes at his most macabre, cf. *Frogs* 117 ff.; and Herakles, unlike most mortals, is a direct blood-relation of the god who has watched him die, and therefore has a valid claim of *philia* upon Zeus. This legitimates Hyllos' unparalleled, bitter attack on the gods in the closing lines: 1264 ff. The hope that the supreme god even cares for the fate of his own children is destroyed, and the normal assumption from other versions of the myth, that Herakles would be taken up to Olympos, is eliminated during the final minutes of Sophokles' drama (cf. Silk and Stern, *Nietzsche on Tragedy*, 255). *Women of Trachis* is one of the bleakest of all tragedies; the ending rivals those of *King Lear* and *Kát'a Kabanová*.

24. *Sophocles: Women of Trachis* trans. E. Pound (London 1969) 66.

25. This point needs emphasis, given the propensity to see Oidipous as doom-laden and predestined. As soon as that is implied, the tragic effect is lost, and a comic dimension intrudes even on this appalling myth; cf. Aristophanes' skittish fun with the opening lines of Euripides' *Antigone* (*Frogs* 1182 ff.), and Berkoff's brilliant rehandling of the myth in *Greek*.

26. Cf. e.g. the opening scene of *Agamemnon*, esp. 11, 34–5—and 248 ff.

27. This point is rightly stressed by B. Knox in *Sophocles: The Three Theban plays*, trans. R. Fagles (Harmondsworth 1984) 137 ff. R. Rehm, *The Greek Tragic Theatre* (London 1993) 115–16 is excellent on the dangers for Sophokles and the mid- to late fifth-century audience of a random, *tuchê*-dominated universe; note the elders' perverse desire to have even this horrible oracle fulfilled, so there is some minimal order in the universe (if the gods say something will happen, it will) to which they can cling. Cf. also the detailed analysis of 897 ff. in Winnington-Ingram, *Sophocles: An Interpretation*, 197 ff.

28. Halliwell, *Poetics of Aristotle*, 13–14, cf. 119, objects strongly to the over-humanizing tenor of Knox's justly famous interpretation of the drama (restated in *Sophocles*, trans. Fagles, 149–53). But the thrust of Knox's interpretation is basically right. (Some qualifications, which do not affect my argument, are entered by Vickers, *Towards Greek Tragedy*, 498.) Unlike Aischylean gods and *daimones*, Sophocles' Apollo never intervenes to link one human-originated action to another, either before or during the events dramatized in the drama itself. Sophocles even frees the original prediction from the wrongdoing by Laios, explaining *why* he was cursed with this appalling oracle, which is found in all other known versions of this myth. Sophocles' Delphi simply predicted, without giving any reason, that *if* Laios had a child it *would* kill its father and marry its mother. He did beget a child, and so, and choosing freely, it did violate two of mankind's deepest taboos. This is just like Homeric *moira*.

29. Cf. Lattimore, *Story Patterns in Greek Tragedy*, 41, and also 7–8, where, writing about Aischylos' *Seven against Thebes*, Lattimore amplified his concept of a 'right order—a sense of necessity, of must-be-so' in tragedy; when Eteokles leaves to confront his brother, choosing to accept the opponent given to him by the sequence of speeches, 'the curse, the fate, the action and the choice coincide'.

30. In Aristotelian terms, it would be *miaron*, offensive, if at this point Oidipous decided not to know, and broke off his enquiry. Cf. Aristotle's point (53ª36–9) that it will not do for myths to be changed so that e.g. Aigisthos and Orestes go off as friends; by the climax of *Libation Bearers*, both story and plot (*praxis* and *muthos*) demand that Orestes murder the usurpers.

31. This effect is too marked to be a coincidence; quite simply, Euripides' extant dramas and Sophokles' last three plays are not written on the assumption that mankind lives in, and interacts with, an animate universe. The divine is treated ironically, cynically, or sceptically in most of Euripides and in Sophokles' *Elektra*; where it is taken seriously in drama after 430 (*Hippolytos, Bakchai, Oidipous at Kolonos*), individual gods and goddesses manifest their power in a world which otherwise might as well be godless. Nietzsche's analysis of this 'death of tragedy' (*The Birth of Tragedy*, §§11 ff.) is well discussed in Silk and Stern, *Nietzsche on Tragedy*, 153 ff., esp. 157–9.

32. The *History* is the first major work of Greek literature written from a completely sceptical viewpoint. Thoukydides himself reflects on the decline of belief in Athens after the plague of 430 in a famous passage: 2. 53.

33. Cf. e.g. Talthybios at Eur. *Hekabe* 488 f.

34. *Poet.* 51ª12 and 38, 51ᵇ9 and 35, 52ª1 and 24, and 54ª34–6.

35. Halliwell, *Poetics of Aristotle*, 106–7.

36. Aristotle's phrasing ('probability *or* necessity') makes it unlikely that he intended these two terms as complementary alternatives to a hypothetical drama wholly composed of random, chance events—*pace* H. House, *Aristotle's Poetics* (London 1956) 59, and J. Lawlor, *The Tragic Sense in Shakespeare* (London 1969) 74–6.

37. Dramas of *Catastrophe Survived*, in A. Pippin Burnett's apt and precise title (Oxford 1971; on *Iphigeneia*, see 13 and 47 ff.). They include e.g. *Ion, Helen, Philoktetes*, both *Elektras*, and above all *Orestes*. Steiner, *Death of Tragedy*, 7–8, would even disqualify from true tragedy *Oidipous at Kolonos* and *Eumenides*: see now his hardly less compromising position in the present volume, below, pp. 534–46. The whole subject of happy endings has been severely clouded both by Aristotle's self-contradictory advice (*Poet.* 53ª22–6, 54ª4–9), and by the overwhelming influence of the Elizabethan and Jacobean

preference for a corpse-strewn finale in which only a slight hope—if any—is extended for the future. Cf. Lattimore, *Story Patterns in Greek Tragedy*, 76–7 and n. 39.

38. I argue in 'Racine's *Phèdre*' that even French neo-classical tragedy does not satisfy 'classic' Greek conditions.

39. Cf. of course the rise and fall of Aigisthos in the *Oresteia*. There are obvious analogies between Lady Macbeth's monstrously hypocritical reception of Duncan in I. vi and Klytaimnestra's of Agamemnon.

40. G. K. Hunter, *Shakespeare: Macbeth* (Harmondsworth 1967) 39.

41. Ibid. Cf. e.g. A. Harris, *Night's Black Agents: Witchcraft and Magic in Seventeenth Century English Drama* (London 1980) 88; 'the aura of superhuman wickedness that surrounds the witches'.

42. *Hamlet*, II. ii. 596 ff.

43. As Hunter correctly notes ad loc. (*Macbeth*, 143; cf. 11–12). Given the way the events subsequently unfold, Macbeth is either self-deceiving, or simply wrong, in his aside, 'if chance will have me king, why chance may crown me/without my stir' (I. iii. 143–4). He recognizes more truthfully at II. i. 42 that the vision of the dagger 'marshall'st me the way that I was going'.

44. This is analysed (ruthlessly) by his Lady at I. v. 1 ff. Aristotle would have regarded it as a touch of *êthos* (characterization), which is 'needed to explain personal choice when that is not obvious' [sc. from the events] (50^b8–9: the text is corrupt; this interpretation is developed from Jones, *On Aristotle and Greek Tragedy*, 33). From a Greek perspective, the main difference between Shakespearean and classical tragedy is that the outcome in Shakespearean tragedy rests to a greater extent on choices made because of the individual character of the central figure, to a lesser extent on choices whose outcome becomes seen as inevitable because of his or her status and situation.

45. I. i. 9: 'Fair is foul, and foul is fair.' The abnormality of Macbeth's Scotland, its opposition to the natural order, and the divine displeasure manifested in nature's protests, are heavily stressed; see esp. II. ii. 15 ff., iii. 51 ff., iv. 16 ff.

46. Cf. esp. *The Tragedy of King Richard III*.

47. It is relevant to note that parts of this scene, and Hecat's appearance in III. v, were probably interpolated for a revival by the King's Men at the Blackfriars Theatre in or after 1609.

48. Hdt. 1. 46–91.

49. Cf. Ewans, *Aeschylus: Oresteia*, 161, 164–70. In *Macbeth*, this point is explicitly made by the Lord at III. vi. 29 ff.

50. There is therefore a supreme irony when Claudius later expounds an ideology which legitimates his kingship by reference to *to theion*: 'There's such divinity doth hedge a king', IV. v. 125 f.

51. *Form and Meaning in Drama*, 248–338.
52. *English Literature in our Time and the University* (Cambridge 1969) 162, cf. Mason, *Tragic Plane*, 164.
53. Kitto, *Form and Meaning in Drama*, 330.
54. *'Hamlet' and other Shakespearian Essays* (Cambridge 1979) 21 ff.
55. Mason, *Tragic Plane*, 164.
56. There is a striking contrast in the nineteenth-century German tradition: Schelling, Nietzsche, and even Hegel (Bradley's mentor) readily included Shakespeare, as well as the Greeks, in discussions of tragedy which are fully attuned to its metaphysical dimension. Cf. Silk and Stern, *Nietzsche on Tragedy*, chs. 7–9, esp. 280, 305 ff., and 323.
57. Cf. esp. T. McAlindon, *Shakespeare's Tragic Cosmos* (Cambridge 1991) 102–5. For parallels in the *Oresteia*, cf. C. Macleod, *Collected Essays* (Oxford 1983) 340.
58. On the Greeks, cf. Ewans, 'Racine's *Phèdre*', esp. 89–95; on the Elizabethans, Steiner, *Death of Tragedy*, 114–15. Frequently in tragedy of al' periods *to theion* is used to impart to the action the feeling which is often called 'poetic justice' (cf. Aristotle's discussion in *Poet.* 9). When Orestes returns to Argos on the morning after Klytaimestra's dream, when Gertrude drinks from the poisoned chalice meant for Hamlet, and when the ice melts and Jenufa's murdered baby is discovered on her wedding day, the same vital force is at work.
59. Jones, *On Aristotle and Greek Tragedy*, 29.

26

Tragic Language:
The Greek Tragedians and Shakespeare

M. S. SILK

I

Attempts to elucidate tragic language have been few and brief, and this despite the immense weight and variety of known discussions of tragedy, Greek and other. The claim may seem surprising, even astonishing. After all, the immense weight and variety of known discussions of Greek tragedy includes innumerable commentaries on, surveys of, and insights into, the linguistic usages of the tragedians; while comparable work on (say) Shakespeare, albeit crowded into fewer centuries, is hardly less extensive or less multifarious overall. From the wit of Aristophanes to the sophistications of post-structuralism, from ancient scholarship to modern scholarship, there is no shortage of secondary literature.

And yet virtually all of this literature is concerned *either* with the specificities of single authors, or indeed single works, *or else* with what one may reasonably (and with no belittlement) call the contingent features of one or other phase or tradition of tragic drama.[1] Greek antiquity itself is, no doubt, the effective progenitor of both kinds of discussion. Aristophanes' contrastive critique of the linguistic peculiarities of Aeschylus and Euripides points one way; Aristotle's prescriptions for tragic idiom—of course, *Greek* tragic idiom—point the other. And yet, over and above such contrastive features and such contingent features, I propose that there is such a thing as tragic language, which remains essentially to be defined, towards which the language of all tragedy tends, and the definition of which (given the prime importance of language within tragic, as within most other, drama) promises to assist our understanding of tragedy as a whole.[2]

My discussion, which cannot pretend to be exhaustive or

comprehensive, seeks to provide some groundwork and to offer some pointers towards this end. It concentrates on a few, significant, and (I suggest) representative passages, mostly taken from a few representative tragedies. The passages are drawn from Shakespeare as well as from the Greeks:[3] because the two sets of examples are mutually illuminating; because the Shakespearean presence has the advantage of greater immediacy; and because the transcultural premise of 'tragic language' insists on a practical demonstration. To say that there is such a thing as 'tragic language', and that the language of all tragedy tends towards it, presupposes, no doubt, a more, rather than a less, restrictive notion of what counts as 'tragedy' within the Western tradition or traditions.[4] I do not mean, however, that within some charmed circle of plays tragic drama can be shown to work to a formula. Far from it. I mean that tragic drama has a common logic so powerful as to generate equivalent configurations—equivalent modalities, equivalent mechanisms—even across languages and cultures. And the existence of variations both within and between different traditions of tragedy (some of which will shape my own argument) does not affect these equivalencies.

First: what *has* been said in elucidation of these issues hitherto? The answer in a nutshell is that the language of tragedy is generally supposed (*a*) to be stylized and, specifically, elevated, and also (*b*) to be complex or intensified. Both of these suppositions (let me make clear) are broadly true, both are important, and both are, like so much else, prefigured by Aristotle. Tragic verbalization (*lexis*),[5] says the philosopher, should be 'clear' but not 'low' or 'everyday' (σαφῆ καὶ μὴ ταπεινήν, *Poetics* 22, 1458ᵃ18). Language in tragedy, therefore, is, or should be, elevated by removal from a notional vernacular norm; and the 'not low' is duly explained with reference to the use— evidently the stylized use—of 'alien expressions' (τὰ ξενικά, 1458ᵃ21–2). Such stylization is indeed a familiar feature of Greek tragedy and (*pace* Aristophanes and, in his wake, Nietzsche) only marginally, if at all, attenuated in Euripides.[6] At *Bacchae* 1084, for instance, the messenger describes the ominous still in the air before the women's discovery of the voyeur Pentheus: σίγησε δ' αἰθήρ, 'And the air was still': except that αἰθήρ is verse diction, rather than everyday diction, for 'air';[7] and that, by an archaizing convention familiar to all readers of Greek poetry (and ultimately referable to the usage of Homer), the 'the', the definite article that would be there, again, in ordinary Greek, is not there. Such stylization is likewise, of course, a familiar feature of Shakespearean writing. Take *Macbeth*, v. v, 'Out, out, brief candle!', with its classicizing apostrophe and epithet.[8] But then again in Shakespeare the sudden attenuation of such stylization is equally familiar—'Out, out, brief candle! | Life's but a walking shadow'—where (as modern usage still attests) colloquial force is associated both with the contraction ('Life's') and with the cast of the following phrase (cf. 'walking encyclopaedia', 'walking disaster', etc.).[9] An overall impression of elevated idiom, nevertheless, and certainly of access to elevation, remains the Shakespearean norm.

Aristotle's 'alien expressions', however, are not a straightforward category. That 'alien' is glossed by reference to such elevating mechanisms as 'the archaism' ($\gamma\lambda\hat{\omega}\tau\tau\alpha$)[10] and 'the lengthened form' ($\dot{\epsilon}\pi\dot{\epsilon}\kappa\tau\alpha\sigma\iota\varsigma$), yet also to 'metaphor' ($\mu\epsilon\tau\alpha\phi\rho\acute{\alpha}$, 1458[a]22–3). Metaphor, however, is not, or is only accidentally, associated with elevation: witness 'walking shadow', or the fact that one of the most metaphor-loving poets of ancient Greece is the 'low' Aristophanes,[11] and so on. In itself, metaphor makes for complexity, for intensification, for heightening rather than elevation.[12] Witness, again, 'walking shadow' and also Euripides' $\sigma\acute{\iota}\gamma\eta\sigma\epsilon$, which is not actually 'was still' so much as a more eerie personification, 'went quiet' ('and the lotos rose, quietly, quietly').[13] Tragic poetry, certainly, like most high-style poetry, is particularly given to complexity (or intensification); and Aristotle's intuition in relating this complexity to stylization serves to make his prescription both more plausible than it otherwise would be and, incidentally, more relatable to modern positions. In the first place, his category of 'alien expressions' strikingly anticipates the formalist concept of 'defamiliarization'. That principle, whereby poetic language, by virtue of its non-normal features, is felt to disturb its recipients into a new perception, is one that has much more to do with the absolute non-normality of (say) metaphor than with the conventional stylization of (say) poetic archaism. Then again, the inference of a relationship between the complex-intense and the stylized is strikingly echoed in a classic discussion of tragic idiom by F. R. Leavis, who drew upon the poetic-dramatic experience of Yeats to argue that the tragic requires 'the poetic use of language' and that 'poetry, with attendant non-naturalistic conventions . . . is necessary in order to provide the distance and the frame without which there can be no intensity of the right kind'.[14]

At the same time, it is quite clear that, as a formula for tragic language, Aristotle's prescription, or anytning like it, is inadequate and bound to be so. Stylization and complexity-intensification will prove to be *necessary* for tragedy: they are not *sufficient*. No combination of the two can account for the language of tragedy, because any such combination will be more or less equally characteristic of much other poetry, in fact of most other high-style poetry. In Greece, for instance, the language of Homeric epic, the language of Pindaric lyric, and the language of tragedy are broadly distinguishable in specifiable ways (from dialect mix to phraseological patterns), but they are all broadly stylized and broadly complex (or open to complexity).[15] This point (let me stress) applies to some of the most discussed kinds of semantic intensification that modern critics (reasonably) associate with tragedy, Greek or Shakespearean, such as patterns of recurrent imagery: these one finds equally in (for instance) Homeric and Miltonic epic. Again, it applies to the way that key words, perhaps 'plain words', like 'honest' in *Othello* or 'know' in *Oedipus Tyrannus*, are progressively invested with a complex significance by contrastive and cumulative usages over the course of the work.[16] There is nothing decisively tragic about that kind of intensification. On the contrary, it is a feature of most sizeable works of poetry, from Homer's *Iliad* to Eliot's *Four Quartets*.[17]

Conversely, anyone still hankering after a general formula for tragic language based exclusively on stylization and complexity-intensification should note how differently the *most* complex and intensified language is distributed in our two fields of reference. In Greek tragedy, most of the highest peaks occur in choral reflection and response. Aeschylus' Clytemnestra says

τί ἐστὶ χρῆμα;
What is the matter?
(*Choephori* 885)

and his Orestes says

φιλεῖς τὸν ἄνδρα;
You love your 'husband'?
(894)

but his chorus says (or rather, sings)

διπλοῦς λέων, διπλοῦς Ἄρης

Twin-headed lion, twin-headed kill.

(938)

This chorus, however, like most tragic choruses, is a bystander and neither the agent of tragic misfortune nor even a prime victim of tragic suffering. In Shakespeare, by contrast, the stylistic peaks are commonly scaled by the agent-victims. It is not the bystanders or the incidental victims in *Macbeth*—not the lesser thanes or the porters or doctors or gentlewomen—who have the most complex and the most intensified language. It is Macbeth himself:

> If it were done when 'tis done, then 'twere well
> It were done quickly. If th' assassination
> Could trammel up the consequence, and catch
> With his surcease success; that but this blow
> Might be the be-all and the end-all here—
> But here upon this bank and shoal of time—
> We'd jump the life to come.

(I.vii)

There are indeed analogues to such rich speech—in Aeschylus, in particular, whose Cassandra, for instance, would certainly be a match for Macbeth. But then again, no character in Aeschylus, not even a Cassandra, can compare—for sheer, sustained complexity— with the chorus of *Agamemnon* in its long opening song.

The demands on an audience's understanding that are imposed by such linguistic richness have a further bearing on Aristotle's prescription. If judged as a formula for tragedy, the prescription in its full form is still less satisfactory, though also more thought-pro- voking, than I have yet suggested. *Lexis* (Aristotle assures us) should not only be 'not low', it should be 'clear'. This requirement would accommodate most of Homeric epic (though not all of Milton), but it would tend to exclude some of the most notable moments in Shakespeare ('here upon this bank and shoal of time'), as well as the word-plays that so offended Dr Johnson;[18] and it would certainly disqualify great swathes of extant Greek tragedy, including choral lyrics, prophetic utterances (from Cassandra in *Agamemnon* to Tiresias in *Oedipus Tyrannus*), and arguably at least some 'ordinary' dialogue too. That 'arguably' conceals an impor- tant argument. Consideration of Greek tragedy, especially in its later, Sophoclean-Euripidean, phase, has led a number of contemporary critics to reinterpret what Nietzsche (in deceptively neo-Aristotelian fashion) saw as the 'simple transparency' of the 'Apolline' dialogue. 'The language of Sophocles' heroes surprises us by its Apolline precision and lucidity, so that we feel we are looking into the innermost ground of their being':[19] this nineteenth-century reading of tragic *logos*, though not repudiated, is in our own day often problematized. Alongside this orderly Apollinity, articulated by conventional elevation, the revisionist reading detects signs of linguistic disorder; the same tragic dialogue that seems to offer transparency *also* readily deceives. And indeed it can hardly be denied that (even?) in Sophocles, it is often the case that 'logical argument fails. . . . Civilized discourse gives way . . . Instead of mediating between mind and world, language becomes entangled in a series of conflicts which confuse and obscure perception of reality.'[20]

And yet this modern, or post-modern, view of tragic language does not, on reflection, seem to bear so closely on our enquiry. Could one argue that it sheds much light on (say) Aeschylus' *Persians* or (even?) Shakespeare's *Antony and Cleopatra*? And even where 'civilized discourse' does 'give way', even where 'language is not just the medium of tragedy [but] an element in the tragic situation', even where (as in—say—*Antigone*) language does become 'entangled in conflicts'—even there, it is not clear that 'the tragic situation' is dependent on this entanglement nor, therefore, that the entanglement is inherently 'tragic'. Furthermore: to grant that in some plays language fails in its 'proper' communicative role *between* the *dramatis personae* is not to say that there, let alone in tragic drama as a whole, language fails to communicate to *us*, its audiences and readers. There is a difference between a play about failure and a failed play. Yet some of the readings of tragic non-communication on-stage come dangerously close to treating it as non-communication *per se*: 'because tragic knowledge eludes the boundaries of ordinary language, it needs visual dramatization'; 'the tragic message . . . is precisely that there are zones of opacity and incommunicability in the words men exchange'; 'language itself appears as a distortion and displacement'.[21] Such formulations are not wholly new. From an earlier generation one recalls Emil Staiger's suggestion that 'the tragic never comes clearly and immediately to verbal expression',[22] and, before that, Nietzsche's dictum that the heroes of Greek tragedy, and likewise Hamlet, the archetypal figure of modern tragedy, 'talk more superficially than they act'.[23] As against such claims, one would do better to reaffirm the exceptional competence and penetration of tragic language, alike in its Greek and its Shakespearean forms, and insist, in particular, on the unrivalled power, vested in the speaking (or singing) characters (or choruses), to *realize* the most comprehensive claims about their and our condition: 'Life's but a walking shadow . . .' At all events, the sense of 'tragic language' that we seek to articulate is based on this perceived power, not on that alleged incapacity, in tragedy as we know it.

II

All we have established so far is that the language of tragedy—of classical tragedy as we know it from the Greeks, from Shakespeare, and putatively from elsewhere—is both stylized-elevated and complex-intensified. If we are to get beyond this point, we must draw on a variety of traditions—traditions as various as those of Vernant and Knox, or those of Nietzsche, Hegel, and Aristotle—and construct a larger argument. The first step is to remind ourselves *why* the language of tragedy should have its two properties. Summarily, let us note that elevation is appropriate: *both* to the universal, even metaphysical, vastness of tragedy's concerns; *and* then also to the high status of its significant human players by virtue of which they have the scope and the dignity to act and suffer in the tragic universe. These acting and suffering players, however, are individuals. As individuals they strive: they assert themselves, they make decisions, and they collide with other individuals, with society, with the very order of the universe itself. The special nature of these strivings and the special experience of the individuals involved can only be articulated, or 'realized', through complex and intensified language.[24] These are general truths, which stand irrespective of the particularities which different poetic languages may exhibit. Irrespective also of the 'heroic' quality of the striving. The striving individual may be, but is not necessarily, a 'tragic hero', either in the sense of one possessing, or earning, some special moral authority, or by virtue of an exclusive centrality to the tragic action. In *Antigone* both Creon and Antigone are striving individuals; in *Bacchae* Cadmus and Agave, as well as Pentheus, come under this heading; so too in *Macbeth* do Macbeth and Lady

Macbeth and at least some of their various victims and opponents. The specific question, which of these are 'tragic heroes', the general question, what is a 'tragic hero', and the semi-specific question, how far does this essentially Renaissance concept assist a sensitive response to earlier (or indeed to any) tragedy, are not questions we need consider here.[25]

From these principles we can move to a second step. Consider Creon, agreeing, against all his convictions, to free Antigone:

οἴμοι· μόλις μέν, καρδίας δ' ἐξίσταμαι
τὸ δρᾶν· ἀνάγκῃ δ' οὐχὶ δυσμαχητέον.

I back off, hard though it is—but still
We must not fight against necessity
(Sophocles, *Antigone* 1105–6)

and the chorus of Oceanids rebuking Prometheus

ἰδίᾳ γνώμᾳ σέβῃ θνατοὺς ἄγαν, Προμηθεῦ

By your own will you reverence man too much, Prometheus

(?Aeschylus, *Prometheus,* 543)[26]

and Cleopatra responding to Antony's resolve to fight on in a hopeless cause

It is my birthday,
I had thought t' have held it poor; but since my lord
Is Antony again, I will be Cleopatra.
(*Antony and Cleopatra*, III. xiii)

Beyond all the variable specifics of action and agents, myth and history, *polis* and *genos*, dynasties and ideologies, tragedy (Greek and Shakespearean) is propelled by a small set of irreducible determinants of which three seem to be of special importance: compulsion, excess, and identity. In concrete linguistic terms, tragedy tends to foreground *must* and *too* and the *name*.[27] 'Must' as opposed to merely 'might' or 'can': the striving individual *must* assert himself or herself or (like Creon) *must* give way. 'Too' in contradistinction to proportion and restraint and sufficiency: in a universal perspective the self-assertive go too far. And the *name*: the striving individual is a special someone with an identity, which must, by his or her striving, be lived up to, in a sense created, certainly *realized*. He or she must, in Pindar's words, 'become what you are' and thus (as we say) live up to their name.[28] In that living-up-to is the compulsion to strive and all the risk or reality of excess. Lesser thanes and porters and doctors and gentlewomen in *Macbeth* are not striving individuals. On a tragic level they take no risks and so they have no name. Likewise the guard in *Antigone*, the nurse in *Hippolytus* and, above all, the members of the tragic chorus. They are, in Vernant's words, a 'collective and anonymous presence' from whose 'ordinary condition' the 'individual character' is always 'more or less estranged'—[29]estranged by his (or her) compulsions, by his excess, by his name. For the striving individual, 'my lord is Antony again' (with all the attendant tragic entailment) and so (with the same entailment) 'I will be Cleopatra', where *will* implies not only decision, but necessity as well.[30]

Instances, of course, do not always take exactly the same form, nor do comparable forms of words always mean exactly the same thing. It is already obvious that *must* encapsulates different sorts of compulsion. We (or the individuals involved) may perceive the compulsion of internal resolve, or the compulsion of external fate, or both; and 'both' is a familiar possibility in Greek drama in particular, where the tradition of 'double determination' produces a variety of conflicts and alignments.[31] Consider *Oedipus at Colonus*, for instance, where despite Oedipus' curse Polynices *must* challenge his brother, even though he knows it means his own death (1437–8) and the further ruin of his house. His language is all compulsion:

1418	οὐχ οἷόν τε	('it cannot be')
1426	οὐχὶ συγχωρητέα	('I must not give in')
1441	εἰ χρή, θανοῦμαι	('if I must, I shall die')
1442	ἃ μὴ δεῖ	('what must not be')

But while Antigone condenses all this into 'your decision' (ταῦτά σοι δεδογμένα, 1431), Polynices himself is equally prepared to talk the language of 'fate' (τῷ δαίμονι, 1443). Othello in his great speech ('It is the cause, it is the cause, my soul', *Othello*, v. ii) talks the language of external necessity,

> When I have plucked thy rose
> I cannot give it vital growth again,
> It *needs must* wither . . .

but ultimately with reference to the consequence of his own resolve:

> Yet she *must* die, else she'll betray more men.

Hamlet's insistence on following his father's ghost seems to be both resolve and external necessity, with the external agency presented as dominant, but the human choice as final.

—You shall not go, my lord.
　　　　　　—Hold off your hands.
—Be ruled, you shall not go.
　　　　　　—My *fate* cries out,
And makes each petty arture in this body
As hardy as the Nemean lion's nerve:
Still am I *called* . Unhand me, gentlemen:
By heaven, I'll make a ghost of him that lets me:
I say, away! Go on; *I'll* follow thee.

(*Hamlet*, I. iv)

The same might be said of Agamemnon, in the face of Artemis' demand, '*stooping to* the strap of *compulsion* '

ἀνάγκας ἔδυ λέπαδνον
(Aeschylus, *Agamemnon* 218)

in the decision to sacrifice his daughter.[32]

Compulsion, either internal or external, is often weighed in a simple question. So it is with Creon, faced with Tiresias' warnings in *Antigone* (1099): τί δῆτα χρὴ δρᾶν; 'What, then, must I do?' Compare: 'What shall Cordelia speak? Love and be silent' (*King Lear*, I. i), Cordelia's first fateful words that set in motion Lear's tragedy and her own. Here, as elsewhere, a *must* that betokens a tragic individual's decision is disguised with a question and also a *will*. Compare Orestes at a uniquely awesome moment of personal crisis: Πυλάδη, τί δράσω; μητέρ' αἰδεσθῶ κτανεῖν; 'Pylades, what *do* I do? *Am* I to spare my mother?' (Aeschylus, *Choephori* 899)—in effect, '*must* I kill her, now that I see and feel what it involves?'[33] And Pylades, with allusion to an explicit external-metaphysical frame, answers one question with another, *yes*: ποῦ δαὶ τὸ λοιπὸν Λοξίου μαντεύματα; 'Apollo's oracles—what will become of them?' (900). Yet in spite of the frame, it remains Orestes' decision. 'The decision that he "must" kill his mother was taken before the play began, but now it has to be taken again, and it remains his own.'[34]

The striving individual goes *too* far and generally comes to acknowledge it. Othello:

When you shall these unlucky deeds relate,
Speak of me as I am . . .

.   .   .   .

Of one that loved not wisely, but *too* well;
Of one not easily jealous, but, being wrought,
Perplexed *in the extreme.*

(*Othello*, v. ii)[35]

Contrast the insight of Cadmus in *Bacchae*, aware (unlike Agave) that the 'animal' head in her arms is actually the head of her son, Pentheus. In his eyes, excess, far from merely afflicting some special individual, is built into the metaphysical reality that is the very condition of individual existence itself: ὡς ὁ θεὸς ἡμᾶς ἐνδίκως μὲν ἀλλ' ἄγαν . . . ἀπώλεσ' . . . ('The god has ruined us—justly, but *too much*,' 1249–50).[36] At one unguarded moment, a similar response to reality afflicts Hamlet: 'The slings and arrows of *outrageous* fortune' (*Hamlet* III. i). In Greek tragedy, the Apolline principle of 'nothing in excess' (μηδὲν ἄγαν: Apolline both literally and in Nietzsche's extended sense) is constantly activated from the perspective of the orderly anonymous survivors, who see a cosmic problem only in the sense of fearing the dangers of any incautious striving. The nurse in *Hippolytus* speaks for many who (unlike the poet Blake) do not believe that 'the road of excess leads to the palace of wisdom':

> οὕτω τὸ λίαν ἧσσον ἐπαινῶ
> τοῦ μηδὲν ἄγαν·
> καὶ ξυμφήσουσι σοφοί μοι.
>
> Extremes I have less
> Time for than the 'nothing in excess',
> And all the sages back me
>
>   (264–6)

and many a tragic chorus shudders, like the Thebans in *Oedipus Tyrannus*, at the thought of success, even, that is 'over' limits (εἰ πολλῶν ὑπερπλησθῇ μάταν, 873–4).[37] Everything 'over' is suspect, however 'good' in itself: it was Oedipus, after all, who shot 'over' the limits when he so impressively solved the Sphinx's riddle (καθ' ὑπερβολὰν τοξεύσας, *OT* 1196–7). The case may be more lurid when 'too' and 'over' lead to crime, as with Macbeth's 'vaulting ambition which *o'er*leaps itself' (*Macbeth*, I. vii), or to madness, as with Euripides' Heracles or Shakespeare's Lear ('be Kent unmannerly, When Lear is *mad* . . . check | This hideous *rashness*', *King Lear*, I. i): it is no different in principle.

It is no coincidence that when the striving individual who has gone too far comes to recognize his striving for what it is, the recognition will have come ὀψέ, '*too late*'. This 'too' evokes not only the poignancy of such moments[38] but the excess that made them inevitable (and the poignancy itself is ultimately another comment on the unrestrainedness of the causal order of things). So it is in *Antigone* when the chorus eventually says to Creon

οἴμ᾽ ὡς ἔοικας ὀψὲ τὴν δίκην ἰδεῖν

It seems you recognized justice too late

(1270)

and Creon can only reply

ἔχω μαθὼν δείλαιος

I have learned and suffered.

(1272)

So too with the Theban royal house in *Bacchae*,

Διόνυσε, λισσόμεσθά σ᾽, ἠδικήσαμεν

Dionysus, we beseech you, we have done wrong

(1344)

where Dionysus' answer reflects the *must* that Pentheus in particular ignored:

ὄψ᾽ ἐμάθεθ᾽ ἡμᾶς, ὅτε δ᾽ ἐχρῆν οὐκ ᾔδετε

Too late you knew me: when you *should* you knew me not.

(1345)

The 'too late' can be uttered, with ironic perversity, by the striving individual against the powerless, as Clytemnestra throws it against the chorus in *Agamemnon*:

γνώσῃ διδαχθεὶς ὀψὲ γοῦν τὸ σωφρονεῖν

You'll learn to know your place, maybe too late

(1425)[39]

and more brutally still by the individual against the very object of his misplaced energies, as by Othello against Desdemona

D. Kill me tomorrow; let me live tonight.

.   .   .   .

O. It is too late.

(*Othello*, v. ii)

or (worse still?) against an unintended victim, as when Gertrude drinks the poison meant for Hamlet: 'It is the poisoned cup; it is too late' (*Hamlet*, v. ii). In all these different contexts the sense of excess remains.

Their compulsions and their excess are integral to the striving individuals' identity; and their identity is peculiarly strong. For all the vacillations of a Hamlet or the elusiveness of a Heracles, we tend to feel that in a very special sense they are, as Hegel said, 'that which they will and accomplish... they are that which they are'.[40] 'Speak of me as I am,' says Othello; and the striving individuals tend to show a preoccupation with how, and what, and who, they are.[41] They are what Nietzsche called 'truly-in-and-for-themselves': they claim 'the right to answer all accusations with an eternal "that's me".'[42] They may, like Creon and Antigone, like Macbeth and Lady Macbeth, have a set place in a social order, but by virtue of their self-asserting they are never wholly containable within an order and instead will tend to create their own isolation or dislocation from it.[43] And throughout the plays, our and their sense of their individual being is marked and enforced by appropriate linguistic indicators, above all the *name* and related formulations. The name—'that mark of recognition' by which 'society places' its members—[44] seems to embody all the endeavour that isolates them from society, so that any belated compromise with the social order can induce, ironically enough, a distancing from the name as well. Witness, for instance, Othello. At the end of the play—and at *his* end—he speaks of himself and his name from a strange new perspective: 'That's he that was Othello—here I am' (*Othello*, v. ii). Conversely, for Creon, faced with the final horror of his wife's suicide, the 'I' on whose integrity he insisted throughout his conflicts with Antigone and Haemon is seen as the decisive agent of even this most recent calamity:

> ἐγὼ γάρ σ', ἐγώ σ' ἔκανον, ὦ μέλεος,
> ἐγώ, φάμ' ἔτυμον
> I am your killer, I am, I am
> In truth the one
>   (Sophocles, *Antigone* 1319–20)

whereas now, relinquishing that integrity, he is (literally?)

> τὸν οὐκ ὄντα μᾶλλον ἢ μηδένα
> one who exists but as non-entity.
>   (1325)

The revelation of Oedipus' identity induces a kind of stylized hysteria among the old men at Colonus (Sophocles, *OC* 214–24), as does, in more rhetorical idiom, Macbeth's announcement of his name to young Siward in the final battle for the crown (*Macbeth*, v. vii); while in the conventional 'recognition' scene that figures in various Greek tragedies, revelation of identity generally provokes an explosion of joy as well as furthering an intrigue. Exciting as they may be, though, such moments are more or less tangential to the inner causalities of tragic action, the individual strivings and their consequences.[45] In some plays, however, names and associated titles take on a causal significance of an obviously relevant kind. In *Macbeth* (I. iii) it is the witches' address to the Thane of Glamis as *also* Thane of Cawdor and as 'king hereafter' that serves as symbol and spring of Macbeth's fatal ambition. In *Antony and Cleopatra* (III. xiii) the moment of resolution when Antony 'is Antony again' and (so) 'I will be Cleopatra', is one link in a chain of moments which, right up to the two lovers' deaths, make it seem not only plausible but necessary that (as Cleopatra puts it) 'none but Antony Should conquer Antony (IV. xv) and that she, on her side, should remain 'noble to myself' (v. ii).[46] In *Oedipus Tyrannus*, on an even grander scale, the famous hero's name is famously 'placed' with reference both to sight (*Oidipous: eidon*), which Oedipus once had but, in an act bordering on self-destruction, chooses not to have—and again to knowledge (*Oidipous: oida*), which Oedipus thought he had, but did not have. In his own richly ironic words he is: ὁ μηδὲν εἰδὼς Οἰδίπους, 'Know-nothing Oedipus' (397).[47]

In *Bacchae* the issue of identity is probed no less disturbingly. The implication, latent in Pentheus' name, that he is 'man of *grief*' (*penthos*) is spelt out by Tiresias (367) and restated by Dionysus (506–8):[48]

Δι. οὐκ οἶσθ' . . . ὅστις εἶ.
Πε. Πενθεύς, ᾿Αγαύης παῖς, πατρὸς δ' ᾿Εχίονος.
Δι. ἐνδυστυχῆσαι τοὔνομ' ἐπιτήδειος εἶ.

DIO. You know not who you are . . .
PEN. Pentheus—son of Agave and Echion.
DIO. You have a name fit for calamity.

By interpreting the name, the god effectively dismembers Pentheus' identity, as the women will dismember his body; the self-asserter, meanwhile, clings to the name as a token of meaning in itself. Eventually, the two dismemberments are brought together in the messenger's account of Pentheus' death and, before it, the description of his brief and belated awakening to the reality of his nightmarish situation. In this long speech (1043–1152) Pentheus' name occurs seven times, first as the name of an assertive individual, a lord and master of his fate:

Πενθεύς τε κἀγὼ (δεσπότῃ γὰρ εἱπόμην)

Pentheus and I (of course I followed master)

(1046)

later as the name of the helpless son of a possessed woman

ἐγώ τοι, μῆτερ, εἰμί, παῖς σέθεν
Πενθεύς

Mother, it is I, your son
Pentheus

(1118–19)

finally as the label attached to the remains of a body

πᾶσα δ' ᾑματωμένη
χεῖρας διεσφαίριζε σάρκα Πενθέως

And one and all, blood all upon their hands,
Played catch-the-ball with bits of flesh of Pentheus.

(1135–6)

Between them, these seven enunciations of the name construct a simple but telling pattern. The first six (while Pentheus still lives) are all placed at the assertive beginning of the verse, and the seventh and last (when Pentheus is now dead and his identity is extinguished) at the submissive end.[49]

III

Compulsion, excess, identity: the *must*, the *too*, the *name*. These crucial markers may pervade the dramatic text or they may surface in a more restricted way. In either case they tend to occupy the linguistic foreground, and not randomly, but at representative moments of crisis for the individuals in question. Tragedy (if we may appeal to a familiar schematization) tends to involve configurations of action in which one or more striving individuals assert themselves, and from that assertion find, or create, catastrophe, and in the catastrophe they, or others on their behalf, find a recognition that this whole sequence from assertion to catastrophe is (as any Aristotelian would insist) a necessary one; catastrophe is sometimes averted, of course, but, even when averted, is still, in a strict sense, necessary.[50] The assertion will tend to take one or both of two forms: a decision, into which it is articulated; or a collision with others in which it is embodied. *Decision*, because the assertion, with all its fateful, and generally irrevocable, consequences[51] may be construed as mistaken (ἁμαρτία), or may be made in ignorance, but is unlikely to be accidental: ἕκων ἕκων ἥμαρτον ('I did wrong *on purpose, on purpose*', *Prometheus* 266) is a familiar tragic cry. *Collision*, because the assertion will commonly be identified and assessed by its encroachment on the domain of others. We thus have a set of elemental moments centring on the catastrophe and leading up to it or following from it. For the individuals involved the catastrophe itself is not so much a moment of crisis as a moment of fulfilled pain. The true critical moments are those that lead up to it or follow from it: assertive moments of decision or collision before the event and retractive moments of recognition afterwards;[52] and it is these moments of crisis around which the determinative linguistic markers tend to cluster. Given that some tragedies fall short of recognition (like *Trojan Women*), or assume rather than stage crucial decisions (like *Antigone*),[53] or represent collisions in action rather than in verbal confrontation (like *Macbeth*), there can of course be nothing like a predictable pattern of critical moments, let alone a predictable pattern of linguistic clusters around them. None the less, the markers do tend to cluster around these moments and, by their clustering, mark them off as special in turn: Creon deciding to free Antigone; Antony and Cleopatra resolving to fight on; Pentheus in collision with Agave, which is *his* moment of recognition; Othello brushing aside Desdemona's plea; Orestes recognizing the enormity of his commitment to kill his mother.

These and other critical moments are marked by names and titles, by too muches and too lates, by musts and wills. And yet a comparable sense of identity, excess, compulsion, can sometimes be created without such markers. What can happen is that, at the critical moments, the logic of identity or excess or compulsion is not stated explicitly but is enacted by appropriate stylistic means (of which intensified poetic language provides a plentiful supply);

or alternatively, explicit statement is enforced by such means. Either way, it is characteristic that the decisive and elemental quality of the crisis is mediated through decisive and elemental language, which (despite the requisite intensification of tragic language as a whole) is generally language of stylized simplicity; such language will be prominent, even if not pervasive, at these moments; and what this language will in any case tend to do is—by the classic defamiliarizing process—mark itself off from a maybe more elaborate linguistic norm in the surrounding text.[54]

The specific mechanisms, of course, will vary: not randomly, however, but in accordance with the determinative logic of the moment in question. A moment of crisis, for instance, can be marked by *dislocation* in a way that focuses sharply on an individual identity. Consider again, in more detail, the moment in *Choephori* when Orestes prepares to kill his mother and she pleads for her life—and Orestes, in sudden consternation, turns to a third party for advice:

Κλ.   ἐπίσχες, ὦ παῖ, τόνδε δ' αἴδεσαι, τέκνον,
       μαστόν, πρὸς ᾧ σὺ πολλὰ δὴ βρίζων ἅμα
       οὔλοισιν ἐξήμελξας εὐτραφὲς γάλα.
Ορ.   Πυλάδη, τί δράσω; μητέρ' αἰδεσθῶ κτανεῖν;
ΠΥΛΑΔΗΣ
       ποῦ δὴ τὸ λοιπὸν Λοξίου μαντεύματα
       τὰ πυθόχρηστα, πιστά τ' εὐορκώματα;
       ἅπαντας ἐχθροὺς τῶν θεῶν ἡγοῦ πλέον.
Ορ.   κρίνω σε νικᾶν, καὶ παραινεῖς μοι καλῶς.

CLYT.   Wait, my son! my child, regard my breast!
       Here, how often once you used to drowse,
       And squeeze the nourishing milk out with your gums.
OR.   Pylades, what do I do? Am I to spare my mother?
PYL.   Apollo's oracles—what will become of them,
       The word of Delphi and the covenant?
       Make men your enemies, but not the gods.
OR.   You give me good advice. I judge you win.

(896–903)

Two features of the writing are notable. In the first place, there is the striking ('defamiliarizing') switch from the relatively ornate language of the mother (note the transferred 'ornamental' epithet εὐτραφές, 'nourishing') to the crushingly simple question of the son. Secondly, these are the first and only words spoken by Orestes' companion Pylades in the play, though he has been on-stage for much of the action. What we have, as far as the two men are concerned, is a startling conversion of monologue into dialogue; and the dislocating effect of this serves not only to focus attention onto the moment of crisis but to project what has hitherto been, and will subsequently again be, Orestes' undivided commitment, as momentarily challenged. The challenge is in effect to his whole identity. By virtue of *who* he is, he must both *not* kill Clytaemnestra and *yet* kill Clytaemnestra. It is as if his mother were saying: who are you, after all? are you not my son? The answer has to be: yes, but also my father's son, therefore his avenger. The *must* implicit in that answer is duly articulated by Pylades in terms of oracles and sacred agreements and Orestes' purpose is duly restored. The momentary division of the words between speakers thus symbolizes the momentary division in Orestes' own mind, and the very fact that he should at this juncture appeal to another is made to seem an indicator, and even an enactment, of what we, in a special sense might well call 'a crisis of identity'.

Compare and contrast the sequence in *Bacchae* 809–12 where Pentheus, after a fruitless argument with Dionysus, eventually loses patience

Πε.   ἐκφέρετέ μοι δεῦρ' ὅπλα, σὺ δὲ παῦσαι λέγων

PEN.   Bring me my armour here!—and you be quiet

only to be startled into a quite new response by the god's invitation to see the maenads in action:

Δι.   ἆ.
       βούλῃ σφ' ἐν ὄρεσι συγκαθημένας ἰδεῖν;
Πε.   μάλιστα . . .

DIO.   Stop!
       You want to *see* them sitting on the hillside?
PEN.   I do, yes . . .

Pentheus, maybe to his own surprise, 'decides' to be tempted. Of special importance here is the isolated, *extra metrum* ἆ ('stop') that introduces the tempting question.[55] It constitutes (we might say) a challenge to the orderly line-structure and the orderly exchange of lines in the stichomythia which, up to this point, has been on Pentheus' terms, because dictated by his orderly, and ordering, royal self. But which 'self' is he now? We have here (in Dodds's classic reading) 'the beginning of a psychic invasion, the entry of

the god into his victim, who was also in the old belief his vehicle',
and in these lines (in Dodds's words again) 'his self-mastery van-
ishes'.[56] The challenging monosyllabic interruption (we may add)
marks the moment of rupture within Pentheus' whole being.

Contrast, again, *Macbeth* II. ii:

MACB. I have done the deed. Didst thou not hear a noise?
LADY M. I heard the owl scream and the crickets cry.
Did not you speak?
MACB.   When?
LADY M.   Now.
MACB.   As I descended?
LADY M. Ay.
MACB.   Hark! Who lies i' th' second chamber?
LADY M. Donalbain.
MACB.   This is a sorry sight.
LADY M. A foolish thought to say a sorry sight.
MACB. There's one did laugh in's sleep, and one cried 'Murder!'
That they did wake each other. I stood and heard them.

The sudden disintegration of the verse into staccato exchanges
(*antilabe* in an extreme form) of course sums up the high tension
that momentarily afflicts both Macbeth and his wife, but especially
Macbeth, after the murder of Duncan and 'those of his chamber'.
Beyond that, however, it hints at the disintegration of self-
stability[57] on Macbeth's side which is written into the agitated
conversation that follows:

MACB. But wherefore could not I pronounce 'Amen'?
.   .   .   .
LADY M. These deeds must not be thought
After these ways; so, it will make us mad.
MACB. Methought I heard a voice cry, 'Sleep no more . . .
.   .   .   .
Glamis hath murdered sleep; and therefore Cawdor
Shall sleep no more—Macbeth shall sleep no more'

and now the roll-call of Macbeth's titles has a dissociative, not a
cumulative, ring,

I am afraid to think what I have done
.   .   .   .
What hands are here? Ha! they pluck out mine eyes

and mind and hands, hands and eyes, seem fragmented—until
finally:

To know my deed, 'twere best not know myself.

It is more than a play on words to suggest that the elemental quality of so much of the language in this sequence (heavily monosyllabic, as often in Shakespeare at such moments) helps to realize the
terrible nightmare: elements of human selfhood threatened with
their dissolution.

If identity can be evoked—or challenged—by stylistic mechanisms of dislocation, excess is often associated with effects of
contradiction or paradox: 'not only, but also', but in contexts
where *either* the 'not only' *or* the 'but also' would make adequate
sense, and their combination evokes instead a disturbing super-
fluity. In the simplest of instances paradox is actually built into
the explicit formulation of excess itself. Thus *Bacchae* 1249–50:
ὡς ὁ θεὸς ἡμᾶς ἐνδίκως μὲν ἀλλ' ἄγαν . . . ἀπώλεσ', 'The god has
ruined us—justly, but too much.' Excess is explicit and paradox
unmistakable—and this, of course, near the climax of a play in
which excess, madness, and paradox on a vaster scale are never
far away. The same can be said of *Hamlet*, in which what the king
calls 'Hamlet's transformation' (II. i) marks the point from which
madness, feigned madness, more commonplace eccentricity (like
Polonius'), and 'ordinarily' extravagant endeavours jostle bewil-
deringly. Not the least extraordinary feature of the play is the
alarming variation of tone and register within single scenes, so
that the scene (III. i) that brings on Hamlet contemplating life
and death in high verse ('To be or not to be . . .') soon has him
bemusing Ophelia in plain prose:

HAM. Are you honest?
OPH. My lord?
HAM. Are you fair?
OPH. What means your lordship?
HAM. That if you be honest and fair, your honesty should admit no dis-
course to your beauty.
OPH. Could beauty, my lord, have better commerce than with honesty?
HAM. Ay, truly: for the power of beauty will sooner transform honesty
from what it is to a bawd than the force of honesty can translate beauty
into his likeness. This was sometime a paradox, but now the time gives
it proof. I did love you once.
OPH. Indeed, my lord, you made me believe so.
HAM. You should not have believed me; for virtue cannot so inoculate our
old stock but we shall relish of it. I loved you not.

In this most painful of human collisions, and amidst such a swirl of contradiction ('I did love you once': 'I loved you not'), it seems only appropriate that whatever was 'sometime a paradox' should 'now' be subject to 'proof'. The thought that paradox can be proved would have commended itself to Aeschylus, when formulating Agamemnon's dilemma: ἀνάγκας ἔδυ λέπαδνον, 'Compulsion's strap he stooped to' (*Agamemnon* 218). To sacrifice Iphigenia was *both* a choice ('stooped to') *and* a non-choice ('compulsion'), and the contradiction is shown to be such by the reciprocal killings—his own and Clytemnestra's—that are engendered in the wake of that first shedding of blood.

In some instances paradox is itself one of two alternative possibilities. Witness *Macbeth* II. ii again:

> What hands are here? Ha! they pluck out mine eyes.
> Will all great Neptune's ocean wash this blood
> Clean from my hand? No; this my hand will rather
> The multitudinous seas incarnadine,
> Making the green one red.

Where Lady Macbeth, in the face of the horror of the moment, can calmly suggest that 'a little water clears us of this deed', Macbeth suffers the agony of recognition, and the perceived excess of his deed translates itself into the most extravagant of conceits: the oceans themselves will take on the colour of the blood of his victims. Within his speech, two contradictory stylistic registers fight for control—not only 'wash . . . clean . . . hands' and 'making . . . green . . . red', but also 'Neptune's ocean' and 'multitudinous . . . incarnadine'—but it is the simpler idiom that wins, and its victory only serves to make contradiction worse. 'Making the green one red': even the colour of life will be perverted (as the murderers themselves already are) by the deed.

Compare the contrastive styles of utterance at *Oedipus Tyrannus* 435–8:

Τε. ἡμεῖς τοιοίδ᾽ ἔφυμεν, ὡς μὲν σοὶ δοκεῖ,
    μῶροι, γονεῦσι δ᾽, οἵ σ᾽ ἔφυσαν, ἔμφρονες.
Οι. ποίοισι; μεῖνον. τίς δέ μ᾽ ἐκφύει βροτῶν;
Τε. ἥδ᾽ ἡμέρα φύσει σε καὶ διαφθερεῖ.

TIR. To you I am a born fool, but to those
    Parents who gave you birth I would sound wise.

OED. Parents? Wait: who is it gave me birth?
TIR. This day will give you birth and dissolution.

At the height of the clash between a restless Oedipus and a reluctant Tiresias, the flow of the king's anger is suddenly checked by the old prophet's talk of 'parents'. The staccato three-sentence line that it provokes, highly unusual and arresting in itself,[58] engenders in its turn a remark of prophetic paradox—'this day will give you birth'—completed by the hardly less disconcerting, 'and dissolution'. It is not surprising, then, that Oedipus' exasperated rejoinder should make the hero himself the victim (rather than the hidden cause) of excess: ὡς πάντ᾽ ἄγαν αἰνικτὰ κἀσαφῆ λέγεις, 'Your words are all too full of mystery' (439).

The moment of Antony's resolution that we glanced at earlier (*Antony and Cleopatra*, III. xiii) is a prime instance of a critical moment around which specific linguistic markers form a cluster. A fuller citation will make the point:

ANT. There's hope in't yet.
CLEO.   That's my brave lord!
ANT. I will be treble-sinewed, hearted, breathed,
     And fight maliciously. For when mine hours
     Were nice and lucky, men did ransom lives
     Of me for jests: but now I'll set my teeth,
     And send to darkness all that stop me. Come,
     Let's have one other gaudy night. Call to me
     All my sad captains; fill our bowls once more.
     Let's mock the midnight bell.
CLEO.   It is my birthday,
     I had thought t'have held it poor; but since my lord
     Is Antony again, I will be Cleopatra.
ANT. We will yet do well.
CLEO. Call all his noble captains to my lord.

Here, as everywhere, the great lovers live and breathe beyond the normal rules ('If it be love indeed, tell me how much.'— 'There's beggary in the love that can be reckoned', I. i). For all the protestations of requisite intent—'I will be treble-sinewed', 'I'll set my teeth', 'I will be Cleopatra', 'We will yet do well'— that 'yet' and, particularly, Antony's 'one other' and 'once more', hint at a recognition that even their defiance of the rules is coming to an end. Connoting, seemingly, both 'one last' and 'one too many', it is as if this high equivalent of the modern 'one for the road' summed up the extravagance against which the orderly rationality of Caesar must be triumphant. The recognition, then, has more than a touch of *amor fati*: 'Komm du, du letzter, den ich anerkenne . . .'[59] Amidst these expansive markers, however, are signs of unstable contradiction. Antony will in one phrase 'send to *darkness*' everyone in his path, and in the next make himself 'one other *gaudy night*'; and both the clash of 'darkness' (figurative) and 'night' (literal) and the strangeness of the collocation 'gaudy night' itself[60] seem to sum up his, and Cleopatra's, immoderation and its instability. One notes, again, the haunting displacement, 'sad captains', where the shape of the phrase seems to entail a generic epithet (like Cleopatra's 'noble captains' a few lines later), not the specific 'sadness' that Antony means to remove—and the result is a new set of contradictory alignments: 'gaudy' and 'sad', 'sad' and 'fill our bowls'. The simplicity of the language that encases the paradoxes ('I'll set my teeth', 'Come, Let's have', 'call to me', 'fill our bowls') is as marked as ever.

Compulsion, the *must* of tragedy, is perhaps evoked most readily. There is one characteristic mechanism: intensifying repetition or some other kind of parallel structuring: as if to say, anything once *can* be anything; anything twice *must* be as it is.[61] In various of the instances already discussed a sense of the inevitable, or (often) an irresistible movement towards the inevitable, is created in such a way. In our *Antony and Cleopatra* passage (yet again) an insidious pattern of assonance envelops the assertions of identity and the paradoxes and seems to present us, and the lovers, with compulsion at the heart of things: 'And send to darkness *all* that stop me. . . . *call* to me | *All* my sad captains; *fill* our *bowls* once more. . . . but since my lord | Is Antony again, I *will* be Cleopatra. | We *will* yet do *well*. | *Call all* . . .' In such a sequence the balancing of 'Antony' and ' Cleopatra' in the one line has its own irresistible logic.

Consider in this context the repetitive phraseology that marks Macbeth's crisis of decision (*Macbeth*, I. vii):

> If it *were done* when '*tis done*, then '*twere* well
> It *were done* quickly

and more intensively, the first phase of his recognition (II. ii):

MACB. Methought I heard a voice cry, '*Sleep no more*;
   Macbeth does murder *sleep*'—the innocent *sleep*,
   Sleep that knits up the ravelled sleave of care,
   The death of each day's life, sore labour's bath,
   Balm of hurt minds, great nature's second course,
   Chief nourisher in life's feast.
LADY M.   What do you mean?
MACB. Still it cried, '*Sleep no more*', to all the house;
   'Glamis hath murdered *sleep*; and therefore Cawdor
   Shall *sleep no more*—Macbeth shall *sleep no more*'.

Here the overall frame formed by the repetition of 'Sleep no more' contains a series of subsidiary progressive parallel structures, notably the set of appositional phrases to 'sleep', itself subsuming the assonantal series, '*death . . . day's life . . . labour's bath, ba*lm', that stretches out from 'death' towards images of hope: elusive images, as the grim repetition of 'sleep no more' makes plain.

Alongside that last passage one could set Macbeth's great last speech, in which his 'recognition' reaches its final phase. Seyton brings the news of Lady Macbeth's death and then a messenger news from the front (V. v):

SEY. The Queen, my lord, is dead.
MACB. She should have died hereafter;
   There would have been a time for such a word.
   Tomorrow, and tomorrow, and tomorrow,
   Creeps in this petty pace from day to day
   To the last syllable of recorded time,
   And all our yesterdays have lighted fools
   The way to dusty death. Out, out, brief candle!
   Life's but a walking shadow, a poor player,
   That struts and frets his hour upon the stage,
   And then is heard no more; it is a tale
   Told by an idiot, full of sound and fury,
   Signifying nothing.
                Enter a messenger
   Thou com'st to use thy tongue; thy story quickly.

As befits such a definitive statement of the inevitable, the speech is constructed around a plangent series of aural inevitables, some involving the repetition of sounds and sound clusters, some whole

words: 'tomorrow and tomorrow and tomorrow', 'petty pace', 'day
to day', 'dusty death', 'out, out', 'poor player', 'struts and frets',
'tale told', '*full* of *sound* and *fury*, *signifying*'. And here too is the
linguistic token of excess, the flat contradiction between 'signifying nothing' in the general and (bizarrely!) 'thy story quickly' in
the particular. In Macbeth's irredeemable universe, communication is as urgent as it is futile; and the only real 'message' left is the
superfluousness of messages *tout court*.

Many of the most familiar moments in Shakespeare (one can
hardly help noting) fall into this category of the stylistic inevitable
at the moment of crisis. To those examples already discussed we
may add as many more, from Hamlet's 'To be or not to be'
(*Hamlet*, III. i) to the moments at the beginning and end of *King
Lear* when Cordelia (I. i) answers her father's demand for public
protestations of love with

COR. Nothing, my lord.
LEAR. Nothing!
COR. Nothing.
LEAR. Nothing will come of nothing. Speak again

(but all the *again* that matters has just taken place)—and then when
Lear distracts Albany from his well-meant proclamation and
finally accepts that Cordelia is dead (V. iii):

ALB.   All friends shall taste
    The wages of their virtue, and all foes
    The cup of their deservings. O, see, see!
LEAR. And my poor fool is hanged! No, no, no life!
    Why should a dog, a horse, a rat have life,
    And thou no breath at all? Thou'lt come no more,
    Never, never, never, never, never.
    Pray you, undo this button. Thank you, sir.
    Do you see this? Look on her. Look, her lips.
    Look there, look there!

In this final, painful sequence, an overwhelming series of parallelisms begins with 'no, no, no life', ends with 'look there, look
there' (the moment of Lear's death), and reaches its climax on
'never, never'. Rather as in Macbeth's 'tomorrow' speech, the terrible irreversibility of the 'nevers' goes hand in hand with a jarring
contradiction, this time between 'their deservings' and 'why
should a dog'. The importance of elemental language in this

instance (centred, here, on a sequence of thirty monosyllables, from 'And my' to 'no more') needs no demonstration.

On the Greek side—and insisting again on the way that critical moments gain force and direction from clusters of linguistic features and associated mechanisms—we may look back to several passages discussed earlier. First, to the simple combination of paradox and repetition in Prometheus' cry, 'I did wrong on purpose, on purpose' (*Prometheus* 266).[62] Likewise to the see-saw exchange between Oedipus and the paradox-monger Tiresias (*OT* 435–8):

TIR. I am a *born* fool to you, but to those
    Parents who *gave you birth* I would sound wise.
OED. Parents? Wait: who is it *gave me birth*?
TIR. This day will *give you birth*

in which one labours to find an English equivalent for the insidious sequence: ἔφυμεν . . . γονεῦσι δ᾽ οἵ σ᾽ ἔφυσαν . . . ἐκφύει . . . φύσει σε.

Then again to *Antigone* 1319–20, where the repetition is too conclusive to be lost in any translation: ἐγὼ γάρ σ᾽, ἐγώ σ᾽ ἔκανον, ὦ μέλεος | ἐγώ, φάμ᾽ ἔτυμον, 'I am your killer, I am, I am | In truth the one.' Then again, on a larger scale, to the parallel placing of the six-fold 'Pentheus' at the start of the verse in the messenger's speech in *Bacchae*.[63] The effect of that particular pattern might be seen as a subliminal one. In contrast the same speech contains two short sequences, both more immediately striking, in the terrible lull before the storm that sees Pentheus' death. First, the stranger, Dionysus, gives his victim a miraculous means of access to the sights he insists on seeing (1064–5):

λαβὼν γὰρ ἐλάτης οὐράνιον ἄκρον κλάδον
κατῆγεν, ἦγεν, ἦγεν ἐς μέλαν πέδον·

He took the top branch of a fir sky-high
And bent it, bent it, bent it to the ground.

Greek literature in general, and Greek tragic dialogue in particular, does not cultivate repetitions of this kind. 'The threefold repetition . . . suggests the slow descent of the tree-top' (Dodds ad loc.). So, no doubt, it does, but over and above such a purely local enactment, the eeriness of the moment (Dionysus is exercising a more-than-human power, ἔργματ᾽ οὐχὶ θνητὰ δρῶν, 1069) and the

inexorability of the larger sequence of events are conveyed at the
same time. Then, a little later, once Dionysus has called out to
the women that their enemy is among them, comes the passage we
excerpted earlier (1084–5):

> σίγησε δ' αἰθήρ, σῖγα δ' ὕλιμος νάπη
> φύλλ' εἶχε, θηρῶν δ' οὐκ ἂν ἤκουσας βοήν.

> The air went quiet; held the wood quiet its leaves;
> No sound of any creature could be heard.

The repetition this time carries additional literary allusions to the
world of lyric poetry, specifically to a passage in the poet Alcman
(fr. 89),

> εὕδουσι δ' ὀρέων κορυφαί . . .
> εὕδουσι δ' οἰωνῶν φῦλα . . .

> They sleep, the mountain peaks . . .
> They sleep, the breed of birds . . .

and another that echoes it in Simonides (frs. 38, 21–2), a vignette
of Danae soothing the infant Perseus with a lullaby:

> εὗδε βρέφος,
> εὑδέτω δὲ πόντος, εὑδέτω δ' ἄμετρον κακόν

> Baby, sleep;
> Sea, sleep;
> All immeasurable evil, sleep.[64]

By means of this unexpected evocation of soothing lullabies and
natural harmony, Euripides constructs what Eduard Fraenkel
called a 'contrast that intensifies the horror':[65] a paradox of an
unusual kind but unmistakable in its impact. Yet over and above
the evocation, the repetitions exercise their due effect. The awful
irreversibility of Pentheus' situation is translated into an 'objective
correlative' (in Eliot's time-honoured phrase), not only in the
action depicted but in the language that depicts it.

If one seeks a Greek tragedy in which repetition and parallelism are
most intensively at work as markers of compulsion, it must be that
ultimate drama of necessity and necessities, *Oedipus Tyrannus*.[66] We
have already said something of the Oedipus–Tiresias encounter,
where indeed language used in the specified way is more pervasive
than we have shown.[67] Perhaps the single most telling sequence in the
play, though, is Oedipus' agonizing encounter with the herdsman

which forces the recognition he is so afraid of and, at the same time, so insistent on provoking. As the truth looms closer and the sense of crisis mounts, linguistic markers put any question of evasion or further delay out of court. What must come must come:

Θε. τῶν Λαΐου τοίνυν τις ἦν γεννημάτων.
Οι. ἢ δοῦλος, ἢ κείνου τις ἐγγενὴς γεγώς;
Θε. οἴμοι, πρὸς αὐτῷ γ' εἰμὶ τῷ δεινῷ λέγειν.
Οι. κἄγωγ' ἀκούειν· ἀλλ' ὅμως ἀκουστέον.
Θε. κείνου γέ τοι δὴ παῖς ἐκλῄζεθ'· ἡ δ' ἔσω
  κάλλιστ' ἂν εἴποι σὴ γυνὴ τάδ' ὡς ἔχει.
Οι. ἦ γὰρ δίδωσιν ἥδε σοι; Θε. μάλιστ', ἄναξ.
Οι. ὡς πρὸς τί χρείας; Θε. ὡς ἀναλώσαιμί νιν.
Οι. τεκοῦσα τλήμων; Θε. θεσφάτων γ' ὄκνῳ κακῶν.
Οι. ποίων; Θε. κτενεῖν νιν τοὺς τεκόντας ἦν λόγος.
Οι. πῶς δῆτ' ἀφῆκας τῷ γέροντι τῷδε σύ;
Θε. κατοικτίσας, ὦ δέσποθ', ὡς ἄλλην χθόνα
  δοκῶν ἀποίσειν, αὐτὸς ἔνθεν ἦν· ὁ δὲ
  κάκ' ἐς μέγιστ' ἔσωσεν. εἰ γὰρ αὐτὸς εἶ
  ὅν φησιν οὗτος, ἴσθι δύσποτμος γεγώς.
Οι. ἰοὺ ἰού· τὰ πάντ' ἂν ἐξήκοι σαφῆ.
  ὦ φῶς, τελευταῖόν σε προσβλέψαιμι νῦν,
  ὅστις πέφασμαι φύς τ' ἀφ' ὧν οὐ χρῆν, ξὺν οἷς τ'
  οὐ χρῆν ὁμιλῶν, οὕς τέ μ' οὐκ ἔδει κτανών.

H. The child was someone of the house of Laius.
O. A slave? Or one of his own family?
H. No more! I am at the grim edge of speech.
O. And I of hearing; yet it must be heard.
H. The child was known as his; but she could tell
 You best, the lady in the house: your wife.
O. Why—she gave it to you?
H.   Yes, my lord.
O. With what in mind?
H.   That I should put it down.
O. Its own mother?
H.   Frightened of the prophecy.
O. Which was?
H.   He'd be his father's murderer.
O. Then why give him to this old man?
H. Pity, sir. I thought he'd take the child
 Home with him to another land. Instead
 He saved it for the worst. Know this: if you
 Are the one he spoke of, you were cursed at birth.

o. It has come true, all of it! No, no!
  Light, for the last time let me look at you.
  Shown up! I am son, consort, killer of those
  I must not, must not, never should have been.
                                    (1167–85)[68]

As so often in Greek tragedy, 'debate' follows the conventional stylization of largely alternating lines in stichomythia. The inherent parallelism of this form (the relevance of which as a compulsive element for Greek tragedy as a whole should not be discounted), hugely accentuated by the contrastive modes of the two speakers, dominates the exchange. Oedipus' words are questions, the herdsman's are statements, and the two points at which Oedipus stops asking questions are the two particular points of crisis when he has the truth in his sights ('And I of hearing') and then finally face to face ('It has come true'). At these two moments of relative arrest, parallelism is intensified with two triads. In the first of these the parallel sequence enforces explicit compulsion: from 'speech' (λέγειν) to 'hearing' (ἀκούειν) to 'must be heard' (ἀκουστέον).[69] In the second triad—that is, in Oedipus' last words, that centre on οὐ χρῆν, οὐ χρῆν, οὐκ ἔδει ('not', 'not', 'never')—parallelism reaches its height. In elemental and heavily monosyllabic language (something not commonly sought or achieved in ancient Greek) inevitability is evoked in the most conclusive way, with οὐ χρῆν protesting, 'no: must not', and the repetition insisting, 'yes: had to be'. Between these two points of concentration parallelism remains powerfully operative in a different way. The switch of speakers within the line (*antilabe*) that begins at 1173 and ends at 1176 is so organized as to make Oedipus' questions shorter and shorter, as if to suggest a progressive closing-in on him as his own questions intensify, until formal balance is restored for the last sombre exchange of four-line speeches (1178–81~1182–5).

The choral verses that follow these words are, as usual, at an elevated distance from the immediacy of this or any individual's suffering. And yet, as if the echoes of Oedipus' terrible crisis were still reverberating, the repetitions continue, strangely, until, soon enough, enacting parallels and explicit *must* converge (1186–95):

> ἰὼ γενεαὶ βροτῶν,
> ὡς ὑμᾶς ἴσα καὶ τὸ μη-

δὲν ζώσας ἐναριθμῶ.
τίς γάρ, τίς ἀνὴρ πλέον
τᾶς εὐδαιμονίας φέρει
ἢ τοσοῦτον ὅσον δοκεῖν
καὶ δόξαντ᾽ ἀποκλῖναι;
τὸν σόν τοι παράδειγμ᾽ ἔχων,
τὸν σὸν δαίμονα, τὸν σόν, ὦ
τλᾶμον Οἰδιπόδα, βροτῶν
οὐδὲν μακαρίζω.

Oh mortal generations,
How close to nothing are your lives:
Make audit.
Is there a man, is there,
Picks up more happiness
Than seeming and, having seemed,
Than ruin?
Yours gives proof,
Your fate, unhappy Oedipus, yours:
Nothing can be blest
That's mortal.[70]

First, τίς/τίς (in the English, 'is there'/'is there'): identity, for the moment, is absent.[71] Then δοκεῖν/δόξαντ᾽ ('seeming'/'seemed'). And then what one commentator rightly calls a 'stylistic rarity',[72] the triple τὸν σόν ('yours'), not at first interpretable, then explained as 'your fate, yours'; but specification of identity now brings no comfort. With the elucidation of this 'yours', one becomes aware of a simple overarching repetition that encapsulates the previous set, εὐδαιμονίας/δαίμονα (approximated in the English by 'happiness'/'unhappy'); and then, with the close of the stanza, another that encapsulates it all: βροτῶν . . . μηδέν/βροτῶν οὐδέν ('mortal . . . nothing'/'nothing . . . mortal'), at which point the symbolic failure of striving, assertive identity is seen to be complete: nothing . . . and . . . nothing. With the completion of the stanza, one becomes aware, too, of an unusually intense parallelizing within its metrical structure. We have here a three-part aeolic stanza (of three lines, four lines, and another four) in which each subsection ends, as commonly, on a 'pendant' resolution (with the normal 'blunt' cadence, ∪ −, 'resolved' by ∪ − −), but where—quite unexpectedly—the three resolving words of each subsection are themselves parallel in metrical shape and, indeed, in grammatical status, namely the three quadrisyllabic verbs, ἐναριθμῶ, ἀποκλῖναι, μακαρίζω (of which the English trisyllabic phrases, 'make audit', etc., offer a feeble equivalent). Horrible as the sense is, it does all make sense, and definitively: *it must be so.*[73]

IV

The critical moments of tragedy—the moments of assertion and recognition—are moments when the striving individual experiences change at its most decisive and immediate. They touch directly on that irreversible condition of all human existence, 'the pathos of becoming'. Perhaps, then, if these distinctive tragic moments are so close to the irreversible, it follows that *must*, compulsion, be it inner or outer, is tragedy's ultimate determinant. Brecht, certainly, would have agreed, when he contrasted the message of tragedy (or 'dramatic theatre') with the positive promise of his own 'epic theatre': the tragic lesson, 'the sufferings of this man appal me, because they are *inescapable*', and the 'epic', 'the sufferings of this man appal me, because they are *unnecessary*'.[74] The same un-Brechtian message would seem to be implicit in all the formal regularities of tragic verse—more scrupulously maintained in classical and neo-classical tragedy than in Shakespeare, but essential to both.

Is this, then, the ultimate meaning of tragic stylization? Beyond all its Apolline transparency, does it, after all, point to a dead end?—line after parallel line, cadence after cadence, elevation after elevation: *it must be so*. As if to say: struggle we may, but the elemental *must* is what we are reduced to, as Oedipus is reduced to 'nothing . . . nothing . . .' and Lear to 'never, never . . .'. Or is this conjunction of the transparent and the impassable the ultimate paradox? And is it therefore rather paradox, and excess, and the 'just too much' that paradox points to, that has the last word? Or could one even give this special, ultimate weight to identity?—to the name that is extinguished in the 'nothing' and the 'never', and yet survives *per contra*, in evocation, to give the 'nothing' and the 'never' their specific meaning.[75] Better, no doubt, to stay with all three determinants, with compulsion, excess, and identity, with the *must*, the *too*, and the *name*, and conclude that in their many configurations, and their many guises, we may locate the distinctive language of tragedy.[76]

Notes

1. I mean the kind of discussion represented by (parts of) W. Jens, *Die Bauformen der griechischen Tragödie* (Munich 1971).
2. Without excluding the possibility of comparable 'tragic' language outside drama, I see good reasons for associating such language with tragic drama above all; compare and contrast Silk and Stern, *Nietzsche on Tragedy*, 278–9, on the tragic effect.
3. For Shakespeare I use the Alexander text (1951), and for the Greek tragedians the latest Oxford Classical Texts (by Page, Lloyd-Jones and Wilson, and Diggle). Translations are my own.
4. See above, pp. 2–8.
5. See M. S. Silk, 'The "Six Parts of Tragedy" in Aristotle's *Poetics*: Compositional Process and Processive Chronology', *PCPS* 40 (1994) 108–15.
6. For Nietzsche, see *Birth of Tragedy*, §11 and for Aristophanes, *Frogs* 939–58. A glance at, say, W. Breitenbach, *Untersuchungen zur Sprache der euripideischen Lyrik* (Stuttgart 1934), shows how firmly Euripidean lyrics, in particular, remain within the bounds of traditional elevated-idiom. It is symptomatic that P. T. Stevens, *Colloquial Expressions in Euripides* (Wiesbaden 1976), should have thrown up so little that is demonstrably unelevated—and one tends to suspect that comparably systematic researches into the other tragedians would throw up as little and as much (cf. Stevens himself, ibid. 8).
7. Cf. the distribution of usage in LSJ s.v.
8. Both are enshrined in classical rhetoric: see e.g. Quintilian, 9. 2. 38, on *apostrophe* (exemplified by, *inter alia*, 'vos . . . Albani tumuli atque luci') and 8. 2. 10 on *epitheta* ('cum dentibus albis').
9. See *OED* s.v. 'Walking: ppl.5'. Authorities argue about the exact nature, or extent, of Shakespearean colloquialism and Shakespearean elevation. Otto Jespersen noted 'the proximity of his poetical diction to ordinary prose' (in *Literary English since Shakespeare*, ed. G. Watson [Oxford 1970] 77, orig. in Jespersen's *Growth and Structure of the English Language* [Oxford 1948]). N. F. Blake suggests that 'Shakespeare's language was less colloquial than that of many contemporaries' (*Shakespeare's Language: An Introduction* [London 1983] 29). There is no doubt, though, that Shakespeare's tragedies use a lower and a higher range of styles ('[in Shakespeare] Latinate vocabulary is used for the high style', Blake, ibid. 43). It was precisely his use of 'low' language in high tragic contexts which (thanks to an intervening shift in socio-linguistic fashion) shocked Dr Johnson about *Macbeth* (*The Rambler*, 168: Raleigh, *Johnson on Shakespeare*, 202–6).

10. Subsuming (for Aristotle) words borrowed from some other dialect of Greek: cf. M. S. Silk, 'LSJ and the Problem of Poetic Archaism: From Meanings to Iconyms', *CQ* 33 (1983) 303.

11. Documented in J. Taillardat, *Les Images d'Aristophane* (Paris 1965).

12. On the distinction, cf. M. S. Silk, 'Aristophanes as a Lyric Poet', *YCS* 26 (1980) 120.

13. T. S. Eliot, *Four Quartets* ('Burnt Norton', I).

14. 'Tragedy and the "Medium"', in F. R. Leavis, *The Common Pursuit* (London 1952) 130–1; see Silk and Stern, *Nietzsche on Tragedy*, 277–8. 'Greek tragedy is poetry' is the robust claim of Lattimore, *Story Patterns in Greek Tragedy*, 13.

15. In Aristotle's own defence, indeed, it can be said that his thoughts are actually offered as a formula for tragedy in particular, but for all serious poetry in general: hence references in *Poet.* 22 to dithyrambic and epic poetry.

16. For 'honest' in *Othello*, see Rosenmeyer, below, p. 519, and W. Empson, *The Structure of Complex Words* (London 1964) 218 ff.; for 'know' in *OT*, see e.g. Calame and Buxton in this volume (above, pp. 19–25, 40–3). I borrow 'plain words' from an unpublished paper by Professor P. E. Easterling, based on her introduction to a forthcoming commentary on Soph. *OC*; cf. also her article, 'Repetition in Sophocles', *Hermes* 101 (1973) 14–34.

17. *Iliad*—*timê* etc.; Eliot—'time' etc.

18. *Preface to Shakespeare*: 'a quibble, poor and barren as it is, gave him such delight that he was content to purchase it by the sacrifice of reason, propriety and truth' (Raleigh, *Johnson on Shakespeare*, 23–4). D. Attridge, *Peculiar Language: Literature as Difference from the Renaissance to James Joyce* (London 1988) 188–209, puts Johnson's criticisms into an interesting perspective.

19. *Birth of Tragedy*, §9.

20. Segal, *Tragedy and Civilization*, 53. Helene Foley's discussion of *Antigone* in this volume (above, pp. 49–73) is one of various notable contributions to this view of Sophoclean drama. Cf. also Calame, above, pp. 28–9.

21. Segal, *Tragedy and Civilization*, 58; J.-P. Vernant in Vernant and Vidal-Naquet, *Tragedy and Myth in Ancient Greece*, 18; B. E. Goff, *The Noose of Words: Readings of Desire, Violence and Language in Euripides' Hippolytos* (Cambridge 1990) 46.

22. Quoted by Segal, *Tragedy and Civilization*, 58.

23. *Birth of Tragedy*, §17: Silk and Stern, *Nietzsche on Tragedy*, 281, 365–7.

24. Cf. Silk and Stern, *Nietzsche on Tragedy*, 276–8; Steiner, *Death of Tragedy*, 238–318 *passim*; Frye, *Anatomy of Criticism*, 37, 210. On the

metaphysical affinities of tragedy, see further Ewans, above pp. 439–57.

25. On 'the hero' as a Renaissance concept, see (still) Jones, *On Aristotle and Greek Tragedy*. The great value of Knox's *Heroic Temper*, which is centred on a discussion of recurrent linguistic 'formulas' (p. 9), is somewhat compromised by his insistence on *heroic* specifications and his corresponding emphasis on the 'single dominating character' which (with some reason, of course) he associates particularly with Sophocles (see above all ch. 1, pp. 1–27), albeit himself well aware (e.g. p. 2) that it is the Senecan-Renaissance tradition that established this emphasis. Regarding *moral* authority: with characters like Macbeth in mind, it is worth stressing that the striving—and suffering—individual, *however vitiated* can make us 'see feelingly', can be our 'scapegoat', in the terminology of Berger and Girard (see Mitchell-Boyask, above pp. 426–37).

26. On the text, see West ad loc.

27. From this point on, the scheme of my argument is new, though obviously there are all sorts of pointers elsewhere—like Frye on the tragic 'this must be' (*Anatomy of Criticism*, 284–5), Nietzsche on Dionysiac 'excess' (*Birth of Tragedy*, §4 etc.), Knox on tragic-heroic 'identity' (*Heroic Temper*, 8 etc.,), and T. S. Eliot on the self-dramatization of the Shakespearean individual in a frame of reference that looks forward to Nietzsche and back to Seneca ('Shakespeare and the Stoicism of Seneca', in *Selected Essays*[3] [London 1951] 129–32). Knox also points the way with his interest in linguistic 'formulas' (*Heroic Temper*, 9 etc.), albeit his 'formulas' are restricted to focal 'heroes' in Sophocles (cf. above, n. 25). By way of clarification of my overall position, note the following: I suppose that the coincidence of the three determinants is peculiar to tragedy. I do not suppose that tragedy is 'about' compulsion, excess, or identity. Nor do I suppose that the three, singly, are only to be found in tragedies, though I think I do suppose that none of them, even singly, characterizes any other genre *as a whole*. One could say a good deal about identity as a determinant of (say) Beckett's *Waiting for Godot*, but hardly as a determinant of tragicomedy (or whatever genre one takes *Godot* to belong to) as a whole. Likewise, one could discuss compulsion as a determinant of (say) Virgil's *Aeneid* ('sed me iussa deum', 6. 461), but hardly as a specific determinant of epic poetry as a whole (the *Odyssey*? the *Faerie Queene*?). One could indeed see the Bergsonian rigidities of character in much of the world's comedy as determinative compulsions; but then again, many comic figures (from Philocleon in *Wasps* onwards) are strikingly free, or freed, of any such compulsions (on which cf. Silk, 'The People of Aristophanes', in C. B. R. Pelling [ed.],

Characterization and Individuality in Greek Literature [Oxford 1990], *passim*).

28. γένοι᾽ οἷος ἐσσί (μαθών): Pind. *Pyth*. 2. 72. 'Du sollst der werden, der du bist', as Nietzsche puts it (*The Gay Science*, 270). The current fashion is to simplify and/or trivialize this classic, open-ended maxim: see e.g. the review of modern interpretations by G. W. Most, *The Measures of Praise* (Göttingen 1985) 101–3. But then what can one expect of a generation that is content to see this most exploratory of Greek poets as a sort of advertising agency? On 'living up to': contrast my discussion of Homeric character (with its fixed qualities) in 'The People of Aristophanes', 165.

29. In Vernant and Vidal-Naquet, *Tragedy and Myth in Ancient Greece*, 10. Cf. Gould, above p. 222.

30. Knox, *Heroic Temper*, 10 (and elsewhere) saw the first-person singular future as characteristic of the Sophoclean 'resolve to act'. Elsewhere I have argued that it is characteristic of (*inter alios*) gods and uncharacteristic of (*inter alios*) old men: see M. S. Silk, 'Heracles and Greek Tragedy', in I. McAuslan and P. Walcot (edd.), *Greek Tragedy* (Oxford 1993) 124, 127–8, 136–7, and 'Nestor, Amphitryon, Philocleon, Cephalus: The Language of Old Men in Greek Literature from Homer to Menander', in F. de Martino and A. H. Sommerstein (edd.), *Lo spettacolo delle voci* (Bari 1995), 165–214 ('parte seconda'). Plainly, first-person futures can mean all sorts of things; they do not mean 'necessity' *per se*.

31. On 'double determination', see Mogyoródi in this volume, pp. 369–70, and cf. her whole argument about *Antigone*, pp. 358–76.

32. On the phraseology, cf. Silk, *Interaction in Poetic Imagery*, 166; on the sacrifice, cf. van Erp Taalman Kip and Garvie in this volume, pp. 119–48.

33. With subjunctives (δράσω, αἰδεσθῶ) rather than futures: cf. Garvie ad loc. αἰδεσθῶ is not easy to put into plausible English (literally, 'am I to let a proper sense of shame/respect constrain me from killing my mother').

34. Garvie ad loc.

35. My discussion is not, I think, affected by the possibility that 'Speak of them as they are' (Quarto), and not 'Speak of me as I am' (Folio), may be Shakespeare's original version, nor by the reasonable thought that 'loved . . . too well' does not *by itself* account for Othello's gullibility: his extremity is not in doubt. More generally, it is worth adding that the tragic *too* may be labelled at the outset as the problem that engenders the tragedy, as it is in *Antony and Cleopatra* ('If it be love indeed', cf. above, p. 479). Conversely, it may itself be problematized in the course of the drama, as it is by

Euripides in *Medea*, where the heroine can say (of herself) οὐκ ἄγαν σοφή (305) and (of 'the plausible villain') οὐκ ἄγαν σοφὸς ὡς καὶ σύ (sc. Jason) (583–4).

36. Cf. Soph. *Ajax* 951 and Eur. *HF* 1087–8 (ὦ Ζεῦ, τί παῖδ' ἤχθηρας ὧδ' ὑπερκότως | τὸν σόν;), and the Odyssean echo in that second passage (τί νύ οἱ τόσον ὠδύσαο, Ζεῦ; *Od.* 1. 62) only serves to point up the contrast of self-destructive tragic excess with an epic ordeal which did, and was always bound to, sort itself out in the end.

37. *OT* 874 evokes an archaic 'Apolline' fear of material κόρος, on which see e.g. Dawe on 872–3, and cf. e.g. Aesch. *Agam.* 1011 f.

38. On which see R. B. Rutherford, 'Tragic Form and Feeling in the *Iliad*', *JHS* 102 (1982) 148–9.

39. The conjunction of ὀψέ and allusion to the 'Apolline' virtue of σωφροσύνη is not unique: cf. e.g. the attenuated insult in Eur. *Or.* 99 ὀψέ γε φρονεῖς εὖ (Electra to Helen).

40. Hegel, *Ästhetik*, ed. F. Bassenge (Berlin 1955), iv. 1086. Though the Hegelian formula is meant to characterize the 'heroes' of Greek tragedy, and especially those of Aeschylus and Sophocles, precisely in contradistinction to those of 'modern' tragedy, such as Hamlet (see Silk and Stern, *Nietzsche on Tragedy*, 322–5), I would argue that if we put the stress on *identity*, rather than *character*, the formula holds good for tragedy as a whole.

41. Knox, *Heroic Temper*, 36: 'in the Sophoclean hero the sense of identity, of independent, individual existence, is terribly strong'. For a more subtle, neo-Girardian, formula for 'heroic' identity, see Mitchell-Boyask, above pp. 426–37.

42. *The Gay Science*, 23. Nietzsche ascribes the saying about 'the right' to Napoleon.

43. Cf. Knox, *Heroic Temper*, 36: 'The centre of tragedy is in the hero's isolation': Frye, *Anatomy of Criticism*, 208.

44. Goldhill, *Reading Greek Tragedy*, 19.

45. It is noteworthy that the emotional climax of 'recognition' scenes often bypasses the actual name or names: see e.g. Eur. *El.* 581 and Soph. *El.* 1222.

46. The 'chain' begins in 1. i with Cleopatra's 'Antony will be himself' and Philo's 'sometimes when he is not Antony'.

47. See Calame in this volume, p. 22.

48. See Stanford, *Ambiguity,* 176. The principle here, as in *OT*, is that of the *nomen omen*, on which see e.g. Dodds ad loc.; Stanford, *Ambiguity*, 34–42, and *Aeschylus in his Style* (Dublin 1942) 72–5; W. Kranz, *Stasimon* (Berlin 1933) 287 ff; and C. P. Segal, '*Nomen Sacrum*: Medea and Other Names in Senecan Tragedy', *Maia* 34 (1982) 241–6.

49. The seven occurrences in full are: 1046, 1058, 1070, 1100, 1113, 1119, 1136. Elsewhere in the play the positioning of Pentheus' name is, by contrast, random. For instance, in Tiresias' speech (266–327) it comes twice, once in fifth foot (309), once in second/third (320); in the Agave-Cadmus stichomythia (1263–301) three times, twice in first foot (1276, 1301), once in second/third (1284).

50. '*Pathos* or catastrophe, whether in triumph or in defeat, is the archetypal theme of tragedy': Frye, *Anatomy of Criticism*, 192.

51. A. Rivier, *Essai sur le tragique d'Euripide* (Lausanne 1944) 33, speaks of 'une décision capitale, souvent mortelle, toujours irrevocable'.

52. 'Recognition', of course, in a more profound sense than Aristotle mostly means by ἀναγνώρισις, which is largely to do with 'recognition of people' not 'realization of circumstances' (Lucas on *Poet.* 11, 52ᵃ29 ff.). For Aristotle 'the moment of recognition' in *Choephori* would be the moment when Electra recognizes Orestes.

53. In *Tro.* Hecuba has her moment of higher understanding (1240 ff.), but as the victim, not as the agent, of any relevant decision or collision. For *Ant.* cf. Mogyoródi in this volume, pp. 360–2.

54. These generalizations are not to be treated as a formula. Quite apart from variations from play to play, the specifics of the 'elemental language', the 'prominence', and the 'marking-off' depend on the particular stylistic norms of the tragic tradition in question. For instance, to take the obvious differentia: in Greek tragedy any 'stylized simplicity' is to be placed against the greater richness of the collective choral lyric as well as the lesser richness of the 'normal' dialogue of the individual characters; in Shakespeare, the extreme contrast would be with the rich language of the excessive individuals at their most expansive. Apropos the formalist concept of defamiliarization, it is worth stressing that—*pace* some formalist discussions themselves—no established linguistic norm can be *per se* defamiliarizing; only the unexpected, the breach of a norm, can be that. Hence 'poetic language' in the sense of a stylized elevation cannot itself defamiliarize, unless it is unexpected (which it never is in verse tragedy).

55. On ἆ see Dodds ad loc. and cf. Dover on Ar. *Ran.* 759.

56. Dodds ad loc.: on the tempting scene, p. 172; on 810–12, p. 175.

57. Contrast the effect of a comparable arrangement of dialogue in Racine's *Bérénice* II. 5, where (in the closing couplet of the scene) Titus announces his decision to the queen and the normal flow of the verse collapses into fivefold *antilabe*: '(T) Mais . . . (B) Achevez (T) Hélas (B) Parlez (T) Rome . . . L'Empire . . . | (B) Hé bien? (T) Sortons, Paulin: je ne lui puis rien dire.' The effect there is more one of irreversible parallelism (see above, pp. 480–8).

58. Cf. Soph *Ant.* 1099 (Creon's τί δῆτα χρὴ δρᾶν; φράζε· πείσομαι δ' ἐγώ) at a moment of comparable crisis.

59. The first line of the last, unfinished draft of Rilke's last notebook (Dec. 1926).

60. 'Gaudy night' was seemingly coined for this passage on the analogy of, and in ironic contradistinction to, the usual 'gaudy day' (see *OED*[2] s.vv). The collocation also evokes the usual sense of 'gaudy' = 'bright' (*OED*[2] s.v. a[2].3a, e.g. Cowley, 'The gaudy heaven'ly bow') and maybe also the now archaic 'gaudy-green' (a bright, yellowish, i.e. day-time, colour), still current in Spenser and others: *OED*[2] s.v.

61. For the logic, cf. e.g. P. Furia, *The Poets of Tin Pan Alley* (Oxford 1990) 78, on the song-writer Gus Kahn: 'Kahn turned out three romantic laments in 1924, and in each he cleverly let the repetitiveness of the music suggest the motif of fate.' (The 'laments' in question included the classic, 'It Had to Be You'.)

62. Socrates, in particular (οὐδεὶς ἑκὼν ἐξαμαρτάνει: Pl. *Tim.* 345d), would have found Prometheus' ἑκὼν ἑκὼν ἥμαρτον a paradox. Cf. Antigone's ὅσια πανουργήσασ' (Soph. *Ant.* 74, on which see Mogyoródi in this volume, p. 363).

63. On these passages, see above, pp. 473, 478–9, 470, 471–2, and add (*inter alia*) Aesch. *Cho.* 896 ff. (above, p. 474) where—untranslatably—the exchange between mother and son involves a crucial parallelism and sound-echo between her αἴδεσαι, τέκνον and his αἰδεσθῶ κτανεῖν: the phrases are metrically aligned and almost anagrammatic.

64. On the Simonides passage, see Silk, *Interaction in Poetic Imagery*, 164, 167, and to the whole sequence add Theoc. 2. 38–9 (σιγῇ . . . σιγῶντι . . . σιγῇ) and 24. 7–8 (εὕδετ' . . . εὕδετ' . . .).

65. See Silk, *Interaction in Poetic Imagery*, 6.

66. Cf. Mogyoródi and Evans in this volume, pp. 358 and 443–5.

67. In particular: the scene begins with Tiresias' ominous words, φεῦ, φεῦ, φρονεῖν . . . φρονοῦντι (316–7), whose sound parallelism is duly echoed in the prophet's last words at the scene's end (φάσκειν . . . φρονεῖν, 462). The effect of the inexorable which, in context, this remarkable pattern carries is shared by Oedipus' angry words in 371, so often quoted for their sound-pattern and so rarely *interpreted* with reference to it: τυφλὸς τά τ' ὦτα τόν τε νοῦν τά τ' ὄμματ' εἶ. The alliteration does of course, as critics tend to say, lend itself to a 'contemptuous staccato effect' in an actor's delivery (the phrase is that of W. B. Stanford, *The Sound of Greek* [Berkeley 1967] 143). More significantly, it marks the self-propelling nature of the fraught collision between blind seer and unseeing king. The monumental and monosyllabic quality of the diction is (in a language like Greek) astonishing, and helps to give this particular line special prominence. The same may be said to a lesser

degree of 430–1 (οὐκ . . . οὐχὶ . . . ἄψ- . . . ἀπ- . . . ἄπ- . . .). In contrast to this stridently echoey rhetoric of Oedipus, it is Tiresias' words that have the ultimate authority, but the connotation of *what must be* that the repetitions carry is all the stronger for that.

68. For obvious reasons I have tilted this translation towards a version that, however palely, reflects the stylistic features under discussion.

69. On this ἀκουστέον, cf. the comments of Lattimore, *Story Patterns in Greek Tragedy*, 41 and Knox, *Heroic Temper*, 10; and Ewans, above, p. 445.

70. Among various apparent eccentricities in this translation, I have eliminated the quasi- (though only quasi-) personal element in ἐναριθμῶ and μακαρίζω because in modern English it is difficult to preach authoritatively (unless with irony, *à la* Eliot) in the first person.

71. Cf. the insidious repetition at 1098, τίς σε, τέκνον, τίς σ᾽ ἔτικτε; in the Greek, of course, each of these τίς words is 'who', not 'any(one)', but as far as non-identity is concerned, it comes to the same thing.

72. Dawe ad loc.

73. By contrast there is nothing of this in the responding antistrophe, 1196 ff.: no quadrisyllabic, or any other, significant parallelisms and no *must*. The markers return at 1204 ff.

74. From 'Vergnügungstheater oder Lehrtheater?', in *Brecht on Theatre*, 71.

75. Eur. *Tro.* 1322–4: ὄνομα δὲ γᾶς ἀφανὲς εἶσιν· ἄλλᾳ δ᾽ | ἄλλο φροῦδον, οὐδ᾽ ἔτ᾽ ἔστιν | ἁ τάλαινα Τροία.

76. My thanks to Pat Easterling, John Kerrigan, Laurel Silk, and audiences in Oxford and St Andrews, for various comments and suggestions on which I have gratefully drawn.

27

Ironies in Serious Drama

THOMAS G. ROSENMEYER

I want to talk about ironies in drama, rather than dramatic irony. Dramatic irony is an idea coined by Bishop Thirlwall, in response to his experience of reading Sophocles.[1] Both his terminology and his perceptions, echoing directly the thinking of some of the German Romantics around the start of the nineteenth century, set a fashion and in the end blocked progress. For his focus on the large tensions and the calculated disharmonies which emerge from *Oedipus Tyrannus* must blind us to other, often less obvious strategies. The effect of the German Romantics upon modern and postmodern criticism remains overwhelming. The counter-classical notion that irony is a matter of total reverberation remains in force. From the New Critics[2] to Northrop Frye[3] to the latest deconstructionist,[4] irony is a concept expanded rather than inspected. Frye, who comes from a study of romance, starts by defining irony as a way of looking, a species of cool appraisal. But as his argument continues, other qualities get mixed in, until the term becomes a pregnant catch-all for a vast array of things. One New Critic, Robert Heilman, in his fretwork investigation of *Othello*, uses the term irony to establish all sorts of linkages, until irony becomes, as it does in Thirlwall, virtually indistinguishable from tragedy.[5] The same is, roughly speaking, true of the work of Bert O. States.[6]

There are honourable exceptions. D. C. Muecke's *The Compass of Irony*, Wayne Booth's *A Rhetoric of Irony*, and books by D. J. Enright, J. A. Dane, and others, have contributed greatly to an understanding of how distinct ironies work, especially in narrative fiction;[7] and theoretical treatments coming out of linguistics and speech-act theory have raised new issues.[8] But as the present generation of students of literature has come to know the term, in the wake of Roland Barthes and Paul De Man and generally the poststructuralists, Schlegel's globalization of irony has ballooned further. We now find that irony is the gap between signifier and signified, the resistance to closure, the statutory impossibility of fixed communication, the fractured identity of the subject, supplementarity, *sous rature*, and much else.[9] In its first guise, if semiotic deferral is a property of the literary text, irony must be both a good thing and inescapable. No worthwhile text can be imagined to open itself up without intimations of this constitutive irony. But on these grounds irony comes to be useless as a critical label. In a social and aesthetic universe in which irony is endemic, the success (or lack of success) of works of literature cannot be judged by their handling of irony. Postmodernism would grant this, in the sense that a special status for literature is disavowed. But for those of us who still hope that literature and, especially, drama are circumscribable entities, the postmodernist appeal to irony must be faulted on two scores: it stipulates that all texts are equally subject to the shiftiness of textuality; and it tends to reduce all kinds of irony to the master figure required by that stipulation.

The Romantic ballooning found its early critics. Lewis Campbell, in his great work on Sophocles, comments witheringly on the meaninglessness of 'irony',[10] and suggests that whenever people talk of 'the irony of Sophocles', the truth is 'better explained by speaking separately (1) of the power of God as an element in Greek tragedy;[11] (2) of the effect of contrast in exciting wonder, and intensifying pity and fear; (3) of the subtle use of language in pointing contrasts through *litotes*, double meanings, and suggestions of the truth; (4) of the ethical genius of Sophocles, unobtrusively making felt the full meaning of every situation; and (5) of the pathetic force with which by a few simple touches he stirs the deepest springs of feeling'.[12] What is clear in this litany of substitutes is that those who talk of irony often mean different things, and that we cannot restore meaning to the term unless we specify what these various things are and how they co-operate in the text. I do not think they are precisely what Campbell proposes, and I want to submit my own tabulation, different from that of Muecke, who remains the master tabulator, though drama figures less prominently in his scheme than narrative and lyric. Moreover, a concept that has had so much vigorous critical energy invested in it cannot be abandoned like an unwanted child. Common speech-habits won't allow it, nor will, one assumes, future critics who continue to bank on the resonance of a broad understanding in popular speech.

It might be argued that irony, in the English-speaking tradition at least, is more easily cornered in narrative than in drama. Swift, Fielding, Gibbon: these are the names that come immediately to mind, and when the term was first detached from the rhetorical context typified by Puttenham and his successors, it was the early eighteenth-century prose-writers who played the leading role. In Germany, August Wilhelm Schlegel wrote that it is assumed that 'whenever the tragic takes root everything like irony immediately ceases'.[13] And Goethe, whose *Wilhelm Meister* was thought by its contemporaries to be the most impressive embodiment of everything that was understood by irony, is felt by some modern critics to have been incapable of writing tragedy. And yet, what is *Faust II*, if not a headlong, perhaps cruel, demonstration of innumerable ironies, small and big? The old notion, that narratorial irony is not available to the drama, has long been exploded. Pirandello and Ionesco are ironists to no lesser degree than Sterne or Diderot, and they are by no means the first.

That in the modern consciousness irony is associated with the drama as much as with the novel is clear from the language of Reinhold Niebuhr. According to him, a sense of irony in history is engendered in us if we visualize history as drama; 'the ironic nature of our conflict with communism sometimes centers in the relation of power to justice and virtue',[14] that is, the range of issues we associate with high drama more than with narrative. Niebuhr's remarks point to an important advantage enjoyed by drama: the novel, by its richness, by its mimesis of the confusions and imbrications of the lived life, and with its admixture of interior monologue, narrated conversation, and the back and forth movement between narrator and characters, is often too complex to leave much room for those ironies which move us powerfully. Drama is a shaped structure, more condensed ($\dot{\alpha}\theta\rho o\acute{\omega}\tau\epsilon\rho o\nu$); its beginning and its end can be felt to relate to each other. A large group of ironies, as I hope to indicate, depend for their effect upon audience response, not reader tracking, via hindsight and anticipation, which a novel cannot be said to stimulate with equal efficiency or economy (though a lyric, of course, can).

It is also possible to argue the other way round. Taking various kinds of speech act—command, statement, persuasion, question, concession—and structuring them via such categories as 'addressee', 'intention', 'intender', and 'signified', one may ask whether drama allows relations, or distances, that are less obvious in the novel, or in the epic, and whether this makes for ironic responses. Another point, first hinted at by Aristotle, though in a different context (*Poetics* 24, 1460ª14–17): in the epic, the act of Achilles pursuing Hector in combat is a certain configuration, drawing on the resources of dream psychology and simile for its power. The same scene acted out on the stage would lack this power, and its dynamics would be γελοῖα, 'ludicrous'. Now we could paraphrase 'ludicrous' by saying that with the added elements of chorus, spectacle, and audience, the dramatic blocking ridiculed by Aristotle might be used to increase the potential for complication and refraction. Superimposed upon the characters of the incident, there would be actors to help corrupt the illusion of unmediated experience. The dramatic event is more palpable than that of narrative, and less pure. The gain for possible ironies is substantial. In the novel, the reader listens in to what the characters have to say to each other. In drama, the actor-character addresses the audience, sometimes over the heads of his fellow characters, sometimes through them. And from the very beginning the boundary between what is an actor and what is a character is not entirely clear.

The drama offers yet another advantage. As Muecke puts it: 'plays are more frequently ironical than narratives. . . . The reason is that only in the theatre does the observer . . . watch actual people who *cannot* know they are being watched.'[15] The characters' necessary ignorance of audience, playwright, and production invites ready victimization. Other features of the drama add to the scope for irony. When we speak of theatricality, we include a tendency on the part of the dramatic hero (less so the heroine) to engage in self-dramatization, often at the point where his weakness or the misfortune that holds him captive is most apparent. When Othello is about to kill himself, or when Oedipus is on the verge of finding out who he really is, they have some of their most ringing verses of self-acclaim. This disproportion between rhetorical energy and personal disintegration is a source of powerful irony, which is, by and large, unavailable to the writer of narrative, not only because climactic undoings are not what the novel strives for, but more especially because the novel lacks the ability to trace a character's progress or decline by the gauge of shaped, public speech.

A word of caution: the irony that goes with self-acclaim, the irony of big speech and fatal weakness, comes off properly only in the hands of certain dramatists. Such false pretension is a close neighbour to the braggadocio of the Roister-Doisters of comedy, who have at best a very limited stake in irony. Moreover, it can, if it is handled without restraint, smother itself. This is what happens in much neo-classical drama, where big speech turns into a signal of generic commitment rather than retaining its function as a tool of climax. In the *Oedipus* of Dryden and Lee, the scene between Oedipus and Iocasta is managed so grandly that all the delicate implications and unspoken forebodings of the Sophoclean text are articulated and worked to death. Those crucial ironies—Oedipus cursing the killer, Iocasta loving Oedipus like a son—are trumpeted until melodrama and manner have choked them. Irony, it appears, requires restraint, a refinement of touch which imitators of the classical canon often choose to sacrifice.

But the time has come to make some distinctions.[16] I shall be laying out four general classes of irony, each with its special subdivisions. My survey will have to be rapid, and formalistic; there is no time for canvassing the multitude of issues—psychological, rhetorical, anthropological, philosophical—which irony provokes. The first type I shall take up is what I call forensic irony, the irony of attack and defence. Let me start with a passage from *Othello* (III. iii. 134 ff.). Iago, pressed by Othello to express his thoughts, replies that he has the same rights as a slave—that is, he does not have to speak his inmost thoughts, particularly if they happen to be disagreeable.

> Utter my thoughts? Why, say they are vile and false,
> And where's that palace whereinto foul things
> Sometimes intrude not? Who has that breast so pure
> But some uncleanly apprehensions
> Keep leets and law days, and in sessions sit
> With meditations lawful?

Iago admits the likelihood that his thoughts are impure.[17] The syntax is clever; rhetorical questions, conditional clauses, concessions, along with general propositions, conspire to persuade Othello to persevere in his belief in Iago's integrity. Iago states the truth about himself, but in such a way that Othello cannot be made to accept it. This is a type of forensic irony which I call 'Henry', after Mr Kissinger: deliberately telling the truth in such a way that nobody will believe it. In what follows, Iago pursues the same line of persuasion (144–54), but now coming down hard on the personal application of what he had advanced as a general premise. As Iago zeroes in on his own personal worth, seeming to plead for his unworth, he falls back on a second form of forensic irony, of the type 'Theophrastus', which Puttenham calls 'diminishing': understating and soft-pedalling the case for what the ironist wants his interlocutor to believe. In both cases, Iago victimizes himself as well as Othello, but the self-victimization is a lesser and momentary device, organized to achieve a more profound violation.

There is a great deal of forensic irony in drama, and it occurs in a variety of shapes and effects, from voicing the position of your victim in order to undercut it, to expressing a Socratic diffidence about certainty, to declaring a sportive unconcern with commitment. It is triggered by the encounter between a disdainful master-handler of speech and the unlucky butt of his experimentation. It should be understood that the victim may be the audience, or the ironist himself, or, especially in narrative fiction, a character or an event submitted to the author's jovial or bitter condescension. Forensic irony can be concentrated in one word or one sentence, or it can represent the informing pattern of a sustained sequence or a complete text, as it does in Swift's *Proposal* or in Meredith's *Egoist*. In drama, the more concentrated and occasional use is more common, though Wilde, and Meredith himself with his dramatic adaptation of *The Egoist*, offer counter-evidence.

Forensic irony is designed less to deceive than to deflate the victim or to perform an end-run around one's self-approbation. Such ironies are relatively easy to decipher, and rewarding to study, for they rely more heavily than other kinds of irony on the complex natural stratagems of language. Linguists and speech-act theorists are concerned exclusively with this type of irony, and have devised interesting theories to explain the naturalness of its indirection of speech. Forensic irony is the only kind studied by the ancients, though an extension of Socratic irony to designate the life and career of Socrates put Quintilian close to intuiting a larger application of the term.[18] The Romantics and their postmodern successors fail to recognize that the rhetorical masters of irony are supremely confident of the power of language. Forensic irony is based on the assumption that the process of inversion or deflection, provoked by delivery, context, and inference, is fully, if not always immediately, registered by the addressee and the listener or reader, and hence is symptomatic of the intelligibility and veracity of communal speech.[19] In spite of the recent flare-up of interest in the subject, and in the face of a flood of exploitations, what happens between enunciation and perception, via inference, remains a mystery. Perhaps metaphor furnishes the closest analogy; one might compare Donald Davidson's 'distinction between what words mean and what they are used to do'.[20] Or again, for certain kinds of forensic irony, one might look to music, to the natural relation between overtones and fundamental sounds, for an instructive if proximate parallel. But these are hazardous guesses. I am less concerned with the epistemological and semiological identification of irony than with the plotting of its conceivable manifestations.

The occurrences of the Greek word for irony (*eirôneia*) and its derivatives in the earliest texts, and analyses from Plato on, suggest that the ironical man is a scornful man. He looks down on his victim, either to unsettle him or to treat him curtly. Compare Aristotle's view that irony is an instrument of scorn and more in the spirit of the free citizen than vulgar slapstick ($\beta\omega\mu\omega\lambda\omega\chi\ell\alpha$). In conversation with his inferiors, the proud man may use irony.[21] In Theophrastus' *Characters* Aristotle's free speaker is dropped in favour of the prevaricator of the earlier texts, and the social relation between ironist and victim is modified, but the disdain remains. The social or intellectual gap between ironist and victim would seem to argue against the prominence of forensic irony in Greek tragedy, where the characters are generally of comparable standing.[22] And in fact such irony appears prevalent only where intrigue or comic angling has corroded the social parity of the agents, or, as in Seneca, where the central characters regard themselves as uprooted from the consensus of the community. But much as one would like to unravel the social implications, not to mention the gender entailments, of forensic irony, the ancient evidence can be deceiving. For instance, Demosthenes (who uses the term *eirôneia* in the old sense of 'shamming') rarely has recourse to irony, perhaps because in his relation with his adversaries, whom he treats as pariahs, he usually affects to be too angry to muster the necessary coolness. Still, at best, social frame and social space might supply the semiotic parameters for an analysis of the conditions under which forensic irony could be expected. For the Greek texts, the best hope for achieving results would seem to lie with comedy.[23] More generally speaking, a transcultural analysis of forensic ironies would have to take account of the differences between modes of response and intonation in the various speech-communities. I am not competent to pursue this avenue.

After forensic irony, the second type is that of blind irony: revealing one's nature without being aware of doing so, or expressing an unintentional *double entendre*, or unknowingly pronouncing a prophetic truth which the addressee does not, and the audience may or may not, accept.[24] Here, as in forensic irony, the contribution is by a single character, and the formulation may be cumulative rather than limited. But there is no attempt at dissembling or simulation, the social frame is immaterial because speaker and victim are one, and the irony comes into being because of the context within which the character speaks. When Cadmus in *The Bacchae* chooses to support Dionysus because, as he puts it, it is good to *pretend* that a member of the family is a god (333–6), we must assume, from the way Euripides has constructed Cadmus' role in the play, that the old man is entirely serious about it. The disproportion between this piece of petty snobbery and the catastrophic invasion of Dionysiac power is such that Cadmus' *cosa nostra* argument emerges as a case of blind irony. Another example, of a more subtle kind: when Cressida takes her first leave from Troilus (*Troilus and Cressida*, III. ii. 147 ff.), she says: 'I have a kind of self resides with you; | But an unkind self, that itself will leave | To be another's fool.' This has a slight air of 'Henry' about it, except that there is no dissembling (I am not convinced by those who debunk Cressida's character). Cressida is telling the truth, Troilus does not believe it, as he is perhaps expected by her not to believe it; both of them, and the audience with them, will later find out that the truth is in fact even more compelling than Cressida, in her diffidence about herself, assumed in the act of speaking. Hindsight, or again the audience's familiarity with the material, is a crucial factor in the identification of this species of blind irony. In Seneca's *Agamemnon* (290) Clytaemestra objects to Aegisthus' continued counsel of conspiracy: 'scilicet nubet tibi, | regum relicto rege, generosa exuli? ('Am I to leave my king of kings, compromise my status, and marry a runaway?') The queen offers this insulting proposition, an insult close to forensic irony, as something quite implausible. The audience knows it will come true.

Some cases of blind irony—Cressida's is one of them—shade off into a third type, to which I now turn; let us call it structural irony.

Blind irony differs from structural irony in that we associate the former with a particular character—clearly Oedipus' error about himself and about others falls under this heading—while structural irony is produced by the text or the plot rather than by a specific speaker, though the voices are, naturally, those of the speakers. Its formulation is more pervasive, and its effect more lasting. This is the irony of tension starred or belaboured by the New Critics. Audience perception is never as immediate as it always is with forensic irony, and as it sometimes is with blind irony. To the extent that the play *Oedipus* or a Euripidean sociodrama is felt to be ironic, structural irony, appreciated fully only when the play is complete, supports the specific blind ironies of the agents. This teleological implication of structural irony is radically opposed to the post-structuralist notion of irony, whose workings spill beyond the confines of a single artefact. What has been called irony of circumstances, and again Helene Foley's ritual irony,[25] come under this rubric, but they are only two of a large number of possibilities. For this is, probably, the richest class, and at the same time the one most difficult to subdivide into subcategories. It is also the one most vulnerable to Lewis Campbell's attack. There is the irony I call 'Godot': the irony that triggers the feeling that in spite of the progress of the action, nothing has changed. Or, more closely wedded to the level of language, the irony I call 'Cratylus', a function of the significant ambivalence of a prominent term or manner of speaking used in the course of the play. The role of the word 'honest' in *Othello* is a celebrated instance.[26] Structural irony is more easily isolated in drama than in narrative fiction or the lyric, where the voice of the author is felt to be virtually accessible, thus rendering the interpretive choice between forensic and structural more difficult.

The Romantic thinkers whose fragmentary formulations made us most keenly aware of the power of structural irony were influenced less by the dramatists than by Plato.[27] When, at the end of the *Protagoras*, Socrates ruefully comments that he and Protagoras have reversed positions; and when, in *The Sophist* and *The Politicus*, the participants look for the sophist and, willy nilly, hit on the philosopher, structural irony as an artistic procedure is already fully developed. And when Northrop Frye distinguishes between comedy and tragedy—comedy sets up an arbitrary law and then organizes an action to break or evade the law; and tragedy presents the reverse process, of narrowing a relatively free life into a chain of causation—we seem to be looking at ironic descriptions of what happens, in its own ironic way, in the *Phaedo* or the *Timaeus*. The irony which arises from an implicit questioning of the 'law,' *nomos*, and of the relation of the human *nomos* to a larger *nomos*, and the showing that *nomos* 'law' and *phusis* 'nature' are in important ways indistinguishable, is as important to the Platonic quest as it is to the dramatic undertaking. But with this we are sliding into the collapsing of the notions of irony and tragedy against which Campbell tried to warn us.

One more question concerning structural irony. It will, on occasion, operate without the agency of speech. Ironies invested in musical compositions and in pictorial work, including films, demonstrate this. Aristotle's tale of the statue of Mitys at Argos falling and killing the man who had killed Mitys (*Poetics* 9, 1452^{a}8) may be cited as a case of structural irony, though of course Aristotle says nothing about that. But a serious play does not feature a statue falling and killing a character. What it does is to talk about it. Everything that is important about a play, and that includes its ironies, depends on speech. Whether the structures are symbolic, or thematic, or semantic, they function within the drama by virtue of the speech put in the mouth of characters and choruses and, perhaps, a narrator. Irony of fate, and irony of events, are projected by means of what people say. A drama built on the principles offered by Artaud or Gordon Craig is less likely to contain ironies, or at least not the ironies that lend substance to the dramatic effect.

The fourth and final type, I suggest, is *Fiktionsironie* (a cumbrous English equivalent might be the irony of skewed orders of reality). I use the German term because this type is the most flamboyant progeny of the German Romantic tradition of Tieck, Grabbe, and others. Here the contribution is neither by a sole speaker nor by the text but, directly or indirectly, by the creative intelligence felt to operate through the play. When the world of characters and the world of actors are confused or dovetailed; or the audience is given a passport into the world of the characters, as happens in *The Knight of the Burning Pestle*; or when the character ponders his own fictive status, as in much of Pirandello, the notion of structural irony is no longer adequate to the tonal and hierarchic complexities. *Fiktionsironie* is at least as old as Aristophanes'

Peace, where Trygaeus turns to the stage-hands and asks them to be careful about the handling of the crane by which he and his beetle are to ascend to the sky.[28] But it has since generated a massive array of stratagems, and vastly complicated our expectations of the links between author, artefact, audience, and levels of reality within the play. Moreover, the Romantic impulse has bred a type of play that defies expectation of structure, and thus appears to remove the rug from under the potential for structural irony. Ionesco's *Bald Soprano*, and Handke's *Kaspar*, are examples. In such plays the hunt for blind ironies or structural ironies is frustrated by the author's refusal to be held accountable for any constant save the absurd. But we could say that the frustration of audience-tracking by the withholding of an anticipated structural logic is itself a species of structural irony, one which I therefore call 'Bobby', after Bobby Smith, the ubiquitous absentee character of *Bald Soprano*. The clash, and the click, between audience disorientation and what is darkly felt to be the play's internal logic is compelling evidence.

Friedrich Schlegel, in one of his more radical moments, thought he could dispense with the audience. 'Mancher redet so vom Publikum, als ob es jemand wäre, mit dem er auf der Leipziger Messe im Hotel de Saxe zu Mittag gespeist hätte. Wer ist dieses Publikum?—Publikum ist gar keine Sache, sondern ein Gedanke, ein Postulat, wie Kirche.'[29] If I may be permitted a free, modernizing translation—a virtual necessity with most of Schlegel's dicta—it would run something like this: 'Many people talk of the audience as if it was somebody you met at a JCC luncheon at the Ritz. Who is this audience? It isn't anything concrete, but a thought, a postulate, like "The Church".' Schegel's erasure of the role of the audience, like the grafting of the audience into the inner workings of the play by Beaumont and Holberg and Tieck, answers to the contextualist demand that the tensions be internal to the work of art. But then Schlegel wrote no plays, and was in fact lampooned by some of the active playwrights of the time. It is certain today, and really always has been, that an investigation of irony and ironies cannot proceed without noting the various ways in which an audience responds to measurable stimuli. The disorientation of the audience in the face of the complexities of *Marat/Sade* is as crucial for the production and testing of ironies as the complicity of the audience in the face of the lean purposefulness of *Oedipus Tyrannus*.

I prefer to list under *Fiktionsironie* certain items that others might wish to count under structural irony. One such is the kind I call 'Helen': a character's or scene's latent appeal to an authoritative myth or work or author of which the audience is made to feel that its significance within the play is intimately related to the bias of the author. Initially, of course, the citing of a myth has little enough to do with authorial intrusion. It is, in fact, unavoidable in classical drama, and an important trigger of both blind and structural ironies, especially through the use of the Euripidean prologue. The prologue of *The Trojan Women* assures us that the Greeks will suffer. Hence, whatever the Greeks say in the course of the drama must be understood in the light of our awareness of what they do not, or refuse to, understand. This species of irony is almost automatic in a tragedy based on a well-known myth. Here structural irony is appreciated by anticipation rather than hindsight. Compare also the misleading prologue, as in *Ion*, and contrast the uninformative prologue, as in *Troilus and Cressida*.

A special situation arises, however, when the author turns critic of his precursors. In his *Electra*, Sophocles suppresses Aeschylus' motif of the footprints. This reticence is not sufficient to alert us to anything unusual. But when Euripides has his Electra comment scathingly on the idea of footprints being used in evidence, we sit up and take notice. The reference is not to a myth, but to a document, a particular version of the myth. This gets us very close to Senecan dramaturgy, where, as Wilamowitz put it, the characters' lines suggest, not that they act out privileged parts in a well-known tale, but that they have read the version by Sophocles or Astydamas and are trying to improve on it. Seneca and Euripides in this vein exemplify the ironic interpolation of the authorial voice that we associate with the modern French updatings of classical drama or, in the novel, with Thomas Mann's recreations of scripture.

More radically, however, the figure I call 'Helen' can make for a degree of authorial confession. Marlowe's tendency to create characters who mirror his own Faustian being is well known. What Marlowe does is to adopt images, or fall back on myths or traditions, which help him put the identification across. The audience is made dimly aware of the virtual entry of the playwright into his work. The old cliché that the dramatist remains outside his *œuvre* is not borne out. 'Was this the face that launched a thousand ships'

has, for me, the force of an irony whose scope encompasses a receptiveness to the voice of the master of the revels sounding through
the embodied language of the plot. The shock of the apparition, the
clash between expectation and appearance, issues in a question that
compounds booklearning with disenchantment, and thus takes its
place alongside other ironies affecting the hero about to be
unheroed. There is even a touch of forensic irony, with
Mephistopheles as the victim. But without the echo of the author's
private voice ringing in the phrase, the power of the question
would be greatly reduced. Tieck, with his introduction of the poet
as a *dramatis persona* in his version of *Puss in Boots* and in *Die
verkehrte Welt*, merely completed the process, and made the irony
more evident.

So much for my four classes, and a few of the subheadings.
Much more could be said about them, and about their intricate
coexistence in dramatic literature. In each case, to evaluate the
force of the irony, or to ask whether the case merits the label irony
at all, we ought to ponder the presence and degree of simulation or
dissimulation, the kind of wit perceived, the victimization and
hurt—who is it that is hurt?—and the stages and levels of catching-
on. But I must confess that I have not yet touched on the most
important issue. Once a listener or reader or critic has isolated various types of irony, and hazarded guesses about the collaboration
of the various types, a larger question presents itself: what this may
tell us about the kind of play in which they occur. Only if we can
show how irony, or ironies, go along with the other stratagems
used by the playwright, how ironies contribute to the total effect of
the play, can we say that we have got beyond the scholastic exercise
conducted in this paper. A purely quantitative procedure is not
sufficient. The fact that a play has a larger or smaller admixture of
forensic irony or of blind irony, or that it allows for an unusual
degree of anticipation, or that 'Svejk' and 'Penguin' are more pervasive in it than 'Brutus' and 'Ludwig', is obviously important.
But the most we can hope for is a loose correlation of some such
quantitative determinations with other judgements. If, in *Othello*
or Sophocles' *Electra*, we find that anticipatory knowledge is
allowed a greater scope than hindsight, and that forensic irony,
through Iago and Orestes, looms large, this will, in a rather
obvious way, support the identification of the drama as a revenge
play. But in addition, the varieties of blind and structural ironies

that link Othello with Desdemona suggest further that the principals are not merely the passive agents of a vicious plot, but that they, in their fashion, creatively participate, as active dupes, in the tragic experience. In the end the tracking of irony can proceed only by a constant process of qualification and revision, whereby the concepts of victimizer and victim are shown to be subject to all sorts of modifying and reciprocal pressures. Perhaps irony will turn out to be a largely heuristic handle, to be abandoned as soon as it has served its first usefulness. But this ironic conclusion—please check under 'Brabantio'—I mean to resist.

APPENDIX: SOME SPECIES OF IRONY (NOT RESTRICTED TO DRAMA)

'It might perhaps be prudent not to attempt any formal definitions. Since, however, Erich Heller, in his *Ironic German*, has already quite adequately *not* defined irony, there would be little point in not defining it all over again': Muecke, *Compass of Irony*, 14. Irony differs from other kinds of discourse in combining within it elements of verbal deflection or cunning; detachment and wit (the latter in its larger eighteenth-century sense); a delayed response (Booth, *Rhetoric of Irony*: click); and victimization and hurt. Irony involves: (1) a disparity between manifest speech and pertinent perception. (2) The perceived disparity is appreciated for its social or aesthetic wit. (3) There is a click of recognition, on the part of the victim or the audience. (4) The wit is hurtful; irony cannot do without at least one bruised or unsettled victim, one whose status and feelings as a participant in a normal system of communication are adversely affected. (This same formulation, of course, applies to other speech-relations, such as abuse, or hectoring; but that does not invalidate its application to irony.)

The list of ironies below is necessarily selective, approximate, and eminently revisable, begging for subtler and broader entries. Cf. the caveats of Muecke (*Compass of Irony*, 66–7) on 'drawing the moon from the millpond'. Taxonomy is an arid exercise and by its nature unstoppable, but it has its uses where significant distinctions are widely ignored. Normally, cases of III (*Structural Irony*) and IV (*Fiktionsironie*) are reinforced by cases of I (*Forensic Irony*) and II (*Blind Irony*), and vice versa. Ideally, cases of types II, III, and IV gain their right to the label 'irony' from their affinity to, or collapsibility into, cases of type I. Cases of *a*, *b*, etc. may be covered by more than one of the subheadings. The names of the subheadings (in italics) are drawn from various contexts, not always explained by the (complete or incomplete) references cited. Booth's 'unstable ironies' are unstable in the sense that often they cannot be located securely in any one of the slots below. Luckily, serious public drama does not, as a rule, favour some of the more recondite or complex varieties of irony found in the eighteenth-century satirists from whom Muecke gets much of his material.

I

Forensic Irony

Aggressive or defensive dissembling, simulation, or affectation, contributed by a single character, via a single formulation or a unitary posture, designed to hurt a victim. Audience perception clicks in almost immediately; the victim also is intended to catch on without delay. In some cases ironist and victim are identical.

a *Theophrastus*: Seneca, *Troades* 209–10: saying less to achieve more or remain uninvolved.

a^1 *Pandarus*: Plutarch, *Adulator* 58b–c: using understatement to gain advantage.

a^2 *Socrates*: Euripides, *Electra* 1124: claiming uncertainty or ignorance to safeguard truth and deflate victim's assumptions.

a^3 *Jane*: Euripides, *Ion* 542: simulating naïvety playfully.

a^{3a} *Anatole*: France, *Penguin Island*, ch. 1: simulating inability to recognize probabilities or observe the law of the excluded middle (cf. IIi and IIIe^1).

a^4 *Anaximenes*: *Rhet. ad Alexandrum* 21: pretending not to say what one is actually saying: *praeteritio*.

b *Crassus*: Cicero, *De Oratore* 2. 65. 262: voicing victim's position to undercut it.

b^1 *Medea*: Euripides, *Medea* 509 ff.: rampant flattery; victim may or may not catch on.

b^2 *Barabas*: Marlowe, *Jew of Malta*, 2. 3. 40: victimizing oneself.

c^1 *Dido*: Virgil, *Aeneid* 4. 381: voicing other than or the contrary of what is intended or expected; victim to catch on.

c^2 *Scipio*: Cicero, *De Oratore* 2. 67. 272: voicing other than or the contrary of what is intended or expected; victim to understand dimly.

c^3 *Iago*: Shakespeare, *Othello*, 3. 3. 216–17: voicing other than or the contrary of what is intended or expected; victim not to catch on.

c^4 *Bérénice*: Racine, *Bérénice*, 5. 5. 1328: bidding or forbidding or conceding the contrary of what is desired.

c^5 *Jonathan*: Swift, *A Modest Proposal*: voicing the contrary of what is desired and reducing *ad absurdum* latent implications.

d^1 *Henry*: Shakespeare, *Othello*, III. iii. 134–9: voicing the truth in such a way that the victim does not catch on.

d^2 *Cassandra*: Aeschylus, *Agamemnon* 1107–13: voicing the truth mysteriously; victim does not catch on, but audience does.

d^3 *Gregory*: Vlastos, *Socrates*, ch. 1: stating a case that is both untrue and true (complex irony); victim not to catch on.

d^4 *Mark*: Twain, 'How to Tell a Story': saying things seriously in such a way that their silliness or humour becomes apparent.

e^1 *Laelius*: Cicero, *De Oratore* 2. 71. 86: engaging in intentional *double entendre*; victim to catch on (NB: not all *double entendres* are ironic!).

e^2 *Clytemnestra*: Euripides, *Helen* 1288 ff.: engaging in intentional *double entendre*; victim not to catch on. Prominent in intrigues.

f *Caius*: Shakespeare, *Merry Wives*, 2. 3. 9–11: boasting or (self-)dramatizing from weakness.

g^1 *Holofernes*: Shakespeare, *Love's Labour's Lost*, IV. ii. 13 ff.: engaging in clever talk to unnerve the victim.

g^2 *Feste*: Shakespeare, *Twelfth Night*, II. iv. 74–9: engaging in light banter, to conceal profundity or concern or anguish.

g^3 *Armado*: Aeschylus, *Agamemnon* 866–73: speaking gravely or grandiloquently of mundane or uncertain matters.

g^4 *Creusa*: Euripides, *Ion* 881–906: using language such as to undermine the spirit of what is said.

h *Ithamore*: Marlowe, *Jew of Malta*, IV. II. 106 ff.: engaging in *sermocinatio*: assuming a persona.

h^1 *Hinze*: Tieck, *Gestiefelte Kater*: (of animals on stage) using human speech.

h^2 *Genie*: Disney, *Aladdin*: (of demons or spirits on stage) using human speech.

i *Achilles*: Shakespeare, *Troilus and Cressida*, II. iii. 81 ff.: allowing a work, myth, or tradition external to the drama to deflect the speech (cf. III*j* and IV *g*).

II

Blind Irony

'Dramatic irony' showing up the ignorance of the agent/victim. Contributed by a single character, via a single formulation or a chain of them. No dissembling or simulation is involved. Audience perception varies from almost immediate to delayed. There is no manifest ironist, though the speaker might be regarded as the victim of a hidden forensic irony issuing from the argument, or Fate, or the author.

a^1 *Cadmus*: Euripides, *Bacchae* 333 ff.: revealing one's nature without being aware of doing so.

a^2 *Lyssa*: Euripides, *Heracles* 849 ff.: revealing another's nature without being aware of doing so.

b *Cressida*: Seneca, *Phaedra* 241: knowingly telling the truth, which is later understood more fully.

c^1 *Deianeira*: Sophocles, *Trachiniae* 602–15: making statements indicative of, or acting on the basis of, ignorance about the present.

c^2 *Menelaus*: Euripides, *Helen* 277–9: making statements indicative of, or acting on the basis of, ignorance about the future.

c^3 *Teucer*: Euripides, *Helen* 116–22: making statements indicative of, or acting on the basis of, ignorance about the past.

d^1 *Oedipus*: Sophocles, *Oedipus Tyrannus* 1080–5: making statements indicative of, or acting on the basis of, ignorance about one's own role or nature.

d^2 *Bussy*: Chapman, *Bussy D'Ambois*, 1.1: making statements at odds with one's actions.

e *Agave*: Euripides, *Bacchae* 1212–15: making statements indicative of, or acting on the basis of, ignorance about personal identities.

f *Othello*: Shakespeare, *Othello*, III. iv. 39: making statements indicative of, or acting on the basis of, a wrong evaluation of the purposes of others.

g *Theseus*: Sophocles, *Oedipus Coloneus* 606: making statements known by the audience to clash with extradramatic reality.

h *Pentheus*: Euripides, *Bacchae* 814: engaging in unintentional *double entendre*.

i *Svejk*: Hasek, *The Good Soldier Svejk*: ingénu's sad or amusing inability to recognize proprieties or observe the law of the excluded middle.

i^1 *Eugene*: Ionesco, *Rhinoceros*: taking conflicting stances.

j *Yorick*: Shakespeare, *Hamlet*, v. i: expressing views or mood at odds with context or expectations.

k *Logician*: Ionesco, *Rhinoceros*, I: *Aneinandervorbeisprechen*: dialogue glancing off addressee.

III
Structural Irony

Enactment of systemic disparity. Contributed by the text or the argument rather than by a character (though the voice is, naturally, that of a character or characters), via a more pervasive or lasting formulation. The text or argument reveals a disparity between passages or actions or events or insights. No dissembling or simulation is involved. The audience perception is slow, energized by hindsight more often than by anticipation. The audience frequently joins the character(s) *in loco victimae*, but also identifies with an implied ironist (Fate or the like) located above the level of the action.

a^1 *Cratylus*: Plato, *Cratylus*: argument conveys significant ambivalence.

a^2 *Heraclitus*: Sophocles, *Oedipus Coloneus* 1211 ff.: argument suggests that a reputable or confidently asserted proposition equals or turns into its contrary.

a^3 *Protagoras*: Plato, *Protagoras* 361a–c: argument issues in cross-over, i.e. reciprocal change of positions.

b^1 *Umbrella*: Aeschylus, *Agamemnon* 367–402: argument suggests that the condemnation of a character also applies to the speaker's side.

b^2 *Christian*: Grabbe, *Don Juan und Faust*: argument discloses that two or more dissimilar characters are in an important sense alike.

c^1 *Penguin*: France, *Penguin Island*, ch. 1: argument suggests that the law of the excluded middle does not apply (cf. Ia^{3a}).

c^2 *Bobby*: Ionesco, *Bald Soprano*: argument frustrates the audience's expectation of logical or empirical structure.

d *Godot*: Beckett, *Godot*: argument suggests that in spite of seeming progress nothing has changed.

e^1 *Aeschylus*: A. Lebeck, *Oresteia*: argument discloses concrete implementation of earlier, often figurative clue.

e^2 *Brabantio*: Euripides, *Medea* 1081–1115: argument discloses the inadequacy (by shortfall or excess) of a speech segment.

f^1 *Maia*: Euripides, *Helen* 115–25: argument suggests that appearance and reality are not easily matched.

f^2 *Creon*: Sophocles, *Antigone* 481: argument suggests that nature and convention are not easily matched.

f^3 *Antonin*: Artaud, *Theatre and its Double*: argument suggests that bad equals, or implies, good.

g^1 *Apollo*: Euripides, *Ion* 1553–70: argument suggests a hidden order or causal chain underlying seeming randomness.

g^2 *Atropos*: Muecke, *Irony*, 44: argument suggests that choice is neutralized by doom.

g^3 *Tyche*: Euripides, *Ion*: argument suggests that order is vitiated by chance.

h^1 *Mitys*: Aristotle, *Poetics* 1452^{a}8: argument discloses that personal initiative leads to the contrary of what is intended.

h^2 *Brutus*: Shakespeare, *Julius Caesar*: argument discloses that the outcome is adversely determined by the complexity of the agent's character or history.

h^3 *Frédéric*: Flaubert, *Education Sentimentale*: argument discloses a character failing to live up to self-projection.

i *Bronx*: Horovitz, *Indian Wants the Bronx*: argument features characters victimized by lack of communication.

j *Jean-Paul*: Sartre, *The Flies*: argument or character defeats audience expectation relative to classical text or norm.

IV
Fiktionsironie

Rupture of dramatic illusion. Contributed directly or indirectly by the ironist author or characters. There is some degree of dissembling or simulation. The audience perception varies from almost immediate to perplexed. The audience is always, the character(s) sometimes, *in loco victimae*.

a   *Denis*: Diderot, *Paradoxe sur le Comédien*: actor is detached from character acted.

b   *Charenton*: Weiss, *Marat/Sade*: world of characters and world of actors (and of author-director) are dovetailed or confused.

*b*¹   *Trygaeus*: Sophocles, *Oedipus Tyrannus* 895: character reverts to status as actor.

*b*²   *Ludwig*: Tieck, *Gestiefelte Kater*: author-director invades the world of characters.

*b*³   *Prospero*: Shakespeare, *Tempest*, IV. i. 35–42: character takes on functions of author-director.

c   *Rosencrantz*: Stoppard, *Rosencrantz and Guildenstern are Dead*: disclaimer of the seriousness or 'reality' of the fiction.

d   *Nathanael*: Tieck, *Gestiefelte Kater*, I. ii: character defends lack of realism by saying the drama needs it.

e   *Nell*: Beaumont and Fletcher, *Knight of the Burning Pestle*: audience is admitted into the world of the characters.

f   *Luigi*: Pirandello, *Sei personaggi in cerca d'autore*: character ponders his own fictive status.

*f*¹   *Fischer*: Tieck, *Gestiefelte Kater*: action perceived as a stage-play, with character-actors being watched and critiqued by other character-actors.

g   *Thomas*: Mann, *Joseph und seine Brüder*: external authority qualifies the autonomy of the argument.

*g*¹   *Helen*: Goethe, *Faust* II: myth, or tradition, or model author or work, pressures or gainsays character's speech or stance.

*g*²   *Pooh*: Crews, *Pooh Perplex*: parody.

Notes

1. C. Thirlwall, 'On the Irony of Sophocles', *The Philological Museum* 2 (1833) 483–536. Here and elsewhere I take the liberty of citing some materials from my 'Irony and Tragic Choruses', in J. H. D'Arms and J. W. Eadie (edd.), *Ancient and Modern: Essays in Honor of Gerald F. Else* (Ann Arbor 1977) 31–44.

2. For a trenchant critique of New Critical irony, see R. S. Crane, 'The

Critical Monism of Cleanth Brooks', in id. (ed.), *Critics and Criticism* (Toronto 1952) 83–107. Also A. Ford in *Arion* 1 (1991) 128.

3. Frye, *Anatomy of Criticism*, 40 ff., 61, 219, 270 ff., 366.

4. See C. D. Lang, *Irony/Humor: Critical Paradigms* (Baltimore 1988) 50–69, on De Man, Derrida, Barthes, Lyotard, Lacan, and Deleuze.

5. R. Hellman, *Magic in the Web: Action and Language in 'Othello'* (Lexington, Mass. 1956).

6. B. O. States, *Irony and Drama: A Poetics* (Ithaca, NY 1971).

7. Muecke, *Compass of Irony*; Booth, *Rhetoric of Irony*; D. J. Enright, *The Alluring Problem: An Essay on Irony* (Oxford 1986); Dane, *Critical Mythology of Irony*. I am indebted to Muecke, and to others before him, for some of my illustrative texts. In addition to recent works on irony cited here and elsewhere in these notes, the following should be mentioned: *Poétique* 36 (1978), esp. the essays by groupe μ and by Sperber and Wilson; *Poetics Today* 4/3 (1983); B. Allemann, *Ironie und Dichtung*[2] (Pfullingen 1956); E. Behler, *Klassische Ironie— Romantische Ironie—Tragische Ironie* (Darmstadt 1972); W. Boder, *Die sokratische Ironie in den platonischen Frühdialogen* (Amsterdam 1973); C. Brooks, 'Irony as a Principle of Structure', in M. D. Zabel (ed.), *Literary Opinion in America*[3] (New York 1962) 729–41; H. H. Clark and R. J. Gerrig, 'On the Pretense Theory of Irony', *Journal of Experimental Psychology* 113/1 (1984) 121–76; J. Culler, *Flaubert: The Uses of Uncertainty* (London 1974); P. Friedländer, *Platon*[2] i (Berlin 1954) ch. 7; L. R. Furst, *Fictions of Romantic Irony* (Cambridge, Mass. 1984); F. Garber (ed.), *Romantic Irony* (Budapest 1988); G. J. Handwerk, *Irony and Ethics in Narrative: From Schlegel to Lacan* (New Haven 1985); R. Jancke, *Das Wesen der Ironie* (Leipzig 1929); V. Jankelevitsch, *L'Ironie, ou la Bonne Conscience*[2] (Paris 1950); G. M. Kirkwood, *A Study of Sophoclean Drama* (Ithaca, NY 1958) ch. 6; D. Knox, *Ironia: Medieval and Renaissance Ideas on Irony* (Leiden 1989); N. Knox, *The Word Irony and its Content, 1500–1755* (Durham, NC 1961); D. C. Muecke, *Irony* (London 1970); id., 'Irony Markers', *Poetics* 7 (1978) 363–75; id., 'Images of Irony', *Poetics Today* 4/3 (1983) 399–413; R. Rorty, *Contingency, Irony, and Solidarity* (Cambridge 1989); G. G. Sedgwick, *Of Irony: Especially in Drama*[2] (Toronto 1948); R. B. Sharpe, *Irony in the Drama* (Chapel Hill 1959); I. Strohschneider-Kohrs, *Die romantische Ironie* (Tübingen 1960); A. R. Thompson, *The Dry Mock: A Study of Irony in Drama* (Berkeley 1948); Vernant and Vidal-Naquet, *Mythe et tragédie en Grèce ancienne*, ch. 5; G. Vlastos, *Socrates* (Cambridge 1991) ch. 1 (rev. A. Nehamas, *Arion* 2 [1992] 157–86); R. Warning, 'Ironiesignale und ironische Solidarisierung', in W. Preisendanz and R. Warning (edd.), *Das Komische: Poetik und Hermeneutik* 7 (Munich

1976) 416–23; A Wilde, *Horizons of Assent: Modernism, Postmodernism, and the Ironic Imagination* (Baltimore 1981).

8. C. Kerbrat-Orrecchioni, 'Problèmes de l'ironie', *Linguistique et sémiologie: Travaux du Centre de recherches ling. et sém. de Lyon* (1976/2) 9–45 (see also *Poétique* 41 [1980] 108–27); D. Sperber and D. Wilson, 'Les Ironies comme mentions', *Poétique* 36 (1978) 399–412, now corrected in Sperber and Wilson, *Relevance* (Oxford 1986) 237–43 (mention has been abandoned in favour of echo) (see also Sperber and Wilson in P. Cole [ed.], *Radical Pragmatics* [New York 1981] 295–318); H. P. Grice, 'Logic and Conversation', in id., *Studies in the Way of Words* (Cambridge, Mass. 1989) 34, and 'Further Notes on Logic and Conversation', esp. 53–4. It may be worth mentioning that drama, taken as a joint voice of dramatist and character, may cast some doubt on Grice's view, ibid. 54, that 'while I may without any inappropriateness prefix the employment of a metaphor with *to speak metaphorically*, there would be something very strange about saying, *to speak ironically, he is a splendid fellow*'. Eward Albee's *A Delicate Balance*, for instance, is full of speech directions including 'ironically'.

9. A rudimentary bibliography of post-structuralist irony would include: R. Barthes, *Critique et vérité* (Paris 1966) 74–5; P. De Man, *Blindness and Insight* (New York 1971) 192–7, 203; id., *Allegories of Reading* (New Haven 1979) 116, 301 (where De Man, as usual, miswrites 'parabasis' for 'parecbasis', which is Schlegel's term); J. Derrida, *Marges de la philosophie* (Paris 1972) 296, on Valéry; J. V. Smyth, *A Question of Eros* (Tallahassee, Fla. 1986) ch. 4; S. A. Tyler, *The Unspeakable* (Madison, Wis. 1987), p. xiii; T. Eagleton, *The Ideology of the Aesthetic* (Oxford 1990) ch. 7, on Kierkegaard; J. Schwartz, *Irony and Ideology in Rabelais* (Cambridge 1990) 198; H.-T. Lehmann, *Theater und Mythos* (Stuttgart 1991) 136–8, 169; S. Goldhill, *The Poet's Voice* (Cambridge 1991) 94. It should be added that in his later, more decidedly deconstructionist writings, De Man uses the term 'irony' sparingly. But according to E. Behler, *Irony and the Discourse of Modernity* (Seattle 1990) 101, De Man 'came to a position which equated irony with any type of text'.

10. L. Campbell, *Sophocles*[2] (2 vols.; Oxford 1879) i, 126–33, esp. 132. Cf. W. Empson's review of Booth, *Rhetoric of Irony*, in *The New York Review of Books* 20/10 (1975) 37–9, and his conclusion: 'A good book . . . I found it all the more extraordinary that what I had long thought "irony" to mean does not get mentioned at all.' U. Japp, *Theorie der Ironie* (Frankfurt/M. 1983) is another anti-expansionist.

11. This is how irony is understood by K. Reinhardt in his *Sophocles*[3] (Frankfurt/M. 1947) 131, 133. See also H. Weinstock, *Sophokles*[3] (Wuppertal 1948) 253–61.

12. See now also the reservations of T. C. W. Stinton, *Collected Papers on Greek Tragedy* (Oxford 1990) 489. For the views of the Romantics on the different demands of drama and narrative fiction, see Stroh-schneider-Kohrs, *Die romantische Ironie, passim.*

13. A. W. Schlegel, *Kritische Schriften und Briefe*, vi, ed. E. Lohner: *Vorlesungen über dramatische Kunst und Literatur*, ii (Stuttgart 1967) 127. Schlegel himself, as he continues, radically qualifies the assumption.

14. R. Niebuhr, *The Irony of American History* (London 1952) 5.

15. Muecke, *Compass of Irony*, 223.

16. My inventory of ironies, set forth in the appendix that precedes these notes, is designed to be orderly, economical, and practical. It is less qualified, less subtle, less discursive than Muecke's beautifully erudite account. It excludes much that Muecke calls irony, and which I believe does not quite deserve the label. And its purpose is to cover drama, which Muecke brings in only sporadically. Even under the rubrics 'dramatic irony' and 'dramatized irony', Muecke's examples are often from outside drama.

17. For this cf. H. P. Grice, 'Logic and Conversation' (undated manuscript) III. 19, who disputes the capacity of irony to voice adverse judgements 'unless there is some *shadow* of justification for a straightforward application' (my emphasis). (This is not in the printed version cited above, n. 8.)

18. Quintil. 9. 2. 46. The distinction which Quintilian makes at 9. 2. 44 ff. between irony as trope and irony as figure appears disregarded at 8. 6. 54, where the examples provided for tropes look very much like examples given for figures at 9. 2. For ancient discussions of irony, see O. Ribbeck, 'Über den Begriff des εἴρων', *Rh.Mus.* 21 (1876) 381–400; W. Büchner, 'Über den Begriff der Eironeia', *Hermes* 76 (1941) 339–58; and L. Bergson, 'Eiron und Eironeia', *Hermes* 99 (1971) 409–22, who considers the approaches of Ribbeck and Büchner too limited.

19. For what I call 'registering' or 'catching-on', Booth (*Rhetoric of Irony*) prefers the term 'reconstruction', which seems to me too cerebral, more suited to the response of the critic than to that of the audience or the ironist's butt.

20. D. Davidson, 'What Metaphors Mean', *Critical Inquiry* 5 (1978) 33. Davidson's distinction is, of course, indebted to Wittgenstein.

21. καταφρονητικόν (*Rhet.* 2.2.1379^{b}31), ἐλευθεριώτερον (3.18.1419^{b}7); *Nic.Eth.* 4.8.1124^{b}30–1. Elsewhere in the *Rhetoric*, and generally in the *Poetics* and the ethical treatises, Aristotle offers a less class-conscious and less positive evaluation of εἰρωνεία. See Dane, *Critical Mythology*, 45 ff., for a good summary of irony in Aristotle and

Theophrastus. For irony as 'public school manner' in Margaret Atwood, see Swearingen, *Rhetoric and Irony*, 216–18.

22. The pedagogical function of irony, derived from Socrates and codified in Philodemus, περὶ παρρησίας, p. 13, no. 26 Olivieri, suits itself to the Stoic conception of drama.

23. For the complexity of forensic irony, see also J. Schaeffer, 'Ironic Discourse and the Creation of the Secular', *Soundings* 66 (1983) 319–30.

24. For prophetic irony, see F. M. C. Turner, *The Element of Irony in English Literature* (Cambridge 1926) 11–12 *et passim*.

25. See Foley, *Ritual Irony*.

26. In II. iii and III. iii 'honest', a key-word in the ironic exchanges between Othello and Iago, is variously used in the senses of 'truthful', 'virtuous', and 'simple-minded'.

27. See the paean to Plato in Booth, *Rhetoric of Irony*, 269–76.

28. For this kind of irony in Aristophanes, see K. Dover, *Aristophanes* (London 1972) ch. 4.

29. *Friedrich Schlegel: Kritische Schriften*, ed. W. Rasch (Munich 1956) 8.

28

Tragic and Homeric Ironies:
Response to Rosenmeyer

N. J. LOWE

Surveys of irony are commonly of inverse value to their length; Professor Rosenmeyer's seems to me one of the very finest, and in particular a significant advance on the canonical Mueckean taxonomy.[1] Its fuller recognition of the unusual status of drama in the cladistics of the ironic makes it possible, in a way that Muecke's analysis does not, to address the central question of what—if anything—is distinctive about the ways of irony in ancient tragedy, and how thinking about ironies might help us to frame or circumscribe at least the ancient world's notion of 'the tragic' itself. Rosenmeyer has fingered four peculiarities that sharpen the ironic possibilities open to theatre: the much tighter structural economy of drama; the interpolation of the actor into the process of fiction as a mediating presence between character and audience to replace the deleted narrator; the blatant asymmetry of the one-way mirror that is the fourth-wall window; the extra load carried by public speech in the characters' self-definition. I want, in picking up the gauntlet tossed down in his closing paragraphs, to use these very points as the basis for one possible definition of 'the tragic' that may in turn help us to pin down the nature of the special relationship we continue to see between Greek tragedy and what we find it convenient to call irony.

As the historians of ironology remind us, the perception of such a relationship does not pre-date the Romantic critics; but it is a relationship that, though variously defined and constructed, has never since been seriously doubted. Thirlwall's seminal essay, from which the later notion of 'dramatic irony' is usually argued to derive, was itself, as Rosenmeyer notes, an attempt to define an essential but then-unnamed quality in the art of Sophocles, and the centrality of the notion of irony to our perception of the essence of ancient tragedy is still reflected in the titling of famous books on Euripides: *Ironic Drama* (implying there is some drama that is not?); *Ritual Irony* (a phrase that itself aptly and knowingly invites a variety of semantic linkages between qualifier and noun).[2] At stake may be not merely a definition of the tragic but a whole ideology of interpretation; Euripidean criticism, in particular, has been notoriously subject to global 'ironic' readings of Booth's 'stable' type, those where the reader's or audience's search for an ironic subtext terminates in a single, finite interpretation, as opposed to 'unstable' ironies, whose ironic ripples spread out indefinitely to undercut everything, including the decipherability of the ironic message itself. Alongside the prevailing readings of Euripides as a destabilizing ironist whose challenging juxtapositions of speech and action, speech and speaker, speech and result, endlessly defer finality of understanding, a vocal minority-tradition of *stable* Euripidean ironics has, from Verrall to Vellacott, invoked the respectable language of irony to argue the very unrespectable critical heresy that the text intends exactly what the critic wants it to mean, however cranky, and that if it says something to contradict him, then that passage must be understood as 'ironic'. We may well feel uncomfortable with this conscription of irony as an intentionalists' charter; but if we wish to resist it, we need a model that makes clear why it is illegitimate.

I return to this, and to my own nine-oxen's worth of reflection on irony in general, at the close. But I should state here that, like Rosenmeyer, I accept the three central propositions of the classical, Mueckean model of irony: that 'irony' is a term with a long history of complex shifts in usage, and that the present diversity of applications carries the genetic imprint of this ancestry; that there is nevertheless a family resemblance between the effects we find it comfortable to label with the term; and that this resemblance is accessible to reasonably successful classification and analysis in terms of semiotic, pragmatic, and speech-act models. It is possible—perhaps unavoidable—to subscribe to this catechism while still attaching the obligatory ironic caution that the term 'irony' may be nearing the end of its evolutionary span of usefulness.[3] (Balloons are most interesting at the precise moment when they seem about to pop.) My own reading of the litany leans further towards formalism than does Rosenmeyer's wider, wiser perspective, but I hope it may be seen as complementary.

One of the ironic attractions of Rosenmeyer's elegant and powerful taxonomy is that it deliberately sidelines three influential but problematic epithets spawned by the Romantic reinvention of the term, and whose histories intersect in Thirlwall's 1833 essay on Sophocles. In chronological order, 'tragische Ironie' seems to have been coined first by Adam Müller in 1806, and makes its first English appearance, albeit inconspicuous and undefined, in Thirlwall;[4] 'Sophoclean irony' was substituted for Thirlwall's own 'practical irony' in later nineteenth-century English usage; 'dramatic irony' is the twentieth-century synonym, generally attributed to Thirlwall though his text uses neither the actual term nor, it has recently been pointed out, the modern concept.[5] Without proposing to reinstate these labels, I should nevertheless like, by revisiting our common understanding of what each might connote, to show how an attempt to define a distinctively *tragic* irony might help to point us towards a formulation of 'the tragic' itself.

When we speak, if we dare to, of 'tragic irony' today, we normally mean something rather different from Müller (who wanted to create a category that would give equal time to a notion of irony as serious, as part of his argument with Schlegel's contention that all irony was a species of the comic) or indeed from Thirlwall (who seems to mean by the phrase no more, and perhaps less, than the use in tragedy of the whole repertory of verbal and practical ironies). Our 'tragic irony' would not, I think, refer primarily to a species of the forensic genus—although the sophisticated usage of such expressions as 'ironically' in the tragic scholia[6] testifies to an early interest in the forensic varieties of 'ironic' speech acts (the only species recognized by the ancient term) as a characteristic device of the genre. Nor, I think, would we locate the notion of 'tragic irony' in the category of *Fiktionsironie*, except in the extended sense where theatricality is seen as an *allegory* for some larger process of narrating the world in which we, the audience, are ourselves the narrative creation of a transcendent author and audience whose motives may be no more noble or caring than ours are in the writing and watching of plays. While in contrast to Aristophanic and Plautine comedy there may be a variety of shades of subtler theatrical self-reference in ancient tragedy, there is no irresistibly explicit *Fiktionsironie*.[7]

Rather, where Old Comedy is characterized by Rosenmeyer's types I and IV (forensic and *Fiktionsironie*), tragedy is dominated by the blind and structural ironies II–III. Forensic irony entails the deliberate assertion of power relationships, the ironist's freedom to turn others into the victims of a more or less humiliating asymmetry; while *Fiktionsironie* entails the acknowledgment by the characters themselves that they and all values asserted within the text are no more than arbitrary narrative constructs. Both are peculiarly at home in the Aristophanic model of the universe. By contrast, Aristophanic comedy has relatively little use for tragedy's prominent blind and (especially) structural ironies, in part because the shape and course of events to come is so much less predictable than it is in tragedy. It is very rare in Old Comedy for the audience to know things that none of the characters do; on the contrary, Aristophanic comedy is generally careful to take its time over releasing the heroes' plans for the play, and furthermore often forces significant revision of those plans in the course of attempting to put them into effect. In itself, this is close to the model pursued in the second half of the *Odyssey*, where the ironist's advantage lies with the hero, and is closely linked to his larger programme of remodelling the existing structure of power relationships in a way that will allow him to triumph over his vastly more powerful enemies.

But a moment's reflection bears out Rosenmeyer's caution that the 'tragicness' of ironies in tragedy cannot be reduced to a mere mixture of classes, for any such convenient polarization between the ironic systems of tragedy and comedy breaks down with the classical New Comedy of Menander and Terence (even if it arguably continues to work quite well for Plautus). In Menander we do usually know by the end of the first act how the configuration of relationships has to come out; we do know things that no individual character has yet discovered or collated; we do hear unintended resonances in the words of characters of which the speakers themselves remain unaware, and notice structurally significant links between words or events that have not yet dawned on the people directly affected. There are, as in tragedy, gods who know more than the humans, and an audience who has access to both. What, then, is different about the ironies of New Comedy, and why do they not strike us as 'tragic'?

The answer, surely, lies in the special relationship fifth-century tragedy seeks with Homer, by virtue of its special reading of Homeric epic. For us, 'tragic irony' is most often a way of using the intermeshed forms of blind and structural irony to highlight the gap between individual and cosmic value—the ways in which things that mean a great deal to individuals become futile or infinitesimal when viewed in the objective proportions of time, multitudes, or divinity. And it is by now a familiar truism that this particular 'ironic' image of the universe goes quite directly back to the *Iliad*.[8] For it is the *Iliad* that offers the model of a bipartite cosmos, in which the individual mortal characters are framed in an immortal perspective where will, time, accident, and power are all illusory, and in which the narrativity of human experience is annihilated in an atemporal view of all time and space as simultaneously accessible to apprehension. In the Homeric model, we are constantly being reminded of the different narrative vistas of the same events as perceived by the mortal characters, the gods, and the audience. There is an immensely complex combinatorial array of ways in which narrative information can be withheld between these three intelligences; only the voice of the bard has unrestricted access to all, and it is precisely this voice that is deleted in the translation of epic into drama. But one paradoxical implication of this is that 'dramatic irony', in its traditional sense of the audience knowing what the characters do not, seems neither original nor exclusive to the drama. And if 'tragic irony' is then the specific use of such multiple perspectives to problematize the values we assign under our own restrictedly earthly, timebound, and personal view of the world, then this too is already part of the epic repertoire emulated by early tragedy.

But why, in that case, is Menander not 'tragic'? We might reasonably feel that the sanction of laughter makes for an essential difference between the kinds of ironic response available to the audience; but it is not easy to define what the difference *is* that laughter makes, or how it comes to make it. A more sophisticated answer might be that New Comedy evokes an interpretation of the world that is Odyssean rather than Iliadic, and that we traditionally refuse the label 'tragic' to the Odyssean model on the grounds that human access to absolute value is affirmed rather than problematized. Yet if that really were all, we ought to consider abandoning the terms 'tragedy' and 'comedy' altogether, speaking instead of Iliadic and Odyssean drama; and in any case, 'tragic' irony is already deeply Odyssean, in that even if tragedy's underlying world-model is Iliadic, it is nevertheless the *Odyssey* that has supplied tragedy with most of its repertoire of particular ironic effects. Between the human cast of the *Iliad* there is no disguise, no recognition, no intrigue, no ironies of identity, no speaking of lies, very little deception. It is arguable that the absence of these particular ironic elements contributes in some way to the *Iliad*'s intimation of the tragic, by refusing humans even the power to control the perceptions of others. But in that case, what does tragedy have to do to assimilate these manipulative Odyssean ironies into its manipulated Iliadic world?

I believe these questions can be met, but only at the cost of venturing a slightly cumbersome definition of 'the tragic' itself. I would suggest something on these lines: '*the tragic' is the fifth century's reading of Homer, generalized across the entire corpus of myths, concentrated by filtration from* diegêsis *into* mimêsis, *and subsequently fixed by the cultural canonization of fifth-century tragedy itself*. Elements of this reading include: an obsessive reproduction of favoured Homeric situations and motifs; a purging of 'cyclic' narrative qualities;[9] a privileging of the Iliadic world-picture over the Odyssean, whose own narrative devices are cannibalized and assimilated in a new model that suggests the hermeneutics of deception are built into the structure of the world; a resistance to contemporary settings and invented characters; and (especially relevant for the ironics of tragedy) a construction of the narrative universe as a dualistic system of worlds. New Comedy shares many, but not all, of these preoccupations; in particular, it reverses the relationship between the Iliadic and Odyssean world-models, privileging law over force and order over entropy in a universe whose upper chamber is morally benign. In fifth-century tragedy, these narrative values are abstracted from the epics as a set of generic narrative templates to which other, and eventually all, available heroic legends can be adapted; every extant tragedy, no matter what its myth, is built centrally around plot patterns unmistakably recycled from one or both epics. But at the same time the transition from telling to showing imposes a number of strictures that heighten certain narrative priorities and motifs: the elision of any authoritative narratorial presence; a strong distinction between dramatized and reported action; casts in single figures rather than hundreds of thousands; an emphasis on cognition rather than action; increased weight given to the expression of emotion and the interrogation of language; the removal of the superhuman plane from more than incidental view.

These are more claims than I can develop here; let me focus
those most relevant to my argument with a single concrete example of the 'irony of Sophocles'. At *Ajax* 91–117 the audience sees
and overhears three characters outside the shelter: Athena,
Odysseus, and Ajax himself. A remarkable generic hierarchy of
semipermeable perceptual filters operates between these three:
Athena can see and hear both Odysseus and Ajax; Odysseus can see
and hear Ajax, but can only hear Athena; Ajax too can hear Athena,
but does not register Odysseus at all. Odysseus embodies a normal,
or slightly privileged, state of human consciousness: he is fully
alert to his earthly surroundings, and vouchsafed an awareness of
the presence of divinity, but he cannot see the goddess's form, and
his knowledge of her is limited to what she volunteers in words.
Below Odysseus in the cognitive hierarchy, Ajax is deluded, hallu-
cinating a false reality and unaware of his enemy standing before
him. And above them both, Athena embodies the perspective of
Homeric Olympus: omnipercipient, watching and overhearing the
mortal characters, but also commanding direct access to their
unspoken thoughts. God, mortal, madman: this hierarchy of sen-
tience is fundamental to tragedy's image of the structure of its
world. But there are two further tiers to add to the chain of perception. Outside the fourth wall, an audience of which even
Athena remains unconscious is watching and listening, aware of
events that have not yet taken place in the world of the stage; while
behind the *skênê* lies a vast hidden world that (unlike all the others)
is *screened* from the direct perception of that audience, and mediated to them entirely by the language of the characters.

I want to make two general points about this hierarchy of
worlds.[10] First, what in Homer is wholly abstract and conceptual
is in tragedy vividly *reified* in performance space. The metaphysical relationships between audience, gods, and humans may be fundamental already to the Homeric world-structure; but in the
Sophoclean period of tragedy they become more sharply insistent
through their concrete visualization in the coding of space (a coding significantly *not* shared by Aristophanic comedy). *Ajax* is the
earliest extant text in which all these relations can be seen with reasonable confidence to operate simultaneously, but they are part of
the basic semiotic apparatus of the mature genre from at least the
Oresteia onwards. The horizontal axis divides the space into three
zones: the outside world of the audience, which terminates at the

edge of the *orchêstra*; the visible world of the stage, which reaches
to the front wall of the *skênê*; and the verbalized world 'off-stage',
which is projected behind the *skênê* door and away down the *parodoi*, though (as the incompatible 'off-stage' worlds of Ajax and
Odysseus remind us) its truer locus is inside the characters'
heads.[11] At the same time, the vertical axis marks a metaphysical
separation between two planes of existence within the stage world:
the groundling level of the mortals, and the supernal plane of the
gods.[12] Thus the very space of tragic performance is in effect a
sophisticated epistemological map of tragedy's metaphysical structure, marked out into four perceptual domains: the theatre audience; the divine characters; the human characters; and the unseen
inner worlds of those characters' beliefs and desires, created for us
by their language.

But more important still is the astonishing complexity of 'ironic'
juxtapositions mapped out in a scene such as this. What the audience sees, what a god sees, what a mortal sees, and what a madman
sees are already four quite different versions of the same interior
and exterior reality; but the hierarchical nesting of audience frames
means that the constellation of worlds is indefinitely *extensible* by
concatenation, embedding, and multiplication. Each character's
imperfect picture of reality contains within it an imperfect picture
of all the other characters' pictures, and all their pictures of his or
her own picture, and so on indefinitely in a recursive *mise en abîme*,
so that even with tragedy's upper limit of three speaking characters
the proliferation of worlds can be arbitrarily complex.[13] And
beyond even this, the very one-way mirror between frames of perception that makes ironic effects possible is itself suggestively, and
ironically, mirrored at three or four levels (between audience and
characters, goddess and mortals, eavesdropper and speaker, the
hero's public words and the private reality that only he can see), so
that each link in the chain—each sentient denizen of the tragic universe—is simultaneously the audience of a spectacle and the spectacle of an unseen higher audience, with no guarantee that the chain
of spectation even terminates with the theatre audience itself.[14]

Such an intricate matrix of simultaneous contrasts between the
contents of different vantages and consciousnesses is peculiarly ill-
comprehended by the crudely bipolar handbook-definition of 'dramatic irony', which distinguishes merely between what the
characters 'know' and what the audience knows. Even knowledge

itself is only one modality among many relevant to the ironic
matrix: there are also desires, emotions, senses of obligation, perceptions of possibility, inviting us to compare not only the worlds
characters believe but the constellations of virtual worlds they each
hope for, fear, or dismiss. With all this in mind, how many different 'ironies', in the sense of pointed disjunctions of world-model
between participants, can we find in this scene? We could begin
anywhere, without even starting to address the finer-scale ironies
in the dialogue: Ajax and Odysseus hold fatally different pictures
of what is inside the shelter; the visible and the reported Odysseus
are contrasted by being outside/inside Ajax's perception and
power, alive/moribund; of the three nested audiences observing
Ajax, Ajax is aware only of Athena, and only partly of her; Athena
is not Ajax's 'ally' (117), but his destroyer; her questions are not
the ingenuous requests for information Ajax hears, but a brutal
demonstration for the edification of Odysseus . . . But can such a
list ever in fact be complete, when its contents are limited only by
our sensitivity and imagination as readers? Is 'irony' even a finite
quantity at all?

It is anxieties of this kind that have tended to shift perceptions
of irony in drama away from the closed and authorly towards the
open and readerly. In particular, the last quarter-century has
largely accepted Vernant's attempt to substitute for 'irony', as the
defining characteristic of the Greek 'tragic message', the more
nuanced notion of 'ambiguity'. Yet it seems to me that 'irony' after
all is the term we really want, because it more readily allows that
the structure of meaning may reside not just, or even primarily, in
the word, but in the world. Tragedy's irony is not merely verbal
but, in Thirlwall's original terminology, 'practical'; it problematizes issues of knowledge and teleology not by textual play alone,
but by its vivid concretization of the Homeric hierarchy of modal
worlds amongst which language can move and meaning shift.
There is an important difference between tragedy and other forms
here. In ordinary discourse, we deal with such bewildering inter-
ference-patterns by *intentionalizing*: by representing piquant contradictions in the information reaching us as the product of an act
of willed communication, its meaning programmed by an outside
intelligence, an 'ironist'. (This *may*, of course, coincide more or
less closely with an actual person's actual purpose.) Our classification of the kind of irony perceived will depend to a great extent on

where in the imagined path of the ironic 'message' we locate this ironizing purpose. Forensic ironies will tend to be seen as originating with the speaker; blind and structural ironies with a controlling teleology, a god or fate, within the fictional world; *Fiktionsironie* with an outside author; while postmodern, transcendental ironies will have their point of origin in the wider world of language, signs, and ideas in which author and audience are embedded. And one major difference between tragic and Homeric ironies is the agnostic *elision* of the figure of the ironist. The fifth line of the *Iliad* ('and the plan of Zeus was accomplished') issues a blanket certificate of intention for its myriad structural ironies as an all-inclusive *'boulê* of Zeus'; but tragedy, in off-staging Zeus altogether,[15] allows the very identity and purpose of the demiurgic ironist to recede into indeterminacy.

For the central embarrassment with trying to isolate irony has always been that this figure of the ironist is in the last resort dispensable; that not merely all language, but all experience, is ironic if read in the proper way. In the end, 'irony' is a mode of reading, which can of course be deliberately solicited by the text or its producer, but which ultimately depends on the reader's or listener's own willingness to find pointed meaning in a tacit dissonance between content and context—more precisely, between the literal content of the text and the sense required by the larger act of communication and interpretation of which the text is the principal vehicle: a speech act in the case of verbal texts, an act of interpretative processing in the case of pure events. And even the term 'text' here necessarily includes the non-verbal: any structure of events or their signifiers that can carry referential content, which need not be narrative or even propositional (think of the ways in which instrumental music can be 'ironic'). The diffusion of irony as a critical term, both in its usage and its range of reference, reflects our increasing sensitivity to such dissonances in an environment of ever greater informational density.

In this light, just as important and revealing as the question of how irony works may be the question of how we manage to *suspend* our ironic mechanism in so many of our everyday dealings with language and the world in general. Further exploration of the frontier between irony and the comic may have much to teach us here: I suspect the next major impulse to ironology will come from the already much more progressive and interdisciplinary field of humour studies, where there has been considerable interest in the construction of cognitive schemata to model what happens in the particular ironic response that expresses itself in the physiological impulse to laughter.[16] This psychological approach has implications for the study of irony in general. There certainly appears to be in the human animal an inbuilt need to see language and meanings as single and simple, even though we know perfectly well when we think about it that they are nothing of the kind. It may be part of our basic childhood machinery of learning language—indeed, of making sense of experience—that on the one hand we can recognize the openness and plurality of meanings, while on the other we instinctively desire the relationship between signs and things to be univocal; and that may be why we have such an inexhaustible capacity for pleasurable or painful surprise each time we are forced to recognize that it is not. As Raymond Queneau wrote at the end of his long career as a professional ironist, 'Every sentence contains an infinity of words; we perceive only a tiny few, the rest being at infinity or imaginary.'[17] Our momentary glimpses of that infinity may be what makes the ironic experience so powerful.

If that is the case, of course, the makers and consumers of classical tragedy were peculiarly well trained to focus on infinity in this way, because immersion from childhood in the *Iliad* and *Odyssey*—and particularly in their speeches—is surely the most intensive grounding in ironics any tutor could design. As we read or listen to a Homeric speech, our ear is progressively tuned to the rich harmonic overtones that give timbre and resonance to all speech acts, the meanings that hide between the lines of words. Some elementary examples are partly worked out for us, with the narrator explaining that the intention is different from the words. 'So she spoke; for she was ashamed to mention her happy marriage to her own father; but he understood everything, and made a speech in reply'—in which Alcinous makes no mention of Nausicaa's marriage either, or even the fact that he realizes that her speech, which is ironic but hardly 'ambiguous', is really about something else.[18] But one of the peculiarities of reading Homer is that such direct narratorial nudges in the ribs are the very infrequent exception, and that most of the time the text simply presents us with a silent invitation to measure the distance between words and intentions from such clues as we can find in the content, the context, and our putative understanding of human nature. By constructing a supposedly authoritative role for the narrating voice, by contrasting that authority with the openness and indeterminacy of the embedded voices of the characters, and finally by withholding the voice of narratorial authority from the normal presentation of embedded speech, the epics in effect train their audience to see meaning as multiple, rather than unitary, and to leave the mechanism that registers such multiplicity switched permanently on. And by deleting the narratorial voice altogether, tragedy in turn presents us with an epic from which all illusion of singleness of textual meaning has been systematically stripped away. This stark exposure of the sinews of Homeric irony surely lies behind the special role we feel for classical tragedy in the anatomy of irony, and for irony in the anatomy of tragedy.

Notes

1. Other important short treatments to append to Rosenmeyer's own bibliog.: N. Knox, 'On the Classification of Ironies', *Modern Philology* 70 (1972) 53–62; Muecke, *Irony and the Ironic*, superseding *Irony* (1970); J. E. Seery, *Political Returns: Irony in Politics and Theory from Plato to the Antinuclear Movement* (Boulder, Col. 1990) 161–225. On classical ironies, see now D. P. Fowler, 'Postmodernism, Romantic Irony, and Classical Closure', in I. J. F. De Jong and J. P. Sullivan (edd.), *Modern Critical Theory and Classical Literature* (Leiden 1994) 231–56.

2. P. H. Vellacott, *Ironic Drama* (Cambridge 1975); Foley, *Ritual Irony*.

3. 'It is not inconceivable that "irony", now a key concept in literary criticism, will follow into limbo the concept of "sublimity", so indispensable to earlier centuries' (Muecke, *Irony and the Ironic*, 13).

4. C. Thirlwall, 'On the Irony of Sophocles', *Philological Museum* 2 (1833) 493, 535–6; see Dane, *Critical Mythology of Irony*, 122–6, 130.

5. Dane, *Critical Mythology of Irony*, 126–9.

6. Alongside the many laconic glosses of the form *eirônikôs, kat' eirôneian*, etc., there are numerous extended discussions in which the ironic subtext is paraphrased or the speech-act function analysed; see e.g. the longer notes on *Prometheus* 937 and 985, *OT* 402, *Orestes* 93, *Andromache* 203. On *Ajax* 666 the hero's famous announcement that 'In future, I shall know to yield to the gods, and shall learn to revere the Atreidae' is glossed in the older scholia: 'a grudging remark, inverting the relationship in irony; he ought to have said "revere the gods, and yield to the Atreidae", but says the opposite as if the Atreidae were now the real *theomachoi*.'

7. Cf. more fully Taplin's chapter in this volume (pp. 188 ff.). The nearest and most notorious moment is the one instanced under 'Trygaeus' in Rosenmeyer's anatomy. But even there we have to do with a 'subliminal' metatheatricality (P. Wilson and O. Taplin, 'The "Aetiology" of Tragedy in the *Oresteia*', *PCPS* 39 [1993] 169–80; cf. N. T. Croally, *Euripidean Polemic: The Trojan Women and the Function of Tragedy* [Cambridge 1994] 235–48); and it would sound odd to call this irony 'tragic'.

8. Two canonical discussions are R. B. Rutherford, 'Tragic Form and Feeling in the *Iliad*', *JHS* 102 (1982) 145–60; John Gould, 'Homeric Epic and the Tragic Moment', in T. Winnifrith, P. Murray, and K. W. Gransden (edd.), *Aspects of the Epic* (London 1983) 32–45.

9. J. Griffin, 'The Epic Cycle and the Uniqueness of Homer', *JHS* 97 (1977) 39–53; J. Herington, *Poetry into Drama: Early Tragedy and the Greek Poetic Tradition* (Berkeley 1985) 133–44.

10. In what follows, I use this term in the Leibnitzian sense current in possible-worlds narratology: 'a set of entities (objects, persons) organised and related in specific ways (through situations, events and space-time)' (R. Ronen, *Possible Worlds in Literary Theory* [Cambridge 1994] 8). Cf. esp. M.-L. Ryan, 'The Modal Structure of Narrative Universes', *Poetics Today* 6 (1985) 717–55, rev. in id., *Possible Worlds, Artificial Intelligence, and Narrative Theory* (Bloomington, Ind. 1991) 109–23. The most useful general synopsis of possible-world models in dramatic theory remains K. Elam, *The Semiotics of Theatre and Drama* (London 1980) 99–119; to discussions cited there add also T. G. Pavel, *Fictional Worlds* (Cambridge, Mass. 1986); G. Currie, *The Nature of Fiction* (Cambridge 1990).

11. See esp. R. Padel, 'Making Space Speak', in Winkler and Zeitlin (edd.), *Nothing to Do with Dionysos?*, 336–65.

12. I assume here that Athena, and other gods in Sophocles and Euripides who appear undisguised while mortals are on-stage, use either roof, *theologeion*, or *mêchanê*; for present purposes it does not matter which, but see D. J. Mastronarde, 'Actors on High: The Skene Roof, the Crane, and the Gods in Attic Drama', *CA* 9 (1990) 247–94; H.-J. Newiger, 'Ekkyklema und Mechané in der Inszenierung des griechischen Dramas', *WJA* 16 (1990) 33–42.

13. For simplification's sake I use a prologue scene; most scenes, of course, include an additional ironizing layer in the presence of the chorus, who normally arrive after the audience has had privileged sight of the opening. There is thus visible throughout the main body of the play a surrogate audience whose view of the action is a pointedly restricted subset of the view available to their real-world counterparts.

14. When Odysseus concludes (125 f.) 'I see that we, as many as live, are nothing more than images, empty shadow', his first-person plural with its indefinite gloss invites the audience to include itself in his insight, and his equation of the subject of seeing with its precarious object (*eidôla*, 'images/ghosts/illusions') is a reflexive comment on the ironic structure of the tragic universe itself, in which the relationship between spectacle and spectator images that between the spectator himself and the higher powers or perspectives that view his own life.

15. Taplin, *Stagecraft of Aeschylus*, 431–2.

16. See esp. S. Attardo, *Linguistic Theories of Humor* (Berlin 1994) (with index s.v. 'irony'); V. Raskin, *Semantic Mechanisms of Humor* (Dordrecht 1985); and the continuing series of papers by these authors and their collaborators in *Humor*.

17. *Les Fondements de la littérature d'après David Hilbert* (Paris 1976) 12.

18. *Odyssey* 6. 57–70.

29

Tragedy, Pure and Simple

GEORGE STEINER

I

'Tragedy and the tragic' . . .: the excess of literary, scholarly, philosophical attention and the prodigality of magisterial treatments—from Aristotle to Dr Johnson, from Johnson to Nietzsche and Walter Benjamin—contrast strikingly with the paucity of first-order theoretical examinations of comedy. Very likely comedy is the more difficult, and the more elusive, of the two genres. And from this contrast arises a first, vexing question: why does human sensibility, in its creative and analytic motions, find the tragic to be more elevated, more fascinating, more conducive to major aesthetic forms and metaphysical suggestion, than it does the comic? Is there something in 'tragedy' which not only seduces imagination and intellect but *flatters* them, as 'comedy' does not? The ennobling solicitations of sorrow, of mourning, of drastic loss, have been explored by psychologists and philosophers as diverse as Boethius, Hume, and Freud. But there is a question which is much more embarrassing and very rarely asked, almost a taboo question, about the self-flattery, the self-aggrandizement in grief. Even where it is deeply personal, acute, and scarring (there, perhaps, most)—why is it that something in us feels good when we report disaster? Why is it that, deep within us, even the sickness of a child or the death of one close to us flatters, where the comic does not? The comic does not flatter sensibility. It does not bribe consciousness. We recount tragic experiences in which we have been involved, to which we have been witness, with an altogether different intonation of *dignitas* and pathos than we do their comic counterparts.

The 'cut' between these two registers runs deep. There are a few instances—few and inexhaustible to our reception—in which the distinction is seemingly meaningless. Where tragedy and comedy move to an identical vanishing-point on the horizon of human perception: this conjunction is aimed at in Socrates' lost proof of the generative sameness of the tragic and the comic at the close of the *Symposium*. There are moments of tragic laughter and laughing desolation in Rabelais, during the parody of the Crucifixion. Which of our two labels attaches to the close of Mozart's *Figaro* or (even more challengingly) to *Così Fan Tutte?* To the plays of Chekhov? Reading the *Metamorphosis* to a circle of friends, Franz Kafka doubles over with helpless laughter and is wholly amazed at the numb horror, the paralysis, of his listeners. Such 'uncertainty principles' have, as we shall note, nothing to do with 'tragicomedy', a scenic genre whose conventions are, as in melodrama, those of four acts of latent or temporary catastrophe followed by fortunate resolution and felicity. Vishnievsky's *Optimistic Tragedy*, in which death is followed by collective communist triumph and the promise of social redemption, is a programmatic statement of the tragicomic mechanism in human history. The authentic *Aufhebung* of the ontological differentiations between tragedy and comedy is, as I have said, rare and resistant to diagnosis.

II

Despite the plethora of commentary on tragedy, rigorous definition seems as elusive as ever. More particularly: in the Anglo-American world, the spate of recent studies of Greek tragic drama—be they anthropological, ritual, structural, post-structural, deconstructionist, feminist, linguistic, or scenic in orientation (of the making of such books there is no end)—does little to articulate, let alone clarify, the fundamental issue. Which is one of a religious-metaphysical point of view: of the vision of man's circumstance which tragedy, and ancient tragedy in particular, is meant to represent, to enact, possibly to generate—where 'representation' (*mimêsis*), 'enactment' (the staging of the myth in a full Aristotelian sense), and 'generation' (the invention of a myth-fiction, as may have been the case in Sophocles' *Antigone*) are three distinct, but overlapping, categories.[1]

Let me put forward one possible definition of 'tragedy' in its pure or absolute mode. 'Tragedy' is a dramatic representation, enactment, or generation of a highly specific world-view. This world-view is summarized in the adage preserved among the elegies ascribed to Theognis, but certainly older, and present also in Middle Eastern sacred texts: 'It is best not to be born, next best to die young.' This dictum is a transparent shorthand for a larger conception. It entails the view that human life *per se*, both ontologically and existentially, is an affliction. That non-existence or early extinction are urgent desiderata. The proposition implies that men and women's presence on this earth is fundamentally absurd or unwelcome, that our lives are not a gift or a natural unfolding, but a self-punishing anomaly. We are unwelcome guests, old enough at the moment of birth (as Montaigne says) to be a corpse and blessed only if this potentiality is realized as swiftly as it can be. A 'normal' life-span, let alone old age, are sadistic misfortunes. It follows that the engendering of children, the willed continuation of human beings, is folly or deliberate cruelty. It follows also—and this is a key issue—that suicide is both logical and economically advantageous in the root sense of the word 'economic'. Or to cite Camus: 'suicide is the only serious philosophic question'.

This view can be clearly stated. Its formal and substantive consequences can be clearly drawn. It can be shown or, as Shakespeare would put it, 'bodied forth' in discursive, in narrative, in poetic or dramatic configurations. It can—I am saying that it does—provide a rigorous, working definition for tragic drama in its purest and simplest form. Theognis' maxim will be restated on a number of key textual occasions in Greek theatre; in the affirmation in *King Lear* whereby humans are mere homicidal sport for the gods, as 'flies to wanton boys'; and then in Kafka's forever haunting *summa*: 'there is abundance of hope, but none for us'.

The tragic postulate, in this pure and defining expression, cannot, in any strict sense, be 'lived'. Adhered to stringently, it must lead to suicide and/or to the renunciation of child-bearing, be it by collective abortion. To indulge life, while proclaiming its unbearable tenor, is to exhibit paradoxicality or falsehood. In rare fact, the imperative of abolute negation as voiced by Theognis *has* been acted upon. There have been individual or group suicides on grounds of ontological despair. There have been attempts to suspend human generation. Children have been aborted or killed so as to guard them from the foreseeable blackness of life. Certain Auschwitz survivors have either committed suicide in the zero-light of their experience (long after, like Primo Levi) or abstained from having children lest something of their unendurable insights and previsions be transmitted to their offspring.

But the translation of the pure tragic axiom into a performative act is infrequent. It is exceedingly difficult to document. Motives invite sceptical enquiry. And the intellectual convictions or psychic states or 'moods' (Heidegger's *Stimmungen*) which would dictate self-annihilation tend, except in psychotic lesions, to be brief and intermittent. 'Black holes' are formidably difficult to locate; they yield little testimony, not only in astrophysics.

III

This is the obvious but consequential reason why our literatures contain so very few 'absolute' tragedies. Why should a man or woman bent on death, on the arrest of the human species, bother to write a play? Why should audiences be willing to endure the presentation of what is, in essence, a sentence of and to death? Why volunteer to be told, to be shown, that (as the grim adage in Irish literature has it) only 'where there is death there is hope'?

The question as to whether there are any pure, absolute tragedies in the extant corpus of Attic drama is, I believe, almost intractable. With one exception, the plays which have come down to us are not trilogies. Even where we know the titles of the two accompanying dramas, the texts we know come to us more or less artificially isolated. We can, therefore, only conjecture as to the cumulative treatment of the material, if any: the three units in a trilogy could, of course, touch on entirely distinct subjects. In a number of instances, we may be dealing with the closing part of the triptych—but this is by no means always established. It is, moreover, in the nature of Greek myths to be open-ended, to be part of a complex dynamic reaching forward into further or variant situations. The plays which we have—few as they are—reflect this central fact: thus the transfigurative miracle, the *commedia* (in Dante's use of the term), at the end of *Oedipus at Colonus* is at once counterpointed by a second coda (possibly a later addendum) on the return to Thebes of Oedipus' daughters—a return which the audience knows to be fraught with horror.

But there is another constraint on our perception. In no single case do we have a trilogy together with its satyr-play. We do know that certain (but how many? how regularly?) of these comic,

subversive, parodistic epilogues bore on the material of the preceding tragic dramas. We know absolutely *nothing* as to the psychological effects aimed at or achieved. Was the satyr-play meant
to (did it?) dispel, relativize, the impact of the tragic spectacle? Did
it challenge the validity, the representative legitimacy of the tragic
view in some pivotal, subversive way?[2] We are almost totally in the
dark on this decisive issue.

If we look at them in (probably) artificial isolation from the textual and performative context, a number of Greek tragedies do
approach the absolute despair, the nihilism in respect of hope,
which I have adduced in my definition. Of the epic cycles, two—
the Trojan and the Theban—yield arguments of total despair.
Stripped of its Virgilian promise, the destruction of Troy and the
devouring consequences of this destruction on both the victors and
the vanquished generate an irreparable triumph of the inhuman.[3]
The metamorphosis of Hecuba points up the regress of men and
women to a bestial estate, as does the blood-sacrifice, so long dwelt
on, of young children. As Lucan had it, the ruins of Troy are then
themselves ruined—and Lucan knew whereof he spoke, in time of
fratricidal, homicidal civil war. Massacre, rape, enslavement,
infanticide, and a chain of sadistic retribution converge towards an
essential nightmare and dehumanization. Euripides' *Hecuba* and
Trojan Women (is there really any puzzle about Aristotle's *tragikôtatos?*) come near to a *degré zéro* of existential vision: an approach
underlined by Sartre's adaptations of Euripides, in times which
were again those of systematic torture and massacre. Elsewhere, I
have tried to analyse the tragic weight of Sophocles' *Antigone*.
There is peculiar, calculated horror in the fact that Creon's fatal
delay in arriving at the rock-tomb is brought about by his desperate good deed, the symbolic reburial of Polyneices.[4] Eurydice's
suicide in recollection of the sacrificial slaying of Creon's other and
eldest son, before Haemon, adds deliberately to the effect of complete closure on hope or consolation.

The crux is that offered by the *Bacchae*. The aura of suggestion
which emanates from this text is almost excessive. We have reason
to believe that this is Euripides' last play and one produced under
stress of exile and isolation in a savage ambience. It may be the last
in date, or one of the last in date, of all the Greek tragic dramas
which have come down to us. This fact induces an illusion of retro-
spection and finality, as if Euripides' use of the Pentheus episode

constituted a sombre review of the whole genre and even of the sociology of Greek theatrical celebrations and of their relations to Dionysus. It was as if the *Bacchae* asked of itself, of the poet and of the spectator: what price in felt suffering, in the release of unreason, must be paid, has been paid, for the seventy years of supreme dramatic presentment since Aeschylus?

The termination of this play presses towards total despair, towards annihilating terror far transgressing any plausible moral or compensatory motives. The ruin and dispersal of Cadmus' house, the reduction of even the marginally implicated to animal status, as they come on top of and after Agave's unspeakable awakening to her blind deed, accumulate to absolute, incomprehensible horror. The gods do not only kill us for their sport, as Lear has it: they torture and humiliate us *in extremis*, when we are totally defeated, when we grovel before them. Challenged, in a characteristically Euripidean vein, to justify his uttermost sadism, Dionysus backtracks from one untenable stance to the next: he, the god, was much aggrieved; his father Zeus had willed this insensate chastisement; fate and necessity had programmed these inhumanities from times immemorial. In turn, each apologia worsens the situation and seems to pass on mankind a long sentence of death and absurdity. Here, indeed, we stand at the blind eye of the hurricane of pure tragedy, here at the self-destructive climax of the most profound, the most incommensurable, of Greek tragic texts. The problem is, of course, that the entire last part of the *Bacchae* has come down to us in mutilated form, that there are destructive lacunae and uncertainties in what is always a reconstructed reading and an editorial choice. None the less, any listing of the rare absolute tragedies in the Western legacy will have Euripides' last play very near to its centre.

IV

It is largely misread tags out of Aristotle's *Poetics*,[5] propositions from Horace, distant rumours concerning Ovid's lost *Medea*, and, above all, the rediscovery of Seneca, which inspire what we have of medieval beliefs about tragedy, about its 'sad song', in Chaucer's laconic, haunting phrase. It is the example of Seneca which inflects the Western theatrical and academic-theatrical practice towards violent melodrama, towards the almost unexamined identification of tragedy with horror in high places. It is the plays of Seneca which initiate the unresolved tension between physical savagery and recitation, between histrionic enactment on the stage and indirect rhetorical evocation. A play such as Shakespeare's early *Titus Andronicus* illustrates the one extreme; the tragedies of Racine, the other.

But the mature Shakespeare is not, or is only very exceptionally, a 'tragedian'. Dr Johnson held comedy to be Shakespeare's natural idiom. I would put it otherwise. The Shakespearean sense of reality, of man's works and days, is conceptually and pragmatically tragicomic. Shakespeare *knows*, in every fibre of his compendious being, that a child is being born next door, a birthday celebrated below stairs, in the very instant of the murder of Agamemnon or the blinding of Oedipus. He *knows*, overwhelmingly, that the facts of the world are hybrid, that desolation and joy, destruction and generation are simultaneous. The sum of the extant is never in one key, it is never one thing only. Fortinbras will be a sounder king than Hamlet could ever have been. Scotland will flower after the slaying of Macbeth. Cassio will govern justly in Cyprus. The plays tell us that, explicitly. Concomitantly, there is a sadness, as of summer rain, in the merriment which concludes *Twelfth Night,* and a sadness in the nuptials which crown the *Merchant of Venice.* Only twice, I believe, does Shakespeare 'monotonize' his dramatic ontology (and I am using the word in its proper sense of musical single notes): only twice does he abandon his tragicomic faith. *Lear can* be read as ending in darkness (though redemptive hints are also notable). *Timon of Athens* is pure tragedy. Not, primarily, because of its eloquent condemnation of the cosmos as irremediably corrupt, of society as leprosied unto extinction, of the generation of children as a bestial folly. Not because the sun is slandered and men and women are made ludicrous, lecherous animals filled with venereal disease. No, for a very precise textual reason: near the end of the play, Timon bids 'language cease'. The trope is immensely reinforced by the fact that his epitaph is meant to be washed away by the sea, so that there can be no textuality left. This injunction appears nowhere else in the entire corpus. It has nothing to do with the wonderful meditations on silence by Volumnia or Cordelia; it is something quite different. It is, in and for Shakespeare, the zero point, the black hole of hope. In no other consciousness of which we have certain record, was language as central, as charged with the articulate totality of the world. Once and once only, do words cry out for their own self-annihilation. Not only let language cease: let the script, the epitaph, be washed away for ever by the sea. After which, Shakespeare moves, as if in suppression of a singular terror, into the magical music of forgiveness and recuperation which is that of the four last romance-plays.

After the *Bacchae*, it is Racine who is the 'absolutist' in Western tragic drama. His uses of Jansenism, a current of tragic dissent or heresy within Christianity, allow him to conceive of a human condition in which Christ endures in agony till the end of time. As Pascal says (in unconscious echo of *Macbeth*), 'how can you sleep?'—when Christ hangs in agony until the end of the world. More specifically, Racine fixes on the paradox (a taboo subject among Christians) of Jesus's temporality, of his entry into history at a specific date and place. It follows, for Racine, that those damned prior to that date, like the characters of Greek myth, are damned irremediably.[6] Phèdre, Athalie, Andromaque are damned for ever in a quite specific way that defines their aptitude for the tragic, as no character can be for whom there might be the forgiveness of God at the end of time. Hence the *gravamen* of pure tragedy. Precisely as Shakespeare will not, Racine brings the universe (*univers* is a key word) to a single point of total compaction. As the tragic plot unfolds, all else in nature and existence seems to hold its breath. Eternity is gathered in an hour (this is the fundamental meaning of Racine's effortless adoption of neo-Aristotelian unities of action, place, and time).[7] No irony, no distant flicker of comedy, no possible exit from disaster (and *disaster*, we tend to forget, means literally the fall of the stars out of a last blackness) intrudes on the muted purity of total loss. Had I to choose the ultimate 'moment of truth' in Western tragedy, it would be that of the almost unspoken adieu at the finale of *Bérénice* (and too often we forget that 'adieu' has in it 'God'). A man and a woman who have loved each other unspeakably, unutterably, and will never see each other again, walk off the stage out of two doors. No 'hurricanoes spout', no woods march on a castle, no drop of blood is spilled. Those are vulgar contingencies by an Elizabethan working playwright. A single ordinary word, spoken in flawless civility between a man and a woman on a perfectly bare stage, marks the horizon from which there can be no return of hope, and makes of 'tout l'univers' an emptiness, a desert for the human soul. No one prior to Racine, no one after, has, I believe, matched that economy of the absolute.

One further step needed to be taken. From Aeschylus to Racine, the agents in tragedy are an élite marked out for desolation by their high social station and, even more importantly, by their eloquence, their *paideia*: whatever their enmities, they share that *paideia*. It is comedy which extends to the lower orders. Büchner's *Wozzeck* presents the systematic torment and humiliation of an almost illiterate nobody. We witness the harrying to hallucination and death of a human being scarcely articulate. The derisive verbosity of Wozzeck's persecutors mocks the inhumanity latent in high-flown speech. Wozzeck's suffering is the more universal, the more of an indictment of the human circumstance, because he can barely express it. In the play, the hysterical laughter of children sees out an unendurable reality. From the inarticulacy of Wozzeck to the linguistic minimalism of Beckett, the line and logic are direct. Step by step, in Beckett's last experiments for the stage, language is snuffed out. We end with an open mouth, a black hole, screaming its way into silence.

Thus, as we look back, the list of tragedies 'pure and simple' is very short. A handful of ancient Greek plays (about whose qualifying context we cannot be certain): Marlowe's *Faustus* if we subtract the comic sub-plot; *King Lear*, perhaps, and, most certainly, *Timon*; the three or four supreme plays of Racine; Büchner's *Wozzeck*; some moments in Ibsen and, perhaps, Strindberg; the metaphysical *guignol* of Beckett. Elsewhere, as in the texture of our common lives and biology, the fundamental rhythms are tragicomic. The curtain-line belongs to hope:

> So thanks to all at once, and to each one,
> Whom we invite to see us crown'd at Scone.

The rise to preponderance of the modern prose-novel, and of such derivatives as the film, have made the concept of tragedy diffuse. The contours are today so loose as to be almost meaningless. They comport 'horror', in the Senecan-Jacobean lineage of the 'horror movie'; the macabre, for example, when the epithet 'tragic' attaches to chronicles and graphic documents of crime or political violence. Often 'tragedy' is used for domestic *tristesse*, for physical or mental affliction, for the collapse of social-economic hopes. Dreiser's *American Tragedy* is so apt a title just because the events narrated are of so banal and contingent a kind. Modern literature, in the form of the novel, has indeed penetrated to the heart of desolation—witness a Dostoevsky or a Conrad—and I would set Franz Kafka next to Racine in the connoisseurship of pure despair. Strikingly, however, it is twentieth-century opera which comes nearest to the absolute tragedies which I have cited. And it does so in returning to some of those very texts: as in Enesco's and in Stravinsky's *Oedipus*, in Strauss's *Elektra*, in Alban Berg's *Wozzeck* first and foremost, or in Henze's version of the *Bacchae* (*The Bassarids*).

V

One asks: will there be new 'pure and simple' tragedies in anything like the old sense? Prediction in such matters is always hindsight masked. But my guess would be 'No'.

It has long been manifest that tragedy, closely defined, evolves from a context of felt, or challenged, religious beliefs. The mythological matter of the tragic draws on the dynamics of the supernatural. No *Hamlet* without its Ghost; no *Macbeth* without Witches; no *Phèdre* outside the vengeful reach of an afterlife ('Minos juge aux Enfers tous les pâles humains'). A negative theology can, in exceptional hands, yield a tragic world-view. It does so in the cold, uncannily luminous miniature of Yeats's *Purgatory* and in those parables of Beckett which owe so much to that Yeats fragment:[8] observe the absent presence of Golgotha in *Endgame*.[9] But it is difficult to imagine a renascence of high tragic theatre in a positivist climate of consciousness, in a mass-market society, more and more of whose thinking members regard the question of the existence of God, let alone of demonic agents intervening in mundane affairs, as archaic nonsense. That master of ironic, scrupulous reason, Immanuel Kant, held evil to be an incarnate presence in human affairs: we don't.

The mythologies which now inform our perceptions of the self and of reality are therapeutic. Vishnievsky's *Optimistic Tragedy* stages the heroic deaths of Bolshevik fighters. Their fate *is* worthy of lamentation, but it will serve the ineluctable victory of justice. Mankind must step over its dead in order to reach the great dawn. Freud's reading of the individual psyche and of history is stoic and unsparingly ironic. But its trust in science, in the advance of scientific knowledge and its ameliorating applications, remains unwavering. *Wissenschaft*, disinterested exploration, are stronger than death. Socialism, psychoanalysis, the programme of the free market and, above all, the triumphalism of the sciences turn on a core of messianic secularism. How else would mankind keep going after what it has experienced and continues to experience today in so many 'locales' of abomination?

There is a last point. Modernity has made us alert, as never before, to the autonomous weight of semantic-poetic forms. Textuality itself looms large in our aesthetic response. We are, in consequence, more observant than were earlier sensibilities of the plain fact that absolute 'pure' tragedies, enactments or articulations of the death of hope, do, in a sense, contradict or deconstruct themselves, just because they exist, because they are there for us to ponder or stage. Why compose, let alone publish or commit to public performance, a pure tragedy? Why wax eloquent if 'language must cease'? Why expend fantastically 'artful' poetry on life-denying horror, on Agave holding aloft the bloody head of her own son? By virtue of its bare existentiality, the absolute tragic statement implies positive values of survivance, of formal beauty or innovation, of repeatability. In some ways, it cheats. No one wrote tragedies in the extermination camps. (Music was composed, but that is another, and exceedingly difficult, question.)

Our current politics are, in many parts of the earth, openly bestial. The phenomenology of AIDS has triggered atavistic intimations of the demonic, of a world in which we are indeed unwelcome or parasitic lodgers. The possibilities of a thermonuclear or bacterial process of self-destruction remain in force, as do possibilities of mass starvation. Yet none of these apocalyptic scenarios has occasioned the major reflex of imaginative construction exemplified by great tragic drama. Our fictions fall trivially short of the fact. Treatments of the Holocaust have, with one or two exceptions, beggared belief in their inadequate vulgarity. As Heidegger foresaw, the cosmetic and the pharmaceutical can even despoil us of our own death. Our culture bids us to 'get on with it'—where the 'it' remains, of course, the unasked question. All the more reason to turn back to *Antigone* or the *Bacchae*, to *Bérénice* or to *Wozzeck*, and be humbled by their strangeness.

Notes

1. Nothing isolates British classical studies from those on the Continent more obviously than the absence in these studies of any normal resort to the major philosophic texts on Greek tragedy. Hölderlin, Hegel, Schelling, Nietzsche, Walter Benjamin, and Heidegger play almost no part in British academic-professional discussions of Greek tragic drama. They are, of course, of the essence. [*In an aside during the spoken version of his paper at the King's conference, Professor Steiner was kind enough to exempt the present editor from this charge*: Ed.]

2. During the Second World War, at one of its worst points, in '42, to help British war-relief, the British government sent the Old Vic to make a tour of American cities. My father took me as a very young boy. A then still fairly young Laurence Olivier was playing Oedipus the King. As blinded, blood-dripping Oedipus, with both eyes streaming with blood, with hands filled with blood, at the end he cascaded down the stage (it was one of his great physical, athletic *coups de théâtre*), down a long flight of steps, rolling over and over, the blood pouring onto the steps. The house lights were kept down, and there was no applause: only a total numbness at the immensity of the performance at that moment. The house lights blaze up, the curtain rises—on Olivier in the dandy's costume of Sheridan's Mr Puff. And the house exploded, stood and roared in a kind of numb relief and strangeness, but also resentment. It's as near as I've come to some silly, primitive guess as to what *might* have been the *Stimmung* of the audience as it leaves the theatre of Dionysus in Athens after a satyr-play mocking, contravening, deconstructing the tragic play before it.

3. The first play staged with Allied permission in Berlin in 1945 was Hauptmann's version of the *Oresteia*, against a vast photograph of the ruins of Berlin. The audience couldn't bear it. Many of them collapsed. And when the word 'Troy' rang out, it named Berlin and every other city.

4. Even Shakespeare couldn't handle this. The closely analogous hanging of Cordelia is caused by the fact that the messenger arrives thirty seconds too late, does not run fast enough after the Edmund/Edgar duel. It is an unbearable mishap (though that is too simple a word), very different from the logic of the autonomous self-punishment of Creon.

5. As I listen, endlessly, to debates on the *Poetics* and the new editions (of these, too, there is no end), I am prepared to wager that the young man who took the notes at Aristotle's lecture was sitting very near the door on a very noisy day.

6. One of the most sadistic paradoxes, one which Christianity cannot cope with. Bossuet wrote endlessly on it: *what of those before the coming of*

Jesus? It is the heretical modern therapeutic ecumenism of Coca-Cola to tell us, 'it'll all be all right, nevertheless': not theologically it won't.

7. There is no forcing for Racine. The twenty-four-hour single play, single action, is to him the breath of reality, completely natural. Most other neo-classical dramatists chafe and struggle and cannot come to terms with this spurious convention of containment.

8. In that fragment, one of the great tragic texts in Western literature, Yeats has a man kill his son lest the son perpetuate the psycho-genetics of evil and of inherited crime.

9. So often missed: every name in the play is the Crucifixion. Hamm is the hammer and Clov is the nails ('les clous'). *Endgame* re-enacts what Racine and Pascal knew, that Jesus hangs on that cross till the end of time.

Bibliography of Abbreviated Works

The following list contains only works of secondary literature referred to in abbreviated form in the notes of one or more of the chapters of the book. Standard commentaries (referred to by the commentator's name) and a few other standard works of reference are not included here except where confusion might otherwise result.

ADKINS, A. W. H., *Merit and Responsibility* (Oxford 1960).

BARLOW, S. A., *The Imagery of Euripides* (London 1971).

BELFIORE, E. S., *Tragic Pleasures: Aristotle on Plot and Emotion* (Princeton 1992).

BERGER, H., '*King Lear:* The Family Romance', *Centennial Review* 23 (1979) 348–76.

—— 'Text against Performance: The Gloucester Family Romance', in P. Erickson and C. Kahn (edd.), *Shakespeare's Rough Magic: Renaissance Essays in Honor of C. L. Barber* (Newark, Del. 1985).

BERS, V., 'Tragedy and Rhetoric', in I. Worthington (ed.), *Persuasion: Greek Rhetoric in Action* (London 1994) 176–95.

BLUNDELL, M. W., *Helping Friends and Harming Enemies: A Study in Sophocles and Greek Ethics* (Cambridge 1989).

BOLLACK, J., *L'Oedipe roi de Sophocle: Le Texte et ses interprétations* (4 vols.; Lille 1990).

BOOTH, W. C., *A Rhetoric of Irony* (Chicago 1974).

BRECHT, B., *Brecht on Theatre: The Development of an Aesthetic*, ed. and trans. J. Willett (London 1964).

—— *The Messingkauf Dialogues*, trans. J. Willett (London 1965).

BREMER, J. M., RADT, S. L., and RUIJGH, C. J., *Miscellanea Tragica in Honorem J. C. Kamerbeek* (Amsterdam 1976).

BURKE, K., *Language as Symbolic Action: Essays on Life, Literature and Method* (Berkeley 1966).

BURKERT, W., 'Greek Tragedy and Sacrificial Ritual', *GRBS* 7 (1966) 87–121.

BUXTON, R., 'Blindness and Limits: Sophokles and the Logic of Myth', *JHS* 100 (1980) 22–37 (reprinted in H. Bloom (ed.), *Sophocles: Modern Critical Views* [New York 1990] 105–26).

CALAME, C., 'De la poésie chorale au stasimon tragique: Pragmatique de voix féminines', *Métis* (forthcoming).

CARRARA, P., *Eretteo* (Florence 1977).

CHANTRAINE, P., *Dictionnaire étymologique de la langue grecque* (Paris 1968).

DANE, J. A., *The Critical Mythology of Irony* (Athens, Ga. 1991).

DAWE, R. D., *Studies on the Text of Sophocles* (3 vols.: i–ii, Leiden 1973; iii, Leiden 1978).

DODDS, E. R., *The Greeks and the Irrational* (Berkeley 1951).

DORJHAN, A. P., 'Poetry in Athenian Courts', *CP* 22 (1927) 85–93.

DUPONT-ROC, R., and LALLOT, J., *Aristote: La Poétique* (Paris 1980).

EASTERLING, P. E., 'Tragedy and Ritual: "Cry 'Woe, woe', But May the Good Prevail" ', *Métis* 3 (1988) 87–109.

—— 'Tragedy and Ritual', in R. Scodel (ed.), *Theater and Society in the Classical World* (Ann Arbor 1993) 7–23.

ELSE, G. F., *Aristotle's Poetics: The Argument* (Cambridge, Mass. 1967).

EUBEN, J. P. (ed.), *Greek Tragedy and Political Theory* (Berkeley 1986).

EWANS, M., 'Racine's *Phèdre* and Greek tragedy', *Prudentia* (suppl.vol. 1993) 89–102.

—— *Aeschylus: Oresteia* (London 1995).

FOLEY, H. P., *Ritual Irony: Poetry and Sacrifice in Euripides* (Ithaca, NY 1985).

FRIEDRICH, R., 'Drama and Ritual', in J. Redmond (ed.), *Themes in Drama*, v: *Drama and Religion* (Cambridge 1983) 159–223.

FRYE, N., *The Anatomy of Criticism* (Princeton 1957).

GAUGER, B., *Gott und Mensch im Ion des Euripides* (Bonn 1977).

GELLIE, G. H., *Sophocles: A Reading* (Melbourne 1972).

GENTILI, B., and PRETAGOSTINI, R. (edd.), *Edipo: Il Teatro greco e la cultura europea* (Rome 1986).

GILLIGAN, C., *In a Different Voice* (Cambridge, Mass. 1982).

—— WARD, J. V., and TAYLOR, J. M., *Mapping the Moral Domain* (Cambridge, Mass. 1988).

GIRARD, R., *Violence and the Sacred*, trans. P. Gregory (Baltimore 1977) (= *La Violence et le sacré* [Paris 1972]).

GOHEEN, R. F., *The Imagery of Sophocles' Antigone: A Study in Poetic Language* (Princeton 1951).

GOLDHILL, S., *Reading Greek Tragedy* (Cambridge 1986).

—— 'The Great Dionysia and Civic Ideology', in Winkler and Zeitlin (edd.), *Nothing to Do with Dionysos?* (below), 97–129.

GRIFFITHS, F. T., 'Girard on the Greeks / The Greeks on Girard', *Berkshire Review* 14 (1979) 20–36.

HALL, E., *Inventing the Barbarian: Greek Self-definition through Tragedy* (Oxford 1989).

SNELL, B., *The Discovery of the Mind*, trans. T. G. Rosenmeyer (Cambridge, Mass. 1953).

SOMMERSTEIN, A. H., HALLIWELL, S., HENDERSON, J., and ZIMMERMAN, B. (edd.), *Tragedy, Comedy and the Polis* (Bari 1993).

SORUM, C. E., 'The Family in Sophocles' *Antigone* and *Electra*', *CW* 75 (1982) 201–11.

SOURVINOU-INWOOD, C., 'Assumptions and the Creation of Meaning: Reading Sophocles' *Antigone*', *JHS* 109 (1989) 134–48.

STANFORD, W. B., *Ambiguity in Greek Literature* (Oxford 1939).

—— *Greek Tragedy and the Emotions* (London 1983).

STEINER, G., *The Death of Tragedy* (London 1961).

SWEARINGEN, C. I., *Rhetoric and Irony* (Oxford 1991).

SYNGE, J. M., *Collected Works*, ed. R. Skelton (Oxford 1962–8), ii: *Prose*, ed. A. Price; iii. Plays I, ed. A. Saddlemyer; iv. Plays II, ed. A. Saddlemyer.

SZONDI, P., *Versuch über das Tragische*, in *Schriften* i (Frankfurt/M. 1978).

TAPLIN, O. P., *The Stagecraft of Aeschylus: The Dramatic Use of Exits and Entrances in Greek Tragedy* (Oxford 1977).

—— *Greek Tragedy in Action* (London 1978).

—— *Comic Angels and other Approaches to Greek Drama through Vase-Paintings* (Oxford 1993).

TRONTO, J. C., *Moral Boundaries* (New York 1993).

UNAMUNO, M. DE, *The Tragic Sense of Life* (London 1921).

VAHLEN, J., *Beiträge zu Aristoteles' Poetik*, ed. H. Schöne (Leipzig 1914) (originally in *SWAW* 52 [1866]).

VERNANT, J.-P., 'Ambiguité et renversement: sur la structure énigmatique d'*Œdipe-Roi*', in Vernant and Vidal-Naquet, *Mythe et tragédie en Grèce ancienne* (below), 101–31.

—— 'The God of Tragic Fiction', in J.-P. Vernant and P. Vidal-Naquet, *Myth and Tragedy in Ancient Greece*, trans. J. Lloyd (New York 1988) 181–8.

—— and VIDAL-NAQUET, P., *Mythe et tragédie en Grèce ancienne II* (Paris 1986).

—— *Tragedy and Myth in Ancient Greece*, trans. J. Lloyd (Brighton 1981) (= *Mythe et tragédie en Grèce ancienne* [Paris 1972]).

VICKERS, B., *Towards Greek Tragedy* (London 1973).

VOEGELIN, E., *Order and History* (5 vols.; Baton Rouge, La. 1956, 1957, 1957, 1974, 1987).

WILSON, P. J., 'Leading the Tragic *Khoros*: Tragic Prestige in the Democratic City', in C. Pelling and C. Sourvinou-Inwood (edd.), *Greek Tragedy and the Ancient Historian* (Oxford, forthcoming).

WINKLER, J. J., and ZEITLIN, F. I. (edd.), *Nothing to Do with Dionysos? Athenian Drama in its Social Context* (Princeton 1990).

HALLIWELL, S., *Aristotle's Poetics* (London 1986).

—— *The Poetics of Aristotle: Translation and Commentary* (London 1987).

HEATH, M., *The Poetics of Greek Tragedy* (London 1987).

HEGEL, G. W. F., *Sämtliche Werke*, ed. L. Boumann *et al.*, rev. H. Glockner (20 vols.; Stuttgart 1949–59: Jubiläumsausgabe).

HEIDEN, B., *Tragic Rhetoric: An Interpretation of Sophocles' Trachiniae* (New York 1989).

HENRICHS, A., 'Greek Maenadism from Olympia to Messalina', *HSCP* 82 (1978) 121–60.

—— 'Loss of Self, Suffering, Violence: The Modern View of Dionysus from Nietzsche to Girard', *HSCP* 88 (1984) 205–40.

—— 'Dancing for Dionysus: Choral Self-referentiality and Dionysiac Ritual in Euripides' (forthcoming).

HESTER, D. A., 'Sophocles the Unphilosophical: A Study in the *Antigone*', *Mnemosyne* 24 (1971) 11–59.

HOLST-WARHAFT, G., *Dangerous Voices: Women's Laments and Greek Literature* (Ithaca, NY 1992).

HUNTER, G. K. (ed.), *Shakespeare: Macbeth* (Harmondsworth 1967).

IZARD, C. E., KAGAN, J., and ZAJONC, R. B. (edd.), *Emotions, Cognition and Behaviour* (Cambridge 1984).

JONES, J., *On Aristotle and Greek Tragedy* (London 1962).

JUST, R., *Women in Athenian Law and Life* (New York 1989).

KITTO, H. D. F., *Form and Meaning in Drama* (London 1956).

—— *Greek Tragedy*[3] (London 1961).

—— 'Greek Tragedy and Dionysus', in J. Gassner and R. G. Allen (edd.), *Theatre and Drama in the Making* (Boston 1964) 6–20.

KITZINGER, R., 'Stylistic Methods of Characterization in Sophocles' *Antigone*' (Diss. Stanford 1976).

KNOX, B. M. W., *The Heroic Temper: Studies in Sophoclean Tragedy* (Berkeley 1964).

—— *Word and Action: Essays on the Ancient Theater* (Baltimore 1979).

—— 'Sophocles and the *Polis*', in J. de Romilly (ed.), *Sophocle* (Entretiens Hardt 29, Geneva 1982) 1–27.

KOHLBERG, L., *The Philosophy of Moral Development* (San Francisco 1981).

—— *The Psychology of Moral Development* (San Francisco 1984).

LADA, I., ' "Empathic Understanding": Emotion and Cognition in Classical Dramatic Audience-Response', *PCPS* 39 (1993) 94–140.

LATTIMORE, R., *Story Patterns in Greek Tragedy* (London 1964).

LAZARUS, R. S., *et al.*, 'Emotions: A Cognitive-Phenomenological Analysis', in R. Plutchik and H. Kellerman (edd.), *Emotion: Theory, Research, and Experience*, i: *Theories of Emotion* (New York 1980) 189–217.

LEBECK, A., *The Oresteia: A Study in Language and Structure* (Cambridge, Mass. 1971).

LEINIEKS, V., *The Plays of Sophocles* (Amsterdam 1962).

LESKY, A., *Göttliche und menschliche Motivation im homerischen Epos* (Heidelberg 1961).

LINFORTH, I. M., 'Antigone and Creon', *UCPCP* 15 (1961) 183–260.

LLOYD-JONES, H., *The Justice of Zeus* (Berkeley 1971).

LORAUX, N., *The Invention of Athens: The Funeral Oration in the Classical City*, trans. A. Sheridan (Cambridge, Mass. 1986).

MASON, H. A., *The Tragic Plane* (Oxford 1985).

MATTHIESSEN, K., *Elektra, Taurische Iphigenie und Helena* (Göttingen 1964).

—— 'Der Ion: Eine Komödie des Euripides?', *Sacris Erudiri* (*Jaarboek voor Godsdienstwetenschappen* 31 [1989–90]) 271–91.

MITCHELL, R. N., 'Miasma, Mimesis and Scapegoating in Euripides' *Hippolytus*', *CA* 10 (1991) 98–122.

MUECKE, D. C., *The Compass of Irony* (London 1969).

—— *Irony and the Ironic* (London 1982).

MÜLLER, G., *Sophokles: Antigone* (Heidelberg 1967).

MURNAGHAN, S., '*Antigone* 904–920 and the Institution of Marriage', *AJP* 107 (1986) 192–207.

NEUBERG, M., 'How Like a Woman; Antigone's "inconsistency" ', *CQ* 40 (1990) 54–76.

NIETZSCHE, F. W., *The Birth of Tragedy* (= *Die Geburt der Tragödie* [Leipzig 1872]).

NORTH, H., 'The Use of Poetry in the Training of the Ancient Orator', *Traditio* 8 (1952) 22–7.

NUSSBAUM, M., *The Fragility of Goodness* (Cambridge 1986).

—— 'Tragedy and Self-sufficiency: Plato and Aristotle on Fear and Pity', *Ox.Stud.Anc.Phil.* 10 (1992) 133–7.

OBER, J., and STRAUSS, B., 'Drama, Political Rhetoric, and the Discourse of Athenian Democracy', in Winkler and Zeitlin (edd.), *Nothing to Do with Dionysos?* (below), 237–70.

O'CASEY, S., *The Complete Plays*, i (London 1949).

ONIANS, R. B., *The Origins of European Thought* (Cambridge 1954).

ORTONY, A., CLORE G. L., and COLLINS, A., *The Cognitive Structure of Emotions* (Cambridge, Mass. 1988).

OUDEMANS C. W., and LARDINOIS, A. P. M. H., *Tragic Ambiguity: Anthropology, Philosophy and Sophocles' Antigone* (Leiden 1987).

PAGE, D. L., *Further Greek Epigrams* (Cambridge 1981).

PERLMAN, S., 'Quotations from Poetry in Attic Orators of the Fourth Century BC', *AJP* 85 (1964) 155–72.

PICKARD-CAMBRIDGE, A., *The Dramatic Festivals of Athens*[2], rev. J. Gould and D. M. Lewis (corr. edn.) (Oxford 1988).

POOLE, A., *Tragedy: Shakespeare and the Greek Example* 1987).

PORTER, E. J., *Women and Moral Identity* (North Sydney 1991).

PUCCI, P., *Oedipus and the Fabrication of the Father: Oedipus Tyra. Modern Criticism and Philosophy* (Baltimore 1992).

RALEIGH, W., *Johnson on Shakespeare* (Oxford 1908).

REINHARDT, K., *Sophokles*, trans. H. and D. Harvey (Oxford 1979).

ROBERTS, D. H., 'Sophoclean Endings: Another Story', *Arethus.* (1988) 177–96.

ROSENBLOOM, D., 'Shouting "Fire" in a Crowded Theater: Phryniche *Capture of Miletos* and the Politics of Fear in Early Greek Traged *Philologus* 137 (1993) 159–96.

ROSENMEYER, T. G., *The Art of Aeschylus* (Berkeley 1982).

SEAFORD, R. A. S., 'On the Origins of Satyric Drama', *Maia* 28 (1976 209–21.

—— 'Dionysiac Drama and Dionysiac Mysteries', *CQ* 31 (1981) 252–75.

—— 'Dionysus as Destroyer of the Household: Homer, Tragedy, and the Polis', in C. Faraone and T. H. Carpenter (edd.), *Masks of Dionysus* (Ithaca, NY 1993) 115–46.

—— *Reciprocity and Ritual: Homer and Tragedy in the Developing City-State* (Oxford 1994).

SEALE, D., *Vision and Stagecraft in Sophocles* (London 1982).

SEGAL, C. P., *Tragedy and Civilization: An Interpretation of Sophocles* (Cambridge, Mass. 1981).

—— *Dionysiac Poetics and Euripides' Bacchae* (Princeton 1982).

—— *La Musique du Sphinx: Poésie et Structure dans la Tragédie Grecque* (Paris 1987).

—— *Euripides and the Poetics of Sorrow: Art, Gender, and Commemoration in Alcestis, Hippolytus, and Hecuba* (Durham, NC 1993).

—— *Oedipus Tyrannus: Tragic Heroism and the Limits of Knowledge* (New York 1993).

—— 'Sophocles' *Oedipus Tyrannus*: Freud, Language and the Unconscious', in P. L. Rudnytsky and E. H. Spitz (edd.), *Freud and Forbidden Knowledge* (New York 1994) 72–95.

—— *Sophocles' Tragic World: Divinity, Nature, Society* (Cambridge, Mass., forthcoming).

SEIDENSTICKER, B., *Palintonos Harmonia* (Göttingen 1982).

—— - 'Peripetie und tragische Dialektik: Aristoteles, Szondi und die griechische Tragödie', *Drama* 1 (1991) 240–63.

SILK, M. S., *Interaction in Poetic Imagery* (Cambridge 1974).

—— 'The autonomy of comedy', *Comparative Criticism* 10 (1988) 3–37.

—— and STERN, J. P., *Nietzsche on Tragedy* (Cambridge 1981 [corr.edn. 1983]).

WINNINGTON-INGRAM, R. P., *Sophocles: An Interpretation* (Cambridge 1980).
—— *Studies in Aeschylus* (Cambridge 1983).
XANTHAKIS-KARAMANOS, G., *Studies in Fourth-Century Tragedy* (Athens 1980).
ZEITLIN, F. I., 'Mysteries of Identity and Designs of Self in Euripides' *Ion*', *PCPS* 35 (1989) 144 ff.
—— 'The Theater of Self and Society in Athenian Drama', in Winkler and Zeitlin (edd.), *Nothing to Do with Dionysos?* (above), 130–67.

Index I

Tragic Passages

This index lists significant discussions of extant plays by Aeschylus, Euripides, and Sophocles, and of specified passages from those plays. For all other discussions of the three Greek tragedians, and all other playwrights, Greek or non-Greek, see Index II. It should be noted that, in the case of overlapping or sequential passages, compendious references have sometimes been used. Thus the reference to *Agam.* 49–62 subsumes discussions of 49ff. (on p. 122), 50 (p. 136), 59–62 (p. 141). Throughout the index, specified line references are in brackets.

Index II
General

The following categories of items are not in general covered by this index: names of modern classical scholars (and/including contributors to this volume); passing references to Aristotle and to one or other of the three Greek tragedians, especially in the notes; comments on tragic or tragic-related topics in the notes, where these merely amplify an item, already indexed, in the text; and references to, and passages from, extant plays by the three tragedians (for which see Index I). Where no ambiguity results, various post-classical authors and authorities are cited by surname alone.